QlikView: Advanced Data Visualization

Discover deeper insights with Qlikview by building your own rich analytical applications from scratch

Miguel Ángel García

Barry Harmsen

Stephen Redmond

Karl Pover

BIRMINGHAM - MUMBAI

QlikView: Advanced Data Visualization

First published: December 2018

Production reference: 1191218

Published by Packt Publishing Ltd.
Livery Place
35 Livery Street
Birmingham B3 2PB, UK.

ISBN 978-1-78995-599-6

www.packtpub.com

`mapt.io`

Mapt is an online digital library that gives you full access to over 5,000 books and videos, as well as industry leading tools to help you plan your personal development and advance your career. For more information, please visit our website.

Why subscribe?

- Spend less time learning and more time coding with practical eBooks and Videos from over 4,000 industry professionals
- Learn better with Skill Plans built especially for you
- Get a free eBook or video every month
- Mapt is fully searchable
- Copy and paste, print, and bookmark content

PacktPub.com

Did you know that Packt offers eBook versions of every book published, with PDF and ePub files available? You can upgrade to the eBook version at `www.PacktPub.com` and as a print book customer, you are entitled to a discount on the eBook copy. Get in touch with us at `service@packtpub.com` for more details.

At `www.PacktPub.com`, you can also read a collection of free technical articles, sign up for a range of free newsletters, and receive exclusive discounts and offers on Packt books and eBooks.

Contributors

About the authors

Miguel Ángel García is a Business Intelligence consultant and Qlik Solutions Architect from Monterrey, Mexico. Having worked throughout many successful Qlik implementations, from inception through implementation, and performed across a wide variety of roles on each project, his experience and skills range from pre-sales to applications development and design, technical architecture, system administration, as well as functional analysis and overall project execution. He currently holds the QlikView Designer, QlikView Developer, and QlikView System Administrator Certifications.

Barry Harmsen is a Business Intelligence Consultant based in the Netherlands. Here he runs Bitmetric, a boutique consulting firm specialized in the Qlik product suite. Originally from a background of traditional business intelligence, data warehousing, and performance management, in 2008 Barry made the shift to Qlik and a more user-centric form of Business Intelligence. Since then, he and his team have helped many clients get the most out of their investments in the Qlik platform.

Barry is one of the four Qlik experts teaching at the Masters Summit for Qlik, an advanced 3-day training for experienced Qlik professionals. He also runs the Amsterdam chapter of the Qlik Dev Group, an open and informal gathering where Qlik professionals can share knowledge and experiences.

Stephen Redmond is the CTO and Qlik Luminary at CapricornVentis - a QlikView Elite Partner. He is the author of several books, including QlikView for Developers Cookbook and QlikView Server and Publisher, both published by Packt Publishing. He is also the author of the popular DevLogixseries for SalesLogix developers. In 2006, after many years of working with CRM systems, reporting and analysis solutions, and data integration, Stephen started working with QlikView. Since then, CapricornVentis has become QlikView's top partner in the UK and Ireland territories, and with Stephen as the head of the team, they have implemented QlikView in a wide variety of enterprise and large-business customers across a wide range of sectors, from public sector to financial services to large retailers. In 2014, Stephen was awarded the Luminary status by Qlik in recognition of his product advocacy. He regularly contributes to online forums, including the Qlik Community.

Karl Pover is the owner and principal consultant of Evolution Consulting, which provides QlikView consulting services throughout Mexico. Since 2006, he has been dedicated to providing QlikView presales, implementation, and training for more than 50 customers. He is the author of Learning QlikView Data Visualization, and he has also been a Qlik Luminary since 2014.

Packt is Searching for Authors Like You

If you're interested in becoming an author for Packt, please visit authors.packtpub.com and apply today. We have worked with thousands of developers and tech professionals, just like you, to help them share their insight with the global tech community. You can make a general application, apply for a specific hot topic that we are recruiting an author for, or submit your own idea.

Table of Contents

Preface

QlikView is one of the most flexible and powerful business intelligence platforms around, and if you want to transform data into insights, it is one of the best options you have at hand. Use this Learning Path, to explore the many features of QlikView to realize the potential of your data and present it as impactful and engaging visualizations.

Each chapter in this Learning Path starts with an understanding of a business requirement and its associated data model and then helps you create insightful analysis and data visualizations around it. You will look at problems that you might encounter while visualizing complex data insights using QlikView, and learn how to troubleshoot these and other not-so-common errors. This Learning Path contains real-world examples from a variety of business domains, such as sales, finance, marketing, and human resources.

With all the knowledge that you gain from this Learning Path, you will have all the experience you need to implement your next QlikView project like a pro.

Who this book is for

This Learning Path is designed for developers who want to go beyond their technical knowledge of QlikView and understand how to create analysis and data visualizations that solve real business needs. To grasp the concepts explained in this Learning Path, you should have a basic understanding of the common QlikView functions and some hands-on experience with the tool.

What this book covers

Chapter 1, Performance Tuning and Scalability, is where we look at understanding how QlikView stores its data so that we can optimize that storage in our applications. We will also look at topics such as Direct Discovery and testing implementations using JMeter.

Chapter 2, QlikView Data Modeling, looks in detail at dimensional data modeling and learning about fact and dimension tables and using best practices from Ralph Kimball in QlikView. We also learn about how to handle slowly changing dimensions (SCDs), multiple fact tables, and drilling across with document chaining.

Chapter 3, Best Practices for Loading Data, is where we look at implementing ETL strategies with QVD files. We also introduce QlikView Expressor.

Chapter 4, Advanced Expressions, is where we look at areas such as the Dollar-sign Expansion, set analysis, and vertical calculations using Total and Aggr.

Chapter 5, Advanced Scripting, looks at optimizing loads, Dollar-sign Expansion in the script, and control structures. We also introduce the concept of code reuse.

Chapter 6, What's New in QlikView 12, presents a summary of the changes in the QlikView software, as well as in the Qlik ecosystem in general, that happened since the previous version of this book was published in 2012. In this chapter, we will bring you up to speed with the changes over the past few years.

Chapter 7, Styling Up, will help us learn how to style our QlikView documents. We will learn about the various document and sheet properties and will use them to manage the visual style of our document. We will also take a closer look at some of the most fundamental objects and learn how we can change their appearance.

Chapter 8, Building Dashboards, introduces us to the three basic types of QlikView users, and how we can best cater to their needs. We will learn about the various charting options that are available in QlikView, and will see how we can add interactivity to our QlikView documents. We will also be introduced to basic calculations.

Chapter 9, Advanced Data Transformation, returns to the topic of data transformation. We will learn about the most commonly used data architectures that can ease QlikView development and administration. Next, we will take a close look at aggregating and sorting data in the data model. In the fi nal part of the chapter, we will learn how to take advantage of some of QlikView's most powerful data transformation capabilities.

Chapter 10, Security, shows how to secure our QlikView documents. We will see how we can allow only authorized users to open our documents and will learn how we can limit what a user can do and see within our document.

Chapter 11, Data Visualization Strategy, begins our journey to create a data-driven organization using QlikView.

Chapter 12, Sales Perspective, explains the data model's importance to data visualization, and shows us how to create advanced analyses, such as customer stratifi cation, churn prediction, and seasonal trends.

Chapter 13, Financial Perspective, illustrates the usage of metadata to format an income statement, a balance sheet, and a cash flow statement.

Chapter 14, Marketing Perspective, walks us through various types of visualization that reveal customer profiles, potential markets, social media sentiment, and the sales pipeline.

Chapter 15, Working Capital Perspective, describes how to analyze days sales of inventory, days sales outstanding, and days payable outstanding, at both a high and a detailed level. It also explains how they are important in order to determine customer stratification.

Chapter 16, Operations Perspective, shows us how to analyze our service levels, predict supplier lead times, and investigate whether on-time deliveries depend on the supplier.

Chapter 17, Human Resources, reveals how to visualize personnel productivity and personal behavior analysis.

Chapter 18, Fact Sheets, demonstrates an ad hoc design method to create a customer fact sheet that includes bullet graphs, sparklines, and a customized UX.

Chapter 19, Balanced Scorecard, details a more formal design method to build an information dashboard containing balanced scorecard metrics.

Chapter 20, Troubleshooting Analysis, takes a look at resources and methods to debug problems in our QlikView applications.

Chapter 21, Mastering Qlik Sense Data Visualization, explains what Qlik Sense means to a QlikView developer and proposes a plan to master Qlik Sense data visualization.

To get the most out of this book

To use this book, you primarily need the QlikView Desktop software. With regards to computer requirements, you will need a PC with at least Windows XP (or better), 2 GB of hard disk space, and 2 GB of RAM. A 64-bit machine is required if you want to use QlikView 12 or a higher version, and is the recommended environment for this book and QlikView development in general. If you prefer to use a 32-bit machine, you can install QlikView 11 instead.

For best understanding, a general knowledge of BI and its terminology is required. Basic understanding of databases and SQL is preferred, but not compulsory for this book.

Download the example code files

You can download the example code files for this book from your account at `http://www.packtpub.com`. If you purchased this book elsewhere, you can visit `http://www.packtpub.com/support` and register to have the files emailed directly to you.

You can download the code files by following these steps:

1. Log in or register at `http://www.packtpub.com`.
2. Select the **SUPPORT** tab.
3. Click on **Code Downloads & Errata**.
4. Enter the name of the book in the **Search** box and follow the on-screen instructions.

Once the file is downloaded, please make sure that you unzip or extract the folder using the latest version of:

- WinRAR / 7-Zip for Windows
- Zipeg / iZip / UnRarX for Mac
- 7-Zip / PeaZip for Linux

The code bundle for the book is also hosted on GitHub `https://github.com/PacktPublishing/QlikView-Advanced-Data-Visualization`. We also have other code bundles from our rich catalog of books and videos available at `https://github.com/PacktPublishing/`. Check them out!

Conventions used

There are a number of text conventions used throughout this book.

CodeInText: Indicates code words in text, database table names, folder names, filenames, file extensions, pathnames, dummy URLs, user input, and Twitter handles. For example; "In the QVScriptGenTool_0_7 64Bit\Analyzer folder there is a ZIP file called FolderTemplate.zip."

A block of code is set as follows:

```
Sales:
Load * INLINE [
Country, Sales
USA, 1000
UK, 940
Japan, 543
];
```

When we wish to draw your attention to a particular part of a code block, the relevant lines or items are set in bold:

```
Sales:
Load * INLINE [
Country, Sales
USA, 1000
UK, 940
Japan, 543
];
```

Any command-line input or output is written as follows:

```
C:\Program Files\QlikView\qv.exe
```

New terms and important words are shown in bold. Words that you see on the screen, for example, in menus or dialog boxes, appear in the text like this: "Click on the **Execution** tab."

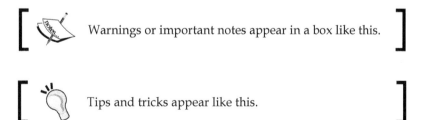

Warnings or important notes appear in a box like this.

Tips and tricks appear like this.

Get in touch

Feedback from our readers is always welcome.

General feedback: Email `feedback@packtpub.com`, and mention the book's title in the subject of your message. If you have questions about any aspect of this book, please email us at `questions@packtpub.com`.

Errata: Although we have taken every care to ensure the accuracy of our content, mistakes do happen. If you have found a mistake in this book we would be grateful if you would report this to us. Please visit, `http://www.packtpub.com/submit-errata`, selecting your book, clicking on the Errata Submission Form link, and entering the details.

Piracy: If you come across any illegal copies of our works in any form on the Internet, we would be grateful if you would provide us with the location address or website name. Please contact us at `copyright@packtpub.com` with a link to the material.

If you are interested in becoming an author: If there is a topic that you have expertise in and you are interested in either writing or contributing to a book, please visit `http://authors.packtpub.com`.

Reviews

Please leave a review. Once you have read and used this book, why not leave a review on the site that you purchased it from? Potential readers can then see and use your unbiased opinion to make purchase decisions, we at Packt can understand what you think about our products, and our authors can see your feedback on their book. Thank you!

For more information about Packt, please visit `packtpub.com`.

1
Performance Tuning and Scalability

"The way Moore's Law occurs in computing is really unprecedented in other walks of life. If the Boeing 747 obeyed Moore's Law, it would travel a million miles an hour, it would be shrunken down in size, and a trip to New York would cost about five dollars. Those enormous changes just aren't part of our everyday experience."

— Nathan Myhrvold, former Chief Technology Officer at Microsoft, 1995

The way Moore's Law has benefitted QlikView is really unprecedented amongst other BI systems.

QlikView began life in 1993 in Lund, Sweden. Originally titled "QuickView", they had to change things when they couldn't obtain a copyright on that name, and thus "QlikView" was born.

After years of steady growth, something really good happened for QlikView around 2005/2006 — the Intel x64 processors became the dominant processors in Windows servers. QlikView had, for a few years, supported the Itanium version of Windows; however, Itanium never became a dominant server processor. Intel and AMD started shipping the x64 processors in 2004 and, by 2006, most servers sold came with an x64 processor — whether the customer wanted 64-bit or not. Because the x64 processors could support either x86 or x64 versions of Windows, the customer didn't even have to know. Even those customers who purchased the x64 version of Windows 2003 didn't really know this because all of their x86 software would run just as well (perhaps with a few tweaks).

But x64 Windows was fantastic for QlikView! Any x86 process is limited to a maximum of 2 GB of physical memory. While 2 GB is quite a lot of memory, it wasn't enough to hold the volume of data that a true enterprise-class BI tool needed to handle. In fact, up until version 9 of QlikView, there was an in-built limitation of about 2 billion rows (actually, 2 to the power of 31) in the number of records that QlikView could load. On x86 processors, QlikView was really confined to the desktop.

x64 was a very different story. Early Intel implementations of x64 could address up to 64 GB of memory. More recent implementations allow up to 256 TB, although Windows Server 2012 can only address 4 TB. Memory is suddenly less of an obstacle to enterprise data volumes.

The other change that happened with processors was the introduction of multi-core architecture. At the time, it was common for a high-end server to come with 2 or 4 processors. Manufacturers came up with a method of putting multiple processors, or cores, on one physical processor. Nowadays, it is not unusual to see a server with 32 cores. High-end servers can have many, many more.

One of QlikView's design features that benefitted from this was that their calculation engine is multithreaded. That means that many of QlikView's calculations will execute across all available processor cores. Unlike many other applications, if you add more cores to your QlikView server, you will, in general, add more performance.

So, when it comes to looking at performance and scalability, very often, the first thing that people look at to improve things is to replace the hardware. This is valid of course! QlikView will almost always work better with newer, faster hardware. But before you go ripping out your racks, you should have a good idea of exactly what is going on with QlikView. Knowledge is power; it will help you tune your implementation to make the best use of the hardware that you already have in place.

The following are the topics we'll be covering in this chapter:

- Reviewing basic performance tuning techniques
- Generating test data
- Understanding how QlikView stores its data
- Looking at strategies to reduce the data size and to improve performance
- Using Direct Discovery
- Testing scalability with JMeter

Reviewing basic performance tuning techniques

There are many ways in which you may have learned to develop with QlikView. Some of them may have talked about performance and some may not have. Typically, you start to think about performance at a later stage when users start complaining about slow results from a QlikView application or when your QlikView server is regularly crashing because your applications are too big.

In this section, we are going to quickly review some basic performance tuning techniques that you should, hopefully, already be aware of. Then, we will start looking at how we can advance your knowledge to master level.

Removing unneeded data

Removing unneeded data might seem easy in theory, but sometimes it is not so easy to implement—especially when you need to negotiate with the business. However, the quickest way to improve the performance of a QlikView application is to remove data from it. If you can reduce your number of fact rows by half, you will vastly improve performance. The different options are discussed in the next sections.

Reducing the number of rows

The first option is to simply reduce the number of rows. Here we are interested in `Fact` or `Transaction` table rows—the largest tables in your data model. Reducing the number of dimension table rows rarely produces a significant performance improvement.

The easiest way to reduce the number of these rows is usually to limit the table by a value such as the date. It is always valuable to ask the question, "Do we really need all the transactions for the last 10 years?" If you can reduce this, say to 2 years, then the performance will improve significantly.

We can also choose to rethink the grain of the data—to what level of detail we hold the information. By aggregating the data to a higher level, we will often vastly reduce the number of rows.

Reducing the number of columns

The second option is to reduce the width of tables – again, especially `Fact` or `Transaction` tables. This means looking at fields that might be in your data model but do not actually get used in the application. One excellent way of establishing this is to use the **Document Analyzer** tool by Rob Wunderlich to examine your application (`http://robwunderlich.com/downloads`).

As well as other excellent uses, Rob's tool looks at multiple areas of an application to establish whether fields are being used or not. It will give you an option to view fields that are not in use and has a useful **DROP FIELD Statements** listbox from which you can copy the possible values. The following screenshot shows an example (from the default document downloadable from Rob's website):

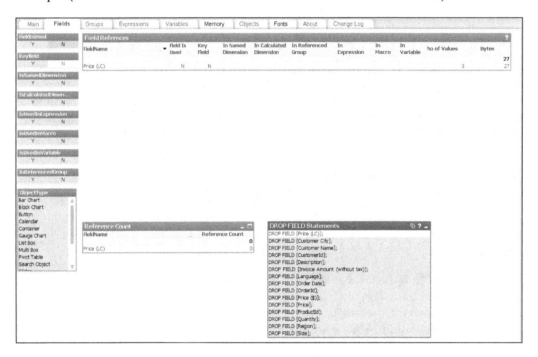

Adding these `DROP FIELD` statements into the end of a script makes it very easy to remove fields from your data model without having to dive into the middle of the script and try to remove them during the load – which could be painful.

There is a potential issue here; if you have users using collaboration objects – creating their own charts – then this tool will not detect that usage. However, if you use the `DROP FIELD` option, then it is straightforward to add a field back if a user complains that one of their charts is not working.

Of course, the best practice would be to take the pain and remove the fields from the script by either commenting them out or removing them completely from their load statements. This is more work, because you may break things and have to do additional debugging, but it will result in a better performing script.

Replacing text keys with numbers

Often, you will have a text value in a key field, for example, something like an account number that has alphanumeric characters. These are actually quite poor for performance compared to an integer value and should be replaced with numeric keys.

 There is some debate here about whether this makes a difference at all, but the effect is to do with the way the data is stored under the hood, which we will explore later. Generated numeric keys are stored slightly differently than text keys, which makes things work better.

The strategy is to leave the text value (account number) in the dimension table for use in display (if you need it!) and then use the AutoNumber function to generate a numeric value—also called a surrogate key—to associate the two tables.

For example, replace the following:

```
Account:
Load
    AccountId,
    AccountName,
    …
From Account.qvd (QVD);

Transaction:
Load
    TransactionId,
    AccountId,
    TransactionDate,
    …
From Transaction.qvd (QVD);
```

With the following:

```
Account:
Load
    AccountId,
```

```
    AutoNumber(AccountId) As Join_Account,
    AccountName,
    ...
From Account.qvd (QVD);

Transaction:
Load
    TransactionId,
    AutoNumber(AccountId) As Join_Account,
    TransactionDate,
    ...
From Transaction.qvd (QVD);
```

The `AccountId` field still exists in the `Account` table for display purposes, but the association is on the new numeric field, `Join_Account`.

We will see later that there is some more subtlety to this that we need to be aware of.

Resolving synthetic keys

A synthetic key, caused when tables are associated on two or more fields, actually results in a whole new data table of keys within the QlikView data model.

The following screenshot shows an example of a synthetic key using **Internal Table View** within **Table Viewer** in QlikView:

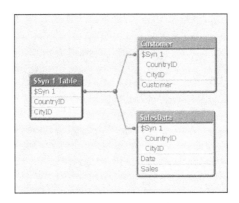

In general, it is recommended to remove synthetic keys from your data model by generating your own keys (for example, using `AutoNumber`):

```
Load
    AutoNumber(CountryID & '-' & CityID) As ClientID,
    Date,
```

```
    Sales
From Fact.qvd (qvd);
```

The following screenshot shows the same model with the synthetic key resolved using the `AutoNumber` method:

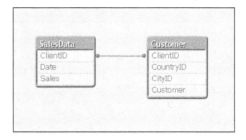

This removes additional data in the data tables (we'll cover more on this later in the chapter) and reduces the number of tables that queries have to traverse.

Reviewing the basics

So, with a basic understanding of QlikView development, you already have a good idea of how to improve performance. After reading the rest of this chapter, you will have enough information to seriously move forward and master this subject.

Generating test data

It is enormously useful to be able to quickly generate test data so that we can create QlikView applications and test different aspects of development and discover how different development methods work. By creating our own set of data, we can abstract problems away from the business issues that we are trying to solve because the data is not connected to those problems. Instead, we can resolve the technical issue underlying the business issue. Once we have resolved that issue, we will have built an understanding that allows us to more quickly resolve the real problems with the business data.

We might contemplate that if we are developers who only have access to a certain dataset, then we will only learn to solve the issues in that dataset. For true mastery, we need to be able to solve issues in many different scenarios, and the only way that we can do that is to generate our own test data to do that with.

Generating dimension values

Dimension tables will generally have lower numbers of records; there are a number of websites online that will generate this type of data for you.

The following screenshot demonstrates setting up a **Customer** extract in Mockaroo:

This allows us to create 1,000 customer records that we can include in our QlikView data model. The extract is in the CSV format, so it is quite straightforward to load into QlikView.

Generating fact table rows

While we might often abdicate the creation of test dimension tables to a third-party website like this, we should always try and generate the Fact table data ourselves.

A good way to do this is to simply generate rows with a combination of the AutoGenerate() and Rand() functions.

For even more advanced use cases, we can look at using statistical functions such as NORMINV to generate normal distributions. There is a good article on this written by Henric Cronström on *Qlik Design Blog* at http://community.qlik.com/blogs/qlikviewdesignblog/2013/08/26/monte-carlo-methods.

We should be aware of the AutoGenerate() function that will just simply generate empty rows of data. We can also use the Rand() function to generate a random number between 0 and 1 (it works both in charts and in the script). We can then multiply this value by another number to get various ranges of values.

In the following example, we load a previously generated set of dimension tables — Customer, Product, and Employee. We then generate a number of order header and line rows based on these dimensions, using random dates in a specified range.

First, we will load the Product table and derive a couple of mapping tables:

```
// Load my auto generated dimension files
Product:
LOAD ProductID,
     Product,
     CategoryID,
     SupplierID,
     Money#(CostPrice, '$#,##0.00', '.', ',') As CostPrice,
     Money#(SalesPrice, '$#,##0.00', '.', ',') As SalesPrice
FROM
Products.txt
(txt, utf8, embedded labels, delimiter is '\t', msq);


Product_Cost_Map:
Mapping Load
   ProductID,
   Num(CostPrice)
Resident Product;

Product_Price_Map:
Mapping Load
```

```
        ProductID,
        Num(SalesPrice)
    Resident Product;
```

Now load the other dimension tables:

```
    Customer:
    LOAD CustomerID,
         Customer,
         City,
         Country,
         Region,
         Longitude,
         Latitude,
         Geocoordinates
    FROM
    Customers.txt
    (txt, codepage is 1252, embedded labels, delimiter is '\t', msq);

    Employee:
    LOAD EmployeeID,
         Employee,
         Grade,
         SalesUnit
    FROM
    Employees.txt
    (txt, codepage is 1252, embedded labels, delimiter is '\t', msq)
    Where Match(Grade, 0, 1, 2, 3);  // Sales people
```

We will store the record counts from each table in variables:

```
    // Count the ID records in each table
    Let vCustCount=FieldValueCount('CustomerID');
    Let vProdCount=FieldValueCount('ProductID');
    Let vEmpCount=FieldValueCount('EmployeeID');
```

We now generate some date ranges to use in the data calculation algorithm:

```
    // Work out the days
    Let vStartYear=2009;        // Arbitrary - change if wanted
    Let vEndYear=Year(Now()); // Generate up to date data
    // Starting the date in April to allow
    // offset year testing
    Let vStartDate=Floor(MakeDate($(vStartYear),4,1));
    Let vEndDate=Floor(MakeDate($(vEndYear),3,31));
    Let vNumDays=vEndDate-vStartDate+1;
```

Run a number of iterations to generate data. By editing the number of iterations, we
can increase or decrease the amount of data generated:

```
// Create a loop of 10000 iterations
For i=1 to 10000

    // "A" type records are for any date/time

    // Grab a random employee and customer
    Let vRnd = Floor(Rand() * $(vEmpCount));
    Let vEID = Peek('EmployeeID', $(vRnd), 'Employee');
    Let vRnd = Floor(Rand() * $(vCustCount));
    Let vCID = Peek('CustomerID', $(vRnd), 'Customer');

    // Create a date for any Time of Day  9-5
    Let vOrderDate = $(vStartDate) + Floor(Rand() * $(vNumDays)) +
((9/24) + (Rand()/3));

    // Calculate a random freight amount
    Let vFreight = Round(Rand() * 100, 0.01);

    // Create the header record
    OrderHeader:
    Load
        'A' & $(i)      As OrderID,
        $(vOrderDate)   As OrderDate,
        $(vCID)         As CustomerID,
        $(vEID)         As EmployeeID,
        $(vFreight)     As Freight
    AutoGenerate(1);

    // Generate Order Lines

    // This factor allows us to generate a different number of
    // lines depending on the day of the week
    Let vWeekDay = Num(WeekDay($(vOrderDate)));
```

```
        Let vDateFactor = Pow(2,$(vWeekDay))*(1-(Year(Now())-
Year($(vOrderDate)))*0.05);

        // Calculate the random number of lines
        Let vPCount = Floor(Rand() * $(vDateFactor)) + 1;

        For L=1 to $(vPCount)
            // Calculate random values
            Let vQty = Floor(Rand() * (50+$(vDateFactor))) + 1;
            Let vRnd = Floor(Rand() * $(vProdCount));
            Let vPID = Peek('ProductID', $(vRnd), 'Product');
            Let vCost = ApplyMap('Product_Cost_Map', $(vPID), 1);
            Let vPrice = ApplyMap('Product_Price_Map', $(vPID), 1);

            OrderLine:
            Load
                'A' & $(i)        As OrderID,
                $(L)           As LineNo,
                $(vPID)           As ProductID,
                $(vQty)           As Quantity,
                $(vPrice)        As SalesPrice,
                $(vCost)        As SalesCost,
                $(vQty)*$(vPrice) As LineValue,
                $(vQty)*$(vCost) As LineCost
            AutoGenerate(1);

        Next

        // "B" type records are for summer peak

        // Summer Peak - Generate additional records for summer
        // months to simulate a peak trading period
        Let vY = Year($(vOrderDate));
        Let vM = Floor(Rand()*2)+7;
        Let vD = Day($(vOrderDate));
        Let vOrderDate = Floor(MakeDate($(vY),$(vM),$(vD))) + ((9/24) +
(Rand()/3));

        if Rand() > 0.8 Then

            // Grab a random employee and customer
            Let vRnd = Floor(Rand() * $(vEmpCount));
            Let vEID = Peek('EmployeeID', $(vRnd), 'Employee');
            Let vRnd = Floor(Rand() * $(vCustCount));
```

```
Let vCID = Peek('CustomerID', $(vRnd), 'Customer');

// Calculate a random freight amount
Let vFreight = Round(Rand() * 100, 0.01);
// Create the header record
OrderHeader:
Load
    'B' & $(i)        As OrderID,
    $(vOrderDate)     As OrderDate,
    $(vCID)          As CustomerID,
    $(vEID)          As EmployeeID,
    $(vFreight)      As Freight
AutoGenerate(1);

// Generate Order Lines

// This factor allows us to generate a different number of
// lines depending on the day of the week
Let vWeekDay = Num(WeekDay($(vOrderDate)));
Let vDateFactor = Pow(2,$(vWeekDay))*(1-(Year(Now())-
Year($(vOrderDate)))*0.05);

// Calculate the random number of lines
Let vPCount = Floor(Rand() * $(vDateFactor)) + 1;

For L=1 to $(vPCount)

    // Calculate random values
    Let vQty = Floor(Rand() * (50+$(vDateFactor))) + 1;
    Let vRnd = Floor(Rand() * $(vProdCount));
    Let vPID = Peek('ProductID', $(vRnd), 'Product');
    Let vCost = ApplyMap('Product_Cost_Map', $(vPID), 1);
    Let vPrice = ApplyMap('Product_Price_Map', $(vPID), 1);

    OrderLine:
    Load
        'B' & $(i)        As OrderID,
        $(L)            As LineNo,
        $(vPID)          As ProductID,
        $(vQty)          As Quantity,
        $(vPrice)        As SalesPrice,
        $(vCost)         As SalesCost,
        $(vQty)*$(vPrice) As LineValue,
        $(vQty)*$(vCost) As LineCost
    AutoGenerate(1);
```

```
      Next

    End if
Next

// Store the Generated Data to QVD
Store OrderHeader into OrderHeader.qvd;
Store OrderLine into OrderLine.qvd;
```

Understanding how QlikView stores its data

QlikView is really good at storing data. It operates on data in memory, so being able to store a lot of data in a relatively small amount of memory gives the product a great advantage—especially as Moore's Law continues to give us bigger and bigger servers.

Understanding how QlikView stores its data is fundamental in mastering QlikView development. Writing load script with this understanding will allow you to load data in the most efficient way so that you can create the best performing applications. Your users will love you.

A great primer

A great primer on how QlikView stores its data is available on *Qlik Design Blog*, written by Henric Cronström (http://community.qlik.com/blogs/qlikviewdesignblog/2012/11/20/symbol-tables-and-bit-stuffed-pointers).

 Henric joined QlikView in 1994, so he knows quite a bit about exactly how it works.

Looking at things from a simple level

From a simple level, consider the following small table:

First name	Surname	Country
John	Smith	USA
Jane	Smith	USA
John	Doe	Canada

For the preceding table, QlikView will create three symbol tables like the following:

Index	Value
1010	John
1011	Jane

Index	Value
1110	Smith
1111	Doe

Index	Value
110	USA
111	Canada

And the data table will look like the following:

First name	Surname	Country
1010	1110	110
1011	1110	110
1010	1111	111

This set of tables will take up less space than the original data table for the following three reasons:

- The binary indexes are bit-stuffed in the data table—they only take up as much space as needed.

- The binary index, even though repeated, will take up less space than the text values. The Unicode text just for "USA" takes up several bytes—the binary index takes less space than that.

- Each, larger, text value is only stored once in the symbol tables.

So, to summarize, each field in the data model will be stored in a symbol table (unless, as we will see later, it is a sequential integer value) that contains the unique values and an index value. Every table that you create in the script—including any synthetic key tables—will be represented as a data table containing just the index pointers.

 Because the data table indexes are bit-stuffed, and because data is stored in bytes, adding another bit or two to the indexes may not actually increase the overall width of a data table record.

Exporting the memory statistics for a document

To help us understand what is going on in a particular QlikView document, we can export details about where all the memory is being used. This export file will tell us how much memory is being used by each field in the symbol tables, the data tables, chart objects, and so on.

Perform the following steps to export the memory statistics for a document:

1. To export the memory statistics, you need to open **Document Properties** from the **Settings** menu (*Ctrl + Alt + D*). On the **General** tab, click on the **Memory Statistics** button, as shown in the following screenshot:

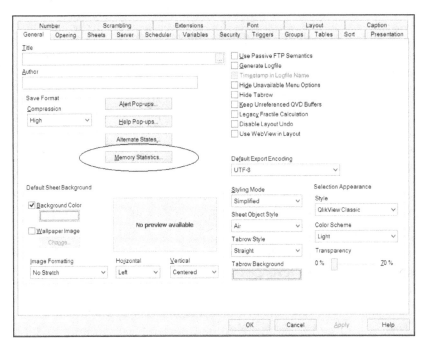

2. After you click on the button, you will be prompted to enter file information. Once you have entered the path and filename, the file will be exported. It is a tab-delimited data file:

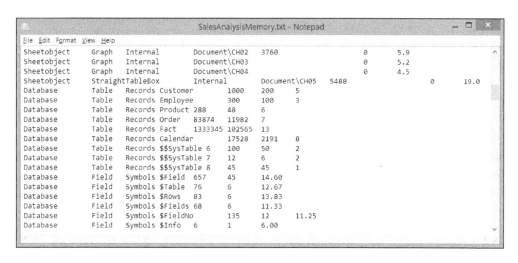

3. The easiest way to analyze this file is to import it into a new QlikView document:

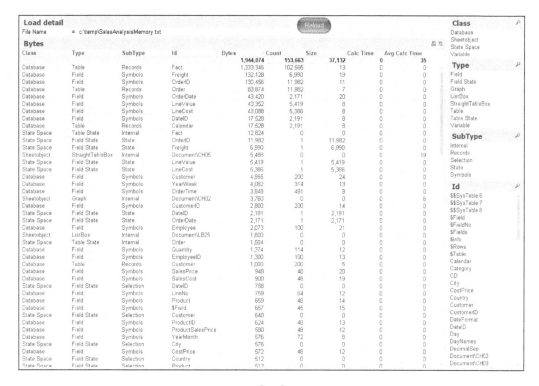

We can now see exactly how much space our data is taking up in the symbol tables and in the data tables. We can also look at chart calculation performance to see whether there are long running calculations that we need to tune. Analyzing this data will allow us to make valuable decisions about where we can improve performance in our QlikView document.

One thing that we need to be cognizant of is that the memory usage and calculation time of charts will only be available if that chart has actually been opened. The calculation time of the charts may also not be accurate as it will usually only be correct if the chart has just been opened for the first time—subsequent openings and changes of selection will most probably be calculated from the cache, and a cache execution should execute a lot quicker than a non-cached execution. Other objects may also use similar expressions, and these will therefore already be cached. We can turn the cache off—although only for testing purposes, as it can really kill performance.

Strategies to reduce the data size and improve performance

Using some of the test data that we have generated, or any other data that you might want, we can discover more about how QlikView handles different scenarios. Understanding these different situations will give you real mastery over data load optimization.

Optimizing field values and keys

To begin with, let's see what happens when we load two largish tables that are connected by a key. So, let's ignore the dimension tables and load the order data using a script like the following:

```
Order:
LOAD OrderID,
     OrderDate,
     CustomerID,
     EmployeeID,
     Freight
FROM
[..\Scripts\OrderHeader.qvd]
(qvd);
```

```
OrderLine:
LOAD OrderID,
     LineNo,
     ProductID,
     Quantity,
     SalesPrice,
     SalesCost,
     LineValue,
     LineCost
FROM
[..\Scripts\OrderLine.qvd]
(qvd);
```

The preceding script will result in a database memory profile that looks like the following. In the following screenshot, Database has been selected for Class:

Class	Type	SubType	Id	Bytes	/ Count
				1,710,383	**156,919**
Database	Table	Records	OrderLine	923,085	102,565
Database	Field	Symbols	OrderDate	346,140	11,982
Database	Field	Symbols	Freight	132,128	6,990
Database	Field	Symbols	OrderID	130,456	11,982
Database	Table	Records	Order	83,874	11,982
Database	Field	Symbols	LineValue	43,352	5,419
Database	Field	Symbols	LineCost	43,088	5,386
Database	Field	Symbols	CustomerID	2,800	200
Database	Field	Symbols	Quantity	1,374	114
Database	Field	Symbols	SalesPrice	948	48
Database	Field	Symbols	SalesCost	900	48
Database	Field	Symbols	LineNo	759	64
Database	Field	Symbols	ProductID	624	48
Database	Field	Symbols	EmployeeID	481	37
Database	Field	Symbols	$Field	174	12
Database	Field	Symbols	$FieldNo	88	8
Database	Field	Symbols	$Rows	31	2
Database	Field	Symbols	$Table	26	2
Database	Field	Symbols	$Fields	22	2
Database	Table	Records	$$SysTable 2	13	13
Database	Table	Records	$$SysTable 4	12	12
Database	Field	Symbols	$Info	6	1
Database	Table	Records	$$SysTable 3	2	2

There are some interesting readings in this table. For example, we can see that when the main data table—OrderLine—is stored with just its pointer records, it takes up just 923,085 bytes for 102,565 records. That is an average of only 9 bytes per record. This shows the space benefit of the bit-stuffed pointer mechanism as described in Henric's blog post.

The largest individual symbol table is the `OrderDate` field. This is very typical of a `TimeStamp` field, which will often be highly unique, have long decimal values, and have the `Dual` text value, and so often takes up a lot of memory — 28 bytes per value.

The number part of a `TimeStamp` field contains an integer representing the date (number of days since 30th December 1899) and a decimal representing the time. So, let's see what happens with this field if we turn it into just an integer — a common strategy with these fields as the time portion may not be important:

```
Order:
LOAD OrderID,
     Floor(OrderDate) As DateID,
     . . .
```

This changes things considerably:

Class	Type	SubType	Id	Bytes	Count
				1,381,608	147,108
Database	Table	Records	OrderLine	923,085	102,565
Database	Field	Symbols	Freight	132,128	6,990
Database	Field	Symbols	OrderID	130,456	11,982
Database	Table	Records	Order	83,874	11,982
Database	Field	Symbols	LineValue	43,352	5,419
Database	Field	Symbols	LineCost	43,088	5,386
Database	Field	Symbols	DateID	17,368	2,171
Database	Field	Symbols	CustomerID	2,800	200

The number of unique values has been vastly reduced, because the highly unique date and time values have been replaced with a much lower cardinality (2171) date integer, and the amount of memory consumed is also vastly reduced as the integer values are only taking 8 bytes instead of the 28 being taken by each value of the `TimeStamp` field.

The next field that we will pay attention to is `OrderID`. This is the key field, and key fields are always worth examining to see whether they can be improved. In our test data, the `OrderID` field is alphanumeric — this is not uncommon for such data. Alphanumeric data will tend to take up more space than numeric data, so it is a good idea to convert it to integers using the `AutoNumber` function.

`AutoNumber` accepts a text value and will return a sequential integer. If you pass the same text value, it will return the same integer. This is a great way of transforming alphanumeric ID values into integers. The code will look like the following:

```
Order:
LOAD AutoNumber(OrderID) As OrderID,
     Floor(OrderDate) As DateID,
     . . .


OrderLine:
LOAD AutoNumber(OrderID) As OrderID,
     LineNo,
     . . .
```

This will result in a memory profile like the following:

Database	Field	Symbols	$Table	26	2
Database	Field	Symbols	$Fields	22	2
Database	Table	Records	$$SysTable 2	13	13
Database	Table	Records	$$SysTable 4	12	12
Database	Field	Symbols	$Info	6	1
Database	Table	Records	$$SysTable 3	2	2
Database	Field	Symbols	OrderID	0	11,982

The `OrderID` field is now showing as having 0 bytes! This is quite interesting because what QlikView does with a field containing sequential integers is that it does not bother to store the value in the symbol table at all; it just uses the value as the pointer in the data table. This is a great design feature and gives us a good strategy for reducing data sizes.

We could do the same thing with the `CustomerID` and `EmployeeID` fields:

```
Order:
LOAD AutoNumber(OrderID) As OrderID,
     Floor(OrderDate) As DateID,
     AutoNumber(CustomerID) As CustomerID,
     AutoNumber(EmployeeID) As EmployeeID,
     . . .
```

That has a very interesting effect on the memory profile:

Class	Type	SubType	Id	Bytes	Count
				1,345,623	147,108
Database	Table	Records	OrderLine	923,085	102,565
Database	Field	Symbols	Freight	132,128	6,990
Database	Field	Symbols	OrderID	95,856	11,982
Database	Table	Records	Order	83,874	11,982
Database	Field	Symbols	LineValue	43,352	5,419
Database	Field	Symbols	LineCost	43,088	5,386
Database	Field	Symbols	DateID	17,368	2,171
Database	Field	Symbols	CustomerID	1,600	200
Database	Field	Symbols	Quantity	1,374	114
Database	Field	Symbols	SalesPrice	948	48
Database	Field	Symbols	SalesCost	900	48
Database	Field	Symbols	LineNo	759	64
Database	Field	Symbols	ProductID	624	48
Database	Field	Symbols	EmployeeID	296	37
Database	Field	Symbols	$Field	171	12

Our `OrderID` field is now back in the `Symbols` table. The other two tables are still there too. So what has gone wrong?

Because we have simply used the `AutoNumber` function across each field, now none of them are perfectly sequential integers and so do not benefit from the design feature. But we can do something about this because the `AutoNumber` function accepts a second parameter — an ID — to identify different ranges of counters. So, we can rejig the script in the following manner:

```
Order:
LOAD AutoNumber(OrderID, 'Order') As OrderID,
     Floor(OrderDate) As DateID,
     AutoNumber(CustomerID, 'Customer') As CustomerID,
     AutoNumber(EmployeeID, 'Employee') As EmployeeID,
     ...


OrderLine:
LOAD AutoNumber(OrderID, 'Order') As OrderID,
     LineNo,
     ...
```

This should give us the following result:

Database	Table	Records	$$SysTable 2	13	13
Database	Table	Records	$$SysTable 4	12	12
Database	Field	Symbols	$Info	6	1
Database	Table	Records	$$SysTable 3	2	2
Database	Field	Symbols	CustomerID	0	200
Database	Field	Symbols	EmployeeID	0	37
Database	Field	Symbols	OrderID	0	11,982

This is something that you should consider for all key values, especially from a modeling best practice point of view. There are instances when you want to retain the ID value for display or search purposes. In that case, a copy of the value should be kept as a field in a dimension table and the AutoNumber function used on the key value.

 It is worth noting that it is often good to be able to see the key associations — or lack of associations — between two tables, especially when troubleshooting data issues. Because AutoNumber obfuscates the values, it makes that debugging a bit harder. Therefore, it can be a good idea to leave the application of AutoNumber until later on in the development cycle, when you are more certain of the data sources.

Optimizing data by removing keys using ApplyMap

For this example, we will use some of the associated dimension tables — Category and Product. These are loaded in the following manner:

```
Category:
LOAD CategoryID,
     Category
FROM
[..\Scripts\Categories.txt]
(txt, codepage is 1252, embedded labels, delimiter is '\t', msq);

Product:
LOAD ProductID,
     Product,
     CategoryID,
     SupplierID,
     CostPrice,
     SalesPrice
FROM
[..\Scripts\Products.txt]
(txt, codepage is 1252, embedded labels, delimiter is '\t', msq);
```

This has a small memory profile:

Class	Type	SubType	Id	Bytes	Count
				3,160	302
Database	Field	Symbols	Product	659	48
Database	Field	Symbols	ProductID	624	48
Database	Field	Symbols	SalesPrice	580	48
Database	Field	Symbols	CostPrice	572	48
Database	Table	Records	Product	192	48
Database	Field	Symbols	SupplierID	140	10
Database	Field	Symbols	$Field	105	7
Database	Field	Symbols	Category	67	5
Database	Field	Symbols	$FieldNo	66	6
Database	Field	Symbols	CategoryID	55	5
Database	Field	Symbols	$Table	27	2
Database	Field	Symbols	$Rows	23	2
Database	Field	Symbols	$Fields	22	2
Database	Table	Records	$$SysTable 2	8	8
Database	Table	Records	$$SysTable 4	7	7
Database	Field	Symbols	$Info	6	1
Database	Table	Records	Category	5	5
Database	Table	Records	$$SysTable 3	2	2

The best way to improve the performance of these tables is to remove the `CategoryID` field by moving the `Category` value into the `Product` table. When we have small lookup tables like this, we should always consider using `ApplyMap`:

```
Category_Map:
Mapping
LOAD CategoryID,
     Category
FROM
[..\Scripts\Categories.txt]
(txt, codepage is 1252, embedded labels, delimiter is '\t', msq);

Product:
LOAD ProductID,
     Product,
     //CategoryID,
     ApplyMap('Category_Map', CategoryID, 'Other') As Category,
     SupplierID,
     CostPrice,
     SalesPrice
FROM
[..\Scripts\Products.txt]
(txt, codepage is 1252, embedded labels, delimiter is '\t', msq);
```

By removing the `Symbols` table and the entry in the data table, we have reduced the amount of memory used. More importantly, we have reduced the number of joins required to answer queries based on the `Category` table:

Class	Type	SubType	Id	Bytes	Count
				3,044	284
Database	Field	Symbols	Product	659	48
Database	Field	Symbols	ProductID	624	48
Database	Field	Symbols	SalesPrice	580	48
Database	Field	Symbols	CostPrice	572	48
Database	Table	Records	Product	192	48
Database	Field	Symbols	SupplierID	140	10
Database	Field	Symbols	$Field	89	6
Database	Field	Symbols	Category	67	5

Optimizing performance by removing keys by joining tables

If the associated dimension table has more than two fields, it can still have its data moved into the primary dimension table by loading multiple mapping tables; this is useful if there is a possibility of many-to-many joins. You do have to consider, however, that this does make the script a little more complicated and, in many circumstances, it is a better idea to simply join the tables.

For example, suppose that we have the previously mentioned `Product` table and an associated `Supplier` table that is 3,643 bytes:

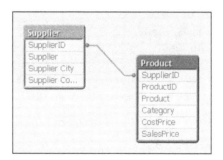

By joining the `Supplier` table to the `Product` table and then dropping `SupplierID`, we might reduce this down to, say, 3,499 bytes, but more importantly, we improve the query performance:

```
Join (Product)
LOAD SupplierID,
```

```
Company As Supplier,
...

Drop Field SupplierID;
```

Optimizing memory by removing low cardinality fields

Joining tables together is not always the best approach from a memory point of view. It could be possible to attempt to create the ultimate joined table model of just having one table containing all values. This will work, and query performance should, in theory, be quite fast. However, the way QlikView works is the wider and longer the table you create, the wider and longer the underlying pointer data table will be. Let's consider an example.

Quite often, there will be a number of associated fields in a fact table that have a lower cardinality (smaller number of distinct values) than the main keys in the fact table. A quite common example is having date parts within the fact table. In that case, it can actually be a good idea to remove these values from the fact table and link them via a shared key. So, for example, consider we have an Order table loaded in the following manner:

```
Order:
LOAD AutoNumber(OrderID, 'Order') As OrderID,
     Floor(OrderDate) As DateID,
     Year(OrderDate) As Year,
     Month(OrderDate) As Month,
     Day(OrderDate) As Day,
     Date(MonthStart(OrderDate), 'YYYY-MM') As YearMonth,
     AutoNumber(CustomerID, 'Customer') As CustomerID,
     AutoNumber(EmployeeID, 'Employee') As EmployeeID,
     Freight
FROM
[..\Scripts\OrderHeader.qvd]
(qvd);
```

This will give a memory profile like the following:

Class	Type	SubType	Id	Bytes	Count
				258,644	33,524
Database	Field	Symbols	Freight	132,128	6,990
Database	Table	Records	Order	107,838	11,982
Database	Field	Symbols	DateID	17,368	2,171
Database	Field	Symbols	YearMonth	576	72
Database	Field	Symbols	Day	248	31
Database	Field	Symbols	Month	156	12
Database	Field	Symbols	$Field	115	9
Database	Field	Symbols	$FieldNo	99	9
Database	Field	Symbols	Year	54	6

We can see the values for Year, Month, and Day have a very low count. It is worth noting here that Year takes up a lot less space than Month or Day; this is because Year is just an integer and the others are Dual values that have text as well as numbers.

Let's modify the script to have the date fields in a different table in the following manner:

```
Order:
LOAD AutoNumber(OrderID, 'Order') As OrderID,
     Floor(OrderDate) As DateID,
     AutoNumber(CustomerID, 'Customer') As CustomerID,
     AutoNumber(EmployeeID, 'Employee') As EmployeeID,
     Freight
FROM
[..\Scripts\OrderHeader.qvd]
(qvd);

Calendar:
Load Distinct
     DateID,
     Date(DateID) As Date,
     Year(DateID) As Year,
     Month(DateID) As Month,
     Day(DateID) As Day,
     Date(MonthStart(DateID), 'YYYY-MM') As YearMonth
Resident
   Order;
```

We can see that there is a difference in the memory profile:

Class	Type	SubType	Id	Bytes	/ Count
				243,344	**35,695**
Database	Field	Symbols	Freight	132,128	6,990
Database	Table	Records	Order	83,874	11,982
Database	Field	Symbols	DateID	17,368	2,171
Database	Table	Records	Calendar	8,684	2,171
Database	Field	Symbols	YearMonth	576	72
Database	Field	Symbols	Day	248	31
Database	Field	Symbols	Month	156	12
Database	Field	Symbols	$Field	115	9
Database	Field	Symbols	$FieldNo	55	5
Database	Field	Symbols	Year	48	6

We have all the same symbol table values that we had before with the same memory. We do have a new data table for Calendar, but it is only quite small because there are only a small number of values. We have, however, made a dent in the size of the Order table because we have removed pointers from it. This effect will be increased as the number of rows increases in the Order table, whereas the number of rows in the Calendar table will not increase significantly over time.

Of course, because the data is now in two tables, there will be a potential downside in that joins will need to be made between the tables to answer queries. However, we should always prefer to have a smaller memory footprint. But how can we tell if there was a difference in performance?

Testing chart performance for different load options

As well as information about memory use in each data table and symbol table, we can recall that the **Memory Statistics** option will also export information about charts—both memory use and calculation time. This means that we can create a chart, especially one with multiple dimensions and expressions, and see how long the chart takes to calculate for different scenarios.

Let's load the Order Header and Order Line data with the Calendar information loaded inline (as in the first part of the last example) in the following manner:

```
Order:
LOAD AutoNumber(OrderID, 'Order') As OrderID,
     Floor(OrderDate) As DateID,
     Year(OrderDate) As Year,
     Month(OrderDate) As Month,
```

```
        Day(OrderDate) As Day,
        Date(MonthStart(OrderDate), 'YYYY-MM') As YearMonth,
        AutoNumber(CustomerID, 'Customer') As CustomerID,
        AutoNumber(EmployeeID, 'Employee') As EmployeeID,
        Freight
FROM
[..\Scripts\OrderHeader.qvd]
(qvd);



OrderLine:
LOAD AutoNumber(OrderID, 'Order') As OrderID,
     LineNo,
     ProductID,
     Quantity,
     SalesPrice,
     SalesCost,
     LineValue,
     LineCost
FROM
[..\Scripts\OrderLine.qvd]
(qvd);
```

Now we can add a chart to the document with several dimensions and expressions like this:

YearMonth	CustomerID	Sales $	Cost $	Margin $	Margin %	Cum. Sales $	# Orders	Product 101	Prod 102-106
		288,715,597.09	224,772,646.40	63,942,950.69	22.15%	0.00	11,982	2,209	10,782
2009-01	3	7,327.89	5,139.47	2,188.42	29.86%	7,327.89	1	0	0
2009-01	4	7,461.18	5,747.95	1,713.23	22.96%	14,789.07	1	0	0
2009-01	5	31,006.99	22,125.30	8,881.69	28.64%	45,796.06	1	0	1
2009-01	6	834.17	571.97	262.20	31.43%	46,630.23	1	0	0
2009-01	8	36,277.85	28,574.83	7,703.02	21.23%	82,908.08	2	0	1
2009-01	11	9,503.71	7,827.08	1,676.63	17.64%	92,411.79	1	0	1
2009-01	14	27,987.96	21,175.78	6,812.18	24.34%	120,399.75	2	0	1
2009-01	15	1,985.20	1,689.20	296.00	14.91%	122,384.95	1	0	0
2009-01	18	211,142.18	165,958.56	45,183.62	21.40%	333,527.13	2	2	6
2009-01	20	1,248.00	883.08	364.92	29.24%	334,775.13	1	0	0
2009-01	22	12,054.08	9,593.32	2,460.76	20.41%	346,829.21	2	1	1
2009-01	24	561.47	550.16	11.31	2.01%	347,390.68	2	0	0
2009-01	25	155.64	104.79	50.85	32.67%	347,546.32	1	0	0
2009-01	26	39,663.59	28,990.80	10,672.79	26.91%	387,209.91	3	0	1
2009-01	27	5,147.72	4,169.82	977.90	19.00%	392,357.63	1	0	1
2009-01	28	4,346.76	3,632.64	714.12	16.43%	396,704.39	1	1	0
2009-01	32	51,051.31	36,570.48	14,480.83	28.37%	447,755.70	1	0	0
2009-01	33	11,036.71	7,828.78	3,207.93	29.07%	458,792.41	1	0	2
2009-01	34	9,400.57	7,083.08	2,317.49	24.65%	468,192.98	2	0	0
2009-01	35	92,789.84	73,302.02	19,487.82	21.00%	560,982.82	2	0	4
2009-01	36	3,593.34	2,658.95	934.39	26.00%	564,576.16	1	0	0
2009-01	39	34,587.67	26,552.92	8,034.75	23.23%	599,163.83	3	1	5
2009-01	40	12,406.63	9,591.38	2,816.25	22.69%	611,570.46	1	0	0
2009-01	41	35,689.54	27,310.42	8,379.12	23.48%	647,260.00	1	0	1
2009-01	43	3,780.12	3,116.78	663.34	17.55%	651,040.12	1	0	0
2009-01	45	92,960.09	73,108.00	19,852.09	21.36%	744,000.21	2	0	5

We have used `YearMonth` and `CustomerID` as dimensions. This is deliberate because these two fields will be in separate tables once we move the calendar fields into a separate table.

The expressions that we have used are shown in the following table:

Expression Label	Expression
Sales $	Sum(LineValue)
Sales $ Color	ColorMix1(Sum(LineValue)/Max(total Aggr(Sum(LineValue), YearMonth, CustomerID)), White(), ARGB(255, 0, 128, 255))
Cost $	Sum(LineCost)
Margin $	Sum(LineValue)-Sum(LineCost)
Margin %	(Sum(LineValue)-Sum(LineCost))/Sum(LineValue)
Cum. Sales $	RangeSum(Above(Sum(LineValue),0,RowNo()))
# Orders	Count(DISTINCT OrderID)
Product 101	Sum(If(ProductID=101,1,0))
Product 102-106	Sum(If(Match(ProductID,102,103,104,105,106), 1, 0))

Turning the cache off

The cache in QlikView is enormously important. Calculations and selections are cached as you work with a QlikView document. The next time you open a chart with the same selections, the chart will not be recalculated; you will get the cached answer instead. This really speeds up QlikView performance. Even within a chart, you might have multiple expressions using the same calculation (such as dividing two expressions by each other to obtain a ratio) — the results will make use of caching.

This caching is really useful for a working document, but a pain if we want to gather statistics on one or more charts. With the cache on, we need to close a document and the QlikView desktop, reopen the document in a new QlikView instance, and open the chart. To help us test the chart performance, it can therefore be a good idea to turn off the cache.

 Note that you need to be very careful with this dialog as you could break things in your QlikView installation. Turning off the cache is not recommended for normal use of the QlikView desktop as it can seriously interfere with the performance of QlikView. Turning off the cache to gather accurate statistics on chart performance is pretty much the only use case that one might ever come across for turning off the cache. There is a reason why it is a hidden setting!

Examining the chart calculation time for different scenarios

Now that the cache is turned off, we can open our chart and it will always calculate at the maximum time. We can then export the memory information as usual and load it into another copy of QlikView (here, the **Class** of **Sheetobject** is selected):

Class	Type	SubType	Id	Bytes	Count	Calc Time	Avg Calc Time
				2,033,840	0	265	265
Sheetobject	StraightTableBox	Internal	Document\CH01	2,033,840	0	265	265

What we could do now is make some selections and save them as bookmarks. By closing the QlikView desktop client and then reopening it, and then opening the document and running through the bookmarks, we can export the memory file and create a calculation for **Avg Calc Time**. Because there is no cache involved, this should be a valid representation.

Now, we can comment out the inline calendar and create the `Calendar` table (as we did in a previous exercise):

```
Order:
LOAD AutoNumber(OrderID, 'Order') As OrderID,
     Floor(OrderDate) As DateID,
//     Year(OrderDate) As Year,
//     Month(OrderDate) As Month,
//     Day(OrderDate) As Day,
//     Date(MonthStart(OrderDate), 'YYYY-MM') As YearMonth,
     AutoNumber(CustomerID, 'Customer') As CustomerID,
     AutoNumber(EmployeeID, 'Employee') As EmployeeID,
     Freight
FROM
[..\Scripts\OrderHeader.qvd]
(qvd);


OrderLine:
//Left Join (Order)
LOAD AutoNumber(OrderID, 'Order') As OrderID,
     LineNo,
     ProductID,
     Quantity,
     SalesPrice,
     SalesCost,
     LineValue,
     LineCost
```

```
FROM
[..\Scripts\OrderLine.qvd]
(qvd);

//exit Script;

Calendar:
Load Distinct
    DateID,
     Year(DateID) As Year,
     Month(DateID) As Month,
     Day(DateID) As Day,
     Date(MonthStart(DateID), 'YYYY-MM') As YearMonth
Resident
    Order;
```

For the dataset size that we are using, we should see no difference in calculation time between the two data structures. As previously established, the second option has a smaller in-memory data size, so that would always be the preferred option.

Optimizing performance by creating counter fields

For many years, it has been a well-established fact among QlikView consultants that a Count() function with a Distinct clause is a very expensive calculation. Over the years, I have heard that Count can be up to 1000 times more expensive than Sum. Actually, since about Version 9 of QlikView, this is no longer true, and the Count function is a lot more efficient.

 See Henric Cronström's blog entry at http://community. qlik.com/blogs/qlikviewdesignblog/2013/10/22/ a-myth-about-countdistinct for more information.

Count is still a more expensive operation, and the recommended solution is to create a counter field in the table that you wish to count, which has a value of 1. You can then sum this counter field to get the count of rows. This field can also be useful in advanced expressions like **Set Analysis**.

Using the same dataset as in the previous example, if we create a chart using similar dimensions (YearMonth and CustomerID) and the same expression for Order # as done previously:

```
Count(Distinct OrderID)
```

This gives us a chart like the following:

YearMonth	CustomerID	# Orders (Sum)
		11,982
2009-01	3	1
2009-01	4	1
2009-01	5	1
2009-01	6	1
2009-01	8	2
2009-01	11	1
2009-01	14	2
2009-01	15	1
2009-01	18	2
2009-01	20	1
2009-01	22	2
2009-01	24	2
2009-01	25	1
2009-01	26	3
2009-01	27	1
2009-01	28	1
2009-01	32	1
2009-01	33	1
2009-01	34	2
2009-01	35	2
2009-01	36	1
2009-01	39	3
2009-01	40	1
2009-01	41	1
2009-01	43	1
2009-01	45	2

After running through the same bookmarks that we created earlier, we get a set of results like the following:

Class	Type	SubType	Id	Bytes	Count	Calc Time	Avg Calc Time
				301,168	0	31	24
Sheetobject	StraightTableBox	Internal	Document\CH02	301,168	0	31	24

So, now we modify the `Order` table load as follows:

```
Order:
LOAD AutoNumber(OrderID, 'Order') As OrderID,
    1 As OrderCounter,
    Floor(OrderDate) As DateID,
    AutoNumber(CustomerID, 'Customer') As CustomerID,
    AutoNumber(EmployeeID, 'Employee') As EmployeeID,
    Freight
FROM
[..\Scripts\OrderHeader.qvd]
(qvd);
```

Once we reload, we can modify the expression for `Order #` to the following:

```
Sum(OrderCounter)
```

We close down the document, reopen it, and run through the bookmarks again. This is an example result:

Class	Type	SubType	Id	Bytes	Count	Calc Time	Avg Calc Time
				301,104	0	16	9
Sheetobject	StraightTableBox	Internal	Document\CH02	301,104	0	16	9

And yes, we do see that there is an improvement in calculation time — it appears to be a factor of about twice as fast.

The amount of additional memory needed for this field is actually minimal. In the way we have loaded it previously, the `OrderCounter` field will add only a small amount in the symbol table and will only increase the size of the data table by a very small amount — it may, in fact, appear not to increase it at all! The only increase is in the core system tables, and this is minor.

> Recalling that data tables are bit-stuffed but stored as bytes, adding a one-bit value like this to the data table may not actually increase the number of bytes needed to store the value. At worst, only one additional byte will be needed.

In fact, we can reduce this minor change even further by making the following change:

```
    . . .
    Floor(1) As OrderCounter,
    . . .
```

This forces the single value to be treated as a sequential integer (a sequence of one) and the value therefore isn't stored in the symbol table.

Optimizing performance by combining fact tables?

If we load all of our tables, the data structure may look something like the following:

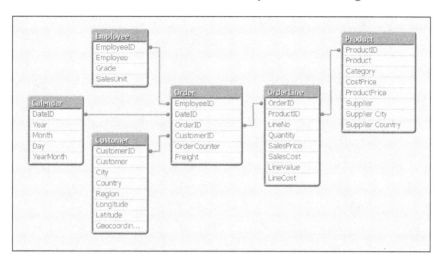

In this format, we have two fact tables—Order and OrderLine. For the small dataset that we have, we won't see any issues here. As the dataset gets larger, it is suggested that it is better to have fewer tables and fewer joins between tables. In this case, between Product and Employee, there are three joins. The best practice is to have only one fact table containing all our key fields and associated facts (measures).

In this model, most of the facts are in the OrderLine table, but there are two facts in the Order table—OrderCounter and Freight. We need to think about what we do with them. There are two options:

1. Move the EmployeeID, DateID, and CustomerID fields from the Order table into the OrderLine table. Create a script based on an agreed business rule (for example, ratio of line Quantity) to apportion the Freight value across all of the line values. The OrderCounter field is more difficult to deal with, but we could take the option of using Count (Distinct OrderID) (knowing that it is less efficient) in the front end and disposing of the OrderCounter field.

    This method is more in line with traditional data warehousing methods.

2. Move the EmployeeID, DateID, and CustomerID fields from the Order table into the OrderLine table. Leave the Order table as is, as an Order dimension table.

    This is more of a QlikView way of doing things. It works very well too.

Although we might be great fans of dimensional modeling methods (see *Chapter 2, QlikView Data Modeling*), we should also be a big fan of pragmatism and using what works.

Let's see what happens if we go for option 2. The following is the addition to the script to move the key fields:

```
// Move DateID, CustomerID and EmployeeID to OrderLine
Join (OrderLine)
Load
    OrderID,
    DateID,
    CustomerID,
    EmployeeID
Resident
    Order;

Drop Fields DateID, CustomerID, EmployeeID From Order;

// Rename the OrderLine table
RENAME Table OrderLine to Fact;
```

So, how has that worked? The table structure now looks like the following:

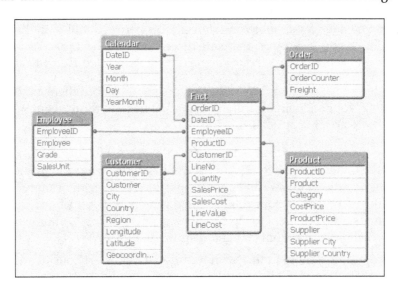

Our expectation, as we have widened the biggest data table (OrderLine) and only narrowed a smaller table (Order), is that the total memory for the document will be increased. This is confirmed by taking memory snapshots before and after the change:

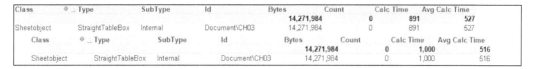

Class	Type	SubType	Id	Bytes	Count	Calc Time	Avg Calc Time
				1,270,370	150,494	0	0
Database	Table	Records	OrderLine	923,085	102,565	0	0
Database	Field	Symbols	Freight	132,128	6,990	0	0
Database							

Class	Type	SubType	Id	Bytes	Count	Calc Time	Avg Calc Time
Database				1,644,732	150,498	0	0
Database	Database	Table	Records	Fact	1,333,345	102,565	0	0
Database	Database	Field	Symbols	Freight	132,128	6,990	0	0
Database	Database	Table	Records	Order	47,928	11,982	0	0
Database	Database	Field	Symbols	LineValue	43,352	5,419	0	0
Database	Database	Field	Symbols	LineCost	43,088	5,386	0	0
Database	Database	Field	Symbols	DateID	17,368	2,171	0	0
Database	Database	Table	Records	Calendar	8,684	2,171	0	0

But have we improved the overall performance of the document?

To test this, we can create a new version of our original chart, except now using Customer instead of CustomerID and adding Product. This gives us fields (YearMonth, Customer, and Product) from across the dimension tables. If we use this new straight table to test the before and after state, the following is how the results might look:

Class	Type	SubType	Id	Bytes	Count	Calc Time	Avg Calc Time
				14,271,984		0	891	527
Sheetobject	StraightTableBox	Internal	Document\CH03	14,271,984		0	891	527

Class	Type	SubType	Id	Bytes	Count	Calc Time	Avg Calc Time
				14,271,984		0	1,000	516
Sheetobject	StraightTableBox	Internal	Document\CH03	14,271,984		0	1,000	516

Interestingly, the average calculation has reduced slightly. This is not unexpected as we have reduced the number of joins needed across data tables.

Optimizing your numbers

QlikView has a great feature in that it can sometimes default to storing numbers as Dual values—the number along with text representing the default presentation of that number. This text is derived either by applying the default formats during load, or by the developer applying formats using functions such as Num(), Date(), Money(), or TimeStamp(). If you do apply the format functions with a format string (as the second parameter to Num, Date, and so on), the number will be stored as a Dual. If you use Num without a format string, the number will usually be stored without the text.

Thinking about it, numbers that represent facts (measures) in our fact tables will rarely need to be displayed with their default formats. They are almost always only ever going to be displayed in an aggregation in a chart and that aggregated value will have its own format. The text part is therefore superfluous and can be removed if it is there.

Let's modify our script in the following manner:

```
Order:
LOAD AutoNumber(OrderID, 'Order') As OrderID,
     Floor(1) As OrderCounter,
     Floor(OrderDate) As DateID,
     AutoNumber(CustomerID, 'Customer') As CustomerID,
     AutoNumber(EmployeeID, 'Employee') As EmployeeID,
     Num(Freight) As Freight
FROM
[..\Scripts\OrderHeader.qvd]
(qvd);



OrderLine:
LOAD AutoNumber(OrderID, 'Order') As OrderID,
     LineNo,
     ProductID,
     Num(Quantity) As Quantity,
     Num(SalesPrice) As SalesPrice,
     Num(SalesCost) As SalesCost,
     Num(LineValue) As LineValue,
     Num(LineCost) As LineCost
FROM
[..\Scripts\OrderLine.qvd]
(qvd);
```

The change in memory looks like the following:

Class	Type	SubType	Id	Bytes	Count	Calc Time	Avg Calc Time
				220,088	17,891	0	0
Database	Field	Symbols	Freight	132,128	6,990	0	0
Database	Field	Symbols	LineValue	43,352	5,419	0	0
Database	Field	Symbols	LineCost	43,088	5,386	0	0
Database	Field	Symbols	SalesPrice	948	48	0	0
Database	Field	Symbols	CostPrice	572	48	0	0

Class	Type	SubType	Id	Bytes	Count	Calc Time	Avg Calc Time
				143,316	17,891	0	0
Database	Field	Symbols	Freight	55,920	6,990	0	0
Database	Field	Symbols	LineValue	43,352	5,419	0	0
Database	Field	Symbols	LineCost	43,088	5,386	0	0
Database	Field	Symbols	CostPrice	572	48	0	0
Database	Field	Symbols	SalesPrice	384	48	0	0

We can see that there is a significant difference in the `Freight` field. The smaller `SalesPrice` field has also been reduced. However, the other numeric fields are not changed.

Some numbers have additional format strings and take up a lot of space, some don't. Looking at the numbers, we can see that the `Freight` value with the format string is taking up an average of over 18 bytes per value. When `Num` is applied, only 8 bytes are taken per value. Let's add an additional expression to the chart:

Expression label	Expression
`Avg. Bytes`	`Sum(Bytes)/Sum(Count)`

Now we have a quick indicator to see whether numeric values are storing unneeded text.

Optimizing chart calculation times

Once we have optimized our data model, we can turn our focus onto chart performance. There are a few different things that we can do to make sure that our expressions are optimal, and we can use the memory file extract to test them.

Some of the expressions will actually involve revisiting the data model. If we do, we will need to weigh up the cost of that performance with changes to memory, and so on.

It will be useful to begin with an explanation of how the QlikView calculation engine works.

The QlikView calculation engine

QlikView is very clever in how it does its calculations. As well as the data storage, as discussed earlier in this chapter, it also stores the binary state of every field and of every data table dependent on user selection—essentially, depending on the green/white/grey state of each field, it is either included or excluded. This area of storage is called the **state space** and is updated by the QlikView logical inference engine every time a selection is made. There is one bit in the state space for every value in the symbol table or row in the data table—as such, the state space is much smaller than the data itself and hence much faster to query.

There are three steps to a chart being calculated:

1. The user makes a selection, causing the logical inference engine to reset and recalculate the state space. This should be a multithreaded operation.

2. On one thread per object, the state space is queried to gather together all of the combinations of dimensions and values necessary to perform the calculation. The state space is being queried, so this is a relatively fast operation, but could be a potential bottleneck if there are many visible objects on the screen.

3. On multiple threads per object, the expression is calculated. This is where we see the cores in the task manager all go to 100 percent at the same time. Having 100 percent CPU is expected and desired because QlikView will "burst" calculations across all available processor cores, which makes this a very fast process, relative to the size and complexity of the calculation. We call it a *burst* because, except for the most complex of calculations, the 100 percent CPU should only be for a short time.

Of course, the very intelligent cache comes into play as well and everything that is calculated is stored for potential subsequent use. If the same set of selections are met (such as hitting the Back button), then the calculation is retrieved from the cache and will be almost instantaneous.

Now that we know more about how QlikView performs its calculations, we can look at a few ways that we can optimize things.

Creating flags for well-known conditions

We cannot anticipate every possible selection or query that a user might make, but there are often some quite well-known conditions that will generally be true most of the time and may be commonly used in calculations. In this example, we will look at Year-to-Date and Last Year-to-Date—commonly used on dashboards.

The following is an example of a calculation that might be used in a gauge:

```
Sum(If(YearToDate(Date), LineValue, 0))
/Sum(If(YearToDate(Date,-1), LineValue, 0))
-1
```

This uses the `YearToDate()` function to check whether the date is in the current year to date or in the year to date period for last year (using the `-1` for the offset parameter). This expression is a sum of an `if` statement, which is generally not recommended. Also, these are quite binary—a date is either in the year to date or not—so are ideal candidates for the creation of flags. We can do this in the `Calendar` table in the following script:

```
Calendar:
Load Distinct
    DateID,
    -YearToDate(DateID) As YTD_Flag,
    -YearToDate(DateID,-1) As LYTD_Flag,
    Date(DateID) As Date,
    Year(DateID) As Year,
    Month(DateID) As Month,
    Day(DateID) As Day,
    Date(MonthStart(DateID), 'YYYY-MM') As YearMonth
Resident
    Order;
```

 Note the - sign before the function. This is because `YearToDate` is a Boolean function that returns either true or false, which in QlikView is represented by `-1` and `0`. If the value is in the year to date, then the function will return `-1`, so I add the `-` to change that to `1`. A `-` sign before `0` will make no difference.

In a particular test dataset, we might see an increase from 8,684 bytes to 13,026—not an unexpected increase and not significant because the `Calendar` table is relatively small. We are creating these flags to improve performance in the frontend and need to accept a small change in the data size.

The significant change comes when we change the expression in the chart to the following:

```
Sum(LineValue*YTD_Flag)/Sum(LineValue*LYTD_Flag)-1
```

In a sample dataset, we might see that the calculation reduces from, say, 46 to, say, 16—a 65 percent reduction. This calculation could also be written using **Set Analysis** as follows:

```
Sum({<YTD_Flag={1}>} LineValue)/Sum({<LYTD_Flag={1}>} LineValue)-1
```

However, this might only get a calc time of 31—only a 32.6 percent reduction. Very interesting!

If we think about it, the simple calculation of `LineValue*YTD_Flag` is going to do a multithreaded calculation using values that are derived from the small and fast in-memory state space. Both `If` and `Set Analysis` are going to add additional load to the calculation of the set of values that are going to be used in the calculation.

In this case, the flag field is in a dimension table, `Calendar`, and the value field is in the fact table. It is, of course, possible to generate the flag field in the fact table instead. In this case, the calculation is likely to run even faster, especially on very large datasets. This is because there is no join of data tables required. However, the thing to bear in mind is that the additional pointer indexes in the `Calendar` table will require relatively little space whereas the additional width of the fact table, because of the large numbers of rows, will be something to consider. However, saying that, the pointers to the flag values are very small, so you do need a really long fact table for it to make a big difference. In some cases, the additional bit necessary to store the pointer in the bit-stuffed table will not make any difference at all, and in other cases, it may add just one byte.

`Set Analysis` can be very powerful, but it is worth considering that it often has to go, depending on the formula, outside the current state space, and that will cause additional calculation to take place that may be achieved in a simpler manner by creating a flag field in the script and using it in this way. Even if you have to use `Set Analysis`, the best performing comparisons are going to be using numeric comparisons, so creating a numeric flag instead of a text value will improve the set calculation performance. For example, consider the following expression:

```
Sum({<YTD_Flag={1}>} LineValue)
```

This will execute much faster than the following expression:

```
Sum({<YTD_Flag={'Yes'}>} LineValue)
```

So, when should we use `Set Analysis` instead of multiplying by flags? Barry Harmsen has done some testing that indicates that if the dimension table is much larger relative to the fact table, then using `Set Analysis` is faster than the flag fields. The reasoning is that the multiply method will process all records (even those containing 0), so in larger tables, it has more to process. The `Set Analysis` method will first reduce the scope, and apply the calculation to that subset.

Of course, if we have to introduce more advanced logic, that might include AND/OR/NOT operations, then `Set Analysis` is the way to go—but try to use numeric flags.

Sorting for well-known conditions

Any time that you need to sort a chart or listbox, that sort needs to be calculated. Of course, a numeric sort will always be the fastest. An alphabetic sort is a lot slower, just by its nature. One of the very slowest sorts is where we want to sort by expression.

For example, let's imagine that we wish to sort our `Country` list by a fixed order, defined by the business. We could use a sort expression like this:

```
Match(Country,'USA','Canada','Germany','United Kingdom','China','India
','Russia','France','Ireland')
```

The problem is that this is a text comparison that will be continually evaluated. What we can do instead is to load a temporary sort table in the script. We load this towards the beginning of the script because it needs to be the initial load of the symbol table; something like the following:

```
Country_Sort:
Load * Inline [
Country
USA
Canada
Germany
United Kingdom
China
India
Russia
France
Ireland
];
```

Then, as we won't need this table in our data, we should remember to drop it at the end of the script—after the main data has been loaded:

```
Drop Table Country_Sort;
```

Now, when we use this field anywhere, we can turn off all of the sort options and use the last one—Load Order. This doesn't need to be evaluated so will always calculate quickly:

Using Direct Discovery

Traditionally, QlikView has been a totally in-memory tool. If you want to analyze any information, you need to get all of the data into memory. This has caused problems for many enterprise organizations because of the sheer size of data that they wanted to analyze. You can get quite a lot of data into QlikView—billions of rows are not uncommon on very large servers, but there is a limit. Especially in the last few years where businesses have started to take note of the buzz around Big Data, many believed that QlikView could not play in this area.

Direct Discovery was introduced with QlikView Version 11.20. In Version 11.20 SR5, it was updated with a new, more sensible syntax. This syntax is also available in Qlik Sense. What Direct Discovery does is allow a QlikView model to connect directly to a data source without having to load all of the data into memory. Instead, we load only dimension values and, when necessary, QlikView generates a query to retrieve the required results from the database.

Of course, this does have the potential to reduce some of the things that make QlikView very popular—the sub-second response to selections, for example. Every time that a user makes a selection, QlikView generates a query to pass through to the database connection. The faster the data connection, the faster the response, so a performative data warehouse is a boon for Direct Discovery. But speed is not always everything—with Direct Discovery, we can connect to any valid connection that we might normally connect to with the QlikView script; this includes ODBC connectors to Big Data sources such as Cloudera or Google.

Here we will get an introduction to using Direct Discovery, but we should read the more detailed technical details published by the Qlik Community, for example, the SR5 technical addendum at `http://community.qlik.com/docs/DOC-3710`.

Direct Discovery restrictions

There are a few restrictions of Direct Discovery that will probably be addressed with subsequent service releases:

- **Only one direct table is supported**: This restriction has been lifted in QlikView 11.20 SR7 and Qlik Sense 1.0. Prior to those versions, you could only have one direct query in your data model. All other tables in the data model must be in-memory.

- **Set Analysis and complex expressions not supported**: Because the query is generated on the fly, it just can't work with the likes of a `Set Analysis` query. Essentially, only calculations that can be performed on the source database — `Sum`, `Count`, `Avg`, `Min`, `Max` — will work via Direct Discovery.

- **Only SQL compliant data sources**: Direct Discovery will only work against connections that support SQL, such as ODBC, OLEDB, and custom connectors such as SAP and JDBC. Note that there are some system variables that may need to be set for some connectors, such as SAP or Google Big Query.

- **Direct fields are not supported in global search**: Global search can only operate against in-memory data.

- **Security restrictions**: Prior to QlikView 11.20 SR7 and Qlik Sense 1.0, Section Access reduction can work on the in-memory data, but will not necessarily work against the `Direct` table. Similarly, `Loop` and `Reduce` in `Publisher` won't work correctly.

- **Synthetic keys not supported**: You can only have native key associations. `AutoNumber` will obviously not be supported on the direct table.

- **Calculated dimensions not supported**: You can only create calculated dimensions against in-memory data.

- **Naming the Direct table**: You can't create a table alias. The table will always be called `DirectTable`.

It is also worth knowing that QlikView will use its cache to store the results of queries. So if you hit the Back button, the query won't be rerun against the source database. However, this may have consequences when the underlying data is updated more rapidly. There is a variable — `DirectCacheSeconds` — that can be set to limit the time that data is cached. This defaults to 3600 seconds.

Direct Discovery syntax

The most important statement is the opening one:

```
DIRECT QUERY
```

This tells QlikView to expect some further query components. It is similar to the SQL statement that tells QlikView to execute the subsequent query and get the results into the memory. The DIRECT QUERY is followed by:

```
DIMENSION  Dim_1, Dim_2, ..., Dim_n
```

We must have at least one dimension field. These fields will have their values loaded into a symbol table and state space. This means that they can be used as normal in listboxes, tables, charts, and so on. Typically, the DIMENSION list will be followed by:

```
MEASURE  Val_1, Val_2, ..., Val_n
```

These fields are not loaded into the data model. They can be used, however, in expressions. You can also have additional fields that are not going to be used in expressions or dimensions:

```
DETAIL  Note_1, Note_2, ..., Note_n
```

These DETAIL fields can only be used in table boxes to give additional context to other values. This is useful for text note fields.

Finally, there may be fields that you want to include in the generated SQL query but are not interested in using in the QlikView model:

```
DETACH other_1, other_2, ..., other_n
```

Finally, you can also add a limitation to your query using a standard WHERE clause:

```
WHERE x=y
```

The statement will, of course, be terminated by a semicolon.

We can also pass valid SQL syntax statements to calculate dimensions:

```
NATIVE('Valid SQL ''syntax'' in quotes') As Field_x
```

If your SQL syntax also has single quotes, then you will need to double-up on the single quotes to have it interpreted correctly.

Looking at an example Direct Query

The following is an example of a Direct Query to a SQL server database:

```
DIRECT QUERY
dimension
    OrderID,
    FLOOR(OrderDate) As DateID,
    CustomerID,
    EmployeeID,
    ProductID
measure
    Quantity,
    SalesPrice,
    LineValue,
    LineCost
detail
    Freight,
    LineNo
FROM QWT.dbo."Order_Fact";
```

This results in a table view like the following:

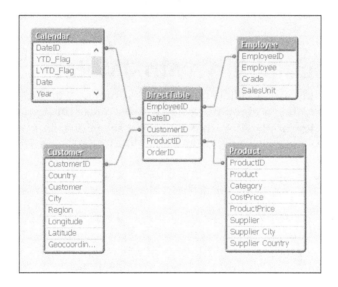

You will note that the list of fields in the table view only contains the dimension values. The measure values are not shown.

You can now go ahead and build charts mostly as normal (without, unfortunately, **Set Analysis**!), but note that you will see a lot more of the hourglass:

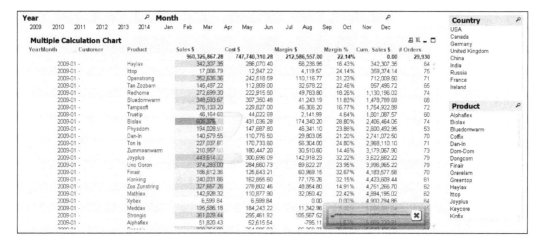

The **X** in the bottom corner of the chart can be used to cancel the execution of the direct query.

Testing scalability with JMeter

JMeter is a tool from Apache that can be used to automate web-based interactions for the purpose of testing scalability. Basically, we can use this tool to automatically connect to a QlikView application, make different selections, look at different charts, drill up and down, and repeat to test how well the application performs.

JMeter first started being used for testing QlikView about 3 years ago. At the time, while it looked like a great tool, the amount of work necessary to set it up was very off-putting.

Since then, however, the guys in the Qlik scalability center have created a set of tools that automate the configuration of JMeter, and this makes things a lot easier for us. In fact, almost anyone can set up a test—it is that easy!

Obtaining the scalability tools

The tools needed to test scalability are made available via the Qlik community. You will need to connect to the Scalability group (`http://community.qlik.com/groups/qlikview-scalability`).

Search in this group for "tools" and you should find the latest version. There are some documents that you will need to read through, specifically:

- `Prerequisites.pdf`
- `QVScalabilityTools.pdf`

Installing JMeter

JMeter can be obtained from the Apache website:

`https://jmeter.apache.org/`

However, the prerequisites documentation recommends a slightly older version of JMeter:

`http://archive.apache.org/dist/jakarta/jmeter/binaries/jakarta-jmeter-2.4.zip`

JMeter is a Java application, so it is also a good idea to make sure that you have the latest version of the Java runtime installed — 64-bit for a 64-bit system:

`http://java.com/en/download/manual.jsp`

It is recommended not to unzip JMeter directly to `C:\` or `Program Files` or other folders that may have security that reduces your access. Extract them to a folder that you have full access to. Do note the instructions in the `Prerequisites.pdf` file on setting heap memory sizing. To confirm that all is in order, you can try running the `jmeter.bat` file to open JMeter — if it works, then it means that your Java and other dependencies should be installed correctly.

Microsoft .Net 4.0 should also be installed on the machine. This can be downloaded from Microsoft. However, it should already be installed if you have QlikView Server components on the machine.

Installing the scalability tools

Depending on your system, you may find that the ZIP file that you download has its status set to **Blocked**. In this case, you need to right-click on the file, open the properties, and click on the **Unblock** button:

If you don't, you may find that the file appears to unzip successfully, but the executables will not run. You might see an error like this in the Windows Application Event Log:

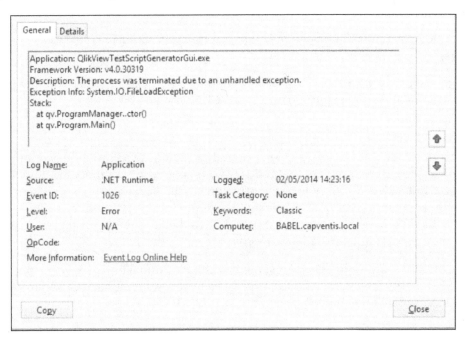

After you have made sure that the ZIP file is unblocked, you can extract the scalability tools to a folder on your system. Follow the instructions in the Prerequisites.pdf file to change the configuration.

Hitting *Start + R* and then typing `perfmon` will allow you to run the **Performance Monitor** tool to import the profile as set out in the documentation.

About the scalability tools

The toolset consists of the following separate parts:

- **Script generator**: Used to generate the JMeter script
- **Script executor**: Executes the generated script
- **Analyzer**: A QlikView document that reads various logs to give you results

Running an example execution

Running a session is actually quite straightforward, and a lot easier than having to craft the script by hand.

There are a couple of steps that we need to do before we can generate a test script:

1. We need to open the target application in QlikView desktop and extract the layout information:

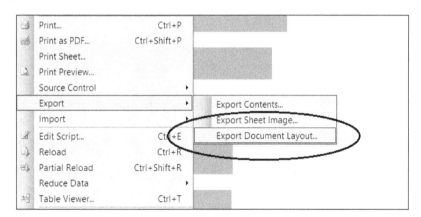

   This exports all of the information about the document, including all of the objects, into XML files that can be imported into the script generator. This is how the script generator finds out about sheets and objects that it can use.

2. Copy the `AjaxZfc` URL for the application. We need to give this information to the script builder so that it knows how to connect to the application:

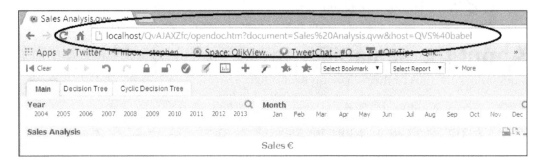

3. Clear the existing log files from the QVS. These files will be in the `ProgramData\QlikTech\QlikViewServer` folder. Stop the QlikView Server Service and then archive or delete the `Performance*.log`, `Audit*.log`, `Events*.log`, and `Sessions*.log` files. When you restart the service, new ones will start to be created:

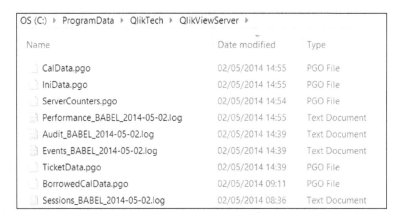

 Note that you should be careful not to delete the PGO files in the same folders – these are copies of the server's license information files.

4. Start the Performance Monitor using the template that you configured earlier. Double-check that it starts to create content in the folder (for example, `C:\PerfLogs\Admin\New Data Collector Set\QlikView Performance Monitor`).

Once those steps have been completed, we can go ahead and create a script:

1. Execute the script generator by running `QlikViewTestScriptGeneratorGui.exe` from the `ScriptGenerator` folder.

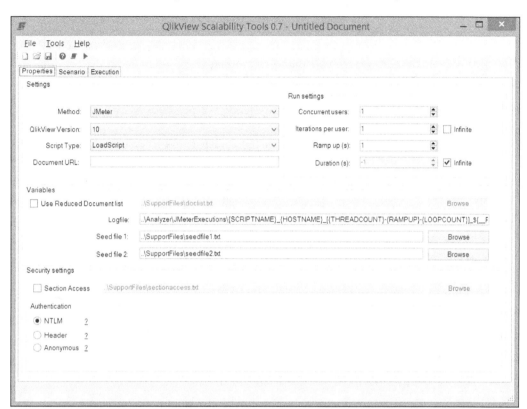

2. There are some properties that we need to set on this page:

Property	Value
QlikView version	11.
Document URL	Paste the URL that you recorded earlier.
Security settings	Choose the right authentication mechanism for your QlikView server (more details discussed later).
Concurrent users	How many users you want to run concurrently.
Iterations per user	How many times each user will run through the scenario. If you set this to **Infinite**, you need to specify a **Duration** below.
Ramp up	What time should there be before all users are logged in. 1 means that all users start together.

Property	Value
Duration	How long the test should be run for. If you set this to **Infinite** then you must set a number of **Iterations per user** above it.

> If you use NTLM, then you cannot use more than one concurrent user. This is because the NTLM option will execute under the profile of the user running the application and each concurrent user will therefore attempt to log in with the same credentials. QVS does not allow this so each concurrent user will actually end up killing each other's sessions.
>
> If you want to simulate more than one user, then you can turn on Header authentication in the QVWS configuration and make use of the `userpw.txt` file to add a list of users. The QVS will need to be in DMS mode to support this. Also bear in mind that you will need to have an appropriate number of licenses available to support the number of users that you want to test with.

3. Save the document in the `ScriptGenerator\SourceXMLs` folder. Note that you should not use spaces or non-alphanumeric characters in the XML filename. It is a good idea to make the filename descriptive as you might use it again and again.

4. Click the **Scenario** tab. Click the **Browse** button and navigate to the folder where you save the document layout information earlier. Save the template (it's always a good idea to save continually as you go along). Change the **Timer Delay Min** to 30 and the **Max** to 120:

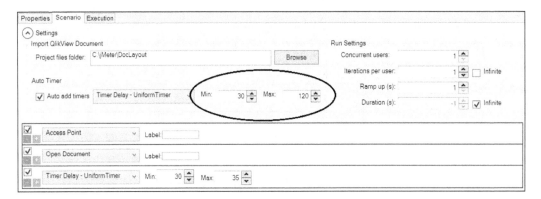

This setting specifies the range of delay between different actions. We should always allow an appropriate minimum to make sure that the application can update correctly after an action. The random variation between the minimum and maximum settings gives a simulation of user thinking time.

5. By default, there are three default actions—open AccessPoint, open the document, and then a timer delay. Click on the green + button on the left-hand side of the bottom timer delay action to add a new action below it. Two new actions will be added—an unspecified **Choose Action** one and a timer delay containing the settings that we specified above. The **Auto add timers** checkbox means that a timer delay will be automatically added every time we add a new action.

6. Build up a scenario by adding appropriate actions:

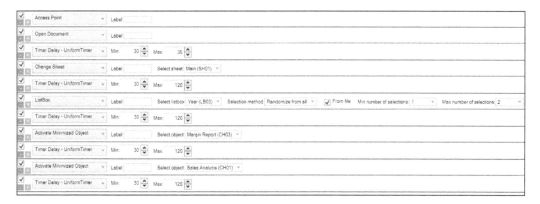

Remember to keep saving as you go along.

7. Click on the **Execution** tab. Click on **Yes** in answer to the **Add to execution** prompt. Expand the **Settings** option and click on **Browse** to select the JMeter path:

When you click on **OK**, you will be prompted on whether to save this setting permanently or not. You can click on **OK** in response to this message:

1. Right-click on the script name and select **Open in JMeter**:

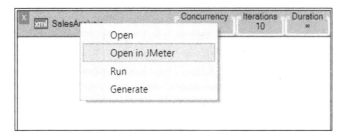

2. Click on **OK** on **OutputPopupForm**. When JMeter opens, note the entries that have been created in the test plan by the script generator.

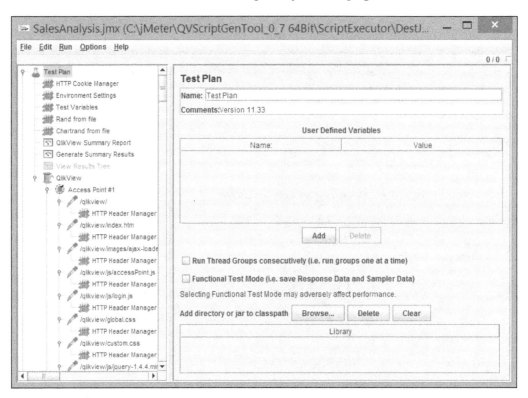

3. Close JMeter. Back in the script generator, right-click on the script again and select **Run** from the menu. The **Summary** tab appears, indicating that the script is executing:

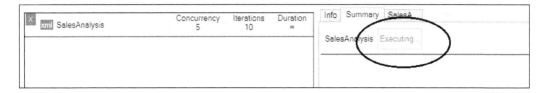

Once you have executed a test, you will want to analyze the results. The scalability tools come with a couple of QVW files to help you out here. There are a couple of steps that you need to go through to gather all the files together first:

1. In the QVScriptGenTool_0_7 64Bit\Analyzer folder, there is a ZIP file called FolderTemplate.zip. Extract the FolderTemplate folder out of the ZIP file and rename it to match the name of your analysis task—for example, SalesAnalysis. Within this folder, there are four subfolders that you need to populate with data:

Subfolder	Data source
EventLogs	These are the QVS event logs—Events_servername_*.log
JMeterLogs	These are the JMeter execution logs that should be in QVScriptGenTool_0_7 64Bit\Analyzer\JMeterExecutions
ServerLogs	These are the CSV files created—SERVERNAME_Processes*.csv
SessionLogs	These are the QVS session logs—Sessions_servername_*.log

2. Open the QVD Generator.qvw file using QlikView Desktop. Set the correct name for the subfolder that you have just created:

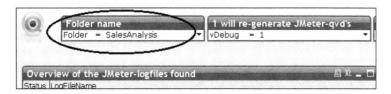

3. Reload the document.

4. Once the document has reloaded, manually edit the name of the server using the input fields in each row of the table:

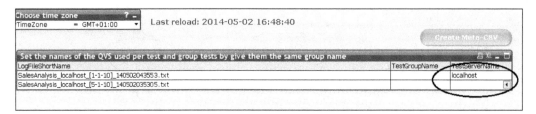

5. Once you have entered the data, click on the **Create Meta-CSV** button. You can then close the QVD Generator.

6. Open the SC_Results - DemoTest.qvw file and save it as a new file with an appropriate name—for example, SC_Results - SalesAnalysis.qvw. Change the **Folder Name** variable as before and reload.

Now you can start to analyze your server's performance during the tests:

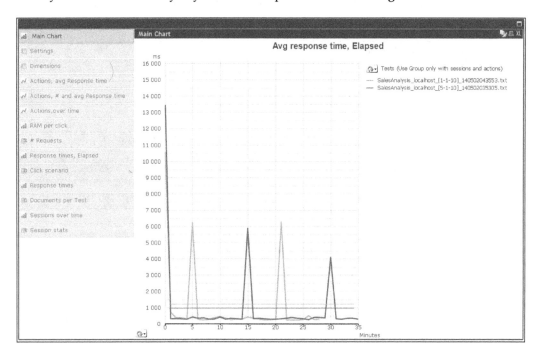

Because you can run multiple iterations of the test, with different parameters, you can use the tool to run comparisons to see changes. These can also be scheduled from the command line to run on a regular basis.

One thing that these JMeter scripts can be used for is a process called "warming the cache". If you have a very large QlikView document, it can take a long time to load into memory and create the user cache. For the first users to connect to the document in the morning, they may have a very poor experience while waiting for the document to open — they may even time out. Subsequent users will get the benefit of these user actions. However, if you have a scheduled task to execute a JMeter task, you can take the pain away from those first users because the cache will already be established for them when they get to work.

Summary

There has been a lot of information in this chapter, and I hope that you have been able to follow it well.

We started by reviewing some basic performance improvement techniques that you should already have been aware of, but you might not think about. Knowing these techniques is important and is the beginning of your path to mastering how to create performative QlikView applications.

We then looked at methods of generating test data that can be used to help you hone your skills.

Understanding how QlikView stores its data is a real requisite for any developer who wants to achieve mastery of this subject. Learning how to export memory statistics is a great step forward to learn how to achieve great things with performance and scalability.

We looked at different strategies for reducing the memory profile of a QlikView application and improving the performance of charts.

By this stage, you should have a great start in understanding how to create really performative applications.

When it gets to the stage where there is just too much data for QlikView to manage in-memory, we have seen that we can use a hybrid approach where some of the data is in-memory and some of the data is still in a database, and we can query that data on the fly using Direct Discovery.

Finally, we looked at how we can use JMeter to test our applications with some real-world scenarios using multiple users and repetitions to really hammer an application and confirm that it will work on the hardware that is in place.

Having worked through this chapter, you should have a great understanding of how to create scalable applications that perform really well for your users. You are starting to become a QlikView master!

In the next chapter, we will learn about best practices in modeling data and how that applies to QlikView.

2
QlikView Data Modeling

"It is a capital mistake to theorize before one has data. Insensibly one begins to twist facts to suit theories, instead of theories to suit facts."

— Sherlock Holmes (Arthur Conan Doyle), A Scandal in Bohemia

In data warehousing and business intelligence, there are many approaches to data modeling. We hear of personalities such as Bill Inmon and Ralph Kimball. We talk of normalization and dimensional modeling. But we also might have heard about how QlikView can cut across all of this—we don't need to worry about data warehousing; we just load in all the data from source systems and start clicking. Right?

Well, that might be right if you want to load just a very quick application directly from the data source and aren't too worried about performance or maintainability. However, the dynamic nature of the QlikView script does not mean that we should throw out all of the best practices in data warehouse design that have been established over the course of many years.

In this chapter, we are going to look at the best practices around QlikView data modeling. As revealed in the previous chapter, this does not always mean the best performing data model. But there are many reasons why we should use these best practices, and these will become clear over the course of this chapter and the next.

The following are the topics we'll be covering in this chapter:

- Reviewing basic data modeling
- Dimensional data modeling
- Handling slowly changing dimensions
- Dealing with multiple fact tables in one model

Reviewing basic data modeling

If you have attended QlikView training courses and done some work with QlikView modeling, there are a few things that you will know about, but I will review them just to be sure that we are all on the same page.

Associating data

QlikView uses an associative model to connect data rather than a join model. A join model is the traditional approach to data queries. In the join model, you craft a SQL query across multiple tables in the database, telling the **database management system (DBMS)** how those tables should be joined — whether left, inner, outer, and so on. The DBMS might have a system in place to optimize the performance of those queries. Each query tends to be run in isolation, returning a result set that can be either further explored — Excel pivot tables are a common use case here — or used to build a final report. Queries might have parameters to enable different reports to be executed, but each execution is still in isolation. In fact, it is the approach that underlies many implementations of a "semantic layer" that many of the "stack" BI vendors implement in their products. Users are isolated from having to build the queries — they are built and executed by the BI system — but each query is still an isolated event.

In the associative model, all the fields in the data model have a logical association with every other field in the data model. This association means that when a user makes a selection, the inference engine can quickly resolve which values are still valid — possible values — and which values are excluded. The user can continue to make selections, clear selections, and make new selections, and the engine will continue to present the correct results from the logical inference of those selections. The user's queries tend to be more natural and it allows them to answer questions as they occur.

It is important to realize that just putting a traditional join model database into memory, as many vendors have started to do, will not deliver the same interactive associative experience to users. The user will probably get faster running queries, but they will still be isolated queries.

Saying that, however, just because QlikView has a great associative model technology, you still need to build the right data model to be able to give users the answers that they don't know and are looking for, even before they have asked for them!

Automatically associating tables

We should know that QlikView will automatically associate two data tables based on both tables containing one or more fields that match exactly in both name and case. QlikView fields and table names are always case sensitive—Field1 does not match to FIELD1 or field1.

Suppose that we run a very simple load statement such as the following:

```
Customer:
Load * Inline [
CustomerID, Customer
1, Customer A
2, Customer B
];

Sales:
Load * Inline [
Date, CustomerID, Value
2014-05-12, 1, 100
2014-05-12, 2, 200
2014-05-12, 1, 100
];
```

This will result in an association that looks like the following:

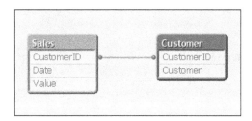

If you read the previous chapter, you will know that this will generate two data tables containing pointer indexes that point to several symbol tables for the data containing the unique values.

Understanding synthetic keys

A **synthetic key** is QlikView's method of associating two tables that have more than one field in common. Before we discuss the merits of them, let's first understand exactly what is happening with them.

For example, consider the following simple piece of script:

```
Budget:
Load * Inline [
CustomerID, Year, BudgetValue
1, 2013, 10000
2, 2013, 15000
1, 2014, 12000
2, 2014, 17500
];

Sales:
Load * Inline [
Date, Year, CustomerID, Value
2013-01-12, 2013, 1, 100
2013-02-25, 2013, 2, 200
2013-02-28, 2013, 1, 100
2013-04-04, 2013, 1, 100
2013-06-21, 2013, 2, 200
2013-08-02, 2013, 1, 100
2014-05-12, 2014, 1, 100
2014-05-12, 2014, 2, 200
2014-05-12, 2014, 1, 100
];
```

This will produce an **Internal Table View** like the following:

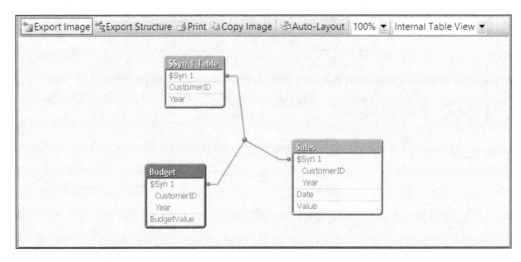

It is worth noting that QlikView can also represent this as a **Source Table View**, showing the association in a more logical, database way, like the following:

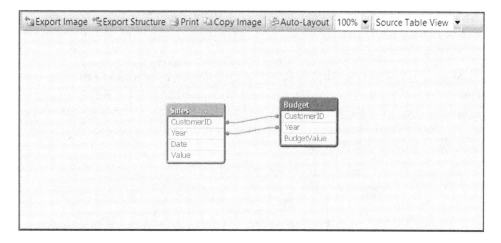

We can see from **Internal Table View** that QlikView has moved the common fields into a new table, **$Syn 1 Table**, that contains all the valid combinations of the values. The values have been replaced in the original tables with a derived composite key, or surrogate key, that is associated with **$Syn 1 Table**.

To me, this is perfectly sensible data modeling. When we look at our options later on in the chapter, we will begin to recognize this approach as **Link Table** modeling. There are, however, some scare stories about using synthetic keys. In fact, in the documentation, it is recommended that you remove them. The following is quoted from *QlikView Reference Manual*:

> *When the number of composite keys increases, depending on data amounts, table structure and other factors, QlikView may or may not handle them gracefully. QlikView may end up using excessive amounts of time and/or memory. Unfortunately, the actual limitations are virtually impossible to predict, which leaves only trial and error as a practical method to determine them.*

> *An overall analysis of the intended table structure by the application designer. is recommended, including the following:*

Forming your own non-composite keys, typically using string concatenation inside an AutoNumber script function.

Making sure only the necessary fields connect. If, for example, a date is used as a key, make sure not to load e.g. year, month or day_of_month from more than one internal table.

The important thing to look at here is that it says, "When the number of composite keys increases…"—this is important because you should understand that a synthetic key is not necessarily a bad thing in itself. However, having too many of them is, to me, a sign of a poor data modeling effort. I would not, for example, like to see a table viewer looking like the following:

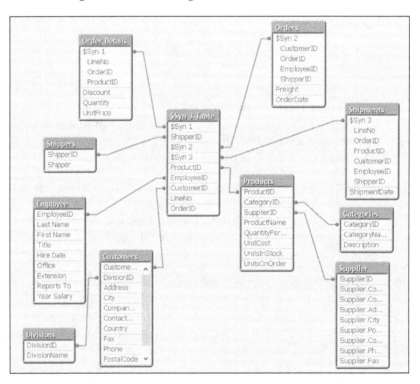

There have been some interesting discussions about this subject in the Qlik community. John Witherspoon, a long time contributor to the community, wrote a good piece entitled *Should we stop worrying and love the Synthetic Key* (http://community.qlik.com/thread/10279).

Of course, Henric Cronström has a good opinion on this subject as well, and has relayed it in *Qlik Design Blog* at http://community.qlik.com/blogs/qlikviewdesignblog/2013/04/16/synthetic-keys.

My opinion is similar to Henric's. I like to see any synthetic keys resolved in the data model. I find them a little untidy and a little bit lazy. However, there is no reason to spend many hours resolving them if you have better things to do and there are no issues in your document.

Creating composite keys

One of the methods used to resolve synthetic keys is to create your own composite key. A composite key is a field that is composed of several other field values. There are a number of ways of doing this, which we will examine in the next sections.

Using string concatenation

The very simplest way of creating a composite key is to simply concatenate all the values together using the & operator. If we were to revisit the previously used script and apply this, our script might now look like the following:

```
Budget:
Load
    CustomerID & Year as BudgetKey,
    BudgetValue
Inline [
CustomerID, Year, BudgetValue
1, 2013, 10000
2, 2013, 15000
1, 2014, 12000
2, 2014, 17500
];

Sales:
Load
    Date,
    Year,
    CustomerID,
    CustomerID & Year as BudgetKey,
    Value
Inline [
Date, Year, CustomerID, Value
2013-01-12, 2013, 1, 100
2013-02-25, 2013, 2, 200
2013-02-28, 2013, 1, 100
2013-04-04, 2013, 1, 100
2013-06-21, 2013, 2, 200
2013-08-02, 2013, 1, 100
```

```
2014-05-12, 2014, 1, 100
2014-05-12, 2014, 2, 200
2014-05-12, 2014, 1, 100
];
```

When we reload this code, the table viewer will look like the following screenshot:

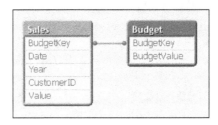

The synthetic key no longer exists and everything looks a lot neater.

 We will ignore any potential data issues with this particular dataset for now — we will cover more on that later in this chapter.

To see the composite key in action, I like to use a table box with values from both tables, just to see that the association works:

CustomerID	Year	Value	BudgetKey	BudgetValue
1	2013	100	12013	10000
1	2014	100	12014	12000
2	2013	200	22013	15000
2	2014	200	22014	17500

A table box works very well for this use case. I utilize them all the time when testing key associations like this. It is almost the only time that I use table boxes these days! In a normal user interface, a table box can be useful to display transaction-level information, but you can also use a straight table for this and have far more control with the chart than with the table. Totals, set analyses in expressions, and visual cues are all things that you can have in a straight table that you can't have in a table box.

We need to concern ourselves with key collision potentials; in this case, the key value of **12013**, composed of the **CustomerID** value of **1** and the **Year** value of **2013**. Let's imagine a further set of values where the **CustomerID** value is **120** and the **Year** value is **13**. That would cause a problem because both combinations would be **12013**. For that reason, and this should be considered a best practice, I would prefer to see an additional piece of text added between the two keys like the following:

```
. . .
CustomerID & '-' & Year as BudgetKey,
. . .
```

If we do that, then the first set of values would give a key of **1-2013** and the second would give a key of **120-13** — there would no longer be a concern about key collision. The text that you use as the separator can be anything — characters such as the hyphen, underscore, and vertical bar are all commonly used.

> Note that if you use keys like this in calculations or Dollar-sign Expansion (which would not be a good practice), then a hyphen could be interpreted as a minus sign. We shouldn't really use keys like that though.

Using one of the Hash functions

A **Hash** function takes the number of fields as a parameter and creates a fixed length string representing the hash of those values. The length of the string, and hence the possibility of having key collisions, is determined by the hash bit length. There are the following three functions:

* `Hash128()`
* `Hash160()`
* `Hash256()`

The number at the end of the function name (`128`, `160`, or `256`) represents the number of bits that will be used for the hash string. We don't really need to worry too much about the potential for key collision — in his blog post on the subject, Barry Harmsen, co-author of *QlikView 11 for Developers*, *Packt Publishing*, worked out that the chance of a collision using `Hash128()` was one in 680 million (`http://www.qlikfix.com/2014/03/11/hash-functions-collisions/`).

Of course, if you do have a large dataset where that risk becomes greater, then using the `Hash256()` function instead will reduce the possibility to, effectively, zero. Of course, a longer hash key will take up more space.

If we were to use a Hash function in our script, it would look like the following:

```
Budget:
Load
    Hash128(CustomerID, Year) as BudgetKey,
    BudgetValue
    . . .
```

```
Sales:
Load
    Date,
    Year,
    CustomerID,
    Hash128(CustomerID, Year) as BudgetKey,
    Value
    . . .
```

Notice that the function just takes a list of field values. The Hash functions are deterministic—if you pass the same values to the function, you will get the same hash value returned. However, as well as having the same values, the order that the fields are passed in the function must also be identical.

This load will produce values that look like the following in my table box:

CustomerID	Year	Value	BudgetKey	BudgetValue
1	2013	100	DYL1<51`_X(R6[2_R8#>50	10000
1	2014	100	HBFK;#0]KWHI;T<V^SI>5(	12000
2	2013	200	H8L0(A@3FW8N%C=3G8+>5$	15000
2	2014	200	L!FJ'/?02XXD*<G*SSQ>5,	17500

The other thing that is important to know about the Hash functions is that their deterministic nature should transcend different reloads on different machines. If you run the same script as I did, on the same version of QlikView, you should get the same result.

Using the AutoNumber function

One of the problems with both of the two previously mentioned approaches is that the keys that are generated are string values and, as we saw in the previous chapter, they will take up a lot of space. It is far more efficient to use integer keys—and especially sequential integer keys (because they are not stored in the symbol tables). The AutoNumber function will do that for us.

The AutoNumber function will accept a string value and return an integer. How it works is that during the brief lifetime of a load script execution, QlikView maintains an internal database to store the passed string values. If you pass exactly the same value, then you will get exactly the same integer returned. It can be said to be deterministic (given the same input, you will get the same output), but only within the current execution of the script.

This last point is important to note. If I pass "XXX" and get a return of 999 today, I cannot guarantee that "XXX" will return 999 tomorrow. The internal database is created anew at each execution of the script, and so the integer that is returned depends on the values that are passed during the load. It is quite likely that tomorrow's dataset will have different values in different orders so will return different integers.

AutoNumber will accept two possible parameters—a text value and an AutoID. This AutoID is a descriptor of what list of sequential integers will be used, so we can see that we have multiple internal databases, each with its own set of sequential integers. You should always use an AutoID with the AutoNumber function.

When creating a composite key, we combine the AutoNumber function with the string concatenation that we used previously.

 There is a "hybrid" function of AutoNumber and Hash (128 and 256) that will generate the hash value and then use that string in the AutoNumber calculation. This is useful, but it does not have the facility to pass the AutoID.

If we modify our script to use AutoNumber, then it should look something like the following:

```
Budget:
Load
    Year, CustomerID,
    AutoNumber(CustomerID & '-' & Year, 'Budget') as BudgetKey,
    BudgetValue
    . . .


Sales:
Load
    Date,
    Year,
    CustomerID,
    AutoNumber(CustomerID & '-' & Year, 'Budget') as BudgetKey,
    Value
    . . .
```

The table box will look like the following:

CustomerID	Year	Value	BudgetKey	BudgetValue
1	2013	100	1	10000
1	2014	100	3	12000
2	2013	200	2	15000
2	2014	200	4	17500

We now have a sequential integer key instead of the text values.

One thing that is interesting to point out is that the string values for keys make it easy to see the lineage of a key—you can discern the different parts of the key. I will often keep the keys as strings during a development cycle just for this reason. Then, when moving to production, I will change them to use `AutoNumber`.

Realizing that facts are calculated at the level of their table

One thing that new QlikView developers, especially those with a SQL background, have difficulty grasping is that when QlikView performs a calculation, it performs it at the correct level for the table in which the fact exists. Now, I know what I just wrote might not make any sense, but let me illustrate it with an example.

If I have an `OrderHeader` table and an `OrderLine` table in SQL Server, I might load them into QlikView using the following script:

```
OrderHeader:
LOAD OrderID,
   OrderDate,
   CustomerID,
   EmployeeID,
   Freight;
SQL SELECT *
FROM QVTraining.dbo.OrderHeader;

OrderLine:
LOAD OrderID,
   "LineNo",
   ProductID,
   Quantity,
   SalesPrice,
   SalesCost,
   LineValue,
   LineCost;
SQL SELECT *
FROM QVTraining.dbo.OrderLine;
```

Note that there are facts here at different levels. In the `OrderLine` table, we have the `LineValue` and `LineCost` facts. In the `OrderHeader` table, we have the `Freight` fact.

If I want to look at the total sales and total freights by a customer, I could create a chart like the following:

Dimension	Total Freight Expression	Total Sales Expression
CustomerID	Sum(Freight)	Sum(LineValue)

This would produce a straight table that looks as follows:

CustomerID	Total Freight	Total Sales
	1,498,116.84	998,296,382.35
1001	7,630.71	3,360,064.06
1002	7,916.07	4,639,691.47
1003	8,188.87	4,963,990.16
1004	7,879.04	5,678,877.59
1005	7,413.66	3,827,835.46
1006	7,856.24	5,470,773.01
1007	7,843.42	4,819,726.77
1008	7,295.45	4,360,783.45
1009	7,110.83	4,509,171.42
1010	7,406.63	5,519,946.07
1011	7,324.32	5,066,749.68
1012	6,653.31	4,068,364.91
1013	7,207.09	4,704,212.66
1014	7,562.32	4,808,996.39
1015	6,999.62	4,725,484.66
1016	7,629.47	5,446,577.47
1017	8,447.81	5,128,596.12

Now, this is actually correct. The total freights and sales values are correctly stated for each customer. The values have been correctly calculated at the level that they exist in the data model.

If I were to do something similar in SQL, I might create a query like the following:

```
SELECT
    OH.CustomerID,
    CAST(Sum(OH.Freight) As money) As [Total Freight],
    CAST(SUM(OL.LineValue) As money) As [Total Sales]
FROM OrderHeader OH
INNER JOIN OrderLine OL
ON OH.OrderID=OL.OrderID
GROUP BY OH.CustomerID
ORDER BY 1
```

The result might look like the following screenshot:

	CustomerID	Total Freight	Total Sales
1	1001	55790.16	3360064.06
2	1002	92202.98	4639691.47
3	1003	80287.23	4963990.16
4	1004	93817.77	5678877.59
5	1005	77836.41	3827835.46
6	1006	96574.37	5470773.01
7	1007	95090.42	4819726.77
8	1008	69295.74	4360783.45
9	1009	81225.48	4509171.42
10	1010	92216.97	5519946.07
11	1011	77006.00	5066749.68
12	1012	77694.56	4068364.91
13	1013	82742.20	4704212.66
14	1014	99173.56	4808996.39
15	1015	82172.07	4725484.66

We can see that the sales values match with QlikView, but the freight values are totally overstated. This is because the freight values have been brought down a level and are being totaled with the same freight value repeated for every line in the one order. If the freight value was $10 for an order and there were 10 order lines, QlikView would report a correct freight value of $10 while the SQL query would give us an incorrect value of $100.

This is really important for us to know about when we come to data modeling. We need to be careful with this. In this instance, if a user were to drill into a particular product, the freight total will still be reported at $10. It is always worth checking with the business whether they need those facts to be moved down a level and apportioned based on a business rule.

Joining data

As part of basic training, you should have been introduced to the concepts of join, concatenate, and `ApplyMap`. You may have also heard of functions such as `Join` and `Keep`. Hopefully, you have a good idea of what each does, but I feel that it is important to review them here so that we all know what is happening when we use these functions and what the advantages and disadvantages are of using the functions in different scenarios.

Understanding Join and Keep

Even though the QlikView data model is an associative one, we can still use joins in the script to bring different tables together into one. This is something that you will do a lot when data modeling, so it is important to understand.

As with SQL, we can perform inner, left, right, and outer joins. We execute the joins in a logically similar way to SQL, except that instead of loading the multiple tables together in one statement, we load the data in two or more statements, separated by Join statements. I will explain this using some simple data examples.

Inner joins

An **inner join** will join two tables together based on matches across common key values. If there are rows in either table where there are no matches, then those rows will no longer exist in the final combined table. The following is an example load:

```
Table1:
Load * Inline [
FieldA, FieldB, FieldC
1, A, 1A
2, B, 2B
3, C, 3C
];

Inner Join (Table1)
Load * Inline [
FieldA, FieldD, FieldE
2, X, 2X
3, Y, 3Y
4, Z, 4Z
];
```

This will result in a single table with five fields and two rows that looks like the following:

FieldA	FieldB	FieldC	FieldD	FieldE
2	B	2B	X	2X
3	C	3C	Y	3Y

I describe an inner join as destructive because it will remove rows from either table. Because of this, you need to think carefully about its use.

Note that in all the examples of `Join`, we will use the option to include the table name—as in `Join (TableName)`—as a parameter to `Join`. If you don't include it, then the join will be assumed to be to the last loaded table. It is always be best practice to explicitly state it.

Left and right joins

I use left joins quite frequently, but rarely a right one. Which is which? Well, the first table that you load is the left table. The second table that you use the `Join` statement on is the right table.

The left join will keep all records in the left, or first, table and will join any matching rows from the right table. If there are rows in the right table that do not match, they will be discarded. The right join is the exact opposite. As such, these joins are also destructive as you can lose rows from one of the tables.

We will use the previous example script and change `Inner` to `Left`:

```
. . .
Left Join (Table1)
. . .
```

This results in a table that looks like the following:

FieldA	FieldB	FieldC	FieldD	FieldE
1	A	1A	-	-
2	B	2B	X	2X
3	C	3C	Y	3Y

Note that the first row has been retained from the left table, despite there being no matches. However, `FieldD` and `FieldE` in that row are null.

Changing from `Left` to `Right` will result in the following table:

FieldA	FieldB	FieldC	FieldD	FieldE
2	B	2B	X	2X
3	C	3C	Y	3Y
4	-	-	Z	4Z

In this case, the row from the left table has been discarded while the unmatched row from the right table is retained with null values.

Outer joins

An **outer join** will retain all the rows from all the tables. Matching rows will have all their values populated whereas unmatched rows will have null values in the appropriate fields.

For example, if we replace the `Left` or `Right` join in the previous script with the word `Outer`, then we will get a table similar to the following:

FieldA	FieldB	FieldC	FieldD	FieldE
1	A	1A	-	-
2	B	2B	X	2X
3	C	3C	Y	3Y
4	-	-	Z	4Z

 The keyword `Outer` is not mandatory. This means that `Outer Join (Table1)` and `Join (Table1)` are the same join.

Cartesian joins

For newbie QlikView developers who have come from the world of SQL, it can be a struggle to understand that you don't get to tell QlikView which fields it should be joining on. You will also notice that you don't need to tell QlikView anything about the datatypes of the joining fields.

This is because QlikView has a simple rule on the join—if you have fields with the same field names, just as with the associative logic, then these will be used to join. So you do have some control over this because you can rename fields in both tables as you are loading them.

The datatype issue is even easier to explain—QlikView essentially doesn't do datatypes. Most data in QlikView is represented by a **dual**—a combination of formatted text and a numeric value. If there is a number in the dual, then QlikView uses this to make the join—even if the format of the text is different.

But what happens if you don't have any fields to join on between the two tables? What we get in that scenario is a **Cartesian join**—the product of both tables. Let's have a look at an example:

```
Rene:
Load * Inline [
Field1, Field2
1, A
2, B
3, C
];
```

```
Join (Rene)
Load * Inline [
Field3, Field4
4, X
5, Y
6, Z
];
```

This results in a table like the following:

Field1	Field2	Field3	Field4
1	A	4	X
1	A	5	Y
1	A	6	Z
2	B	4	X
2	B	5	Y
2	B	6	Z
3	C	4	X
3	C	5	Y
3	C	6	Z

We can see that every row in the first table has been matched with each row in the second table.

Now this is something that you will have to watch out for because even with moderately sized datasets, a Cartesian join will cause a huge increase in the number of final rows. For example, having a Cartesian join between two tables with 100,000 rows each will result in a joined table with 10,000,000,000 rows! This issue quite often arises if you rename a field in one table and then forget to change the field in a joined table.

Saying that though, there are some circumstances where a Cartesian product is a desired result. There are some situations where I might want to have every value in one table matched with every value in another. An example of this might be where I match every account number that I have in the system with every date in the calendar so that I can calculate a daily balance, whether there were any transactions on that day or not.

Understanding the effect of duplicate key values on joins

If you have some understanding of joins, you will be aware that when one of the tables has rows with duplicate values of the join key — which is common with primary to foreign key joins — then the resultant table will also have multiple rows. A quick example to illustrate this is as follows:

```
Dimension:
Load * Inline [
```

```
KeyField, DimensionValue
1, One
2, Two
3, Three
];

Left Join (Dimension)
Load * Inline [
KeyField, Value
1, 100
2, 200
3, 301
3, 302
];
```

This will result in a table like the following:

KeyField	DimensionValue	Value
1	One	100
2	Two	200
3	Three	301
3	Three	302

We have two rows for the `KeyField` value 3. This is expected. We do need to be careful though that this situation does not arise when joining data to a fact table. If we join additional tables to a fact table, and that generates additional rows in the fact table, then all of your calculations on those values can no longer be relied on as there are duplicates. This is definitely something that you need to be aware of when data modeling.

What if there are duplicate key values in both tables? For example, suppose that the first table looked like the following:

```
Dimension:
Load * Inline [
KeyField, DimensionValue
1, One
2, Two
3, Three.1
3, Three.2
3, Three.3
];
```

This will lead us to a table that looks like the following:

KeyField	DimensionValue	Value
1	One	100
2	Two	200
3	Three.1	301
3	Three.1	302
3	Three.2	301
3	Three.2	302
3	Three.3	301
3	Three.3	302

The resulting number of rows is the product of the number of keys in each table. This is something that I have seen happen in the field and something that you really need to look out for. The symptoms will be a far-longer-than-expected load time and large amounts of memory consumed. Have a look at this, perhaps silly, example:

```
BigSillyTable:
Load
    Floor(Rand()*5) As Key1,
    Rand()*1000 As Value1
Autogenerate(1000);

Join
Load
    Floor(Rand()*5) As Key1,
    Rand()*1000 As Value2
AutoGenerate(1000);
```

There are only 1,000 rows in each table with a low cardinality key that is duplicated (so there is an average of 200 rows per key). The resulting table will have approximately 200,000 rows!

This may seem a bit silly, but I have come across something similar.

Understanding Keep

The Keep syntax is quite interesting. It operates in a similar way to one of the destructive joins—it must take an inner, left, or right keyword—that means it will remove appropriate rows from the tables where there are no matches. However, it then leaves the tables as separate entities instead of joining them together into one.

As a use case, consider what might happen if you have a list of account numbers loaded and then used left Keep to load a transaction table. You would be left with the account and transaction tables as separate entities, but the transaction table would only contain rows where there was a matching row in the account table.

Concatenating rows

Concatenation in QlikView is quite similar to the Union All function in SQL (we can make it like a simple union by using the Distinct keyword when loading the tables). As with many things in QlikView, it is a little easier to implement than a union, in that you don't have to always ensure that both tables being concatenated have the same number of fields. If you concatenate tables with different numbers of fields, QlikView will go ahead and add any additional fields and populate nulls into any fields that didn't already have values. It is useful to review some of the aspects of Concatenate because we use it very often in data modeling.

Reviewing Concatenate

If you have come across concatenation before, you should be aware that QlikView will automatically concatenate tables based on both tables having the exact same number of fields and having all fields with the same names (case sensitive). For example, consider the following load statements:

```
Table1:
Load * Inline [
A, B, C
1, 2, 3
4, 5, 6
];

Table2:
Load * Inline [
A, C, B
7, 8, 9
10, 11, 12
];
```

This will not actually end with two tables. Instead, we will have one table, Table1, with four rows:

A	B	C
1	2	3
4	5	6
7	9	8
10	12	11

If the two tables do not have identical fields, then we can force the concatenation to happen using the Concatenate keyword:

```
Table:
Load * Inline [
A, B, C
1, 2, 3
4, 5, 6
];

Concatenate (Table1)
Load * Inline [
A, C
7, 8
10, 11
];
```

This will result in a table like the following:

A	B	C
1	2	3
4	5	6
7	-	8
10	-	11

You will notice that the rows where there were no values for field **B** have been populated with null.

There is also a NoConcatenate keyword that might be useful for us to know about. It stops a table being concatenated, even if it has the same field names as an existing table. Several times, I have loaded a table in a script only to have it completely disappear. After several frustrating minutes debugging, I discovered that I have named the fields the same as an existing table—which causes automatic concatenation. My table hadn't really disappeared, the values had just been concatenated to the existing table.

Differentiating Concatenate and Join

Sometimes it can be difficult to understand what the effective difference is between Concatenate and Join and when we should use either of them. So, let's look at a couple of examples that will help us understand the differences.

Here are a couple of tables:

Key	Value1
1	100
2	200
3	300

Key	Value2
1	1000
2	2000
3	3000

Now, if I load these tables with `Concatenate`, I will get a resulting table that looks like the following:

Key	Value1	Value2
1	100	-
1	-	1000
2	200	-
2	-	2000
3	300	-
3	-	3000

If I loaded this table with `Join`, the result looks like the following:

Key	Value1	Value2
1	100	1000
2	200	2000
3	300	3000

We will have a longer data table with `Concatenate`, but the symbol tables will be identical. In fact, the results when we come to use these values in a chart will actually be identical! All the QlikView functions that we use most of the time, such as `Sum`, `Count`, `Avg`, and so on, will ignore the null values, so we will get the same results using both datasets.

So, when we have a 1:1 match between tables like this, both `Join` and `Concatenate` will give us effectively the same result. However, if there is not a 1:1 match — where there are multiple key values in one or more of the tables — then `Join` will not produce the correct result, but `Concatenate` will. This is an important consideration when it comes to dealing with multiple fact tables, as we will see later.

 It is worth considering that if you need to calculate something like *Value1/Value2* on every line, then they will need to be matched with `Join` (or `ApplyMap` as discussed in the following section).

Mapping data with ApplyMap

This is one of my favorite functions in QlikView — I use it all the time. It is extremely versatile in moving data from one place to another and enriching or cleansing data. Let's review some of the functionality of this very useful tool.

Reviewing the basic functionality of ApplyMap

The basic function of ApplyMap is to move data — usually text data — from a mapping table into a dimension table. This is a very normal operation in dimensional modeling. Transactional databases tend to be populated by a lot of mapping tables — tables that just have a key value and a text value.

The first thing that we need to have for ApplyMap is to load the mapping table of values to map from. There are a few rules for this table that we should know:

- A mapping table is loaded with a normal Load statement that is preceded by a Mapping statement.
- The mapping table can only have two columns.
- The names of the columns are not important — only the order that the columns are loaded is important:
    - The first column is the mapping lookup value
    - The second column is the mapping return value
- The mapping table does not survive past the end of the script. Once the script has loaded, all mapping tables are removed from memory.
- There is effectively no limit on the number of rows in the mapping table. I have used mapping tables with millions of rows.
- Mapping tables must be loaded in the script before they are called via ApplyMap. This should be obvious, but I have seen some confusion around it.

As an example, consider the following table:

```
Mapping_Table:
Mapping
Load * Inline [
LookupID, LookupValue
1, First
2, Second
3, Third
];
```

There are a couple of things to note. First, let's look at the table alias—Mapping_Table. This will be used later in the ApplyMap function call (and we always need to explicitly name our mapping tables—this is, of course, best practice for all tables). The second thing to note is the names of the columns. I have just used a generic LookupID and LookupValue. These are not important. I don't expect them to associate to anything in my main data model. Even if they did accidentally have the same name as a field in my data model, there is no issue as the mapping table doesn't associate and doesn't survive the end of the script load anyway.

So, I am going to pass a value to the ApplyMap function—in this case, hopefully, either 1, 2, or 3—and expect to get back one of the text values—First, Second, or Third.

In the last sentence, I did say, "hopefully." This is another great thing about ApplyMap, in that we can handle situations where the passed ID value does not exist; we can specify a default value.

Let's look at an example of using the mentioned map:

```
Table:
Load
    ID,
    Name,
    ApplyMap('Mapping_Table', PositionID, 'Other') As Position
Inline [
ID, Name, PositionID
101, Joe, 1
102, Jane, 2
103, Tom, 3
104, Mika, 4
];
```

In the ApplyMap function, we have used the Mapping_Table table alias of our mapping table—note that we pass this value, in this case, as a string literal. We are passing the ID to be looked up from the data—PositionID—which will contain one of 1, 2, 3, or 4. Finally, we pass a third parameter (which is optional) to specify what the return value should be if there is no match on the IDs.

Note that you don't always have to pass a string literal—anything that returns a string that matches to a previously loaded mapping table will work.

This load will result in the following table:

ID	Name	Position
101	Joe	First
102	Jane	Second
103	Tom	Third
104	Mika	Other

We can see that **Joe**, **Jane**, and **Tom** were successfully mapped to the correct position, whereas **Mika**, whose ID was **104**, did not have a matching value in the mapping table so ended up with **Other** as the position value.

Mapping numbers

Something that many people don't think about, but which works very well, is to use the mapping functionality to move a number from one place to another. As an example, imagine that I had a product cost table in my database that stored the averaged cost for each product per month. I want to use this value in my fact table to calculate a margin amount per line. My mapping load may look something like the following:

```
Product_Cost_Map:
Mapping Load
    Floor(MonthStart(CostMonth)) & '-' & ProductID As LookupID,
    [Cost Value] As LookupValue;
SQL SELECT * From [Monthly Product Cost];
```

A good thing to note here is that we are using a composite key for the lookup ID. This is quite common and never an issue—as long as you use the exact same syntax and value types in the `ApplyMap` call.

 Recall that the `Floor` function will take any numeric value, remove any decimal part—without rounding—and return just the integer part. The `MonthStart` function will always return the first of the month for any date passed to it.

Once we have this table loaded—and, depending on the database, this could have millions of rows—then we can use it in the fact table load. It will look something like this:

```
Fact:
Load
    ...
    SalesDate,
```

```
    ProductID,
    Quantity,
    ApplyMap('Product_Cost_Map', Floor(MonthStart(SalesDate)) & '-'
            & ProductID,0)
            *Quantity As LineCost,
    . . .
```

In this case, we use the `MonthStart` function on the sales date and combine it with `ProductID` to create the composite key.

Here, we also use a default value of 0 — if we can't locate the date and product combination in the mapping table, then we should use 0. We could, instead, use another mapping to get a default value:

```
Fact:
Load
    . . .
    SalesDate,
    ProductID,
    Quantity,
    ApplyMap('Product_Cost_Map',
            Floor(MonthStart(SalesDate)) & '-' & ProductID,
            ApplyMap('Default_Cost_Map', ProductID, 0))
            *Quantity As LineCost,
    . . .
```

So, we can see that we can nest `ApplyMap` calls to achieve the logic that we need.

Using ApplyMap instead of Join with duplicate rows

We saw earlier in the discussion on joins that where there are rows with duplicate join IDs in one (or both) of the tables, the join will result in more rows in the joined table. This is often an undesired result — especially if you are joining a dimension value to a fact table. Creating additional rows in the fact table will result in incorrect results.

There are a number of ways of making sure that the dimension table that you join to the fact table will only have one row joined and not cause this problem. However, I often just use `ApplyMap` in this situation and make sure that the values that I want to be joined are sorted to the top. This is because in a mapping table, if there are duplicate key values, only the first row containing that key will be used.

As an example, I have modified the earlier basic example:

```
Mapping_Table:
Mapping
Load * Inline [
```

```
LookupID, LookupValue
1, First
2, Second.1
2, Second.2
3, Third.1
3, Third.2
3, Third.3
];
```

We can see that there are now duplicate values for the 2 and 3 keys. When we load the table as before, we will get this result:

ID	Name	Position
101	Joe	First
102	Jane	Second.1
103	Tom	Third.1
104	Mika	Other

We can see that the additional rows with the duplicate keys are completely ignored and only the first row containing the key is used. Therefore, if we make sure that the rows are loaded in the order that we want—by whatever order by clause we need to construct—we can just use ApplyMap to move the data into the fact table. We will be sure that no additional rows can possibly be created as they might be with Join.

Dimensional data modeling

There are several methodologies for implementing a data warehouse or data mart that might be useful to consider when implementing QlikView in an organization. However, for me, the best approach is dimensional modeling—often called **Kimball dimensional modeling**—as proposed by Ralph Kimball and Margy Ross in the book *The Data Warehouse Toolkit, John Wiley & Sons*, now available in its third edition.

Some other methodologies, most noticeably that proposed by Bill Inmon, offer a "top-down" approach to data warehousing whereby a normalized data model is built that spans the entire enterprise, then data marts are built off this to support lines of business or specific business processes. Now, QlikView can sit very readily in this model as the data mart tool, feeding off the **Enterprise Data Warehouse (EDW)**. However, QlikView cannot implement the normalized EDW.

In my opinion, Kimball dimensional modeling, on the other hand, is right up QlikView's street. In fact, I would suggest that you can build almost all elements of this type of data warehouse using just QlikView! The difference is that Kimball's approach is more "bottom-up"—the data marts (in our case, QlikView applications) are built first and then they can be combined to build a bigger data warehouse. Also, with this approach, we can build a data framework that power users can make use of to build their own analyses, beyond what might be achievable with other tools.

In this chapter, I am going to talk about some of the concepts of Kimball dimensional modeling, but I will not be going into deep detail on Kimball's concepts. I will describe the concept at a high level and then go in to detail on how that can be applied from a QlikView point of view. To find out more information on Kimball dimensional modeling, I recommend the following:

- Buy and read *The Data Warehouse Toolkit*
- Check out the Kimball Group's online resources at `http://www.kimballgroup.com/data-warehouse-business-intelligence-resources`

There are some key fundamental concepts that we should understand about dimensional modeling. You may already be familiar with some of the terminology. Ralph Kimball didn't create the concepts of facts and dimensions, and you will come across those terms in many contexts. However, he has created a solid methodology for modeling data in multiple different scenarios.

Differentiating between facts and dimensions

Essentially, facts are numbers. They are numbers that we will add up, average, count, or apply some other calculation to. For example, sales value, sales quantity, and monthly balance are all facts.

Dimensions are the values that give context to our facts. So, customer or product are both examples of dimensions. Date is also a good example of a dimension—almost every fact that you will come across will have a date context.

We store dimensions in a table of attributes. For example, a customer table might have attributes of name, city, or country. A date table will have attributes such as year, month, quarter, and week.

We will store one or many facts in a table along with the keys to associate them to the dimensions. An example of a row in a sales fact table might look like the following:

RowID	DateID	CustomerID	ProductID	StoreID	Quantity	Sales Value	Sales Cost	Sales Margin
2345	20140520	2340000563	1929	34	20	120.00	100.00	20.00

What this row of data tells us is that on a particular date, in a particular store, a particular customer purchased 20 units of a particular product that had a sales value of $120.00. We can find out what product was sold by looking for **ProductID** 1929 in the `Product` dimension table.

Of course, this is not a normal query! Typically, we might start by selecting a store and then that would select for us all the fact rows that are associated with that row. We then have a calculation to add up all the sales values from that set of rows to give us the total sales for that store.

Understanding the grain

The single row in the previous fact table represents the **grain** of the data — the lowest level — that we are going to report on. Typically, for best results, you want the grain to be the lowest transaction level. In this case, it might not be. This customer might have bought the same product several times on the same day, so this row would actually represent an aggregated view of the data. If we added in a new field for, say, transaction number or perhaps transaction time, then we would increase the number of rows in the fact table, lowering the level of the data and changing the grain.

When we are designing the model, we need to understand what grain we want the data to be at. The business requirement will define the grain for us — if it is important for us to know the times of transactions, then we may want to have the grain at a lower level. If not, then a higher level is good. Of course, we need to consider that part of the joy of QlikView is to answer those questions that haven't been asked, so we may need to consider that, while the business does not need that grain now, they will perhaps need it in the future. We also need to balance that against the number of transaction rows in the fact table, which will be the primary driver of the size of our in-memory document and the speed of results for our users.

Understanding star schemas

Once we have loaded the fact table and the four dimension tables discussed previously, our schema might look something like the following:

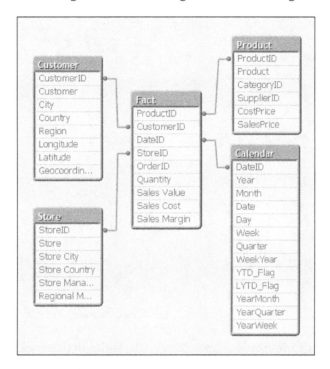

This structure, with one fact table and several dimension tables, with the dimensions all being at one level, is a classic **star schema**.

If we look at the `Product` table here, we will note that there is a `CategoryID` field and a `SupplierID` field. This would lead us to understand that there is additional data available for `Category` and `Supplier` that we could load and end up with a schema like the following:

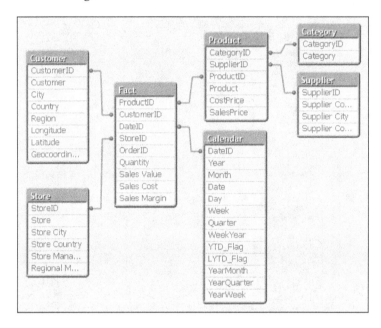

This is no longer a "pure" star schema. As we add tables in this way, the schema starts to become more like a snowflake than a star—it is called a **snowflake** schema.

We discussed in the previous chapter about the potential issues in having many tables in a schema because of the number of joins across data tables. It is important for us to understand that it isn't necessary for the snowflake to remain and that we should actually move the data from the `Category` and `Supplier` tables into the `Product` table, returning to the star schema. This is not just for QlikView; it is as recommended by Kimball. Of course, we don't always have to be perfect and pragmatism should be applied.

By joining the category and supplier information into the `Product` table, we will restore the star schema and, from a QlikView point of view, probably improve performance of queries. The `Product` table will be widened, and hence the underlying data table would increase in width also, but we also have the option of dropping the `CategoryID` and `SupplierID` fields so it probably will not have a very large increase in size. As dimension tables are, generally, relatively smaller than the fact tables, any additional width in the data table will not unduly increase the size of the overall document in memory.

Summing with facts

There are some complications with facts when it comes to the types of calculations that we can perform on them. The most basic calculation that we can do with any fact is to add up the values in that field using the Sum function. But not all facts will work correctly in all circumstances.

Luckily, most facts will probably be fully **additive**. This means that we can perform a Sum function using that field and we will get a sensible and correct answer no matter what context we apply — no matter what selections we make or charts we use that calculation in. For example, the Sales Value field is usually going to be additive across all dimensions and give us a correct answer as we make different selections.

Some facts are only **semi-additive**. These facts can be summed, but only across some of the dimensions. For other dimensions, it does not make sense to sum them, for example, a monthly balance field. It makes sense to select a month and then sum these balances across accounts, territories, cities, and so on, but it doesn't make sense at all to sum a balance across months. If the balance in my checking account is about $100 at the end of every month, it doesn't mean that it will be $1,200 at the end of the year (though I really wish it did!).

Yet other facts won't be additive at all. These are called **non-additive** facts. Any ratio or percent value would not be additive. For example, if we stored the sales margin percent (the sales margin divided by the sales value) in the fact table, then this could not be sensibly added up in any way. If possible, we shouldn't have such ratios in the fact table and should, instead, always retain the original additive facts. It is perfectly sensible to calculate a margin percent expression like this in QlikView:

```
Sum([Sales Margin])/Sum([Sales Value])
```

Because both of the facts involved are additive, the expression will calculate correctly across all dimensions.

Discovering more about facts

There are a few different types of fact tables that we will encounter reasonably regularly. These are as follows:

- Transaction
- Periodic snapshot
- Factless

The following sections give a brief description of these and how you may need to deal with them in QlikView.

Transaction fact tables

The **transaction fact table** is by far the most common type that you will encounter. At the lowest grain, each row in the table represents one event that has happened; for example, a sale of a particular product in a particular store to a particular customer at a particular time by a particular operator at a particular till. Another example might be the scanning of a product as it is placed into a pick basket in a warehouse automated pick system.

Each of these is an atomic event — it is the lowest level of detail that we can have about the process in question. It also gives us more flexibility from a QlikView point of view in that we can calculate our results over many different dimensions.

Because this transaction represents one event, there are generally relatively few facts associated with it. We might, for example, just have quantity and value. If the system gives us the information, we might also have cost and perhaps a derived margin, but that would be all.

Periodic snapshot fact tables

We can, as we have already discussed, aggregate transactions to a higher level. If the retailer does not care about which customer bought a product or at what till, we might remove the customer, till, time, and operator from the transaction and then roll up the values to just date, store, and product, summing up the facts appropriately.

Often, this is done for a performance benefit because less rows will equal less memory used by QlikView. However, when we change the grain and reduce the number of dimensions, we also have the opportunity to add other facts to the table from other events. For example, retailers often throw out unsaleable items — this is called **waste**. This event would also have a date, store, and product associated with it so we could join the two fact tables to create a new, wider fact table. Any other events in the store that have a date and product associated with them could equally be joined in.

The fact tables are called **periodic snapshot** fact tables. Usually they have a period associated with them such as a particular day or rolled up to week or month.

In the previous example, the periodic snapshot table will have the same structure as a transaction fact table and it is fair to say that it still counts as a transaction fact table for modeling purposes. The facts are rolled up from the underlying facts and can be treated the same. However, there are periodic snapshot tables that will represent the end of period position for a value — for example, an account balance or an inventory level — and we need to be careful with these because the facts will be semi-additive.

Factless fact tables

There are fact tables that record an atomic event that doesn't have any particular amount or other measure associated with it. For example, many retailers will have a person on the shop floor who has the task of wandering around checking for empty shelves. If they find a shelf where all the stock has been sold, they scan the product bar code off the shelf and this goes into the backend system. This "gap count" just records the date, time, shelf number, and product. There is no quantity or value involved.

Quite often, we will create a fact—usually just with a value of 1—to be used in calculations.

Dealing with nulls in fact tables in QlikView

Because QlikView isn't too hung up on referential integrity of data, we as designers should always be thinking about it because we shouldn't really allow a disconnect between dimension tables and fact tables. Null values in fact fields are not a problem for QlikView. They will get completely ignored in the majority of calculations, and this is the correct behavior that we want.

Null values in dimension keys are a different matter. QlikView will allow them, but this causes us a problem when it comes to charts. Let's look at a very simple example:

```
Dimension:
Load * Inline [
CustomerID, Customer, Country
1, Customer A, USA
2, Customer B, USA
3, Customer C, UK
4, Customer D, UK
];

Fact:
Load
*
Inline [
Date, CustomerID, Sales Value
2014-01-01, 1, 100
2014-01-01, 2, 100
2014-01-01, 3, 100
2014-01-01, 4, 100
2014-01-01, , 100
2014-01-02, 1, 100
2014-01-02, 2, 100
2014-01-02, 4, 100
];
```

Note that this inline statement won't actually produce a null value; it will instead produce a zero length string. However, this is good enough for the example.

If we create a chart for the sum of sales value by country, it will look like the following:

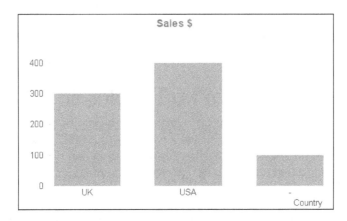

We have a bar that shows an amount associated with a null value. We can't select this bar to find out any other information. I can't drill down to discover the transactions that are not associated to a country.

The way to handle this is to actually create an additional row in the dimension table with a default value and key that we can use in the fact table:

```
Dimension:
Load * Inline [
CustomerID, Customer, Country
0, Missing, Missing
1, Customer A, USA
2, Customer B, USA
3, Customer C, UK
4, Customer D, UK
];

Fact:
Load
    Date,
```

```
    If(Len(CustomerID)=0, 0, CustomerID) As CustomerID,
    [Sales Value]
Inline [
Date, CustomerID, Sales Value
2014-01-01, 1, 100
2014-01-01, 2, 100
2014-01-01, 3, 100
2014-01-01, 4, 100
2014-01-01, , 100
2014-01-02, 1, 100
2014-01-02, 2, 100
2014-01-02, 4, 100
];
```

We now have a value in the `Country` field that we can drill into to discover fact table rows that do not have a customer key:

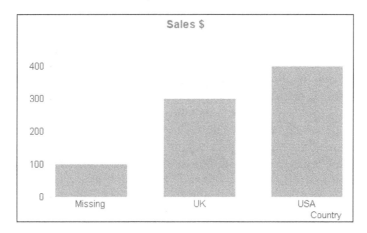

There may actually be cases where the key is not missing but is just not applicable. In that case, we can add an additional "Not Applicable" row to the dimension table to handle that situation.

Designing dimension tables

We have a good idea now about fact tables, but we have only briefly talked about the dimension tables that create the context for the facts.

Denormalizing dimensions and conformed dimensions

We discussed star schemas previously, and we discussed that snowflake schemas are not ideal for QlikView and also not recommended by Kimball.

Snowflaking dimensions is akin to the normalization process that is used to design transactional databases. While it may be appropriate for transactional databases, where insert speed is the most important thing, it is not appropriate for reporting databases, where retrieval speed is the most important thing. So denormalizing the dimension tables, by joining the lower level tables back into the main table (joining category and supplier into product in the previous example), is the most efficient method — and this applies for QlikView as well as any database warehouse.

There is another excellent reason for creating a single table to represent a dimension. We are generally not going to build only one QlikView document. We will probably have many business processes or areas that we will want to cover with our applications. These QlikView documents might share dimensions, for example, both a sales and a purchases application will have a product dimension. Depending on the organization, the product that you buy might be the same as the products that you sell. Therefore, it makes sense to build one product dimension, store it to QVD, and then use it in any documents that need it.

Dimensions created that will be shared across multiple dimensional models are called **conformed dimensions**.

Understanding surrogate keys

In Kimball dimensional modeling, there is the concept of replacing the original primary key values of dimensions, in both the dimension and fact tables, with a sequential integer value. This should especially be the case where the primary key is made up of multiple key values.

We should recognize this immediately in QlikView as we already discussed it in *Chapter 1, Performance Tuning and Scalability* — we use the **AutoNumber** function to create a numeric key to associate the dimension with the fact table.

If necessary, we can retain the original key values in the dimension table so that they can be queried, but we do not need to retain those values in the fact table.

Dealing with missing or late arriving dimension values

A late arriving dimension value is a value that does not make it into the dimension table at the time that we load the information into QlikView. Usually, this is a timing issue. The symptoms are the same as if the dimension value doesn't exist at all—we are going to have a referential integrity issue.

Let's look at a quick example:

```
Dimension:
Load * Inline [
CustomerID, Customer, Country
1, Customer A, USA
2, Customer B, USA
3, Customer C, UK
4, Customer D, UK
];

Fact:
Load * Inline [
Date, CustomerID, Sales Value
2014-01-01, 1, 100
2014-01-01, 2, 100
2014-01-01, 3, 100
2014-01-01, 4, 100
2014-01-01, 5, 100
2014-01-02, 1, 100
2014-01-02, 2, 100
2014-01-02, 4, 100
];
```

We can see that we have four rows in the dimension table, but we have five distinct key values in the fact table. We need to add additional rows to the dimension table derived from the fact table:

```
Concatenate (Dimension)
Load Distinct
    CustomerID,
    'Missing ' & CustomerID As Customer,
    'Missing ' & CustomerID As Country
Resident
    Fact
Where Len(Lookup('CustomerID', 'CustomerID', CustomerID,
'Dimension'))=0;
```

You might wonder why I am not using a `Not Exists` function here. `Exists` will check in the symbol table to see whether a value has already been loaded. We only have one symbol table per field and, in this case, both tables have the same field name—`CustomerID`—and hence will have the same symbol table. Because the fact table has been loaded, the symbol table will be fully loaded with all of the available values, so a `Not Exists` function will never return true and no additional values will be loaded.

Defining Kimball's four-step dimensional design process

Now that we know a bit more about the definitions around facts and dimensions, we can talk about Kimball's dimensional design process. This, as a basic tenet, can be applied to almost every QlikView application that you might build.

The four steps are as follows:

- Select the business process
- Declare the grain
- Identify the dimensions
- Identify the facts

Selecting the business process

There are often two ways that developers choose to pick the subject of their QlikView documents. One is line-of-business—for example, Sales, HR, Finance, and so on. The other is by business process. A **business process** is a set of activities that a business performs that may generate a set of metrics, for example, process orders, ship orders, or order stock. Each process will generate one set of facts.

The difference between a line-of-business application and a process-based application is sometimes so subtle that you'll feel there isn't really a difference at all! This is especially true where the identified line-of-business appears to only really have one process within an organization.

Take selling for example. In some organizations, the only thing that is important about selling is the taking orders process. If you are asked to build a sales application for that organization, the line-of-business and the process will be the same. In other organizations, however, they will also be looking for information on customer and prospect contacts—visits, phone calls, and so on.

The line-of-business application will probably want to try and load the facts from both processes so as to compare them and answer business questions about the relationship between visits and orders. The process-based application will tend to just focus on the one set of facts.

In a "pure" Kimball dimensional model, we focus on the process model and one fact table. Where we are building a more line-of-business application with multiple fact tables, we should apply this four step sequence for each process. We will discuss later how we handle a QlikView model with multiple fact tables.

So, the first step is to select that business process.

Declaring the grain

We have already learned what is meant by grain—the level of detail in the fact table. By declaring the grain, we are specifying what level of aggregation we want to deal with.

In almost every situation, the best choice of grain is the atomic choice—the transactional data at the lowest level of detail. Going atomic means that our users can slice and dice the information by whatever dimensions they want. By making a choice to aggregate the fact table, we remove some choice from the user. For example, if we aggregate the retail sales to day, store, and product, we remove the ability of the users to interrogate the data by till, operator, or time of day.

Identifying the dimensions

The dimensions that will be used will pretty much fall out of grain declaration. The complication here is where we are doing a line-of-business app; while we are doing this step by step for one process at a time, we need to be aware of those dimensions that are shared, and we should be sure to have a conformed dimension.

Identifying the facts

We need to specify what facts—what numbers in the data—we are going to use. We also need to think about any derived facts that might be necessary. For example, if we have a quantity and price, do we need to derive the line value?

Learning some useful reusable dimension methods

There are a couple of things that you will come up against repeatedly in creating QlikView documents. One that you will pretty much use in all QlikView documents is the creation of a calendar dimension. Another, that you might not use in every application but will come in useful, is dealing with hierarchies. Lastly, we will look at the practice of creating dimensional facts.

Creating a calendar dimension

Almost every fact table that we will come across will have a date of some sort—at least one, there may be more. Quite often, the source system that we will be extracting the data from may have a calendar table that we can use as the dimension table, but sometimes it doesn't and we need to derive one ourselves.

The basic idea of creating a calendar dimension is to first establish the bounds—what are the earliest and latest dates that should be included. Once we have that, we can generate a row for every date between those bounds (inclusive) and use QlikView functions to derive the date parts—year, month, week, and so on.

In training, you may have come across some methods to establish the minimum and maximum values of the date by querying the fact table. For example, you may have seen something like the following:

```
MinMaxDates:
Load
    Min(OrderDate) As MinDate,
    Max(OrderDate) As MaxDate
Resident
    Fact;

Let vStartDate=Peek('MinDate');
Let vEndDate=Peek('MaxDate');

Drop Table MinMaxDates;
```

There are some problems with this method, so I rarely use it outside the classroom.

One of them is that once you get past a million fact table records, the time taken to calculate the min and max values becomes more and more perceptible and unacceptable in a well-designed script.

However, for me, the main issue is that it is a pointless exercise. The minimum date will rarely, if ever, change—it is a well-known value and can therefore be stated in the script without having to try and calculate it every time. The maximum date, depending on the business, is almost always going to be today, yesterday, or some derivation thereof. Therefore, it is easily calculable without having to scan down through a data table. My calendar script is almost always going to start off something like the following:

```
Let vStartDate=Floor(MakeDate(2009,1,1));
Let vEndDate=Floor(Today());
Let vDiff=vEndDate-vStartDate+1;
```

So, I am stating that the first date for my data is January 1, 2009. The end date is today. When working with dates, I will always transform them to integer values, especially when used with variables. Integers are a lot easier to deal with. I will also always calculate the number of dates that I will need in my calendar as the last date minus the first date plus 1. The rest of my script might look like the following:

```
Calendar:
Load *,
    Date(MonthStart(DateID), 'YYYY-MM') As YearMonth,
    Year & '-' & Quarter As YearQuarter,
    WeekYear & '-' & Num(Week, '00') As YearWeek;
Load
    DateID,
    Year(DateID) As Year,
    Month(DateID) As Month,
    Date(DateID) As Date,
    Day(DateID) As Day,
    Week(DateID) As Week,
    'Q' & Ceil(Month(DateID)/3) As Quarter,
    WeekYear(DateID) As WeekYear,
    -Year2Date(DateID) As YTD_Flag,
    -Year2Date(DateID, -1) As LYTD_Flag;
Load
    RecNo()-1+$(vStartDate) As DateID
AutoGenerate($(vDiff));
```

There are a couple of preceding loads here, which I quite like to use to make scripts more readable. If you haven't come across preceding loads, any load statement that is just a list of field names and functions, terminated with a semicolon, will load its data from the next statement down in the script.

In this case, at the bottom of the pile is an `AutoGenerate` function that will generate the required number of rows. We use a calculation based on the current record number and the start date to calculate the correct date that we should use. The preceding load directly above it will create all the date parts—year, month, week, and so on, and a couple of year-to-date flags that we can use in calculations. The topmost preceding load will use fields created in the middle part to create additional fields.

If you really need a script to derive the calendar table from the data, I can highly recommend the script published on the Qlik community website by Torben Seebach from itelligence in Denmark at `http://community.qlik.com/docs/DOC-6662`.

Unwrapping hierarchies

Way back in the day, there was a piece of script going around that would unwrap a hierarchical relationship in data. It was the most complicated piece of script that you could imagine—but it worked. It was so popular that Qlik decided to create new functions in QlikView to do the operation. There are two—`Hierarchy` and `HierarchyBelongsTo`.

Creating leaves with Hierarchy

The `Hierarchy` function will unwrap the hierarchy and create multiple leaf nodes for each level of the hierarchy. Let's create a very simple hierarchical table:

```
Load * Inline [
NodeID, Location, ParentID
1, World,
2, EMEA, 1
3, Americas, 1
4, AsiaPac, 1
5, USA, 3
6, Canada, 3
7, Brazil, 3
8, UK, 2
9, Germany, 2
10, France, 2
11, China, 4
12, Japan, 4
13, New York, 5
14, Texas, 5
15, California, 5
```

```
16, London, 8
17, Greater Manchester, 8
18, Manchester, 17
19, Bavaria, 9
20, Munich, 19
21, New York, 13
22, Heuston, 14
23, San Francisco, 15
];
```

Each row has a node key, a name, and a parent key that refers to the node key of the level above. So, USA's parent key is 3, which refers to the node key of the Americas.

The first three parameters of the Hierarchy function are mandatory. The other parameters are optional. The parameters are as follows:

Parameter	Description
NodeID	This is the unique key for each row in the input table.
ParentID	This is the key that refers to the parent's node key.
NodeName	This is the field that has the name of the node.
ParentName	If we want to create a new field to store the name of the node's parent, we can pass a string value here (that means the text is passed in single quotes).
PathSource	If we want a path field — a single field containing the full hierarchical path — then we need to tell the functions which field contains the text. Usually, this will be the same as the NodeName field, and if you leave it blank, then the NodeName field will be used.
PathName	Again, if we want a path field, we need to specify a name for it — this is a string value, so the text must be in single quotes.
PathDelimiter	For the path field, this specifies the value that should separate each of the values — a string value in single quotes.
Depth	We can have a field created to store the level in the hierarchy. We pass the desired name of the new field as a string value in single quote marks.

We don't need to have the path or the depth fields created, but they can be useful to have.

To change the preceding table into a full hierarchy, we add the `Hierarchy` statement above the `Load` statement:

```
Hierarchy(NodeID, ParentID, Location, 'Parent Location', 'Location',
'PathName', '~', 'Depth')
Load * Inline [
...
```

This will produce a table that looks like the following:

NodeID	Location	ParentID	Location1	Location2	Location3	Location4	Location5	Parent Location	PathName	Depth
1	World		World	-	-	-	-		World	1
2	EMEA	1	World	EMEA	-	-	-	World	World~EMEA	2
3	Americas	1	World	Americas	-	-	-	World	World~Americas	2
4	AsiaPac	1	World	AsiaPac	-	-	-	World	World~AsiaPac	2
5	USA	3	World	Americas	USA	-	-	Americas	World~Americas~USA	3
6	Canada	3	World	Americas	Canada	-	-	Americas	World~Americas~Canada	3
7	Brazil	3	World	Americas	Brazil	-	-	Americas	World~Americas~Brazil	3
8	UK	2	World	EMEA	UK	-	-	EMEA	World~EMEA~UK	3
9	Germany	2	World	EMEA	Germany	-	-	EMEA	World~EMEA~Germany	3
10	France	2	World	EMEA	France	-	-	EMEA	World~EMEA~France	3
11	China	4	World	AsiaPac	China	-	-	AsiaPac	World~AsiaPac~China	3
12	Japan	4	World	AsiaPac	Japan	-	-	AsiaPac	World~AsiaPac~Japan	3
13	New York	5	World	Americas	USA	New York	-	USA	World~Americas~USA~N...	4
14	Texas	5	World	Americas	USA	Texas	-	USA	World~Americas~USA~T...	4
15	California	5	World	Americas	USA	California	-	USA	World~Americas~USA~C...	4
16	London	8	World	EMEA	UK	London	-	UK	World~EMEA~UK~London	4
17	Greater Manc...	8	World	EMEA	UK	Greater Manch...	-	UK	World~EMEA~UK~Greater...	4
18	Manchester	17	World	EMEA	UK	Greater Manch...	Manchester	Greater Manchester	World~EMEA~UK~Greater...	5
19	Bavaria	9	World	EMEA	Germany	Bavaria	-	Germany	World~EMEA~Germany~...	4
20	Munich	19	World	EMEA	Germany	Bavaria	Munich	Bavaria	World~EMEA~Germany~...	5
21	New York	13	World	Americas	USA	New York	New York	New York	World~Americas~USA~N...	5
22	Heuston	14	World	Americas	USA	Texas	Heuston	Texas	World~Americas~USA~T...	5
23	San Francisco	15	World	Americas	USA	California	San Francisco	California	World~Americas~USA~C...	5

If the `PathName` field is added as a listbox, the **Show as TreeView** option can be specified on the **General** properties tab:

With this option turned on, the listbox will be presented in a tree view:

Creating parent associations with HierarchyBelongsTo

The HierarchyBelongsTo function is slightly different in that it unwraps the link from parent to child and makes it navigable in QlikView. Each child node is associated with its parent, grandparent, and so on. We can also create a field to capture the depth difference between node and ancestor.

The parameters are as follows—only the DepthDiff parameter is optional:

Parameter	Description
NodeID	This is the unique key for each row in the input table.
ParentID	This is the key that refers to the parent's node key.
NodeName	This is the field that has the name of the node.
AncestorID	This is a string value, passed in single quote marks, to specify a name for the field to store the ancestor key.
AncestorName	This is a string value, passed in single quote marks, to specify a name for the field to store the name of the ancestor.
DepthDiff	If you want this field created, pass a string value, in single quote marks, for the name that you want for the field.

Taking the inline table of the previous locations, we can replace the Hierarchy function with a HierarchyBelongsTo function as shown:

```
HierarchyBelongsTo (NodeID, ParentID, Location, 'AncestorID',
'AncestorName', 'DepthDiff')
Load * Inline [
...
```

Then, we will obtain a table that looks like the following:

NodeID	Location	AncestorID	AncestorName	DepthDiff
1	World	1	World	0
2	EMEA	1	World	1
2	EMEA	2	EMEA	0
3	Americas	1	World	1
3	Americas	3	Americas	0
4	AsiaPac	1	World	1
4	AsiaPac	4	AsiaPac	0
5	USA	1	World	2
5	USA	3	Americas	1
5	USA	5	USA	0
6	Canada	1	World	2
6	Canada	3	Americas	1
6	Canada	6	Canada	0
7	Brazil	1	World	2
7	Brazil	3	Americas	1
7	Brazil	7	Brazil	0
8	UK	1	World	2
8	UK	2	EMEA	1
8	UK	8	UK	0
9	Germany	1	World	2
9	Germany	2	EMEA	1
9	Germany	9	Germany	0
10	France	1	World	2
10	France	2	EMEA	1
10	France	10	France	0
11	China	1	World	2
11	China	4	AsiaPac	1
11	China	11	China	0
12	Japan	1	World	2
12	Japan	4	AsiaPac	1
12	Japan	12	Japan	0
13	New York	1	World	3
13	New York	3	Americas	2
13	New York	5	USA	1

This table has all the nodes associated to their parents and vice versa.

Creating dimensional facts

Most of the facts that we deal with in the fact table are numbers that we will calculate and recalculate based on a user's selections. It can sometimes be useful for us to precalculate some values in the script that are less dependent on other dimensions and store them in the dimension table. Some examples are:

- Customer balance
- Number of orders this year
- Number of orders last year
- Current stock quantity

These values should all be calculable from the fact table, but having them precalculated in the dimension table means that performance can be improved. Having them in the dimension table also makes them easier to use as dimension type values—we can query and group by them.

Creating these facts in the script is as simple as loading and grouping from the fact table, for example:

```
Left Join (Customer)
Load
    CustomerID,
    Count(OrderID) As [Orders This Year],
    Sum([Line Value]) As [Sales This Year]
Resident Fact
Where Year(OrderDate)=Year(Today())
Group by CustomerID;
```

Handling slowly changing dimensions

For many dimensions, we are not usually worried about changes being made in the underlying system. If a salesperson gets married and their surname changes from "Smith" to "Jones," we just reload the QlikView document and the new surname will appear in the selectors. However, if the same person changes from the inside sales team to the northwest sales team, just updating the data means that sales attributed to that salesperson will no longer get attributed to the correct team.

These changes to the dimensions do not happen very frequently and are called **slowly changing dimensions (SCDs)**. Kimball defines eight different methods of handling SCDs, from Type 0 to Type 7. The first example discussed previously, the change of surname, is an example of Type 1—simply update the value (Type 0 says to use the original value). The second change, where the sales team is updated, should be handled by Type 2—add a new row to the dimension table. Type 1 and Type 2 will be, by far, the most common ways of handling SCDs.

For a full list of the SCD handling types with descriptions, see *The Data Warehouse Toolkit* or go to http://www.kimballgroup.com/data-warehouse-business-intelligence-resources/kimball-techniques/dimensional-modeling-techniques/.

The rest of this section will talk about Type 2. If we are lucky, either the underlying dataset or the ETL that loads the data warehouse where we are getting our data from will already record start and end dates for the validity of the records, for example, something like the following:

SalesPersonID	Name	Territory	From	To
1	Joe Bloggs	NE	01/01/2009	
2	Jane Doe	Inside	01/01/2009	12/31/2013
2	Jane Doe	NW	01/01/2014	

Let's discuss different methods of how we can handle this.

Taking the most recently changed record using FirstSortedValue

The first method that can be used is just to transform the Type 2 data into Type 1 data and treat it as if the additional records were just updates.

We can use a function in QlikView called `FirstSortedValue`. The function can be used within a `Group By` load expression and will return the first value of a field based on the grouped fields and a sort field. Let's look at an example, just using the three rows mentioned previously:

```
Data:
Load * Inline [
SalesPersonID, Name, Territory, From, To
1, Joe Bloggs, NE, 2009-01-01,
2, Jane Doe, Inside, 2009-01-01, 2013-12-31
2, Jane Doe, NW, 2014-01-01,
];

Inner Join (Data)
Load
    SalesPersonID,
    FirstSortedValue(Distinct Territory, -From, 1) As Territory
Resident
    Data
Group by SalesPersonID;
```

The magic is in the `FirstSortedValue` function. The parameters are as follows:

Parameter	Meaning
Distinct	When you sort the values in a dataset, it is possible that there might be more than one row with the same sort. The default functionality is to return a null value in this case. When we specify `Distinct`, one of the values will be returned, although we can only assume that the value returned will be based on load order.
Territory	This is the field value that we want to be returned after the sort is performed.
-From	This is the field (in this case a date field) that defines the sort order. Sort order is lowest to highest. By adding a minus sign before the field name, we change the sort order to highest to lowest—this is what we want in this case because we want the latest date.
1	This is an optional parameter and `1` is the default value. This specifies which row we want after the values are sorted.

The result of this join is shown in the following table:

SalesPer...	Name	Territory	From
1	Joe Bloggs	NE	2009-01-01
2	Jane Doe	NW	2014-01-01

Of course, this is not what we really want in this situation, and we need to look at further alternatives.

Using IntervalMatch with SCDs

QlikView has a great function called `IntervalMatch` that works very well in situations where we have start and end dates and we want to match this to a dimension such as a calendar.

To see it in action, let's load some data. First, we will load the tables as separate entities. We should create a unique key in the salesperson table to associate into the fact table. We also need to back-fill the `To` date with a value if it is blank—we will use today's date:

```
SalesPerson:
Load
    AutoNumber(SalesPersonID & '-' & Territory & '-' & From, 'SP') As
SP_ID,
    SalesPersonID,
    Name,
```

```
    Territory,
    From,
    If(Len(To)=0, Today(), To) As To
Inline [
SalesPersonID, Name, Territory, From, To
1, Joe Bloggs, NE, 2009-01-01,
2, Jane Doe, Inside, 2009-01-01, 2013-12-31
2, Jane Doe, NW, 2014-01-01,
];

Fact:
Load * Inline [
OrderDate, SalesPersonID, Sales Value
2013-01-01, 1, 100
2013-02-01, 2, 100
2014-01-01, 1, 100
2014-02-01, 2, 100
];
```

Now, this will create a false association:

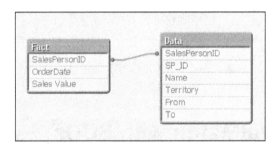

If we do a calculation based on the **Sales Person** column, we will actually get the correct result:

Sales Person	Sales $
	400
Jane Doe	200
Joe Bloggs	200

However, if we calculate on **Territory**, the result is incorrect:

Territory	Sales $
	400
Inside	200
NE	200
NW	200

The result actually doesn't look like it makes any sense—although it is perfectly logical if we think about it.

At this stage, we can introduce `IntervalMatch`:

```
LinkTable:
IntervalMatch(OrderDate, SalesPersonID)
Load
    From,
    To,
    SalesPersonID
Resident
    SalesPerson;
```

This will create a table, called `LinkTable`, with four fields—`OrderDate`, `SalesPersonID`, `From`, and `To`—containing the logical association between the order date, sales person, and the from and to dates.

Now, we are not finished because we also have a synthetic key that we should remove. What we need to do is join the `SP_ID` field from the salesperson table into this link table and then we can join `OrderDate`, `SalesPersonID`, and `SP_ID` from the link table into the fact table. Once that is done, we can drop the link table and also drop `SalesPersonID` from the fact table (as the association will be on `SP_ID`).

This will look like the following:

```
Left Join (LinkTable)
Load
    From,
    To,
    SalesPersonID,
    SP_ID
Resident
    SalesPerson;

Left Join (Fact)
Load
    OrderDate,
    SalesPersonID,
    SP_ID
Resident
    LinkTable;

Drop Table LinkTable;
Drop Field SalesPersonID From Fact;
```

The resulting table structure will look like the following:

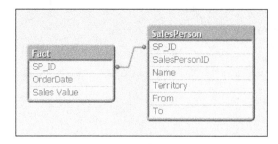

The straight table of sales by territory will now look like the following:

Territory	Sales $
	400
Inside	100
NW	100
NE	200

Using hash to manage from/to dates

The from/to dates that we have in the data source should hopefully be managed by either the source application or an ETL tool. However, sometimes QlikView is the ETL tool, and we need to manage those from/to dates as best we can.

One method we can do is to load the data with a hash key (see *Using one of the Hash functions* earlier in this chapter) that encapsulates all the field values in each row. We can then store the data to QVD. Using this key, we should be able to detect when the data changes. If it changes, we can then load the new data and add to the data in the QVD.

We can load the initial set of data, with an initial start date, in the following manner:

```
SalesPerson:
LOAD
    Hash256(SalesPersonID, Name, Territory) As HashKey,
    SalesPersonID,
    Name,
    Territory,
    '2009-01-01' As From
FROM
[..\Scripts\SalesPersonList_Initial.txt]
```

```
(txt, codepage is 1252, embedded labels, delimiter is ',', msq);

Store SalesPerson into SalesPerson.QVD;
```

Now, once we have the QVD built, we can have a daily reload process that loads the QVD, loads the current salesperson file, and compares for hashes that don't already exist. If there are a few that don't exist, we can add them with today as the `From` date in the following manner:

```
SalesPerson_Temp:
LOAD HashKey,
    SalesPersonID,
    Name,
    Territory,
    From
FROM
SalesPerson.QVD
(qvd);

Concatenate (SalesPerson_Temp)
LOAD
    Hash256(SalesPersonID, Name, Territory) As HashKey,
    SalesPersonID,
    Name,
    Territory,
    Date(Today(), 'YYYY-MM-DD') As From
FROM
[..\Scripts\SalesPersonList_Current.txt]
(txt, codepage is 1252, embedded labels, delimiter is ',', msq)
Where Not Exists(HashKey, Hash256(SalesPersonID, Name, Territory));

Store SalesPerson_Temp into SalesPerson.QVD;
```

As long as the data in the current dataset doesn't change, the existing QVD will stay the same. If it does change, the new or updated rows will be added to the QVD.

 If we are using QlikView data files to store slowly changing dimensions in this way, we need to be aware that QVDs are not considered to be a resilient persistent storage method. Appropriate backups need to be put in place because if you lose these QVDs, then you lose the change information.

Now, you may have noticed that I have called the table `SalesPerson_Temp`. This is because I am not finished with it yet. I need to now calculate the `To` date. I can do this by sorting the list by salesperson and date, with the date in descending order — that means that the first row for each salesperson will be the most recent date and therefore the `To` date will be today. On subsequent rows, the `To` date will be the previous row's `From` date minus one day:

```
SalesPerson:
Load
    SalesPersonID,
    Name,
    Territory,
    From,
    Date(If(Previous(SalesPersonID)<>SalesPersonID,
        Today(),
        Previous(From)-1), 'YYYY-MM-DD') As To
Resident
    SalesPerson_Temp
Order by SalesPersonID, From Desc;

Drop Table SalesPerson_Temp;
```

Now, we have our table with to/from dates that we can use with an interval match as demonstrated in the previous section.

Dealing with multiple fact tables in one model

In data models designed around business processes, we will often have just one source fact table. If we have additional fact tables, they tend to be at a similar grain to the main fact table, which is easier to deal with. Line-of-business documents may have fact tables from lots of different sources that are not at the same grain level at all, but we are still asked to deal with creating the associations. There are, of course, several methods to deal with this scenario.

Joining the fact tables together

If the fact tables have an identical grain, with the exact same set of primary keys, then it is valid to join, using a full outer join, the two tables together. Consider the following example:

```
Fact:
Load * Inline [
Date, Store, Product, Sales Value
2014-01-01, 1, 1, 100
2014-01-01, 2, 1, 99
2014-01-01, 1, 2, 111
2014-01-01, 2, 2, 97
2014-01-02, 1, 1, 101
2014-01-02, 2, 1, 98
2014-01-02, 1, 2, 112
2014-01-02, 2, 2, 95
];

Join (Fact)
Load * Inline [
Date, Store, Product, Waste Value
2014-01-01, 1, 1, 20
2014-01-01, 2, 1, 10
2014-01-02, 2, 2, 11
2014-01-03, 2, 1, 5
];
```

This will produce a table that looks like the following:

Date	Store	Product	Sales Value	Waste Value
2014-01-01	1	1	100	20
2014-01-01	1	2	111	-
2014-01-01	2	1	99	10
2014-01-01	2	2	97	-
2014-01-02	1	1	101	-
2014-01-02	1	2	112	-
2014-01-02	2	1	98	-
2014-01-02	2	2	95	11
2014-01-03	2	1	-	5

We know from our previous discussion about null values in fact tables that QlikView will perfectly handle these values for all calculations.

Concatenating fact tables

Concatenation of tables instead of joining them is often a go-to strategy for the creation of combined fact tables. It works well because logically we end up with the same result as joining. Also, if there is any suspicion that there are duplicate keys (so, in our example, two or more rows for the same date, Store and Product — which may be valid), then concatenation will still work where a join will not. In the previous example, if we were to concatenate rather than join, then the table would look like the following:

Date	Store	Product	Sales Value	Waste Value
2014-01-01	1	1	100	-
2014-01-01	1	1	-	20
2014-01-01	1	2	111	-
2014-01-01	2	1	99	-
2014-01-01	2	1	-	10
2014-01-01	2	2	97	-
2014-01-02	1	1	101	-
2014-01-02	1	2	112	-
2014-01-02	2	1	98	-
2014-01-02	2	2	95	-
2014-01-02	2	2	-	11
2014-01-03	2	1	-	5

One thing that we need to consider is that this table is longer than the previous one while still being as wide. Therefore, it will take up more space in memory.

It can also work to concatenate fact tables that have a different grain. In that case, it is a good idea to populate the key values that are missing with a key value pointing to the "not applicable" value in the dimension, as we discussed earlier.

Changing the grain of a fact table

We mentioned previously that we can reduce the granularity of a fact table by aggregating the facts to a smaller subset of dimensions — for example, removing transaction time and aggregating to transaction date. There may be other occasions, and good business reasons, where you have a fact table at one grain and want to make it more granular to match with another fact table. For example, suppose that I have sales data by date and have budget data by week; I may want to split the budget down to the day level to give me more granularity in my day-by-day analysis.

Imagine a scenario where we are going to load the weekly budget but we want to apportion that over the days in a different ratio—to reflect general trading conditions. The percentages that we want per day are as follows:

Day	Percentage
Monday	10%
Tuesday	13%
Wednesday	15%
Thursday	17%
Friday	20%
Saturday	25%
Sunday	0%

We can load a mapping table with this information and then use that to calculate the correct daily value:

```
Budget_Day_Percent:
Mapping Load * Inline [
Day, Percentage
0, .10
1, .13
2, .15
3, .17
4, .20
5, .25
6, 0
];

Budget:
Load
    YearWeek,
    Store,
    Product,
    [Budget Value] As WeekBudget
From Budget.qvd (QVD);

Left Join (Budget)
Load
    YearWeek,
    Date
From Calendar.qvd (QVD);
```

```
Left Join (Budget)
Load
    Date,
    Store,
    Product,
    WeekBudget
       * ApplyMap('Budget_Day_Percent', WeekDay(Date), 0)
       As [Budget Value]
Resident
    Budget;

Drop Field WeekBudget;
```

Linking fact tables of different grains

If the fact tables have different grains, especially where they have quite different dimension keys, only sharing a few, it often doesn't make sense to concatenate them — we just create a wide and long fact table that has many null values. In that case, it makes more sense to create a link table to associate the two tables.

A link table is pretty much exactly like a synthetic key table, except that we are controlling the creation of composite keys. There are a couple of simple rules for the creation of link tables:

- Create a key in each fact table that will associate the rows in the fact table to the link table. This will mostly be a combination of the keys that we are going to use in the link table using `AutoNumber`.
- Use a mixture of concatenation and joins to create the link table.
- Drop the key fields that have been added to the link table from the fact tables.

I did once have a different approach to this, using primary keys for each fact table, but the preceding approach is far simpler.

Let's look at an example. We will return to retail sales and budgets, but this time we will have very different grains that are not easily changeable. We will have a date, store, and product, but the sales information will be down to till, operator, and time. There is very little chance of us manipulating the budget data down to this level.

Now, it is valid to concatenate these tables as we discussed earlier. Once you have used both techniques a number of times, you will be able to make a good judgment of which one to use on a case-by-case basis. Most often, the overriding consideration should be memory size and lower memory equals lower cache and better performance for more users.

The following is the example load:

```
Sales:
LOAD
    AutoNumber(Floor(Date) & '-' & Store & '-' & Product, 'SB_Link') As
SB_Link,
    *
INLINE [
  Date, Store, Product, Till, Operator, Time, Sales Quantity, Sales
Value
  2014-01-01, 1, 1, 1, 1, 09:00:00, 1, 12.12
  2014-01-01, 1, 2, 1, 1, 09:01:30, 2, 3.33
  2014-01-01, 2, 1, 3, 5, 10:11:01, 4, 17.88
  2014-01-01, 2, 2, 5, 5, 12:02:22, 1, 1.70
];


Budget:
LOAD
    AutoNumber(Floor(Date) & '-' & Store & '-' & Product, 'SB_Link') As
SB_Link,
    *
INLINE [
  Date, Store, Product, Budget Value
  2014-01-01, 1, 1, 20.00
  2014-01-01, 1, 2, 3.00
  2014-01-01, 2, 1, 20.00
  2014-01-01, 2, 2, 3.00
];

Link_Table:
Load Distinct
    SB_Link,
    Date,
    Store,
    Product
Resident
    Sales;

Join (Link_Table)
Load Distinct
    SB_Link,
    Date,
    Store,
```

```
        Product
Resident
        Budget;

    Drop Fields Date, Store, Product From Sales;
    Drop Fields Date, Store, Product From Budget;
```

This will produce a model like the following:

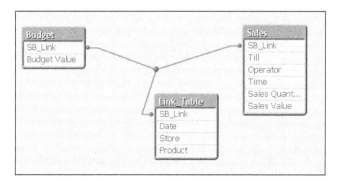

In this case, we happen to have all the fields that we are using in the link table in both tables. What happens if we have a different table in the mix that only has two of those fields? For example, if we have a table containing the current stock levels for each product by store, we can add this to the link table in the following manner:

```
Store_Stock:
Load
    AutoNumber(Store & '-' & Product, 'SS_Link') As SS_Link,
    *
Inline [
Store, Product, Stock Level
1, 1, 12.00
1, 2, 2.00
2, 1, 6.00
2, 2, 2.00
];

Join (Link_Table)
Load Distinct
    SS_Link,
    Store,
    Product
Resident
    Store_Stock;

Drop Fields Store, Product from Store_Stock;
```

The data model will now look like the following:

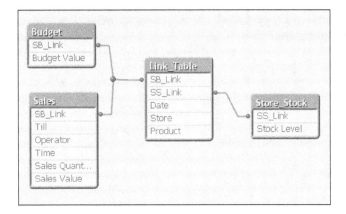

We can continue to add keys to this table like this—either joining or concatenating. We can also, if necessary, build two or three link tables and then concatenate them together at the end.

Drilling across with document chaining

One of the basics of dimensional modeling is the ability to drill between models to answer questions. There are a few situations in QlikView that make this an important consideration, for example:

- We might have multiple data models, with some shared dimensions, that might be difficult technically, or even excluded by license, to associate within one QlikView document.

- Most analysis for most users can be performed on an aggregated, low-memory-footprint data model, but for some users on some occasions, they need to drill down to a lower level of detail.

- In some situations, the number of applications is not a consideration, and we create multiple applications within different business areas but want users to have some options to link between them.

QlikView handles this quite well with the document chaining function. As with any other system where you need to drill across, the ability to do so is entirely dependent on the use of conformed dimensions.

To enable document chaining with the ability to drill across, we need to add an action to a suitable object (button, text object, gauge chart, or line object) with an **External** action type of **Open QlikView Document**. We can see the settings for this in the following screenshot:

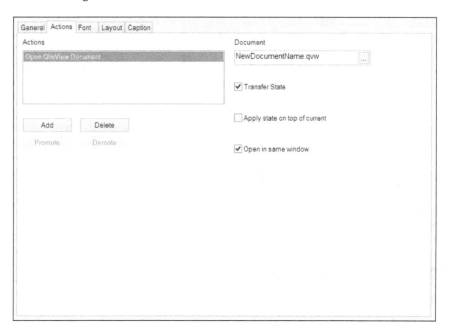

The **Transfer State** option will pass the current selections from this QlikView document to the document being opened. This is based on field name and the values. This is why it is important to use conformed dimensions because they ensure that both the field names and field values are the same between all the documents that are sharing those dimensions.

Summary

This chapter has had a lot of really important information. We started by reviewing what you should already know about associating data. You learned important information about keys and autonumbering and the level of calculations used in QlikView. We also reviewed the different methods of stitching data together—join, concatenate, and mapping.

We then moved on to talk about dimensional data modeling, fact and dimension tables, and best practices from Ralph Kimball. You learned how to handle SCDs and multiple fact tables and how to drill across tables.

The previous chapter dealt with loading data for performance. The next chapter will help us continue our learning of how best to load data, building QVD layers, to support a dimensional modeling approach.

3
Best Practices for Loading Data

"Data! Data! Data!" he cried impatiently. "I can't make bricks without clay."

— Sherlock Holmes (Arthur Conan Doyle), The Adventure of the Copper Beeches

In this chapter, beginners to QlikView development will be shown how to connect to different data sources with the QlikView script, load tables of data, transform that data, and create charts and other objects. However, in the real world of QlikView application development, it will be very rare that you will create an application that contains the whole process, from data source to final visualizations, within one QlikView document.

Extract, transform, and load (ETL) is a standard process within data warehousing; moving and transforming data from different data locations into the final dimensional model tables.

In this chapter, we will be looking at creating best practice ETL techniques using QlikView tools. Initially, we will look at how to do this using the QlikView script. At the end of this chapter, we will look at using QlikView's graphical ETL tool — **Expressor** — to provision data for QlikView.

These are the topics that will be covered in this chapter:

- Reviewing data load and storage concepts
- Understanding why to use an ETL approach
- Using an ETL approach to create QVD data layers

- Mastering loading techniques:
    - Incremental load
    - Partial load
    - Binary load
- Using QlikView Expressor for ETL

Reviewing data loading concepts

There are a few things that we need to remind ourselves of before we can fully grasp the concepts covered in this chapter.

Getting data from anywhere

QlikView is data-agnostic. It doesn't care where the data comes from, all QlikView cares about is whether the data is numeric or alphanumeric, and if it is numeric, does it have an alphanumeric representation that needs to be stored. Hence, for practical discussion purposes, there are only two datatypes in QlikView — numeric and dual.

> QlikView does actually recognize both integer and float values and stores them accordingly, with floats taking up more storage bytes. If the numeric values have a format, then they are stored as duals — with the number and the formatted string stored together. The Floor function will not only remove decimals from a number, leaving just an integer, but it will also remove any formatting so it will reduce the amount of space needed to store the values.

This is sometimes difficult for people coming from a database world, where there can be great difficulty in moving data from one place to another. Database ETL designers will have to worry about whether the source data is one length of string versus the target. In QlikView, we need not worry; it is just going to be text.

There are sometimes issues due to this, such as when there is an ambiguity about what the data is, but it does save a lot of time. This is especially true when we need to bring data together from multiple data sources. We may have sales information coming from an ERP system, user information coming from an HR system, and customer contact information coming from a CRM system. Then, add to that budget information from Excel. Because we don't care about the strict datatypes, QlikView can handle all of this data easily. We can start building our applications and delivering results very quickly.

One of the reasons that QlikView can be better than traditional reporting solutions is that QlikView takes a snapshot of the data into the memory and users will query that snapshot. This takes a load off the core systems because the users' queries are not continually running against a production database. However, to make this an even better situation, we need to make sure that QlikView plays nicely with the database and we are not attempting to load 20 million transaction records every 30 minutes. That is behavior that makes us very unpopular with DBAs very quickly.

The data-from-anywhere ability of QlikView is also a great advantage over many other systems, where you might be limited to only connecting to one data source at a time and are forced to write ETL to move other data sources into the common source. Some other systems have the ability to combine data from multiple sources, but often not in such a straightforward way. One of the reasons ETL has developed as a software category is the ability to report on data from multiple sources. Companies had no option but to move the data into a central warehouse where reports could be run. There are, of course, some very good techniques and practices that have come out of ETL processing that we can apply to QlikView implementations—techniques that will save us from the wrath of the DBA!

Loading data from QlikView

One technique that is often quickly forgotten by QlikView developers, if they ever knew about it in the first place, is the BINARY load. This statement will load all of the data of a QlikView file (.qvw) into another—the data tables, symbol tables, and so forth. Once they have been loaded into the new file, you can use it as is, add additional data, remove and reload tables, or perform any other processing that you want.

Because you are loading another file's data tables, symbol tables, and other tables into a new file, there is one restriction in that the BINARY statement must be the very first statement in the script, as shown in the following screenshot:

```
Main   Connection  SubRoutine  Inline Table  DIMS  Fact  Info

  1   BINARY ..\Apps\DailySales.qvw;
  2
  3   SET ThousandSep=',';
  4   SET DecimalSep='.';
  5   SET MoneyThousandSep=',';
  6   SET MoneyDecimalSep='.';
  7   SET MoneyFormat='€#,##0.00;-€#,##0.00';
  8   SET TimeFormat='hh:mm:ss';
  9   SET DateFormat='DD/MM/YYYY';
 10   SET TimestampFormat='DD/MM/YYYY hh:mm:ss[.f
 11   SET MonthNames='Jan;Feb;Mar;Apr;May;Jun;Jul
 12   SET DayNames='Mon;Tue;Wed;Thu;Fri;Sat;Sun';
```

Using this technique, you might have a chain of binary loading documents, each one loading from the one before, but then adding some new data or even removing rows or whole tables, to make it more unique. Another use case is to have completely different documents from a frontend visualization point of view, with different audiences, that share the same data model — one document can load the data while the other documents simply binary load from the original.

Loading similar files with concatenation

We already talked about automatic and manual concatenation in the *Joining data* section *Chapter 2, QlikView Data Modeling*. We will recall that if two tables with the same number of identically named fields are loaded, then QlikView will automatically concatenate those tables.

If we load data from file-based sources using wildcards in the filenames, QlikView will attempt to load each of the matching files. As long as the files contain the same set of fields, the rows in each file will be automatically concatenated, for example:

```
Load Field1, Field2, Field3
From File*.txt (txt, utf8, embedded labels, delimiter is ',',
  msq);
```

As long as every file that matches the wildcard `File*.txt` contains the three fields listed, they will all be concatenated.

 The wildcards available are the standard Windows ones — * to represent zero or many characters and ? to represent just one character.

Loading dissimilar files with Concatenate and For Each

So, if similar files can be loaded using a simple wildcard, what if there are differences, perhaps even just a field or two, but you would still like to concatenate the fields? This might be a common use case if you are loading files that have been generated over time but have had new fields added to them during that period. The older files won't have the fields, so rather than try and retro-fit those files, we can handle them like this:

```
// Assign a variable with blank text
Set vConcatenateOrders='';
FOR Each vFilename in FileList('c:\Data\Filter*.txt')
  Orders:
```

```
$(vConcatenateOrders)
LOAD *
FROM
$(vFilename)
(txt, utf8, embedded labels, delimiter is ',', msq);
// Update the variable with a concatenate statement
Set vConcatenateOrders='Concatenate  (Orders)';
```

```
Next
```

The For Each statement combined with the FileList function will loop through all of the values that are returned by the file specification. The full absolute path (for example, C:\Data\OrderExport2.csv) will be assigned to the vFilename variable.

 There is also a function called DirList that will return a list of folders. Both FileList and DirList will return their values in dictionary order.

Understanding QlikView Data files

A **QlikView Data (QVD)** file is a file format that QlikView uses to store a table of data to disk. Only one table can be stored in each QVD file.

A QVD contains three parts:

- An XML header, which describes the data contained in the QVD. This XML file also contains useful information about the date and time that the QVD was created, the name of the document that created the QVD file, the name of the table in QlikView, and lineage information about where the data originated from — which database queries or table files made up the table in QlikView before the data was stored to QVD.

- The symbol tables for each field in the data in a byte-stuffed format. Byte stuffing helps remove potentially illegal characters from the data. Although this can increase the size of the stored data over the original data, it is usually not significant for symbol tables.

- A bit-stuffed data table is a table of index pointers that points to the symbol table values (as we discussed in *Chapter 1, Performance Tuning and Scalability*).

So, basically the QVD file is an on-disk representation of how that data is stored in memory. For this reason, loading data from a QVD file back into memory is very fast. In fact, if you do no transformation to the data in the load script, then the load is essentially straight from disk into memory. This is the fastest way of getting a single table of data into QlikView.

Even if you need to transform the data, or use `where` clauses, the data load is still very fast—as fast as from any other table files. There are a couple of operations that can be performed on a QVD that do not interfere with the fastest, most optimized load:

- Rename fields using `As`
- A `Where` clause using a single `Exists`

Storing tables to QVD

When we have loaded data into a table, we can store that table to an external file using the `Store` command. The basic syntax of the command is like this:

```
Store TableName into path_to_file (format);
```

This is the syntax that would be used 99 times out of 100. There is a slightly more advanced syntax, where we can specify the fields to be stored:

```
Store Field1, Field2, Field3 from TableName into path_to_file (format)
```

The path will be any valid absolute, relative, or UNC path to the file that you wish to create. The format is one of three values:

Format	Description
qvd	This creates a file of type QVD as described previously.
txt	This creates a comma-separated Unicode text file.
qvx	An XML-based table format that QlikView can read. Because this is an open format, it is often used by third-party organizations to export data to be loaded into QlikView.

If the format is omitted, `qvd` will be used. Because of that, you will usually see `Store` statements without the format specified. A best practice would be to always include the format, even if it is QVD.

Some examples of valid `Store` statements are:

```
Store Sales into D:\QlikView\QVD\Sales.qvd;
Store OrderID, OrderDate, CustomerID, ProductID, SalesValue
From Sales into ..\QVD\Sales.qvd (qvd);
Store Customer into \\qvserver\data\Customer.qvx (qvx);
Store Product into ..\csv\Product.csv (txt);
```

Using QVD files

One of the things that new developers often ask about QVDs is, "why?". They wonder why they need to use QVDs. They know that they can connect to a database and read data and they feel that they can do that again and again and don't see any reason why they need to bother writing the data to a QVD file first. There are, however, several very good reasons to store data in QVDs:

- Speeding up loads by storing data that doesn't change, or doesn't change very frequently. Loading data from a database is relatively much slower than loading data from a local QVD. For example, if you have 2-year-old transactions, that won't change; you could have those in QVDs, and then load newer transactions from the database and concatenate the two sets of data. Of course, this also reduces the load on the database server because we are only looking for relatively few rows of data on each SQL call.

- Combining data from multiple different sources. For example, we could have a new ERP system in place but we also want to add in sales information from an old system. If we keep the old data in QVD, we don't need to have the old database online, so it can be decommissioned.

- Incremental load is the ultimate use of QVDs to load transactional information in the minimum amount of time possible. Basically, we load only the newest data from the database, combine with the older data from locally stored QVDs, and then update the QVDs.

> There is an excellent section on this in both the QlikView Reference Manual and in the QlikView Help file—search for `Using QVD Files for Incremental Load`. We will run through an example of this later in this chapter.

- As discussed in *Chapter 2, QlikView Data Modeling*, dimensional modeling approaches say that we should use conformed dimensions where dimensions are shared across different models. This is an excellent use of QVDs—we create the QVD once and then can share it across many QlikView documents. Even if we are not following a strict dimensional modeling approach, we can still use QVDs to reuse data in more than one application.

- Implementing data quality when preparing data for users. A cleaned set of QVD files, that are centrally created and controlled, can be provisioned for users with confidence that data is correct.

Just from a development point of view, you will find that you are performing reloads again and again as you are perfecting your data model. If you are reloading from a slow database connection, this can be painful. If you create local QVDs, then your development efforts will proceed a lot faster.

Understanding why you should use an ETL approach

Hopefully, from the preceding section, you might start to see why the majority of expert QlikView developers use some kind of an ETL approach to data loading using QVDs.

There are several advantages to using an ETL approach to just load all the data directly from data sources, such as:

- Speeding up overall data loading and reducing of load on database servers by archiving data to QVD

- Reusing extracted data in multiple documents

- Applying common business rules across multiple documents: one version of the truth

- Creating conformed dimensions across multiple business processes, supporting a dimensional modeling approach

- Provisioning a data layer that allows QlikView users to self-serve, without it being necessary to have database skills

Speeding up overall data loading

As mentioned in the previous section, it doesn't make sense to constantly load data from a database that doesn't change. It makes much more sense for the data that doesn't change to be stored locally in QVD files, and then we only need to go to the database server for the data that has changed since the last time that we queried for it.

This approach makes your network engineers and DBAs very happy because the database isn't over-taxed and the amount of network traffic is reduced.

As data volumes increase, it often becomes critical to make sure that reloads are as short as possible so as to fit inside a reload window. By having as much of the data as possible stored locally on the QlikView server in QVD files, we can make sure that we have the shortest reload times possible.

Reusing extracted data in multiple documents

It is not uncommon for the same data table to be used in many places. For example, you may have a staff list that is extracted from an HR system but is used right across all areas of the business. You may also have a global calendar table, which will be used by almost every application, which can be loaded from the finance system.

By extracting the data once into QVD, you are, again, reducing network traffic and database load. If this data is not updated on a very frequent basis, it is also not necessary to re-extract that from the database frequently during the day to feed into a more real-time application. A table like the calendar might only be refreshed monthly.

 Real time means different things to different people, but I would define it as the periodicity of the reload that gives the business the information that it needs to make decisions now. For some businesses that demand a refresh every minute, for others, once a week will do.

Applying common business rules across multiple documents

From a *one version of the truth* point of view, it is critical that measures are calculated the same way across all documents that use them. If two people use different calculations for, say, margin, then they will get different answers and drive, potentially, different actions.

By using an ETL approach, the same calculation can be used to feed the same measure to multiple fact tables, which helps ensure that the same result is obtained across the business.

Creating conformed dimensions

Conformed dimensions are a fundamental of dimensional modeling. What this means is that we create one dimensional table to represent the same entity across the entire business.

For example, we sell a product to customers, our sales people visit prospects, and we order from suppliers. All of these are examples of organizations. By creating a single organization dimension that can be shared across multiple dimensional models, we can gain insight that would otherwise be difficult to achieve.

In the Kimball dimensional modeling approach, there is a technique called the Enterprise Data Warehouse Bus Architecture that helps you identify dimensions that will be shared across multiple models. For more information, see *The Data Warehouse Toolkit* by Ralph Kimball and Margy Ross or their website:

```
http://www.kimballgroup.com/data-warehouse-business-intelligence-
resources/kimball-techniques/kimball-data-warehouse-bus-architecture/
```

Provisioning a self-service data layer

By adopting an ETL approach, we can make our fact table and dimension table QVDs available for users to load into QlikView to create their own analyses, without having to have any database expertise or database connection credentials.

In fact, you can create a QlikView application that will create a script that will read the appropriate QVDs for a process into a new QlikView application, which means your power users do not even have to have any QlikView scripting knowledge.

Using an ETL approach to create QVD data layers

We now know that there are very good reasons for adopting an ETL approach to loading data in QlikView. Now we need to learn how we should go about implementing the approach.

Each part—Extract, Transform, and Load—has its own set of recommendations because each part has a very different function.

Essentially, the approach looks like this:

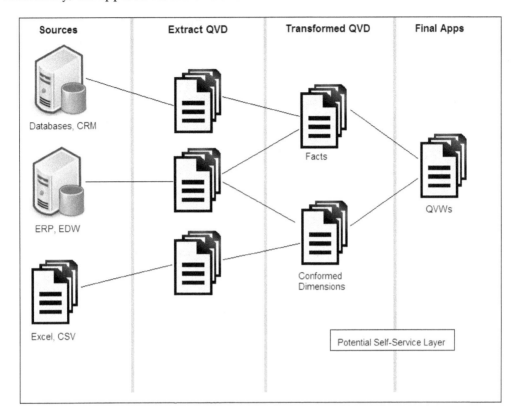

The approach can be explained as follows:

1. Extract the data from data sources into QVDs.

2. Transform the data from the initial QVDs into transformed fact tables and conformed dimensions.

3. Load the transformed QVDs into the final applications.

The final two layers, the transformed QVDs and the final applications, become potential sources for a user's self-service. We can have confidence that users who load data from these layers will be getting access to clean, governed data.

Creating a StoreAndDrop subroutine

When we are loading data to create QVDs, we will end up calling the `Store` statement quite frequently. Also, we tend to drop tables once we have stored them as we don't need that data in the QVW file that has created them. So, we will also call the `Drop` statement quite often.

Anytime that we do something quite frequently in the script, it is a good idea to put that into a subroutine that we can call. Here is an example of a script that will perform the `Store` and the `Drop` operations:

```
Sub StoreAndDrop(vTableName, vPrefix, vQVDFolder)
  Store [$(vTableName)] into
    [$(vQVDFolder)\$(vPrefix)$(vTableName).qvd];
  Drop Table [$(vTableName)];
End Sub
```

The subroutine gets passed the name of the table that we want to store, a prefix that we might want to add to the QVD files, and a folder that we want to put the files in—again, this is absolute, relative, or UNC.

Here are some examples of calling this subroutine:

```
Call StoreAndDrop('Table1', 'E_', 'C:\Temp');
Call StoreAndDrop('Table2', 'EX_', '.\');
```

This is an example of a function that you might want to have in an external text file that can be included in all of your scripts, the advantage being that we can have a central place for the maintenance and support of functions.

To include an external file, you would have a statement like this (this one can be created by using the menu in the script editor—**Insert | Include Statement**):

```
$(Include=..\scripts\storeanddrop.qvs);
```

Now, there is a slight problem with this directive in that if the file doesn't exist or there is some other problem reading the file, QlikView will then just ignore the directive (silent fail). Therefore, we should probably think about modifying the statement to read as follows:

```
$(Must_Include=..\scripts\storeanddrop.qvs);
```

This will throw an error in the script if there is a problem reading the file—which we probably want to have happen. The script failure will throw an error on the desktop or cause an automated task to fail on the server—unless we are handling the error using the `ErrorMode` and `ScriptError` variables.

Extracting data

The goal of extracting data is to connect to our database or other sources, and move the required data from source to QVD as quickly as possible. To this end, we will do basically no transformation of the data at all.

Creating an extractor folder structure

To keep things well organized, we should adopt a practice of keeping to a folder structure for our extraction files and the QVDs that they generate.

Within our `Extractors` folder, there should be a subfolder for each data source. For example, we will have a subfolder for our `Sales Database` and `HR System`. We might also have a subfolder for a set of budget files that are stored in Excel somewhere. We will very often have a `Shared` subfolder that will contain useful scripts and QVDs that will be shared across multiple sources. For example, we might store our `StoreAndDrop` script in the `Shared` subfolder structure. Our folder structure may look like the following screenshot:

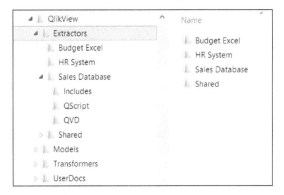

It is worth noting that if there was only going to be one budget Excel file and it is related to sales, it is perfectly correct to do the practical thing and handle it alongside the other sales data instead of creating a separate set of folders.

Unless an Excel file requires a load process such as `CrossTable`, I probably wouldn't create a QVD from it at all. The overhead counteracts any benefits.

Within each subfolder, there will be three new subfolders:

Subfolder	Purpose
`Includes`	This folder will hold `include` text files containing a QlikView script. A common use of such files is to store connection strings or variable declarations that might be shared across multiple files. By keeping such information in a separate `include` file, we can quickly change values without having to edit multiple QVWs.
`QScript`	This folder will hold either QVW files that will be executed by a server/publisher reload task or text files (usually with a QVS extension) containing a script that we will run via a publisher task. In either case, the purpose of the script will be to connect to the data sources, load the data, and store the data into QVD files.
`QVD`	The destination folder for the data generated by the scripts.

Differentiating types of scripts

While all extractor scripts will connect to a data source, load the data, then store to QVD, there are some logical differences based on the way that they will operate and the frequency that they will be executed. The following table describes this:

Script type	Description
Low frequency	The data that is being loaded does not change frequently or at all. Therefore, there is little point in refreshing the QVD on a very frequent (for example, daily) basis. A good example of this might be a calendar table, which we can use to calculate many years into the past and many years into the future. Another example may be a department structure that doesn't really change very frequently. We can refresh the QVD every so often, automatically or manually, but not frequently. The complexity of the script is irrelevant because it runs so infrequently.
Simple, high frequency	Common for dimensional data, we will connect to the data source, load the data, and store straight to QVD with little or no additional calculation. We will do this frequently because we need to make sure that any changes in such data are reflected in the models. However, the size of these dimension tables (relatively small compared to the fact tables) means that loading the entire table every time is not unfeasible.

Script type	Description
Complex, high frequency	Usually applied to fact tables where loading the entire table every time is unfeasible, we need to apply additional logic so as to only load from the database those records that we need to get now. We will then combine those records with records that we already have in a QVD so as to create the final extract QVD.

It is important to analyze your loads for these characteristics because you need to appropriately combine or split scripts based on when you should be performing reloads. It is pointless, for example, to include a low frequency script along with a high frequency script in the one script module. Also, it would be good practice to have your simple scripts in a separate module to your complex scripts.

In an environment where there are data batch jobs running—for example, data warehouse ETL processes or financial account processing—we are often limited in our Qlik reloads to a certain time window. In those circumstances, we need to be even more certain that we are not loading unnecessary data.

Executing the extractors

Execution of the extractors should be very straightforward. Each of the scripts will connect to the data source, load the data, and write the data to a QVD in the QVD folder. At the end of execution, you should have an up-to-date set of QVDs for that data source, ready for transformations.

As a best practice, it is a good idea to also adopt a naming convention for the QVD files that are produced. It can be a good idea to prefix the files with a letter or abbreviation—such as E_ or EX_ —so as to quickly distinguish an extractor QVD from any other. Including the table name in the filename is mandatory. Adding the data source or abbreviation would also be a good step, for example:

```
E_SalesData_Customer.qvd
```

Transforming data

The transformation step is where all the magic happens. We will take QVD data (and possibly simple Excel data) and transform that data into conformed dimensions and fact tables.

Creating a transformer and model folder structure

When transforming, we are going to make use of two folder structures. One will hold the transformation scripts and include files that will actually perform the transformations. The other folder structure will hold the QVDs that are output from those transformations. The reason we split into `Transformers` and `Models` is that, in theory, we should only have one transformer that creates a QVD, such as a conformed dimension, but that QVD may need to be written out to more than one `Model` subfolder.

The subfolders under `Transformers` and `Models` should be based on the modeling that you have performed in advance — either process or line-of-business based. Have a look at the following screenshot:

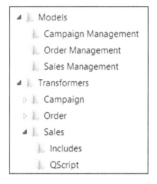

 It is worth remembering that when we are using a structured folder arrangement like this, then we should use relative paths in our script so that we can move files from development servers, where we will have established identical paths, to test or production servers without having to change the script.

Executing transformers

The only rule that we can specify about execution of transformers is that they need to be appropriately scheduled after the extractors that create the QVDs that the transformers depend on. Other than that, we will be applying different business rules to that data and those rules are context-specific.

This is a good point to add a reminder that when creating surrogate keys using the AutoNumber function, the keys generated can only be relied upon within the same script. We can't create surrogate keys in a QVD in one script and expect them to match surrogate keys created in a different script, even if the original keys were identical. We can, however, use a function such as Hash256 to create consistent surrogate keys between different loads, remembering to apply AutoNumber on them when loading data into the final application.

It is a good practice to apply a naming convention to the files that are generated in the Models folders. A common convention is to apply a prefix of FACT_ to a fact table and DIM_ to a dimension table. A source name would not be appropriate here as there may be multiple sources, so just the prefix plus the table name will suffice, for example:

```
FACT_Sales.qvd;
DIM_Organization.qvd;
DIM_Calendar.qvd;
```

For operational reasons, you may wish to partition your fact tables, so a partition indicator would be appropriate:

```
FACT_Sales_2012.qvd;
FACT_Sales_2013.qvd;
FACT_Sales_2014.qvd;
```

Loading data

If the transformation step has been carried out correctly, there should be very little to do in the UserApp folder other than to load the QVDs.

Creating a UserApp folder structure

As with the other operations, it is a best practice to create a UserApp folder structure with a subfolder structure that represents either the business process or line-of-business for the apps within it.

This whole UserApp folder can be mounted on a QlikView server, or each subfolder could be mounted separately.

Executing the load step

The load step could be as simple as the following:

```
LOAD * FROM ..\Models\Campaign Management\FACT_Sales.qvd (QVD);
LOAD * FROM ..\Models\Campaign Management\DIM_Organization.qvd (QVD);
LOAD * FROM ..\Models\Campaign Management\DIM_Calendar.qvd (QVD);
```

If the transformation step has been correctly implemented, then the tables should load (optimized load) and all the tables should be associated correctly with no synthetic keys.

The one allowable transformation (which does cause an unoptimized load) that might be performed in this step is the use of the `AutoNumber` function to generate surrogate keys. Using it at this stage will ensure that the generated keys will associate correctly as they are all being generated within the same script.

Mastering loading techniques

There are a few techniques for data loading that you need to spend some time learning to be a true master of the subject. We will have a look at some examples of them in this section.

It has already been mentioned that there is an excellent article on incremental load in both the help file and the reference manual. We will work through some examples here to help give you a good grounding in the subject. We will also look at a couple of other load techniques that will be very useful in your arsenal — binary load and partial load.

Loading data incrementally

The basic process of an incremental load is to have most of the data stored in QVDs on the server and then connect to the database to just obtain those records that are needed to update the QVDs to be concurrent.

Thinking about this, there must be a few pieces that are needed before we can implement the strategy:

- There will need to be an initial load of the data. This may be a complete load of the data table into one QVD or it may be a partitioned load of the data in several QVD files based on, most likely, a date field.

- We will need to be able to establish which field in the data identifies new or updated records. If the data is transactional, with only new rows being ever added, a sequential ID field will work for this purpose. A create date can also be used. However, if the data might be modified, we will need to have a `date` field that stores the modified date and time.

- We need to have a primary key for the data stored. We can use this value in an `Exists` clause or we can use it with joins to the source data to handle deletions.

- We will need to establish a way of storing the last time that we ran the extraction process. I like to use a variable for this as their values will persist with a given QVW file. However, we can also add some resilience by storing the value to a QVD.

Note that because we are using QVD files to persist data, it is a good idea to ensure that those QVD files are backed up on a regular basis. Although they can, in theory, be recreated from the original data source, it may be a lot quicker to just restore the files from an archive. In the case where the original data is no longer available, backup becomes even more critical.

Establishing the script for the basic process

The script for the basic process will be as follows:

1. Establish the date and time that the extraction was last run:

```
// When was the last load?

// Do we have a value in our variable?
If Len('$(vLastExtractionDate)')=0 Then

  // Do we have a QVD with the date?
  Let vFileLen=FileSize('..\QVD\Sales.Transactions.
LastQVDExtractionDate.qvd');
  if Len('$(vFileLen)')=0 Then
    // Set the last extraction date to an arbitrary date.
    // For example, the first day of this year
    Let vLastExtractionDate=
        TimeStamp(YearStart(Today()), 'YYYYMMDD HH:mm:ss');
  Else
    LastExtraction:
    Load
      LastExtractionDate
    From
```

```
          [..\QVD\Sales.Transactions.LastQVDExtractionDate.qvd]  (QVD);

      Let vLastExtractionDate=Peek('LastExtractionDate');

      Drop Table LastExtraction;

      // It is possible that there was no date in the file
      if Len('$(vLastExtractionDate)')=0 Then
        Let vLastExtractionDate=YearStart(Today());
      End if
    End if


  End if
```

2. Record the current date and time:

```
// Record the current date and time
Let vCurrentExtractionDate=TimeStamp(Now(), 'YYYYMMDD HH:mm:ss');
```

3. Extract the records from the database where the modified date lies between the two dates:

```
// Load the modified records
Orders:
LOAD OrderID,
     OrderDate,
     CustomerID,
     EmployeeID,
     Freight;
SQL SELECT *
FROM QVTraining.dbo.OrderHeader
Where OrderDate >= '$(vLastExtractionDate)'
and OrderDate < '$(vCurrentExtractionDate)';
```

4. Concatenate data from the stored QVD — if it exists — where we have not already loaded that row:

```
// Concatenate QVD data - if it exists
Let vFileLen=FileSize('..\QVD\E_Sales.Transactions.qvd');
// Note that if the file doesn't exists, vFileLen will be blank
If Len('$(vFileLen)')>0 Then

  Concatenate (Orders)
  Load *
  From
```

```
   [..\QVD\Sales.Transactions.LastQVDExtractionDate.qvd] (QVD)
   Where Not Exists(OrderID);
```

```
End if
```

5. Store the entire table back to the QVD:

    ```
    // Store the data back to the QVD
    Store Orders into [..\QVD\E_Sales.Transactions.qvd] (QVD);
    ```

    ```
    Drop Table Orders;
    ```

6. Update the date and time for the last extraction:

    ```
    // Update the Last Extract date
    Let vLastExtractionDate=vCurrentExtractionDate;
    ```

    ```
    // Persist the value to QVD
    LastExtraction:
    Load
      '$(vLastExtractionDate)' As LastExtractionDate
    AutoGenerate(1);
    ```

    ```
    Store LastExtraction into [..\QVD\Sales.Transactions.
    LastQVDExtractionDate.qvd] (QVD);
    ```

    ```
    Drop Table LastExtraction;
    ```

Running an incremental load when data is only added

In many transactional systems, rows are only allowed to be added to the system. This is true for many bookkeeping systems. If you make a mistake, you are not allowed to edit or delete the row: you need to add a new transaction to correct the error.

In that case, our basic process is actually too complex. It will work perfectly as it is, but we can modify it to remove the Not Exists clause when loading the QVD. In theory, the QVD should never contain records that we have loaded within the date range. However, in the real world, it is always better to leave the check in place — Exists does not impact an optimized load from the QVD.

Loading incrementally when data might be modified

Other systems allow users to make adjustments directly to the transactional data. If they do, they will usually (although not universally!) have a field that contains the timestamp for when the modification was made.

In this case, our basic script should work perfectly. You just need to modify the extraction query and make sure that you include a where clause on the field that contains the modified date.

Handling deletions from the source system

It could be possible that the system that you are reading data from may allow transaction rows to be deleted. The problem for us is that we may have one of the deleted rows already stored in our QVD and we will get no indication (because there can be no modified date on a deleted row!) that the row is gone.

In that situation, we will add an Inner Join load of the primary key value from the data source, just after we have concatenated the rows from the QVD to the modified rows, but just before we store the data to QVD. The Inner Join load will remove any rows from the in-memory table that do not exist in the data source. We can then store the table to file and the deleted rows will no longer exist, for example:

```
// Check for deleted records
Inner Join (Orders)
SQL SELECT OrderID
FROM QVTraining.dbo.OrderHeader
Where OrderDate >= '20140101';
```

Note that there is a date on this. We are assuming here that previous years' data is stored in separate QVD files, so we would not be modifying this.

Handling situations where there is no modify date

Handling situations when there is no modify date present is tricky and you will need to utilize the assistance of the local DBA or application developer. Often the system will keep a log of changes and you may be able to query this log to obtain a list of the primary keys for the records that have changed in the period since the last extraction.

If there is no such set of records, you may be able to get the DBA or developer to create a database trigger that creates a separate record in a table when a row is inserted or modified. You can then query this table to obtain your list of primary keys.

Whatever the situation, there is often some kind of solution available.

Partially reloading only one part of the data model

Partial reload in QlikView is a very useful feature. It allows us to either completely replace a whole table in the data model or add new rows to a table, without modifying the data in any of the other tables. This can be used to really speed up data loads for more real-time applications.

A partial reload can be executed from the **File** menu in QlikView desktop, or by selecting the **Partial** checkbox when configuring the reload schedule in QlikView Server or publisher. When the partial reload is executed, it will completely ignore tables that are loaded normally and will not modify them in any way. However, tables that have a load statement prefixed with the `Replace` or `Add` keyword will be modified. During a normal reload, these keywords are ignored.

 Mapping tables will have been removed from the original data after the load, so if we are going to use them in the partial load, we will also need to reload them with the `Replace` keyword.

Replacing a table

To completely replace a whole table, we put the `Replace` keyword before the load statement for that table, for example:

```
Orders:
Replace
Load *
From [..\QVD\Orders.qvd] (QVD);
```

In this case, we assume that the QVD has already been updated (perhaps using the incremental load process) and we need to replace the whole table.

Adding new rows to a table

We can also add new rows to a table without having to remove the table. By placing the `Add` keyword before the load statement, we can leave what we have already loaded and then just add new rows. This can be an effective method of running incremental loads:

```
Orders:
Add
LOAD OrderID,
    OrderDate,
```

```
        CustomerID,
        EmployeeID,
        Freight;
SQL SELECT *
FROM QVTraining.dbo.OrderHeader
Where OrderDate>'$(vLastReloadTime)';
// Update the last reload time
Let vLastReloadTime=Timestamp(Now(), 'YYYYMMDD HH:mm:ss');
```

Managing script execution in partial reloads

In the last example, the final step was to update a variable. We may notice, however, that there was no option to say whether this should happen if the load is a partial load or a normal reload. All such assignments will happen either way. We can, however, manage this process by using the `IsPartialReload` function, which returns `true` or `false`, depending on the reload type:

```
If IsPartialReload() Then
   // Do partial reload stuff
Else
   // Do normal reload stuff
End if
```

Loading the content of another QVW

We can extract the entire contents of one QVW into another using a process called `Binary` load. The `Binary` statement takes the path to a QlikView QVW file and loads all of the data tables, symbol tables, and so forth into the loading document.

Because this process essentially creates a new data model in the loading document, there is a rule about `Binary`, in that it must be the very first statement executed in the script. Also, we can have only one `Binary` statement in any one application.

Once the `Binary` load has completed, you can then add additional script to do whatever you need to do. For example, you may wish to add a new table. Another thing that you may want to do is extract tables from the original data into QVD files. You may also want to drop tables.

One use case that I have for this is for the creation of several documents that have an identical data model but will have different UIs. You may want to give a more structured UI with locked down ability to add new objects, or export data, to one set of users, while giving a different UI with full collaboration and export to another set of users.

Henric Cronström from Qlik has written an excellent blog post on how the cache in QlikView Server works that indicates that because the QlikView Server cache is global, there are actually cache efficiencies that mean that this approach is not necessarily a bad thing for your server:

```
http://community.qlik.com/blogs/qlikviewdesignblog/2014/04/14/the-
qlikview-cache
```

Using QlikView Expressor for ETL

In June 2012, Qlik announced the purchase of Expressor Software. The press release talked about a **metadata intelligence** solution for data lineage and data governance, but what exactly is this product?

There are a couple of parts to the technology that are interesting. The main business of Expressor Software was the creation of an ETL tool that could connect to multiple different data sources, read data, and write it out to different locations. As part of this, they happened to create connectors that could connect to QlikView files—QVW, QVD, and QVX—and read both data and metadata from those files. They also created connectors to write out data in QVX format. Obviously, they felt that the QlikView market was worth going after.

Almost as a side effect, they were able to create the genesis of what is today the QlikView Governance Dashboard. Using their technology, they were able to connect to QlikView files and read enough metadata to create a full governance solution about a QlikView implementation. This was actually a big deal because governance was something that Qlik was getting beaten about with by competitors. Now there was an effective solution—Qlik liked it so much, they bought the company.

Introducing Expressor

Expressor is actually formed of three major components:

- **Studio**: This is the desktop tool used to build the ETL packages.
- **Data integration engine**: This is a GUI-free service that actually runs the packages, either on demand or on a schedule (it is a special version of this engine that is used by the Governance Dashboard).
- **Repository**: This is a source repository based on the subversion versioning and revision control system. This allows multiple developers to work on the same project.

As an ETL tool, Expressor Studio is quite intuitive for those who have experience with other ETL tools. It has some differences but many similarities.

Most ETL tools will have some kind of scripting/development language to enable the building of business rules to be applied to data during the transformation stage. With Expressor, that language is Lua:

```
http://www.lua.org
```

One thing that Expressor has, that makes it different, is its ability to partition data on the fly during data loads and make the data loading process multithreaded. Most Qlik developers will be familiar with data being loaded and processed one row at a time. Expressor will intelligently partition the entire load into separate sets of rows and then load each of these partitions simultaneously. This can make a huge impact on data load times, significantly reducing them.

Understanding why to use Expressor for ETL

Why, when QlikView and Qlik Sense already have a rich and powerful scripted ETL ability (as we have seen already), would we consider using Expressor instead?

The very simple answer is, control. By using Expressor or any other ETL tool to create the QVD or QVX data model layer, we are taking control of the data provisioning and centrally controlling it. Policies and security are put in place to make sure that QlikView users, no matter what ability, cannot get enterprise data other than via the QlikView data layer.

This could be seen as a downside by QlikView developers, who may be anxious to get applications built and deployed. However, granting such access to the enterprise data systems is not seen as a good practice in data governance. We extract the data, apply common business rules, and deploy the QlikView data layer from a central tool.

We can still, probably, make the argument that the data layer could still be provisioned using QlikView. However, there are still very good reasons to use Expressor instead:

- **It isn't QlikView**: The people who will be responsible for provisioning the data layer may not be QlikView developers. If they are experienced database developers, then they will be much more comfortable with Expressor than with QlikView scripts.
- **Speed**: The ability to automatically partition data loads and run multithreaded data loads make Expressor extremely quick for getting data.
- **Repository**: This helps in allowing multiple users to work on the same projects and gives versioning control to projects.

When reading on further, it will be useful to have a copy of Expressor installed on your workstation. The installation is very straightforward and the application will run, without license, on Windows 7 and 8 desktops.

Understanding workspaces, libraries, projects, and artifacts

Within QlikView Expressor, we will partition our own work into different organization units to better manage what we are doing. The terminology is very different from QlikView, so we need to understand that now.

Creating a workspace

A workspace is a collection of related projects. As with most things in this regard, there are no hard-and-fast rules about how many workspaces you need to create. Some organizations may have one. Others have one for every project. The norm is somewhere in between the two. We will probably have a workspace for related areas of ETL—perhaps by line-of-business or by data source.

There are two types of workspaces—standalone and repository. A standalone workspace will be stored locally on the developer's workstation. The repository workstation is stored in the Expressor repository. A standalone workspace can be converted to a repository workspace.

When we first open QlikView Expressor, we are presented with some options for workspaces:

When we select the **New Workspace...** option, we are presented with the following screen:

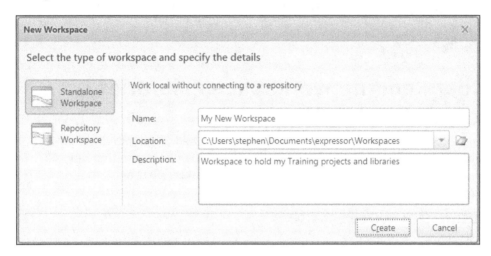

We can pick that our new workspace is either **Standalone Workspace** or **Repository Workspace**. If we select **Standalone Workspace**, we can specify the path to where the workspace will be stored. If we select **Repository Workspace**, we will give the connection information to where the repository is stored.

The repository is an Expressor implementation of the Subversion versioning system. This will be available with an Expressor server and is useful for multideveloper environments.

> Anyone who has used Subversion may note that the default port that Expressor uses is 53690, whereas the default Subversion port is 3690. Note that you should not update the version of svn that Expressor uses to the latest version available as you will probably break the repository.

Managing extensions

In QlikView Expressor, extensions are code libraries that allow Expressor to read and write to different file types and databases. There are some extensions that are installed out-of-box (such as the **QlikView Extension**), but we need to make sure that they are enabled. We need to access the **Manage Extensions...** option from the **Desktop** menu:

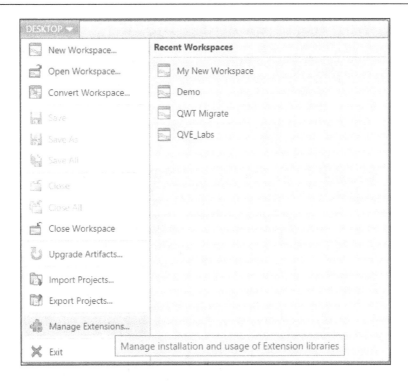

When we select the menu option, the **Manage Extensions** dialog opens:

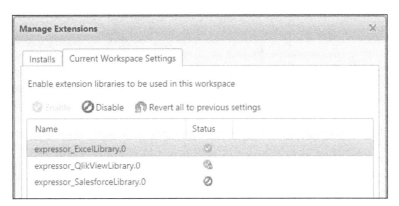

Within this window, we can use the **Current Workspace Settings** tab to enable or disable extensions. We can use the **Installs** tab to install a new extension or uninstall an existing one.

Working with libraries and projects

Basically, a library and a project are the same thing. Both of them are storage locations for other objects, such as data flows, connection information, and so forth. The only difference is that a library cannot contain a deployment package—only a project can produce one of these packages for the integration engine.

A library is used to hold objects, or artifacts as they are called in Expressor, which will be shared among other projects.

To add a new project or library, you can select the **Project** or **Library** buttons on the ribbon bar or you can right-click on the workspace name:

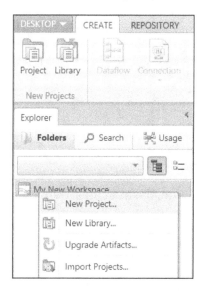

To add either, we just need fill in a name and description in the dialog and click on the **Create** button:

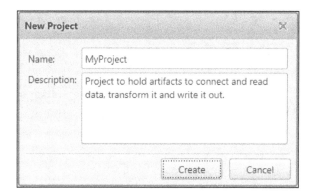

Note that the name of the project, as with all other artifacts, cannot have spaces in it. It can only consist of letters, numbers, and the underscore symbol. It must begin with a letter.

Understanding artifacts

When we create the project, we will see several folders — one for each of the types of artifact that may make up our project:

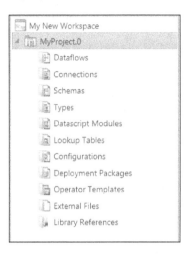

The different artifacts are as follows:

Artifact	Description
Dataflows	A **Dataflow** artifact is the actual flow of data, in one or more steps, that is the actual ETL process. They are defined via a drag-and-drop visual interface.
Connections	The **Connections** artifacts tell Expressor how to connect to the data. We can have file connections — basically a path to a folder, database connections, or QVX connector connections — a connection to a package that will generate a QVX.
Schemas	**Schemas** map the source or target data to the datatypes that are understood by Expressor. They may encapsulate transformations.
Types	The **Types** artifact will contain semantic type information about data. We have two types of semantic type, atomic — mapping data type and constraints for one piece of data, and composite — essentially mapping an entity of atomic types.

Artifact	Description
Datascript Modules	The artifacts will contain Lua functions that can be called from transformation scripts or can be used to implement a custom data read.
Lookup Tables	Not dissimilar to mapping tables in QlikView, these are locally stored tables that we can use to map values as part of a transformation.
Configurations	**Configurations** can contain multiple parameters that we can then use throughout the other artifacts. A large number of the settings can be parameterized. By having multiple configurations, it allows us to set up things such as Dev/Test/UAT/Production without having to reconfigure every artifact.
Deployment Packages	Packages are compiled dataflows, along with their associated artifacts, that will be executed by the integration engine—either scheduled or on demand.
Operator Templates	Within a dataflow, we can configure Read, Write, and Transformation operators. Once configured, we can save that operator as a template to be reused.
External Files	These are basically any type of file that might be used by data scripts.
Library References	When we add a reference to a library, all that library's artifacts will become available within the project as if they were part of the project.

Configuring connections

Before we can read or write data with QlikView Expressor, we need to configure a connection. We have a choice of three different connections. To add a connection, we can either right-click on the Connections folder under the project or we can click on the **Connection** button in the ribbon bar:

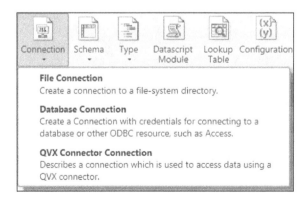

Here is a description of the different connection types:

Connection	Description
File	The **File** connection allows us to connect to a folder on the filesystem—either a local folder or a server share. We can use this folder to both read and write data. Typically though, read will be from one connection and write will be to another.
Database	The **Database** connection allows us to connect to different databases using an ODBC driver. Drivers are supplied for some of the more common databases and you can use an existing DSN for others. The connection can be read and/or write. As with the **File** connection, the typical implementation will have different connections for read and for write, or you will read from a database connection and write to a file connection.
QVX Connector	The **QVX** connection allows us to use the installed QlikView Expressor connector—the same one that you can use from within QlikView—to execute an existing package and read the QVX data. This is a read-only connection.

Configuring a File connection

Configuring a **File** connection is quite straightforward. We just need to know the path to the folder:

After clicking on the **Next** button, we can enter a name (remember, no spaces) for the connection and a description:

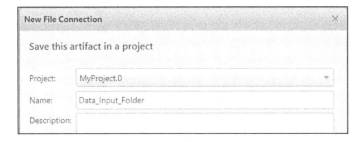

We continue adding **File** connections for every folder that we are going to read from or write to.

If we are going to have many projects reading from or writing to the same set of folders, the connections should be configured in a library.

Connecting to a database

The connection to a database is fairly straightforward. Expressor comes with drivers installed for the following:

- Apache Hive
- Cloudera Impala
- IMB DB2
- Microsoft SQL Server
- MySQL Enterprise Edition
- Oracle Database
- PostgreSQL
- Sybase ASE
- Teradata

In addition, Expressor will natively support (can use its own property dialogs to configure the connection) the following drivers if they are installed from the vendor websites:

- Informix
- MySQL Community Edition
- Netezza

Finally, Expressor will also support other ODBC drivers, but a DSN will need to be configured outside of Expressor.

To add the database connection, we first need to select the correct driver to use:

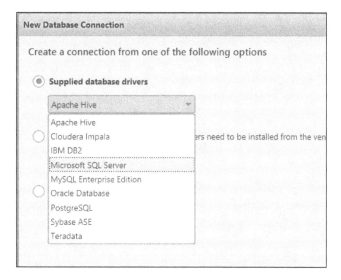

We then fill in the database specific connection information (Expressor will test the connection before allowing you to continue) and then give the connection a name.

Creating a QVX Connector Connection

The **QVX Connector Connection** uses the same connector that we would use in QlikView to connect to an on-demand package. The only packages that can be used are those that will generate a QVX output.

There is a slightly different approach here in that we name the connection before we enter the connection details:

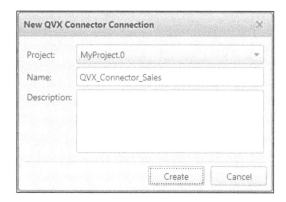

When we click on the **Create** button, Expressor will go ahead and save the connection and open the properties for us to edit.

We select the **QlikViewExpressorConnector.exe** option as the connector to use (you may also see the governance connector in the list, if you have the Governance Dashboard installed on the same machine). Click on the **Actions** button and select **Build Connection String**:

The following instructions are seen in the dialog box:

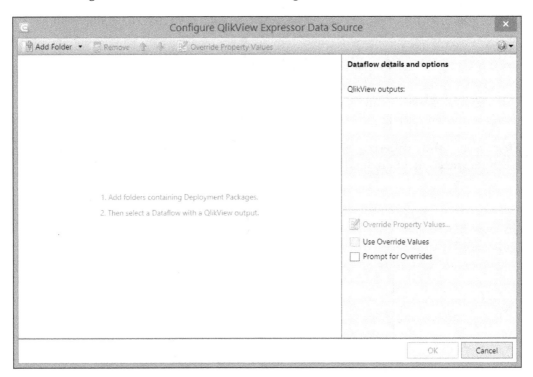

The instructions are as follows:

1. **Add folders containing Deployment Packages**: Click on the **Add Folder** button and browse for a folder that contains a workspace (the default folder for workspaces is `c:\users\username\documents\expressor\Workspaces`) and select a `Project` folder that contains a package (the dialog won't let you select a folder unless there is a package in it).

2. Then select a Dataflow with a QlikView output:

Configuring types and schemas

As we just mentioned, we have two kinds of types, **Atomic** and **Composite**.

Adding additional Atomic types

At its simplest, an **Atomic** type is simply a basic type such as string, date, number, and so forth. We can extend these basic types by adding constraints, such as length or value, to those basic types—implementing business rules.

We add a new **Atomic** type by right-clicking on the `Types` folder under the project and/or by clicking on **Type** in the ribbon bar:

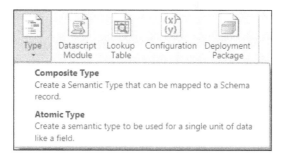

We can now give a name to our **Atomic** type and Expressor will open the properties page for us to enter basic type and constraint information:

Depending on the base datatype, we can set different levels of constraint. If the constraint rule fails, we can set different corrective actions to be performed. The default is that the type should **Escalate** the breach of the constraint, which would normally throw an error in the dataflow.

Once we have set our constraints, we can save the **Atomic** type.

Creating Composite types

A **Composite** type is a collection of types that we can map our data onto. So, for example, we can create an order **Composite** type that represents exactly how we think an order should look. When we import external data, we can map that external data to our Composite type. By mapping everything to a **Composite** type, which can also encapsulate data constraints, we ensure consistency.

We create a **Composite** type by right-clicking on the Types folder under the project or by clicking on **Type** on the ribbon bar, as with the **Atomic** type. We name the artifact as usual and Expressor will open the properties window:

We can click on the **Add** button to add a new **Atomic** type to our **Composite** type:

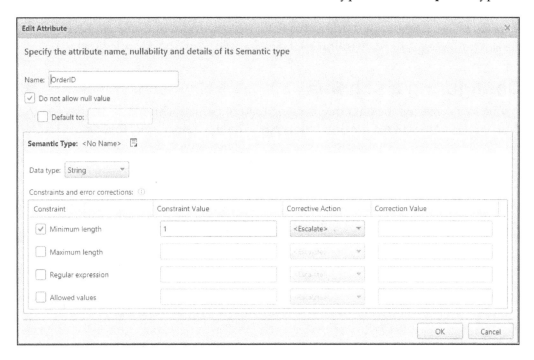

For each attribute, we can assign a datatype and any constraints. We can also assign a **Semantic Type** (**Atomic** type) that we have previously configured (**Shared**) or create a new **Atomic** type (**New (local)**) that will be added to the current project):

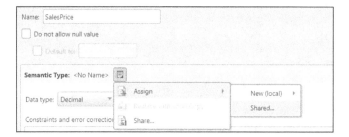

If we do assign a **Semantic Type** to the field, the constraint options will become grayed out because the constraints will be inherited from the **Atomic** type.

Configuring a schema

A schema represents the data that is being read or being written. We can have different types of schema for different types of data. For example, text data is handled differently than database data, which is handled differently from QlikView data. A schema can be configured from either the data itself—which is the usual way—or from a **Composite** type that we have already configured.

To configure a schema, we can either right-click the schemas folder under the project or click on the **Schema** button in the ribbon bar:

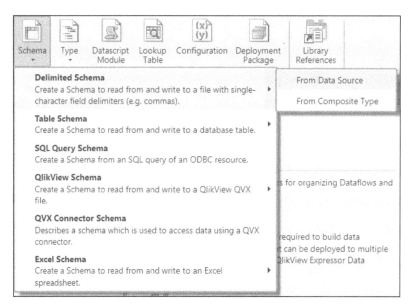

A wizard will open that will allow us to configure the schema from the data. For file sources, we can either browse to the file or we can just paste some sample rows (browsing for the file will just load the first 10 rows):

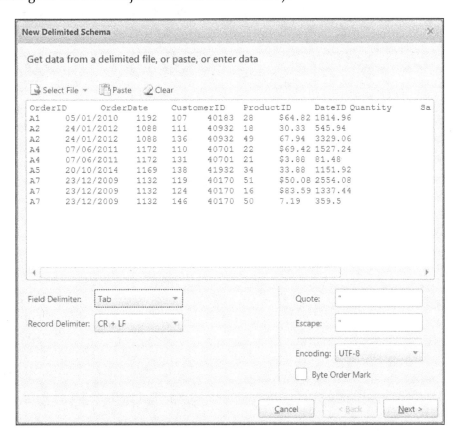

We then specify the **Field Delimiter** value and the **Record Delimiter** value, any quote information, and the **Encoding** type. When we click on **Next**, the dialog will preview the data and show us the column headings. We can use the first row of the data for column headings by clicking on the **Set All Names from Selected Row** button:

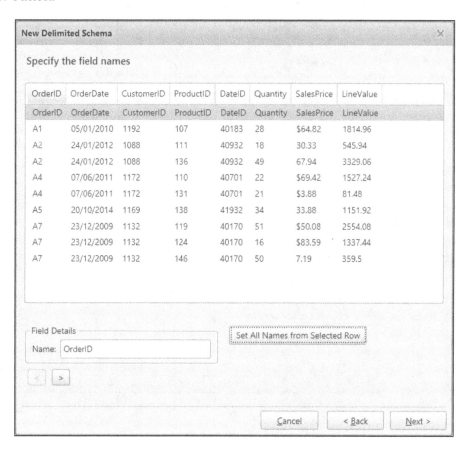

After clicking on **Next** again, we can give a name to the schema (usual artifact name rules apply) and click on **Finish** to save the schema. Once we have saved the schema, we need to edit the details — we right-click on it and select **Open**:

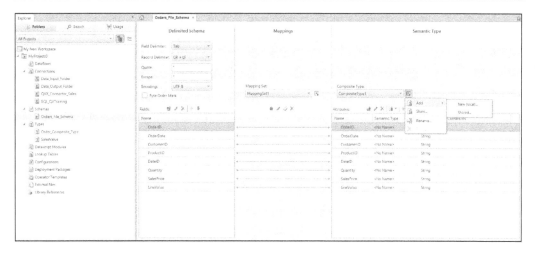

We note that the schema has been assigned a generated **Composite** type (**CompositeType1**) and that the input fields are mapped to it. However, we want to assign our **Composite** type that we have already configured.

On clicking the **Actions** button to the right-hand side of **CompositeType1**, we can select to add a **Shared** type. When we select our **Composite** type, we will be prompted to generate a new mapping:

We would normally choose **Yes** to allow the system to make the mappings for us:

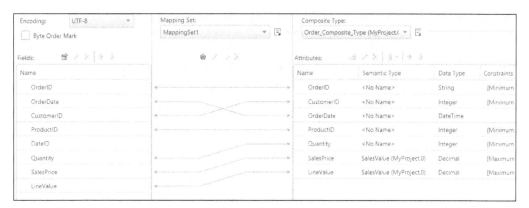

We do need to tweak a couple of the mappings. If you click on the link from **OrderDate to OrderDate** and then click on the pencil icon above it (or just double-click on the link), we can enter the correct format string for Expressor to interpret the text:

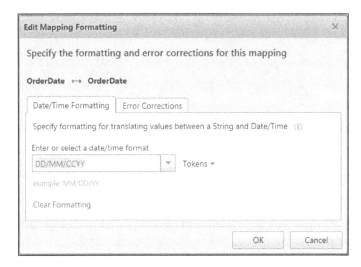

In this case, the data is in UK date format, so we need to specify **DD/MM/CCYY**, where **D** represents day, **M** represents month, **C** represents century, and **Y** represents year.

We should also edit the mapping for the sales price field because there is a dollar symbol. Expressor allows us to take care of that:

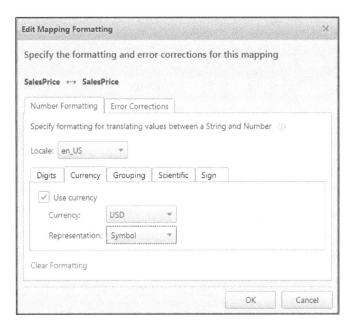

We can now select the **CompositeType1** type from the drop-down menu and use the **Actions** button to delete it. Hit the **Save** button to save the schema.

This schema that we have just created can be used to either read or write text files. In fact, it is a good idea to design your schemas based on the required output rather than the inputs.

Creating and packaging a basic dataflow

Now that we have configured connections, types, and schemas, we can create a simple dataflow to move data from a text object into a QVX file for consumption by QlikView.

Understanding the dataflow toolbox

When creating a dataflow, we have a toolbox available of different operators that we can use within the dataflow. There are four categories:

- Inputs
- Outputs
- Transformers
- Utility

Inputs

The **Inputs** toolbox contains eight options (depending on what extensions you have turned on), each used to read data:

This table describes each of the read operators:

Operator	Description
Read File	The **Read File** operator will connect to a file using one of the file connections and one of the schemas that we have built
Read Table	The **Read Table** operator will connect to a table using a database connection and read the data
SQL Query	The **SQL Query** operator will execute a query that has been defined in a schema against a database connection
Read Custom	**Read Custom** allows you to run a data script to read and generate data that can be passed to another operator — this is an extremely powerful option
Read Lookup Table	This operator reads a lookup table that has been populated by another dataflow step
Read Excel	This is part of the Excel extension that allow us to read data from Excel files
Read QlikView	This QlikView operator is part of the QlikView extension and can read from QVW, QVD, and QVX
Read QVX Connector	The **Read QVX Connector** operator can read data from a QVX connector

Outputs

The **Outputs** toolbox contains nine operators (depending on what extensions you have turned on), each used to write data in different ways:

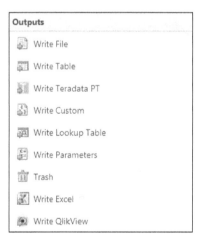

This table describes each of the write operators:

Operator	Description
Write File	The **Write File** operator will write data to a text file in a folder specified by a file connection.
Write Table	**Write Table** uses a database connection to write a database table. We can specify that a table should be created in the database if it does not exist.
Write Teradata PT	This allows you to write data to Teradata using **Parallel Transporter**. Note that you will need to download additional client libraries—TTU v13.10 or later.
Write Custom	**Write Custom** allows you to write data out using a data script. This is a powerful feature.
Write Lookup Table	This is used to populate an Expressor lookup table—not unlike a QlikView mapping table.
Write Parameters	This allows us to generate a `parameters` file that can be used to pass parameters to other options in the dataflow.
Trash	This is an interesting option—**Trash** takes an input and does nothing with it, it is as if you had thrown it away. It can be useful during development and troubleshooting.
Write Excel	This uses the Excel extension to create Excel output.
Write QlikView	This uses the QlikView extension to generate QVX output.

Transformers

Transformers are operators that allow us to transform data. As such, they will form a central part of almost any dataflow. There are six operators available:

This table describes each of the transformer operators:

Operator	Description
Aggregate	This operator allows you to perform grouping and aggregation on data
Join	The **Join** operator allows us to join—inner, left, right, and outer—data tables together
Transform	This is the core transformation operator, where we perform many of the applications of business rules
Multi-Transform	The multi operator will allow multiple transformations to be performed and up to nine different output streams
Pivot Row	This is similar to the CrossTable function in QlikView that takes data in columns and generates a new row for each column
Pivot Column	The **Pivot Column** operator is the opposite of **Pivot Row**—it takes multiple rows and creates one row with multiple columns

Utility

The **Utility** operators contain several operators that operate on data in ways that are not transformative, but are useful in an ETL system. There are six operators available:

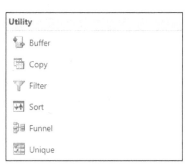

This table describes each of the utility operators:

Operator	Description
Buffer	This is a useful operator where there may be issues with the timing of arrival of records to a multi-input operator (such as a **Join**). It will temporarily buffer data to disk until the next operator is ready to process it.
Copy	The **Copy** operator will take one input stream and allow us to split that into up to 10 output streams, each containing the same data.

Operator	Description
Filter	The **Filter** operator allows us to create rules to filter data into multiple different output streams.
Sort	The **Sort** operator does what we expect: it sorts the data. We can assign a certain amount of memory for the operator to use as well as disk storage if it needs it.
Funnel	**Funnel** is similar to QlikView's **Concatenate** but more like **SQL Union**—it accepts multiple input streams and returns the union in one output stream.
Unique	The **Unique** operator will return one row for multiple values of a key field.

Creating the dataflow

We add a new dataflow in a similar manner to other artifacts—right-click or use the ribbon. When the dataflow is first added, a blank workspace appears:

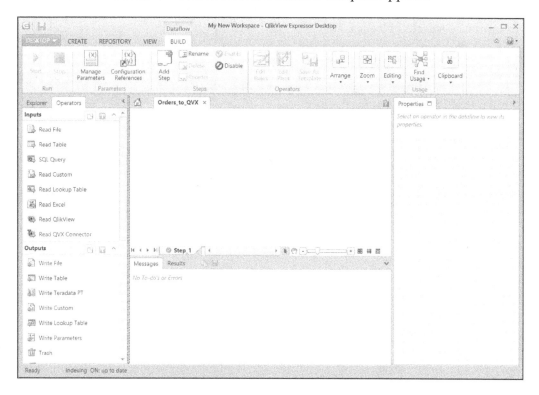

To the left-hand side, we have the operator panel. We can click-and-drag any operator from the panel onto the dataflow workspace:

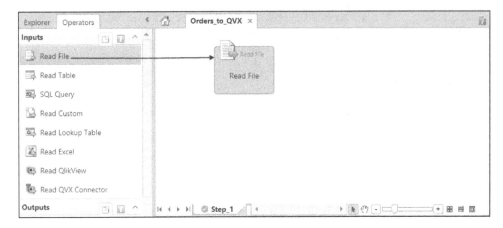

On the right-hand side is a properties panel that allows us to set the properties for the currently selected object.

Configuring a Read File operator

After we have dragged an operator such as **Read File** onto the dataflow, we need to modify its properties:

The properties that you need to fill out are as follows:

Property	Description
Name	Free text name that we want to apply to the operator.
Connection	The file connection from which you want to read the file. All available connections will be in the dropdown.
Schema	The name of the schema that you will use.
Type	The **Composite** type that the schema will map to.
Mapping	The mapping set that will be used.
File name	The name of the file.
Quotes	Choose **May have quotes** or **No quotes** – depending on whether the file will have quotes or not.
Skip rows	If your text file has a header row, you will want to set this to 1.
Error handling	Either abort the dataflow, skip the record, reject the record, skip remaining records, or reject the remaining. Rejected records are put out the rejected records stream.
Show errors	Set whether the errors are shown or not.

Adding a Transformation operation

If we drag a **Transformation** operator from the **Transformation** panel onto the dataflow, we can then click on the output of the **Read File** operator and drag the mouse to the input of the **Transformation** operator:

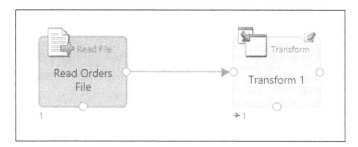

The **Read File** operator should now change to green because it is complete and doesn't need us to do anything else. If it doesn't, we need to look at the messages panel to find out what we have forgotten!

If we click on the **Edit Rules** button on the **Transformation** operator's properties panel (or double-click on the **Transformation** operator), then the edit rules dialog opens:

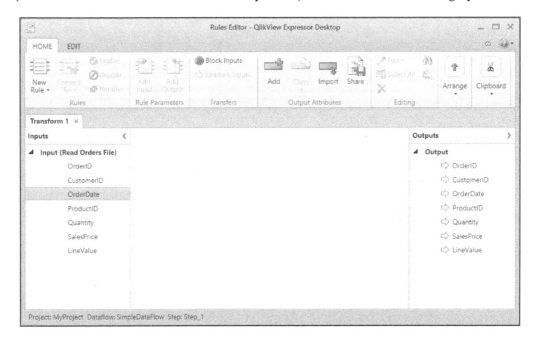

The list of fields on the left-hand side is the list from the incoming stream. The list on the right-hand side is the list of fields that will be output. With nothing else changed, we see that the lists match. Every input field will be output. The white arrow to the left of each output field indicates that they are being output because they are input fields.

We can block an input field from being output by selecting that field in the left-hand side list and clicking on the **Block Inputs** button on the ribbon bar. If we do that for the **LineValue** field, the lists will look like this:

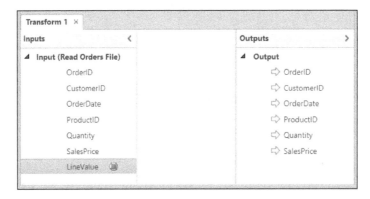

If we want to actually output a field that contains the line value, we can calculate it from the **Quantity** and **SalesPrice** fields. We need to first click on the **Add** button on the ribbon bar to add a new attribute to the **Outputs** list—for example, **LineSalesAmount**.

We then click on the **New Rule** button on the ribbon bar and select **Expression Rule**. We drag **Quantity** and **SalesPrice** onto the **Add Input** side of the rule and we drag our new **LineSalesAmount** field onto the **Add Output** side of the rule. In the expression area, we can replace `nil` with `Input.Quantity*Input.SalesPrice`:

Creating a QVX output

Once we have configured the **Transformation** operator, we can now drag a **Write** QlikView operator from the **Outputs** panel to dataflow and connect the output of the **Transformation** operator to the input of the **Write** QlikView operator.

> QVX is an open format to allow any developer to extract data into a file or data stream that QlikView and Qlik Sense can read. Like QVD files, QVX files only contain one table of data. At time of writing, the only Qlik format that Expressor can write is QVX.

We then set the properties of the output. Now, we haven't defined a schema for the output file, but Expressor has a nice facility where it can generate a new schema from the output of the previous operator. Clicking on the **Actions** button to the right-hand side of the **Schema** dropdown gives us a menu where we can select this option.

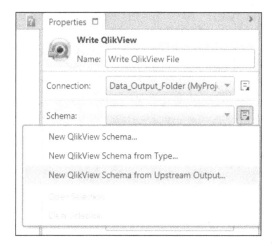

Once all the operators have been configured, they should all turn green. Now we can save it and test it. If all goes well, we should have a QVX file in the output folder.

Packaging the dataflow

Now that we have a working dataflow, we can package it up.

We simply add a new deployment package to the project and we can drag our dataflow into the **Compiled Dataflows** section.

That's it! The package can now be used in Expressor connectors and also with the integration engine on a schedule.

Summary

This chapter has been a very important one from a data loading point of view. As a QlikView developer, you should now have a great understanding of QVDs and why and how we should use them to implement an ETL approach. The folder structure model here will support an implementation from small business to enterprise.

We also looked at implementing really important techniques such as incremental load and partial load.

Finally, we had an introduction to Qlik's ETL tool, QlikView Expressor, and understand why it might be implemented instead of the QVD approach. There is a lot more to learn about Expressor and hopefully this introduction will spur you on to learn more about the product.

4
Advanced Expressions

"The general who wins a battle makes many calculations in his temple before the battle is fought. The general who loses a battle makes but few calculations beforehand. Thus do many calculations lead to victory, and few calculations to defeat: how much more no calculation at all! It is by attention to this point that I can foresee who is likely to win or lose."

— Sun Tzu, The Art of War

There is a great skill in creating the right expression to calculate the right answer. Being able to do this in all circumstances relies on having a good knowledge of creating advanced expressions. This is what this chapter aims to teach you. Of course, the best path to mastery in this subject is actually getting out and doing it, but there is a great argument here for regularly practicing with dummy or test datasets.

When presented with a problem that needs to be solved, all the QlikView masters will not necessarily know immediately how to answer it. What they will have though is a very good idea of where to start, that is, what to try and what not to try. This is what I hope to impart to you here. Knowing how to create many advanced expressions will arm you to know where to apply them — and where not to apply them.

This is one area of QlikView that is alien to many people. For some reason, they fear the whole idea of concepts such as Set Analysis and Aggr. However, the reality is that these concepts are actually very simple and supremely logical. Once you get your head around them, you will wonder what all the fuss was about.

The following are the topics we'll cover in this chapter:

- Reviewing basic concepts
- Using range functions
- Understanding Dollar-sign Expansion

- Using advanced Set Analysis
- Calculating vertically

Reviewing basic concepts

Before we set off on the journey of advanced expressions, it is a good idea to step back and look at some of the simpler methods of doing things. Set Analysis only arrived in Version 8.5 of QlikView, so those of us who worked with the versions before that will have done things in a few different ways.

Searching in QlikView

Field searching in QlikView is one of the most powerful features. It is a feature that has been added and enhanced over the years. Many users will be familiar with the search icon on a listbox:

Clicking on this icon will open the search box for that field:

When we enter search text, the results are highlighted in the listbox. We can choose to click on any of the results to make a selection, press the *Enter* key to select all of the matching results, or press *Ctrl + Enter* to add the matching results to the existing selections.

There are some other ways that we can call up the search box for a listbox. The easiest way is to actually just click on the listbox's caption and just start typing, and the default search type for that listbox will get activated. The other way that you can activate a search is by right-clicking on the listbox and selecting the required search from the menu:

Field searches can also be activated in other sheet objects. Search will be on by default in the multibox but can also be enabled in the table box, current selections box, straight table, and pivot table (using the **Dropdown Select** option in the **Presentation** tab). They can be identified from the small black down arrow alongside the field caption:

Clicking on this down arrow will show a captionless listbox. You can select in this listbox just as with a normal listbox. If you start typing, the search box will appear, just as when you click on the caption of a normal listbox. If you right-click on this pop-up listbox, you will get the same options as if you right-click on a normal listbox.

There are several search types that we need to understand; they are discussed in the upcoming sections.

Searching for text

Text-based searches are the most frequently used. There are two main options for text-based search: **normal** and **wildcard**. The default setting for the search mode is specified in the **Presentation** tab under **Document Properties**:

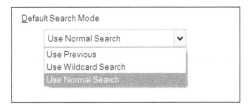

There is a third option in these properties: **Use Previous**. What this means is that whatever the user has done last will be the default. The user can override the search type that is presented, so this setting remembers whatever they have done.

Wildcard search

A wildcard search uses one of the two wildcard characters, in whatever combination we desire, to search for text. The characters are as follows:

Character	Description
*	This wildcard replaces zero or more characters
?	This wildcard replaces exactly one character

Some example searches are shown in the following table:

Example search	Example results in country
g	Germany, Gabon, British Guiana, United Kingdom, Argentina
g*	Germany, Gabon
*on	Lebanon, Gabon
*o?	Gabon, United Kingdom, Lebanon
f*e	France

Wildcards are extremely flexible, but can be very expensive if used to search a lot of data.

If the default search is not a wildcard, you can start typing the * or ? character and QlikView will automatically switch to a wildcard search.

 We should consider that the search will start working immediately when we start typing. There can be a delay with fields that have many values, so we need to be careful about the default search options.

Normal search

A normal search doesn't use wildcards at all. Instead, it tries to match the beginning of words in the data to what the user is typing. This is actually a more natural type of search for users because they will often type the start of what they are looking for and might be confused by wildcard options. If the user types multiple words, separated by a space, all of the words are used to attempt a match.

The following are some example searches:

Example search	Example results in country
g	Germany, Gabon, British Guiana
ger	Germany
k	Kenya, United Kingdom
un kin	United Kingdom
blah king	United Kingdom

If the default search is wildcard, you can switch to the normal search by simply deleting the wildcard characters and then typing. QlikView will automatically switch to the normal search.

Fuzzy search

Fuzzy search isn't a text comparison. Instead, it applies a phonetic algorithm to the search term and the data and then sorts the listbox based on the search score. Words that are a better phonetic match will be sorted to the top and those that are not a good match will be at the bottom.

Associative search

The associative search option will search for a value across other fields, not including the field that you are searching in. When you select the value in the associative search, it then selects the values in the field that you are searching in that are associated with the value that you have selected. Ok, that sounds like a bit of a mouthful, so I will give an example. When I click on the search button, say, the **Country** field, I can see a double chevron (**>>**) button. Clicking on this button activates the associative search, as follows:

If I type 2009 into this search box now, it doesn't search in **Country**; it searches every other field except **Country**. I can see that it has found a value under **Year**; if I select this and then press *Enter*, it will select all of the countries that are associated with the value 2009 in **Year**.

Let's put this functionality in a little more perspective; to achieve the same result without an associative search, we would need to select **2009** in the **Year** field, select the possible values from the **Country** field (there is a right-click option to select possible values), and then clear the **Year** field. It is a pretty cool search function!

Of course, it is not always logical that an associative search should look in every single field. For example, in the preceding screenshot, we see that the field **DI.Year** is searched. This is a field in a data island table (for more information on data islands, refer to the *Data islands* section) and so will not be associated. Also, there are many fields in the dataset, for example, keys and numeric values, that should not be searched. It is possible, in the listbox properties, to select those fields that should be included rather than looking at all fields.

In the **General** tab of the listbox properties, there is a button called **More Search Settings** that will open a dialog box to allow us to configure this:

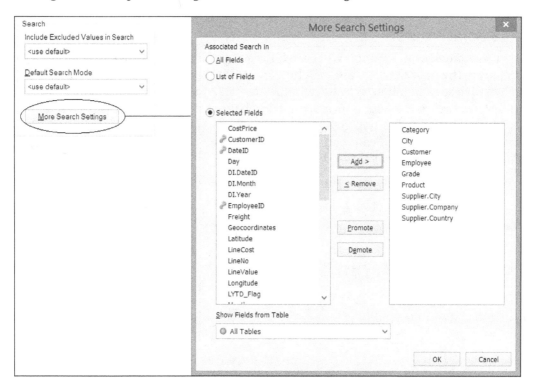

Advanced search

The advanced search feature in QlikView is actually incredibly powerful. It allows us to search for values in a field based on the comparison of an expression. It is as if we create a simple straight table with the searched field as the dimension and the expression that we want to calculate, then select those dimensions in the chart that meet whatever criteria we choose.

To open the advanced search dialog, we can right-click on a listbox and select **Advanced Search** from the menu:

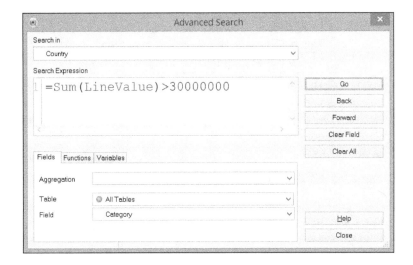

We enter the = sign, which indicates that this is an advanced search, and then the expression that we want to calculate. When we click on the **Go** button, this expression is evaluated against all the values in the field (in this case, **Country**), and where it is true, these values are selected.

The really powerful thing about this is that this expression can be as complex as we need it to be. As long as it is valid QlikView syntax, it can be used in an advanced search. All that is needed is that the expression will return a Boolean response: true or false.

Searching numeric fields

All of the text searching options mentioned previously — wildcard, normal, fuzzy, associative, and advanced — also work with numeric fields. Additionally, we can also use a numeric search with numeric fields.

Numeric search

The numeric search option allows us to use combinations of >, <, and = to perform numeric searches. The following are some example combinations:

Example search	Description
>99	This searches for all values that are greater than 99
<99	This searches for all values that are less than 99
>=99	This searches for all values that are greater than or equal to 99
<=99	This searches for all values that are less than or equal to 99
>99<199	This searches for all values that are greater than 99 but less than 199
>=99<=199	This search for all values that are greater than or equal to 99 but less than or equal to 199

When we type the search expression into the numeric listbox, it will react in a way similar to that of a text-based search:

Automatic interpretation of searches

This is quite clever. When we use a search box, we can do any of the standard searches—normal, wildcard, numeric, fuzzy, and advanced—and QlikView will automatically interpret what type of search it is based on what we type. Consider the following scenarios:

- If we just type text, without any special characters, QlikView will perform a normal search

- If we use wildcards, *or ?, then QlikView will perform a wildcard search

- If we start the search with a ~ sign, then QlikView will perform a fuzzy search

- If we start the search with an = sign, then QlikView will perform an advanced search

- If we use a < or > sign, then QlikView will perform a numeric search

- If we enclose in parentheses and use a pipe symbol, QlikView will expect multiple values

Multiple values search

We can pass multiple values to a search by enclosing them in parentheses and separating the multiple values using a pipe symbol, for example:

```
(Germany|China)
(*ge*|*ch*)
(>=2009<=2011|>=2013<=2014)
(>=2009<=2011|*14)
```

Any valid search syntax will be acceptable within the different values. QlikView will automatically interpret the search based on the rules mentioned.

 It is worth noting that this syntax can also be used to pass multiple values when using a **Select in Field** action.

Searching in multiple listboxes

If we select multiple listboxes either by dragging across them or by clicking on them while holding down the *Shift* key and then start typing, the subsequent search will be performed across all of the selected listboxes:

 Note that you cannot use the *Enter* key here to make a selection. You can only now make a selection by clicking the mouse in one of the listboxes.

Understanding bookmarks

We should know that a bookmark is a saved set of selections. When we save a bookmark, all of the current selections will be stored. It is important to note that this will include any advanced searches, so bookmarks can be used to store advanced logic.

A bookmark can be recalled by the user, but they can also be used to set the parameters for reports and alerts and can be used in Set Analysis.

Saving a bookmark

We can save a bookmark using the menu options or if there is a bookmark object added to the user interface, we can use that to create it. Either way, the **Add Bookmark** dialog will appear:

The options for the bookmark are as follows:

Option	Description
Make this bookmark a document (server) bookmark	This tells QlikView to store the bookmark in the document for use by all users (or on the server if using a server document, where we also have the option to share with other users).
Share Bookmark with Other Users	This option is for server bookmarks only; we can choose to share them with other server users.
Include Selections in Bookmark	This will normally be a default option—you usually want your selections to be stored in the bookmark! Of course, there are use cases where you might not, such as only storing the layout state or input field values.
Make bookmark apply on top of current selection	By default, this is off and the bookmark's store selections will completely replace whatever current selections we have when the bookmark is recalled. If this option is on, only the fields that have stored values in the bookmark will have their values changed and all other selections will be retained.
Include Layout State	This will retain information about which tab is open and which charts are currently active. When recalled, the same tab and charts should be opened.
Include Scroll Position	If your chart is a tabular chart, the bookmark will retain information about how far you have scrolled down the chart. Worth noting is the fact that this will always be a "best guess" effort as the data will probably change in the meantime.
Include Input Field Values	This will cause any input field values to be stored in the bookmark. This is actually the only way to share input field values between different users.
Info Text	This could be just information that we want to store to remind ourselves about what this bookmark contains. It will be the text displayed if the pop-up option is selected.
Pop-Up Message	If this is selected (and I strongly recommend that it should not be!), every time the bookmark is recalled, **Info Text** will be displayed in a message box. It becomes very annoying after a while.

Managing bookmarks

The **More** option from the **Bookmarks** menu (*Ctrl + Shift + B*) allows us to manage our bookmarks:

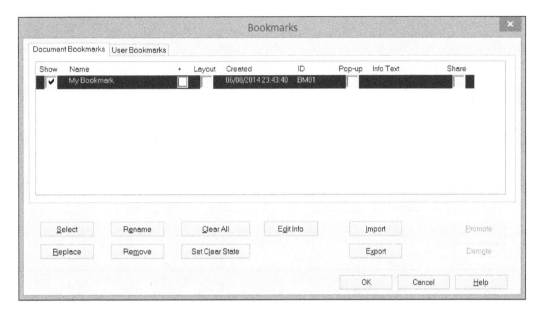

Possibly, the most interesting option here is the **Export** and **Import** buttons. These allow us to export bookmarks to an XML file and then import them into different documents later.

Using variables in QlikView

Many calculations will rely on a variable. This can be a simple value, such as an exchange rate entered into an input box, a percentage entered using a slider, or a more complex calculation.

SET versus LET

We are probably aware that variables can be entered either in the QlikView script via the **Variables** tab under **Document Properties** or using the **Variable Overview** dialog.

When creating a variable in the script, we do this using either the SET or LET keywords. For example, to create the v1 and v2 variables, use:

```
SET  v1=1+1;
LET  v2=1+1;
```

The SET keyword will assign the text on the right-hand side of the equals sign to the variable. The LET keyword will instead evaluate the text on the right-hand side of the equals sign and then assign the result to the variable. If we load this script in the QlikView debugger, we will see the following result:

```
Main    variables.qvs
1
2 // SET versus LET
3 SET  v1=1+1;
4 LET  v2=1+1;
5
6

LET  v2=1+1



--- Script Finished ---        v2      2
                                v1      "1+1"
                                DayNames    "Mon;Tue;Wed;Thu;Fri;S.
                                MonthNames    "Jan;Feb;Mar;Apr;M
```

We can see that v1 has been assigned the text "1+1", whereas for v2, the text has been evaluated and the value of 2 has been assigned to the variable.

We can achieve a similar result when using the **Variables** tab under **Document Properties** or using the **Variable Overview** dialog, to create a variable. When we add a variable, we can either just enter text in the **Definition** box, in which case just the text is assigned to the variable, or we can begin the definition with an = sign that causes the expression to be evaluated and the result of the calculation gets assigned to the variable, for example, using the **Variable Overview** to create v3 and v4, you get the following:

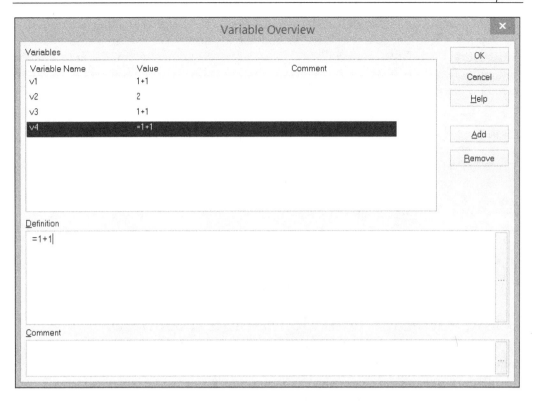

As with v1 and v2, v3 will have the text "1+1" while v4 will evaluate to 2.

There is no difference between using SET in the script and assigning text to a variable in the **Variable Overview** window. There is, however, a difference between using LET in the script and using = at the start of the variable definition. In the script, the result is calculated once during the script execution and the variable will then have a static value. If we use the = sign at the start of the definition, the variable's value will be recalculated every time there is a new selection made by users.

Using variables to hold common expressions

We will quite often use variables to hold commonly used expressions. That way, if the expression needs to change, then we don't need to hunt down every use of the expression; we can just change the variable.

The best practice here is to define these variables in the script with a SET statement. Quite often, these SET statements are stored in a separate QVS that might be shared with several documents, especially if the expressions in question are for color values that will be used throughout the organization. For example, we can have an external variables file with the following lines:

```
// Color expressions
SET cCompanyGreen=ARGB(255,20,228,68);
SET cCompanyBlue=ARGB(200,0,32,200);
SET cCompanyAlert=ARGB(255,255,0,0);
SET cCompanyWarning=ARGB(200,255,126,0);
```

Then, we can load them into our main script using the following:

```
$(Must_Include=..\scripts\variables.qvs);
```

If one of the colors needs to change, we can simply update the file and the change will be updated in every document that uses it on the next reload.

Using variables with Dollar-sign Expansion

We probably have seen variables being used in scripts and expressions and might have come across the concept of **Dollar-sign Expansion**. This function, which we will delve into in much more detail, allows us to access variable values in a way that is not quite intuitive for those who are used to common programming languages. To add to the confusion, we don't always need to use Dollar-sign Expansion with variables; we can use them sometimes just like other programming languages!

With Dollar-sign Expansion, we will wrap the variable name in parentheses preceded by a dollar sign, for example:

```
LET vx=$(vy)*2;
```

When this is processed, what happens is that the value inside the parentheses is evaluated and placed into the expression to replace the dollar sign. Once all the Dollar-sign Expansions have been completed, the whole expression is evaluated with the expanded values. We can think of it as a two-step process, for example, if vy has a value of 2, LET vx=$(vy)*2; becomes LET vx=2*2;.

This is now evaluated and the result, 4, is placed in vx. If we were looking at this script in the debugger window, we would actually see this two-step process in action. The central bar of the debugger will display the line that is about to be executed. If there are Dollar-sign Expansions, then the line that is displayed is with the values already expanded:

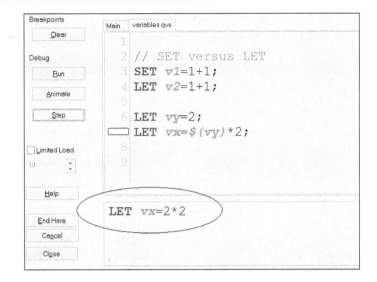

In fact, this is one of the situations where we don't have to use Dollar-sign Expansion. If a variable contains just a numeric value, then it is allowable to just call:

```
LET vx=vy*2;
```

Limiting calculations

There are quite a few ways of restricting a calculation to something other than the current selections. Before we had Set Analysis, we had to do things differently. It is useful to know about these because there are still circumstances in which they are still good to use.

Sum of If

A **Sum of If** means that we are performing an aggregation, such as Sum, on the results of an If statement. Consider the following example:

```
Sum(If(Country='Germany', Sales, 0))
```

In this case, the Sales value will only be summed if Country is equal to Germany.

On a smaller dataset, you will not see much of an issue with this calculation. However, as the dataset increases in size, we will find that this way of performing calculations is relatively inefficient, not least because the comparison is text-based. Also, we need to consider that if a user selects a set of countries, or any other selection that excludes Germany, then the result will be zero, which might not be what you want to happen.

It isn't a QlikView issue, but just a computer issue; however, any comparison that is done using text values is always going to be more expensive than a comparison using numbers.

Flag arithmetic

One of the ways that we can improve performance of a comparison calculation is to create a numeric flag field in the script. For example, we can do the following in the script:

```
Load
    ...
    If(Country='Germany',1,0) As Germany_Flag,
    ...
```

This will create a (quite efficiently stored) field that contains just 1 or 0. We can use this in an expression like the following:

```
Sum(If(Germany_Flag=1, Sales, 0))
```

This expression will perform an order of magnitude better than the equivalent text comparison. However, the following calculation will be even better:

```
Sum(Germany_Flag * Sales)
```

As there is no comparison happening here, it is a fairly straightforward mathematical calculation for the system to calculate, and it will be performed even faster than the Sum of If.

>
> As noted in the *Creating flags for well-known conditions* section of *Chapter 1, Performance Tuning and Scalability*, the flag arithmetic works better if there are relatively fewer rows in the dimension table than in the fact table. Where there are a large number of rows in the dimension table, Set Analysis with the flag field will perform better.

This type of flag arithmetic is very common, and we will always look to create flags like these in the script to improve the efficiency of calculations in chart expressions. Here are a couple of examples of flags that we will often create in fact or calendar tables:

```
Load
    ...
    -YearToDate(DateField)          As YTD_Flag,
    -YearToDate(DateField,-1)       As LYTD_Flag,
    ...
```

In this case, we are using a QlikView function (YearToDate) that returns a Boolean result. In QlikView, Boolean false is always represented by 0. Any non-zero value is Boolean true; however, QlikView functions will always return -1 for true. Hence, the minus sign prefixed to the function will change the -1 result to a 1.

Calculations using variables

On occasions where we might want some flexibility around what we calculate from what the users select, we might ask those users to change variables, usually using the slider or calendar controls, and then use those variables in the expressions.

For example, if we had two variables called vMinDate and vMaxDate, we can add calendar controls to allow the user to modify them:

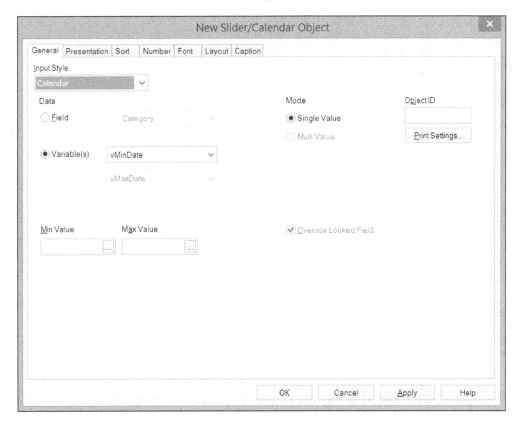

We can now add an expression to calculate the sales between those two values in the following manner:

```
Sum(if(DateID>=$(vMinDate) and DateID<=$(vMaxDate), LineValue, 0))
```

We can also grab the to-date calculation (for example, to calculate a balance) in the following manner:

```
Sum(if(DateID<=$(vMaxDate), LineValue, 0))
```

Data islands

Using a variable or set of variables can be quite flexible but sometimes we might want to give users even more options for selections, while still keeping those selections separate from the main data model. In these circumstances, we can create a completely separate data model, which has full QlikView selectability, and then derive the values from this data model that should be used in the calculations for the main data model. When we create separate data models like this, the non-main data model is called a **data island**. For example, we can load a calendar table in the following manner:

```
// Load the Date Island
Let vMinDate=Floor(MakeDate(2009,1,1));
Let vMaxDate=Floor(MakeDate(2014,12,31));
Let vDiff=vMaxDate-vMinDate+1;

Qualify *;
DI:
Load
    TempDate as DateID,
    Year(TempDate) As Year,
    Month(TempDate) As Month;
Load
    $(vMinDate)+RecNo()-1 As TempDate
AutoGenerate($(vDiff));
Unqualify *;
Set vMinDate="=Min(DI.DateID)";
Set vMaxDate="=Max(DI.DateID)";
```

The `Qualify` statement prefixes the name of the table (`DI`) to each field so that these fields should not be associated to the rest of the data model.

We use the SET statements at the end to add the calculation of minimum and maximum dates to the variables. We can then use those variables in expressions as shown:

```
Sum(if(DateID>=$(vMinDate) and DateID<=$(vMaxDate), LineValue, 0))
```

Otherwise, we can use those variables as shown in the following expression:

```
Sum(if(DateID<=$(vMaxDate), LineValue, 0))
```

This data island does not need to be just a single table. If it makes sense, it can be a small data model in itself and perhaps two separate calendar tables connected via a link table.

We do have to be careful that a data island does not become a separate data model, with its own facts and dimensions, as this can be against the license agreement when using **document licenses**.

Set Analysis

After having done any basic QlikView training, we will have had some sort of introduction to Set Analysis. This is one of the most powerful features of QlikView and allows us to create some great solutions. Of course, like any powerful feature, there is room for misuse and abuse.

In this segment, we will revisit some of the basics of Set Analysis and will explore more advanced topics later on in this chapter.

Explaining what we mean by a set

Understanding a little about sets is the key to understanding how QlikView works. We already know about the symbol tables and the logical inference engine. A simple Venn Diagram can help us understand how they hang together.

When we load data into a QlikView document and we have no selections made, we will have access to all the data points for the purpose of performing calculations, as you can see:

In mathematical terms, this is our universe. It contains all of the entities that we might want to consider. If we perform a simple Sum calculation across a field, we will get the total value of all the values in that field.

Now, let's consider what happens when we make a selection in QlikView. For example, if we were to select the value 2013 in the **Year** field, QlikView would immediately apply the logical inference engine to establish all of the values that are still available, as follows:

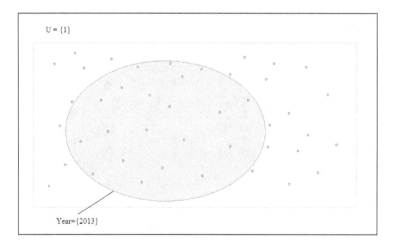

Now, when we perform the same Sum calculation, we only get a result based on the values contained within the shaded area.

If we were to make a further selection, for example, if we select both **China** and **Germany** in **Country**, then QlikView will further reduce the dataset upon which calculations are performed, as follows:

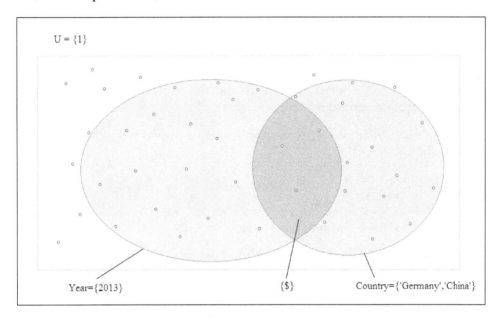

Now, the calculation of the Sum expression is only performed on the shaded area where the two ellipses overlap.

That, in a nutshell, is how QlikView works. It is beautifully simple and a great way of working with data from a data discovery point of view. However, we often want to think about other considerations. For example, if the user has selected **Germany**, what might be the value of everything else that isn't Germany? In the preceding model, we no longer have access to the data about "not Germany" because it has been excluded by selection.

Set identifiers

There are two main SET identifiers in every QlikView document:

Identifier	Description
{1}	This is the universe — the set of all possible values in the document, regardless of any selections
{$}	This represents the set of values based on current selections

Note that the $ sign here is completely unrelated to the $ sign used for Dollar-sign Expansion!

With no selections made in the document, {1} and {$} are identical. As selections are made, {1} will not change while {$} will get smaller.

Other identifiers are possible in a QlikView document. All bookmarks will be a set of the values based on the selections contained in the bookmark. Each Alternate State will also be a set of its current selections.

We write a SET identifier into an expression inside the function to which the set will apply, for example:

```
Sum({1} LineValue)
Sum({$} LineValue)
Sum({BM01} LineValue)
Sum({[My Bookmark]} LineValue)
```

If the SET identifier is not specified (as with most expressions), then the {$} set is used.

Set modifiers

The real power of Set Analysis comes when we can modify a set using modifiers. Any set, such as {1}, {$}, bookmark, and so on, can be modified. We modify a set by specifying an alternate set of values for a field. The values we specify will override the values selected in this field in this set.

Set modifiers are written inside the SET identifier's curly braces using angle brackets. The syntax will look like the following:

```
Function({Set_ID<Field1=NewSet1, Field2=NewSet2>} FieldValue)
```

What can sometimes confuse new users is that NewSet1 in the preceding syntax is often a set of specified values that are written, again, inside curly braces. For example, a set of values for **Year** can be written as follows:

```
{2009,2010,2011}
```

When this is included in a function, it looks like the following:

```
Sum({$<Year={2009,2010,2011}>} LineValue)
```

Otherwise, we can have multiple fields as shown:

```
Sum({$<Year={2011}, Country={'Germany','China'}>} LineValue)
```

There are a lot of different brackets here (not to mention that if the field name has a space, then you will need to use square brackets!) and this can lead to confusion.

There is an old developer's trick that can help you when writing out a set expression: always open and close a pair of brackets before entering the content inside them. This way, you always know that you will have a correctly matching pair. I might write one of the previous expressions in the following steps:

```
Sum()
Sum({})
Sum({$<>})
Sum({$<Year={}>})
Sum({$<Year={2009,2010,2011}>} LineValue)
```

Now, of course, these set modifiers do not have to be static values. We can introduce Dollar-sign Expansion into the expression to provide more dynamic calculations:

```
Sum({$<Year={$(vThisYear)}>} LineValue)
Sum({$<Year={$(vLastYear)}>} LineValue)
```

Understanding Dollar-sign Expansion

Dollar-sign Expansion is a process that allows us to replace text in an expression, or line of script, with either the value of a variable or some other calculation.

Suppose that we have a variable with a value of 10 and we write an expression like the following:

```
Sum(If(Field1=$(vValue), 1, 0))
```

The Dollar-sign expression, $(vValue), will get expanded to its value (10) and the expression that gets executed will be as follows:

```
Sum(If(Field1=10, 1, 0))
```

We can also have a calculation inside the Dollar-sign expression like the following:

```
If(Year=$(=Year(Today())), LightGreen())
```

In this case, the function Year(Today()) will be calculated and its value replaced into the main expression in the following manner:

```
If(Year=2014, LightGreen())
```

We do have to be aware that it is the exact value of the Dollar-sign expression that is replaced into the main expression, and it becomes as if we have typed that value there. Therefore, if it is a string value rather than a numeric value, then we need to make sure that we include the single quotes around the value.

For example, suppose that we have a variable called vCountry with a value of Germany and we have a color expression in a bar chart like the following:

```
If(Country=$(vCountry), LightGreen())
```

We might be surprised to find that the Germany bar is not highlighted. This is not such a surprise if we consider that the Dollar-sign Expansion will result in the following expression:

```
If(Country=Germany, LightGreen())
```

To QlikView, this looks like you are trying to compare the **Country** field to another field called **Germany**. Instead, we should have our original expression as shown:

```
If(Country='$(vCountry)', LightGreen())
```

This will expand out to the following:

```
If(Country='Germany', LightGreen())
```

 Of course, it can be interesting to use Dollar-sign Expansion to put different field names into an expression!

This issue is equally critical with dates. The problem is that sometimes all looks OK, but we need to consider that, without quotes, the value 8/9/2014 will actually be evaluated to 4.413549597263599e-4 (8 divided by 9 and then divided by 2014).

With dates, you can use quotes and then they will be evaluated correctly — as long as the text of the date matches the field's date format. However, it can often be a better practice to use a function like Floor or Num to transform your dates into numbers instead of relying on the text format being correct.

Following the two-step process

As was mentioned in the *Reviewing basic concepts* section, whenever Dollar-expansion is used, there is always a two-step process followed:

1. The expression or variable inside the Dollar-sign Expansion's parentheses is calculated and its value is placed into the expression, or script line, to replace the dollar-sign.

2. The newly formed expression or script line is executed.

Following the steps in the script debugger

We can use the script debugger to follow the two steps of the Dollar-sign Expansion process. For example, suppose that we had a piece of script as shown:

```
Let vMinDate=Floor(MakeDate(2009,1,1));
Let vMaxDate=Floor(MakeDate(2014,12,31));
Let vDiff=vMaxDate-vMinDate+1;

DI:
Load
    TempDate as DateID,
    Year(TempDate) As Year,
    Month(TempDate) As Month;
Load
    $(vMinDate)+RecNo()-1 As TempDate
AutoGenerate($(vDiff));
```

If we run the script debugger and put a breakpoint on the second load statement, we can observe what is happening when the Dollar-sign Expansion happens:

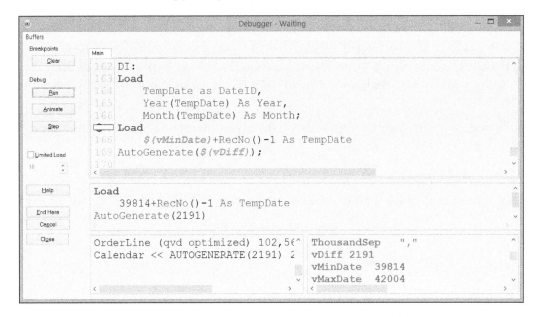

If we look at the central panel, we can see that the Dollar-sign Expansion has replaced $(vMinDate) with 39814 and $(vDiff) with 2191. The original expression is as follows:

```
Load
    $(vMinDate)+RecNo()-1 As TempDate
AutoGenerate($(vDiff));
```

This preceding code is now changed to the following:

```
Load
    39814+RecNo()-1 As TempDate
AutoGenerate(2191);
```

This debugger process is an excellent way of testing our Dollar-sign Expansion in the script.

 We can also use the Trace statement to echo variable values to the **Script Execution Dialog** box and to the document log file.

Following the steps in a chart expression

The best way to follow the steps in a chart expression, and hence to debug the Dollar-sign Expansion, is to use a Straight Table. One of the features of all charts is that if you don't specify a label for an expression, then the expression itself is used as the label, but not just the expression as entered — it is the expression after the first step with the Dollar-sign Expansion complete. This label is the easiest seen in a Straight Table.

For example, I add a Straight Table to my document, with no dimension, and have set the expression to the following:

```
Sum(If(Country='$(vCountry)', 1, 0))
```

Then, I can see the expanded expression by hovering over the label of the expression:

We can also right-click on the label and choose **Copy to Clipboard** | **Cell Value**, which allows us to paste the expression into a text editor (or another chart or text object). This can be useful if the expression is very long.

Understanding when the steps happen in chart expressions

One thing that might become apparent here is that because the first step, the actual expansion, happens before the expression is calculated; this means that the first step is not calculated in reference to the dimensions of the chart. The first step is calculated outside of the chart.

This can be a slight downside because it means that we can't successfully use a chart's dimension value in a Dollar-sign Expansion expression used inside that chart.

Just to illustrate this, suppose that I add a Straight Table with `Country` as a dimension, and then, I add the following expression:

```
'$(=MaxString(Country))'
```

I might expect that this should just calculate out the same value as the dimension on each row. However, this is not what happens:

Country	'United Kingdom'
Canada	United Kingdom
China	United Kingdom
France	United Kingdom
Germany	United Kingdom
India	United Kingdom
Ireland	United Kingdom
Russia	United Kingdom
United Kingdom	United Kingdom
USA	United Kingdom

Because the Dollar-sign Expansion has been calculated outside of the chart, it will just calculate `MaxString` based on the current selections in the document.

Using parameters with variables and Dollar-sign Expansion

We can use parameters in variables and then pass those parameters when we use the Dollar-sign Expansion. This creates a type of macro that can be used in script or in expressions.

A variable parameter is identified with a Dollar-sign and a number. The first parameter will be $1, the second will be $2, and so on.

For example, if I have fields that contain a code and a description separated by a period, I can define a couple of variables in the script in the following manner:

```
// Macros
SET mLefty=Left($1, index($1, '.')-1);
SET mRighty=Mid($1, index($1, '.')+1);
```

Then, I can load my data in the following manner:

```
Test:
Load
    $(mLefty(Field1)) as Field1.Code,
    $(mRighty(Field1)) as Field1.Desc
Inline [
Field1
001.Value one
002.Value two
003.Value three
];
```

I can also call it in an expression, for example:

```
=$(mLefty('004.Field Four'))
```

Of course, this might not work so well in a chart, because of the step order, but it would work well in a text object, caption, and so on.

Using variables in expressions

In many cases, we can just use a variable in an expression as we would in any other programming language:

```
If(Country=vCountry, Sum(LineValue), 0)
```

However, if the variable does not contain a simple value, but instead contains an expression, then it will not work like this and we need to use Dollar-sign Expansion instead.

For example, if we have a variable called `cCompanyWarning` that has a value of `ARGB(200,255,126,0)`, then we cannot simply use this in a color expression because, as far as QlikView is concerned, this is not a color, it is just text. However, suppose that we put it into an expression like the following:

```
=$(cCompanyWarning)
```

We can see that it is no longer just text. The text will get replaced into the expression and then QlikView will evaluate the `ARGB` function as if we had typed it there in the first place.

Using advanced Set Analysis

Basic Set Analysis should be in even the most junior QlikView developer's arsenal of tools. The ability to add modifiers, most frequently to the $ set, allows us to perform some very useful calculations that we either couldn't perform at all without Set Analysis, or that would have required us to do a lot more work.

Identifying the identifiers

We should already know about at least two of the identifiers that we can use in a Set Analysis expression: 1 and $. We also should know that the $ set is the default so that if there is no set identifier specified, then QlikView will use the $ set, which is just for current selections.

The following table shows a list of all the identifiers that you may come across:

Identifier	Description
1	This is the universe—it represents all of the values within the document, ignoring any selections.
$	This is the set that represents the values in the dataset as they are based on current selections. This is the default set.
$n	This set represents the *n*th last set of current selections that you might navigate by clicking on the **Back** button on the navigation toolbar. $1 is the set of selections before you made the most recent selection, $2 is the second last set, and so on. This is rarely used.

Identifier	Description
$_n	This is similar to $n except that it gives access to the *n*th forward set of selections that you might navigate by clicking on the Forward button on the navigation toolbar. Therefore, it is only available if a user has clicked on the **Back** button. This is even more rarely used than $n.
Bookmark (ID or name)	We can use a bookmark as a set identifier, representing the set of values that would be if the bookmark were applied. The identifier can be used as either the bookmark name or bookmark identifier (for example, BM01).
State name	When we use Alternate States in an application, each state name becomes an identifier that represents the current selections in that state. In this case, the $ identifier will still represent the current selections set in the default state, but the default set in an expression will depend on the state of the object containing the expression.

Understanding that modifiers are sets

We know that the true power of Set Analysis comes not just with the ability to specify different identifiers in an expression (although having just that could be quite powerful) but with the ability to modify those sets with our own set of selections.

At this stage, we should be familiar with using a Set Analysis expression with modifiers as shown:

```
Sum({$<Year={2012,2013}>} SalesValue)
```

Here, we appear to have a field called `Year` compared to an element value list of {2012,2013}.

It makes some kind of sense that `Year` is equal to either 2012 or 2013 but actually the = sign here does not actually mean "equals". It can't really because `Year` can't be "equal" to both values.

What we have to understand is that the values on both sides of the = sign are both sets. `Year` is a data field but that is actually a set of values. The {2012,2013} list is also a set. Therefore, the = sign becomes not a direct comparison, but like a union operation between the set of all `Year` values and the set of values in the braces.

We have to be careful about this because I have seen confusion around it. For example, it is valid to have another field instead of an element list (the list of values enclosed in {}) as shown:

```
Sum({$<OrderDate=DeliveryDate>} OrderValue)
```

I have seen this described as being where `OrderDate` is equal to `DeliveryDate`. This is incorrect! This set will give you all values where the `OrderDate` values are in the range of the `DeliveryDate` values. For example, suppose that we have the following dataset:

```
Orders:
Load * Inline [
OrderID, OrderDate, DeliveryDate, OrderValue
1, 2014-08-10, 2014-08-10, 100
2, 2014-08-10, 2014-08-11, 100
3, 2014-08-11, 2014-08-12, 100
4, 2014-08-13, 2014-08-14, 100
];
```

We might expect that the preceding expression would only match for the first order. However, it could match for the first three orders! The union of the values in the `OrderDate` field with the values in `DeliveryDate` will actually only exclude the last order. The order dates in orders 1 and 2 match to the delivery date from order 1, while the order date from order 3 matches to the delivery date from order 2.

> Note that when using a field instead of an element value list, the comparison set of values becomes the selected values in the field, not the possible values. If you want the possible values, you should use a `P()` set (as discussed later).

Set arithmetic

We can use mathematical set arithmetic with any set such as identifier, field, or element list. The operators only work on sets and return a set result. The operators are listed in the following table:

Operator	Description	Venn diagram
+ (Union)	The result is a set that represents the union of the sets.	

Operator	Description	Venn diagram

- (Exclusion)	The result will be all of the values in the first set that are not included in the second set.
	
	- can also be used as a unary operator (just with one set) where it will return the complement set, for example:
	
	`Sum({$<OrderDa`
	`te=-{'2014-08-10'}>} OrderValue)`	

* (Intersection)	The result will be a set of all the values that are common to both sets.	
/ (Symmetric difference)	The result will be a set of all the values that are in either set but not the values that are common to both.	

As stated previously, these sets can be applied to identifiers, fields, and element lists. So we can create a set in the following manner:

```
Sum({$*BM01} SalesValue)
```

This will give us the intersection of current selections and the bookmark `BM01`.

We can also have a set as follows:

```
Sum({$<OrderDate=DeliveryDate-{'2014-08-13','2014-08-11'}>}
OrderValue)
```

We can get quite sophisticated with this set arithmetic. If we do need to have more than one set operators, we should remember to use parentheses because `($*BM01)-BM02` is different from `$*(BM01-BM02)`.

Where there is a set comparison that includes the field that we are modifying, we can make use of some shorthand; this will be familiar to C/C#/Java programmers. For example, if we want every year except for one particular year, we can perform the following:

```
Sum({$<Year=Year-{2013}>} SalesValue)
```

We can shorten the expression in the following manner:

```
Sum({$<Year-={2013}>} SalesValue)
```

We can equally perform similar shorthand with the other operators:

```
+=
*=
/=
```

Using searches in Set Analysis

When we first learned to use Set Analysis, we might have learned that we can use wildcard search within a modifier. This is quite a powerful feature. However, we can really enhance what we can do with Set Analysis when we learn that we can also use advanced search within our modifiers.

Essentially, any exact match, wildcard, or advanced search that we can use in a search dialog in a listbox can be used in a modifier.

For example, if we want to see the sales for Germany, we can use an exact match:

```
Sum({<Country={'Germany'}>} LineValue)
```

If we are looking for sales for years in the 2010s, we might do this:

```
Sum({<Year={"201*"}>} LineValue)
```

If we want sales since 2011, we can do this:

```
Sum({<Year={">=2011"}>} LineValue)
```

How about we check for all sales for those countries that sold more than 5, 000, 000 in 2013:

```
Sum({<Country={"=Sum({<Year={2013}>} LineValue)>5000000"}>} LineValue)
```

We know that if we want to get the sales for a list of countries, we can simply list them in an element value list like this:

```
Sum({<Country={'Germany','China'}>} LineValue)
```

However, we also have the option to use search syntax like this:

```
Sum({<Country={"(Germany|China)"}>} LineValue)
```

And, as we saw in the earlier part of this chapter, that syntax allows us to include multiple search options:

```
Sum({<Year={"(2010|2013|200*)"}>} LineValue)
```

This can also be expressed as follows:

```
Sum({<Year={2010,2013,"200*"}>} LineValue)
```

 There is a convention that we should use single quotes with literal values and use double quotes with wildcard and other searches. However, they are actually interchangeable. This is useful to know if you need to use one or the other in the text of the search.

Using Dollar-sign Expansion with Set Analysis

So far, we have used mostly static values in our example modifiers. However, the most power will come when we combine modifiers and Dollar-sign Expansion.

There is no great magic here. Wherever we might use a static value, we just replace it with a Dollar-sign Expansion. For example, we can use the following:

```
Sum({<Year={$(vMaxYear)}>} LineValue)
```

We can also use the following:

```
Sum({<Year={$(=Max(Year))}>} LineValue)
```

The only thing that we need to really consider here is that when performing an exact match with dates, we need to make sure that the value returned from the Dollar-sign Expansion matches the text of the date's dual value. It isn't such an issue if you are doing a greater-than or less-than comparison, because then you can use either the dual text or numeric format. For example, if we have a Month field that is Dual('Jan',1), Dual('Feb',2), and so on, then we can't do the following:

```
Sum({<Month={3}>} LineValue)
```

Instead, we need to do this:

```
Sum({<Month={'Mar'}>} LineValue)
```

Although the following is also fine:

```
Sum({<Month={">=3<5"}>} LineValue)
```

Comparing to other fields

Quite often, in a set modifier, we will want to compare the field to be modified to the values in a different field. There are a number of different options, and they are discussed in the upcoming sections.

Direct field comparison

We have seen this already, but it is acceptable for the set comparison to be directly against another field. For example:

```
Sum({<Year=DI.Year>} LineValue)
```

We can use set arithmetic on these like this:

```
Sum({<Year=Year+DI.Year>} LineValue)
```

 We must recall that the set of values in the comparison field (in this case, `DI.Year`) is only the selected values – not possible values.

Using Concat with Dollar-sign Expansion

One way that we can get over the limitation of only seeing selected values in the other field is to use the `Concat` function along with Dollar-sign Expansion to derive an element value list, for example:

```
Sum({<Year={$(=Concat(Distinct DI.Year,','))}>} LineValue)
```

This might expand to something like this:

```
Sum({<Year={2011,2012,2013}>} LineValue)
```

With text values, we might need to make use of the `Chr(39)` function, which returns a single quote, to derive the correct list:

```
Sum({<Country={'$(=Concat(Distinct DI.Cntr,Chr(39)&','&Chr(39)))'}>}
LineValue)
```

This might expand to something like the following:

```
Sum({<Country={'France','Germany','Ireland','USA'}>} LineValue)
```

Using the P and E element functions

The `P` and `E` functions, which can only be used in a set modifier expression, will return a set of either the possible or excluded values. As they are functions, they can themselves accept a set identifier and modifier. We can also specify which field we want to return the set of values for. If left out, the field that we are modifying will be returned.

Let's look at some examples. First, if we perhaps want to modify the `Year` field with the years that are selected in a particular bookmark, use:

```
Sum({<Year=P({BM01} Year)>} LineValue)
```

What if we want to modify the `Year` field with all of the values in the `DI.Year` field:

```
Sum({<Year=P({$} DI.Year)>} LineValue)
```

Otherwise, to get all of the values in the `DI.Year` field that are not selected:

```
Sum({<Year=E({$} DI.Year)>} LineValue)
```

Set Analysis with Alternate States

When using Alternate States in a QlikView document, we can now add additional complexity to calculations. The syntax is quite straightforward though.

Using Alternate States as identifiers

When we want to access the values in an Alternate State, we can simply add the Alternate State name as the set identifier:

```
Sum({State1} LineValue)
```

Of course, all of the usual set arithmetic is applicable:

```
Sum({$*State1} LineValue)
```

Comparing fields between states

We can also modify a field in a set expression using the set of values from a field in another state. The syntax uses the state name, a double-colon (::), and the name of the field. For example:

```
Sum({State1<Year=$::Year, Month=$::Month} LineValue)
```

Calculating vertically

One of the most powerful features in QlikView is the ability to create vertical calculations in charts. We normally calculate values horizontally, where all values are in reference to the dimensions in the chart. It is a very important feature for us to also make vertical calculations across those horizontal numbers. For example, we might want to know what the total of all our calculations is so that we can calculate a ratio.

We might want to know the average, or the standard deviation, to draw a line in a chart. We might want to accumulate just the last four results to calculate a rolling average.

Using inter-record and range functions

There are several functions that allow us to compare between different records in a chart. Some work in all charts, but others are specific to a particular chart type, such as a pivot table. In the graphical charts (Bar, Pie, and so on), we should imagine their Straight Table equivalent to understand how these functions will work.

The main functions that we can use here are listed in the following table:

Function	Description
Above	This allows us to access the values in the chart above the current row
Below	Like Above, we get only access to the values below the current row
Before	This is used in a pivot table to access the values before the current column
After	Again, this is used in a pivot table to get access to the values after the current column
Top	This gives us access to the value in the first row of the chart
Bottom	This gives us access to the value in the last row of the chart
First	In a pivot table, this gives us access to the value in the first column of the chart
Last	This gives us the value in the last column in a pivot table
RowNo	This tells us the number of the current row in the chart
ColumnNo	In a pivot table, this tells us the number of the current column
NoOfRows	This tells us how many rows there are in the chart
NoOfColumns	In a pivot table, this tells us the number of columns

The default for the Above, Below, Before, After, Top, Bottom, First, and Last functions are to just return one value that will be, as you would expect, the value in the direction stated in the name of the function. Consider the following example:

```
Above(Sum(LineValue))
```

This will give us the value of Sum(LineValue) in the row directly above it.

These functions also take additional, optional parameters. The second parameter will accept an offset value, defaulting to 1, indicating how many rows above we want to take the value. So, consider the following example:

```
Above(Sum(LineValue),2)
```

This will give us the value two rows above. In fact, we can actually specify 0 as the offset and this will just give us the current row.

The third optional parameter, which defaults to 1, will specify how many row values we want to return. Consider the following example:

```
Above(Sum(LineValue),0,4)
```

This will give us four values, starting with the current row. Now, QlikView cannot handle multiple values like this, and if we try to use this in a chart, it will return null. This is where we need to use the range functions, which will handle a range of values like this. There are several range functions, such as RangeSum, RangeCount, and RangeAvg, that are designed for this purpose. So, if we want the average of the four values above, we would do the following:

```
RangeAvg(Above(Sum(LineValue),0,4))
```

This will give us, if the dimension in this chart were in months, a four-month moving average:

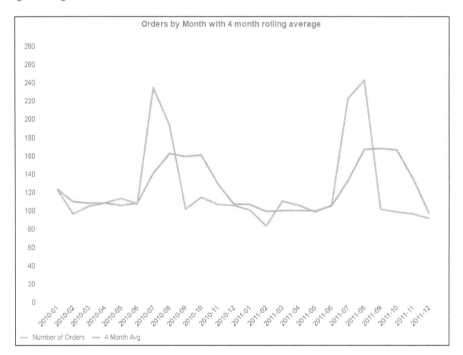

If we include the RowNo function to tell us what row we are on, we can calculate a cumulative value:

```
RangeAvg(Above(Sum(LineValue),0,RowNo()))
```

This might be used in, say, a Pareto analysis:

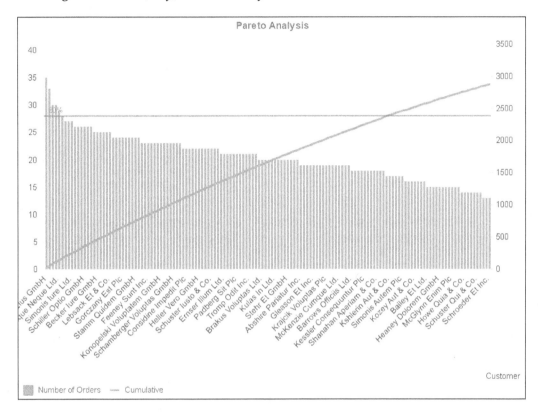

Applying the Total qualifier

By default, of course, expressions in charts will be calculated with respect to the dimensions in the chart. The Sum calculation on the USA row will only calculate for values that are associated with the USA. This is exactly what we will expect.

Sometimes, we will want to override this behavior so that we can create a calculation that ignores the dimensions in the chart. For example, we might want to calculate the percentage of the current value versus the total. When we add the Total qualifier into our expression, then the dimensions will be ignored and the expression will be calculated for the whole chart.

For example, suppose that we have a chart that has the following expression:

```
Sum(LineValue)
```

Now, we add a second expression with the `Total` qualifier:

```
Sum(Total LineValue)
```

We can see the effect of the `Total` qualifier:

Country	Sum(LineValue)	Sum(Total LineValue)
	288,715,597	**288,715,597**
Canada	26,305,874	288,715,597
China	18,349,460	288,715,597
France	18,601,651	288,715,597
Germany	38,453,709	288,715,597
India	7,081,852	288,715,597
Ireland	18,243,189	288,715,597
Russia	19,982,932	288,715,597
United Kingdom	60,134,504	288,715,597
USA	81,562,425	288,715,597

We can see that the dimensions in the chart have been ignored and the same total value has been calculated on each row. We can then change this to divide one by the other:

```
Sum(LineValue)/Sum(Total LineValue)
```

We will get a percentage calculated:

Country	Sum(LineValue)	Sum(LineValue)/Sum (Total LineValue)
	288,715,597	**100.00%**
Canada	26,305,874	9.11%
China	18,349,460	6.36%
France	18,601,651	6.44%
Germany	38,453,709	13.32%
India	7,081,852	2.45%
Ireland	18,243,189	6.32%
Russia	19,982,932	6.92%
United Kingdom	60,134,504	20.83%
USA	81,562,425	28.25%

Now, if we were to add a second dimension to this chart, we would get the percentage of each row in reference to the total as before. However, what if we wanted to see the percentage of the second dimension in reference to the first dimension's total? In this case, we can add a modifier to the Total qualifier to indicate that it should not ignore some dimensions:

```
Sum(LineValue)/Sum(Total<Region>LineValue)
```

Now, only the second dimension is ignored:

Region	Country	Sum(LineValue)	Sum(LineValue)/Sum (Total LineValue)	Sum(LineValue)/Sum (Total<Region> LineValue)
Americas	⊟ Canada	26,305,874	9.11%	24.39%
	USA	81,562,425	28.25%	75.61%
	Total	**107,868,300**	**37.36%**	**100.00%**
Asia/Pac	⊟ China	18,349,460	6.36%	72.15%
	India	7,081,852	2.45%	27.85%
	Total	**25,431,312**	**8.81%**	**100.00%**
Europe	⊟ France	18,601,651	6.44%	11.97%
	Germany	38,453,709	13.32%	24.74%
	Ireland	18,243,189	6.32%	11.74%
	Russia	19,982,932	6.92%	12.86%
	United Kingdom	60,134,504	20.83%	38.69%
	Total	**155,415,986**	**53.83%**	**100.00%**
Total		**288,715,597**	**100.00%**	**100.00%**

Creating advanced aggregations with Aggr

QlikView has a fantastic chart engine. It is no surprise that we can get additional access to this chart engine, inside or outside of a chart, so as to create more advanced calculations. The Aggr function allows us to create a virtual chart—we can imagine it like a Straight Table—and then, we can do something with the set of values that are returned, that is, the expression column in our imaginary Straight Table.

Like a chart, the Aggr function takes an expression as a parameter. It also takes one or more dimensions. It then calculates the expression against the dimensions and returns a set of the results that we generally use in another aggregation function such as Sum, Avg, Max, Stdev, and so on. For example, suppose we were to perform the following Aggr function:

```
Aggr(Sum(OrderCounter), Country)
```

Then, we can imagine the virtual Straight Table that this will create:

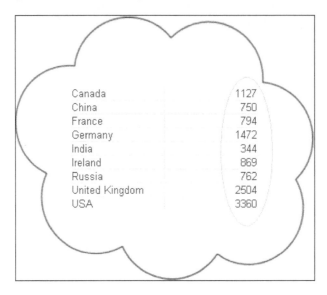

Canada	1127
China	750
France	794
Germany	1472
India	344
Ireland	869
Russia	762
United Kingdom	2504
USA	3360

We might then want to calculate the average of these values:

```
Avg(Aggr(Sum(OrderCounter), Country))
```

When an `Aggr` function is used within a chart, its context is set by the dimensions of the chart. This means that on each row of the chart, the `Aggr` function will only have access to the values that are related to the dimension values for that row. For example, if we want to use the `Aggr` above in a chart that contains the `Country` dimension, we will need to add the `Total` qualifier:

```
Avg(Total Aggr(Sum(OrderCounter), Country))
```

If we didn't, the calculation will respect the dimensionality of the chart and just give us the sum of the `OrderCounter` field on each row:

Country	Sum(OrderCounter)	Avg(Aggr(Sum (OrderCounter), Country))	Avg(Total Aggr(Sum (OrderCounter), Country))
	11,982	1,331.3	1,198.2
Canada	1,127	1,127.0	1,198.2
China	750	750.0	1,198.2
France	794	794.0	1,198.2
Germany	1,472	1,472.0	1,198.2
India	344	344.0	1,198.2
Ireland	869	869.0	1,198.2
Russia	762	762.0	1,198.2
United Kingdom	2,504	2,504.0	1,198.2
USA	3,360	3,360.0	1,198.2

There is an interesting issue present in this table. The average of 1,198.2 does not appear to be correct! The average should be 1,331.3. However, if we turn off the Supress Zero option for the chart, we will find that there is another blank value, Country! If we include this in the average calculation, then we will get 1,198.2 and this is what Aggr is doing. We can exclude the blank value by using a bit of Set Analysis:

```
Avg(Total Aggr(Sum({<Country={*}>} OrderCounter),
Country))
```

Using Aggr to calculate a control chart

Statistical control charts were first proposed by Walter A. Shewhart, a statistician working for Bell Laboratories in the 1920s. They take into consideration that variation is normal in a process and that we should only be concerned with variation outside control limits.

A control chart will often use a combination and a mean of a range of values from a particular period to compare to another period. For example, we might say that we will treat 2012 as a sample for the deviation of our sales figures and then we want to see the trend of our sales figures in 2014.

To do this, we will have to have a calculation of the mean value that includes a Set Analysis statement to limit to the correct period:

```
Avg({$<Year={2012}>} Total Aggr(Sum({$<Year={2012}>} LineValue),
YearMonth))
```

Note that the Set Analysis expression needs to be contained in both the Aggr expressions and in the aggregation function that we use Aggr with.

We can add the upper control value for the control chart:

```
Avg({$<Year={2012}>} Total Aggr(Sum({$<Year={2012}>} LineValue),
YearMonth))
+
2*Stdev({$<Year={2012}>} Total Aggr(Sum({$<Year={2012}>} LineValue),
YearMonth))
```

We can add the lower control as well:

```
Avg({$<Year={2012}>} Total Aggr(Sum({$<Year={2012}>} LineValue),
YearMonth))
-
2*Stdev({$<Year={2012}>} Total Aggr(Sum({$<Year={2012}>} LineValue),
YearMonth))
```

Now we should have a chart that allows us to look at different year's performance versus the 2012 controls:

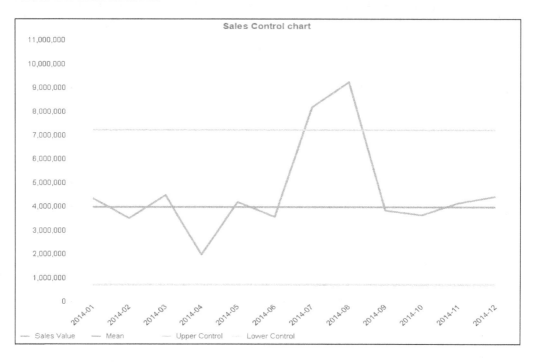

Calculated dimensions

Another use that we can put the `Aggr` function to is to create calculated dimension. Before we had dimension limitations in charts, this was the only way that we can limit some charts to, say, the top 5. In fact, we still need to turn to this to calculate the top *x* dimension values in pivot tables. For example, if we want to have the top 5 customers, we need to add a calculated dimension of the following:

```
=If(Aggr(Rank(Sum(LineValue)), Customer)<=5, Customer, Null())
```

We should also set the **Supress When Value is Null** option for this dimension. We can also add a second dimension such as `Year` to the chart:

Customer	Year	2012	2014	2013	2009	2011	2010	Total
Friesen Error Ltd.		222,947	93,059	1,025,501	305,584	233,207	553,275	2,433,572
McKenzie Cumque Ltd.		317,481	151,162	800,728	775,069	309,961	376,517	2,730,917
Nitzsche Et GmbH		133,538	260,544	426,261	654,781	412,128	443,324	2,330,576
Toy Sint GmbH		692,042	204,039	776,023	505,591	161,493	344,577	2,683,766
Parker In & Co.		196,973	209,892	858,076	341,792	308,938	404,377	2,320,048
Total		1,562,981	918,696	3,886,589	2,582,816	1,425,726	2,122,070	12,498,879

This is a really interesting thing because it is using the calculated virtual chart to provide the values for the dimension, but knows how the dimension values are associated to the data so that it can correctly calculate the totals.

No to nodistinct

The `Aggr` function has as an optional clause, that is, the possibility of stating that the aggregation will be either `distinct` or `nodistinct`.

The default option is `distinct`, and as such, is rarely ever stated. In this default operation, the aggregation will only produce distinct results for every combination of dimensions—just as you would expect from a normal chart or straight table.

The `nodistinct` option only makes sense within a chart, one that has more dimensions than are in the `Aggr` statement. In this case, the granularity of the chart is lower than the granularity of `Aggr`, and therefore, QlikView will only calculate that `Aggr` for the first occurrence of lower granularity dimensions and will return null for the other rows. If we specify `nodistinct`, the same result will be calculated across all of the lower granularity dimensions.

This can be difficult to understand without seeing an example, so let's look at a common use case for this option. We will start with a dataset:

```
ProductSales:
Load * Inline [
Product, Territory, Year, Sales
Product A, Territory A, 2013, 100
Product B, Territory A, 2013, 110
Product A, Territory B, 2013, 120
Product B, Territory B, 2013, 130
Product A, Territory A, 2014, 140
Product B, Territory A, 2014, 150
Product A, Territory B, 2014, 160
Product B, Territory B, 2014, 170
];
```

We will build a report from this data using a pivot table:

Sales Report					🔲 XL
Product	Territory	Year	2013	2014	Total
Product A	Territory A		100	140	240
	Territory B		120	160	280
Product B	Territory A		110	150	260
	Territory B		130	170	300

Now, we want to bring the value in the **Total** column into a new column under each year, perhaps to calculate a percentage for each year. We might think that, because the total is the sum for each `Product` and `Territory`, we might use an `Aggr` in the following manner:

```
Sum(Aggr(Sum(Sales), Product, Territory))
```

However, as stated previously, because the chart includes an additional dimension (`Year`) than `Aggr`, the expression will only be calculated for the first occurrence of each of the lower granularity dimensions (in this case, for `Year = 2013`):

Sales Report							XL
	Year		2013		2014		Total
Product	Territory	Sales $	Aggr Distinct	Sales $	Aggr Distinct	Sales $	Aggr Distinct
Product A	Territory A	100	240	140	0	240	240
	Territory B	120	280	160	0	280	280
Product B	Territory A	110	260	150	0	260	260
	Territory B	130	300	170	0	300	300

The commonly suggested fix for this is to use `Aggr` without `Sum` and with `nodistinct` as shown:

```
Aggr(NoDistinct Sum(Sales), Product, Territory)
```

This will allow the `Aggr` expression to be calculated across all the `Year` dimension values, and at first, it will appear to solve the problem:

Sales Report							XL
	Year		2013		2014		Total
Product	Territory	Sales $	Aggr Nodistinct	Sales $	Aggr Nodistinct	Sales $	Aggr Nodistinct
Product A	Territory A	100	240	140	240	240	240
	Territory B	120	280	160	280	280	280
Product B	Territory A	110	260	150	260	260	260
	Territory B	130	300	170	300	300	300

The problem occurs when we decide to have a total row on this chart:

Sales Report							XL
	Year		2013		2014		Total
Product	Territory	Sales $	Aggr Nodistinct	Sales $	Aggr Nodistinct	Sales $	Aggr Nodistinct
Product A	Territory A	100	240	140	240	240	240
	Territory B	120	280	160	280	280	280
	Total	220 -		300 -		520 -	
Product B	Territory A	110	260	150	260	260	260
	Territory B	130	300	170	300	300	300
	Total	240 -		320 -		560 -	
Total		460 -		620 -		1080 -	

As there is no aggregation function surrounding `Aggr`, it does not total correctly at the `Product` or `Territory` dimensions. We can't add an aggregation function, such as `Sum`, because it will break one of the other totals.

However, there is something different that we can do; something that doesn't involve `Aggr` at all! We can use our old friend `Total`:

```
Sum(Total<Product, Territory> Sales)
```

This will calculate correctly at all the levels:

Sales Report							🖫 XL
	Year		2013		2014		Total
Product	Territory	Sales $	Total	Sales $	Total	Sales $	Total
	Territory A	100	240	140	240	240	240
Product A	Territory B	120	280	160	280	280	280
	Total	220	520	300	520	520	520
	Territory A	110	260	150	260	260	260
Product B	Territory B	130	300	170	300	300	300
	Total	240	560	320	560	560	560
Total		460	1080	620	1080	1080	1080

There might be other use cases for using a `nodistinct` clause in `Aggr`, but they should be reviewed to see whether a simpler `Total` function will work instead.

Summary

This has been a really technical chapter and a very important one on the road to QlikView mastery.

We reviewed some very important concepts that we need to know before we can take on advanced expressions. We had an in-depth look at searching in QlikView, we reviewed bookmarks, we looked at how we use variables, and then discussed how we limit calculations.

Building on these basics, we delved into Dollar-sign Expansion. This feature is used in so many areas, especially Set Analysis, that we really need to have a good grasp of its use.

The *Using advanced Set Analysis* section showed how we can make use of one of QlikView's most powerful features. This is a feature that most QlikView developers will use in most applications.

Finally, we looked at the area of calculating vertically and discussed important functions such as the inter-record functions, the `Total` qualifier, and last but very much not least, the `Aggr` function. We now know that the `Aggr` function is extremely useful, but we don't need to apply it in all circumstances where we have vertical calculations.

In the next chapter, we'll deep dive into the QlikView script and will look at various advanced techniques needed to load data most effectively into QlikView.

Advanced Scripting

5

"In my opinion, the vast majority of scripts written ... are not very original, well-written, or interesting. It has always been that way, and I think it always will be."

— Viggo Mortensen

In anything more than the simplest of QlikView applications, the script is where we spend a very large percentage of our development time.

When we discussed the performance tuning of our applications (*Chapter 1, Performance Tuning and Scalability*), we discussed that almost all of the effort to make our applications more efficient and to consume less memory will be made in the script. Even when we tune expressions in the frontend, then this is more than likely going to be supported by script work.

All data modeling work is going to be in the script. Of course, implementing an ETL process is something that we do in the script. We can use the script to simplify advanced expressions.

Almost everything we discussed in this book so far is either directly script-related or directly influenced by what we do in the script. Therefore, to truly be a QlikView master, you need to master the QlikView script.

This chapter is all about learning great ways of manipulating data in the script. If you can master these methods, then you are well on your way to mastery of the whole product.

These are the topics we'll cover in this chapter:

- Counting records
- Loading data quickly

- Applying variables and the Dollar-sign Expansion in the script
- Using control structures
- Examining advanced Table File Wizard options
- Looking at data from different directions
- Reusing the code

Reviewing the basic concepts

We will have a quick look at some of the basic concepts that we should be aware of when first starting to load data. Anyone who has done basic QlikView training should be familiar with the concepts here, but it is worth reviewing them.

Using Table Files Wizard

We don't have to use Table Files Wizard to load data from file sources, but it is very useful to help us generate the necessary script to load the data correctly. We have some buttons in the script editor that give us access to Table Files Wizard:

These buttons are listed in the following table:

Button	Description
Table Files	This button opens a standard **File Open** dialog. Once a file is selected, the main Table Files Wizard will open with an appropriate file type, based on QlikView's interpretation of the file's content, already selected for us.
QlikView File	This won't actually open the wizard because it only allows a QlikView QVW file to be selected. It will insert a BINARY statement at the beginning of the active tab in the script. We need to be careful here because BINARY, if used, must be the very first statement in the script, so it should be on the very first tab in the script.
Web Files	This allows us to enter a web URI to point at a file source located on the Internet. This can be HTML, but can also be any of the other supported file types.

Button	Description
Field Data	This allows you to point at a field that you have already loaded into the script (therefore, you must have run the script at least once) and parse the contents of the field using a delimiter or fixed record rules.

Some of us might have (accidentally or on purpose) clicked on the **Back** button in the first screen that appears on Table Files Wizard and discovered the actual first page, which corresponds to three of the buttons:

Using relative paths

When we load a file in QlikView, we can either use an absolute or a relative path.

When discussing file paths, an absolute path means the full path to a file starting with either a drive letter or a UNC path, for example, C:\QVDocuments\Finance\Sources\Budget.xls or \\QVServer\QVDocuments\Finance\Sources\Budget.xls.

A relative path means that the path is expressed relative to another path. The default start path is the location of the QlikView QVW file. So, if we have our QVW in:

```
C:\QVDocuments\Finance\Apps
```

Then, the relative path to the source file is:

```
..\Sources\Budget.xls
```

 The . and .. are relative path indicators that have been around since the earliest Unix days. The . indicates the current folder and .. indicates the parent folder. You can concatenate several of them, so ..\.. indicates the parent of the parent folder.

We can also specify an alternate start path using the `Directory` statement. So, if we issue this command:

`Directory 'C:\QVDocuments\Finance';`

Then, the relative path the source file becomes:

```
Sources\Budget.xls
```

Alternatively, you can also use:

```
.\Sources\Budget.xls
```

If we turn on the **Relative Paths** checkbox on the **Data** tab in the script editor, then Table Files Wizard will return the path as a relative path, relative to the document location. It will also automatically add a `Directory` statement like this:

```
Directory;
```

A `Directory` statement without specifying a path is actually superfluous, as it means to just use the default path — the location of the QVW file. Therefore, we can feel free to delete this statement if we don't want to use it.

The main reason why it is preferable to use relative paths instead of absolute paths is transportability — we can move a folder system from one server (for example, a development server) to another (for example, a preproduction system) and all of the paths should still work without having to make any edits to the script.

Delimited files

If the Wizard detects that the file content is just text, it usually guesses that we are dealing with a delimited file and will have a guess at what the delimiter is from the data:

It is often quite good at detecting some of these settings, especially the **Character Set** value, but we might need to tweak these sometimes. Usually, the tweak is just setting the **Labels** option from **None** to **Embedded Labels**.

 The usual options in the **Labels** section that we need to be concerned with are either **None** or **Embedded Labels**. The third option, **Explicit**, is only relevant for certain file types, specifically **Data Interchange Format (DIF)**, which includes a header section that contains explicit labels.

If the first line of the file contains the labels, then we should choose the **Embedded Labels** option. If we choose **None**, then the fields will be named @1, @2, @3, and so forth. We can, of course, rename these fields like this:

```
LOAD
      @1 as SalesPerson,
      @2 as Company,
      @3 as [Sales Value],
      @4 as [Number of Orders]
FROM
[..\Sources\SalesReport.csv]
(txt, utf8, no labels, comment is #, delimiter is ',', msq);
```

To facilitate this, the wizard allows us to change the name in the data display grid, and then it will generate the As statement for us:

Besides changing the **Labels** options, we might also add an entry under **Comment**. Here, we can define a value that might appear at the beginning of a line in the text file (# or // are common), which indicates that this line is a comment and we don't need to load it. Rows beginning with this text will be ignored.

Fixed width files

When the data source has been outputted by a reporting system, it is quite common that the data is in a fixed width format. Every value in each report column takes up the same amount of space, with spaces added wherever necessary to pad the values out to fit. Consider the following example:

```
Country         Sales $  No. Orders
Germany       92,981.20          29
USA           26,265.16          16
France        25,002.56          15
```

To load this in QlikView, we just need to tell the wizard exactly the width each row takes up, and this can be done by a click of the mouse:

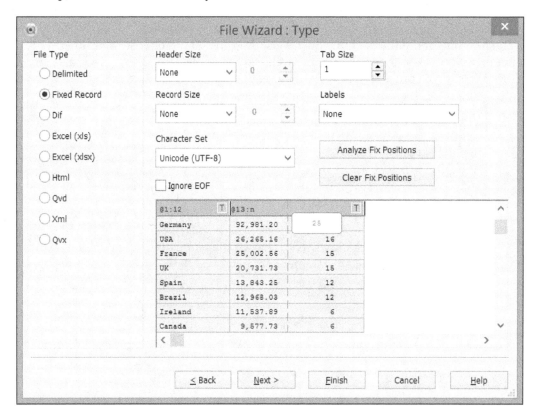

The field names that are generated by the wizard contain the position of the first character and the last character separated by a colon:

```
LOAD @1:12,
     @13:24,
     @25:n
FROM
[..\Sources\CountryReport.txt]
(fix, utf8);
```

The last field will usually have n specified as the ending character. This indicates the end of line position.

We are free to modify these manually, if we need to, as well as adding field aliases. We can even have fixed positions overlapping if it makes sense to do so:

```
LOAD [@1:20] As Field1,
     [@8:24] As Field2,
     [@16:n] As Field3
```

XML files

The wizard is very good at dealing with XML data, from simple tables to more complex relationships. For example, we can have an XML file with data like this:

```
<?xml version="1.0" encoding="utf-8" standalone="yes"?>
<CountryCity>
<Country name="USA">
  <City>New York</City>
  <City>Dallas</City>
  <City>Boston</City>
</Country>
<Country name="Austria">
  <City>Graz</City>
<City>Salzburg</City>
</Country>
<Country name="Belgium">
  <City>Bruxelles</City>
  <City>Charleroi</City>
</Country>
</CountryCity>
```

We can see that the previous data includes values in both tags and elements and also that there is a hierarchy of data between country and city.

When we load this data into Table Files Wizard, the tool automatically recognizes the hierarchies as different tables:

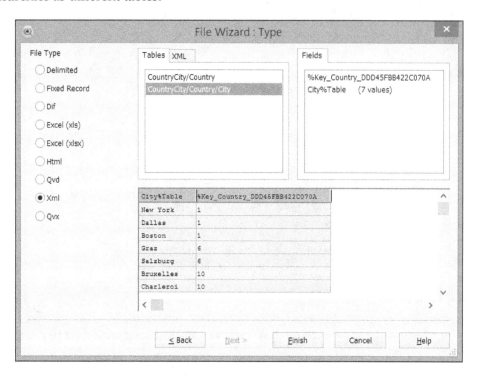

When we click on **Finish** in the wizard, it will generate the code to load each of the tables, with an automatically generated ID field to associate them:

```
// Start of [CountryCity.xml] LOAD statements
City:
LOAD City%Table,
    %Key_Country_DDD45FBB422C070A
// Key to parent table: CountryCity/Country
FROM [..\Sources\CountryCity.xml]
(XmlSimple, Table is [CountryCity/Country/City]);

Country:
LOAD name,
    %Key_Country_DDD45FBB422C070A
// Key for this table: CountryCity/Country
FROM [..\Sources\CountryCity.xml]
(XmlSimple, Table is [CountryCity/Country]);
// End of [CountryCity.xml] LOAD statements
```

Of course, we should probably think about joining these tables together and then dropping the key field.

HTML files

QlikView can handle most HTML files that have tables defined (sometimes, it has difficulty with XHTML). You can either connect to a file locally or a web URL.

For example, if you want to grab the currency conversion rates from the front page of `http://www.xe.com/`, enter the link as follows:

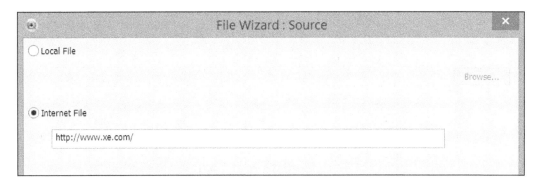

The wizard will connect to the website and retrieve information about all of the tables on the page. In this case, there is just one:

In other cases, you might need to click through the list of tables offered, **@1**, **@2**, **@3**, and so forth, and use the preview window to identify the correct one. The script might look like this:

```
LOAD [Auto-refresh  15x      0 : 59],
     [Auto-refresh  15x      0 : 591],
     USD,
     EUR,
     GBP,
     INR,
     AUD,
     CAD,
     ZAR,
     NZD,
     JPY
FROM
[http://www.xe.com/]
(html, codepage is 1252, embedded labels, table is @1);
```

It could be that the field name that is identified doesn't actually work when you try the reload (as in this case). You could try playing with the spacing—this works here:

```
LOAD [Auto-refresh15x0 : 59],
     [Auto-refresh15x0 : 591],
```

You can replace the fields with just a *:

```
LOAD *
FROM
[http://www.xe.com]
(html, codepage is 1252, embedded labels, table is @1);
```

QVD/QVX files

When it comes to QVD or QVX files, we don't get to modify any settings in the wizard to change the way the file is handled. Setting such as **Embedded Labels**, **Delimiter**, **Header Size**, and so forth, are meaningless when loading a QVD, as all of the information that is needed to interpret the file is already embedded in the file.

Connecting to databases

QlikView can connect to almost every on-premise database system in the world. In fact, the only ones that we might have trouble with are very archaic ones that do not have open drivers.

QlikView can use one of the three different driver types to connect to databases:

Driver type	Description
ODBC	An Open Database Connectivity driver allows us to connect to the majority of the world's database systems because most of the world's database vendors will either issue a driver for free, along with their client tools, or will have licenses for a third party to create a driver. ODBC drivers are configured at the operating system level and their settings are stored in the system registry. Therefore, if documents are moved from development to test/production systems, we need to ensure that the same driver is configured on all systems.
OLEDB	OLEDB is Microsoft's standard for connecting programmatically to databases. It is quite different in implementation from ODBC, but we don't really need to worry about that. Most of the larger database vendors will have an OLEDB driver available as well as the ODBC one. The OLEDB option tends to be faster, especially for Microsoft databases. The configuration information for an OLEDB connection is stored within the QlikView document's CONNECT statement, so it can be a little more portable; we just need to ensure that the drivers are installed on every server that needs them.
Custom	A custom driver can be written, using QlikView's APIs, to allow connections to many more systems. For example, Qlik has custom drivers available for both SAP and SalesForce.com—systems that we cannot otherwise connect directly to. They also have a custom driver that talks to their own server management service and can read information from that into QlikView. In theory, a custom connector can be built for almost any database system that we can think of.

Using the Connect button

When we look at the **Data** tab in the script editor, we see a dropdown that allows us to select the driver type that we want to use:

Once we have selected the driver type that we want to use, we click on the **Connect...** button, which will open a dialog that is appropriate to the selected driver. For ODBC, we don't need to provide any of the connection detail, just the username and password, and the dialog will look like this:

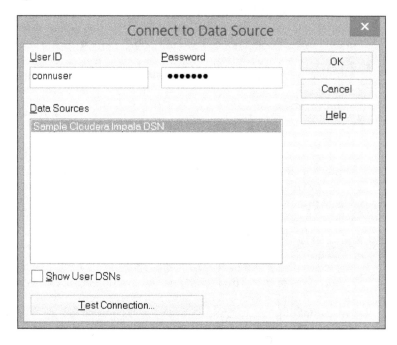

The connection dialog for OLEDB is different because we need to provide connection information. The OLEDB dialog is one that many developers will be familiar with because it comes from the operating system, not from QlikView. We first need to select the correct database driver, and then we can provide connection-specific information. For example, if we used a SQL Server connection, it might look like this:

Any custom connector will have its own dialog. Some have no dialogs at all!

Understanding the Connect To statement

The purpose of all of the dialogs is to generate a `Connect To` statement. This is the statement that tells QlikView how to connect to the driver that is being used.

The `Connect To` statement is usually preceded by an indication of the connection type: `ODBC`, `OLEDB`, or `CUSTOM`. If the connection type is omitted, then `ODBC` is assumed.

Here is an example `ODBC Connect To` statement:

```
ODBC CONNECT TO QVData_ODBC (XUserId is IMcKXZFMCC, XPassword is
GRdHfABOQDbKWZJFeE);
```

We can see that all we need is the ODBC name because the rest of the information necessary to make the connection is already configured within the ODBC connection. We have provided the username and password in the dialog box and QlikView will encrypt them so that casual viewers will not be able to see them.

Compare the ODBC Connect To statement to an OLEDB Connect To statement:

```
OLEDB CONNECT TO [Provider=SQLNCLI11.1;Integrated
Security=SSPI;Persist Security Info=False;User ID="";Initial
Catalog=QVData;Data Source=QVENTSQLWH;Use Procedure for
Prepare=1;Auto Translate=True;Packet Size=4096;Workstation
ID=SRVR1;Initial File Name="";Use Encryption for Data=False;Tag
with column collation when possible=False;MARS
Connection=False;DataTypeCompatibility=0;Trust Server
Certificate=False;Application Intent=READWRITE];
```

In this case, all of the information necessary to make the connection will be listed in the Connect string. This is similar to a Custom Connect To statement:

```
CUSTOM CONNECT TO
"Provider=QvsAdminDataProvider.dll;host=localhost;XUserId=HONSdKD;
XPassword=bfAXSUC;";
```

Explaining the Force 32 Bit option

Prior to QlikView Version 10, if your database vendor only supplied a 32-bit version of its driver, you can only connect to it with a 32-bit version of QlikView. This causes a lot of problems for QlikView customers running 64-bit server versions that could not perform automatic reloads without having to run a 32-bit QlikView desktop from the command line.

In QlikView Version 10.0, the **Force 32 Bit** option was introduced to overcome this problem. Now, along with specifying the connection string, we can also specify whether a 32- or 64-bit connection should be used in the Connect To statement:

```
ODBC CONNECT32 TO [QVData] (XUserId is WAKVcARMNLacWYB);
```

QlikView actually calls separate processes to open the connections and run queries. They are QVConnect32.exe and QVConnect64.exe, which are 32-bit and 64-bit applications, respectively. If we call a Connect To or Connect64 To statement using a 64-bit version of QlikView, QVConnect64.exe will be executed. If we call Connect32 To, then QVConnect32.exe will be executed. QlikView running on a 32-bit system can only execute QVConnect32.exe.

The **Force 32 Bit** option in the **Data** tab will mean that clicking on the **Connect** button will open 32-bit versions of the dialog that have access to 32-bit drivers. These dialogs will also generate a `Connect32 To` statement instead of just a `Connect To` statement.

The Select wizard

Once we have created a connection of any type, its details are cached in the document. This allows us to access the **Select** button and retrieve information about the tables and views in our database:

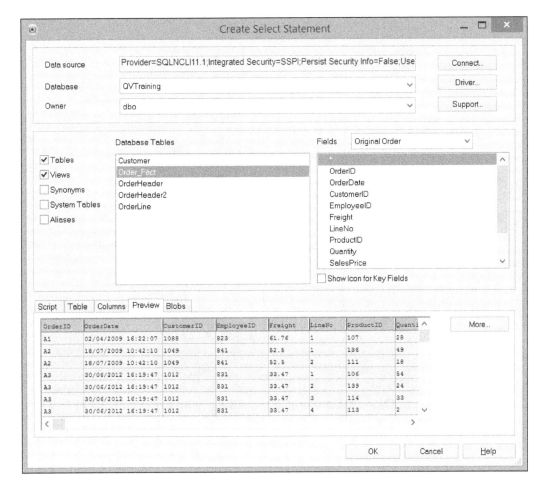

This wizard is a very useful tool because it allows us to interrogate the data structures in the database, preview the data that these tables and views contained, and generate appropriate SQL to retrieve the data.

The default option is for the wizard to generate a very simple `Select *` query to retrieve the data:

```
SQL SELECT *
FROM QVTraining.dbo."Order_Fact";
```

We can also select specific fields from the list of fields to create a more specific, yet still quite simple, query:

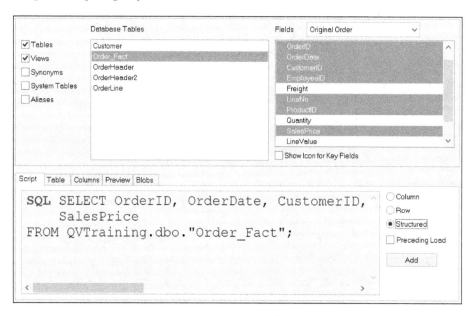

We can also turn on the (highly recommended) **Preceding Load** checkbox. This places a QlikView `Load` statement above the SQL statement. This preceding `Load` statement allows us to apply QlikView functions to the data as we are loading it from the database. A SQL statement with a preceding `Load` statement might look like this:

```
LOAD OrderID,
OrderDate,
CustomerID,
EmployeeID,
//Freight,
    "LineNo",
```

```
ProductID,
    Quantity,
SalesPrice,
LineValue,
LineCost;
SQL SELECT *
FROM QVTraining.dbo."Order_Fact";
```

We might note that even though the SQL query is a very simple `Select *`, we still get the full field list in the preceding `Load` statement.

Note the piece of script that the `Freight` field is commented out. Even though there will be a `Freight` field loaded from the database, if we do not load it in the preceding `Load` statement, then the field will not make it into the final data model.

Counting records

There are two main functions used to count records during load: `RecNo()` and `RowNo()`. After the data has been loaded, we can use another couple of interesting functions: `FieldValueCount()` and `NoOfRows()`. There is also a useful function, `NoOfFields()`, that tells us how many columns there are in a table.

RecNo

The `RecNo()` function gives us the number of the rows in the source table. While the output of the `RecNo` function will always be guaranteed to be ordered, there might be gaps in the sequence because rows may be excluded due to a where clause, for example, this `load` statement:

```
Table1:
Load *, RecNo() As RecNo1
Where Field1<>'C';
Load * Inline [
Field1
A
B
C
D
];
```

Only three rows will be loaded from the source because the row with C as a value is excluded by the Where clause. This results in this table:

Field1	RecNo1
A	1
B	2
D	4

The value 3 is missing in the sequence as the third row was not loaded.

It should also be noted that an additional load from a new source, even if it is concatenating to the same table, will have the numeric sequence restart at 1.

RowNo

The RowNo() function gives us the number of rows in the loaded in-memory table. There should be no gaps in the sequence because the next number is only assigned when the row is actually loaded. For example, if we replace the RecNo() function in the script in the previous example with RowNo(), we will get this result:

Field1	RowNo1
A	1
B	2
D	3

We have to watch out for one aspect of the RowNo() function when using the preceding loads. If we modified the preceding code like this:

```
Table1:
Load *, RowNo() As RowNo1
Where Field1<>'C';
Load *, RowNo() As RowNo2 Inline [
Field1
A
B
C
D
];
```

We will find that RowNo1 will have values as expected; however, RowNo2 will be all zeroes. This is because the RowNo() function only returns correctly in the top loader of a preceding load. It must be like this because each preceding load can have its own Where clause that can modify the number of rows loaded. Only at the topmost load do we actually know that a row is loaded.

RowNo() also differs from RecNo() because as it is the count of the number of rows actually loaded, additional concatenation of rows from different data sources does not reset the counter. So, if we had a couple of loads like this:

```
Table:
Load *, RecNo() As RecNo, RowNo() As RowNo
Inline [
Field
A
B
C
D
];

Load *, RecNo() As RecNo, RowNo() As RowNo
Where Field <> 'G';
Load *
Inline [
Field
E
F
G
H
];
```

The result would look like this:

Field	RecNo	RowNo
A	1	1
B	2	2
C	3	3
D	4	4
E	1	5
F	2	6
H	4	7

The RecNo() function as reset after the first load and skips the number for the excluded rows. The RowNo() sequence is unaffected by the fact of the second load.

FieldValueCount

The `FieldValueCount` function will return the number of values in a field. Be careful that it is not the number of rows in a table that contains the field, but it is the number of unique values in the field. The function takes the name of an existing field as a parameter; however, it needs to be passed as a string:

```
Let x=FieldValueCount('Field1');
```

NoOfRows

The `NoOfRows` function returns the actual number of rows that have been loaded in a table. As with the previous function, the table name is passed as a string value:

```
Let x=NoOfRows('Table1');
```

This function can actually be used inline during a table load. Logically, it will return `RowNo()-1`.

NoOfColumns

The `NoOfColumns` function is similar to the previous one except that it returns the number of columns. As before, we pass the table name as a string:

```
Let x=NoOfColumns('Table1');
```

A use case for both of these table functions is to check whether the expected number of rows and columns are in a table after `Join`.

Loading data quickly

In *Chapter 3, Best Practices for Loading Data*, we discussed fast loading using incremental load and binary load.

The fastest way of loading data into QlikView is to use the `Binary` statement. `Binary` will load the whole data table, symbol tables, and other data from one QVW file (Qlik Sense can binary load from either a QVW or QVF file).

The fastest way of getting a single table into QlikView is from an optimized load QVD because it contains a data table and symbol table.

In this section, we will explore some other options that we need to be aware of to load data quickly.

Understanding compression settings

This might not fit exactly into a chapter on script, but it is something that we need to be aware of and because the script defines the data size, the compression setting will define the on-disk size of the Qlik file. By default, QlikView will compress a QVW file when saving it using a high compression setting. We can change this so that medium compression is used, or we can turn off compression all together.

The main difference, obviously, is the on-disk size of the resultant file. We need to think about the algorithm that is being used to create the compression. It will require additional time for the file to be compressed. For smaller QVW files, this is not really a consideration. However, as the files begin to grow more than 1 GB or more, the compression takes longer and longer and this might become an issue for timings of reloads. For example, a 5 GB application might, depending on the hardware, take 5 minutes or so to compress and save. The same document, when saved without compression, might only take seconds. This is especially a consideration when saving to a network drive.

To change the settings for a particular QlikView document, navigate to **Settings | Document Properties | General | Save Format**:

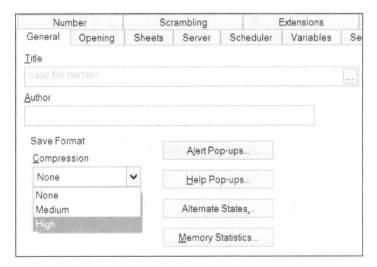

We can also specify this setting at a user level for the creation of new documents, in **Settings | User Preferences | Save**:

If disk space is not an issue, then there is probably no real benefit in allowing compression for larger applications. The applications will save quicker without it. For smaller applications, there is little difference in time.

Obviously, if we are binary loading the data from a QVW that has been compressed, then there will be that extra step of having to decompress the data. The fastest way of getting data into QlikView is by binary loading from an uncompressed QVW on very fast hardware—solid state disks are the best. We always need to balance the speed requirements with the disk space overhead.

Optimal loading from QVD

We have already discussed how the quickest way of loading a table of data is from a QVD file. This load will be listed in the script execution dialog box as **(qvd optimized)**:

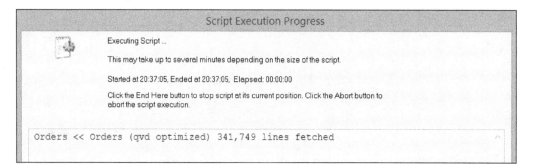

If we perform any additional calculations on this QVD data as it is being loaded — for example, adding additional fields based on QlikView functions, performing most where clauses, and so forth—then the optimized load will be lost and a normal, row-by-row, data load processing will be performed. Of course, if the QVD files are local to your reload engine (either the server or desktop), then that reload will still be quite fast.

There are a few things that we can do when loading QVDs that make sure that as optimal a load as possible will happen.

Using an Exists clause

The only things that we can do to a QVD load that will retain the optimization are:

- Rename fields with the `As` statement
- Use a `Where Exists` or `Where Not Exists` clause

The second option here is interesting because we know that a normal `Where` clause will cause a nonoptimized load. Therefore, if we can think of a way to use existing data, or perform a load of a temporary table that we can use with the `Exists` clause to keep the optimization.

For example, if we are loading some sales order detail lines into a data model in which we have already restricted the sales order headers, we can use an `Exists` clause on the `ID` field that associates them:

```
SalesOrderHeader:
Load *
From SalesOrderHeader.qvd (qvd)
Where Match(Year,2013,2014);

SalesOrderLine:
Load *
From SalesOrderLine.qvd (qvd)
Where Exists(OrderID);
```

In fact, we can replace the `Where` clause in the header table by preloading the years that we want in a temporary table:

```
TempYear:
Load
  2012+RowNo() As Year
AutoGenerate(2);

SalesOrderHeader:
Load *
From SalesOrderHeader.qvd (qvd)
Where Exists(Year);
//Where Match(Year,2013,2014);

SalesOrderLine:
Load *
```

```
From SalesOrderLine.qvd (qvd)
Where Exists(OrderID);

Drop Table TempYear;
```

If we look at the script execution dialog, we will see that the QVDs are optimized in loading:

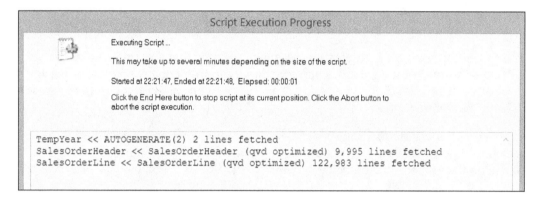

```
TempYear << AUTOGENERATE(2) 2 lines fetched
SalesOrderHeader << SalesOrderHeader (qvd optimized) 9,995 lines fetched
SalesOrderLine << SalesOrderLine (qvd optimized) 122,983 lines fetched
```

Preloading fields into QVDs

Let's imagine a scenario where we want to load sales information from `Sales.QVD` and then concatenate budget information from `Budget.QVD`. The script might look like this:

```
Fact:
Load
  DateID,
  SalesPersonID,
  CustomerID,
  ProductID,
  SalesQty,
  SalesValue
From
  Sales.QVD (QVD);

Concatenate (Fact)
Load
  DateID,
  SalesPersonID,
  CustomerID,
  ProductID,
  BudgetQty,
```

```
    BudgetValue
From
    Budget.QVD (QVD);
```

In this example, the `Sales.QVD` file will load optimized because we are not making any changes to it. The `Budget.QVD` file will not load optimized because it is being appended to the existing table and they do not have the same fields, so QlikView has some work to do.

What happens here is that QlikView will initially load a data table and symbol tables to accommodate the sales information. When we concatenate the budget information, there might be some additional entries into the symbol table but there will be a significant change to the data table, which will have to be widened to accommodate the index pointers for new fields. This change will be barely noticeable on a load of records measured in thousands, but if we have many millions of rows in one or both of the QVDs, then the delay will be significant.

If we were to take a step back and assuming an ETL approach is in place, when generating the QVDs, we should use the `null()` function to add the fields into the `Sales` table from the `Budget` table and add the fields into the `Budget` table into the `Sales` table, then both QVDs will load optimized. For example, in the transformation script, we might have code like this:

```
Sales:
Load
    DateID,
    SalesPersonID,
    CustomerID,
    ProductID,
    SalesQty,
    SalesValue,
    Null() As BudgetQty,
    Null() As BudgetValue
From
    SalesSource.QVD (QVD);

Store Sales into Sales.QVD;
Drop Table Sales;

Budget:
Load
    DateID,
    SalesPersonID,
    CustomerID,
```

```
      ProductID,
      BudgetQty,
      BudgetValue,
      Null() As SalesQty,
      Null() As SalesValue
   From
      BudgetSource.QVD (QVD);

   Store Budget into Budget.QVD;
   Drop Table Budget;
```

Then, when loading into the final document we can do this:

```
   Fact:
   Load * From Sales.QVD;
   Load * From Budget.QVD;
```

Both QVDs will load optimized.

Applying variables and the Dollar-sign Expansion in the script

We had a good discussion in *Chapter 4, Advanced Expressions,* on how to use variables with the Dollar-sign Expansion. Variables are so important to what we do in the script that it is worth just briefly reviewing the topic from a script point of view.

Variables can be assigned in the script using either a Set or Let statement.

A Set statement will assign the text on the right-hand side of the statement to the variable. A Let statement will try and evaluate the text on the right-hand side as an expression and will assign the result of that evaluation (which might be null!) to the variable. For example:

```
   Set v1=1+1;
```

This will result in the v1 variable that contains the value 1+1. Consider the following example:

```
   Let v2=1+1;
```

This will result in the v2 variable that contains the value 2.

A variable can be used simply in assignment to other variables. For example:

```
   Let v3=v2+1;
```

The v3 variable will have the value 3 (2+1). Let's consider another example:

```
Let v4=v1+1;
```

This will not work! That is because v1 contains a string value, so a string plus a number does not make sense. However, we can do this:

```
Let v4=v1&'+1';
```

Now, v4 will have the value 1+1+1.

Generally, we use variables by using the Dollar-sign Expansion. In this case, the variables are wrapped in parentheses and preceded by the dollar sign. There is a two-step execution where the contents of the variable are first expanded and replace the dollar sign, and then, the expression is evaluated as if the value had been typed there in the first place. For example:

```
Let v5=$(v1)+1;
```

In the first step, the value of v1, that is 1+1, will be expanded and will replace the dollar sign:

```
Let v5=1+1+1;
```

In the second step, the expression is evaluated and the value of 3 is assigned to v5. We have seen previously that we can watch this two-step process in action using the central panel in the debug window:

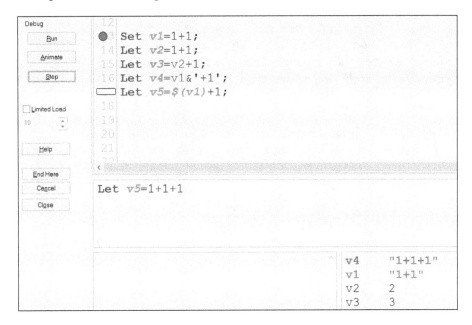

We need to be careful with this because there might be unintended consequences. For example:

```
Let vToday=Today();
Let vYesterday=$(vToday)-1;
```

We might wonder why the `vYesterday` variable has a value of `-0.9998411122145`! This makes sense if we think that the value of `vToday` is something like `8/25/2014` (August 25, 2014), so the second assignment will actually end up being:

```
Let vYesterday=8/25/2014-1;
```

A better way to assign this is:

```
Let vYesterday='$(vToday)'-1;
```

> Note that if you are using dates like this, it is much better to assign the numeric value of the date (for example, `41876` — the number of days since December 30, 1899) rather than the text representation because we have to always be sure that the text value will parse correctly whereas the numeric value is already parsed. `Floor` is a useful function for this as it also removes any time portion.

The following approach is better:

```
Let vToday=Floor(Today());
Let vYesterday=$(vToday)-1;
```

If a variable is assigned a `null` value (either from a failed expression or using the `Null()` function), then the variable will be removed (or not created!). This is useful to tidy up variables at the end of the script.

> Setting variables to null to remove them only applies to variables created within the script execution — variables that have been created in the document interfaces will not be removed by setting them to `null` in the script.

Examining common usage

There are some common use cases of using variables that come up in many applications, so it is worth examining them here.

Holding dates

It is very useful to know which day of the week it is. There is a simple function, `Today()`, that will return the date for today. However, does it really give today's date? It depends! The function can take a parameter:

Parameter value	Description
0	The date when the script was executed
1	The date at the time when the function is called
2	The date when the document was opened

It is interesting that many of us use this function without considering that the default value is 2 — the date when the document was opened. Depending on circumstances, this might not be what we want at all! This is where it can be useful to assign the result of the function to a variable:

```
Let vToday=Floor(Today(1));
```

By placing this call at the beginning of our script, we can then ensure that we are always using the same date throughout the script.

We might also be interested in a timestamp, and the `Now()` function will give us this. However, this function also has parameters that we need to be aware of.

Parameter value	Description
0	The date/time of the previously finished reload
1	The date/time at the time when the function is called
2	The date/time when the document was opened

These are slightly different from the `Today()` function, and the default is also different, which is 1, the time of the function call. We might need to be careful of this because if it is included in a long loop, it will be recalculated many times. It is a much better idea to calculate the value at the beginning of the script:

```
Let vNow=Num(Now(1));
```

As with the `Floor()` function for today, the `Num()` function will transform our timestamp into a numeric value. However, we might not always want the value in this format. We might want to have it in a particular format to use with database queries:

```
Let vCurrentExecution=Timestamp(vNow, 'YYYYMMDD hh:mm:ss');

Orders:
```

```
SQL SELECT OD.* FromvwOrderDetail OD
WHERE OD.TimeStamp>= '$(vPreviousExecution)'
AND OD.TimeStamp< '$(vCurrentExecution)';

Let vPreviousExecution=vCurrentExecution;
```

So, here, I use the `TimeStamp()` function to assign a format to the timestamp value. I can then use this in a SQL query.

In this example, we also have a second variable, which we fill with the current timestamp upon script completion. When the document is saved, we should expect that this variable should be saved with it so that on the next reload, the query should just get the delta change in the orders table. However, what about the very first execution? How can we populate this value if it hasn't been populated before?

A part of the problem is that if a variable hasn't been populated, then it won't exist, so we can't compare it to a value. What we can do, though, is Dollar-sign expand it. If it doesn't exist, the expansion just returns an empty string. We can check the length of this string to see whether it is blank:

```
If Len('$(vPreviousExecution)') = 0 Then
  // Set the variable to an arbitrary date in the past
  Let vPreviousExecution='19990101 00:00:00';
End If
```

Holding paths

We have discussed the uses of relative paths in loading and storing files. This is a generally good idea but there are circumstances where you might need to have absolute paths; for example, when using UNC paths for files, or if you might have changed paths for different purposes.

In these circumstances, rather than relative paths, we will specify the majority of the path using a variable. We might have this in our script:

```
Set vSourcePath='\\QVDataServer\SalesSource';
Set vQVDPath='\\QVServer\QVDPath';
```

Then, we will perform loads like this:

```
Sales:
LOAD *
FROM
[$(vSourcePath)\SalesReport.csv]
(txt, utf8, embedded labels, delimiter is ',', msq);
Store Sales into [$(vQVDPath)\Sales.qvd];
```

If the initial assignment of variables was kept in a separate file, it could be shared amongst several files using an include Dollar-sign Expansion:

```
$(Must_Include=PathVariables.qvs);
```

We use the `Must_Include` syntax here because the include must succeed for the script execution to run successfully.

Examining variable values during reloads

We have seen already that we can examine a variable value in the lower-right panel of the debug window. However, the debug window might not always be where we want it to be when executing a script, especially long running scripts. There is a better way.

The `Trace` statement will echo whatever is typed after it, up to its semicolon statement terminator, to both the script execution dialog and to the document log. As it is a standard statement, we can include variables with the Dollar-sign Expansion and expect their values to be echoed. For example:

```
Trace Previous Execution: $(vPreviousExecution);
Trace Current Execution: $(vCurrentExecution);
```

This will result in something similar to this **Script Execution Progress** dialog:

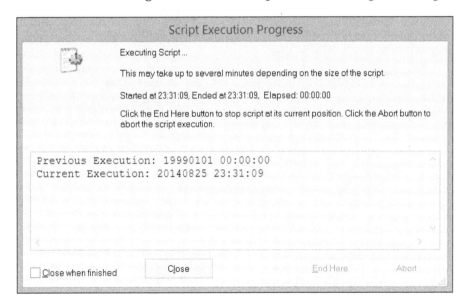

If the **Generate Logfile** option is selected in the **Document Properties**, then the `Trace` result will also be echoed in the logfile:

```
test.qvw.log - Notepad                                    _ □ ×
File  Edit  Format  View  Help
8/25/2014 23:32:44: 0028  Let vYesterday=41876-1
8/25/2014 23:32:44: 0029  Let vNow=Num(Now(1))
8/25/2014 23:32:44: 0030  Let vCurrentExecution=Timestamp(vNow, 'YYYYMMDD hh:mm:ss')
8/25/2014 23:32:44: 0032  Trace Previous Execution: 19990101 00:00:00
8/25/2014 23:32:44: 0032  Previous Execution: 19990101 00:00:00

8/25/2014 23:32:44: 0033  Trace Current Execution: 20140825 23:32:44
8/25/2014 23:32:44: 0033  Current Execution: 20140825 23:32:44
```

There is no real reason as to why we should not generate a logfile. It saves a load of time in troubleshooting reload issues, especially server executed reloads. If the option is turned on, a file called QVWName.qvw.log is created in the same folder as the QVW. If it is a server reload, the logfile is also copied into the Distribution Services log folder for that task.

Nesting Dollar-sign Expansions

It is possible to nest one or more Dollar-sign Expansions. This allows us to create some interesting functionality in scripts.

As an example, consider the variables used for path names. Imagine that we have a separate set of paths to be tested from production. We can do something like this:

```
Set vTestOrProd='Test';
Set vServerTest='\\DataServerTest\Test\Files';
Set vServerProd='\\DataServer1\Production';
Set vSourcePath='$(vServer$(vTestOrProd))\Sources';
Set vQVDPath='$(vServer$(vTestOrProd))\Sources';
```

We will see something like this in the **Debugger** window:

When we nest expansions like this, the inner expansions will be performed first. In this example, the inner expansion sets the name of the variable for the outer expansion.

This might look like a simplified test, but we can actually use something like this, using include files and windows security, to allow only certain people to update the script to start using production files!

Passing parameters to variables – macro functions

We can make a variable calculation a little more intelligent by actually passing parameters to it. This way, it can be like a pseudofunction.

When creating variables with parameters, we can only do so with the Set statement. The Let statement doesn't make any sense here because it tries to evaluate it at the time of assignment, so we can't pass a parameter.

We create parameters by using a dollar sign with a number. We can add multiple parameters; we just need to up the numeric sequence. For example:

```
Set vAdd=($1+$2);
Let vRes=$(vAdd(1,1));
Trace Result of add: $(vRes);
```

This will yield a result of 2. Not terribly complex.

As another example, how about if we wanted a function to format a 10-digit phone number in the (nnn) nnn-nnnn format. We can write a variable like this:

```
Set vPhone='(' &Left($1,3) & ') ' & Mid($1,4,3) & '-' & Right($1,4);

Load Phone, $(vPhone(Phone)) As Formatted Inline [
Phone
2025551234
2125554321
];
```

This is a relatively straightforward calculation but we can have this as complex as we like. Indeed, we can have several of such variables stored in an external file and then include them.

Subroutines

A subroutine is used where we have, generally, a more complex requirement, and we know that we are going to have to repeat it quite often.

A great example of using a subroutine that can be used in most implementations is the repetitive task of storing a table to QVD and then dropping the table that we will have in loader applications. We might implement it like this:

```
Sub StoreAndDrop(vTableName)

   Store [$(vTableName)] into [$(vQVDPath)\$(vTableName).qvd];
   Drop Table [$(vTableName)];

End Sub
```

Then, later in the script, we will call:

```
Call StoreAndDrop('TableName');
```

Note that the subroutine must be loaded in the script before it is called. We can also pass multiple parameters to the subroutine. The parameters become local variables in the subroutine. These are not available outside the subroutine, but variables defined outside the subroutine, global variables, are available.

Using control structures

Any basic development language will include some control structures to either repeat the execution of particular tasks or change what task will happen next based on conditions. QlikView is no different, so in this section we will examine the various options.

Branching with conditional statements

It can be enormously important to be able to execute different sets of statements based on different conditions. It gives us a lot of flexibility in implementing our solutions.

If ... Then ... ElseIf

`If ... Then ... ElseIf` is a fairly fundamental construct in many programming languages. We test a condition, and if it is true, we execute one set of statements. If it isn't true, then we can either execute a different set of statements or perform a new test and keep going.

As an example, if we wanted to test whether a file exists before trying to load it:

```
If Alt(FileSize('c:\temp\Data.qvd'),0)>0 Then

  Data:
  Load *
  From c:\temp\Data.qvd (qvd);

End if
```

 We use `Alt` here because the `FileSize` function returns `null` if the file doesn't exist.

If, instead of not doing anything, we want to load a different file, then we might do this:

```
If Alt(FileSize('c:\temp\Data1.qvd'),0)>0 Then

  Data:
```

```
      Load *
      From c:\temp\Data1.qvd (qvd);

  ELSE

      Data:
      Load *
      From c:\temp\Data2.qvd (qvd);

  End if
```

Of course, we should really check whether this second file exists:

```
  If Alt(FileSize('c:\temp\Data1.qvd'),0)>0 Then

      Data:
      Load *
      From c:\temp\Data1.qvd (qvd);

  ELSEIF Alt(FileSize('c:\temp\Data2.qvd'),0)>0 Then

      Data:
      Load *
      From c:\temp\Data2.qvd (qvd);

  ELSE

      Trace We have no files to load!!!;

  End if
```

A note about conditional functions

There are several functions in QlikView that return a Boolean result. For example, the YearToDate function accepts a date, and some other parameters and will return true or false if that date is in the year-to-date. Unlike other languages, QlikView does not actually have a Boolean type. Instead, Boolean functions will return an integer value— 0 for false and -1 for true. In fact, as far as any condition in QlikView is concerned, 0 is always false and anything that is not 0 means true.

This means that there are several other functions that might not be considered to be strictly conditional and can be used as conditional functions. Any function that returns 0 as an indication of a failure to perform and a nonzero value when it succeeds can be used as a conditional function.

For example, the `Index` function returns the position of a substring in another string. If it fails to locate the substring, then it will return 0. We might think that we should use this in a condition like this:

```
Let vText='ABCDEFG';
Let vSearch='ABC';

If Index(vText, vSearch)>0 Then
   Trace Found $(vSearch) in $(vText);
End if
```

However, as the fail condition returns 0, we can just write the `If` statement like this:

```
If Index(vText, vSearch) Then
   Trace Found $(vSearch) in $(vText);
End if
```

There are a few other functions that return 0. If a function, such as `FileSize`, returns a `null` value for a fail, we can turn this into a zero by wrapping it in the `Alt` function as we did just now. In this case, we included the `>0` test, but we could have written the `If` statement without it:

```
If Alt(FileSize('c:\temp\Data.qvd'),0) Then

   Data:
   Load *
   From c:\temp\Data.qvd (qvd);

End if
```

Switch ... Case

`Switch ... Case` is a less frequently used construct than `If ... Then ... ElseIf`; this will be familiar to C/Java programmers. We test a value and then present several possible options for that value and execute script blocks if there is a match. We can also specify a default if there are no matches.

Here is a very simple example; note that we can pass several values to each `Case` statement:

```
Let vVal='Hello';
SWITCH vVal
CASE 'Hello','Hi'
   Trace Hello there!;
CASE 'Goodbye','Bye'
```

```
    Trace So long!;
DEFAULT
    Trace Glad you are staying;
END Switch
```

When and Unless

When and Unless are the equivalent of a single If ... Then statement. They usually appear as prefixes to a valid statement, but there are some control statements that can have them as suffixes. The statement is followed by a conditional test and then by the statement to execute if the condition is true or false. Consider this example:

```
When Alt(FileSize('c:\temp\Data2.qvd'),0) > 0
    Load * from c:\temp\Data2.qvd (qvd);
```

An example of Unless is:

```
Unless Alt(FileSize('c:\temp\Data1.qvd'),0)=0
    Load * from c:\temp\Data1.qvd (qvd);
```

Looping in the script

Repeating a step several times is something that we will have to do again and again. There are a number of ways of performing loops, depending on requirements.

AutoGenerate

AutoGenerate might not be called a loop by some people but it does actually perform a repeating task, the generation of multiple rows, for a set number of iterations. The statement takes one parameter: the number of rows to generate.

Generating empty rows is not very useful, so we need to combine this AutoGenerate with a function such as RecNo() or RowNo() and other calculations based on them. Often both functions are interchangeable because the number of rows generated as source will usually be the same as the number actually loaded. However, if we are going to use a preceding load, then we will need to use RecNo() as the RowNo() function will return zeroes.

Anywhere that we require to create a sequential list of values, we can think of perhaps using AutoGenerate. A great use case is the generation of a calendar table:

```
// Calendar starts on the 1st January 2010
Let vStartDate=Floor(MakeDate(2010,1,1));
```

```
// Calendar ends on the last day of last month
Let vEndDate=Floor(MonthStart(Today()))-1;
// How many rows do we need to generate?
Let vDiff=vEndDate-vStartDate+1;

// Generate the calendar table
Calendar:
Load
  TempDate as DateID,
  Year(TempDate) As Year,
  Month(TempDate) As Month,
  'Q' &Ceil(Month(TempDate)/3) As Quarter,
  Day(TempDate) As Day,
  Week(TempDate) As Week,
  Date(MonthStart(TempDate), 'YYYY-MM') As YearMonth,
  -YearToDate(TempDate, 0, 1, $(vEndDate)) As YTD_Flag,
  -YearToDate(TempDate, -1, 1, $(vEndDate)) As LYTD_Flag;
// Generate the number of rows required
Load
  RecNo()-1+$(vStartDate) As TempDate
AutoGenerate($(vDiff));
```

This script will generate the number of rows between two dates and use the start date as the first value and increment this by one for each subsequent row. The preceding load then transforms the `TempDate` field into various date values.

Creation of a calendar like this might be a piece of script that you store in a separate text file for inclusion in several QlikView applications.

For ... Next loops

The `For ... Next` type of loops are one of the most common in many programming languages. We assign an initial value to a variable, perform a sequence of statement, increment the variable by a fixed amount, then repeat until we have reached the end point.

Here is a very simple example:

```
For i = 1 to 10
  Trace The value of i is $(i);
Next
```

This will show in the script execution dialog like this:

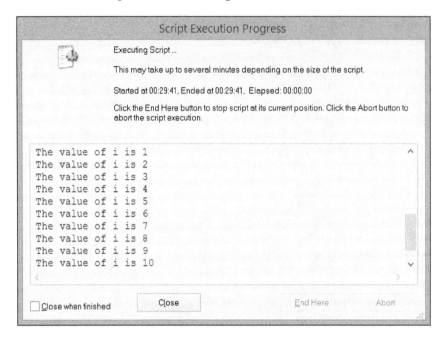

This loop started at 1, echoed the value to the screen, incremented by the default step of 1, and then repeated until it executed for the last value of 10.

If we want to use a step other than the default, we can add the Step to the For statement:

```
For i = 5 to 50 Step 5
   Trace The value of i is $(i);
Next
```

We can even go backwards:

```
For i = 10 to 1 Step -1
   Trace The value of i is $(i);
Next
```

The variable that is generated can be used anywhere that we might use a variable normally in QlikView. Consider this example:

```
For vYear=2010 to Year(Today())
  Data:
  SQL Select *
  From Data
```

```
    Where Year=$(vYear);

    Store Data into $(vQVDPath)\Data$(vYear).qvd;
    Drop Table Data;
Next
```

This script will generate separate QVD files for each year from 2010 to the present year.

We can also nest loops inside each other:

```
For x = 1 to 10
  For y = 1 to 10
    Matrix:
    Load
      $(x) As X,
      $(y) As Y
    AutoGenerate(1);
  Next
Next
```

For Each ... Next loops

Not every loop that we want to make will be based on a sequence of number. The For Each syntax allows us to use a list of any values that we assign:

```
For Each vVar in 'A','B','C'
  Data:
  SQL Select * From Table$(vVar);

  Store Data into $(vQVDPath)\Table$(vVar).qvd;
  Drop Table Data;
Next
```

We can even derive the list of values from the data:

```
Temp:
Load
  Chr(39) &Concat(Field1,Chr(39)&','&Chr(39)) &Chr(39)
    As Temp_Field
Resident Table1;

Let vList=Peek('Temp_Field');

Drop Table Temp;
```

Note the use of Chr(39), which is the apostrophe character. We will also discuss the Peek function later in this chapter.

There are two filesystem-related functions that we can also use with For Each—FileList and DirList.

FileList

The FileList function takes a file mask using wildcards and will return a list containing the full file path of all files that match. We can then loop through that list with For Each and process them. Have a look at this example:

```
For Each vFile in FileList('c:\data\*.csv')
  Let vFileLen=FileSize('$(vFile)');
  Let vFileDate=FileTime('$(vFile)');
  Trace $(vFile) $(vFileLen) $(vFileDate);

  Data:
  LOAD *
  FROM
  [$(vFile)]
  (txt, utf8, embedded labels, delimiter is ',', msq);
Next
```

DirList

The DirList function is similar to FileList except that it returns a list of folders instead of files. This function is very often used with a nested FileList. The following is an example:

```
For Each vFolder in DirList('c:\data\*')
  For Each vFile in FileList('$(vFolder)\*.csv')
    Let vFileLen=FileSize('$(vFile)');
    Let vFileDate=FileTime('$(vFile)');
    Trace $(vFile) $(vFileLen) $(vFileDate);

    Data:
    LOAD *
    FROM
    [$(vFile)]
    (txt, utf8, embedded labels, delimiter is ',', msq);
  Next
Next
```

Do ... Loop

Another very common construction in programming is the Do ... Loop statements, which cause a block of script to be executed either while a condition is fulfilled or until a condition is fulfilled:

```
Let vLetters='ABCDEFGHIJKLMNOPQRSTUVWXYZ';

Do
  Load
    Left('$(vLetters)',1) As Letter,
    RowNo() As LetterIndex
  AutoGenerate(1);

  Let vLetters=Mid('$(vLetters)', 2);
Loop Until Len('$(vLetters)')=0
```

We can also write this by putting a clause at the beginning:

```
Do While vLetters<>''
  Load
    Left('$(vLetters)',1) As Letter,
    RowNo() As LetterIndex
  AutoGenerate(1);

  Let vLetters=Mid('$(vLetters)', 2);
Loop
```

The difference is that a clause at the beginning means that there is potential for the script block to never execute. A clause at the end means that the block will execute at least once.

Exiting

There are a few different circumstances in which we might want to break the execution of the script or a block of script.

Exiting the script

We can exit the entire script by calling the function:

```
Exit Script;
```

The script will terminate normally at this point, as if there were no additional script lines following it.

This can be an enormously useful thing for us to insert into our script to test and troubleshoot. By adding the function at any stage in our script, we can then find out what state our data is in.

We can enhance the troubleshooting functionality by adding a condition to the exit. We can use an `If ... Then` construct, but this is also a case where our conditional functions, `When` and `Unless`, can be appended. For example, if we want to stop our script unless some condition is true, the following code can be used:

```
EXIT Script when FieldValueCount('Letter')<>26;
```

This can also be written like this:

```
EXIT Script unless FieldValueCount('Letter')=26;
```

As another example, we might want the script to end at a certain point unless it is the first day of the month:

```
EXIT Script unless Day(Today())=1;
```

Exiting other constructs

We can also exit other script constructs such as `For/For Each` and `Do` loops and subroutines. The syntax is similar to the aforementioned, but we just need to use the correct keyword for the construct that we are in:

```
Exit For;
Exit Do;
Exit Sub;
```

We can also append conditional expressions:

```
Exit For when vFound=1;
```

Using variables for error handling

Rather than allowing QlikView to throw an error and stopping the execution of a script, there are a number of variables that we can use to handle error situations and allow the script to continue.

ErrorMode

There are three possible values for the `ErrorMode` variable:

ErrorMode	Description
0	QlikView will ignore any errors. The script execution will continue at the next line of script.
1	This is normal error handling. The script will halt and the user will be prompted for an action.
2	In this mode, the user will not be prompted and the script will fail as if the user clicked on **Cancel** on the prompt dialog.

To turn off error handling, we simply set the variable as follows:

```
Set ErrorMode=0;
```

To turn it back on, we set the variable again:

```
Set ErrorMode=1;
```

ScriptError

If we turn off error handling, we will need to do our own error handling by regularly querying the state of the `ScriptError` variable.

The `ScriptError` variable will contain a dual value with the error code as the number and the description as the text. If the error code is zero, then there is no error.

Some of the database errors will generate additional error messaging in the `ScriptErrorDetails` variable.

ScriptErrorCount and ScriptErrorList

If we are interested in the total number of errors and their details, we can query the `ScriptErrorCount` variable, which has the number, and `ScriptErrorList` will have the text of the errors, separated by carriage returns.

Examining advanced Table File Wizard options

The Table Files Wizard is used by many to load a file and generate the load script for it. However, there is a not-so-secret secret button with the word **Next** written on it that is often ignored:

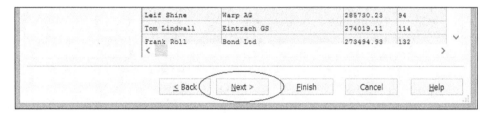

There are some great things in here that are worth looking at.

Enabling a transformation step

When we first hit that **Next** button on the wizard, we are presented with the interesting option, **Enable Transformation Step**:

If we click on this button, it brings us to a new dialog with several tabs:

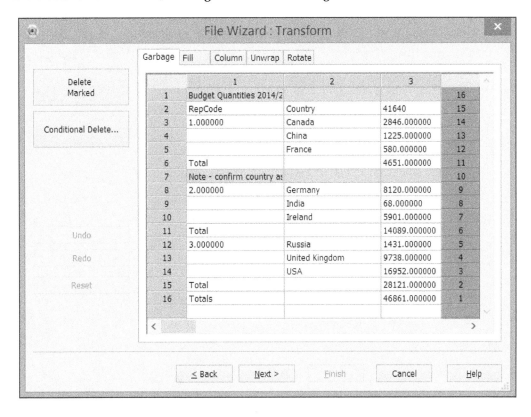

Garbage

The **Garbage** tab allows us to clean out records that are not useful to us. In the preceding screenshot, there are a couple of rows that we can select and click on the **Delete Marked** button to remove. We can also click on the **Conditional Delete...** button and set up a rule to delete particular rows, for example, if they begin with the word **Total**:

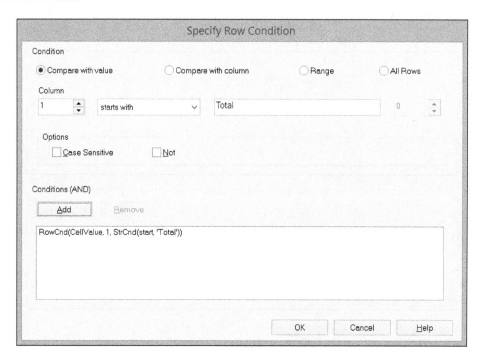

Fill

The **Fill** tab allows us to fill in missing values, or overwrite other values, based on a condition. We can fill data from any direction:

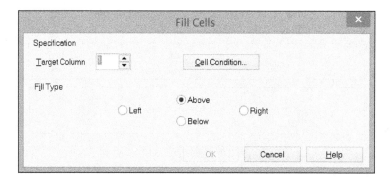

Column

The **Column** feature allows us to create new columns or replace columns, by copying the content of another column:

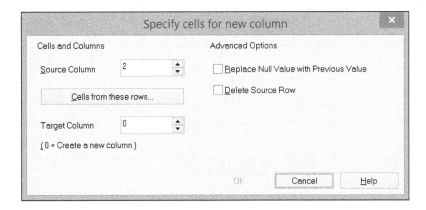

This is quite often used with the **Context** tab because it allows us have two columns: one with the original value and one with the value extracted from the context.

Context

The **Context** tab is only available when working with HTML data. It allows us to extract information from tags in the data. For example, if we go to www.xe.com, we can get a table that lists currencies. In one column, we will have the currency name but this is also a hyperlink. The Context function allows us to interpret the value as HTML and extract the hyperlink href value:

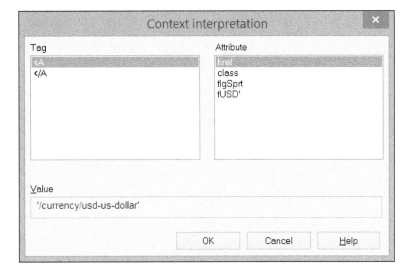

Unwrap

The Unwrap function allows us to take data that might be wrapped across multiple columns and unwrap it. For example, if we have the **Year** and **Value** columns followed by another pair of **Year** and **Value** columns, the Unwrap function will allow us to wrap the second pair of columns back under the first pair where the data should be.

Rotate

The Rotate function allows us to either rotate data to the left-hand side or right-hand side, or transpose the data; that is, columns become rows and rows become columns.

Using the Crosstable wizard

The last couple of pages of Table Files Wizard contain further manipulation options. Probably the most frequently used of these is the **Crosstable** option. This is used, often with Excel files but can also be from any data source, to correct the data where you have what appear to be field names in a two-dimensional matrix and you want to transform them into the field values that they should be. For example, in a budget file, we might have the budget month running across the top of the page:

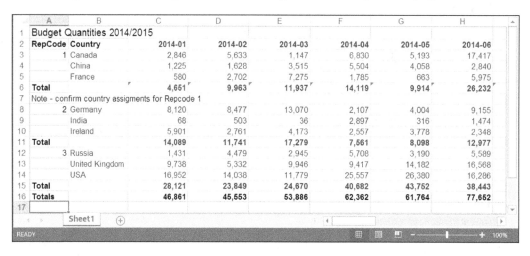

	A	B	C	D	E	F	G	H
1	Budget Quantities 2014/2015							
2	RepCode	Country	2014-01	2014-02	2014-03	2014-04	2014-05	2014-06
3	1	Canada	2,846	5,633	1,147	6,830	5,193	17,417
4		China	1,225	1,628	3,515	5,504	4,058	2,840
5		France	580	2,702	7,275	1,785	663	5,975
6	Total		4,651	9,963	11,937	14,119	9,914	26,232
7	Note - confirm country assigments for Repcode 1							
8	2	Germany	8,120	8,477	13,070	2,107	4,004	9,155
9		India	68	503	36	2,897	316	1,474
10		Ireland	5,901	2,761	4,173	2,557	3,778	2,348
11	Total		14,089	11,741	17,279	7,561	8,098	12,977
12	3	Russia	1,431	4,479	2,945	5,708	3,190	5,589
13		United Kingdom	9,738	5,332	9,946	9,417	14,182	16,568
14		USA	16,952	14,038	11,779	25,557	26,380	16,286
15	Total		28,121	23,849	24,670	40,682	43,752	38,443
16	Totals		46,861	45,553	53,886	62,362	61,764	77,652
17								

Sheet1 ⊕

READY   100%

However, the budget month is actually not a field in itself; it should be a field value. This is where the **Crosstable** wizard comes in:

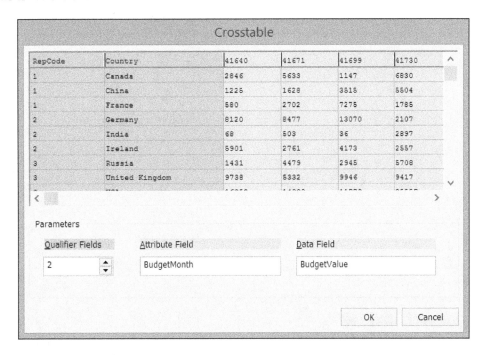

In the wizard, we need to tell it how many fields are **Qualifier Fields**. This means fields that are already correct as field values and don't need to be unraveled. Next, we specify a name that we want to call the new field, for example, BudgetMonth. Finally, we specify a name for the new field that will hold the values that are currently in the matrix, for example, BudgetValue. Luckily, these days, QlikView provides a color coding to show you where each value applies.

When we click on **OK** in the **Crosstable** wizard, we will see a preview of the how the data will look:

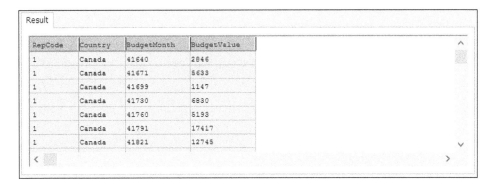

When we now click on **OK**, the script to load the table, along with the **Crosstable** prefix, will be inserted into the script editor:

```
CrossTable(BudgetMonth, BudgetValue, 2)
LOAD RepCode,
     Country,
     [41640],
     [41671],
     [41699],
     [41730],
     [41760],
     ...
     [42309],
     [42339]
FROM
[..\Sources\Budget.xls]
(biff, embedded labels, table is Sheet1$, filters(
Remove(Row, Pos(Top, 1)),
Remove(Row, RowCnd(CellValue, 1, StrCnd(start, 'Total'))),
Remove(Row, Pos(Top, 5)),
Replace(1, top, StrCnd(null))
));
```

We can see that the values that we passed in from the wizard have gone in as parameters. Actually, once we understand what the parameters of the `CrossTable` statement are, we might never use the wizard again!

It is interesting to note that we don't need to actually list all the fields in the file. We can, instead, have a piece of script like this:

```
CrossTable(BudgetMonth, BudgetValue, 2)
LOAD *
FROM
[..\Sources\Budget.xls]
(biff, embedded labels, table is Sheet1$);
```

This will allow different months to be added or removed from the file as time goes on. However, we will need to ensure that the structure of the file doesn't change and no additional columns are added that are not month values (for example, `totals`)

Another thing to note is that if the column names are numeric (as in this example), they will actually be loaded as text. This is correct because QlikView will otherwise just load the column name into all the values! In that case, we might need to add an additional step:

```
Budget_Temp:
CrossTable(BudgetMonth, BudgetValue, 2)
LOAD *
FROM
[..\Sources\Budget.xls]
(biff, embedded labels, table is Sheet1$);
Budget:
NoConcatenate
Load
  RepCode,
  Country,
  Date(Num#(BudgetMonth,'#####')) As BudgetMonth,
  BudgetValue
Resident
  Budget_Temp;

Drop Table Budget_Temp;
```

Looking at data from different directions

Sometimes, we need to consider data from different directions. In this section, we will examine some advanced techniques for data manipulation that will make our lives easier.

Putting things first

We will often come across situations where we need to consider the earliest values in a dataset, either just the first number of rows or the first value in an ordered set. QlikView has functions for this.

First

The `First` statement will precede a load and states the number of records that should be loaded:

```
First 10
Load *
From Data.qvd (qvd);
```

Sometimes, if we want to just get a fixed set of rows from a file, we can use the **Header** option in Table Files Wizard to remove any rows preceding the rows we want and then use the `First` statement to grab the lines that we do want. This can be an effective strategy where there are several datasets in one worksheet in Excel.

FirstSortedValue

`FirstSortedValue` is a very advanced function that can be used both in the script and in charts. We use it to obtain the top value in a sorted list of values.

As an example, say that we want to retrieve `ProductID` with the highest sales value for each order, the following code can be used:

```
TopProd:
Load
  OrderID,
  FirstSortedValue(ProductID, -LineValue) As TopProduct
Resident
  Fact
Group by OrderID;
```

We retrieve the top product based on the order of the `LineValue` field. The minus sign preceding the field name indicates that this is a descending sort, so the first product should correspond to the highest value.

 Note that this is an aggregation function, so in the script, there must be a `Group by` clause.

We can pass some other parameters. For example, if more than one product had the same value, then the default option is to return `null`. If we specify `Distinct` before `ProductID`, then the duplicate situation will be ignored.

We can also pass a third parameter after the sort weight to, say, get the second or third or n^{th} sorted value instead of the first.

Looking backwards

When loading data, it can be a very neat trick to look at data that we have loaded before. There are two great functions that we can use to do this.

Previous

The `Previous` function can look at a value in the previous input row. This can be really useful. In fact, we can nest multiple previous statements together to look even further back!

Mostly, the function will be combined with an `Order By` clause. This means that we can have some kind of expectation of what the previous record held, and therefore, test for that.

As an example, let's look at this simple dataset:

```
Emps:
Load * Inline [
Employee, Grade, StartDate
Brian, 1, 2010-01-04
Jill, 1, 2011-07-19
Graham, 3, 2010-02-02
Miley, 2, 2011-08-20
Brian, 2, 2012-04-03
Jill, 3, 2013-11-01
Miley, 3, 2014-01-30
];
```

We can see that we have a list of employees with the grade that they are at and the date that they started at that grade. What would be good to be able to calculate is the end date for each of the grades (which would be today for the latest grades) so that we can match these employees to events that happened on particular dates (using `IntervalMatch`).

If we sort the data by employee and then the start date in the descending order, we can compare on each row if we are dealing with the same employee as on the previous row. If we are, we can calculate the end date from the previous date. If not, we just use today's date. Here is the code:

```
Employee:
Load
  Employee,
  Grade,
```

```
    StartDate,
    If(Previous(Employee)=Employee,
       Previous(StartDate)-1,
       Today()
    ) As EndDate
  Resident
    Emps
  Order By Employee, StartDateDesc;

  Drop Table Emps;
```

Peek

Peek is the opposite of the Previous function in that Peek will look at data that has been loaded into memory rather than data that is being loaded from a source. From that point of view, it is always available because the data is just there, whereas the Previous function can only operate during a load. This makes Peek very versatile for accessing data from the in-memory tables.

Peek takes up to three parameters:

Parameter	Description
Field name	The name of the field that you want to retrieve the value from. It is passed as text literal, that is, in single quotes.
Row index	The row of the table from which you want to retrieve the field value. This index starts at 0 for row 1 (just to confuse us) and you can also pass a value of -1, which is the default, to retrieve the value from the last row loaded.
Table name	The name of the data table from which you want to retrieve the value. It is passed as a text literal.

If Peek is used with just the field name, then the most recently loaded value into that field, into whatever table, will be returned. If the row index is passed, then you must also pass the table name, as it doesn't make sense without it.

As an example, let's use a loop to cycle through all the records in a table, extract the field values, and display them using a trace:

```
For i=0 to NoOfRows('Employee')-1

  Let vEmp=Peek('Employee', $(i), 'Employee');
  Let vGrade=Peek('Grade', $(i), 'Employee');
  Let vDate=Date(Peek('StartDate', $(i), 'Employee'), 'M/D/YYYY');
```

```
    Trace Employee, $(vEmp), started Grade $(vGrade) on $(vDate);

    Next
```

As a more advanced example of using `Peek`, let's imagine that we had a sale file output from an ERP system that contained both header and line information in the one file. Here is an example:

```
201A0000120140801
202PR0001000005000366
202PR0002000011001954
202PR0003000017000323
202PR0004000001009999
202PR0005000008003287
201A0000220140802
202PR0001000003000360
202PR0002000111000999
```

Lines beginning with `201` are the order header row. They contain the customer number and the order date. Lines beginning with `202` are order lines and they contain a product code, quantity, and price per unit.

Obviously, we might imagine that we could deal with this using Table Files Wizard as it is a fixed width record. However, the problem here is that there are different width values on different lines. This is a perfect place to use `Peek`! Let's have a look at how we build the code for this.

It can be useful to use the wizard to help us get started, especially if there are many fields. In fact, we can run it twice to help build up the script that we need:

```
LOAD @1:3 as LineType,
     @4:9 as CustomerCode,
     @10:n as OrderDate
     . . .
```

The following script has to be run as well:

```
LOAD @1:3 AsLineType,
     @4:9 AsProductCode,
     @10:15 As Quantity,
     @16:n/100 As UnitPrice
     . . .
```

Now, we can combine these. We will use `Peek` to move the `CustomerCode` and `OrderDate` values onto the order line rows:

```
SalesFile_Temp:
LOAD
   @1:3 AsLineType,
  If(@1:3=201,
     @4:9,
     Peek('CustomerCode')
     ) As CustomerCode,
  If(@1:3=201,
     Date#(@10:n,'YYYYMMDD'),
     Peek('OrderDate')
     ) As OrderDate,
If(@1:3=202,@4:9,Null()) As ProductCode,
If(@1:3=202,@10:15,Null()) As Quantity,
If(@1:3=202,@16:n/100,Null()) As UnitPrice
FROM
[..\Sources\SalesFile.txt]
(fix, codepage is 1252);
```

Now, the table will contain a mix of row types, but we only need the ones that are type 202, because they have all the good data now:

```
SalesFile:
Load
   CustomerCode,
   OrderDate,
   ProductCode,
   Quantity,
   UnitPrice,
   Quantity*UnitPrice as LineValue
Resident
   SalesFile_Temp
Where LineType=202;

Drop Table SalesFile_Temp;
```

Reusing code

In various areas of this chapter so far, we've suggested that it can be useful to maintain script elements in separate text files that can be included within the QlikView script using an `Include` or `Must_Include` construct.

Many organizations, when building their own best practices among their QlikView team, will create a library of such scripts.

One such library that any QlikView developer who is interested in increasing their skill levels should look at is the QlikView Components library created by Rob Wunderlich. Refer to `https://github.com/RobWunderlich/Qlikview-Components` for more information.

This library contains a whole host of functions that, even if a developer wasn't to use them, would be worth reviewing to see how things are done.

As a quick example, something that we do in almost every QlikView application is to generate a `Calendar` table:

```
Call Qvc.Calendar(vStartDate, vEndDate, 'Calendar', 'Cal', 1);
```

That is it!

Summary

This chapter has given us a lot of good information on functions that we can use when writing scripts.

After reviewing the basics on loading data, we then went into how to count records and the useful functions that we have for that purpose. We had a discussion on the best way to optimize data loading. We then explored variables and the Dollar-sign Expansion in the script. We talked about fundamental control structures and had a good look at Table Files Wizard, followed by a discussion on using different functions to grab data from different directions.

Finally, we had a very brief discussion on reusing code and the use of libraries such as Rob Wunderlich's QlikView components.

6
What's New in QlikView 12?

If QlikView 12 is your first entry into the world of Qlik then you might be tempted to skip this chapter. However, we highly recommend that, even as a new developer you, at least read the *What is new in the Qlik product portfolio?* section.

We will start with a look at some of the most important changes in QlikView 12. Although QlikView 12 Desktop is the main focus of this book, we will also discuss the changes and improvements in QlikView 12 Server and Publisher.

Next, we will take a look at the broader picture and see how the Qlik product portfolio has changed in the past few years. We will learn what these new products do and how they might fit into your Qlik deployment.

To summarize, in this chapter we will specifically look at:

- What is new in QlikView 12?
- What is new in the Qlik product portfolio?
- How do the products in the Qlik product portfolio fit together?

.How is QlikView 12 different from QlikView 11?

Apart from a restyled application icon, at first glance QlikView 12 looks remarkably similar to its predecessor. Under the hood, however, many improvements and fixes have been realized, and in this section we will take a high level view at some of those changes.

Common QIX Engine

The main difference compared to previous versions is that the underlying engine of QlikView has been replaced with the updated QIX Engine 2.0. This is the same engine that powers the other products in the Qlik portfolio (*Qlik Sense Enterprise and the Qlik Analytics Platform*, discussed later). Besides performance improvements over the previous version, this common engine makes it easier to share data models between QlikView and the other Qlik products, notably Qlik Sense. The shared code base of the engine also ensures that future investments that Qlik does in features, performance, security, and connectivity can be easily back ported to QlikView.

64-bit only

Where previously there were both 32-bit and 64-bit versions of the QlikView software, QlikView 12 desktop and server are only available in the 64-bit version. The 32-bit QlikView desktop version, with its memory limited to 2 GB, has become outdated. If you have a hard requirement to still use a 32-bit version of the software, you will need to fall back to QlikView 11.2.

Online documentation

QlikView 11.2 and earlier included local documentation and help files. With QlikView 12 all documentation and help is found online.

For the English version of QlikView, which we will use in this book, the online help can be found at:

- QlikView 12: `http://help.qlik.com/en-US/qlikview/12.0/Content/Home.htm`
- QlikView 12.1 `http://help.qlik.com/en-US/qlikview/12.1/Content/Home.htm`

You will notice that only the version number is different in the URL.

Downloadable guides can also be found in the online documentation:

- QlikView 12: `http://help.qlik.com/en-US/qlikview/12.0/Content/Guides.htm`

- QlikView 12.1: `http://help.qlik.com/en-US/qlikview/12.1/Content/Guides.htm`

The next changes mainly impact the server side of QlikView, but they are still interesting to take note of.

Security improvements

Although not visible from the outside, Qlik has made significant investments in security around QlikView 12. Improvements include stronger encryption and better encryption handling, centralized client request handling, and XML parsing. These improvements mean that QlikView can now meet some of the more demanding security requirements within the private sector, government, and military.

Mobile touch improvements

With QlikView 12, all the functions that are available in the regular QlikView web client are also accessible on touch devices. Besides consuming applications, this means that you can now also use collaboration capabilities, create and modify objects, and export to Excel on a mobile device. You can also use swiping to scroll, or use a long-press to activate the right-click menus.

Improved clustering and scaling

QlikView 12 supports more nodes in a clustered environment, which means that in multi-node environments QlikView will be able to support more concurrent users.

Clustering improvements in QlikView 12.1

In QlikView 12.1, released in November 2016, even more improvements have been made in the area of clustering, allowing QlikView to scale to even more nodes, users, and documents.

Changes in QlikView 12.1 include improvements for dealing with high-load scenarios, such as shared file caching, offline mode for PGO files, better caching in AccessPoint, and more efficient communication between services.

QlikView 12.1 also has the option to use unbalanced nodes in a cluster (that is, using servers with differences in CPU and RAM in the same cluster). For Publisher, it is now possible to create multiple Publisher (QDS) clusters, referred to as Publisher groups, and to assigns tasks to specific nodes within a cluster.

What is new in the Qlik product portfolio?

Since the publication of the previous version of this book in 2012, the Qlik product suite has changed and expanded significantly, both through acquisitions and the introduction of new products. In this section, we will look at some of the most important changes and we will look at how these fit into the bigger picture.

Qlik Sense Enterprise and the Qlik Analytics Platform

Initially billed as `QlikView.Next` and anticipated to be an update of QlikView, Qlik Sense was launched as a new, separate product in September 2014. Regular users of QlikView will immediately notice that the frontend of Qlik Sense looks very different from QlikView:

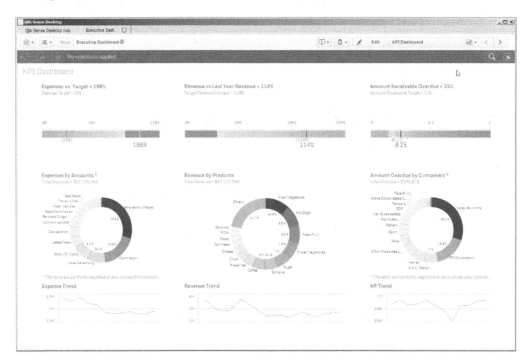

With the introduction of Qlik Sense, Qlik suddenly had two similar products out in the market, which they dubbed the two product strategy. This strategy positions Qlik Sense not as an updated version of QlikView, but rather as a separate self-service visualization solution that co-exists with QlikView. At the same time, QlikView was repositioned as the tool for 'guided analytics'.

The full Qlik marketing mantra is "*Qlik Sense is for Self-Service BI, QlikView is for Guided Analytics*".

As the two product strategy is a major aspect of the Qlik product portfolio and knowing when to apply which product is important, we will have a closer look at the similarities and differences between QlikView and Qlik Sense.

In what way are QlikView and Qlik Sense similar?

Both QlikView 12 and Qlik Sense share the same underlying QIX Engine. They both use the same scripting and expression language. Skills that you have gained (or will gain, using this book) in these areas in QlikView can be directly transferred to Qlik Sense.

In what way do QlikView and Qlik Sense differ?

The main technical differences between QlikView and Qlik Sense are in the frontend presentation and server implementation or, simply put, the things sitting on top of and around the QIX Engine.

Qlik Sense is based on the latest technologies and it employs a web-first approach. It has responsive design, which means that objects automatically adjust to your screen size and device type. This makes it work very well on mobile devices. Qlik Sense also has extensive API's that can be used to automate, extend, or embed the product. All of the development in Qlik Sense takes place on the Qlik Sense Server. As with QlikView, a desktop version, called **Qlik Sense Desktop**, is available. In contrast to QlikView, this desktop version is mainly used as a trial version instead of a development environment. Qlik Sense also has a cloud version, called **Qlik Sense Cloud**.

QlikView is based on proven, but older, technologies. It is Windows-centric and uses a desktop-first approach, with a more pixel-perfect oriented design (that is, if you define a chart to be 500 pixels wide, it will always be 500 pixels wide). Compared to Qlik Sense, a developer can quite easily build very sophisticated, custom-styled applications without any additional programming. For example, QlikView applications can perform specific actions (such as showing or hiding an object, making a selection, selecting a sheet, and so on) when certain conditions are met or events are triggered. QlikView applications are developed in the QlikView Desktop application and deployed to the QlikView Server for consumption by users.

Although Qlik Sense does not have many options for customization or advanced application design out of the box, those who possess web development skills will be able to build very sophisticated applications using the Qlik Sense APIs and the Mashup, Widget, and/or Extension functionalities. The barrier to entry is higher, but a developer who is both skilled in QlikView/Qlik Sense and web development will be able to get far more out of Qlik Sense than they will out of QlikView.

What does this mean for users?

As mentioned before, the distinction between the products, according to Qlik, is that *"Qlik Sense is for Self-Service BI, and QlikView is for Guided Analytics"*. What this means from a user-perspective is that Qlik Sense is more geared towards situations where you do not want to, or cannot, predefine everything upfront. This gives more space to the user to build their own charts, sheets and presentations, and so on, to answer their own questions. Questions that you could possibly not have anticipated. This exploration can be done on either centrally managed, governed data models, or on data that the user adds into Qlik Sense. Building charts and other objects is mainly a drag and drop affair, with very little coding or expression writing. Qlik Sense is an ideal environment for engaged users who want to explore, but have limited technical abilities.

In situations where you need predefined business applications, that is, applications with a thought-out data model, sheets, charts, and calculations that are consumed by end users then QlikView is the preferred option. Qlik refers to this as *"Guided analytics"*. Users can still explore, filter, slice, and dice the data and use it to answer their questions, but adding new visualizations is decidedly less smooth than it is in Qlik Sense.

It is important to keep in mind that the two scenarios described previously mainly relate to the casual user experience. An experienced Qlik developer will just as easily answer a new question with QlikView as with Qlik Sense. In fact, many experienced Qlik developers still say that they prefer QlikView if they want to get something done fast.

What is the Qlik Analytics Platform?

The **Qlik Analytics Platform** (**QAP**) can be considered a 'headless' version of Qlik Sense Enterprise. Or, more accurately, Qlik Sense Enterprise is the QAP with some additions, such as the Qlik Sense Client.

The QAP contains the QIX Engine and API's, but lacks a frontend. From a licensing perspective, it is quite attractively priced compared to Qlik Sense Enterprise. This makes the QAP ideal for (OEM) companies that want to embed the software and create their own frontend.

Qlik NPrinting

Qlik NPrinting used to be offered as a third-party add-on to QlikView, but it was acquired by Qlik in February 2015.

NPrinting is an add-on product that can be used to create and distribute static reports based on data and visualizations from QlikView and Qlik Sense. In contrast to many other report writers, which usually only output to PDF, NPrinting can output to many popular file formats, for example, Microsoft PowerPoint, Excel, and Word, but also HTML and PDF. Reports can be scheduled and automatically distributed through multiple channels. Users can also subscribe to reports using the **Newsstand** portal.

NPrinting received an extensive overhaul in version 17. QlikView 12 is only supported from version 17 and up.

Qlik Web Connectors

Over the past few years, cloud-based data sources have steadily increased in popularity. In order to easily load (some of) these data sources into QlikView or Qlik Sense, Qlik offers the Web Connectors as a separate add-on. The Qlik Web Connectors were sold as a third-party add-on under the name QVSource by Industrial CodeBox, until Qlik acquired the company in May 2016.

The Qlik Web Connectors provide preconfigured connectors to load data from sources such as Facebook, Twitter, Google Analytics, Microsoft Dynamics CRM, MailChimp, or SugarCRM.

Qlik GeoAnalytics

Qlik GeoAnalytics is Qlik's most recent acquisition. It was previously known as **IdevioMaps** and was added to the portfolio in January 2017 when Qlik purchased parent company Idevio. Qlik GeoAnalytics is a separate add-on that adds geospatial visualization capabilities to QlikView and Qlik Sense.

Qlik DataMarket

Acquired by Qlik in November 2014, and relaunched as a Qlik branded product in April 2015, Qlik DataMarket offers data as a service. With Qlik DataMarket, you can easily import external reference data into QlikView (and Qlik Sense) and combine it with internal data. Available data ranges from weather and demographics to exchange rates and financial information.

DataMarket is a subscription-based service, but it also has a free tier. Data from DataMarket is loaded into QlikView using the DataMarket Connector.

How do the products in the Qlik product portfolio fit together?

We have seen that the Qlik product portfolio has expanded significantly in the past few years. At the time of QlikView 11 for Developers, there was only QlikView. Nowadays there is a complete range of products and add-ons.

The following diagram gives a high-level overview of how all the products fit together. The base is QlikView and the QAP, both of these use the same QIX Engine. The QAP underpins Qlik Sense Enterprise, which adds a frontend client and collaboration features. NPrinting can be used for static reporting on either QlikView or Qlik Sense. The Qlik Web Connectors, Rest Connector, and DataMarket let both QlikView and Qlik Sense ingest external, web-based data. Geographical analysis in both QlikView and Qlik Sense can be done with the Qlik GeoAnalytics add-on.

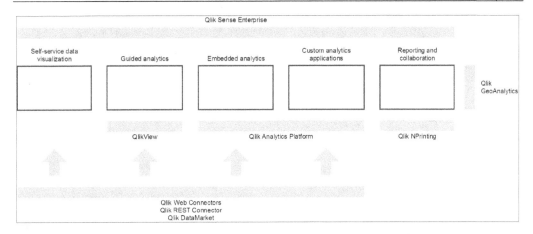

Summary

In this chapter, we've caught up with the most important changes in QlikView 12. We have learned how the Qlik ecosystem has expanded and how all of these products fit together in the bigger picture.

7
Styling Up

Besides presenting useful insights, a very important aspect of a business dashboard is that it should be visually appealing. Our users will be accessing the document every day, so we had better give them something nice to look at while they are drinking their morning coffee.

Our course of action for now will be to take advantage of QlikView's customization flexibility to style up our document, brand it with HighCloud's corporate identity, and set up the general layout on which we will ultimately place our charts.

In this chapter, we will cover the following topics:

- Setting up the workspace
- Understanding and changing the sheet's properties
- Managing our sheet object's appearance
- Using some of the most fundamental objects for selecting and filtering data
- Placing, resizing, and aligning the sheet objects

Design requirements

When we start building the frontend of a QlikView document, we should always begin by defining two fundamental characteristics:

- The screen resolution on which most users will access the document
- The general style and layout of the document

We need to set a standard screen resolution right from the start because it will ultimately determine the placement and size of the objects across the screen. If we build the document targeting a screen resolution higher than that which users have on their machines, they will probably need to use the scroll bars too often. On the other hand, if we target our document to a screen resolution lower than our users' screen resolution, they will see a lot of empty space. Both of these situations will be an inconvenience that our users will need to deal with every day, so we don't want that to happen.

Having a predefined resolution in the document does not keep the user from accessing a document using a lower (or higher) resolution monitor. QlikView allows users to "zoom" a screen to a different size using the **View | Fit Zoom to Window** and **View | Zoom** options. However, using these options can lead to alignment and display issues. It is better to avoid them if possible.

For the HighCloud Airlines document, we will use a screen resolution of 1280 x 1024, since it's the one our primary users (top executives) have set on their monitors.

At the same time, it's been determined that we will divide the frontend layout into four main panels:

- The top panel will be used to place time-related user controls as well as the HighCloud logo
- The left-side panel will hold a majority of the listboxes used to filter the data
- The central area will be used to place the different charts and visualizations
- The right-side panel will have other special objects (that we will discuss later on)

The four main panels are shown in the following diagram:

Time-related user controls and logo		
List boxes used to filter data	Charts and visualizations	Special objects and other controls

The general style of the document should also reflect the HighCloud corporate identity. We will achieve this by:

- Using the official HighCloud logo, seen below. This will be visible at all times and from all worksheets in the document.

- Setting the **Background Color** to white.
- Using the following corporate colors to set different layout object's appearance:

Color name	Color code (RGB)
HighCloud Blue	0, 112, 192
HighCloud Brown	73, 68, 41

The Document Properties window

The **Document Properties** window is where document-level settings are defined. Using this dialog window, we will ensure that HighCloud's logo is embedded into every worksheet of the document. We will also divide the screen space into the panels described previously and set the default **Background Color** option to white.

The **Document Properties** window is shown in the following screenshot:

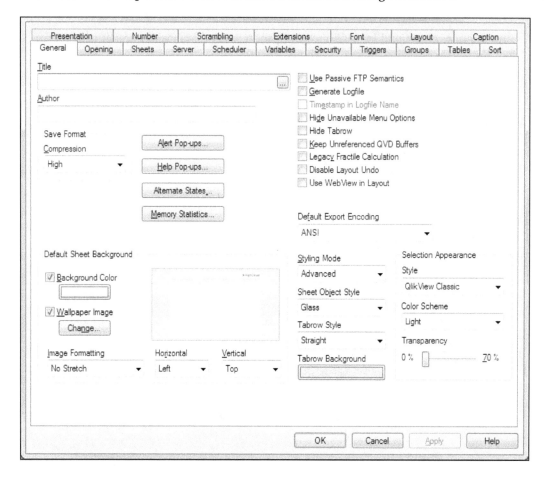

With these design requirements in mind, we will start setting up the document's appearance by following these steps:

1. Open the `Airline Operations.qvw` document we've been working with and go to the **Dashboard** tab.

2. As the document needs to fit the default corporate resolution of 1280 x 1024, select **View** | **Resize Window** | **1280 x 1024** from the menu bar.

3. Then, open the **Document Properties** window by pressing *Ctrl + Alt + D* or by selecting **Settings** | **Document Properties** from the menu bar.

4. Navigate to the **General** tab and enable the **Wallpaper Image** checkbox. Then, click on the **Change...** button.

5. Browse to the `Airline Operations\Design` folder, select the `HighCloud_Background.png` image, and click on **Open**.

6. From the **Default Sheet Background** section of the **Document Properties** window, locate the **Vertical** drop-down and select the **Top** option from the list. The **Horizontal** drop-down will keep the default value, which is the **Left** option.

7. Finally, close the **Document Properties** window by clicking on **OK**.

We've now set the QlikView application window to match the required size of our document. This way, we can ensure that the sheets we design will fit entirely on the target monitors without any scrolling.

> When using the **View | Resize Window** functionality, it is always advisable to also check on the target environment to see if there will be any toolbars or other objects eating into the screen real estate.

Next, we've added a background image which already includes the HighCloud logo, as well as the pre-defined panel divisions that will help us position the objects. All of the sheets we create from now on in our document will automatically have the defined background.

After following the previous procedure, our **Dashboard** sheet should look like the following screenshot:

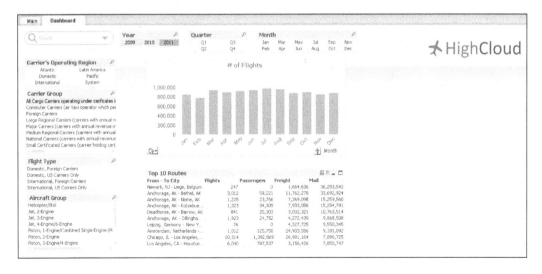

The Sheet Properties dialog

Just as there are document-level properties, we can also set properties at the sheet- and object-level. Let's have a quick look at the **Sheet Properties** dialog.

Open this window by right-clicking on an empty space in the **Dashboard** worksheet and selecting **Properties...**.

The following screenshot shows the **Sheet Properties** dialog:

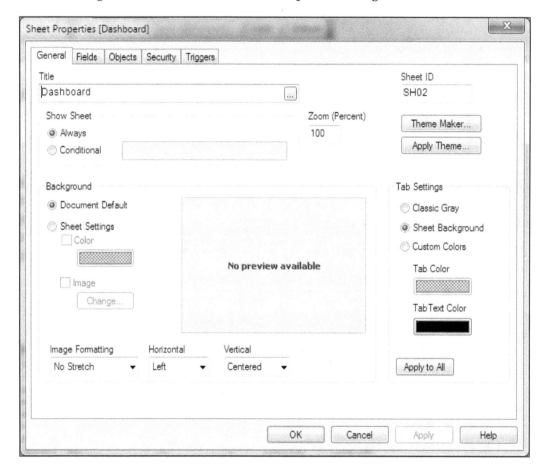

As its name implies, the **Sheet Properties** dialog can be used to set various properties of a worksheet. Let's quickly review the available options.

On the **General** tab, the following properties are of interest:

- **Title**: This property can be used to set the title that appears in the tab row. In addition to static text, this can also be a calculated value.

- **Show Sheet**: This property can be used to conditionally hide/show the sheet. For example, we can use an expression like GetSelectedCount([Carrier Name]) = 1 to only show the sheet when a single carrier is selected.

- **Sheet ID**: This property is the internal ID of the sheet. This ID can be used to reference the sheet from other objects in the document, for example, to activate the sheet by clicking on a button object.

- **Background**: We can either use the **Document Default** option, which we set in the previous section, or override the default by setting a sheet-specific **Color** and/or **Image** selection.

- **Tab Settings**: This property can be used to set any desired **Tab Color** or style.

We've previously worked with the **Fields** tab, which is an easy way to add multiple listboxes to the sheet. Simply select the required fields from the **Available Fields** listbox and double-click (or click **Add >**) to include them in **Fields Displayed in Listboxes**.

The **Objects** tab shows all of the objects that are present on the worksheet, even those that are conditionally hidden. From this tab, we can directly open the individual object's **Properties...** dialog or even **Delete** any of them. The **Objects** tab is shown in the following screenshot:

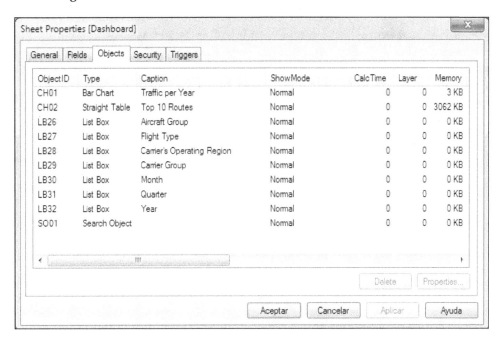

It's also worth noting the **Calc Time** and **Memory** columns in the **Objects** tab. These can be used to optimize our document by identifying which objects have the most impact on performance, or are using up a lot of memory.

The **Security** tab is used to set what users are allowed to do on the corresponding sheet. We are also able to propagate the security settings to all sheets if the **Apply to All Sheets** checkbox is marked. Additionally, when the **Read Only** checkbox is enabled, no selections can be made on the sheet.

Triggers are events to which QlikView can react with **Actions**. When used on sheets, a trigger can be set to respond to events such as activate and deactivate, meaning it will run when entering or leaving the sheet, respectively.

Setting the object properties

It's now time to peek into some of the object-level properties that affect the QlikView document's appearance. The properties we are most interested in at this point are:

- Caption colors
- Caption font

Let's see what these are.

Caption colors and style

By default, almost every object in the QlikView document has a caption bar at the top, unless we choose to explicitly hide it. Since the caption bar will be visible for most of our objects, let's apply a touch of corporate identity by setting the default caption color to **HighCloud Blue** and by selecting a custom styling mode.

Changing the caption colors

Follow these steps to apply a new formatting style to caption bars:

1. Right-click on any of the listboxes on the sheet, for example, **Carrier's Operating Region**.
2. Select **Properties...** and navigate to the **Caption** tab.

Two types of caption colors can be set: one for when the object is **Inactive** and one for when the object is **Active**. An active object is the one on which the user has last clicked, while all of the others are inactive. Since we are not interested in visually identifying the current state of an object, we will apply the same color for both options:

1. Click on the **Background Color** button on the **Inactive Caption** section to open up the **Color Area** dialog window.

2. Make sure the radio buttons corresponding to **Solid Color** and **Fixed Base Color** are selected.

3. Click on the colored square next to the **Fixed** radio button to open the **Color** dialog window.

4. Add the **HighCloud Blue** color to the **Custom colors** section by entering the RGB codes 0, 112, 192 into the respective **Red**, **Green**, and **Blue** inputs and click on the **Add to Custom Colors** button.

5. While we're here, let's also add the **HighCloud Brown** color to the **Custom colors** section. Do this by first selecting the second color placeholder from the left, under the **Custom colors** section, then enter the RGB codes 73, 68, 41 into the **Red**, **Green**, and **Blue** inputs respectively. Finally, click on the **Add to Custom Colors** button.

6. Select the **HighCloud Blue** custom color again from the **Custom colors** section and click on **OK** to close the **Color** dialog window.

7. Click on **OK** to close the **Color Area** dialog window as well.

Now that we've changed the **Background Color** option for the **Inactive Caption** section, we can repeat the same process to set the **Text Color** option of the **Inactive caption** section to white. Once this is done, we've done our fair share of clicking. Fortunately, we can take a different time-saving approach for changing the **Background Color** option of the **Active Caption** section:

1. Right-click on the **Background Color** option in the **Inactive Caption** section and select **Copy**.

2. Right-click on the **Background Color** option in the **Active Caption** section and select **Paste All**.

3. Repeat the same process for the **Text Color** option in the **Active Caption** section.

 Note that the last copied color remains on QlikView's clipboard even when other objects or text are subsequently copied.

The following screenshot shows the **Inactive Caption** and **Active Caption** sections:

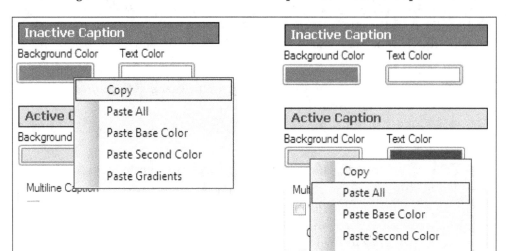

We've now set the colors used by the caption bars for this particular listbox. We will first need to tweak a few other settings before applying this style to every object caption in our document.

The Color Area and Color dialog windows

The **Color Area** and **Color** dialog windows that we've just worked with are used everywhere throughout QlikView to set the color formatting of a variety of object components.

Besides the static, solid color that we used, it is also possible to use gradients of one or two colors. Furthermore, the colors used do not always need to be fixed, they can be based on a dynamic calculation as well. A use case for this is to show a red color when a certain value is below target, and a green one when it is above the target. Calculated colors are set by using an expression with QlikView's color functions, examples of which are `Red()`, `LightGreen()`, `Yellow()`, and so on. In addition to these standard, pre-defined colors, any custom color can be represented using the `RGB()` function.

The following screenshot shows the **Color Area** dialog window:

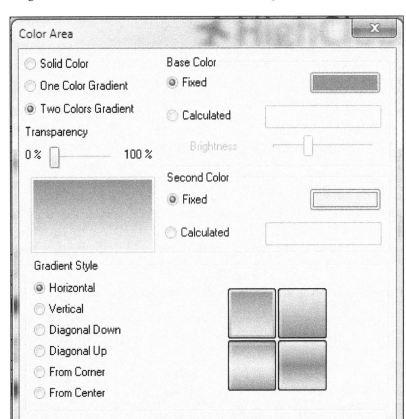

Note that the gradient used in the previous image is an example only, it is inadvisable to use these types of candy-colored gradients in your documents.

Setting the caption font

At 10 points, the default caption font in QlikView is quite big. Let's change the caption font by following these steps:

1. From the **Properties** dialog window of the **Carrier's Operating Region** listbox, click the title's **Font** button on the **Caption** tab.

2. Set the **Size** to 9 in the **Font Dialog**. The font name and font style will be kept as default (**Tahoma, Bold**).

3. Click on **OK** to apply the changes and close the window.

Setting the content font

Besides setting the caption font, we will also change the font used to display the listbox values. To do this, follow these steps:

1. Right-click on the **Carrier's Operating Region** listbox and select **Properties...**.

2. Navigate to the **Font** tab.

3. Change the font **Size** to 9.

4. Click on **OK** to close the **Properties** window.

Setting the global font

An interesting feature in the **Font Dialog** wizard is the option to set a global **Default Font** option, found in the lower-left corner of the **Font Dialog**. By selecting either **List Boxes, Chart, etc.** or **Text Objects/Buttons** under **Default Font**, we can apply the currently selected font to all new objects of the selected class.

The **Font Dialog** window is shown in the following screenshot:

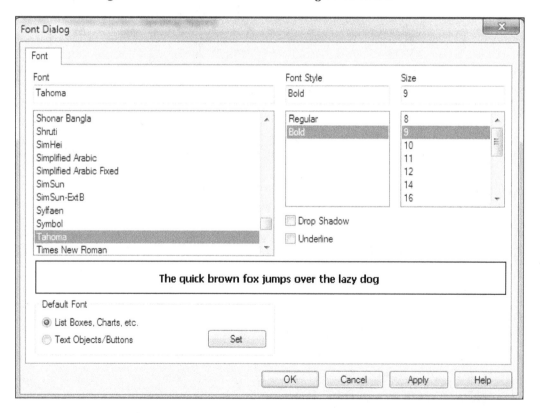

This setting is available from both the caption's font dialog and the content's font dialog.

Propagating the object appearance

By following the previously described procedures, we have set the appearance for a single listbox. To apply the same configuration to all of the remaining listboxes, right-click on the one we already configured, select **Properties...** from the context menu, and go to the **Layout** tab.

At the upper-right corner of the dialog window you will see an **Apply to...** button. Click on it and the **Caption and Border Properties** dialog window will appear. Make sure to mark the following options:

1. The **Apply properties to...** checkbox should be enabled.
2. Select the **Objects in this document** and **All object types** radio buttons.
3. Mark the **Set as default for new objects in this document** checkbox.

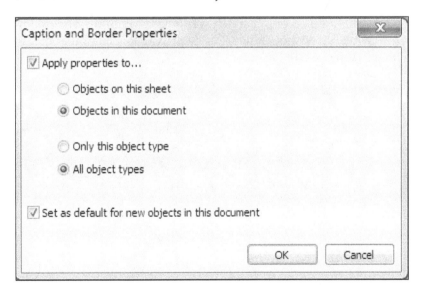

4. Click on **OK** on the two remaining dialog boxes to apply the changes.

Setting the default Sheet Object Style

The captions, as we've styled them now, still have a very basic look. As we noted at the start of this chapter, having a clean, basic style is not necessarily a bad thing, and in many cases is preferred. For now, however, we'll make our presentation a little bit flashier by setting another default **Sheet Object Style**, using the following steps:

1. Open the **Document Properties** dialog by selecting **Settings | Document Properties** or by pressing *Ctrl + Alt + D*.

2. Make sure the **General** tab is active.

3. Set the **Styling Mode** option to Advanced.

4. Set the **Sheet Object Style** option to Glass.

5. Click on **OK** to apply the settings.

The object captions now have a glass-like appearance and rounded corners. The **Advanced** styling mode allows us to make additional changes to an object's style, such as setting rounded corners.

There are several pre-defined object styles available through the **Sheet Object Style** menu. The following screenshot shows how each available combination of **Styling Mode** and **Sheet Object Style** looks:

Hiding captions

Because of the data in them, some of the listboxes, such as **Year**, **Quarter**, and **Month**, do not really need captions. We can hide these captions by right-clicking on the listbox, selecting **Properties...**, and unmarking the **Show Caption** checkbox on the **Caption** tab.

Working with listboxes

Currently, our QlikView document contains the following listboxes in the **Dashboard** sheet:

- **Carrier's Operating Region**
- **Carrier Group**
- **Flight Type**
- **Aircraft Group**
- **Year**
- **Quarter**
- **Month**

Let's see how we can add listboxes and change their properties.

Adding listboxes

Lets add another listbox representing the **Carrier Name** field by right-clicking on the worksheet and selecting **Properties...** (or by pressing *Ctrl + Alt + S*, which is the shortcut for the **Settings | Sheet Properties** menu command). Next, open the **Fields** tab, locate the **Carrier Name** field under the **Available Fields** list, and click on **Add >** to add it as a new listbox.

Many routes lead to Rome

To add an object to a worksheet, there are three basic methods: using the menu, using the toolbar, or using the pop-up menu:

Menu: By selecting **Layout | New Sheet Object**

Toolbar: By using the **design** toolbar

Pop-up: By right-clicking on a blank space within the worksheet and choosing the desired object from the **New Sheet Object** submenu

The examples throughout this book will use a different method each time, but of course you are free to choose your preferred method.

In a moment we will discuss the positioning of the objects we are adding, but for now let's add another listbox, this time using a different method:

1. Right-click anywhere on the sheet and select **New Sheet Object | List Box**.

2. Select **Aircraft Type** from the **Field** drop-down list.

3. Click on **OK** to close the dialog window.

The List Box Properties dialog

Besides the default settings, there are quite a few other options that can be set for listboxes. In this section, we will review the most common of these options. Right-click on any listbox and select **Properties...** to open the **List Box Properties** dialog window.

> While the customization of the listboxes' appearance is quite flexible, one of the options that cannot be changed, at least not out-of-the-box, are the colors used to identify selections. Green always means selected, while white and gray mean associated and excluded values respectively.

The General tab

As the name implies, the **General** tab contains general options for the listbox. Notable options are:

- **Title**: This option is used to set the **Title** label to be different from the default field name. The **Title** label can also be set based on a calculated value.

- **Object ID**: While the title shows the pretty-print frontend name, the **Object ID** option contains the name under which the listbox is known to QlikView. This ID can be used to reference the listbox from other QlikView objects.

- **Always One Selected Value**: This checkbox is only available when a single value is selected at the time we open the **Properties** dialog. This option locks the listbox so that it can only have one value selected at any given time.

- The **Show Frequency** and **In Percent** checkboxes: These options are used to display the absolute number of times that each value appears in the active data set. When **In Percent** is checked, the relative number of appearances versus the total is shown.

The Expressions tab

The **Expressions** tab lets us add calculations and mini charts into listboxes, for example, adding the number of departures to the **Carrier Name** listbox by using the expression Sum([# Departures Performed]). The following screenshot shows the **Carrier Name** listbox with an expression in place:

Carrier Name (# Departures)	
	367
ABSA-Aerolinhas Brasileiras	2,261
ABX Air, Inc.	1,404
ACM AIR CHARTER GmbH	116
Acropolis Aviation Ltd.	24
Aer Lingus Plc	9,821
Aeroflot Russian Airlines	2,744
Aerolineas Argentinas	1,691
Aerolineas Galapagos S A Aerogal	1
AeroLogic GmbH	927
Aeromexico	1
Aeroservices Executive	3
Aerosur	1,159
Aerosvit Ukranian Airlines	1,346
Aerovias Nac'l De Colombia	949
Air-India	2,652
Air Alsie A/S	45

The Sort tab

The **Sort** tab is commonly found across many objects. It offers the option to order the data using any of the following sort orders, outlined in descending order of priority:

- **State**: This option sorts values based on the selection state of the items. Ascending will put all selected or associated items at the top, followed by all non-selected items. Descending performs the opposite sorting. Auto Ascending puts all selected items at the top, but only if the listbox is not big enough to show all of the values at the same time. If all of the values are visible, no sorting has been performed.

- **Expression**: This option sorts the values based on the result of an expression. For example, we could sort carrier names based on the number of departures they have performed.

- **Frequency**: This option sorts the values based on how often the value appears in the dataset.

- **Numeric Value**: This option sorts the values based on the numeric values of each item.

- **Text**: This option sorts the values based on the alphanumerical representation of each item.

- **Load Order**: This option sorts the values based on the order in which the items were loaded into QlikView.

The Presentation tab

The **Presentation** tab lets us change some of the presentation aspects of the listbox. Some of the important options are as follows:

- **Selection Style Override**: This option allows for some (limited) variations on the selection style. For example, it's possible to replace the green background on selected items with a checkbox.

- **Single Column**: This option forces QlikView to use only a single column to list the corresponding field values, even if space is available for multiple columns.

- **Suppress Horizontal Scroll Bar**: When values are longer than the width of a listbox, a horizontal scroll bar is automatically created. Checking this option prevents that from happening.

- **Fixed Number of Columns**: When the **Single Column** checkbox is deselected, this option can be used to set a fixed number of columns for the listbox.

- **Order by Column**: When this option is checked, sorting is performed by column, instead of by row.

- **Alignment**: This option is used to set the alignment of **Text** and **Numbers** within the listbox.

- **Wrap Cell Text**: This option wraps text over multiple lines (as set in the **Height** input box). This can be useful for lengthy instances of text that need to be completely visible.

Suppress Horizontal Scroll Bar

Now might be a good time to suppress the horizontal scroll bar on the **Carrier Group**, **Aircraft Group**, **Aircraft Type**, and **Carrier Name** listboxes.

The Number tab

Like the **Sort** tab, the **Number** tab is used by many different objects. It allows us to control how the listbox content looks by using either predefined or custom formats. For example, if we always want numbers to be displayed with two decimals, we can follow these steps:

1. Check the **Override Document Settings** checkbox.
2. Select the **Fixed to** radio button.
3. Enter 2 in the **Decimals** input box.

By clicking on the **Change Document Format** button, a dialog is opened that lets us set the default number format for every individual field at the document level. This means we will only need to specify the format once, and it will be used everywhere within our document. This option is also available via the **Document Properties** dialog window (**Settings | Document Properties | Number**).

The Font tab

The **Font** tab is also a common one, and its purpose is very straightforward. We already worked with these properties earlier in the chapter while changing the caption font.

The Layout tab

Just as with the others, the **Layout** tab is also one that is used for nearly every object in QlikView. As the name suggests, it allows us to set various layout options.

The different properties available through this tab are directly affected by the document styling mode (**Simplified** or **Advanced**). The **Advanced** styling mode adds more options for styling borders and enables the possibility for rounded corners to be set.

> Since the **Advanced** styling mode is more comprehensive, this section assumes the **Advanced** styling mode is turned on.

Important options on this tab are as follows:

*   **Use Borders**: This checkbox is used to enable/disable the object's border.
*   **Shadow Intensity**: This option selects whether a shadow effect should be added to the object, and if so, specifies its intensity.
*   **Border Width**: This option sets the width of the border, when enabled.

- **Rounded Corners**: This checkbox is used to set whether rounded corners should be used. By (de)selecting individual corners, we can specify which corners should have a rounded effect.

- **Layer**: This option is used to establish the ordering to be used when multiple objects are overlapping. In case of complex, overlapping objects, a **Custom** layer can be used. In this case, higher numbers overlap lower numbers.

- **Apply To...**: This option is used to apply the current format to other objects. We used this function before to apply the same caption layout to every object in the document.

- **Theme Maker** and **Apply Theme**: This option stores the current format in an external theme file. This file can then be used to apply the same format to objects in other documents.

- **Show**: This option allows us to either always show the object, or to apply a condition which must be fulfilled for the object to be shown. An example of this would be to use the expression `GetSelectedCount([Aircraft Group])` `= 1` to the **Aircraft Type** listbox so that it is only visible when a single aircraft group is selected.

- **Allow Move/Size**: Deselecting this option locks the object's size and position.

- **Allow Copy/Clone**: Deselecting this option prevents the object from being copied.

The Caption tab

The **Caption** tab is also a common tab across all QlikView objects. We used it before to set the listbox caption colors and fonts, but it contains a few other interesting options:

- **Multiline Caption**: This option wraps the caption text over the number of lines defined through the **Caption Height** field.

- **X-pos, Y-pos, Width**, and **Height**: While it is easier to just drag, align, and size objects using the mouse, these options let you define the size and location of an object with pixel-level precision. These options can be set for both the **Normal** and the **Minimized** state of the object.

- **Caption Alignment**: This option defines how the display text is aligned in the caption.

- **Special Icons**: This option adds icons to the caption which perform specific actions. An example of these icons would be the one used to send the chart's data to Excel. It is not advisable to add too many icons as this may clutter the interface. When many icons are needed, it is better to select only the **Menu** icon. This option creates an icon that shows a drop-down menu with all of the available actions.

- **Allow Minimize** and **Auto Minimize**: The **Allow Minimize** option enables an object to be minimized. This setting will add a minimize icon to the caption, much like the one on a regular Windows window. When **Auto Minimize** is also marked, different objects with this setting enabled can be interactively and alternately switched between the restored and the minimized states. This means that, when restoring a minimized object, another currently restored object will be automatically switched to the minimized state for the new object to take its place.

- **Allow Maximize**: This option enables an object to be maximized. It adds a maximize icon to the caption, in the same style as in a regular Windows window.

- **Help Text**: This option adds a question mark icon to the caption that, when clicked, will show a pop-up message with the entered help text. The **Help Text** option can contain calculated expressions as well.

This concludes the side-step into the various listbox properties. Don't worry if you didn't memorize all of them at first, we'll encounter them often enough in the rest of the book.

The Multi Box

While listboxes are a very convenient way to quickly make selections, the downside is that they can also take up a lot of space. This is where the multi box offers an alternative. The multi box displays each field on a single line, alongside a drop-down that expands to allow selections to be made.

Let's add a multi box that contains some extra information on flights, by following these steps:

1. Select **Layout | New Sheet Object | Multi Box...**.

2. In the **Title** input field enter `Flight Information`.

3. From the list of **Available Fields**, double-click the fields **From – To City**, **Origin City**, **Origin Country**, **Destination City**, **Destination Country**, and **Distance Interval**.

4. Go to the **Sort** tab and select **Distance Interval** from the list of **Fields**.

5. In the **Sort by** section, uncheck the **Text** option, and mark the **Load Order** checkbox.

6. Click on **OK** to apply the settings and close the **Multi Box Properties** page.

The resulting multi box should look like the one shown in the following screenshot. Notice how the list of values is expandable when clicking on each field. Also note that the sort order for the **Distance Interval** is no longer alphabetical, but uses the order in which the values were loaded into QlikView:

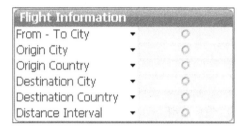

During this exercise, you may have noticed that, unlike the listbox, the **Sort** tab for the multi box contains multiple fields and that we can set different sort orders for each field. This is also the case for the alignment options on the **Presentation** tab and the number format options on the **Number** tab. This is not only true for multi boxes, but for any object that contains multiple dimensions and/or expressions, such as table boxes and charts.

The Current Selections Box

QlikView lets us select data in many different ways: listboxes, clicking in charts and entering search terms, just to name a few. While this is incredibly flexible, it can also become hard to see which information is actually selected at any given moment.

Fortunately, QlikView has an option to show the user exactly which selections are currently applied to the data: the **Current Selections** dialog. To open this dialog, we simply need to press *Ctrl + Q* or select **View | Current Selections** from the menu bar. This floats the **Current Selections** dialog window on top of our worksheet. Once we have had a glance at the **Current Selections** window, we can close the dialog.

It is sometimes useful to permanently display the **Current Selections** dialog. This is where the **Current Selections Box** object comes in handy. To add a **Current Selections Box** object to our **Dashboard** sheet, follow these steps:

1. Select **Layout | New Sheet Object | Current Selections Box**.

2. Click on **OK** to apply the settings and close the **New Current Selections Box** dialog window.

The resulting **Current Selections Box** will look like the following screenshot. Notice how every selection you make is added to the displayed list. Also note that we did not change any of the settings in the **Current Selections Properties** dialog, you may want to review the options yourself at a later time.

Making selections from the Current Selections Box

Besides being a great place to quickly look at the applied filters, the **Current Selections Box** option also allows us to interact with the selections in the following ways:

- Erasing filters: By clicking on the corresponding erase icon for any of the displayed fields, the selection over that field will be cleared.
- Modifying selections: By clicking on the drop-down icon, a list of that corresponding field's values will be displayed, from which we can further refine our selection and select other values, just like with a listbox.
- By right-clicking on each of the displayed filters, we can issue additional commands such as **Select Excluded**, **Select All**, **Clear**, or **Clear Other Fields**.

Adding a Bookmark Object

When using QlikView, we invariably come across some selections that we want to return to at a later time. We can create a bookmark by using the menu (**Bookmarks | Add Bookmark**), using the toolbar, or by pressing *Ctrl + B*. Another option is the **Bookmark Object**. This object lets us create and remove bookmarks from within the worksheet space.

Let's add a bookmark object to our **Dashboard** sheet by following these steps:

1. Right-click anywhere on the worksheet and select **New Sheet Objects | Bookmark Object**.
2. Enter Bookmarks into the **Title** input box.
3. Mark the **Show Remove Button** checkbox.
4. Under **Button Alignment**, select **Vertical**.
5. Click on **OK** to create the bookmark object.

Aligning and resizing sheet objects

When we look at the results so far, we will notice that it looks very unorganized (as seen in the following screenshot). The objects are all over the place and are not aligned with the background. Of course, this is not very convenient for the user, so let's see how we can solve it.

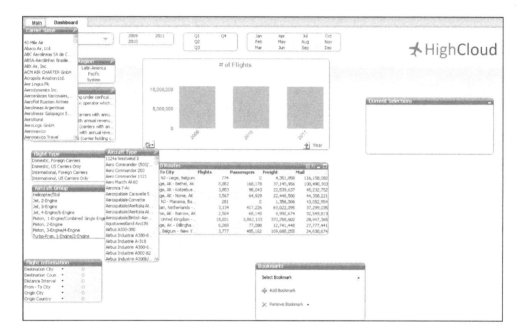

Selecting objects

To select a single object, simply click on its caption. To select multiple objects, activate all of them by either clicking and dragging around them with the mouse cursor ("lassoing"), or by clicking on their captions while keeping the *Shift* key pressed.

Moving objects

Objects (or a selected group of objects) can be moved by clicking on the caption bar and dragging them to the desired location. Objects without a caption (for example, the listboxes showing **Year**, **Quarter**, and **Month** that we created earlier) can be dragged by holding *Alt* and clicking and dragging anywhere on the object. This method also works for objects with a visible caption, and even for objects where **Allow Move/Size** is disabled.

Holding *Ctrl* while pressing the arrow keys moves the active object(s) 1 pixel at a time. Use *Ctrl + Shift* to move them in 10-pixel steps.

Resizing objects

To resize an object, click and drag one of its edges (left, right, top, or bottom) until it fits the required size. You can also use any of the object's corners.

To resize more than one object at once, activate all of them. When resizing one of the selected objects, all of the selected objects will adopt the new size, either vertically, horizontally, or both.

Resizing a Multi Box

Resizing a multi box can be somewhat tricky. Unlike the other sheet objects, if we click and drag one of the object's edges, we can get unexpected results. For example, if we click and drag the right edge and try to make the object smaller, we will, in fact, make it smaller in size but a scrollbar will appear, meaning some part of the object has actually been hidden.

If, on the other hand, we click and drag the right edge and try to make the object larger, it will result in no apparent change.

The key to resizing multi boxes lies in resizing the cells instead. A multi box can be broken into cells, one containing the field label and one containing the field values. By placing the cursor on the right edges of those cells, rather than on the edges of the object, we will be able to click and drag to resize them and, at the same time, resize the entire object.

Hover over the left side of the drop-down icon and watch for when the cursor changes its shape. Click and drag to resize the **Label** cell. Hover over the right edge of the value cell to resize it as well. Resizing cells can be a bit "fiddly," moving the mouse just a little bit may switch between resizing the cell and resizing the object. The following image shows which cursor is associated with which action:

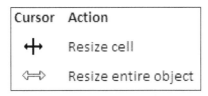

Aligning sheet objects

To align the objects on the screen, activate the desired objects and use the aligning buttons in the design toolbar. Right-clicking on any of the selected objects also brings up the alignment options, seen in the following screenshot:

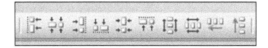

If the design toolbar is not shown in your tool dock (it is turned off by default), you can enable it by selecting **View** | **Toolbars** | **Design** from the menu.

Do a little house keeping

Let's tidy up our current dashboard using the previously described methods. See if you can get the end result to look like the following screenshot:

You may notice in the screenshot that I made some other changes. Besides aligning and sizing the objects, I also fixed the following things:

- Removed the border from the **Search** box.
- Changed the fixed number of columns from the **Quarter** listbox to 4.
- Changed the fixed number of columns from the **Month** listbox to 12.
- Added a caption to the **Traffic per Year** chart.
- Right-aligned the expression labels in the **Top 10 Routes** chart.

See if you can apply these changes as well.

Creating and applying a default color map

Now there is only one thing left to do to finish styling up our document: apply the standard HighCloud color scheme to our charts.

Defining chart colors

We'll start by applying the HighCloud colors to the **Traffic per Year** chart. Follow these steps:

1. Right-click on the bar chart and select **Properties...**.
2. Navigate to the **Colors** tab.
3. From the **Data Appearance** section, click on the first color button under the **Colors 1-6** list, and the already familiar **Color Area** dialog will appear.
4. Change the **Base Color** to the already defined **HighCloud Blue** and close the **Color Area** window.
5. Then, click on the second color button from the color map and change it to **HighCloud Brown**.
6. Click on **OK** to close the **Chart Properties** window.

Once we've changed the color map, our chart will adopt the new colors in the order that was defined. At this time, only one color (**HighCloud Blue**) is used by the chart. However, we will use the same color map for all of our future charts, and some of them will indeed require more of the defined colors.

Setting the default color map

Let's now see how we can use that previous definition and set it as the default scheme for all of our charts:

1. Right-click on the **Traffic per Year** chart again and select **Properties...**.

2. Navigate to the **Colors** tab and click on the **Advanced...** button. You will now see the following dialog:

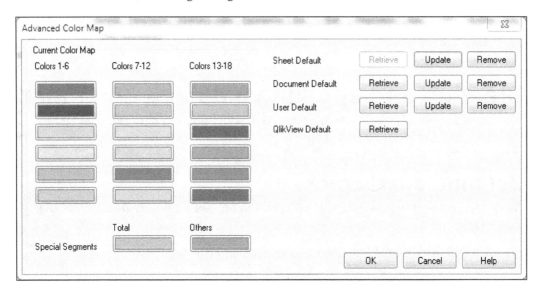

The **Advanced Color Map** dialog window lets us retrieve and update the default color map on a number of levels:

- **Sheet Default**: The color map is only used for objects within this sheet.

- **Document Default**: The color map is used for all of the objects within this document.

- **User Default**: The color map is used for all of the objects that the current user creates. This is very useful when you have a corporate style that you want to apply to all of your charts across all of your documents.

- **QlikView Default**: This is the default QlikView color map.

- These settings can only be retrieved but not overwritten.

Setting a new default color map does not overwrite the color settings on objects that were already created. Those settings would need to be updated manually.

As we only want to apply the color scheme to this document, we will be updating the **Document Default** color map by following these steps:

1. Click on the **Update** button corresponding to **Document Default**.
2. Click on **OK** to close the **Advanced Color Map** dialog.
3. Click on **OK** to close the **Chart Properties** dialog.

The default color map used by the document has been set and it will be automatically applied to all future charts we create.

Summary

We've come to the end of the chapter, in which we learned to set document, sheet, and object properties. We've also learned how to add a background to aid the frontend layout, and also to apply a corporate identity to our document and set a default color map.

We learned how to create and use different objects, such as the listbox, the Current Selections Box, the Multi Box, and the Bookmark Object.

After preparing and setting the style used by the document, we can now continue to create and use the different data visualization objects available in QlikView. In the next chapter, we will look at building the charts and tables which will be used for dashboards, analysis, and reports.

8
Building Dashboards

It's now time to populate our document with charts, tables, and other data visualization objects.

We will first look at the various types of QlikView users, and what they typically look for in a QlikView document. After that we will look at the different chart options available, along with a few other sheet objects, and use them to extend our dashboard. We will also take a more in-depth look at the ways in which we can create basic calculations in the various objects.

Specifically, in this chapter you will learn:

- The three basic types of QlikView users, and how best to cater to their needs
- The various charting options available in QlikView
- Other sheet objects that can be used to add interactivity to our QlikView documents
- How to create basic calculations

Let's get started!

User types

The data model within a single QlikView document can be used to serve the information needs of a wide range of users, from the executive to the operational level. As different user groups have different information needs, QlikView documents are often built using the **Dashboards**, **Analysis**, and **Reports** (**DAR**) approach. Of course, with a limited number of user types, it is inevitable that they are painted with a broad brush. Most QlikView users will fall into more than one user category. Let's take a look at each of them.

Dashboard users

Dashboards offer a quick, bird's-eye view of information. They are often used by executives and middle-management to gauge performance of a limited number of **Key Performance Indicators** (**KPIs**) against predefined targets.

Data displayed in dashboards is usually aggregated at a high level. Drill-downs to more granular data, while technically not a problem in QlikView, are purposely limited. When dashboard users spot an anomaly in the data, they may simply ask an analyst to dig deeper.

Typical data visualization on a dashboard includes speedometers and traffic lights to provide, at a quick glance, the current status of the defined KPIs. The following screenshot depicts a typical, albeit cleanly formatted, dashboard:

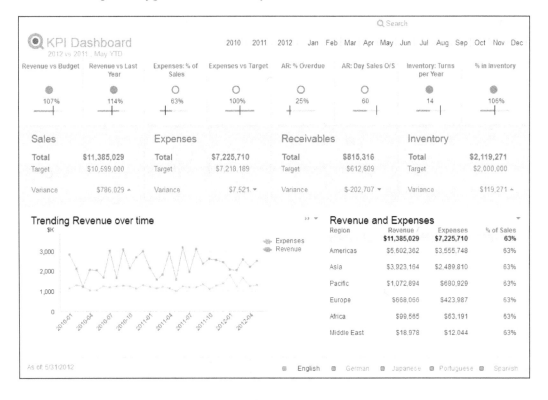

Analysts

While dashboard users commonly want to have a general view on their performance at a glance, analysts are the ones who really dig into the data. They will try to uncover not only what happened, but also why it happened. To do this, they require access to the complete dataset with no detail left out; they also need to be able to query it in many different ways.

In QlikView, this translates to having several listboxes for easy data filtering, along with many different charts offering comprehensive and insightful views of the data. Many analysts will also create their own visualizations whenever they need to answer a specific question, or will make extensive use of **What-If** scenarios to test and predict an outcome based on changes in certain variables.

Typical data visualizations used in analysis include scatter, bar and line charts, and pivot tables. The following screenshot shows an example of a typical analysis sheet:

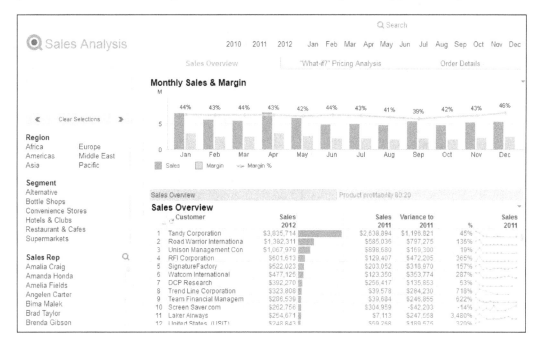

Report users

In QlikView, reports are considered to be more or less static displays of information in a tabular form. Reports can serve multiple purposes; for instance, they can be used to provide users at the operational level with the information they need in their daily activities. They can also be the end-point of an analytical exercise.

Typical data visualizations at the report level are straight tables and pivot tables. The following screenshot shows a typical report:

Number of Orders				14,369					
Order #	Order Date	Customer	Invoice #	Products	Sales Price	Sales / Qty		Revenue	Margin
112683	2010-08-23	Homebound	315436	Great Cranberr	$0.00	27,500		$0.00	-$3,905.00
123888	2010-10-25	Homebound	328968	Great Cranberr	$0.00	27,500		$0.00	-$3,905.00
113727	2010-09-10	Icon	316995	Blue Label Car	$0.00	12,500		$0.00	$0.00
124664	2010-11-12	Icon	330498	Blue Label Car	$0.00	12,500		$0.00	$0.00
213740	2011-08-31	Salamander Junc	117107	Blue Label Car	$0.00	7,500		$0.00	$0.00
211183	2011-09-14	Healtheon	118326	Landslide Hot	$2.28	7,126		$16,247.28	$6,424.80
203053	2011-03-25	Healtheon	103089	Landslide Hot	$2.28	6,480		$14,774.40	$1,982.88
113711	2010-09-11	Scientific Atlanta	317070	Blue Label Car	$0.00	6,250		$0.00	$0.00
113712	2010-09-11	Scientific Atlanta	317105	Blue Label Car	$0.00	6,250		$0.00	$0.00
214783	2011-09-09	Healtheon	118060	Landslide Hot	$2.28	5,834		$13,301.52	$5,259.93
214796	2011-09-20	Healtheon	118892	Landslide Hot	$2.28	5,834		$13,301.52	$5,259.93

Applying the DAR principle to Airline Operations

Now that we've gone through the theoretical part of QlikView use cases and user types, it's time to get practical again. To continue, open the `Airline Operations.qvw` file we've been working on. We will build our exercises upon the previously created data model and frontend.

When we look at the document we have built so far, we will notice that this does not yet cover the Dashboard, Analysis, and Report use cases. That's why, in this section, we will expand on the various charts that are available in QlikView, while also applying the DAR principles.

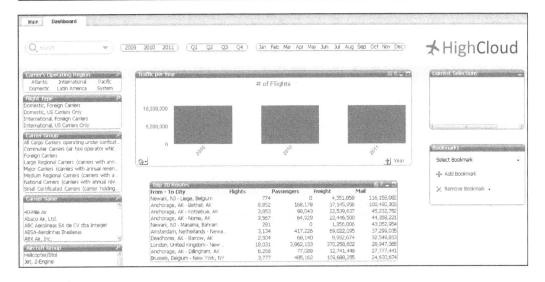

First, though, we need to take a better look at the business requirements set by HighCloud Airlines.

Document requirements

After requirement workshops and interviews with the HighCloud Airlines' executive team, Sara has distilled the following KPIs:

- **Load Factor** %: This gives the number of enplaned passengers versus the number of available seats
- **Performed versus scheduled flights**: This gives the number of flights that were performed versus those that were actually scheduled
- **Air time** %: This gives the time spent flying versus total ramp-to-ramp time
- **Enplaned passengers** (in millions): This gives the number of transported passengers, in millions
- **Departures performed** (in thousands): This gives the number of flights performed, in thousands
- **Revenue Passenger Miles** (in millions): This gives the total number of miles that all passengers were transported, in millions
- **Available Seat Miles** (in millions): This gives the total number of miles that all seats (including unoccupied seats) were transported, in millions
- **Market Share**: This is based on transported passengers

Besides these requirements, there is a need to further analyze the data. While the workshop and interviews weren't conclusive about the exact analytics requirements (they rarely are), there was consensus that at least the following areas should be investigated:

- Trend analysis of the number of flights, transported passengers, freight, and mail through time
- Top 10 routes based on the number of flights, enplaned passengers, freight, and mail
- The number of passengers versus available seats (Load Factor %) across flight types
- The relationship between transported passengers, mail, and the number of flights

In addition, the current metrics currently shown on the **Dashboard** sheet should be moved to the new analysis section.

It was also decided that the following two reports should be available:

- Aggregated flights per month
- KPIs per carrier

Creating the Analysis sheet

The first sheet we will create is the **Analysis** sheet; as the current **Dashboard** sheet already contains a few of the metrics that we want on that sheet, first, let's change the name of the sheet from **Dashboard** to **Analysis**:

1. Right-click anywhere on the sheet workspace and choose **Properties**.
2. Navigate to the **General** tab and enter `Analysis` in the **Title** input field.
3. Click on **OK** to close the **Sheet Properties** dialog.

While we're at it, rename the **Main** sheet to `Associations`. This sheet will help users to find associations on the data across many different fields. We might need to reposition the listboxes to fit our new layout.

Sheet handling

The design toolbar at the top of the screen contains some useful commands for dealing with worksheets.

The first icon on the left adds a new sheet. The second and third icons move the currently active sheet to the left or the right on the tab row. The last icon is used to open the properties dialog for the currently active sheet.

The same functionality can also be found under the **Layout** menu. This menu additionally contains the **Remove Sheet** function, which will remove the currently active sheet.

Just as a quick review to keep our focus, the following requirements were defined for the **Analysis** sheet:

- Trend analysis of the number of flights, enplaned passengers, freight, and mail through time

- Top 10 routes based on the number of flights, enplaned passengers, freight, and mail

- The number of passengers versus available seats (Load Factor %) across flight types

- The relationship between enplaned passengers, mail, and the number of flights

Adding a new chart

Now that we have a general layout to start from, it is time to add another chart to the **Analysis** sheet. A new chart can be added by selecting **Layout | New Sheet Object | Chart** from the menu, right-clicking on the worksheet and selecting **New Sheet Object | Chart**, or clicking on the **Create Chart** button on the toolbar.

This opens the first page of the **Chart Properties** dialog: the **General** tab. On this tab we can set some general settings for the chart, such as what the display text in the caption (**Window Title**) should be, and, more importantly, what **Chart Type** we wish to create.

Another interesting option in this window is the **Fast Type Change** option. This option allows the user to dynamically switch between different types of charts, for example, we may switch between a bar chart and a straight table.

 Yes, pivot tables and straight tables are charts in QlikView

It might seem a little (or very) counter-intuitive, but pivot and regular (straight) tables are considered charts in QlikView.

Bar Chart

One of the required charts in our document should display number of passengers and number of available seats by flight type. We will use a bar chart to visualize this metric. Follow these steps to create it:

1. From the **Chart Type** section in the **New Chart** dialog window, select the **Bar Chart** option (the first one to the left) and click on **Next**.

2. The next dialog is the **Dimensions** dialog. From the list on the left, locate the **Flight Type** field and add it to the **Used Dimensions** list by clicking on the **Add >** button. After that, click on **Next**.

3. We will now enter an expression to get the total number of enplaned passengers. In the **Edit Expression** dialog that opens automatically after clicking on **Next** in the previous window, type the following expression and click on **OK**:

```
Sum ([# Transported Passengers])
```

4. We will assign a label to our expression by typing # of Passengers in the corresponding **Label** field.

5. We will add a second expression to calculate the number of available seats. Do this by clicking on the **Add** button, which will open up the **Edit Expression** window again.

6. Enter the following expression and click on **OK**:

```
Sum([# Available Seats])
```

7. Enter the label # of Available Seats into the **Label** field.

8. Let's have a look at the intermediate result; click on **Finish**.

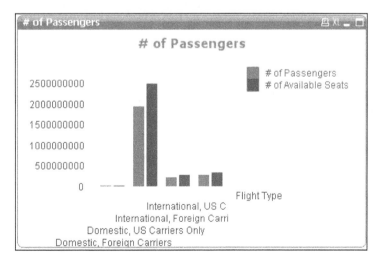

When we look at this chart, we notice that it's quite hard to read. The numbers are really large, all those zeroes occupy a lot of space. Besides that, the title text and caption both say the same thing and do not reference the second expression in the chart.

 We should also note that the corporate colors have been correctly assigned, since the default color map in place was defined in the previous chapter.

Let's correct these issues by changing the following settings in the **Properties** dialog:

1. On the **General** tab, set the **Window Title** field to # of Passengers/ Available Seats (x 1 million) by Flight Type. Next, uncheck the **Show Title in Chart** checkbox.

2. On the **Expressions** tab, select the **# of Passengers** expression and tick the **Values on Data Points** checkbox. Next, highlight **# of Available Seats** and also check the **Values on Data Points** checkbox. Modify both expressions' definition by dividing the result by one million. The expressions will now be:

   ```
   Sum ([# Transported Passengers]) / 1000000
   Sum ([# Available Seats]) / 1000000
   ```

3. On the **Style** tab, change the **Orientation** to horizontal (right icon).

4. On the **Presentation** tab, set the **legend's font format** to **Tahoma**, with a **Regular Font Style**, and with the **Size** set to **8** by first clicking on the **Settings** button, and then clicking on the **Font** button in the **Legend Settings** dialog window.

5. On the **Axes** tab, under **Expression Axes**, check the **Show Grid** checkbox. Change the **Font** format for both **Expression Axis** and **Dimension Axis** to **Tahoma**, with a **Regular Font Style**, and with the **Size** set to **8** using their respective **Font** buttons.

6. On the **Number** tab, hold down the *Shift* key and select **# of Passengers** and **# of Available Seats** from the list of **Expressions**. Next, select **Fixed to** under **Number Format Settings** and set the **Decimals** field to 1.

7. On the **Layout** tab, uncheck the **Use Borders** option.

8. Click on **OK** to close the **Chart Properties** window.

The resulting chart should look similar to the following screenshot:

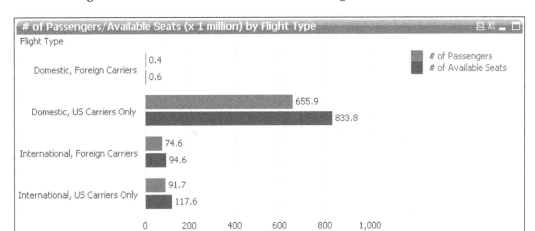

Now that we have formatted our chart, we can copy these settings to another chart using the **Format Painter Tool**. To do this, activate the object for which formatting needs to be copied and then click the **Format Painter Tool** button in the design toolbar. Next, click the target object to apply the format. Use it to copy the formatting options we set previously and apply them to our **Traffic per Year** chart.

Additional bar chart properties

In the previous example we went over the most common bar chart properties. As you may have seen in the various dialog windows, QlikView offers a lot of additional options and settings. Let's look at a few notable options available for bar charts.

Style

On the **Style** tab, you can add a 3D, shadow, or gradient **Look** to your bar chart. Additionally, you can change the **Orientation** option, as we did in the example. Choosing a horizontal orientation can make text labels much more readable. Arguably the most important option on this tab is the **Subtype** option; this lets you change the bar chart from **Grouped**, in which two bars corresponding to one dimension value will be shown side by side, to a **Stacked** arrangement, where the two bars will be stacked on top of each other.

Presentation

Notable options on the **Presentation** tab are the **Bar Distance** option, which controls the distance between bars in a group, and the **Cluster Distance** option, which controls the distance between groups of bars. For the last option to work there needs to be multiple dimensions or expressions.

Expressions and the Edit Expression window

Before we look at the other chart types and objects that QlikView has to offer, it is time to have a more in-depth look at **Expressions** and the **Edit Expression** window.

Expressions

By now you may have noticed that QlikView expressions can be used just about everywhere throughout the program, from chart expressions to expressions for setting colors or window titles. This functionality makes QlikView very flexible. Expressions in QlikView are very similar to formulas that you may know from Excel, or functions that you may know from SQL.

The Edit Expression window

The **Edit Expression** window is used to enter expressions. Whenever you see an ellipsis character (**...**) accompanying an input box, it means you can click on it to enter an expression.

Let's open the **Edit Expression** window now and have a closer look:

1. Right-click the **# of Passengers/Available Seats** chart and choose **Properties....**

2. Select the **Expressions** tab and highlight the **# of Passengers** expression from the list on the left.

3. Click on the **...** button next to the **Definition** input box.

The **Edit Expression** window is shown in the following screenshot:

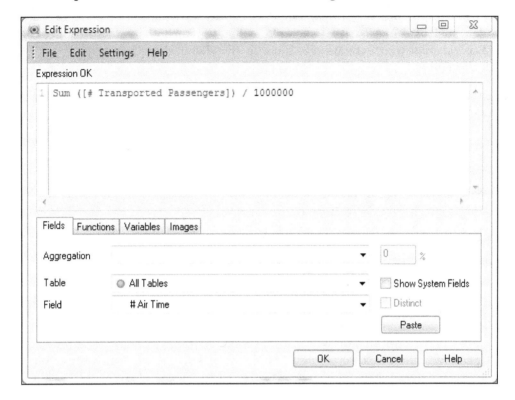

The **Edit Expression** window contains a big input field in which expressions can be entered directly. Once you have familiarized yourself with the various expression functions and their syntax (we'll cover many of them throughout the book), you will realize that this is the fastest way to enter an expression. The **Edit Expression** window automatically checks the syntax of the entered expression; if an error is found, the expression will be underlined with a red squiggly line and the text **Error in expression** will be displayed.

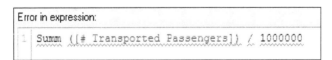

Be aware that the automatic syntax check does not always work flawlessly; with advanced expressions, the editor will sometimes indicate that an error is present when in fact there is none.

At the bottom of the expression editor, a few tabs can be found. Let's quickly see what each of these tabs does.

Fields

The **Fields** tab enables "clicking together" an expression by selecting an **Aggregation** function, such as sum, avg, min, max, and the field to which it should be applied. The **Table** dropdown can be used to filter the field list to those belonging to a particular table.

When the **Distinct** checkbox is marked, only unique values will be considered in the aggregation. This can be useful when, for example, we want to count the number of distinct customers, instead of their total number of appearances in the database.

When all selections have been made, the expression can be entered into the **Edit Expression** input field by clicking on the **Paste** button. Note that the code will be pasted where the cursor presently is, and will replace any highlighted text in the expression.

Functions

While the **Fields** tab makes it possible to create expressions using just the mouse, it is fairly limited in the type of expressions it can create. The **Functions** tab, however, contains a comprehensive list of available functions, grouped by **Function Category** and **Function Name**.

Selecting a particular function will display its syntax in a box. The selected function can be entered into the expression input field by clicking on the **Paste** button, but the corresponding parameters have to be set manually.

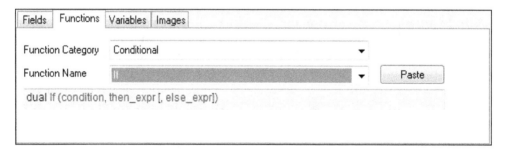

Variables

As we will see later in this chapter, variables can be used to store expressions and values. The advantage of this approach is that we can use an expression in many places, while only maintaining it in a single place.

If, for example, instead of directly typing the # of Passengers expression into the input field we had created a variable containing its definition, we would be able to select that variable from the drop-down list on the **Variables** tab and achieve the same result.

Images

A QlikView expression does not always have to be text or a calculation. There are some objects, for example, the **Text Object** or even a **Straight Table**, that are also able to display the result of an expression as an image.

The **Images** tab makes it easy to select images that are built into QlikView, or which have been bundled into the document via script. Simply select an image name from the **Image** drop-down list or, more conveniently, from a visual menu of images by clicking on the **Advanced** button.

Clicking on the **Paste** option will enter a string referencing the corresponding image into the expression input field. These string values can also be used within expressions. For example, the following expression will compare the **Target** field using the `if` function. If the value is greater than 100, a green upwards arrow will be displayed, otherwise a red downwards arrow will be shown.

```
if(Target > 100, 'qmem://<bundled>/BuiltIn/arrow_n_g.png',
'qmem://<bundled>/BuiltIn/arrow_s_r.png')
```

Click on **Cancel** in the **Edit Expression** dialog window to close it without saving any changes and close the **Chart Properties** window as well.

The Expression Overview window

With expressions in so many locations, it can be hard to keep track of them all. This is where the **Expression Overview** window comes in handy; it offers a central location to manage all expressions being used in our QlikView document.

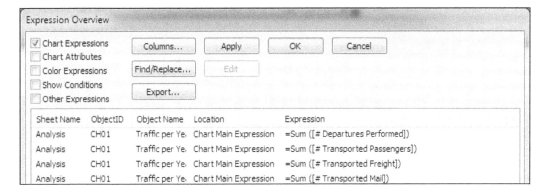

The **Expression Overview** window can be opened by pressing *Ctrl + Alt + E* or by selecting **Settings | Expression Overview** from the menu bar.

By default, only **Chart Expressions** in the QlikView document are shown. This list can be expanded or narrowed down by (de)selecting the checkboxes for each expression type.

It is possible to edit an individual expression by highlighting it from the list and clicking the **Edit** button. Bulk updates are possible, using the **Find/Replace** button. Be very cautious when using this function, as unintended changes can occur.

Line Chart

The **Line Chart** works very much like the bar chart that we looked at earlier. So, instead of creating a new line chart, we will convert one of the already built bar charts into one.

Bar charts versus line charts

While bar and line charts are considered interchangeable by many, there are actually specific use cases in which it is advisable to use one over the other. **Bar charts** are best used to compare different categories, for example, for comparing different Flight Types. **Line charts** are best used to detect trends in series that have an order, such as dates or steps within a process.

Let's follow these steps to convert the **Traffic per Year** chart from a bar chart into a line chart:

1. Right-click the **Traffic per Year** chart and select **Properties…**.
2. On the **General** tab, under **Chart Type** select **Line Chart** (second icon from the top left).
3. Click on **OK** to apply the settings.

The resulting line chart is shown in the following picture.

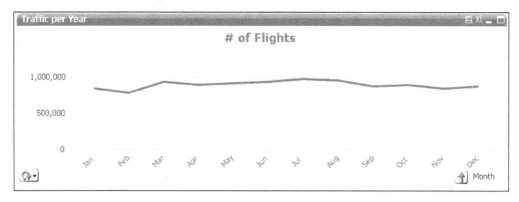

Notice we have to select a year for the months to be shown. In this case, we have selected `2011` in the **Year** listbox.

While this already looks quite nice, we will make a few extra changes:

- As we are more interested in the trend than in the exact values, the axis does not necessarily need to start at **0**
- We will add dots on the actual data points so it is clear for the user where to point their mouse cursor in case they do want to see the exact values
- The numbers on the Y-axis are quite big; we will format the numbers so that they are shown in thousands, millions, or billions depending on the selection

Follow these steps to apply the changes:

1. Right-click on the **Traffic per Year** chart and select **Properties....**
2. Navigate to the **Axes** tab and deselect the **Forced 0** checkbox.
3. Activate the **Expressions** tab and click on the plus icon next to the circular arrow to display the list of expressions.
4. For each expression, individually mark the **Symbol** checkbox under the **Display Options** section and select **Dots** from the drop-down list.
5. Open the **Presentation** tab and set the **Symbol Size** option to **4pt** under the **Line/Symbol Settings** section; this sets the size of the dots.
6. Open the **Number** tab and select all expressions by clicking on the first expression (`# of Flights`) and then holding *Shift* while clicking on the last expression (`Transported Mail`). All expressions will be highlighted.
7. In the **Thousand Symbol** input field enter `x Thousand`.
8. In the **Million Symbol** box enter `x Million`.
9. In the **Billion Symbol** box enter, you guessed it, `x Billion`.
10. Click on **OK** to apply the changes and close the **Chart Properties** dialog.

The resulting line chart is shown in the following screenshot:

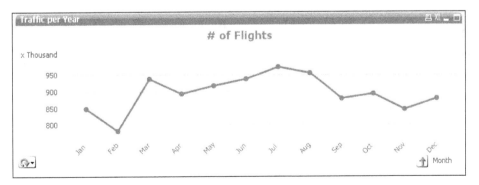

As you can see, the actual trend can be easily perceived and the individual data points are much more visible. Additionally, the scale on the y axis now contains much shorter numbers. The advantage of setting values for thousands, millions, and billions is that the y axis scale will automatically adjust to the appropriate range when updating the chart based on user selections.

Additional line chart properties

While in the previous example we looked at the most common line chart attributes, there are some additional settings in the **Chart Properties** dialog that are interesting to take note of.

Expressions

On the **Expressions** tab, the **Accumulation** option can be used to display a moving total. This means that instead of presenting individual values, each new value is added to the sum of all previous values. In the following chart, instead of the individual amount of flights for each month, we see the total cumulative amount of flights as of each period:

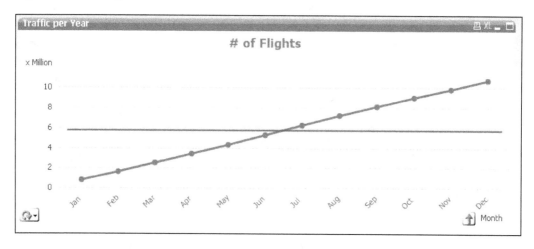

The other line you see in the chart represents the **Average**; this option and is set under the **Trendlines** section.

Style

On the **Style** tab, you can change the **Look** option of the line chart. Besides some 3D effects, an interesting visualization is the area chart (fourth icon from the top). Another useful setting, though admittedly not as useful as it is for bar charts, is the **Orientation** option. This allows you to change the orientation from vertical to horizontal.

Presentation

The **Presentation** tab offers options to change how the data is presented within the chart. Useful options are under the **Line/Symbol Settings** section; with these options we can change the **Line Width** option of the chart as well as the size of the symbols (as we saw when we added the dots in the previous chart).

For charts that have many values on the X-axis, a useful option is the **Chart Scrolling** option. By checking the **Enable X-Axis Scrollbar** checkbox and setting a value for the **When Number of Items Exceeds** parameter, a scrollbar is added to the chart whenever the number of values on the X-axis exceeds the specified amount.

Arguably the most useful option in this tab, however, is found under the **Reference Lines** section. This option can be used to integrate additional, straight lines to the line chart. A practical example would be to add a target reference to compare each data point to a predefined objective.

By clicking on the **Add** button, the **Reference Lines** dialog opens. Here we can set an expression for the reference line, set its label, and change some other settings with regard to formatting. The following screenshot shows an example of a static 900,000 flights target line, but of course a dynamic target could also be used if it is included in the data model:

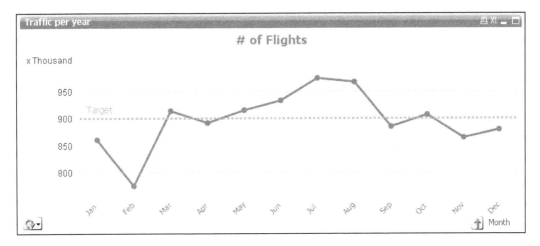

Combo Chart

Though it sounds fancy, the Combo Chart is nothing more than a combination of the bar and line charts that we used earlier. It brings together all the properties of both charts.

Let's look at how this combined chart works by converting the **# of Passengers /
Available Seat (x 1 million) by Flight Type** chart that we created earlier:

1. Right-click on the bar chart and select **Properties....**

2. From the **General** tab, change the **Chart Type** option from **Bar Chart** (top left
   icon) to **Combo Chart** (third icon from the left).

3. On the **Expressions** tab select the **# of Passengers** expression. Next, deselect
   the **Line** checkbox under **Display Options** and select the **Bar** checkbox.
   Disable the **Values on Data Points** option as well.

4. Next, select the **# of Available Seats** expression. Then, deselect the **Line**
   checkbox and mark the **Symbol** checkbox. Select the **Diamonds** option
   from the drop-down list on the right. Disable the **Values on Data Points**
   option as well.

5. Click on **Add** to open the **Edit Expression** window and enter the following
   new expression and then click on **OK** to close the editor:

   ```
   Column(1) / Column(2)
   ```

6. Enter `Load Factor` as this expression's **Label**.

7. With the new expression highlighted from the expressions' list, deselect the
   Line checkbox and enable the **Values on Data Points** option.

8. Navigate to the **Presentation** tab and set the **Symbol Size** option to **4 pt**.

9. On the **Number** tab, select the **Load Factor** expression and set the **Number
   Format Settings** option to **Fixed to 1 Decimals** and mark the **Show in
   Percent (%)** option.

10. Click on **OK** to close the **Chart Properties** dialog.

The end result should look like the following chart:

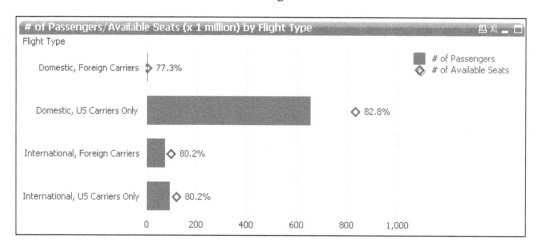

One thing you may notice is that while we entered three expressions, only two are visible in the chart. This happens because we did not select any display mode for the **Load Factor** expression. However, we did activate the **Values on Data Points** checkbox, and that is why the value for **Load Factor** is shown in the chart.

You may also wonder about the expression that we used to calculate the **Load Factor** value:

```
Column(1) / Column(2)
```

This expression tells QlikView to divide the result of the first expression by the result of the second expression. You will understand that the order of the expressions should not be changed in order for this to work reliably.

Container

By now, with three charts already created, our worksheet is becoming somewhat cluttered again. Time to do another round of reorganizing. The option of choice this time will be a container object in which we will group multiple objects together in the same screen space. The user will then be able to interactively switch between objects.

Let's put all three charts (or, two charts and a table) into the container object by following these steps:

1. Go to **Layout | New Sheet Object | Container** in the menu bar.
2. On the **General** tab, select the three items corresponding to our charts from the **Existing Objects** list (**Traffic per Year**, **Top 10 Routes**, and **# of Passengers**).

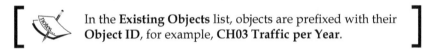

In the **Existing Objects** list, objects are prefixed with their **Object ID**, for example, **CH03 Traffic per Year**.

3. Click on **Add** to place them in the **Objects Displayed in Container** list to the right.
4. Go to the **Presentation** tab and select **Tabs at bottom** from the **Appearance** drop-down menu.
5. Go to the **Layout** tab and deactivate the **Use Borders** option.
6. Click **OK** to close the **Container Properties** dialog and create the new object.

The resulting container is shown in the following image. Notice how we can switch between charts by clicking the tabs on the bottom row.

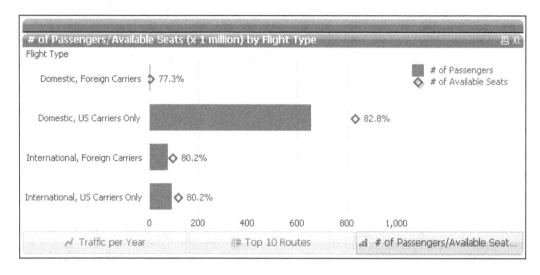

You will also notice that the original charts are still on the worksheet, making it look even messier. We will remove these old objects by right-clicking on each of them and selecting the **Remove** option. A pop-up window will appear asking to confirm deletion of either only the selected object or all linked objects. Click on the **Delete Selected** button as shown in the screenshot below:

The reason this dialog message appears is that there are now two instances of the same object, and QlikView treats them as linked objects (one object sharing the same properties and IDs, but in different locations). We will look at linked objects in more detail later on in this chapter.

After we've removed all the duplicate charts and have properly aligned the container object, we will remove the container's caption by following these steps:

1. Right-click on either the container's caption or one of the buttons on the bottom row and select **Properties...**.

2. Go to the **Caption** tab and deselect the **Show Caption** option.

3. Click on **OK** to apply the settings and close the dialog window.

It is important to click on the container heading or buttons; otherwise we would not be opening the container properties but the properties of the currently active chart. Now we have space to add even more charts!

Scatter Chart

One of the analysis requirements we have to meet is to provide an insight into the relationship between the number of passengers, number of transported mail, and the number of performed departures at the carrier level. To visualize this we will add a scatter chart by following these steps:

1. Go to **Layout | New Sheet Object | Chart** in the menu.

2. From the **New Chart Object** window, set the **Window Title** to:

   ```
   Transported passengers vs mail
   ```

3. Disable the **Show Title in Chart** option and select the **Scatter Chart** (bottom left icon) option in the **Chart Type** section from the **General** tab. Then click on **Next**.

4. Select **Carrier Name** from the **Available Fields/Groups** list and click on the **Add >**button to add it to the **Used Dimensions** list. Click on **Next**.

5. On the **Expressions** tab, select **# Transported Mail** from the **X** listbox and **# Transported Passengers** from the **Y** listbox.

6. Mark the **Bubble Chart** checkbox and enter the following in the **Bubble Size Expression** input field:

   ```
   Sum([# Departures Performed])
   ```

7. Click on **Next** twice.

8. On the **Style** tab, under the **Look** section select the third icon from the top in the right column (above the "glossy" bubbles that are selected by default) and click on **Next**.

9. On the **Presentation** tab, deselect the **Show Legend** checkbox and click on **Next**.

10. On the **Axes** tab, mark the **Show Grid**, **Show Minor Grid**, and **Label Along Axis** checkboxes under X-axis as well as under the y axis. These options add a visible grid to the chart as well as place the labels alongside the axes, which takes less space. Click on **Next**.

11. On the **Colors** tab, enable the **Persistent Colors** checkbox. This setting ensures that dimensions (in our case carriers) keep the same color even when the selection changes. Click on **Next**.

12. On the **Number** tab, select all three expressions and set the **Number Format Settings** option to **Integer**. Enter x 1 thousand in the **Thousand Symbol** field, x 1 million in the **Million Symbol** field, and x 1 billion in the **Billion Symbol** field.

13. Click on **Finish** to apply the settings and close the dialog.

The resulting chart is shown in the following screenshot. The Y-axis shows the number of transported passengers while the X-axis shows the amount of transported mail. The bubble size indicates how many flights (departures) have been performed by each carrier.

We can immediately see there are carriers that only transport mail, such as **United Parcel Service**, and those that only carry passengers, such as **Southwest Airlines Co**. In fact, most carriers seem to either do one or the other, not both.

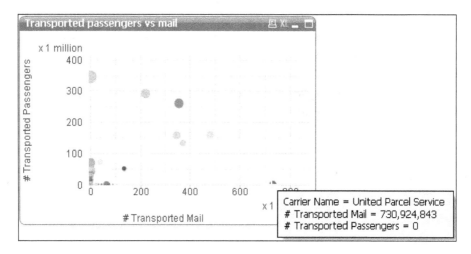

Make a few selections on the **Carrier's Operating Region** listbox and you might gain some interesting insights. Also notice how the unit of the chart's scale changes between selections because we set the **Thousand**, **Million**, and **Billion Symbol** fields.

In our example, we used the **Simple Mode** option to create the expressions for the scatter chart. As the name implies, this allows for only simple expressions to be formulated. We can switch to the Advanced Mode by checking the **Advanced Mode** checkbox on the **Expressions** tab. This will change the view to the regular **Expressions** tab that we saw on earlier charts.

It is important to keep in mind that when dealing with scatter charts the expression that is defined first will be used for the X-axis, the second expression will be used for the Y-axis, and the third expression will always be used to set the bubble size.

Button

Now that we have set up the basic structure and the charts for our analysis sheet, it is time to add a few buttons for the user to interact with. QlikView allows us to execute an action, or a sequence of actions, when a button is clicked.

Let's start with a practical example. During analysis, a user will often want to clear their entire set of selections, or undo and redo single steps in their selection. Follow these steps to add a button that will clear the user's selections:

1. Go to **Layout** | **New Sheet Object** | **Button** in the menu bar.
2. On the **General** tab of the **New Button Object** window, enter Clear Selections in the **Text** input field.
3. Change the **Color** option to *HighCloud brown,* which was defined in the previous chapter and should be part of the custom colors available on the **Color** window.
4. Switch to the **Actions** tab.
5. Click the **Add** button, select the **Clear All** option from the **Action** list on the right, and click on **OK**.
6. Click on **OK** to close the **Button properties** dialog.

We have now created a single button that, when clicked, will clear all current selections.

As we saw while creating the button, there are a wide variety of actions that can be assigned to it. These actions can also be chained, so that one click on a button triggers a sequence of actions. The following screenshot shows a sequence of actions in which we first clear all selections, switch to a predefined sheet, and finally make a selection in a predefined field:

Of course, we still have to create the buttons for undoing and redoing a selection. The corresponding actions are found as **Back** and **Forward**, respectively. Take a minute to create the buttons for these actions as well and align them under the **Current Selections** box. If everything goes correctly, you should end up with something like this:

Test each button to make sure they are doing what they are supposed to do.

Statistics box

A **statistics box** is a convenient way to quickly perform a series of statistics on a single, numeric field. For example, the following shows the total, average, minimum, and maximum distances in a single statistics box.

1. Let's follow these steps to add the statistics box to our analysis sheet: Right-click anywhere on the worksheet and select **New Sheet Object | Statistics Box...**.

2. On the **General** tab, select **Distance** from the **Field** drop-down menu.

3. Double-click on the **Total count** option in the **Displayed Functions** list to remove it, since it will not be relevant.

4. Go to the **Number** tab and select all **Functions** by holding the *Shift* key while clicking on the first and last item in the list. Set their number format to **Override Default Settings** and **Integer**.

5. Click on **OK** to create the statistics box and position it below the buttons we created earlier. Move the bookmark object to a lower position if necessary.

Now whenever we make selections, the **Distance** statistics box will automatically show the various statistics calculated over all the individual records in the fact table.

With the added statistics box object, and after appropriately resizing and positioning objects, the analysis sheet should now look like this:

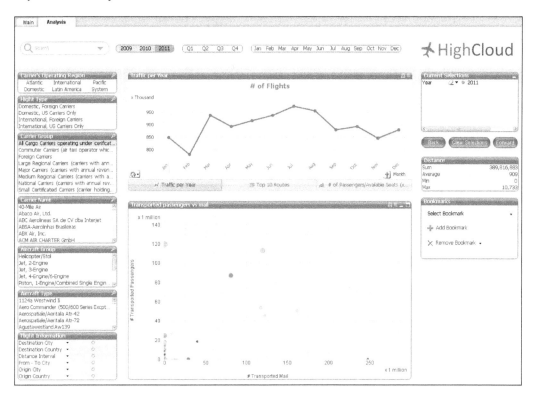

The **Analysis** sheet now meets all the current requirements. The objects we've created while building this sheet are the bar, line, and combo charts, a scatter plot, buttons, and a statistics box. We've also learned how to organize objects using a container and have had a closer look at chart properties, expressions, the expression editor, and expression overview.

Of course, QlikView has many other objects and functions that we can use in our documents. Let's move to our next sheet and discover some more of what QlikView has to offer.

Creating the new Dashboard sheet

Now that we have finished the first iteration of our analysis sheet, it is time to start creating the new Dashboard sheet. As was defined before, we will need to visualize the following KPIs and metrics:

- **Load Factor** %: This gives the number of enplaned passengers versus the number of available seats
- **Performed versus scheduled flights**: This gives the number of flights that were performed versus those that were scheduled
- **Air time** %: This gives the time spent flying versus total ramp-to-ramp time
- **Enplaned passengers** (in millions): This gives the number of transported passengers, in millions
- **Departures performed** (in thousands): This gives the number of flights performed, in thousands
- **Revenue Passenger Miles** (millions): This gives the total number of miles that all passengers were transported, in millions
- **Available Seat Miles** (millions): This gives the total number of miles that all seats (including unoccupied seats) were transported, in millions
- **Market Share**: This is based on enplaned passengers

As we want to have a consistent interface throughout our sheets, let's first set up the new sheet and common objects by following these steps:

1. Add a new sheet by selecting **Layout | Add Sheet...** from the menu.
2. Right-click on the new sheet workspace and select **Properties...**.
3. On the **General** tab, set the **Title** of the sheet to Dashboard and click on **OK** to close the dialog.
4. Right-click on the tab area of the new **Dashboard** sheet and select **Promote Sheet** to place the **Dashboard** sheet to the left of the **Analysis** sheet.

5. Then, navigate to the **Analysis** sheet.

6. Repeat the following process for each of the objects shown in the following screenshot. Right-click and select **Copy to Clipboard | Object**, select the **Dashboard** tab, and right-click on an empty space and select **Paste Sheet Object as Link**.

Now, when we switch between the **Dashboard** and **Analysis** tabs, we can see that the surrounding listboxes, current selection box, buttons, and bookmark object remain consistent; only the contents in the center area of the screen will differ from one tab to the other.

Linked Objects

When we created the **Dashboard** sheet in the previous exercise, we used the **Paste Sheet Object as Link** command instead of **Paste Sheet Object** to paste the copied objects to the new sheet.

The difference between these two options is that using **Paste Sheet Object** creates a copy of the object, which is independent of the source object. The **Paste Sheet Object as Link** option, on the other hand, creates an additional instance (or linked object) of the source object. Any changes made to the layout properties of a linked object will be applied to all other linked objects, with the exception of size and position.

> The size and position of linked objects can be updated manually by right-clicking on the object and selecting **Linked Objects | Adjust Position of Linked Objects**.

When the same object is used in many different places, such as listboxes that appear on every sheet, using linked objects can make maintenance a lot more convenient.

Drag and drop to copy or create linked objects

Objects can also be copied or linked by dragging and dropping.

To copy an object, hold down the *Ctrl* key while clicking on the object's caption and drag the object. A small green plus sign on your cursor will indicate that you are copying an object. Release the mouse cursor on an empty space on the worksheet to create a copy.

Creating a linked object works very similarly to copying an object. Hold down *Ctrl* + *Shift* while clicking on the object's caption. A small chain icon on your cursor indicates that you are linking an object. Drag and release the mouse cursor on an empty space on the worksheet to create the linked object.

Of course, we can also create copies or linked objects on sheets other than the source sheet. To do this, instead of dragging the object to an empty space on the worksheet, drag it to the tab corresponding to the target sheet. The object will appear in exactly the same position as the source object, but on the other sheet.

Let's see how linked objects work by following these steps:

1. On the **Dashboard** tab, create a copy of the **Carrier Name** listbox by holding down the *Ctrl* key, clicking on the header, and dragging the listbox to an empty space on the worksheet.

2. Right-click on the new copy and select **Properties...**.

3. On the **General** tab, set the **Title** of the listbox to `Copy`.

4. On the **Font** tab, set the **Font Style** to **Bold** and the **Font Size** to **16**.

5. Click on **OK** to close the **Properties** dialog.

6. Now, create a linked object of the listbox **Aircraft Group** by holding down *Ctrl + Shift*, clicking on the header, and dragging the listbox to an empty space on the worksheet.

7. Right-click on the new linked object and select **Properties...**.

8. On the **General** tab, set the **Title** to Linked Object.

9. On the **Font** tab, set the **Font Style** to **Bold** and the **Font Size** to **16**.

10. Click on **OK** to close the **Properties** dialog.

The result shows the difference between copied and linked objects. Changes that were made to the copied **Carrier Name** listbox have not been applied to the original, while changes that were made to the linked **Aircraft Group** object were also applied to the original. In fact, they have even been applied to the **Aircraft Group** listbox on the **Analysis** sheet as well.

Let's undo the changes we've made by pressing *Ctrl + Z* until we are back to the original layout.

Beware of deleting linked objects

When deleting a linked object, a popup will ask if you want to only delete the selected object, or if you want to delete all objects. Beware of selecting **Delete All**; all instances of the object will be deleted, even those located on other sheets.

Gauges

After our little detour on linked objects, let's start building the dashboard by adding three gauge charts, one showing a global indicator of **Load Factor** %, the second showing **Performed vs Scheduled Departures ratio** value, and the third showing the **Air Time** % value.

1. Start by adding a new chart object with the **Create Chart** button located on the design toolbar.

2. From the first dialog window, make sure to select **Gauge** as **Chart Type**.

3. In the **Window Title** field, enter Load Factor % as the name of the chart and click on **Next**.

4. This chart type does not make use of dimensions, so we'll skip this window and click on **Next** once more to get to the **Expressions** dialog window.

  If a dimension is present in the gauge chart, the gauge will show the value for the first sorted value in the dimension field. Always ensure, that no dimension is selected. This is especially important to keep in mind when using **Fast Type Change** on charts.

5. Add the following expression in the **Edit Expression** dialog window and click on **OK** to continue:
   ```
   Sum ([# Transported Passengers]) / Sum ([# Available Seats])
   ```

6. The expression that we just created will calculate the percentage of occupied seats compared to those that were available on each flight.

7. The **Label** we'll assign to this expression will be the same as the **Window Title** field that we previously defined: Load Factor %.

8. Click on **Next** three times, until you are at the **Presentation** window, and set the following configuration under the **Gauge Settings** section:
   - **Min** and **Max** values will be 0.5 and 1 respectively
   - From the **Segment Setup** section, we will add two more segments by clicking on the **Add...** button twice
   - Deselect the **Autowidth Segments** checkbox at the bottom of the window

When selected, the **Autowidth Segments** function automatically sizes the segments based on the Min and Max values of the gauge. We want to avoid this as we want to set the values ourselves.

We should now have four segments and will set up each of the four segments is in the following manner:

- **Segment 1**:
  - **Lower Bound**: 0.5
  - **Color** set to **Two Colors Gradient** with the **Base Color** option set to **Red** (R:255; G:0; B:0) and the **Second Color** option set to **Orange** (R:255; G:128; B:0)
  - Color **Gradient Style** option should be set to **Vertical**

- **Segment 2**:
  - **Lower Bound**: 0.625
  - **Color** set to **Two Colors Gradient** with the **Base Color** option set to **Orange** (R:255; G:128; B:0) and the **Second Color** option set to **Yellow** (R:255; G:255; B:0)
  - Color **Gradient Style** option will be set to **Vertical**

- **Segment 3**:
  - **Lower Bound**: 0.75
  - **Color** set to **Two Colors Gradient** with the **Base Color** option set to **Yellow** (R:255; G:255; B:0) and the **Second Color** option set to **Light Green** (R:128; G:255; B:128)
  - Color **Gradient Style** option will be set to **Vertical**

- **Segment 4**:
  - **Lower Bound**: 0.85
  - **Color** set to **Two Colors Gradient** with the **Base Color** option set to **Light Green** (R:128; G:255; B:128) and the **Second Color** option set to **Green** (R:0; G:255; B:0)
  - Color **Gradient Style** option should be set to **Vertical**

In these steps we configured the gauge to display values from 50 to 100 percent. Within this range we defined four separate segments, each with their own color. You may have noticed that we only set the lower boundary for each segment; this is because the upper boundary is automatically defined by the lower boundary of the following segment, or by the upper boundary of the gauge. In our example, **Segment 1** runs from 50 to 62.5 percent (although we specified the limits in decimal form, that is, 0.5 and 0.625), **Segment 2** covers the area ranging from 62.5 to 75 percent, and so on.

The boundaries that we've defined in our example may appear arbitrary. In a real-world situation, ideally we would be setting these boundaries based on targets set by the business.

Let's continue setting up our gauge.

1. Still on the **Presentation** tab, enable the checkboxes corresponding to **Show Scale, Show Labels on Every Major Unit, Hide Segment Boundaries**, and **Hide Gauge Outlines**.

2. Set the value of **Show Scale** to **6 Major Units**, set the value of **Show Labels on Every** to **1 Major Unit**.

3. Click on **Next** three times, until you get to the **Number** dialog window, set the format to **Integer,** and mark the checkbox corresponding to **Show in Percent** (%).

4. Click on **Next** to open the **Font** dialog window and set the **Size** to **8**.

5. Click on **Finish** to create the chart.

The result should be the following gauge chart:

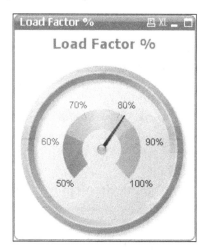

As at this point it's hard to see what exact number the chart is presenting, we'll add a **Text in Chart** attribute to show the corresponding result value using the following steps:

1. Bring up the **Properties...** dialog window again by right-clicking on the **Gauge chart** option and activating the **Presentation** tab.

2. Locate the **Text in Chart** section and click on the corresponding **Add...** button. This brings up the **Chart Text** dialog, which is shown in the following screenshot:

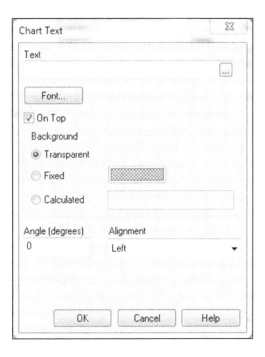

3. We'll add an expression in the **Text** field. Open the **Edit Expression** window by clicking on the **...** button.

4. Type the following expression and click on **OK**:

```
=Num (Sum ([# Transported Passengers]) / Sum ([# Available
Seats]), '##.#%')
```

 It's important to add the equal to sign at the beginning of the expression; otherwise it will not be interpreted as an expression but rather as literal text.

The expression we just created calculates the **Load Factor** % value and formats it as a percentage using the Num() function. Let's finish the text.

5. From the **Chart Text** window, make sure to set the **Alignment** option to **Centered** and change the **Font** option to **Tahoma**, **Font Style** to **Regular**, and **Size** to **14**.

6. Click on **OK** in all of the dialog windows that remain open to apply the changes.

Initially, the added text will be placed at the upper-left corner of the object and we'll need to relocate it. To do that, follow these steps.

1. Activate the gauge object by clicking on the caption. Then, press *Ctrl + Shift*.

   This will show a red border line around the text we want to move as well as around the other chart components (that is, the chart area itself, the legend, if any, and the title).

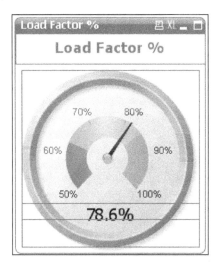

2. Use your mouse to drag the text we added to an appropriate location in the chart and size it accordingly, as shown in the previous screenshot.

> **Resizing chart components**
>
> You can also resize, as well as relocate, other chart components, such as titles and legends, with the *Ctrl + Shift* method described earlier. Be aware that resizing chart component can be a bit "fiddly"; you may have to try a few times before you get it right.

One final adjustment we are going to make to this chart is to remove the caption bar and border and to make the background of the chart fully transparent. To do this we use the following steps:

1. Right-click the gauge chart and select **Properties...**.
2. Navigate to the **Colors** tab and move the **Transparency** slider (under the **Frame Background** option) to **100%**.
3. Navigate to the **Layout** tab and disable the **Use Borders** option.
4. From the **Caption** tab, deselect the **Show Caption** checkbox.
5. Click on **OK** to close the **Chart Properties** window.

The end result should be a gauge chart that looks like this:

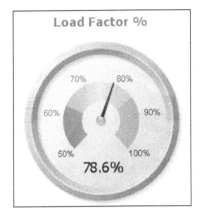

Cloning the object for re-use

Since we have already created a gauge chart with several specific configurations, let's make use of it to create a new one without having to do the whole process over again.

Right-click on the gauge chart we created previously and click on the **Clone** option. A new copy of the object will be created exactly as the previous one; the only thing we will need to do is re-position it and change its expression and title, as well as the text in the chart.

Right-click on the new cloned object and select **Properties...** to make the following changes:

1. In the **General** tab, the **Window Title** field will be Performed vs Scheduled.

2. The expression we will use is:
   ```
   Sum([# Departures Performed]) / Sum([# Departures Scheduled])
   ```

3. The label for the expression is the same as the **Window Title** field: Performed vs Scheduled.

4. On the **Presentation** tab, change the following settings:

   ◦ Set the **Max** value for the gauge to 1.2

   ◦ Set the **Show Scale** value to **8 Major Units**

   ◦ Set the **Show Labels on Every** value to **1 Major Unit**

   ◦ Highlight the **Text in Chart** expression that we added previously and click on the **Edit...** button. Change the expression to:
   ```
   =Num(Sum([# Departures Performed]) / Sum([# Departures Scheduled]), '##.#%')
   ```

Adding Air Time %

The final gauge that we will be creating is the **Air Time** %. Now that you have seen how to create a new gauge and how to clone an existing one, take a chance and see if you can create this gauge yourself:

1. The **Window** and **Expression Title** fields should be `Air Time %`.
2. The expression to calculate the **Air Time** % is as follows:

    ```
    Sum ([# Air Time]) / Sum ([# Ramp-To-Ramp Time])
    ```

3. The **Max** value for the gauge should be `1`.
4. The **Show Scale** value should be set to **6 Major Units**.
5. The **Show Labels on Every** value should be set to **1 Major Unit**.

After applying the changes and rearranging the objects, our dashboard should look like this:

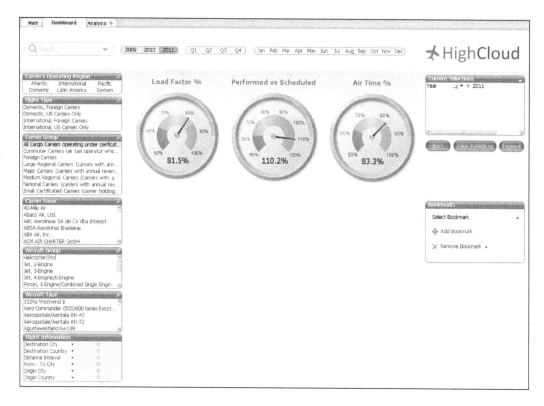

More Gauge styles

While we selected the default speedometer look for our three gauges, QlikView has a few other styles as well. These styles can be selected from the **Styles** tab of the **Chart Properties** dialog.

The following screenshot shows, pictured from left to right and top to bottom, a speedometer, vertical speedometer, thermometer, traffic light, horizontal thermometer, and digital digit gauge. These objects are included in this chapter's solution file on the **Gauge Styles** tab.

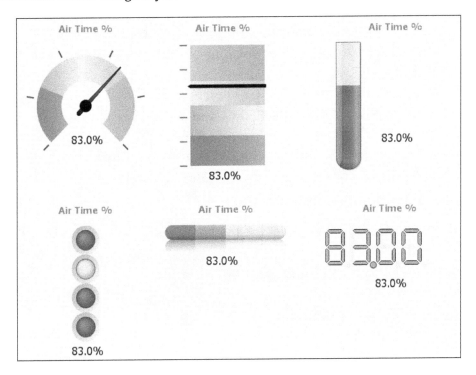

Adding a Text object

Now that we have added the gauges, it is time to add the following four metrics:

- Enplaned passengers (in millions)
- Departures performed (in thousands)
- Revenue Passenger Miles (in millions): the number of miles that paying passengers were transported
- Available Seat Miles (in millions): the total number of miles that paying passengers could have been transported, based on airplane capacity

To display these metrics, we will be using **Text Objects**. A text object can be used to display a static or calculated text and, somewhat counter-intuitively, images as well.

Let's follow these steps to create the first text object that will display Enplaned Passengers:

1. Right-click anywhere on an empty space in the worksheet and select **New Sheet Object | Text Object**.

2. In the **Text** input box enter the following expression:

    ```
    =Num(Sum ([# Transported Passengers]) / 1000000, '#,##0.00')
    ```

3. Move the **Transparency** slider, at the bottom of the window, to **100%**.

4. Go to the **Font** tab and set the **Font** option to **Tahoma**, **Font Style** to **Bold**, and **Size** to **16**.

5. On the **Layout** tab, enable the **Use Borders** checkbox.

6. On the **Caption** tab, check the **Show Caption** checkbox and define the **Title Text** field as `Transported passengers (millions)`.

7. Set the **Horizontal Caption Alignment** option to **Centered**.

8. Mark the **Wrap Text** checkbox under **Multiline Caption**.

9. Click on **OK** to close the dialog window.

After some resizing, the resulting object should look like the following screenshot.

Looking at the steps we went through to create this text object, you may have noticed a few things:

- The expression we used was prefixed with an = (equal to) sign. This is to tell QlikView to treat the entered text as an expression and evaluate it accordingly, instead of treating it as a static text.

- The **Text** object does not have the **Number properties** tab which is often seen on other objects, that is why we used the `Num()` function to properly format the expression output.

- By checking the **Wrap Text** option we can create a multiline caption, this can be very useful when we have long caption texts and limited horizontal space.

Now that we have created the first text object, take a few minutes to create the remaining three. Remember that you can press *Ctrl* and drag the mouse pointer to copy an object, so you do not have to create each text object from scratch. The caption's display and expressions are shown in the following table.

Caption	Expression
Departures performed (in thousands)	=Num(Sum ([# Departures Performed]) / 1000, '#,##0.00')
Revenue Passenger Miles (in millions)	=Num(Sum ([# Transported Passengers] * Distance) / 1000000, '#,##0.00')
Available Seat Miles (in millions)	=Num(Sum ([# Available Seats] * Distance) / 1000000, '#,##0.00')

After creating all four text objects, position them under the gauges in the following manner:

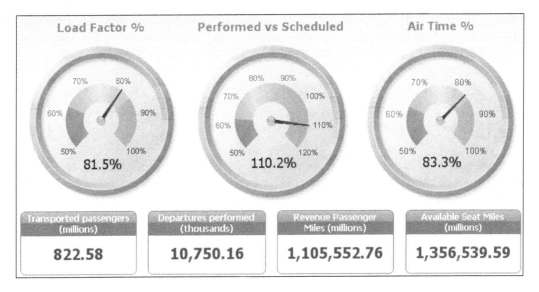

Using a Text Object to display an image

As we said at the start of this section, a text object can also be used to display an image. For example, we may want to display a small "warning" icon on our **Enplaned Passengers** text object whenever the amount of passengers is lower than 1 million. We can achieve that by following these steps:

1. Go to **Layout | New Sheet Object | Text Object** in the menu bar.

2. Do not enter any text; instead, select the **Image** radio button located in the **Background** section and click on **Change...**.

3. Next, navigate to the `Airline Operations\Design` folder and select the `warning.gif` image file.

4. On the **Layout** tab, set the **Layer** to **Top**.

5. Click on **OK** to close the dialog window.

6. Position the warning icon over the **Transported passengers (millions)** text object so that it looks like the following screenshot:

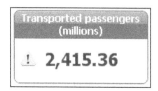

One thing to make note of is the **Layer** setting. By setting it to **Top**, we ensure that the icon is always superimposed over the **Transported passengers (millions)** text object. This is important, otherwise we will not be able to select it using the mouse. Furthermore, if we hadn't set the **100%** transparency in the **Transported passengers** text object, having the icon in a lower layer would prevent it from being visible to the user.

 Remember that we can always access any object's properties via the **Objects** sheet of the **Sheet Properties** dialog (*Ctrl + Alt + S*).

The current result is almost what we want. However, you'll notice that the icon is displayed, even though there are more than 1 million transported passengers, which is the specified limit. Let's take a moment to fix it by using the following steps:

1. Right-click on the warning icon and select **Properties...**.

2. Go to the **Layout** tab and select the **Conditional** radio button under **Show**.

3. Enter the following expression:

```
Sum([# Transported Passengers]) < 1000000.
```

4. Click on **OK** to close the **Text Object Properties** dialog window.

Now the warning icon will only be shown when the specified condition is met; that is, when the number of transported passengers is lower than 1 million. To test it, you can make a few selections, for example, by selecting the year **2011** and **Piston, 1-Engine/Combined Single Engine** from the **Aircraft Group**.

Adding these type of visual cues to our dashboard will make it easier for the users to spot potential issues.

Adding actions to a Text object

Another interesting feature of the Text object is that we can assign actions to it, essentially making it function as a button.

Creating custom-style buttons

By combining a text object with a custom image (or icon) and assigning an action to it, we can create a custom-style button.

We could use this button-like functionality to allow for quick navigation across the document. For example, a text object could be used to switch to a detail sheet when a user clicks on it from a general-level dashboard. In the next example, we will assign an action that will open the **Analysis** sheet when a user clicks on one of the text objects:

1. Go to the **Analysis** sheet.

2. Bring up the **Sheet Properties** window by pressing *Ctrl + Alt + S*.

3. On the **General** tab, set the **Sheet ID** to SH_Analysis and click on **OK** to close the dialog.

4. Go back to the **Dashboard** tab.

5. Right-click on the **Transported passengers (millions)** text object and select **Properties...**.

6. Go to the **Actions** tab and click on the **Add** button.

7. Select the **Layout** option from the **Action Type** section and select the **Activate Sheet** option from the **Action** section. Then click on **OK**.

8. From the **Actions** tab, locate the **SheetID** input box and enter SH_Analysis. Click on **OK**.

9. Repeat steps 5 to 8 for each of the three remaining text objects.

Now, whenever the user clicks on one of the text objects, the **Analysis** sheet will be automatically activated. Note that instead of the sheet's name we used the **Sheet ID** to refer to the **Analysis** sheet. As explained earlier, object IDs are used internally to reference objects.

Gauges can have actions assigned to them as well, using the **Actions** tab of the **Properties** window. A typical use case for this is to let the user drill down to a detailed view for a single KPI or metric. For example, we could create a detailed sheet specifically for the **Load Factor** % metric to analyze it from many different angles (over time, by airline, and so on.) and then reference it from the corresponding gauge chart.

Adding a Pie chart

The final metric that we want to display on our dashboard is Market Share. This metric is based on the number of enplaned passengers per carrier, relative to the total. We will use a **Pie Chart** to visualize this measure. Let's follow these steps:

1. Right-click on an empty space in the sheet and select **New Sheet Object | Chart**.

2. On the **General** tab, select the **Pie Chart** option as the **Chart Type**, the third icon from the left on the bottom row, and click on **Next**.

3. On the **Dimension** tab, select **Carrier Name** from the **Available Fields/ Groups** list and click on the **Add >** button to add it to the **Used Dimensions** list. Click on **Next** to continue.

4. In the **Edit Expression** dialog, enter the following expression and click on **OK**:

   ```
   Sum([# Transported Passengers])
   ```

5. Enter **Market Share** in the **Label** input box.

6. From the **Expressions** tab, enable both the **Relative** and the **Value on Data Points** checkboxes.

7. Click on **Finish** to create the pie chart.

The result should look like the following screenshot:

You will notice that this does not look like a pie chart at all. Maximizing the chart to full screen does show the pie, but it is unusable this way. The reason for this is that there are simply too many dimension values; with hundreds of airlines the chart looks more like a candy-cane than a pie.

Dimension Limits

As the goal of this chart is to display who the big players on the market are, we will modify the chart so that it will only show the airlines that make up 50 percent of the market. All other airlines will be grouped in an **Others** group.

Follow these steps:

1. Right-click on the pie chart and select **Properties...**.

2. Go to the **Dimension Limits** tab.

3. Mark the **Restrict which values are displayed using the first expression** checkbox.

4. Select the **Show only values that accumulate to** radio button and set the corresponding value to **50% relative to the total**. Enable the **Include Boundary Values** checkbox as well.

5. Click on **OK** to close the properties dialog.

The updated pie chart should look like the following screenshot:

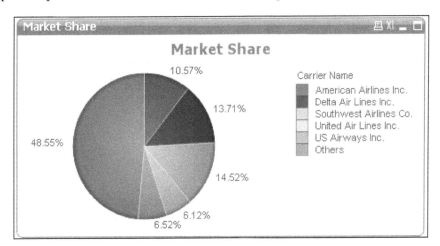

We now see that there are actually only five airlines that, put together, account for 50 percent of transported passengers. Also note that the amounts are shown as a percentage, even though the expression we used returns an absolute number (amount of passengers transported). This is because we have set the **Relative** checkbox on the **Expressions** tab, which makes QlikView automatically calculate the relative amount versus the total amount for each slice.

The **Dimension Limits** option we have used to achieve this is a very useful feature that was introduced in QlikView 11 and enables us to control the number of dimension values handled by a chart.

In the **Dimension Limits** window, all dimensions available in the chart are listed to the left. Simply highlight the desired **dimension** to which the **Dimension Limits** configuration should apply to and select any of the following settings to control the number of dimension values displayed:

- From the **Show only** option we can select **First**, **Largest**, or **Smallest** x values
- From the **Show only values that are** option we can select **Greater than**, **Less than**, **Greater than or equal to**, or **Less than or equal to** a certain value, which can be given as:
  - A percentage relative to the total
  - An exact amount
- From the **Show only values that accumulate to** option we can select a certain value, which can be given as:
  - A percentage relative to the total
  - An exact amount

The difference between the second and the third options is that the former evaluates the individual result corresponding to the dimension's value, while the latter evaluates the cumulative total of that value by either sweeping from largest to smallest or vice versa. This can be used, for instance, in a **Pareto analysis** in which we would present all carriers that make up the 80 percent of the flights, leaving all the rest out.

 Dimension limits can only be set based on the first expression. In case the chart has more than one expression, the rest are not taken into account.

Additional options can be set when working with dimension limits:

- **Show Others**: When this option is enabled, all dimension values that are found off-limits will be grouped into an **Others** category, which will be visible on the chart.
- **Collapse Inner dimensions** can also be used in conjunction with the **Show Others** setting to either hide or display subsequent dimensions' values on the **Others** row, in case the chart has further dimensions than the one highlighted. This is useful mainly on straight tables.

- **Show Total**: When this option is enabled a new total row will be displayed, which is independent from the **Total Mode** control of the **Expressions** tab. This means you can set the **Total Mode** option to perform an operation over the rows, while the **Dimension Total** will hold the actual total, considering on and off-limit dimension values.

 The **Show Total** configuration from the **Dimension Limits** window is virtually treated as a new dimension value. This opens the possibility for having subtotals in a straight table.

- **Global Grouping Mode**: This option determines if the restrictions defined should be calculated considering the inner dimensions or based on a sub total, disregarding the remaining dimensions.

You may have noticed already that this option is not only found on pie charts but on all charts, with the exception of the gauge chart and pivot tables.

Adding the dimension value to the data point values

While looking at the pie chart we created, you may notice that it is somewhat inconvenient to have to switch between the pie slices and the legend to see which slice represents which carrier. Fortunately, there is a little "hack" that we can apply to place the labels on the data points as well. Follow these steps:

1. Right-click on the pie chart and select **Properties...**.

2. Go to the **Expressions** tab, and select **Add** to add a new expression.

3. Enter the following expression:

```
if(count(distinct [Carrier Name]) = 1, [Carrier Name], 'Others')
```

4. For the **Label** field of the expression, enter `Carrier` and enable the **Values on Data Points** option.

5. On the **Presentation** tab, uncheck the **Show Legend** checkbox.

While we're at it, let's apply some extra styling:

1. On the **Font** tab, set the **Size** to **8**.

2. On the **Layout** tab, uncheck the **Use Borders** option.

3. On the **Caption** tab, uncheck the **Show Caption** option.

4. Click on **OK** to close the **Properties** window.

Now the carrier names, along with their respective market share, are shown directly on the pie slices. Since there is no need for a legend anymore, we have disabled it. The expression that we used: `if(count(distinct [Carrier Name]) = 1,` `[Carrier Name], 'Others')` uses a conditional function to check if the current slice corresponds to a single carrier by counting the distinct number of carrier names (`count(distinct [Carrier Name]) = 1`). If the count equals one, the carrier name is used; if not, it must mean that we are looking at the "others" slice of the pie, so the "**Others**" label is applied. Our finished dashboard should now look like the following screenshot:

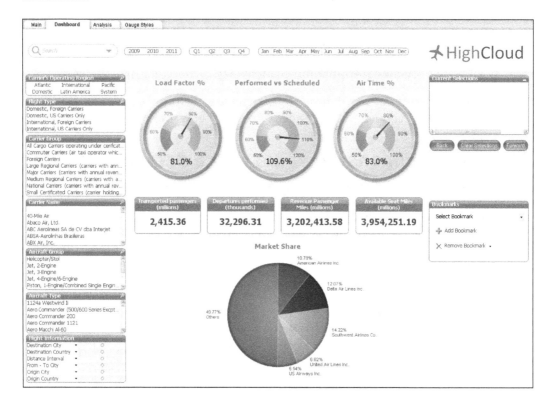

We've now finished the dashboard sheet. We re-used quite a few objects from the **Analysis** sheet, and added gauges, text objects, and a pie chart. Besides creating new objects, we were also introduced to linked objects, actions, and dimension limits.

Let's move on to the last sheet, the **Reports** sheet.

Creating the Reports sheet

Now that we've created our **Dashboard** and **Analysis** sheets, it is time to create the final sheet from our DAR setup: the **Reports** sheet.

As was defined in the requirements, we will be creating the following objects:

- Aggregated flights per month
- KPIs per carrier

But before we begin creating new objects, let's first take a quick look at how we can re-use the expressions that we have created earlier.

Variables

By now you may have noticed that we are using the same expressions in many places. While we could simply type in the same expression every time, this approach has two disadvantages:

- We risk introducing (minor) variations in the way expressions are calculated. For example, one "revenue" expression might contain sales tax while another does not.
- It makes maintenance harder; if the way an expression is calculated changes we'd have to change it in many different places in our document, though the **Expression Overview** window can help us simplify that task.

Enter **variables**. Variables make it easy to store expressions (and other statements, but more on that later) in a central location from where they can be referenced anywhere in our document.

Let's start by creating a variable to store the expression for the **Load Factor** % KPI:

1. Go to **Settings | Variable Overview** in the menu, or click *Ctrl + Alt + V*, to open the **Variable Overview** window.

2. Click on **Add**, enter `eLoadFactor` in the **Variable Name** input box, and click on **OK**.

3. While you would expect it, the new variable is not selected by default after creation. Highlight the **eLoadFactor** variable and enter the following in the **Definition** input box:

   ```
   (Sum ([# Transported Passengers]) / Sum ([# Available Seats]))
   ```

4. In the **Comment** box, enter the description as `The number of transported passengers versus the number of available seats.`

5. Click on **OK** to close the **Variable Overview** window.

6. Go to the **Dashboard** tab.

7. Open the properties for the **Load Factor** % gauge by right-clicking on the object and selecting **Properties...**.

8. On the **Expressions** tab, replace the definition for the **Load Factor** % expression with `$(eLoadFactor)`.

9. On the **Presentation** tab, replace the expression defined in the **Text in Chart** with:

   ```
   =Num($(eLoadFactor), '##.#%')
   ```

10. Click on **OK** to close the **Chart Properties** dialog.

Now, when you look at the **Load Factor** % gauge, you will notice that visually nothing has changed. Behind the scenes, the gauge is now referencing the centrally managed **eLoadFactor** variable. If we were to change this variable in the **Variable Overview** window, the change would automatically be reflected in the gauge.

There are a few points about the steps we used that you will want to take note of:

- **Enclosing the expression in parentheses**: As we want to make sure that the expression always gets calculated in the right order, we enclose it in parentheses. Imagine, for example, we had an expression `vExample` containing `10 + 5` without parentheses. If we were to use that variable in an expression containing a fraction, for example, `$(vExample) / 5`, the wrong result would be returned (`11` instead of `3`).

- **Not prefixing the variable expression with an equals sign**: When the expression in a variable definition is prefixed with an equals sign (=), the variable gets calculated globally. In our example this would mean that the **Load Factor** % value is calculated once for the entire data model. When used in a chart, all dimensions would be ignored and the expression would just return the same global value for each dimension. As we obviously do not want this to happen, in this example we do not prefix our expression with an equals sign.

- **Dollar Sign Expansion**: Enclosing a variable (or an expression) between a dollar sign and parentheses (Dollar Sign Expansion), as we did on the chart's expressions, tells QlikView to interpret the contents, instead of just displaying the contents. For example, `$(=1 + 1)` will not return the static text `1 + 1`, but will return `2`. For now, it's sufficient to note that, when referencing variables, we should use the Dollar Sign Expansion syntax in order for them to be interpreted.

- **The variable name begins with an e**: This is for administration purposes mainly. Having a consistent naming convention helps you, as the developer, as well as any other third-party, to easily identify the purpose of any given variable. We commonly use the following prefixes when naming variables:

    ○ eVariableName: When the purpose of the variable is to serve as an expression definition

    ○ vVariableName: When the purpose of the variable is to store a value, whether static or calculated

The Expression Overview window in action

Of course, creating variables for often-used expressions requires knowing which expressions will be used often. This is not always known beforehand. Fortunately, as we have seen earlier, we can use the **Expression Overview** window to find and replace expressions in a document. Let's see how this approach works by swapping the **Performed vs Scheduled** KPI with a variable:

1. Select **Settings | Variable Overview** from the menu, or click *Ctrl + Alt + V*, to open the **Variable Overview** window.

2. Click on **Add**, enter ePerformedVsScheduled in the **Variable Name** input box, and click on **OK**.

3. Highlight the **ePerformedVsScheduled** variable and enter the following in the **Definition** input box:

    (Sum([# Departures Performed]) / Sum([# Departures Scheduled]))

4. In the **Comment** box, enter Ratio between scheduled and performed flights.

5. Click on **OK** to close the **Variable Overview** window.

6. Open the **Expression Overview** window by selecting **Settings | Expression Overview** from the menu, or by pressing *Ctrl + Alt + E*.

7. Be sure to mark all different expression types from the filtering controls in the window.

8. Click on the **Find/Replace** button.

9. Enter Sum([# Departures Performed]) / Sum([# Departures Scheduled]) in the **Find What** input box.

10. Enter the following in the **Replace With** input box:

    $(ePerformedVsScheduled)

11. Disable the **Case Sensitive** checkbox and click on **Replace All**.

12. Click on **Close** to close the **Find/Replace** dialog.

> Of course, using this method relies on the expressions being entered identically in all places with no spaces out of place. In reality this will not always be the case, you may have to perform a more generic search and perform some manual editing instead of using the **Find/Replace** option.

If everything went well, you should be able to see the updated expressions for the **Performed vs Scheduled** gauge chart on the **Dashboard** sheet.

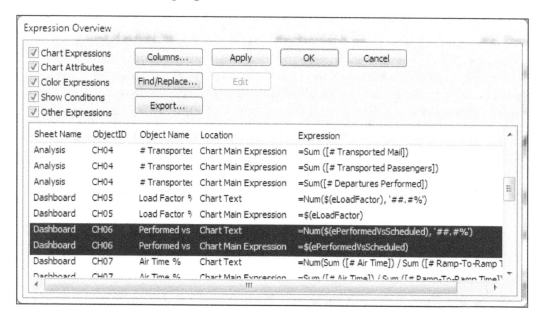

Now that we've seen how to create a new variable and how to retroactively update hard-coded expressions to variables, it is left as an optional exercise to you, the reader, to update the remaining expressions. The rest of this chapter will reference the variables names, but you can also use the expression; the result will be the same.

Should you want to update the remaining expressions, their corresponding definitions are shown in the following table.

Variable name	Expression	Description/Comment
eAirtime	`(Sum ([# Air Time]) / Sum ([# Ramp-To-Ramp Time]))`	Time spent flying versus total ramp-to-ramp time
eEnplanedPassengers	`(Sum ([# Transported Passengers]) / 1000000)`	Total enplaned passengers in millions
eAvailableSeats	`(Sum ([# Available Seats]) / 1000000)`	Total available seats in millions
eDeparturesPerformed	`(Sum ([# Departures Performed]) / 1000)`	Total departures performed in thousands
eRevenuePassengerMiles	`(Sum ([# Transported Passengers] * Distance) / 1000000)`	The total number of miles (in millions) that all passengers were transported
eAvailableSeatMiles	`(Sum ([# Available Seats] * Distance) / 1000000)`	The total number of miles (in millions) that all seats, including unoccupied seats, were transported

Now that we've seen how we can create variables and how we can use them to re-use expressions in our document, let's create the **Reports** sheet.

Copying sheets

While building the **Dashboard** sheet, we created a new sheet and copied linked versions of all the relevant objects. Another approach is to copy an existing sheet and remove all the unnecessary objects from it. We will take this approach to create our initial **Reports** sheet:

1. Go to the **Analysis** sheet.

2. Right-click on an empty space on the worksheet and select **Copy Sheet** from the context menu.

3. Open the **Sheet Properties** window for the new copy of the **Analysis** sheet by pressing *Ctrl + Alt + S*.

4. Rename the sheet by entering `Reports` in the **Title** input box from the **General** tab. Click on **OK** to close the **Properties** dialog.

5. From the new sheet, remove the objects that we do not need: the container object and the scatter chart at the center, and the distance statistics box.

Now we're ready to start adding our reporting objects.

KPIs per airline, origin, and destination country

Our first requirement is to create a table that shows **Load Factor** %, **Performed vs scheduled flights**, and **Air time** %. We also want to be able to alternate the dimension so we can see these KPIs by **Airline**, **Origin Country**, and **Destination Country**.

Cyclic and Drill-down groups

Since we want to be able to switch between dimensions in our table, we will be using a cyclic group. As we saw before, cyclic groups can be used to dynamically switch the dimension of a chart. We can cycle through the dimensions by clicking on the circular arrow, or by selecting a specific dimension by clicking on the drop-down arrow or right-clicking on the circular arrow.

In *Chapter 3, Seeing is Believing*, we described a way to create drill-down and cyclic groups. However, there is another approach, which we will follow here:

1. Select **Settings | Document Properties** from the menu bar to open the **Document Properties** window.

2. Go to the **Groups** tab and click on **New**.

3. Make sure that the **Cyclic Group** radio button is selected in the **Group Settings** dialog window.

4. Enter `Airline_Origin_Destination` in the **Group Name** input box.

5. Select the **Airline, Origin Country**, and **Destination Country** fields from the list of **Available Fields** and click on **Add >** move them under the **Used Fields** list.

6. Click on **OK** to close the **Group Settings** dialog window.

7. Click on **OK** to close the **Document Properties** window.

We have now created a cyclic group called **Airline_Origin_Destination** that we can use as a dimension in our charts.

When creating a cyclic group, make sure to select the **Cyclic Group** radio button from the **Group Settings** dialog window. By default this radio button is set to the **Drill-down Group** value.

A few interesting things to take note of:

- In the **Group Settings** dialog, the **Label** input box can be used to override the display label of the field.

- Besides fields from the data model, an expression can also be used to define a field. This field can be added using the **Add Expression** button and will behave as a calculated dimension.

- In our example, we opened the **Group Settings** dialog via the **Document Properties** window. It can also be opened via the **Edit Groups...** button, which can be found on the **Dimensions** tab of chart objects. This method is probably more convenient, as it fits better into the workflow of creating a new chart object.

A drill-down group is created in the same way as a cyclic group, the only difference is that the fields in the **Used Fields** list are not cycled through, but represent the various levels in a drill-down hierarchy. The top field is the highest aggregation, while the lowest field has the most detail. Our **Traffic per Year** chart uses a drill-down group based on time; its defined hierarchy consists only of two fields: **Year** and **Month**.

It is advisable to ensure that only fields that have a "proper" hierarchy are used for drill-down groups.

Straight table

What is known as a straight table in QlikView is in fact a regular table. It can contain dimensions and calculated expressions, which makes it the ideal candidate to display our KPIs.

> **Straight table versus Table box**
>
> New QlikView developers often confuse the straight table with the table box. While a straight table can contain both dimensions and expressions, a table box, which is created by selecting **Layout | New Sheet Object | Table Box** from the menu bar, can only contain dimensions. This makes it unsuited to display calculated aggregations. The table box can be very useful to display a quick list of possible combinations of fields in the data model, though.

Let's follow these steps to create our KPI straight table:

1. Go to **Layout | New Sheet Object | Chart** in the menu bar.

2. On the **General** tab, select the **Straight Table** option in the **Chart Type** section (bottom right icon).

3. In the **Window Title** input box, place the following expression and click on **Next**:

   ```
   ='KPIs per ' &GetCurrentField(Airline_Origin_Destination)
   ```

4. On the **Dimensions** tab, select the **Airline_Origin_Destination** cycle group from the **Available Fields/Groups** list and double-click on it to move it to the **Used Dimensions** list.

5. Click on **Next** to go to the **Expressions** tab.

6. Create three new expressions using the predefined variables (or enter their expressions directly, if you did not create the variables) and their corresponding labels:
   - **Load Factor %**: $(eLoadFactor)
   - **Performed vs Scheduled flights**: $(ePerformedVsScheduled)
   - **Air time %**: $(eAirTime)

7. Click on **Next** twice to go to the **Presentation** tab.

8. Change the **Alignment** settings for all three expressions so that **Label** and **Data (Text)** are set to **Right** and **Label (Vertical)** is set to **Bottom**.

9. Under the **Totals** section, select the **Totals on Last Row** radio button.

10. Under **Multiline Settings**, mark the **Wrap Header Text** checkbox.

11. Click on **Next** to go to the **Visual Cues** tab.

12. For all three expressions, set the **Upper >=** value to `0.85` and the **Lower <=** value to `0.5`.

13. Click on **Next** to go the **Style** tab.

14. Set **Stripes every Rows** to `1` and click on **Next** to go to the **Number** tab.

15. Set the **Number Format Settings** option for all three expressions to **Fixed to 1 Decimals** and enable the **Show in Percent** (%) checkbox.

16. Click on **Next** three times to go to the **Caption** tab.

17. Tick the **Auto Minimize** checkbox.

18. Click on **Finish** to create the straight table.

The result should look more or less like the following screenshot:

KPIs per Airline			
Airline	Load Factor %	Performed vs scheduled flights	Air time %
Comair Inc.: OH	74.5%	108.6%	71.0%
Seaborne Aviation: SEB	70.6%	97.4%	71.0%
Air Wisconsin Airlines Corp: ZW	71.1%	94.6%	70.7%
Pinnacle Airlines Inc.: 9E	76.3%	96.7%	70.7%
Chautauqua Airlines Inc.: RP	72.6%	96.3%	70.4%
	78.6%	**110.2%**	**83.3%**

Most of the settings will seem pretty straightforward by now, except for the following expression that we used for the **Window Title** input box:

```
='KPIs per ' & GetCurrentField(Airline_Origin_Destination)
```

In this expression, we used the GetCurrentField function. This function takes the name of a cycle or drill-down group, **Airline_Origin_Destination** in our example, and returns the name of the currently active field. When you cycle through the three dimensions, you will notice that the table's caption changes to reflect the active dimension.

 Note that the GetCurrentField function returns the name of the field in the data model, regardless of it being overridden by the **Label** field. If this value needs to be changed, we should either change it directly in the data model or change it by using a conditional function in the expression.

Another thing you may notice in the final result is that some values have a hyphen symbol (–) instead of a value. This happens when the result of the expression is null or missing. We can illustrate this by creating a temporary table box containing the **Airline**, **# Departures Performed**, and **# Departures Scheduled** fields. We will see that, while **40-Mile Air** has actually performed flights, none of them were scheduled. This means that the **Performed vs Scheduled flights** KPI cannot be calculated (division by zero is not possible).

Airline	# Departures Performed	# Departures Scheduled
40-Mile Air: Q5	1.00	0.00
40-Mile Air: Q5	2.00	0.00
40-Mile Air: Q5	3.00	0.00
40-Mile Air: Q5	4.00	0.00
40-Mile Air: Q5	5.00	0.00
40-Mile Air: Q5	6.00	0.00
40-Mile Air: Q5	7.00	0.00
40-Mile Air: Q5	8.00	0.00
40-Mile Air: Q5	9.00	0.00
40-Mile Air: Q5	10.00	0.00
40-Mile Air: Q5	11.00	0.00
40-Mile Air: Q5	12.00	0.00
40-Mile Air: Q5	13.00	0.00
40-Mile Air: Q5	14.00	0.00

Note that, in a table box, each possible combination of values resulting from the enabled fields will occupy one row. All table records in the data model resulting in the same combination of values are grouped into a single row. In our example, **40 Mile Air** could have 10 records with **1.00 Departures Performed** and these will all be grouped into a single row in the table box.

If we want an exact count of the number of rows for each combination of dimensions, we need to use a straight table and include the count function as an expression.

Not all expressions are numbers

A nice feature of straight tables (and pivot tables as well) is that not all expressions need to be numbers. Take a look at the **Expressions** tab of the **Chart Properties** window and you'll see a drop-down menu labeled **Representation**. By default this is set to **Text**, but there are other interesting options:

- Image: This option works in the same way as the text object we used earlier. For example, we could use this setting to display an upward arrow when a certain indicator is showing positive results, or a downward arrow in case of negative performance.

- Circular Gauge: When using this option, we are able to embed a circular gauge chart, similar to the ones we added to the **Dashboard** sheet, into the table cells. The in-cell chart will keep most of the functionality that a typical gauge chart offers.

- Linear Gauge: A circular gauge takes up quite a bit of vertical space, making it less suited for use within tables. The linear gauge, which mainly occupies horizontal space, doesn't share this downside and is therefore better suited for use within table cells.

- Traffic Light Gauge: This option shows a traffic light with the corresponding value lit up. Alternatively, this can show a single light with the associated color of the expression's value.

- LED Gauge: This option shows the expression's value using an LED-style display.

- Mini chart: This option displays a trend using a line-based (sparkline, line with dots, and dots) or bar-based (bars and whiskers) mini chart. It requires an additional dimension on which the trend is based, for example, month.

- Link: This option is used to enable hyperlinking in the table cells. In this case a `<url>` tag must be used within the expression to separate the cell display text and the actual link. For example: `=Company &'<url>'& [Company URL]`.

These options are useful to add visual cues to the otherwise plain table and help the user spot trends quickly within the table.

The following screenshot shows a table with a linear gauge, a traffic light, and mini chart embedded in the cells. This object is included on the **Other representations** tab in this chapter's solution file.

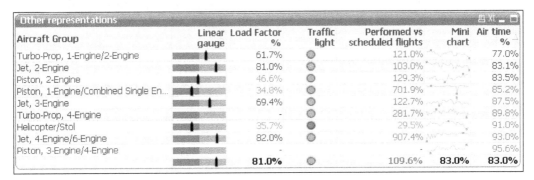

Aircraft Group	Linear gauge	Load Factor %	Traffic light	Performed vs scheduled flights	Mini chart	Air time %
Turbo-Prop, 1-Engine/2-Engine		61.7%		121.0%		77.0%
Jet, 2-Engine		81.0%		103.0%		83.1%
Piston, 2-Engine		46.6%		129.3%		83.5%
Piston, 1-Engine/Combined Single En...		34.8%		701.9%		85.2%
Jet, 3-Engine		69.4%		122.7%		87.5%
Turbo-Prop, 4-Engine		-		281.7%		89.8%
Helicopter/Stol		35.7%		29.5%		91.0%
Jet, 4-Engine/6-Engine		82.0%		907.4%		93.0%
Piston, 3-Engine/4-Engine		-		-		95.6%
		81.0%		109.6%	83.0%	83.0%

Note that when tables are exported to Excel, images such as gauges or mini charts will not be included in the export.

Pivot tables

Moving on to our second requirement for the report sheet, we now have to create a table that shows enplaned passengers and departures performed across the **Carrier Group**, **Airline**, **Year** and **Month** dimensions. This table should show totals for each year, and subtotals for each carrier group.

To create this table we will use a pivot table, which offers more flexibility over a straight table when working with multiple dimensions. Let's follow these steps to create our table:

1. Right-click on an empty space in the worksheet and select **New Sheet Object | Chart**.

2. On the **General** tab, select the **Pivot Table** option in the **Chart Type** section (top-right icon) and click on **Next**.

3. On the **Dimensions** tab, select **Carrier Group, Airline, Year**, and **Month** from the **Available Fields/Groups** list and add them to the **Used Dimensions** section by clicking the **Add>** button.

4. In the **Edit Expression** dialog enter the previously defined expression for **Enplaned Passengers** $(eEnplanedPassengers), and define the **Label** field as Enplaned passengers (millions).

5. Add a second expression to calculate departures performed: $(eDeparturesPerformed), and define the corresponding **Label** as Departures Performed (thousands).

6. Click on **Next** twice to go to the **Presentation** tab.

7. Add a drop-down selection box for the **Carrier Group, Airline**, and **Year** dimensions by selecting them in the **Dimensions** and **Expressions** listbox and checking the **Dropdown Select** checkbox.

8. In the same way, enable the **Show Partial Sums** checkbox for the **Carrier Group** and **Airline** dimensions.

9. The **Enplaned passengers (millions)** and **Departures performed (thousands)** expressions will have the **Alignment** label set to **Right**.

10. Mark the **Wrap Header Text** checkbox and set the **Header Height** option to 3.

11. Click on **Next** three times to go to the **Number** tab.

12. For the **Enplaned passengers (millions)** expression, set the **Number Format Settings** option to **Fixed to** and set it to **3 Decimals**.

13. For the **Departures performed (thousands)** expression, set the **Number Format Settings** option to **Fixed to** and set it to **2 Decimals**.

14. Click on **Next** three times to enter the **Caption** tab.

15. Enable the **Auto Minimize** checkbox.

16. Click on **Finish** to create the pivot table.

Once the pivot chart is created it will initially have all dimension values collapsed, and only the first one will be visible. Use the plus icons to the side of each dimension cell to expand it to the underlying level of aggregation. When a dimension value is expanded, you can use the minus icon to collapse it.

Because we set the **Drop-down Select** option on **Carrier Group**, **Airline**, and **Year**, we can open a pop-up listbox by clicking on the downward arrow in the header of these fields. In big pivot tables, this makes searching for particular dimension values a lot easier.

By right-clicking on the column header and selecting **Expand all** or **Collapse all**, we are able to expand/collapse all corresponding dimension values at once.

One of the advantages of pivot tables is the ability to not only list dimension values as rows, but display them as columns as well, creating a cross-table:

1. Expand any of the **Carrier Group** values to show the **Airline** column.

2. Now, expand any of the **Airline** values to show the **Year** column.

3. Click and drag the **Year** column to place it above the **Enplaned passengers (millions)** column; this should place all the corresponding values at the top horizontally. It is worth noting that it can sometimes require a bit of patience to get the field placed in the right location.

The resulting pivot table should look like the following screenshot.

Enplaned passengers (millions)						
Year		2009		2010		2011
Carrier Group		Enplaned passengers (millions)	Departures Performed (thousands)	Enplaned passengers (millions)	Departures Performed (thousands)	Enplaned passengers (millions)	Departures Performed (thousands)
Commuter Carriers (air...	12.691	749.76	12.531	730.85	12.370	733.96
Foreign Carriers	67.966	561.50	71.336	585.75	75.025	595.57
Large Regional Carriers...	7.605	234.44	1.551	70.46	0.400	41.01
Major Carriers (carriers...	617.952	7,165.88	606.961	6,567.00	599.764	6,129.19
Medium Regional Carri...	0.284	7.84	0.623	17.19	1.201	25.15
National Carriers (carri...	74.068	1,466.55	108.726	2,210.71	130.076	2,663.80
Small Certificated Carri...	5.667	587.45	4.808	590.42	3.740	561.46
-	0.016	0.37	-	-	-	-
Total	786.250	10,773.78	806.536	10,772.38	822.576	10,750.16

In many ways, the pivot table is similar to the straight table. However, you may notice that there are a few differences:

- In a pivot table, expressions can be "rolled up" with subtotals (using the **Show Partial Sums** setting) for different levels.

- It is possible to drilldown to a deeper level by clicking on the expand icons. This can be overridden, however, by enabling the **Always fully expanded** checkbox on the **Presentation** tab, which will make the table to always show all possible dimension values.

- A cross-table can be created by dragging dimensions, like we just did with the **Year** dimension. We can prevent this from happening by unchecking the **Allow Pivoting** checkbox on the **Presentation** tab of the **Chart Properties** window.

Auto minimize

We have now created two chart objects in our **Reports** sheet, a straight table and a pivot table. These two tables do not necessarily need to be consulted at the same time. Additionally, these objects would both benefit from being sized as large as the screen space allows, so it's a good idea to display them one at a time.

Fortunately, while creating the tables we enabled the **Auto Minimize** option (located on the **Caption** tab) for both of these objects. When the **Auto Minimize** option is set for an object, it is automatically minimized whenever another object is restored. For this to work, the corresponding objects must have the **Auto Minimize** option enabled.

Let's make sure that both objects can utilize the maximum amount of space by following these steps:

1. Minimize both the straight table and pivot table.
2. Position and resize the minimized tables in the space between the buttons and the **Bookmarks** object.
3. Now, restore the straight table by double-clicking on its minimized icon.
4. Resize the table so that it occupies all the available space in the center of the screen.
5. Next, restore the pivot table by double-clicking on its minimized icon. At this point, the straight table should be automatically minimized; if it is not, then check the **Auto Minimize** checkbox on the **Caption** tab for both objects.
6. Expand the fields in the pivot table and size it so that it uses all available space in the center of the screen.

The resulting **Reports** sheet should look like the following screenshot:

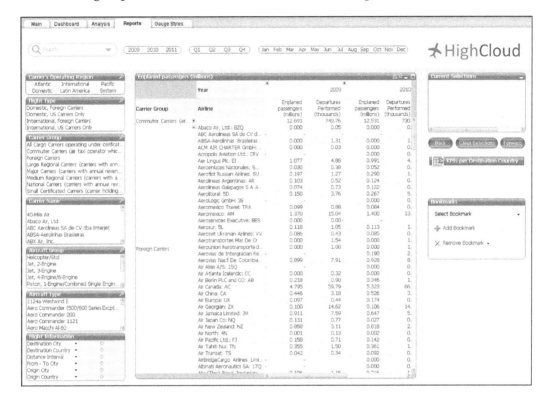

The Report Editor window

Our observant readers may have noticed that the menu bar also includes a **Reports** option. If we did not need it to create these reports, what does it do then?

While the "reports" we created in the **Reports** sheet show detailed information in tabular form, they are limited to single tables. Another disadvantage is that these reports can only be shared with others that have access to the QlikView document, or by exporting them to Excel, in which case proper formatting will be lost.

Enter the **Report Editor**. The **Report Editor** window lets us design static reports that can be used for printed distribution or saved to PDF files. While the Report Editor is far from being a pixel-perfect reporting solution, it can be quite useful to quickly create some static reports.

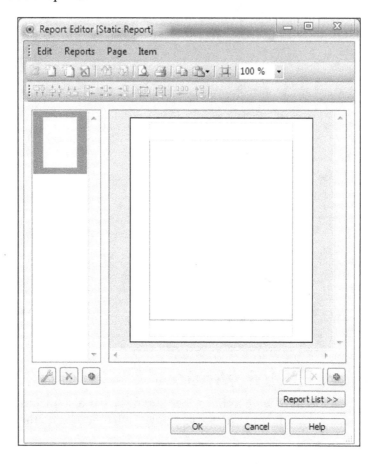

Let's see how the **Report Editor** window works by building a small report:

1. Go to **Reports | Edit Reports** in the menu.

2. From the **Report Editor** window, click the **Add...** button to create a new report.

3. Enter Static Report as the **Name** for our new report and click on **OK**.

4. Click on the **Edit>>** button to begin editing the report.

We are now shown a single, empty report page. We can add objects to this page by simply dragging them from our QlikView document. The implication of this is that, to display an object on our report, it must also exist within our document.

 In the following example, we will be using objects that we have already created on our **Dashboard**, **Analysis**, and **Report** tabs. In your own environment, you might create a separate, hidden tab where you create and store objects that are exclusively used for static reports. Such objects could be formatted differently as well. For example, where we would want sort and selection indicators on our objects used on a dashboard, we would want to suppress these on the "reporting" object. That way, they are not shown in the static report.

We will now add a few objects to our empty report:

1. Drag the **Flight Type** listbox from the app and into the **Report Editor** window.

2. Go to the **Dashboard** tab and drag the **Market Share** pie chart into the **Report Editor** window.

3. Next, go to the **Analysis** tab and drag the **Traffic per Year** line chart into the **Report Editor** window.

4. Select **Page | Page Settings** from the menu bar of the **Report Editor** window.

5. Activate the **Banding** tab and check the **Loop page over possible values in field** checkbox.

6. Select **Flight Type** from the drop-down box and click on **OK**.

7. Click on **OK** to close the **Report Editor** window.

We have now created a very simple report that loops over all values in the **Flight Type** field and creates a single page showing the corresponding **Flight Type**, **Market Share**, and **Number of Flights**. A shortcut to the report is placed under the **Reports** menu.

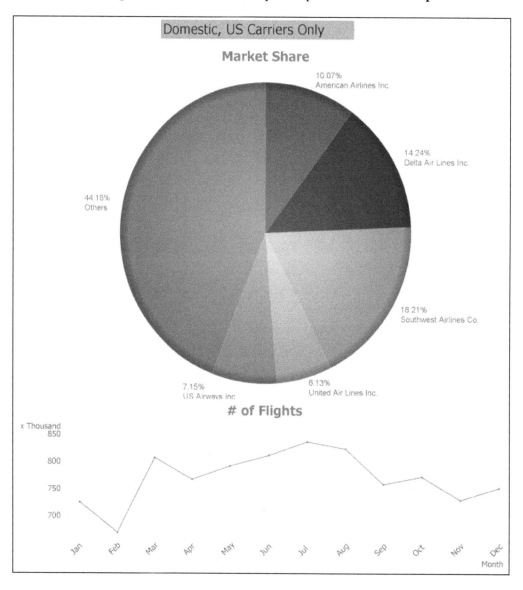

Other options in the **Report Editor** window to take note of:

- **Single versus multi page**: When creating a new page for a report, we can decide if it should be single page, or multi page. The multi page version is useful for printing tables that wrap over multiple pages.

- **Report Settings | Header/Footer**: It is used to set headers and footers for our report. It has a few default variables that can be shown, such as page number, date, time, filename, report name. An image can be included as well; this can be useful to add a logo on our reports.

- **Report Settings | Selections**: Instead of basing our report on the current selection in our document, we can also clear all selections or define a bookmark as a starting point. Besides selections, we can use the `Banding` function to loop the report over all possible values of a field. By setting `Banding` at the report level, instead of applying it to a single report page, it is applied to all pages in the entire report.

Although it is technically a "static report", it's also dynamic because the report output, either a printed page or a PDF file, will be generated the moment the user executes the report by selecting it from the **Reports** menu. This means that all selections the user has in place when creating the report will also be applied to the output, unless otherwise specified via the **Report** settings.

Now that we have created our **Reports** sheet and have created a static report, this chapter is almost at its end. The new objects we encountered in this section are the straight table, table box, and pivot table. Besides these objects, we also learned about variables, cyclic and drill-down groups, auto minimizing, and the Report Editor.

Now let's go to the final part of this chapter, in which we will take a short look at some of the objects that have not been covered in detail.

Other charts

Over the course of this chapter, we looked at the most common charts found within QlikView. There are, however, some charts that we did not use, and we will use this final section to take a quick glance at them. Do not worry though; with the knowledge you picked up earlier in this chapter you should have no problem creating these charts as well. Examples of these charts are also included on the **Other Charts** tab of this chapter's solution file.

Radar Chart

The **Radar Chart** can be used to depict information that is cyclical in nature. For example, the following screenshot illustrates the number of enplaned passengers per month. In this example you can clearly see that travel increases during the summer months:

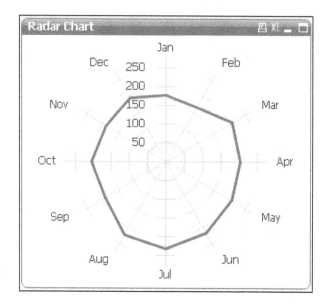

Mekko Chart

The **Mekko Chart** is basically a bar chart with the ability to handle an additional dimension. Our example, shown in the following image, displays the number of enplaned passengers by **Flight Type** and **Year**. The width of the bar is determined by the relative amount versus the total, considering the first dimension: **Flight Type**; and the segment distribution within the bar is determined by the relative amount versus the total, considering the second dimension: **Year**. Looking at this chart we can clearly see that most passengers are being transported on **Domestic, US Carrier Only** flights, and that the number of passengers transported is roughly equally distributed over the years.

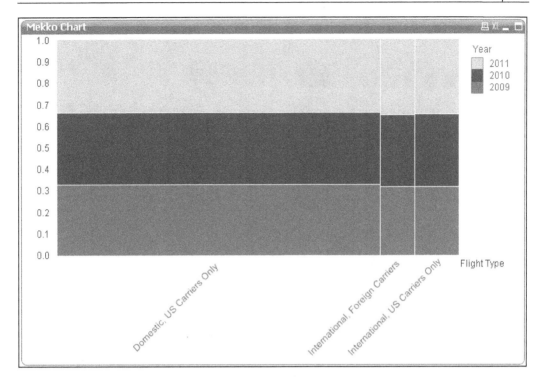

Grid Chart

A **Grid Chart** can contain three different dimensions. In the following example, we've used the **Year**, **Quarter**, and **Flight Type** dimensions. The bubble size represents the number of transported passengers. By taking a closer look, and probably with some imagination, we can spot the same discoveries we made in the first two charts. Bubble sizes are bigger in **Q2** and **Q3**, indicating increased travel during the summer. We can also easily see that most passengers are being transported on **Domestic, US Carriers Only** flights. Additionally, we can see how **Q3** has been smoothly increasing over the last three years.

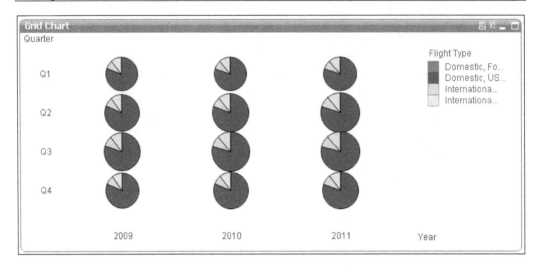

Funnel Chart

A **Funnel Chart** is often used in sales reports to visualize the "sales funnel", that is, which sales opportunities are in which phase of the sales process. The following screenshot shows an example chart that shows the various stages in the sales process and how many clients are present in that phase:

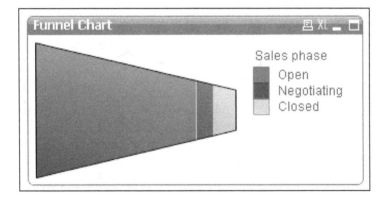

Block Chart

A **Block Chart** can be used to display hierarchical information, by displaying blocks within blocks. In our example, the size of the block corresponds to the number of passengers that were transported. Each block represents a destination city, and they are all grouped into bigger blocks according to their corresponding countries.

In this example we can clearly see that the majority of passengers have arrived somewhere in the **United States**. Within the US, we can see that **Atlanta, GA** and **Chicago, IL** are the most popular destinations.

By comparing blocks within the chart, we can see that the combined total number of people traveling from US to **Canada, Mexico**, and the **United Kingdom** is smaller than the number of people traveling to **Atlanta, GA**.

Trellis Chart

The **Trellis Chart** is not really a separate chart, but a chart option that exists on all charts; with the exception of the straight tables and pivot tables. It creates a grid in which a separate chart is created for each distinct value of the first dimension. To facilitate easy comparisons between charts, each chart's axis uses the same scale.

In the following chart, we have created a chart with two dimensions: **Flight Type** and **Month**. We have enabled the **Trellis Chart** option for the first dimension. The result is a chart that shows, within a grid, a separate chart for each **Flight Type**. Each separate chart shows the **Load Factor** % per **Month**.

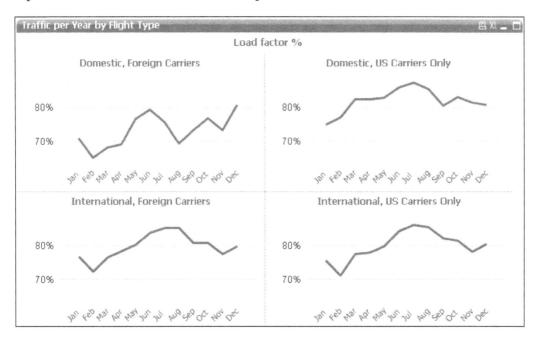

The **Trellis** option can be set by going into the **Chart Properties** of a chart. On the **Dimensions** tab you will find the **Trellis** button; clicking this brings up the **Trellis Settings**, shown in the following screenshot:

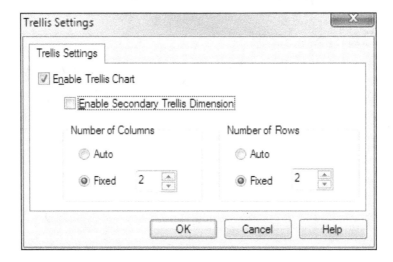

To create a trellis chart, we click on **Enable Trellis Chart**. Optionally, we can manually set the **Number of Columns** and/or **Number of Rows** options.

 With the exception of the trellis and the block chart, you will find that whenever you are thinking of using any of the charts (radar, mekko, funnel, or grid), there is usually a better solution that uses a bar, line, or scatter chart.

Summary

This has been an intense chapter, but you've hopefully achieved a deeper understanding of data visualization in QlikView and familiarized yourself with the basics of building frontend dashboard, analyses, and reports in QlikView.

We started with the **Analysis** sheet, for which we created basic data visualization objects like bar, line, combo, and scatter charts. We also learned how to create container objects, statistics boxes, and buttons, and explored more in-depth chart properties, expressions, the expression editor, and expression overview.

Next we built the **Dashboard** sheet, where we learned how to create gauges, text objects, and pie charts, while also learning about linked objects, actions, and dimension limits.

The final sheet that we built was **Reports**; here we learned how the straight table, pivot table, and table box objects are created. Additionally, we also learned about variables, cyclic and drill-down groups, auto minimizing, and the Report Editor.

We concluded this chapter by looking at some of the chart types that weren't included in our QlikView document, and what the typical use case for these chart types is.

9
Advanced Data Transformation

In this chapter we will dive into advanced transformation functions and techniques available through QlikView's extraction engine. This will allow you, as a developer, to finely process the source data and turn it into a clean design, while at the same time keeping an efficient script.

The goals of this chapter are:

- To provide an overview of the most commonly used data architectures that can ease QlikView's development and administration
- To describe the available functions for data aggregation
- To learn how to take advantage of some of QlikView's most powerful data transformation functions.

Data architecture

Now that we have a decent amount of QlikView development experience under our belt, we will introduce the concept of data architecture. This refers to the process of structuring the different layers of data processing that exist between the source tables and the final document(s). Having a well-designed data architecture will greatly simplify the administration of the QlikView deployment. It also makes the QlikView solution scalable when new applications need to be developed and when the QlikView environment grows. There can be a lot of different data architectures, but in this section we will discuss two of the most commonly used in QlikView enterprise deployments.

Two-stage architecture

The following diagram depicts the two-stage architecture:

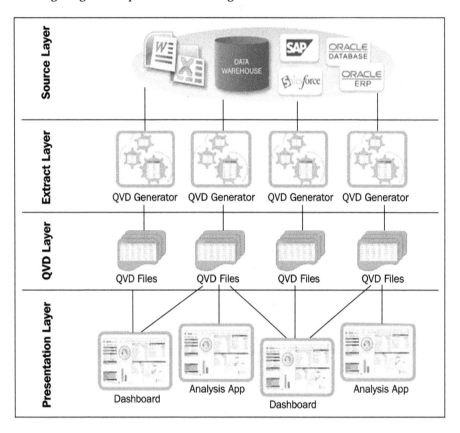

The two-stage architecture is composed of the following layers:

- **Source Layer**: composed of the source databases and original tables.
- **Extract Layer**: composed of QlikView documents, containing mainly script. These are used to pull the data from the source layer and store it into QVD files. The extraction scripts can either create a straight copy of the source tables to store them into the corresponding QVD files, or perform certain transformations before storing the result.

- **QVD Layer**: the set of QVDs resulting from the Extract Layer. These QVDs become the data sources used by the final QlikView document.

- **Presentation Layer**: the set of QlikView documents used to provide the data to the end user. These QlikView files will use the QVDs created in the previous layer as data sources, and sometimes perform additional transformations to create the final data model. No database calls are performed from the presentation layer.

The advantages of using this approach and having a QVD Layer are reuse and consistency. This approach promotes re-use because, in deployments where multiple documents make use of the same source data, the original database (Source Layer) is not overloaded with redundant requests. At the same time, the re-use process ensures consistency across all different QlikView documents that make use of the same data.

 If you look closely, you'll notice that this architecture is the one we've been using in the previous chapters, since we've mainly loaded data into our QlikView document from previously-created QVDs.

This approach is mainly used when the source data is good enough to be included into the QlikView data model with little or no modification. However, when major data transformation is needed, the administration gets a little messy with this architecture since it is not clearly defined at which stage these transformations take place.

Three-stage architecture

Now, let's take a look at the three-stage architecture:

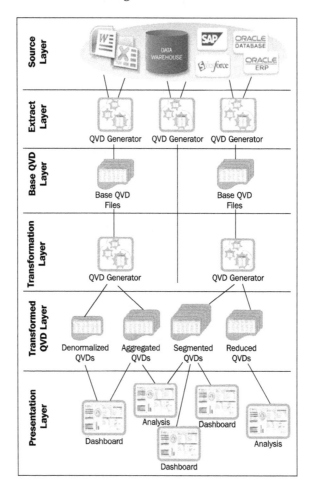

In this architecture, two additional layers are added: **Transformation Layer** and **Transformed QVD Layer**. The role of these two additional layers is to hold all transformations that need to be performed upon the source data before it can be integrated into the target data model.

This also suggests that all base QVDs will ideally keep a straight copy of the source table, which will optimize the extraction process. Then, the Transformation Layer, in which several base QVDs will be combined to create denormalized QVDs, performs any required aggregation or segmentation, and adds new calculated fields or composite keys to prepare the transformed QVDs for a clean and simple load into the final data model.

Since the documents in the Presentation Layer will use the transformed QVDs, and sometimes some base QVDs that required no modification, and will (ideally) read them "as-is", optimized loads will be ensured at this stage.

QVDs can also be reused with this architecture when the data model of two or more QlikView documents require the same source data.

 This approach is the one we will work from this point onwards since new transformations will be made to our base QVDs.

A well-designed data architecture, as those presented in this section, can also enable the possibility of having different QlikView teams working at different stages. For example, IT developers can prepare the base and transformed QVDs, while business teams can make use of those to build the end documents without requiring access to the source database.

Setting up our environment

Now that we've discussed the advantages of using the three-stage architecture, let's take a moment to set up our Windows folder structure following the described guidelines.

By copying the files corresponding to this chapter into your **QlikView Development** folder, you will have a structure like this:

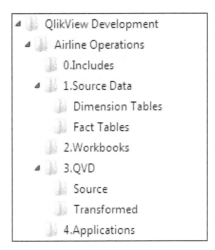

The **0.Includes** folder is used to store re-usable code that is called from the end documents via an `Include` statement. The **1.Source Data** folder represents the Source Layer; this folder is used because our source database is composed of CSV files but wouldn't be required otherwise. The **2.Workbooks** folder holds all QVD Generators (QVW files) for both the Base Layer and the Transformation Layer. The **3.QVD** folder is used to store the resulting QVD files from both the Base Layer (using the **Source** subfolder) and the Transformation Layer (using the **Transformed** subfolder). The **4.Applications** folder represents the Presentation Layer.

Inside these folders, you will find all source tables in CSV format, as well as the extract QVWs and the base QVDs used in previous chapters. We will work directly with the Transformation Layer in the coming sections.

Loading data already stored in QlikView

The first lesson in advanced data transformation will be about optimizing loads when processing data. Now, we will describe yet another way of reading source tables, but this time the "source" will be QlikView itself. There are different cases in which this approach will prove useful and we will describe two scenarios to perform it:

- Accessing data already stored in a QlikView data model (QVW file) from a separate QlikView document. We will call this approach *Cloning a QlikView data model*.

- Accessing data from the same QlikView document in which the data model resides. We will call this approach *Loading from RAM*.

Cloning a QlikView data model

This concept refers to the ability of replicating the data model of an already created QlikView document and placing it into another QlikView document without accessing the original data source. In technical terms, it's a **Binary load**. Once the data model is cloned by the second QlikView document, it can be manipulated further, integrated into a bigger data model (that is, adding more tables to it), or even reduced by removing some of its tables or data.

Suppose we have a QlikView file, with an already constructed data model and all of the composing tables properly associated. We now want to use this same model in another QlikView document, adding just a few more tables. The process for binary loading a QVW is as follows:

1. Create a brand new QlikView document and save it to the disk.

2. Open the **Edit Script** window (*Ctrl + E* or **File | Edit Script...**)

3. Click on **QlikView File...** button, located in the **Data** tab.

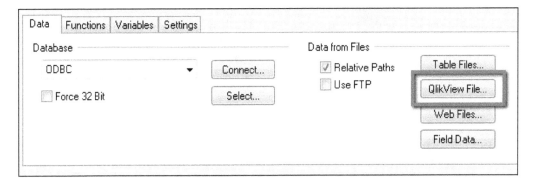

4. Browse to the QlikView file we want to read and click on **Open**.

5. A new script statement will be created at the top of the active script tab, which will be something like `Binary [file name.qvw];`

 The `Binary` statement must be the first statement to be executed in the script, so it has to be always at the top of the first (left-most) script tab. Also, only one binary load is allowed in a QlikView script.

6. At this point, we can add more tables to the already-loaded data model as we would normally do. After reloading the script, the data model will now be in the new QlikView document, along with any other added tables.

 A `Binary` load statement is the fastest way to load data into a QlikView document.

In the environment we've been working throughout the book, can you find a use case for a `Binary` load? Which would it be?

I can think of one. For example, we have an initial QlikView document with the `Airline Operations` data. Based on this initial data model, we can create a new QlikView document, to which we will only add the `Employment` data. As a result, we would have one `Airline Operations` document accessed by certain users, and another with the same data but with additional information about airline employment, which might be treated as confidential and accessed by another group of users.

As a side note, we must point out that binary loads are used in yet another approach to data architecture. We will not discuss it in-depth, but suffice to say that the new layer is composed of QlikView documents consisting of only a data model without any frontend objects, referred to as "QlikMarts". These QlikMarts then become the source for the QlikView documents in the Presentation Layer.

Loading from RAM

In some cases, we will need to read the same table more than once in a single script execution. This means, querying the database (or QVDs) and pulling data from it, and then reprocessing that same data after the first read in order to make it adequate for our data model. Since the data is being stored in RAM after each query during the script execution, we can use that RAM-stored data instead of going directly to the original data source. This is accomplished via a **Resident load**.

Resident load

The keyword `Resident` can be likened to the keyword `From` in a query. The difference is that the `Resident` keyword is used to reference the data in RAM model, that is, all the tables that have been previously read in the preceding queries of the same script. The process for achieving this is as follows:

1. First, we must load data from a data source (any database or table file described in the previous sections), so we create the corresponding query in the script. An example would be:

   ```
   SalesData:
   LOAD
       InvoiceNumber,
       Date,
       SalesPerson,
       Department,
       Amount as InvoiceAmount;
   SQL SELECT * FROM DataBaseName.dbo.Sales;
   ```

Note that we have defined a table name, at the beginning of the query, so that we can use it to reference the table later on. We have also renamed the `Amount` field to `InvoiceAmount`.

2. Next, we add a subsequent query, in the same script, to access the table already in RAM using the `Resident` keyword. In this case, we will also aggregate the data using a `Group By` clause, which is a data transformation technique explained later in this chapter.

```
SalesTotals:
LOAD
   Department,
   Sum(InvoiceAmount) as TotalAmount
Resident SalesData
Group By Department;
```

Note that, when referencing a table that is now part of the QlikView data model, we must use the field names with which they have been defined, which might not necessarily be the same names as in the source table. In this case, we are using `InvoiceAmount`, a name that was defined in the previous query. The same applies for table names.

As a result, we will have two tables in our data model; one with all the data at an atomic level, the product of the first query, and the other as an aggregated version of the `SalesData` table with totals by `Department`, the product of the `Resident`load we constructed in conjunction with the `Group by` statement.

Aggregating data

While QlikView shines in dealing with massive data volumes, sometimes we just do not need to load everything at an atomic level. Data aggregation can, for example, be used in deployments where document segmentation by detail is needed, in which case two documents are created to serve different user groups and analysis needs: one document will have all data with the highest level of detail and another one will have a similar data model but with aggregated (reduced) tables. This way, users are better served by keeping a balance between performance and analysis needs.

In this section, we will implement a document segmentation scenario by aggregating the **Flight Data** table to create a second document intended for executive users, who only require summary data.

Aggregating the Flight Data table

When aggregating data, the first step is always to define which dimension fields will be left out and which ones will be kept in the summarized table. We should analyze this question by looking at the data from the ground up, that is, by reviewing each dimension from the most granular to the most general. The following list shows the most important dimension fields in the Flight Data table, sorted by granularity:

- **Airport (Origin** and **Destination)**
- **City**
- **State**
- **Country**
- **Aircraft Type**
- **Aircraft Group**
- **Airline / Carrier**
- **Carrier Group**
- **Region**
- **Month**
- **Quarter**
- **Year**

If we analyze how removing each dimension would individually affect the result of the summarization process, we can find that the most impact would come from removing the **Airport** dimensions, both Origin and Destination, since those are the ones with the greatest granularity. At the same time, we can say that the **Airport** dimension does not add much value to the analyses we are looking to deliver in our document, so it's a good choice to leave it out.

> Dropping dimensions from the data directly impacts the analyses that can be made in the resulting QlikView document. Therefore, the decision to leave out certain fields for the sake of summarization should always be discussed with the end user.

We could remove additional dimensions, for example, **Aircraft Type** or **Carrier**, but as we move up the detail ladder to the most general dimensions, those dimensions become more and more important to accomplish different analyses.

We must add that leaving dimensions out should be a thorough decision process, thinking both in terms of analytical requirements and the aggregation rate we can achieve. For example, removing the Country dimension would not result in any substantial aggregation if we keep the State field. Also, what happens if we remove the Airport dimensions but keep Origin City and Destination City? What happens is, not surprisingly, that the table will not be significantly reduced since both fields keep a close relation and their granularity is almost the same (there is only one airport in most cities). Therefore, and for the sake of simplicity, we will also leave out all city, state, and country fields.

Finally, before proceeding, we should keep in mind how many records the original table has, in order to be able to measure how much reduction we achieved in the summarization. In our case, the `Flight Data` table originally contains 1,256,075 rows.

Moving on to the aggregation process, follow these steps:

1. Create a new QlikView document and save it inside the `2.Workbooks` folder with the name `Transform - Flight Data.qvw`.

2. Go to the **Script Editor** window, click on the **Table Files...** button in the tool pane and navigate to the `3.QVD\Source` folder.

3. Select the `Flight Data.qvd` file and click **Finish** on the **File Wizard** window.

4. From the generated `Load` script, find the lines corresponding to those fields related to origin and destination airports and erase them. The fields we should remove are:

    ◦ `%Origin Airport ID`
    ◦ `%Origin Airport Sequence ID`
    ◦ `%Origin Airport Market ID`
    ◦ `%Origin World Area Code`
    ◦ `%Destination Airport ID`
    ◦ `%Destination Airport Sequence ID`
    ◦ `%Destination Airport Market ID`
    ◦ `%Destination World Area Code Distance`
    ◦ `Origin Airport Code`
    ◦ `Origin City`
    ◦ `Origin State Code`
    ◦ `Origin State FIPS`
    ◦ `Origin State`
    ◦ `Origin Country Code`
    ◦ `Origin Country`

- Destination Airport Code, Destination City
- Destination State Code
- Destination State FIPS
- Destination State
- Destination Country Code Destination Country
- From - To Airport Code
- From - To Airport ID
- From - To City
- From - To State Code
- From - To State

5. Next, from the list of fields we have kept, we need to identify those that are dimensions and those that are measures. Our measure fields are:

- # Departures Scheduled
- # Departures Performed
- # Payload
- # Available Seats
- # Transported Passengers
- # Transported Freight
- # Transported Mail
- # Ramp-To-Ramp Time
- # Air Time

6. The aggregation functions will be applied to these fields, that is, we will sum the # of Departures, or sum the # Transported Passengers. Identify where each of the listed fields are in the created load statement and replace the field name with the following expression:

Sum (*Field Name*) as *Field Name*

where Field Name represents each of the listed measures.

 Be careful not to remove the comma that separates each field definition and remove the comma from the last listed field, before the From keyword.

7. Finally, we will add a Group By clause to the end of the Load statement, and list *all dimension fields* that have been kept in the script, separated by a comma.

8. We will also add a table name preceding the Load keyword.

9. In the end, the `aggregation` script will look like this:

```
Flights:
LOAD
      [%Airline ID],
      [%Carrier Group ID],
      [%Unique Carrier Code],
      [%Unique Carrier Entity Code],
      [%Region Code],
      [%Aircraft Group ID],
      [%Aircraft Type ID],
      [%Aircraft Configuration ID],
      [%Distance Group ID],
      [%Service Class ID],
      [%Datasource ID],
      [Unique Carrier],
      [Carrier Code],
      [Carrier Name],
      Year,
      Period,
      Quarter,
      [Month (#)],
      Month,
      Sum([# Departures Scheduled]) as [# Departures Scheduled],
      Sum([# Departures Performed]) as [# Departures Performed],
      Sum([# Payload]) as [# Payload],
      Sum([# Available Seats]) as [# Available Seats],
      Sum([# Transported Passengers]) as [# Transported
Passengers],
      Sum([# Transported Freight]) as [# Transported Freight],
      Sum([# Transported Mail]) as [# Transported Mail],
      Sum([# Ramp-To-Ramp Time]) as [# Ramp-To-Ramp Time],
      Sum([# Air Time]) as [# Air Time]
FROM
[..\3.QVD\Source\Flight Data.qvd]
(qvd)
Group By
[%Airline ID], [%Carrier Group ID], [%Unique Carrier Code],
[%Unique Carrier Entity Code], [%Region Code], [%Aircraft Group
ID],
[%Aircraft Type ID], [%Aircraft Configuration ID], [%Distance
Group ID],
[%Service Class ID], [%Datasource ID], [Unique Carrier], [Carrier
Code],
[Carrier Name], Year, Period, Quarter, [Month (#)], Month;
```

10. Next, we will just save the changes and reload the script.

The resulting table will turn our 1,256,075 rows into only 100,091. A brief example of what just happened is shown in the following screenshot:

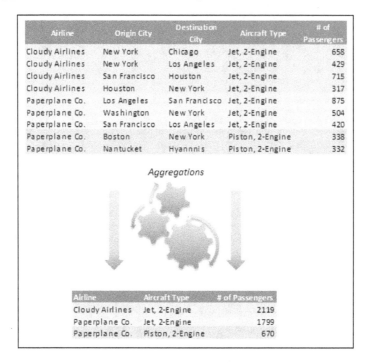

Airline	Origin City	Destination City	Aircraft Type	# of Passengers
Cloudy Airlines	New York	Chicago	Jet, 2-Engine	658
Cloudy Airlines	New York	Los Angeles	Jet, 2-Engine	429
Cloudy Airlines	San Francisco	Houston	Jet, 2-Engine	715
Cloudy Airlines	Houston	New York	Jet, 2-Engine	317
Paperplane Co.	Los Angeles	San Francisco	Jet, 2-Engine	875
Paperplane Co.	Washington	New York	Jet, 2-Engine	504
Paperplane Co.	San Francisco	Los Angeles	Jet, 2-Engine	420
Paperplane Co.	Boston	New York	Piston, 2-Engine	338
Paperplane Co.	Nantucket	Hyannnis	Piston, 2-Engine	332

Aggregations

Airline	Aircraft Type	# of Passengers
Cloudy Airlines	Jet, 2-Engine	2119
Paperplane Co.	Jet, 2-Engine	1799
Paperplane Co.	Piston, 2-Engine	670

Notice how the totals remain the same for both tables.

A smaller table will occupy fewer resources (RAM and CPU) and, therefore, calculations will be faster. If the performance gain attained with data aggregation doesn't mean reducing business value and/or functionality for the end user, then it's a winning approach any day.

The Transformation output

We have loaded the base QVD containing flight data and transformed it by applying aggregations, now what? Well, the next steps would be to store the transformed table, using the store command, into a new QVD file that will reside in the 3.QVDs\ Transformed folder.

After that, a new data model could be created in the Presentation Layer based on the Airline Operations document, but using the newly aggregated QVD and without the Origin and Destination dimensions. This new QlikView document is intended to serve the users who only need summarized information about the Airline Operations document.

Aggregation functions

Of course, QlikView offers more aggregation options than summing. The most commonly used options are shown in the following table:

Function	Explanation	Example
Sum()	Sums numeric expressions. Optionally a DISTINCT qualifier can be added, this will cause the function to ignore duplicate values.	Sum(DISTANCE) Sum(DISTINCT AIR_TIME)
Min()	Returns the lowest value within a numeric range. Optionally a rank can be specified, this will return the nth lowest number. So 2 returns the second lowest number.	Min(DISTANCE) Min(DISTANCE, 2)
Max()	Returns the highest value within a numeric range. Optionally a rank can be specified, this will return the nth highest number. So 2 returns the second highest number.	Max(PASSENGERS) Max(PASSENGERS, 2)
Only()	If the aggregation of a value returns only a single value, that value is returned, otherwise the function returns null. For example, when an expression contains the values {1, 1, 1} then the Only() function will return 1. If an expression contains the values {1, 2, 3} then the Only() function returns null.	Only(SEATS)
MinString()	Similar to the Min() function, but applied to text strings. Also, it does not have the optional rank parameter.	MinString(MANUFACTURER)
MaxString()	Similar to the Max() function, but applied to text strings. Also, it does not have the optional rank parameter.	MaxString(MANUFACTURER)
Concat()	Concatenates all the values of an expression into a single string, which is separated by a delimiter given as a function's parameter. Has an optional DISTINCT qualifier which will set the function to ignore duplicate values.	Concat(AIRPORT_NAME, ';') Concat(DISTINCT MANUFACTURER, ',')
Count()	Counts the number of items in the input expression. Has an optional DISTINCT qualifier that sets the function to ignore duplicate values. Instead of an expression an * (asterisk) can also be used to count the number of rows.	Count(AIRCRAFT_NAME) Count(DISTINCT AIRCRAFT_NAME)

Sorting tables

We will now introduce the `Order By` statement, which is added to a `Load` statement and is used to sort an input table based on certain fields. There is one major condition for the `Order By` statement to work: it must be applied to a `Load` statement getting data from a `Resident` table, not from a table file or any other source.

Some databases can receive `Order By` instructions in the `Select` query, but in this section we will only deal with `Order By` statements on the QlikView side.

The `Order By` statement must receive at least one field name over which the ordering will be performed and, optionally, the sort order (either ascending or descending). If the sort order is not specified along with the field name, the default sort order will be applied, which is ascending.

An example script of an `Order By` statement at play is:

```
Load
  Region,
  Date,
  Amount
Resident SalesTable
Order By Date asc;
```

In this script, we are loading three fields (`Region`, `Date`, and `Amount`) from a previously loaded table, named `SalesTable`, and, as the table is being read, the data is being ordered by `Date` from older to newer records (ascending).

Ordering the Order-By fields

An important point to consider when using the `Order By` statement, is that not only can one field be specified as the sorting value, we can also, for instance, sort the table by `Date` from older to newer and by `Amount` from largest to smallest. The order in which we specify the sorting fields will determine the output of the operation. Take, for example the following two scripts:

```
A:
Load
  Region,
  Date,
  Amount
Resident SalesTable
Order By Date asc,
Amount desc;

B:
Load
```

```
    Region,
    Date,
    Amount
Resident SalesTable
Order By Amount desc,
Date asc;
```

The difference between both scripts is the `Order by` clause. Look closely and you will find that, in script A, the `Date` field takes precedence in the ordering of the data, while in script B, `Amount` is the first ordering field.

Take a moment to think what you would expect as the output of both scripts. You'll discover that the output of each script can be translated to plain English as:

- In script A, the table is first ordered by `Date` from oldest to newest and then, for each date, the corresponding records are sorted by `Amount` in the descending order
- In script B, the table is first ordered by `Amount` of the transaction, biggest amounts at the top, and, for records with the same amount, they get ordered by `Date` from oldest to newest

Normally we will want the table to be sorted by `Date` first and `Amount` as a second sorting value. It's important to take this into account when adding it in to our QlikView scripts.

 As a final remark, remember to drop the table on which the `Resident` load was based if it is no longer needed.

The Peek function

Another tool we'll add to our collection in this set of data transformation techniques is the `Peek` function. The `Peek` function is an inter-record function that allows us to literally peek into previously-read records of a table and use its values to evaluate a condition or to affect the active record (the one being read).

The function takes one mandatory parameter, the field name into which we will "peek", and two optional parameters, a row reference and the table in which the field is located.

For example, an expression like:

```
Peek('Date', -2)
```

This expression will go back two records in the currently-being-read table, take the value on the Date field and use it as a result of the expression.

Or take this other expression:

```
Peek('Date', 2)
```

In this expression instead of "going back" two records, we will take the value in the Date field from the third record from the beginning of the current table (counting starts at zero).

We can also add a table name as the third parameter, as in the following expression:

```
Peek('Date', 0, 'Budget')
```

This expression will return the value that the Date field stores on the first record in the Budget table.

Merging forces

On their own, the Order By statement and the Peek function are already powerful. Now, imagine what happens when we combine both of these tools to enhance our input data. In this section, we will use both of these functions to add a new calculated field to our Employment table.

A refresher

The Employment table provides information regarding the monthly number of employees per airline. The total number is split between part and full time employees, and it also shows the total **FTEs (Full Time Equivalent)**.

The objective

The executives of HighCloud Airlines have asked the QlikView team to create a report that shows the monthly change in number of employees in a line chart to discover and analyze peaks in the employment behavior of each airline.

Getting it done

First, how do we find the total change in number of employees for this month compared to the last? Well, we take the number of employees in the current month and subtract the number of employees we had in the previous month. If the number is zero, it means there was no change (no one fired!), if the number is greater than zero, it means we have new hires in the house; last, and hopefully the least, if the number is less than zero, it means we will be missing some colleagues.

To add this field to our Employment Statistics table, and following the best practices we previously discussed, we will create a new QlikView document, used for transformations, and save it inside the 2.Workbooks folder. Name this file as Transform-Employment Data.qvw. The resulting table will then be saved as QVD inside the 3.QVD\Transformed folder.

Loading the table

Once you have the new QlikView document created, saved and still open, go to the **Edit Script** window (*Ctrl + E*) and perform the following steps:

1. Add a new tab to the script by clicking on the **Tab** menu and selecting **Add Tab...**.

2. From the **Tab Rename Dialog** window, type Initial Load as the name of the new tab and click on **OK**.

3. Use the **File Wizard** dialog to load the **Employment Statistics** table from the corresponding QVD file (T_F41SCHEDULE_P1A_EMP.qvd) stored in the 3.QVD\Source folder.

4. Click on **Finish** on the first dialog window of the **File Wizard** dialog since no alterations will be made to the file on the initial load.

5. Assign the table a name by typing Temp_Employment: before the Load keyword of the generated script. Remove the Directory; statement if necessary.

6. Now, add a new tab to the right of the **Initial Load** tab, by clicking on **Add Tab...** from the **Tab** menu.

7. In the **Tab Rename Dialog** window, type Transformation as the name of the tab and click on **OK**.

8. Once in the **Transformation** tab, we will create the script to load the previously created Temp_Employment table via a Resident load. We will also name this new table as Employment. Write the following code:

```
Employment:
Load
        [%Airline ID],
         Year,
        [Month (#)],
        [# Total Employees],
        Period,
        Month,
        [%Unique Carrier Code],
        [Unique Carrier],
        [Carrier Code],
        [Carrier Name],
        [%Carrier Group ID],
        [# Full Time Employees],
        [# Part Time Employees],
        [# Equivalent FTEs]
    Resident Temp_Employment;
```

We are now ready to add the transformation functions to the table. It's important to note that, if we reload the script at this point, the new employment data will never be created, since both the Temp_Employment table and the Employment table will have exactly the same number of fields as well as the same field names. However, with the functions we will apply, and the new fields we will add, this structural similarity will be lost and we will not need to add the NoConcatenate keyword.

Sorting the table

Using the techniques learned in the *Sorting tables* section of this chapter, we will set the load order of the Resident table using the %Airline ID, Year, and Month # fields. The earlier script will be modified to:

```
Employment:
Load
        [%Airline ID],
        Year,
        [Month (#)],
        [# Total Employees],
        Period,
        Month,
```

```
        [%Unique Carrier Code],
        [Unique Carrier],
        [Carrier Code],
        [Carrier Name],
        [%Carrier Group ID],
        [# Full Time Employees],
        [# Part Time Employees],
        [# Equivalent FTEs]
    Resident Temp_Employment
    Order By [%Airline ID], Year, [Month (#)];
```

Take note of the order in which the sorting fields are defined. The ordering output is: all records will be first sorted by %Airline ID, for each airline, the records will then be sorted by Year in ascending order, and then, for each year, the records will be sorted by Month from first to last. In our case, the %Airline ID sorting can be either ascending or descending, it doesn't matter. However, Year and Month # must be sorted in ascending order, which is the default if no sort order is specified.

Peeking previous records

The final step will be to take the sorted table and start comparing adjacent months to find out the difference in number of employees between them. We've seen how the Peek function will bring a value from previous records, but in our case it gets a little trickier, since we need to be careful not to peek into and compare records corresponding to different airlines. An If expression should be used in conjunction with the Peek function. The adjustment we will make to the previous script will result in:

```
Employment:
Load
    If(
        [%Airline ID] = Peek('%Airline ID', -1),
        [# Total Employees] - Peek('# Total Employees', -1),
        0
        ) as [# Delta Total Employees],
        [%Airline ID],
        Year,
        [Month (#)],
        [# Total Employees],
        Period,
        Month,
        [%Unique Carrier Code],
        [Unique Carrier],
        [Carrier Code],
```

```
      [Carrier Name],
      [%Carrier Group ID],
      [# Full Time Employees],
      [# Part Time Employees],
      [# Equivalent FTEs]
  Resident Temp_Employment
  Order By [%Airline ID], Year, [Month (#)];
```

We are almost ready to reload our script and see the result. We just need to add a
`Drop` statement to remove the `Temp_Employment` table from RAM after using it in the
`Resident load` script. Add the following code at the end of the **Transformation** tab:

```
Drop Table Temp_Employment;
```

After this, save the changes we've made to the QlikView document and hit **Reload**
(or press *Ctrl+R*). The script will perform the transformation and, after it's finished,
we can open the **Table Viewer** window and preview the resulting **Employment**
table. Here is what we'll see:

%Airline ID	Year	Month (#)	# Total Employ...	# Delta Total E...	Period	Month
19386	2009	01	29084	0	200901	Jan
19386	2009	02	29138	54	200902	Feb
19386	2009	03	29084	-54	200903	Mar
19386	2009	04	29849	765	200904	Apr
19386	2009	05	26281	-3568	200905	May
19386	2009	06	27289	1008	200906	Jun
19386	2009	07	26710	-579	200907	Jul
19386	2009	08	26576	-134	200908	Aug

From the **Preview** dialog window, we can see how the very first airline (**19386**) has
had an erratic behavior in their headcount. In February 2009, they had a bump of
54 employees, and in the following month their headcount dropped by the same
amount. Then, a massive reduction of **3568** took place in May 2009.

Now that we've added the # Delta Total Employees field, let's add the corresponding
delta fields for part-time and full-time employees, as well as FTEs. We will also add
the `store` command to save the output table to a QVD file.

Our modified script will be:

```
Employment:
Load
   If(
      [%Airline ID] = Peek('%Airline ID', -1),
      [# Total Employees] - Peek('# Total Employees', -1),
      0
      ) as [# Delta Total Employees],
   If(
      [%Airline ID] = Peek('%Airline ID', -1),
      [# Full Time Employees] - Peek('# Full Time Employees', -1),
      0
      ) as [# Delta Full Time Employees],
   If(
      [%Airline ID] = Peek('%Airline ID', -1),
      [# Part Time Employees] - Peek('# Part Time Employees', -1),
      0
      ) as [# Delta Part Time Employees],
   If(
      [%Airline ID] = Peek('%Airline ID', -1),
      [# Equivalent FTEs] - Peek('# Equivalent FTEs', -1),
      0
      ) as [# Delta Equivalent FTEs],
      [%Airline ID],
      Year,
      [Month (#)],
      [# Total Employees],
      Period,
      Month,
      [%Unique Carrier Code],
      [Unique Carrier],
      [Carrier Code],
      [Carrier Name],
      [%Carrier Group ID],
      [# Full Time Employees],
      [# Part Time Employees],
      [# Equivalent FTEs]
   Resident Temp_Employment
Order By [%Airline ID], Year, [Month (#)];

Drop Table Temp_Employment;
Store Employment into [..\3.QVDs\Transformed\Employment Statistics.
QVD]
```

Adding these fields to our table makes it easier to perform more in-depth analyses, such as the ones shown in the following screenshot:

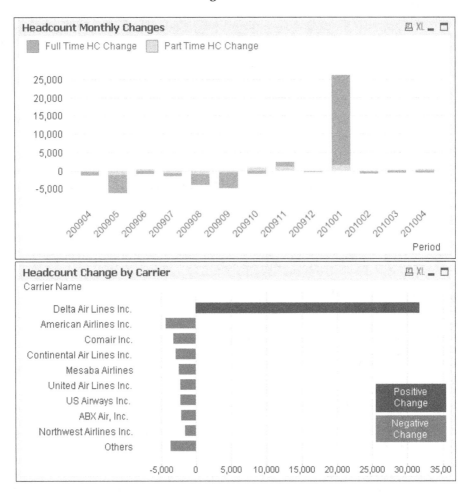

From the previous charts we can see that, while most carriers experienced a downsize in headcount from April 2009 to April 2010 (the selected dataset), **Delta Air Lines Inc.** grew its staff by about 32,000 employees in the same period.

By integrating this data into the final data model, may be able to find correlations between hires, downsizings, # of flights, enplaned passengers, flight occupancy, and so on. This enables the QlikView users at HighCloud Airlines to better make business decisions.

A solo exercise

By now, you are well armed, so what about a little challenge?

We've already added the fields for Monthly Headcount Change. How would we go about adding new fields for Quarterly Headcount Change and Annual Headcount Change? What information can you get from the resulting data?

Dealing with slowly changing dimensions

A slow changing dimension is one whose values vary across undefined time periods, that is, it can have different meanings depending on the time period context.

To illustrate the concept, consider the evolution of Joey, a support technician employee in a given company, over a certain period of time. When Joey joined the company, he had the Junior Support Technician position. Then, after one year, he gets promoted to Senior Technician. And now, one year later, has become the Support Manager.

Now, imagine you want to visualize the number of cases resolved by the entire support team over a three-year period and find out how many of those cases were resolved by junior technicians, how many were resolved by senior technicians, and how many were resolved by the support manager. If, for reporting purposes, we take Joey's current status in the company, all cases he has resolved in the last three years will be logged as if they were resolved by the Support Manager, which is not quite accurate. We should, instead, identify which positions Joey has had and the specific time frame for each of them. Then, count the corresponding number of cases he resolved on each support role and report it. Quite a task if we are dealing with tables of a respectable size.

To tackle challenges like these, we can make use of the `IntervalMatch` script function.

We will adapt our example to the `Airline Operations` data we've been working with, so make sure you have the `Carrier Decode.qvd` file in the `3.QVD\Source` folder.

The Carrier Decode table

Let's start by taking a closer look at the `Carrier Decode` table and its contents. If we were to open the table in Excel this is what we would see:

Airline ID	Carrier Code	Carrier Name	Unique Carrier Code	Unique Carrier Entity	Unique Carrier Name	Carrier World Area	Carrier Group ID	Region Code	Start Date	End Date
20195	WI	Tradewinds Airlines	WI	6884	Tradewinds Airlines	10	4	Domestic	01/02/98	31/12/99
20195	WI	Tradewinds Airlines	WI	16884	Tradewinds Airlines	10	4	International	01/02/98	31/12/99
20195	WI	Tradewinds Airlines	WI	6884	Tradewinds Airlines	10	1	Domestic	01/01/00	31/12/10
20195	WI	Tradewinds Airlines	WI	16884	Tradewinds Airlines	10	1	International	01/01/00	31/12/10
20195	WI	Tradewinds Airlines	WI	6884	Tradewinds Airlines	10	4	Domestic	01/01/11	31/12/11
20195	WI	Tradewinds Airlines	WI	16884	Tradewinds Airlines	10	4	International	01/01/11	31/12/11
20195	WI	Tradewinds Airlines	WI	6884	Tradewinds Airlines	10	1	Domestic	01/01/12	
20195	WI	Tradewinds Airlines	WI	16884	Tradewinds Airlines	10	1	International	01/01/12	

As you can see, the table extract shown in the screenshot contains the data corresponding to one particular carrier: **Tradewinds Airlines**. The first seven columns of the table are not relevant for us right now, so let's focus on the remaining four. We have a **Carrier Group ID** column which tells us if the carrier is catalogued as a Major, Large, Medium Carrier, and so on. We also have a **Region Code** column to indicate if the record corresponds to the domestic or international entity of the carrier (one carrier can perform both types of flights). And last but not least, we have a **Start Date** column and an **End Date** column, which will be the main fields we will use to deal with the slowly changing nature of this particular dimension. Those values indicate in which time frame the particular record is valid.

For example, the first two records shown earlier have a validity period from January 98 through December 99, in which Tradewinds Airlines was catalogued as a Medium Regional Carrier (**Group ID = 4**). Then, from January 2000 all the way through December 2010, the carrier was playing as a Large Regional Carrier (**Group ID = 1**). Afterwards, and until December 2011, it rolled back to the Medium Regional Carrier category but ascended back up as a Large Regional Carrier again for an undefined time.

When reporting Tradewinds Airlines' operations, we must take into account the carrier's classification in place (**Carrier Group ID** field) depending on the time period(s) being analyzed. Dealing with this is not trivial, so let's get going and create some **IntervalMatch** magic.

If we look at the original Flight Data table, we can see that we already have a `%Carrier Group ID` field in it, which is the same to that shown in the `Carrier Decode` table. However, to demonstrate how the `IntervalMatch` function can be useful, let's assume the field is not already in the fact table and that we must obtain it from the `Carrier Decode` table.

IntervalMatch magic

Because of the associative nature of the data model, and the dynamic nature of the queries a QlikView user performs, interval-based dimensions cannot be "queried" as one would with SQL-syntax queries. That's OK, since the associative engine can also handle such dimensions, just with a different, associative-based, approach. Let's see how.

Since the dimension value is dependent upon a time frame, the basic concept is that the key field, through which the dimension is associated with the rest of the data model, must be composed of both the dimension ID and a time element.

We refer to "time element" as the individual pieces into which an interval can be split.

The splitting of intervals means that one interval-based record in a table will be converted to several element-based records. If, for instance, an interval encompasses the equivalent of three time elements, the individual record will then be expanded into three different records, one for each of the corresponding time elements.

Expanding the intervals

The `IntervalMatch` function splits discrete, numeric-based, intervals based on two inputs:

- A table composed of two fields: one for the start of the interval and one for the end of the interval
- A list of values representing the individual data points into which the intervals will be split (the time element), according to their matching

All intervals must be closed, that is, they all must have an end value.

Let's look at a basic example to better illustrate the concept. Suppose we have the following intervals table:

ID	Start	End
A	6	8
B	2	15
C	9	20
D	1	8
E	8	15
F	10	15
G	6	9
H	8	9

We also have a list of the individual data points to associate the data with. The list of data points we will use has 20 values (from 1 to 20).

 Make sure a file called `Intervals.xlsx` is in the `1.Source Data\Examples` folder. It contains both tables described above and is the one we will be using.

To apply the `IntervalMatch` function, follow these steps:

1. Create a new QlikView document, name it `Intervals example.qvw`, and save it inside the `2.Workbooks\Examples` folder.

2. Go to the **Script Editor** window and click on the **Table files...** button to load the table called **Elements** from the `Intervals.xlsx` file.

3. Name the loaded table as `Elements`. The script so far should look as follows:

```
Elements:
LOAD
    Element
FROM
[..\..\1.Source Data\Examples\Intervals.xlsx] (ooxml, embedded
labels, table is Elements);
```

4. Next, create a new `Load` statement under the one we just created, this time loading the **Intervals** table from our Excel file.

5. Modify the `Load` statement by:

   ○ Removing the `ID` field.

   ○ Adding the `IntervalMatch` prefix as follows:

```
IntervalMatch(Element)
```

6. Create a `Drop` statement at the end of the script to remove the `Elements` table from the data model.

7. The final script should look like:

```
Elements:
LOAD
    Element
FROM
[..\..\1.Source Data\Examples\Intervals.xlsx]
(ooxml, embedded labels, table is Elements);

Intervals:
IntervalMatch (Element)
LOAD
    Start,
    End
```

```
FROM
[..\..\1.Source Data\Examples\Intervals.xlsx]
(ooxml, embedded labels, table is Intervals);

Drop Table Elements;
```

8. Now, save the changes and reload the script.

After the script execution, we will end up with one table containing all the expanded intervals and three fields: Element, Start, and End. If we add three listboxes to our workspace, one for each of the fields, and a table box to see the intervals, we will be able to appreciate the associations created by the IntervalMatch function. Some of these associations are depicted in the following screenshots.

When selecting the first interval (**1** through **8**), we see that the elements associated to that interval are all the numbers from **1** through **8**:

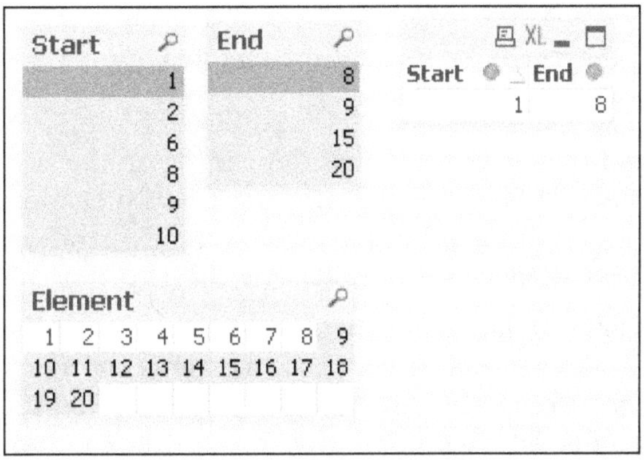

Then, if we select **15** in the **Element** listbox, we will see the four intervals containing that element within. All other intervals are now excluded:

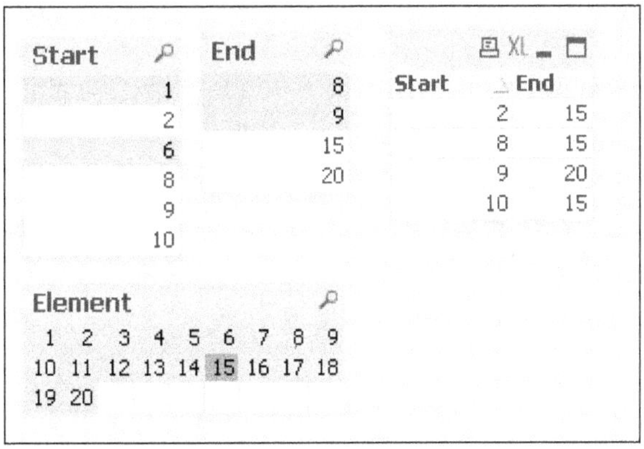

Finally, the actual output table, the one we now have in the data model, looks like this:

Start	End	Element
1	8	1
1	8	2
1	8	3
1	8	4
1	8	5
1	8	6
1	8	7
1	8	8
2	15	2

Some considerations

When working with the IntervalMatch function, it is important to keep the following in mind:

- This function is resource heavy, so, depending on the size of the input intervals table and the elements list, you should first consider if the machine you are working with will be able to handle the operation. Otherwise, you may need to break the work in parts.

- The intervals might enclose elements that are not actually needed in the data model, and we must ensure those elements are not considered when expanding the intervals, so that we save CPU and RAM resources. To do this, the elements list we input in the IntervalMatch function should only contain the required elements.

- Similarly, the intervals table should contain unique records, with no duplicates, to save resources. If one interval is present twice, then the IntervalMatch function will split it twice. Using the Distinct keyword will help us in this matter.

- When using the intervals table, the fields must be specified in the correct order: the start value before the end value.

Applying IntervalMatch to the Carrier Decode table

Now that we've seen an example of how the IntervalMatch function works, we are ready to apply the learned concepts to the Carrier Decode table we discussed earlier.

As a quick recap, our main objective will be to add the `Carrier Group ID` field from the `Carrier Decode` table to the `Flight Data` table. When retrieving the ID value for each of the records in the fact table, we must consider the date on which the corresponding fact took place so that the correct value is assigned. Therefore, the key between the fact table and the `Carrier Decode` table will be composed of a time element (a `Date` field) and the `%Unique Carrier Entity Code` field, which exists in both tables.

Let's follow these steps:

1. Create a new QlikView document; name it as `Transform - Carrier Decode.qvw` and save it inside the `2.Workbooks` folder.

2. Go to the **Edit Script** window and add a new tab. From the **Rename Tab** dialog, type `Facts data` as the tab's name.

3. Once in the new tab, click on the **Table File...** button and browse to the `Flight Data.qvd` file, located inside the `3.QVD\Source` folder.

4. After selecting the file and clicking on **Open**, click on **Finish** in the **File Wizard** window to create the corresponding `Load` statement.

5. Name the table to be loaded as `Flight Data` by typing it before the `Load` keyword and enclosing it within square brackets. Don't forget the colon at the end of the name.

6. Now we will create a new calculated field to build a date representation of the `Period` field. Use the following expression to create the new field:

   ```
   Date#(Period, 'YYYYMM') as Date
   ```

7. We will rename the original `%Carrier Group ID` field from the `Flight Data` table to `OLD_Carrier Group ID`, so that we can use the new field resulting from the transformation instead.

8. The rest of the script will not be modified, so our `Load` statement should be:

   ```
   [Flight Data]:
   LOAD
   Date#(Period, 'YYYYMM') as Date ,
   [%Carrier Group ID] as [OLD_Carrier Group ID],
   [%Airline ID],
       [%Unique Carrier Code],
       [%Unique Carrier Entity Code],
       [%Region Code],
       [%Origin Airport ID],
       [%Origin Airport Sequence ID],
       [%Origin Airport Market ID],
       [%Origin World Area Code],
       [%Destination Airport ID],
       [%Destination Airport Sequence ID],
   ```

```
            [%Destination Airport Market ID],
            [%Destination World Area Code],
            [%Aircraft Group ID],
            [%Aircraft Type ID],
            [%Aircraft Configuration ID],
            [%Distance Group ID],
            [%Service Class ID],
            [%Datasource ID],
            [# Departures Scheduled],
            [# Departures Performed],
            [# Payload],
            Distance,
            [# Available Seats],
            [# Transported Passengers],
            [# Transported Freight],
            [# Transported Mail],
            [# Ramp-To-Ramp Time],
            [# Air Time],
            [Unique Carrier],
            [Carrier Code],
            [Carrier Name],
            [Origin Airport Code],
            [Origin City],
            [Origin State Code],
            [Origin State FIPS],
            [Origin State],
            [Origin Country Code],
            [Origin Country],
            [Destination Airport Code],
            [Destination City],
            [Destination State Code],
            [Destination State FIPS],
            [Destination State],
            [Destination Country Code],
            [Destination Country],
            Year,
            Period,
            Quarter,
            [Month (#)],
            Month,
            [From - To Airport Code],
            [From - To Airport ID],
            [From - To City],
            [From - To State Code],
            [From - To State]
        FROM
        [..\3.QVD\Source\Flight Data.qvd]
        (qvd);
```

9. Now, let's create a new tab by clicking on the **Add new tab** button on the toolbar. The new tab will be named `Intervals`.

10. In this new tab, we will enter the following script:

```
[Carrier Decode]:
IntervalMatch (Date, [%Unique Carrier Entity Code])
LOAD
     [Start Date],
If(Len([End Date]) < 1, Today(1), [End Date]) as [End Date],
     [Unique Carrier Entity] as [%Unique Carrier Entity Code]
FROM
[..\3.QVD\Source\Carrier Decode.qvd]
(qvd);
```

With the preceding script, a new table is being created as the result of the `IntervalMatch` operation. In this case, we are using the extended syntax of the function so that the resulting table has one record for each combination of interval (`Start Date` and `End Date`), data point (`Date`), and dimension (`%Unique Carrier Entity Code`) value.

 When using the extended syntax, all fields specified as the function's parameter must exist in the previouslyloaded fact table, as well as listed in the `Load` statement to which it is being applied.

We are also ensuring that all intervals are closed, which is a requirement of the `IntervalMatch` function, by using a conditional expression. Whenever an open interval is encountered, the date of when the script is executed will be set as the `End Date`field for that interval.

11. Now that we have expanded the intervals, let's associate the dimension value we are interested in (`%Carrier Group ID`) so that we can incorporate it into the fact table. Do this by entering the following code below the previous one:

```
Inner Join ([Carrier Decode])
LOAD
[Start Date],
If(Len([End Date]) < 1, Today(1), [End Date]) as [End Date],
     [Unique Carrier Entity] as [%Unique Carrier Entity Code],
     [Carrier Group ID] as [%Carrier Group ID]
FROM
[..\3.QVD\Source\Carrier Decode.qvd]
(qvd);
```

With the preceding script, we are simply adding the new field (%Carrier Group ID) to the result of the IntervalMatch operation. This leaves us with a table containing all possible combinations of Interval, Date, Unique Carrier Entity ID, and the corresponding %Carrier Group ID value.

12. We will now end the transformation process by joining the expanded-intervals table to the fact table so that the %Carrier Group ID field is added to it. Enter the following script below the previous one:

```
Left Join ([Flight Data])
Load
  Date,
  [%Unique Carrier Entity Code],
  [%Carrier Group ID]
Resident [Carrier Decode];

Drop Table [Carrier Decode];
Drop Field Date;
```

The Join operation is performed by matching both the Date and %Unique Carrier Entity Code fields between the two tables. In the end, we issue a Drop statement to get rid of the Carrier Decode table since we don't need it anymore. We also drop the Date field from the Flight Data table since it was only needed during the IntervalMatch operation.

13. Now that the transformation has taken place and the new %Carrier Group ID field has been added to the fact table, we can store the result into a new QVD file and drop it from RAM with the following two statements:

```
Store [Flight Data] into [..\3.QVD\Transformed\Transformed -
Flight Data.qvd];
Drop Table [Flight Data];
```

Ordering, peeking, and matching all at once

In the earlier sections, we have discussed three different functions commonly used in data transformation. We will now present a use case in which all three functions will complement each other to achieve a specific task.

The use case

We know that the `IntervalMatch` function makes use of closed intervals already defined in a table. What happens if all we have is a start date? To illustrate this scenario, look at the following screenshot:

Airline ID	Carrier Code	Carrier Name	Unique Carrier Code	Unique Carrier Entity	Unique Carrier Name	Carrier World Area Code	Carrier Group ID	Region Code	Start Date
20195	WI	Tradewin(	WI	6884	Tradewinds Airlines	10	4	Domestic	1-Feb-1998
20195	WI	Tradewin(	WI	6884	Tradewinds Airlines	10	1	Domestic	1-Jan-2000
20195	WI	Tradewin(	WI	6884	Tradewinds Airlines	10	4	Domestic	1-Jan-2011
20195	WI	Tradewin(	WI	6884	Tradewinds Airlines	10	1	Domestic	1-Jan-2012
20195	WI	Tradewin(	WI	16884	Tradewinds Airlines	10	4	International	1-Feb-1998
20195	WI	Tradewin(	WI	16884	Tradewinds Airlines	10	1	International	1-Jan-2000
20195	WI	Tradewin(	WI	16884	Tradewinds Airlines	10	4	International	1-Jan-2011
20195	WI	Tradewin(	WI	16884	Tradewinds Airlines	10	1	International	1-Jan-2012

As you can see, the `End Date` field has disappeared. However, there is a way for us to guess it and assign the corresponding value, based on the start date of the immediate following record. That is, if one record starts on 1-Feb-1998 and the immediate following starts on 1-Jan-2000, it means that the first interval ended on 31-Dec-1999, right?

In order for us to calculate the end date, we need to first sort the table values so that all corresponding records are contiguous, then "peek" at the start value from the next (or previous, if ordered backwards) record, subtract one day and that will be our new end date. After that, we are now able to use the `IntervalMatch` function to expand those intervals.

To complete the challenge, make use of the same `Carrier Decode` table we have used previously, only ignore the `End Date` field as if it was not there. You will also be able to compare your results with those we came up with in the previous section.

Good Luck!

Incremental loads

Another important advantage of designing an appropriate data architecture, is the fact that it eases the construction and maintenance of incremental load scenarios, which are often required when dealing with large data volumes.

An incremental load is used to transfer data from one database to another efficiently and avoid the unnecessary use of resources. For instance, suppose we update our Base QVD Layer on a Monday morning, pulling all transactions from the source system and storing the table into a QVD file. The next morning, we need to update our Base QVD layer so that the final QlikView document contains the most recent data, including transactions generated in the source system during the previous day (after our last reload). In that case, we have two options:

1. Extract the source table in its entirety.
2. Extract only the new and/or modified transactions from the source table and append those records to the ones we previously saved in our Base QVDs.

The second option is what we call an **Incremental Load**.

The following diagram depicts the process of an incremental load at a general level, when a Base QVD Layer is used:

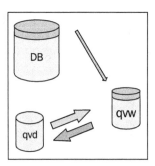

The process of performing an incremental load in QlikView varies in complexity depending on the nature of the source table. At a general-level, we would approach the task by following these steps:

1. We first query the source database using a Where clause with the appropriate logic so that only *new or updated records* are extracted.

2. Once the new records are read, we can *append the ones we previously saved* in QVDs by using the Concatenate function.

   ° In this second load, a Where clause might be required with the appropriate logic so that previously-saved records that were updated in the source table, and therefore read in the first load (step 1), are not read again; by doing so, we will avoid inconsistencies with the data.

3. Finally, once the two tables are concatenated, we save it to the corresponding QVD file, thus replacing the old one.

The basic requirement for an incremental load to be possible is that the new or updated records in the source table can be identified. We can easily identify the target records if the source table has a ModificationTime or Created on field (or similar) and stores the corresponding timestamp or date for each record. This is often the case in production environments, but sometimes this field is not available.

An example pseudocode script that performs the aforementioned procedure is shown as follows:

```
Let vLoadTime = Num(Now( ));

QV_Table:
SQL SELECT
    PrimaryKey,
    Field_A,
    Field_B
FROM Source_Table
WHERE ModificationTime >= $(vLastLoadTime)
AND ModificationTime < $(vLoadTime);


Concatenate (QV_Table)
LOAD
    PrimaryKey,
    Field_A,
    Field_B
FROM OurFile.QVD
WHERE NOT EXISTS(PrimaryKey); /* This where clause is used to
ignore keys that already exist in QV_Table, which are new versions of
existing records. */

If ScriptErrorCount = 0 then

    STORE QV_Table INTO OurFile.QVD;
    Let vLastLoadTime = vLoadTime;

End If
```

In the script we just saw, we use two variables, vLoadTime and vLastLoadTime, to keep track of when the script was last executed and query the database accordingly. These variables are stored as numeric values, rather than using their timestamp representation, to avoid issues regarding date formats. We must ensure the database recognizes the ModificationTime comparison in numeric format, otherwise we should adapt it accordingly. We also use the system variable ScriptErrorCount to ensure that the QVD file and the variable vLastLoadTime are only updated when the previous script is executed without errors.

The process outlined earlier accounts for two scenarios:

- When the source table is only updated by inserting new records (*Insert-Only* scenario)
- When the source table is updated either by inserting new records or by updating existing ones (*Insert and Update* scenario)

There is, however, a third scenario: when the source table can be updated either by inserting new records, updating existing ones, or deleting existing records (*Insert, Update, and Delete* scenario).

When records can be deleted from the source table, the complexity of the incremental load increases and additional steps might be required in the process. One approach that can be implemented, is to perform a second load from the source database, this time pulling the entire list of record IDs (primary keys), without the rest of the fields, and then perform an Inner Join operation with the updated table (the one resulting from the second step in the earlier process) to discard deleted records before saving the new QVD file.

To account for this scenario, the following code should be inserted above the If ... Then ... Else statement in the example script presented previously.

```
Inner Join SQL SELECT PrimaryKey FROM Source_Table;
```

Having an incremental load logic in our *Extract Layer* can help reduce the amount of data being transferred over the network from server to server during the extraction process. It also helps to significantly reduce the time it takes for the extraction to be completed.

When implementing an incremental load, it's essential to monitor and validate the process to ensure that the logic employed in the extraction is appropriate and the data stored in the QlikView document is consistent with the data stored in the source table.

Summary

We've come to the end of an intense chapter. I hope you have followed the topics and, if not, I highly recommend to go back to read those sections which you found most difficult, so that you learn the concepts at full.

In this chapter, we have learned the importance of having a well-designed data architecture, how to load data from another QlikView document or previously loaded table in RAM, and also data aggregation functions and their uses.

We then learned how to order tables during load, how to calculate fields based on previously read records, how to deal with slowly changing dimensions to incorporate those tables into the associative data model, and finally the general process to perform an incremental load.

10
Security

Until now, we have focused our efforts on getting data into QlikView and presenting it in dashboards, analyses, and reports. Our documents were open to anyone with access to QlikView. As QlikView documents can contain huge volumes of sensitive data, in a real world scenario, leaving your data unsecured might be a very risky proposition.

In this chapter, we will focus on how we can secure our QlikView documents. We will first look at how we can make parts of the script only accessible to a limited group of developers. Next, we will see how we can ensure that only authorized users have access to our document. We will finish this chapter by looking at how we can set different permissions for authorized users and can limit which data a user can interact with.

Specifically, in this chapter you will learn:

- How to create a hidden script that is only accessible to a select group of developers
- How to allow only authorized users to open your document
- How to limit what a user can do and see within your document

Time to start locking things down!

Hidden script

When QlikView script is being executed, the results of the actions are written to the **Script Execution Progress** window (and, if enabled, the log file). While this is a very useful feature to see what happened during reload, sometimes you do not want certain things (for example, login credentials) to be visible to everyone. In fact, sometimes you do not even want all developers to have access to the entire script. This is where the **hidden script** comes into play.

The hidden script is a password protected part of the script. It is always the left-most tab (and cannot be moved), so it is executed before the regular script is reloaded. Anything that is executed within the hidden script is not written to the log.

Logging for the hidden script can be turned on by checking the **Show Progress for Hidden Script** checkbox on the **Security** tab of the **Document Properties**. Note that this will allow others to use the debugger to step through the hidden code. Since this defeats a main point for using hidden script, it is not advisable to use this option.

The following screenshot shows us the **Edit Script** window:

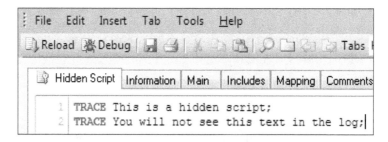

Let's add a hidden script to our document by following these steps:

1. Open our `Airline Operations.qvw` document.
2. Open the **Script Editor** window.
3. Go to **File | Create Hidden Script** in the menu.
4. Enter the password `hidden` twice and click on **OK** to create the hidden script.
5. On the **Hidden Script** tab, enter the following statements:

   ```
   TRACE This is a hidden script;
   ```

6. Save and reload the document.

Notice how the TRACE statement does not show up in the log file.

Reopening hidden script

When the password for the hidden script has been entered, the script remains visible in the **Edit Script** window. The script is hidden when the document is closed and other developers will not be able to see it without entering the password. To reopen a hidden script, select **File | Edit Hidden Script** from the menu and enter the password. Also, be aware that the password for hidden script cannot be recovered, so be sure to keep the password in a safe place.

In the next section, we will see how we can use a hidden script to securely set up user authorization.

Section access

Setting up user authorization under QlikView is generally referred to as **section access**, named after the statement that initiates the authorization section of the script. In section access, fields are loaded with details on which user is allowed which access rights. These fields are loaded in the same way as any other field in QlikView and can be sourced from an inline table, database, or external file.

Better Save than sorry (2)

It is strongly recommended to make a backup copy of your QlikView document before setting up section access. If anything goes wrong during the setup of section access, you will not be able to open your document anymore. Be very careful!

Besides using an inline table, database, or external file, there is also the option of storing and maintaining section access information under QlikView Publisher. Logically, this is no different than storing a table file with section access information in a (semi-)shared folder or, for example, on SharePoint. The data is loaded into the QlikView document as a web file.

As this book is focused on development within QlikView Desktop, storing section access information in QlikView Publisher is out of scope, but it is a good idea to take note of.

Let's start with a simple exercise that protects our QlikView document with a username and password:

1. Press *Ctrl + E* to open the **Edit Script** window.

2. Go to **File | Save Entire Document As** in the menu.

3. Save the file as `Airline Operations SA.qvw`.

4. Now that we've created a separate copy of the file, select the **Hidden Script** tab.

5. Go to **Insert | Section Access | Inline** from the menu.

6. In the **Access Restriction Table Wizard** dialog click on the **Basic User Access Table** button and click on **OK**.

7. In the **Inline Data Wizard** dialog, enter the data from the following table:

ACCESS	USERID	PASSWORD
ADMIN	ADMIN	ADMIN123
USER	USER	USER123

8. Click on **OK** to close the **Inline Data Wizard** dialog.

The following script should have now been generated:

```
Section Access;
LOAD * INLINE [
    ACCESS, USERID, PASSWORD
    ADMIN, ADMIN, ADMIN123
    USER, USER, USER123
];
Section Application;
```

As we can see, the script is started with the `Section Access` statement, which indicates to QlikView that we will be loading user authorization data. This data, `ACCESS`, `USERID`, and `PASSWORD`, is loaded in the next step using an inline table. The script is ended with the `Section Application` statement, indicating that QlikView should return to the regular application script.

We used a hidden script tab to create our section access. When using regular script, any user with privileges to view the script has full access to either the user credentials in plain text (when using an inline table), or to the location of the access files (when using an external table file). By using a hidden script, we can limit who will be able to see the section access script, adding an extra layer of security.

Another thing that you may have noticed is that all field names and field data are written in uppercase. While technically this is not necessary for data loaded from an inline table, any data loaded in section access from an external source must always be in uppercase. For the sake of consistency, it is a good idea to always load all data in uppercase in the section access area.

Now that we've seen how a basic section access example is set up, let's see if it works by following these steps:

1. Save the document by selecting **File | Save Entire Document** in the menu.
2. Click on **OK** to close the **Edit Script** dialog.
3. Close QlikView Desktop by selecting **File | Exit** in the menu.
4. Reopen QlikView and the `Airline Operations SA.qvw` file.
5. In the **User Identification** input box, enter `admin`.
6. In the **Password** input box, enter `admin123`.

If everything was set up ok, you should now be back in the document. Feel free to repeat these steps and enter wrong usernames and passwords to verify that QlikView will deny access to the document.

> QlikView will only verify your user credentials once during each session. You can verify this by closing the document and reopening it, without exiting QlikView Desktop. QlikView will not ask for your username and password the second time. Only when you completely close and reopen QlikView Desktop will you be asked for your credentials again. This is important to remember when changing and testing section access.

Section access fields

Access rights can be defined based on (a combination of) various criteria. In the previous example we used the ACCESS, USERID, and PASSWORD fields, but as we saw in the **Access Restriction Table Wizard** dialog, there are more options, as seen here:

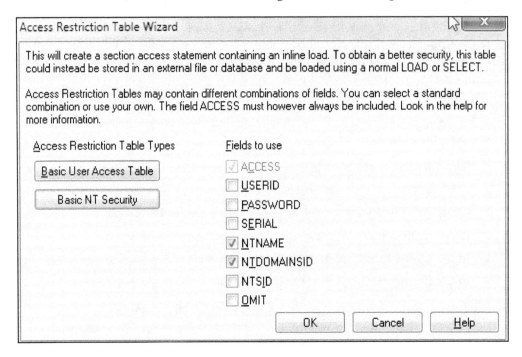

These options, and their description, are listed in the following table:

Field name	Description
ACCESS	A required field that defines the access level for the user. Access level can either be **ADMIN**, for administrator level access with privileges to change anything in the document, or **USER**, for (restricted) user level access.
	Opening the document via QlikView Server ignores the **ACCESS** setting, so every user is treated as having **USER** level access.
USERID	If set, QlikView will prompt for a user ID. This is not the same user ID as the Windows user ID.
PASSWORD	If set, QlikView will prompt for a password. This is not the same password as the Windows password.
SERIAL	A QlikView serial number, this can be used to tie a document to one or more QlikView license numbers.

Field name	Description
NTNAME	An NT Domain User Name or Group Name.
	Please note that the Domain Name needs to be prefixed, so, for example: `DOMAINNAME\NTNAME`
NTDOMAINSID	A Windows NT Domain SID, which is code that identifies the Windows Domain. It uses a value in the form of `S-1-5-21-479397367-1589784404-1244202989`.
	Only users that are logged on to the specified domain will be able to open the document. Be very careful when using this option. An upgrade to your network may mean that you get locked out of your document.
	The value for **NTDOMAINSID** can be entered in the script editor by going to **Insert | Domain SID**.
NTSID	A Windows NT SID, code which identifies a user using a value in the form of `S-1-5-21-479397367-1589784404-1244202989-1234`.
	As with the **NTDOMAINSID** field, be very careful when using this option since a change may lock you out of your document.
	This value can be found by opening command prompt (*Windows Key + R*, entering CMD) and typing `wmic useraccount get name,sid`.
OMIT	The name of a field that should be excluded for the user.

Note that just about any combination of fields is allowable. For instance, if just **NTNAME** and **PASSWORD** is defined, the domain user will need to be logged on correctly and provide the password associated with their domain account in section access. Also, it is valid to just have **USERID**, so only a name needs to be given to get access, regardless of domain user, and there will be no prompt for a password.

Order in which fields are checked

QlikView first checks if the fields SERIAL, NTNAME, NTDOMAINSID, or NTSID grant the user access to the document. Only if no match is found, or if these fields are not set, does QlikView prompt for a USERID and PASSWORD (if set).

In the next section, we'll look at how we can use section access to restrict the data that users can see.

Reduction fields

Besides the fields listed in the previous section, we can associate additional fields with the security fields to reduce the set of data that individual users have access to. Let's follow this example and see how we can limit the flight type (and associated flights) that are available to different users:

1. Open the **Edit Script** dialog and select the **Hidden Script** tab.

2. Update the inline `Section Access` table so it contains the following information:

ACCESS	USERID	PASSWORD	%FLIGHTTYPE
ADMIN	ADMIN	ADMIN123	*
USER	DF	DF123	DOMESTIC_FOREIGN
USER	DU	DU123	DOMESTIC_US
USER	IF	IF123	INTERNATIONAL_FOREIGN

3. Next, place the cursor after the `Section Application` statement.

4. Go to **Insert | Load Statement | Load Inline** in the menu.

5. In the **Inline Data Wizard**, select **Tools | Document** data.

6. In the **Import Document Data Wizard** window, select the field **Flight Type**.

7. Make sure that **Values to import** is set to **All Values** and click on **OK**.

8. Add **Flight Type** as a column header, and add a second column header for %**FLIGHTTYPE**.

9. Fill the table so it looks like the following table:

%FLIGHTTYPE	Flight Type
DOMESTIC_FOREIGN	Domestic, Foreign Carriers
DOMESTIC_US	Domestic, US Carriers Only
INTERNATIONAL_FOREIGN	International, Foreign Carriers
INTERNATIONAL_US	International, US Carriers Only

10. Click on **OK** to close the **Inline Data Wizard** dialog.

The resulting script should look like this:

```
Section Access;
LOAD * INLINE [
    ACCESS, USERID, PASSWORD, %FLIGHTTYPE
    ADMIN, ADMIN, ADMIN123, *
    USER, DF, DF123, DOMESTIC_FOREIGN
```

```
        USER, DU, DU123, DOMESTIC_US
        USER, IF, IF123, INTERNATIONAL_FOREIGN
    ];
    Section Application;

    LOAD * INLINE [
        Flight Type, %FLIGHTTYPE
        "Domestic, Foreign Carriers", DOMESTIC_FOREIGN
        "Domestic, US Carriers Only", DOMESTIC_US
        "International, Foreign Carriers", INTERNATIONAL_FOREIGN
        "International, US Carriers Only", INTERNATIONAL_US
    ];
```

In this script, we've created the %FLIGHTTYPE field. This field exists in both the section access part of the script as well as in the actual data model, thereby acting as a bridge field between these two sections. Through association, we can now limit what a particular user can access within the data model.

Basing an inline table on existing data
One nice feature in the **Inline Data Wizard** dialog is the ability to load the contents of an already loaded field by using **Tools | Document Data**. This can be very useful when we want to group the values of an existing field.

You may notice that for the ADMIN user, we used an asterisk (*) instead of a %FLIGHTTYPE value. When we use an asterisk, it means that the user gets access to all values listed in the reduction field. In this case, that means that ADMIN gets access to the DOMESTIC_FOREIGN, DOMESTIC_US, and INTERNATIONAL_US flight types, but not to the INTERNATIONAL_FOREIGN flight type, since that is not listed in the section access table.

If we want the ADMIN user to be able to access the INTERNATIONAL_FOREIGN flight type as well, we will need to add an additional line referencing the INTERNATIONAL_FOREIGN flight type to the section access inline table. Let's do that now:

1. Create a new line after the line ADMIN, ADMIN, ADMIN123, *.
2. On this new line, enter the following values: ADMIN, ADMIN, ADMIN123, INTERNATIONAL_US.
3. Go to **File | Save Entire Document** to save the document.
4. Click on the **Reload** button to reload the script.

In this exercise, we reduce the data model based on a single field. To reduce the data model on multiple fields, we can simply add another reduction column to the section access table and add a bridge field to the data model.

One important caveat to be aware of in this scenario is that the reduction will be performed over the intersection of all fields. If, for example, we give a user access to the Domestic, US Carriers Only flight type and to the Jet engine type, the user will only be able to see domestic flights carried out by US carriers using a jet-powered aircraft. Any flights that were made using another engine type will be excluded.

Although we have now finished the script part of setting up section access with reduction fields, we will need to make a few more changes before we can see the results. Let's head over to the frontend.

Initial data reduction

We will need to tell QlikView to perform an **Initial Data Reduction** when opening the document. When using initial data reduction, QlikView removes all of the data the user does not have access to, based on the authorizations in section access.

Using initial data reduction is very important. Not using it means that everyone with access to the document has access to all of the data. This means he entire point of using section access is all but lost.

Let's follow these steps to set up initial data reduction for our document:

1. Open the **Document Properties** window by pressing *Ctrl + Alt + D*.
2. Go to the **Opening** tab, and select the **Initial Data Reduction Based on Section Access** checkbox.
3. Make sure that the **Strict Exclusion** checkbox is checked.
4. Check the **Prohibit Binary Load** checkbox (seen in the following screenshot).
5. Click on **OK** to close the **Document Properties** dialog.
6. Go to **File | Save** in the menu to save the document.

We have now set up the document to, upon opening, exclude all of the data that the user does not have access to. Let's have a closer look at the options that we set in the Document Properties:

- **Initial Data Reduction Based on Section Access**: This option enables initial data reduction for the document.

- **Strict Exclusion**: When set, QlikView denies access to users whose data reductions fields cannot be matched to values in the data model. This does not apply to ADMIN users, who will instead get access to the entire data model. It is recommended to always enable this option to prevent unwanted access to data within the document.

- **Prohibit Binary Load**: When set, it is not possible to load the document into another QlikView document using a binary load. It is recommended to always enable this setting unless you are using a multitiered data architecture that uses binary loads, for example, when using QlikMarts.

When a document containing section access is loaded into another document using binary load, the new document will inherit the section access of the original application. Take a minute to try logging in as the DUDF and IF users and see how the data is reduced to show only the authorized flight types. After that, reopen the document and log in as the ADMIN user, we'll need the privileges to make our next changes.

Omitting fields

While looking at the fields in the **Access Restriction Table Wizard**, you may have noticed that there is one field that is a little different from the others: the OMIT field. While all of the other fields are used to identify a user, the **OMIT** field is used to remove fields from the data model for the specified user.

In the next exercise, we will create a new user, NOCARRIER, and will remove the Carrier Name field for this user. Let's follow these steps:

1. Open the script editor by pressing *Ctrl + E* and select the **Hidden Script** tab.
2. Update the section access INLINE table by adding the OMIT field.

3. Set the value of the new OMIT field to null for all existing users, by adding a comma (,) at the end of each ADMIN and USER line.

4. Add a new user at the bottom of the list by entering the following script:

```
USER, NOCARRIER, NOCARRIER123, *, Carrier Name.
```

5. Go to **File | Save Entire Document** to save the document.

6. Click on the **Reload** button to reload the script.

The resulting script should look like this:

```
Section Access;
LOAD * INLINE [
    ACCESS, USERID, PASSWORD, %FLIGHTTYPE, OMIT
    ADMIN, ADMIN, ADMIN123, *,
    ADMIN, ADMIN, ADMIN123, INTERNATIONAL_US,
    USER, DF, DF123, DOMESTIC_FOREIGN,
    USER, DU, DU123, DOMESTIC_US,
    USER, IF, IF123, INTERNATIONAL_FOREIGN,
    USER, NOCARRIER, NOCARRIER123, *, Carrier Name
];
```

We've created a new user, NOCARRIER, whose password is NOCARRIER123. This user has access to all flight types, but cannot see the Carrier Name field.

 Notice that the values in the OMIT column do not need to be in upper case, instead they need to match the exact case of the field names that you want to omit.

We'll test if this works according to plan, but this time we will use another method. Let's follow these steps:

1. Keep your current QlikView application (the program) and document open.

2. Start a second copy of QlikView from the start menu or your quick launch shortcut.

3. If you get an **Auto Recover Files Found** warning, click on **Close** to close it.

4. Go to **File | Open** and select the Airline Operations SA.qvw file.

5. When prompted for a user id and password, enter NOCARRIER and NOCARRIER123 respectively.

If everything went well, we should see that the **Carrier Name** listbox is empty, and that the field is marked as **(unavailable)**.

By opening a second copy of the QlikView software and testing our file in that, we've significantly reduced the risk of getting locked out of our document. If anything is wrong, we can just revert back to the document that we did not close after saving and make the required changes to section access before repeating the process to try again. Using this approach is highly recommended.

Association works in section access too

So far we have been using a single table to store our section access data. However, we can use multiple, associated tables as well.

For example, when we want to OMIT multiple fields for a single user, we need to add each field on a separate line. We can do this within the single table that we've been using so far. However, a better alternative is to remove the OMIT field from the first table and create a second, associated table that contains the USERID and OMIT fields.

Now that we've seen how we can limit who has access to our document, and what they can see, we will now look at how we can restrict what users can do within the document in the next section.

Document-level security

User privileges can be set on two levels within QlikView, at the document level and at the level of individual sheets. We can open the document-level user privileges by pressing *Ctrl + Alt + D* to open the **Document Properties** dialog and selecting the **Security** tab. This tab is shown in the following screenshot:

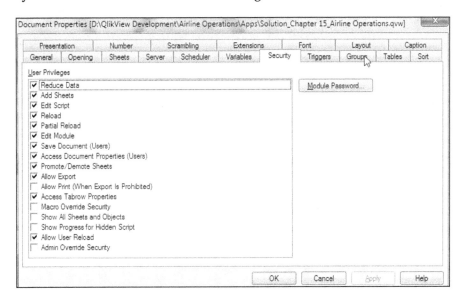

The following table lists and describes the document-level security settings:

User privilege	Description
Reduce Data	Allows users to reduce data using **File | Reduce Data**.
Add Sheets	Allows users to add new sheets by going to **Layout | Add Sheet**.
Edit Script	Allows users to edit the script by going to **File | Edit Script**. It is advisable to not enable this setting.
Reload	Allows a full reload of the document by going to **File | Reload**. As this will always return a full data set, ignoring any section access, it is not advisable to enable this setting.
Partial Reload	Allows users to perform a partial reload by going to **File | Partial Reload**. As this will always return a full data set, ignoring any section access, it is not advisable to enable this setting.
EditModule	Allows users to edit macros by going to **Tools | Edit Module**. It is not advisable to enable this setting.
Save Document (Users)	Allows users with USER privileges to save the document by going to **File | Save**. As this may risk a user overwriting the document with a document containing a reduced data set, it is not advisable to enable this option.
Access Document Properties (Users)	Allows users to open the document properties by going to **Settings | Document Properties**. While it is recommended to disable this setting, even when users have this privilege they will not be able to see the **Sheets**, **Server**, **Scheduler**, **Security** and **Scrambling** sheets.
Promote/Demote Sheets	Allows users to promote and demote sheets by going to **Layout | Promote Sheet** and/or **Layout | Demote Sheet**.
Allow Export	Allows users to export and print data, or to copy it to the clipboard.
Allow Print (When Export Is Prohibited)	If the **Allow Export** checkbox is disabled, setting this option will allow users to still print data.
Access Tab row Properties	Allows users to access the tab row properties.
Macro Override Security	Allows users to bypass all security settings when executing commands from a macro. It is recommended to disable this setting.
Show All Sheets and Objects	Allows users to override all conditional show expressions on sheets and objects by pressing *Ctrl + Shift + S*. It is recommended to disable this setting.
Show Progress for Hidden Script	Shows progress for the hidden script in the **Script Execution Progress** dialog. It is not advisable to enable this setting.

User privilege	Description
Allow User Reload	If the **Reload** checkbox is enabled, selecting this checkbox will prevent users with USER privileges from reloading the document. It is recommended to enable this setting.
Admin Override Security	When set, all security settings for the document and sheets are ignored when a user with ADMIN privileges opens the document, it is advisable to enable this setting.

Besides these settings, the **Module Password** button lets us password protect our macros with a password.

> It is important to note that these user privileges are applied to all users (excluding those with ADMIN privileges). Within QlikView Desktop, it is not possible, for example, to allow one user to export data while not allowing another user to do this.

Besides the document level, we can also set security privileges at the sheet level, as the next section will explain.

Sheet-level security

At the sheet level, we can also determine what actions our users are allowed to make. The sheet-level privileges can be opened by selecting **Settings | Sheet Properties** in the menu and selecting the **Security** tab. This tab is shown in the following screenshot:

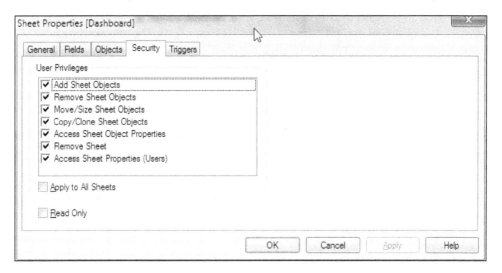

The following table lists and describes the various user privileges that can be set at the sheet level:

User privilege	Description
Add Sheet Objects	Allows users to add new sheet objects.
Remove Sheet Objects	Allows users to remove any of the sheet objects, not just the ones that they created.
Move/Size Sheet Objects	Allows users to move and size sheet objects. On sheets where we do not want the users to move or size any of the objects, this option is a lot more convenient than deselecting **Allow Move/Size** on each individual sheet object.
Copy/Clone Sheet Objects	Allows users to create a copy of existing sheet objects.
Access Sheet Object Properties	Allows users to access the Sheet Properties dialog.
Remove Sheet	Allows users to delete the sheet.
Access Sheet Properties (Users)	Allows users to access the **Properties** pages of objects on the sheet.

By selecting the **Apply to All Sheets** checkbox, we can apply the currently selected privileges to all sheets in the document.

Summary

We have come to the end of this chapter on security, in which we first saw how we can determine which users get access to our document. We then looked at how we can restrict the data that different users have access to. We ended this chapter by looking at how we can set user privileges at the document and sheet levels.

Specifically, in this chapter we learned how to create a hidden script and also that it is very important to create a backup before introducing Section Access.

We also learned how to add Section Access to your document and how to identify users on different criteria, such as **USERID**, **PASSWORD**, but also QlikView's **SERIAL** number or **NTNAME**.

Finally, we learned how we can use Section Access to dynamically reduce the data that is available to the user and how to set user privileges at the document and sheet levels.

11
Data Visualization Strategy

What is the difference between graphic design and data visualization? What distinguishes our actions when we design a website from when we design an executive dashboard? What separates somebody who creates a meaningful icon from another who creates an insightful bar chart?

While both graphic design and data visualization aim to create effective visual communication, data visualization is principally concerned with data analysis. Even though we, who design dashboards and charts, are motivated to create something aesthetically pleasing, we are more passionate about what the data can tell us about our world. This desire to explore our universe via data, and then, communicate our discoveries is the reason that we dedicate our time to learning how best to visualize it.

We start our journey by defining a series of strategies to create and share knowledge using data visualization. In parallel, we propose how we can effectively organize ourselves, our projects, and the applications we develop so that our whole business starts to use insightful visual analysis as quickly as possible. Also, as we survey the entire perspective of our data visualization strategy, we review how we are going to implement it using, arguably, the best data exploration and discovery tool—QlikView.

Let's take a look at the following topics in this chapter:

- Data exploration, visualization, and discovery
- Data teams and roles
- Agile development
- QlikView Deployment Framework

Data exploration, visualization, and discovery

Data visualization is not something that is done at the end of a long, costly **Business Intelligence** (**BI**) project. It is not the cute dashboard that we create to justify the investment in a new data warehouse and several **Online Analytical Processing** (**OLAP**) cubes. Data visualization is an integral part of a data exploration process that begins on the first day that we start extracting raw data.

The importance and effectiveness of using data visualization when we are exploring data is highlighted using Anscombe's quartet. Each of the following scatterplots analyzes the correlation between two variables. Correlation can also be explained numerically by means of *R-squared*. If we were to summarize the correlations of each of the following scatterplots using R-squared, we would discover that the number is be the same for each scatterplot, *.816*. It is only by visualizing the data in a two-dimensional space do we notice how different each correlation behaves:

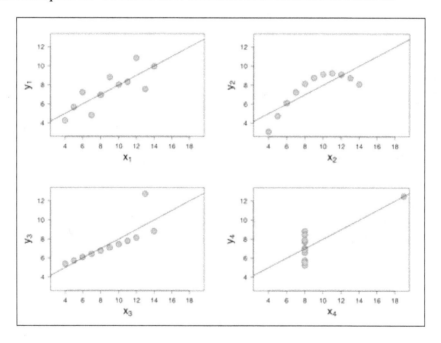

Some tools make it cumbersome to visualize data as soon as it is extracted. Most traditional BI solutions have separate tools for each phase of their implementation process. They have one tool that extracts data, another that creates the OLAP cubes, and yet another that constructs visualizations.

QlikView is a tool that allows us to extract, transform, model, and visualize data within the same tool. Since we can visualize data from the moment it is extracted and throughout the rest of the **extraction, transformation, and load (ETL)** process, we are more likely to discover data anomalies at an earlier stage in the development process. We can also share our discoveries more quickly with business users, and they in turn can give us important feedback before we invest too much time developing analytical applications that don't provide them with real value. Although QlikView is considered a BI software, it stands out amongst its peers due to its extraordinary ability to explore, visualize, and discover data.

In contrast, the implementation of a traditional BI tool first focuses on organizing data into data warehouses and cubes that are based on business requirements created at the beginning of the project. Once we organize the data and distribute the first reports defined by the business requirements, we start, for the first time, to explore the data using data visualization. However, the first time business users see their new reports, the most important discovery that they make is that we've spent a great amount of time and resources developing something that doesn't fulfill their real requirements.

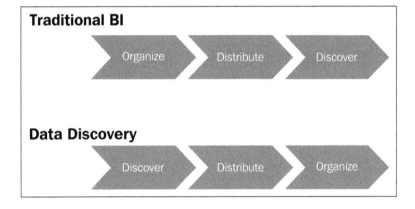

We can blame the business user or the business requirements process for this failure, but nobody can exactly know what they need if they have nothing tangible to start from. In a data discovery tool like QlikView, we can easily create prototypes, or what we later explain as **Minimally Viable Products** (**MVPs**), to allow business users to visualize the data within a matter of days. They use the MVP to better describe their needs, discover data inadequacies, and among other things, confirm the business value of the analysis with their executive sponsors. Only after making and sharing these first discoveries do we invest more of our resources into organizing an iteratively more mature data analysis and visualization.

We've established a general data visualization strategy to support our data exploration and discovery. Now, let's review the strategies that we assign to the teams who are tasked with not only exploring the data directly, but also making sure everyone else in the business can perform their own data exploration.

Data teams and roles

The exact composition of the teams whose principal job is to enable their coworkers to make data-driven decisions will vary as a business's entire data strategy matures. However, many misinterpret what it means to run a mature data-driven business. They believe that at some point all data will and should be governed, and that the team that develops the first QlikView data exploration and discovery projects with will be that governing body.

While a mature data-driven business does count with a large set of governed data and a talented data governance team, it should never be without new, unknown datasets, or without ideas about how to exploit existing datasets in new ways. It is also unrealistic that the same team enforce conformity at the same time that they must strive to innovate. It is for that reason that every mature data-driven business should have both a data research and development (R&D) team, and a data governance team. Each team will have a different data visualization strategy.

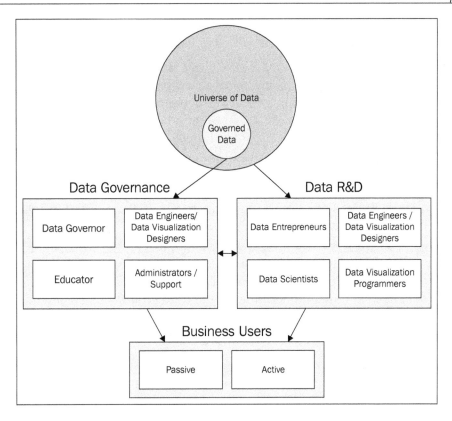

Data research and development

The data R&D team is constantly investigating and creating new solutions to our business problems. When we implement our first data exploration and discovery projects using QlikView, it is common to find out that we are part of a cross-functional, investigative, and proactive team. This team can be the keystone of a more formal data R&D team.

At a minimum, the team should consist of data engineers, data visualization designers, and data entrepreneurs. Data scientists and data visualization programmers may be optional in the beginning, but they become important elements to add as we continue to revolutionize how our business uses data.

It is worth repeating that even though this team will start the data exploration and discovery process, it will not evolve into the data governance team. Instead, this team will continue to look for ever more innovative ways to create business value from data. Once the team develops a stable solution with a long life expectancy, they will migrate that solution and transfer their knowledge to the data governance team.

Our data R&D teams will range in size and capacity, but in general, we aim to cover the following roles within a team that uses QlikView as its primary data exploration tool.

- **Data entrepreneurs**: We look to fill this role with a business analyst who has knowledge of the company, the available datasets, and the business user requirements. We also look for our data entrepreneur to be an early adopter and a cornucopia of ideas to solve the most important problems. They work with all the other team members to develop solutions as the product owner.

- **Data engineers/data visualization designers**: Although this role can be split between two people, QlikView has revolutionized this role. We can now realistically expect that the same person who extracts, transforms, and models data, can also formulate metrics and design insightful data visualization with the data entrepreneur's guidance.

- **Data visualization programmers**: Although this profile is likely not necessary in the beginning, we will eventually need somebody proficient in web development technologies who can create custom data visualizations. For example, we would need this role to create charts that are not native to QlikView like the following cycle plot chart we use for our sales perspective in *Chapter 2, Sales Perspective*. This role can also be outsourced depending on its importance.

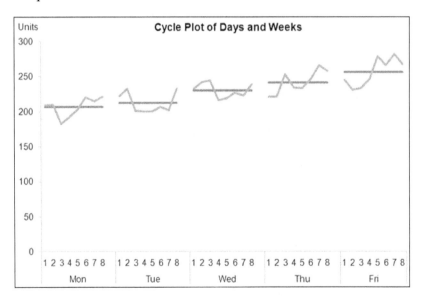

- **Data scientists**: Data science is an ambiguous term. Like many of us who work with data, data scientists are ultimately concerned with extracting knowledge from data. However, they are more focused on using statistics, data mining, and predictive analysis to do so. If they aren't part of the team from the beginning, we should add them later to ensure that the data R&D team continues to innovate.

As far as data visualization is concerned, every member of the data R&D team uses it to make sense of the data and communicate their discoveries with their peers. As such, they should be given space to experiment with advanced data visualization techniques, even when those techniques may appear obscure, or even esoteric. For example, the following scatterplot matrix may not be suitable for most business users, but may help a data scientist create a predictive model:

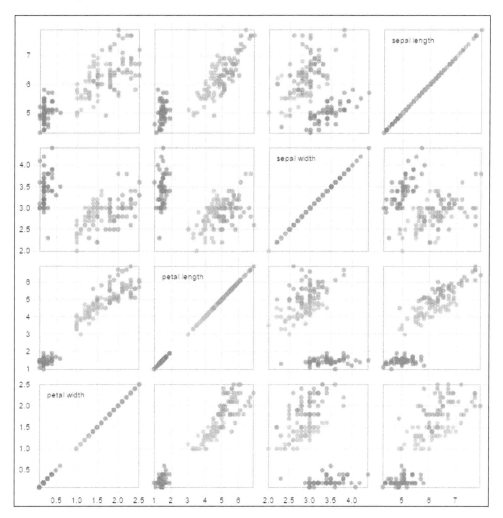

When the data R&D team creates a stable, long-term analytical solution that is going to be used by business users to make their own discoveries, then they should migrate that solution to the data governance team. At this point, both teams should work together to make the data visualization as clear and simple as possible for the business user. While we may be able to train them to use some new data visualization techniques, we will also have to translate other advanced data visualizations into the more commonly used sort.

Data governance team

Data governance is a fundamental part of enabling our entire business to be data driven. The data that is used across the whole company to support common business activities, such as employee performance reviews, financial investments, and new product launches, should be held to a set of standards that ensures its trustworthiness. Among the standards that the data governance team defines and enforces are business rules, data accuracy, data security, and data definitions. The data governance team's job is no less challenging than that of the data R&D team, not the least being because they are the face of the data for most of the business users.

Data governance has a responsibility to make sure data is visualized in a way that is accessible to all business users. Data visualizations should use proper colors, adequate labeling, and approved metrics. The data governance team is also responsible for helping the business users understand data visualization standards, and support those who are going to actively use data to create their own analyses.

Just like our data R&D team, the exact size and makeup of the data governance team will vary. The following list contains the roles that we wish to fill in a team that uses QlikView as its primary data exploration tool:

- **Data governor**: We look for somebody with a similar background as the data entrepreneur in the data R&D team to fill this role. However, the data governor's responsibility is to ensure data quality, uniform business rules, security, and accessible data visualization. They can also be referred to as data stewards. Similar to data entrepreneurs, they help the other team members prioritize pending tasks.

- **Data engineer/data visualization designer**: We create this role to receive solutions from the R&D team and bring them up to the data governance's standards. In addition, they develop QlikView applications for internal control. Even though they don't belong to the R&D team, we expect them to develop innovative ways to visualize the data so that they can enforce the company's data standards more effectively. For example, the following process control chart is an example of the visual analysis that would help them detect data anomalies:

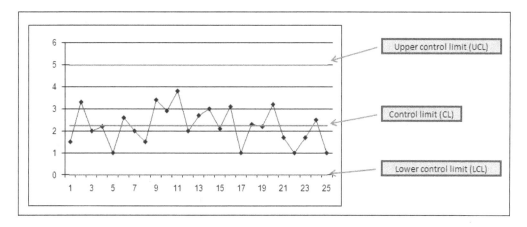

- **Administrator/Support**: This role helps us reduce the distractions our data engineers and data visualization designers face when dealing with daily administration and support issues. Since common QlikView support issues include users unable to access their applications and automatic reload failures, we can often assign the same person to both administrator and support.

- **Educator**: This role performs the never-ending and pivotal job of making business users feel comfortable using the analytical solutions that we develop. Along with teaching business users to use QlikView, they also review the application's content. It is important to note that understanding data visualization is not innate. Therefore, our educators have the responsibility to teach business users how to interpret both simple and advanced data visualizations.

The data governance team may experiment with some data visualization techniques to best analyze , for example, data accuracy or QlikView Server log data. However, for the most part, the data governance team is responsible for establishing and enforcing data visualization standards that create trustworthiness, increase accessibility, facilitate maintenance, reduce training time, and promote clear enterprise communication.

Each team has a separate set of tasks and priorities. However, all data teams should take advantage of agile project management. The data governance team should be especially careful not to confuse data governance with the creation of bureaucratic project management methods. Otherwise, any competitive advantage gained by using QlikView for fast, flexible data exploration and discovery will be wasted.

Agile development

QlikView is software that is best implemented using agile project management methods. This is especially true when we work closely with the business user to deliver data visualization and analysis that provide real value.

The exact agile project management method that we use is not important. The most popular methods are Scrum, *Lean*, and **Extreme Programming** (**XP**). We can find plenty of books and other material that help us decide which method best fits our situation. However, we do take time in this book to review the overall principles that define agile project management:

> "*Manifesto for Agile Software Development*
>
> *We are uncovering better ways of developing software by doing it and helping others do it. Through this work we have come to value:*
>
> *Individuals and interactions over processes and tools*
>
> *Working software over comprehensive documentation*
>
> *Customer collaboration over contract negotiation*
>
> *Responding to change over following a plan*
>
> *That is, while there is value in the items on the right, we value the items on the left more.*
>
> *Kent Beck, Mike Beedle, Arie van Bennekum, Alistair Cockburn, Ward Cunningham, Martin Fowler, James Grenning, Jim Highsmith, Andrew Hunt, Ron Jeffries, Jon Kern, Brian Marick, Robert C. Martin, Steve Mellor, Ken Schwaber, Jeff Sutherland, Dave Thomas*
>
> © *2001, the above authors, this declaration may be freely copied in any form, but only in its entirety through this notice.*"

We take the liberty to mix a few key words from the different agile methods throughout the rest of the book. The following is a list of the most important terms that we will use, and the context in which we will use them. We also reference the specific method that uses the term.

User story

We will describe a series of business user requirements using user stories. A *user story* is common to all agile methods, and describes the business user requirements from the user's perspective in their own words. The following is an example user story from the sales department:

> *"As a salesperson, I would like know who my most important customers are so that I can focus my attention on them."*

An *epic* is a collection of multiple user stories with a common theme.

User stories have a way of helping us look through the eyes of the business users as we develop the best ways to visualize data. This user empathy is important when we create a Minimum Viable Product.

Minimum Viable Product

Henry Ford famously said, "If I had asked people what they wanted they would have said faster horses." If we always ask the business users what they want, they are likely to say prettier Excel tables. We often have to depend on our data entrepreneur, or ourselves as data visualization designers, to develop new ways of analyzing data in QlikView. Then, we have to sell the idea to the business user. In these cases, we are new product developers more than we are software developers.

In his book *Lean Startup*, Eric Ries explains how startups use agile methods for new product development. He recommends building a Minimum Viable Product (MVP), measuring how a customer uses the MVP, and then learning how to improve it.

A QlikView prototype might, for example, only show that it is possible to create a bar chart. A QlikView MVP is a working application that may have only a bar chart, but it displays pertinent information to the user. We can then learn from the user's interaction with the MVP and listen to his or her feedback. We go through the following iterative process each time we decide whether or not to build additional functionality into the MVP. We usually continue this loop pictured here until the value we can add to the MVP is less than the cost to develop it:

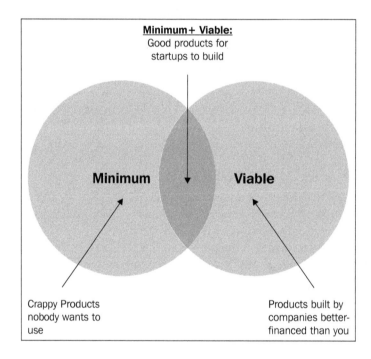

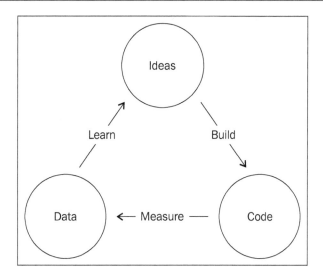

 Even if we have already developed a QlikView application for a department, we should continue to use the MVPs to introduce new functionality.

Whether we realize it or not, we may already follow a process similar to the one in the previous diagram when we develop data visualization and analysis in QlikView. As we begin to master QlikView, we should continue to follow the same iteration, or use a more well-established agile method like Scrum. However, we should avoid using waterfall project management methodologies that don't take advantage of QlikView's flexibility.

We will teach you to create several different visualizations that you can use to create a QlikView MVP using your own business data. Then, you can listen to your business users' feedback and learn how to incrementally improve it based on your business's unique necessities. In this way, we will help you avoid the trap of replicating Excel, or whatever other tool you had previously used, in QlikView.

Along with collaborating closely with the business users and their needs, we also have to be concerned with the overall technical architecture of our solution. Our first technical architecture requirement is to establish a common framework that will make developing QlikView throughout our whole business easier.

QlikView Deployment Framework

The **QlikView Deployment Framework (QDF)** allows us to easily reuse resources and separate tasks between different teams and people. A common folder structure, data, color schemes, and expressions are among the resources that we can share between the data governance team, the R&D team, and active business users.

The QDF is built using a resource container architecture. In the same way that a shipping container on board a ship or stacked in a port can easily be moved from one place to another, QDF containers are independent capsules that can easily be moved and stored in different computers and servers.

When we install QDF, we assign it to a folder where we are going to store these containers. How we define a container depends on how we want to organize the QlikView applications in our business. A container may be a project, it may be a department, or it may define a phase in the **Extraction, Transform, and Load** (ETL) process.

The QDF has two special containers: `0.Administration` and `99.Shared_Folders`. The `0.Administration` container keeps track of the containers that are in the `QDF` folder. It also contains templates that we can use to create our own containers and a few QlikView applications that monitor QlikView usage and governance. The `99.Shared_Folders` container stores all the resources that we want all containers to share.

We can find out more information about the latest version of the QDF in the QDF group in the Qlik Community (`http://community.qlik.com/groups/qlikview-deployment-framework`). Magnus Berg and Michael Tarallo have created an excellent repository of written documentation and step-by-step videos to help us implement the QDF in our business.

We will need to install QDF on our computers before we can perform the advanced analysis exercises.

Exercise 11.1

In order to install the QlikView Deployment Framework, we carry out the following steps:

1. Go to the QlikView Deployment Framework group in Qlik Community (`http://community.qlik.com/groups/qlikview-deployment-framework`).

2. Follow the instructions on the group's home page to install the latest version of QDF and learn more about how to use QDF.

Summary

Our mission is to create a data-driven business, and data visualization plays a key role in accomplishing can perform the advanced analysis exercises. The data visualization strategies that we defined in this chapter are the following:

Data Visualization Strategy 1: Use data visualization as an integral part of data exploration and discovery from the very beginning and all throughout our project.

Data Visualization Strategy 2: Encourage the data R&D team to experiment with new data visualization techniques.

Data Visualization Strategy 3: Enable the data governance team to establish and enforce data visualization standards.

Data Visualization Strategy 4: Collaborate closely with the business user using agile project management methods.

Data Visualization Strategy 5: Propose our own solutions to business problems using new technologies like QlikView and avoid only reproducing legacy reporting methods.

Now, let's begin to apply these strategies and create advanced data analysis in our sales department's QlikView application.

12
Sales Perspective

The success of all businesses is at some point determined by how well they can sell their products and/or services. The large amount of time and money that companies spend on software that facilitates the sales process is testament to its importance. **Enterprise Resource Planning (ERP)**, **Customer Relationship Management (CRM)**, and **Point of Sales (PoS)** software not only ease the sales process, but also gather a large amount of sales-related data. Therefore, it is not uncommon that a company's first QlikView application is designed to explore and discover sales data.

Before we begin to create data visualization and analysis for our sales perspective, let's review the data model that supports it. In the process, we will resolve data quality issues that can either distract users' attention away from a visualization's data or distort how they interpret it. Next, we'll introduce two common sales department user stories and build solutions to stratify customers and analyze customer churn. Finally, let's take our first look at QlikView extensions and overall application design.

In this chapter, let's review the following topics:

- The data model for the sales perspective
- Common data quality issues
- Customer stratification and churn analysis
- QlikView extensions and the cycle plot chart
- QlikView design templates

Let's get started and review the data model that we will use to create our sales perspective in QlikView.

Sales perspective data model

Our company sells gadgets to customers throughout the United States and our sales perspective data model is based on data from an ERP system. The following figure shows the data model that we are going to work with throughout this chapter:

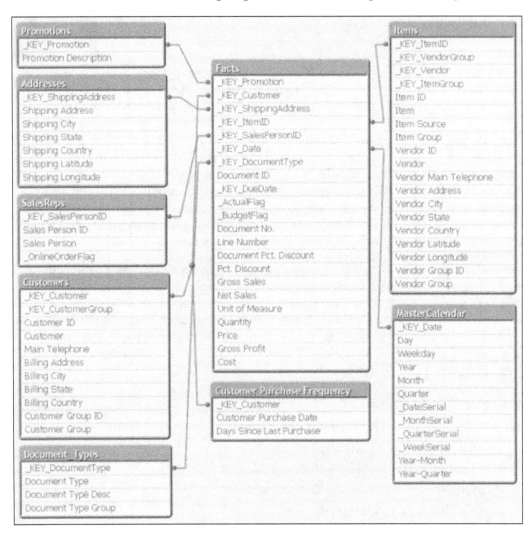

Exercise 12.1

With the following steps, let's migrate the sales perspective container from the book's exercise files to where we've installed QDF on our computers and start to explore the data together:

1. In the `Ch. 2` folder of the book's exercise files, copy the container called `1001.Sales_Perspective` to the `QDF` folder that is located on your computer. By default, the `QDF` folder will be `C:\Qlik\SourceDate`.

2. In the `QDF` folder, open the `VariableEditor Shortcut` in the `0.Administration` container.

3. Click `Container Map Editor`. If the button hangs, then enable the **Open Databases in Read and Write** mode in the **Setting** tab of the **Edit Script** window and try again.

4. In the container map table, go to the empty line after `99.Shared_Folders`, and under the `Container Folder Name` column, click the black arrow indicating that it is an input field.

5. Enter the name of the new container that we just copied, `1001.Sales_Perspective`, into the input field.

6. Continue along the row and enter the `Variable Prefix` as `Sales` and the `Container Comments` as `Container for Sales Perspective`.

7. Click the **Update Map and create Containers** button that is located in the top-left of the container map table, and when prompted, click **Update Container Map**.

8. Save the QlikView file.

Now that we've finished migrating the container to our local QDF, let's open `Sales_Perspective_Sandbox.qvw` in the `1.Application` folder of the `1001.Sales_Perspective` container and explore the sales data in more detail.

The data model that we are using is a star schema and it includes a set of events common to many companies. In the fact table at the center of the model, we store the following events:

- Sales invoices
- Sales credit memos
- Sales budget

 The sales budget may not come from our ERP. It may exist in Excel or in the database of a specific-planning software.

Sales invoices are the principal event of the data model. We don't use the general journal entries that the sales invoices often generate in an ERP system because it does not have the level of detail that a sales invoice does. For example, product details are often not included in the general journal entry.

However, it is important that the total sales amount from our sales invoices matches the total sales that we have in our financial reports. For that reason, it is important to consider any sales cancelation or other sales adjustment.

Finally, we cannot analyze or judge our sales performance without comparing it with something. Basic sales analysis involves comparing current sales with either historical or planned sales. Therefore, we should aim to have at least two years of sales data or the sales budget in our data model. In this data model, we have both historical sales and planned sales data.

 Planned sales can be either a sales budget, a sales forecast, or both.

All of these events are discrete events. In other words, they only exist at a discrete point in time. The fact table that stores discrete events is called a transactional fact table. The date dimension in a transactional fact table holds the date when the event occurred.

Along with the date dimension, we use the 7Ws (who, what, where, when, how many, why, and how) in the following table to describe an example set of metrics and dimensions that we expect to find in a sales perspective data model:

Dimensions		
7Ws	**Fields**	**Comments**
Who	`Customer`	Sometimes, customers are only identifiable by the sales ticket number from a POS system. Otherwise, we hope to have a rich set of attributes that describe our customers as in the case of our data model.
Who	`Sales Person`	In our data model, the sales person is defined at the invoice level. This might also be an attribute of a customer, a product, or an office. We also should include any sales structure hierarchy if it exists.
What	`Item`	Whether it be a product or a service, we should describe what we sell to a customer in a detailed dimension table.
Where	`Billing Address,` `Shipping Address`	The location can either be related to the customer, the sales office, or the store where the sale took place.

Dimensions		
7Ws	**Fields**	**Comments**
When	`Date`	Here, we record the exact date of the sales invoices and credit memos. We don't usually make daily sales budgets, so we assign our monthly budget to the first day of the month.
Why	`Promotion Description`	Giving a possible reason for sales variation versus historical or planned sales is a part of the analytical process. Therefore, we should include any element that is intended to cause variation, such as sales offers and promotions, into the data model.
How	`_OnlineOrderFlag`	We should also include whether we sell our products face to face, online, telephonically, or through any other sales channel.
Metrics		
7Ws	**Fields**	**Comments**
How many	`Net Sales`	The net sales field records an invoice's sales dollar amount after discount. It also stores the net sales budget so we use `_ActualFlag` or `_BudgetFlag` fields to determine whether the amount is actual or budget.
How many	`Quantity`	Sales quantity helps us understand sales in a manner that is independent of any change to the sales price. Quantity can be based on different units of measurement. For example, we can measure hours, kilograms, or pieces.
How many	`Gross Profit`	Although gross profit is not always easy to calculate and might not be available, it is vital to understand the effectiveness of our sales. Like net sales. The amount can also be actual or budget.

For more information on data modeling, read *Data Warehouse Toolkit* by Ralph Kimball, and *Agile Data Warehouse Design* by Lawrence Corr.

Data quality issues

Great data visualization and analysis starts with having a well-built data model that contains high-quality data. If this is our first data exploration and discovery project, one of the most important discoveries that we are going to make is that our data contains a great deal of garbage. One of the most noticeable data-quality issues is the absence of a value in a field.

For example, in Sales_Perspective_Sandbox.qvw, the `Vendor` attribute in the `Items` table does not always have a value. The absence of a value in a field is referred to as a null value. In QlikView, a user can't select a null value. However, we often want to select null values to know which items have missing attributes and send that list of items to whomever is responsible for the catalog's data quality.

In order to select item's with missing vendor information, we replace all the null values in the `Vendor` field with the string `N/A`, by inserting the following code before we load the `Items` table in order to replace all null value in the load script:

```
MappingNULL_NA:
Mapping
LOAD NULL() as NULL,
   'N/A' as Mapped_Value
AutoGenerate (1);
MAP Vendor USING MappingNULL_NA;
```

> Although we have the option to suppress null values in the **Dimensions** tab of a QlikView object, we never use this option unless we understand why the dimension values are null. These null values may indicate a larger problem with our data or the data model.

Missing dimension values

The previous mapping will not get rid of all the null values that we see in our charts because what we perceive in QlikView to be a null value may in fact be a missing value. Unlike missing values, null values can be observed the in the table where they reside. For example, can go to the **Table Viewer**, preview the `Items` table, and see the null values in the `Vendor` field.

However, what if the fact table contains an item key that refers to an item that does not exist in the `Items` table? Or, what if the fact table is missing the item key for some transactions? Despite running our previous null value mapping, we will still see `Vendor` as null in QlikView because the item key that the fact table refers to does exist in the `Items` table. It is a missing value.

The way to give users the ability to select missing items values to replace incorrect and null item keys in the fact table with a key to a fictitious item. The key to the fictitious item is defined as negative one (-1). Our first step to replace incorrect and null item keys is to create a mapping table using the Items table where we map all the existing item keys with their own values:

```
MappingMissingIncorrectItemsKeys:
Mapping
LOAD _KEY_ItemID,
   _KEY_ItemID
FROM
$(vG.QVDPath)\2.Transform\Items.qvd
(qvd);
```

The second step is to save the original value stored in _Key_ItemID in another field and apply this map to the _Key_ItemID field when we load the Facts table:

```
Facts:
LOAD [Document ID],
_KEY_ItemID as Original_ItemID,
      applymap('MappingMissingIncorrectItemsKeys',_KEY_ItemID,-1) as
      _KEY_ItemID,
      _KEY_Date,
      . . .
FROM
$(vG.QVDPath)\2.Transform\Facts.qvd
(qvd);
```

Our final step is to create a fictitious item called 'Missing' with an item key of negative one (-1) in the Items table:

```
Concatenate (Items)
LOAD -1 as _KEY_ItemID,
      'Missing' as [Item ID],
      'Missing' as Item,
      'Missing' as [Item Source],
      'Missing' as [Item Group],
      . . .
AutoGenerate (1);
```

Missing fact values

After the previous two adjustments, we will still encounter some missing values in QlikView. For example, do you notice anything missing from the following chart that shows the monthly net sales for the item *Bamdax 126* in `Sales_Perspective_Sandbox.qvw.`?

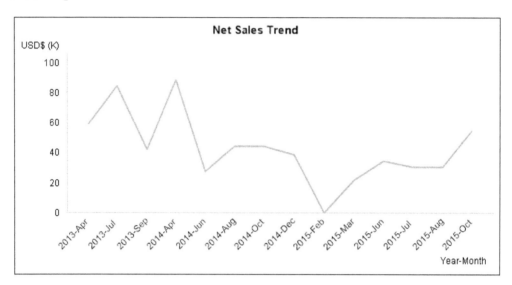

If you noticed that various months do not appear on the horizontal axis, then you are correct. As Bamdax 126 is not sold during every month, there is no relation between Bamdax 126 and the months when the item was not sold. The values are missing, and these missing values distort the line chart.

In order to completely resolve this issue, we would have to complement the fact table with the Cartesian product of any or all dimension key sets, and in effect, measure *nil events*. However, we should take into account that this may cause a severe degradation of our QlikView application's performance. Therefore, we should apply this solution pragmatically to solve specific analytical needs.

In this case, we specifically want to see a more accurate net sales trend for Bamdax 126 that includes the months that we did not sell the item. We do this by adding the following code to our load script after loading the `Facts` table. The code creates a Cartesian product of the `Product` and `Date` dimension key sets and adds it to our `Facts` table:

```
Missing_Facts_Tmp:
Load distinct makedate(Year(_KEY_Date),Month(_KEY_Date)) as _KEY_Date,
    1 as _ActualFlag
Resident Facts;
```

```
Left Join (Missing_Facts_Tmp)
Load distinct _KEY_ItemID
FROM
$(vG.QVDPath)\2.Transform\Items.qvd
(qvd);

Concatenate (Facts)
Load *
Resident Missing_Facts_Tmp;

DROP Table Missing_Facts_Tmp;
```

 In order to reduce the number of rows in the Cartesian product we only use the month and year of the date. We could have optimized it further using the exists() function to concatenate the dimension combinations that don't already exist in the `Facts`.

Finally, we untick the **Suppress Zero-Values** checkbox in the **Presentation** tab of the line chart in order to see the correct net sales trend for Bamdax 126. You will notice that the following line chart shows that Bamdax 126 is purchased almost every two months. It is difficult to make this observation in the previous chart.

 Again, be very careful when creating a Cartesian product in QlikView. We create a Cartesian product by joining two or more tables that do not have a field in common. If the tables are large, then this may cause QlikView to use all the available RAM memory and freeze the computer.

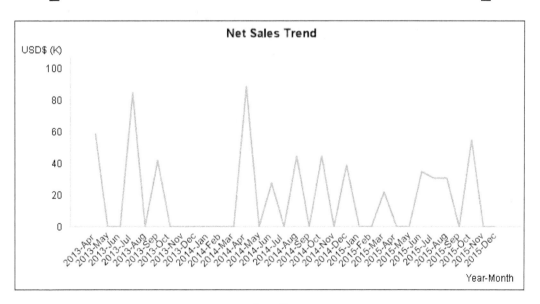

These steps to eliminate null and missing values in the data model will help improve our data analysis and visualization. However, we will most likely not use all the fields in the data model, so we shouldn't waste time to clean every field or create every missing value until they've proven their business value.

Data formatting and standardization

While QlikView is not data-cleansing software, it does allow us to implement some formatting and standardization that makes it easier to visualize data. We perform these actions in the data model load script as best practice. However, we can also use the same QlikView functions directly in any QlikView object.

Case

We read by identifying the overall shape of words. If we use text values with all uppercase letters, then all the words have the same block shape. Which makes words harder to identify and reduces readability. Also, all uppercase text values tend to be less aesthetically appealing.

A quick search in Google reveals that some people have begun to challenge this belief. Hopefully, future scientific studies will soon allow us to make the best decision and confirm how to optimize text readability.

An even worse scenario is when a field has some text values in all uppercase and others in lowercase. This is common when we integrate two data sources, and it is an unnecessary distraction when we visualize data.

First, we use the `capitalize()` function when the field is a proper noun, such as customer name, employee name, or city. The function will return a mixed-case text value with the first letter of every word being a capital letter. Secondly, we use the `upper()` function to standardize text fields that are abbreviations, such as state or units of measurement. Lastly, we use the `lower()` function to standardize all other text fields.

> This solution is not perfect for some text values, such as a street address that contains both proper nouns and abbreviations. For example, Cedar St. NW requires a more nuanced approach. However, a street address is rarely used for analysis, and any extra effort to standardize this or any other field should be weighed against its business value.

Unwanted characters

Text values with strange characters can also be an unnecessary distraction. Characters, such as a number sign (#), an exclamation mark (!), a vertical bar (|), and so on, can sometimes find their way into text descriptions where they don't belong. We can eliminate them with the `purgechar()` function or the `replace()` function.

Also, extra spaces between words in a dimension value can make our charts look sloppy. QlikView tends to eliminate leading and trailing spaces, but it doesn't eliminate extra spaces between words. We can accomplish this using the following expression, preferably in our `load` script:

```
replace(replace(replace(FieldName,' ','<>'),'><',''),'<>',' ')
```

> Hopefully, in the future, regular expressions will be native to QlikView, and we will have a greater ability to clean and standardize data. Barry Harmsen has created custom script functions that allow us to use regular expressions in the load script (http://www.qlikfix.com/2010/10/18/regular-expressions-in-the-load-script/). A third-party tool called QVSource also allows us to use regular expressions in the load script (http://wiki.qvsource.com/Using-Regular-Expressions-In-QlikView.ashx).

Dates and time

Finally, we make sure that all date fields have the same format. This is especially the case when we extract data from different data sources. We use the `date()` or `time()` function to change the format to the default date format that we define in the list of system variables at the beginning of the script.

When we create analysis that is intended for an international audience where some users use the MM/DD/YYYY format and others use the DD/MM/YYYY format, we should consider using the YYYY/MM/DD format. This format won't leave users guessing whether 11/1/2016 refers to November 1, 2016 or January 11, 2016.

Master calendar

Along with formatting field values, we also standardize the use of whole dimension in order to facilitate analysis of tables. Those that we reuse between different data models are called conformed dimensions. The date dimension is ubiquitous and serves as a great example to create the first conformed dimension.

The range of dates that we use in each data model may change, so instead of using the exact same table for each data model, we create a master calendar reusing the same script. We call these reusable scripts subroutines, and in QDF we store script subroutines in the following file path:

```
C:\Qlik\SourceData\99.Shared_Folders\3.Include\4.Sub
```

Although QDF has a master calendar subroutine, we will use the master calendar subroutine that is available from QlikView Components (`http://qlikviewcomponents.org`). Qlikview Components is a library of script subroutines and functions that were developed by Rob Wunderlich and Matt Fryer. We prefer this mastercalendar subroutine because it automatically creates several calendar-based set-analysis variables that we can use in our charts.

QDF is not the end but rather the means. It is designed to be flexible so that we can adapt it to our needs. We can create, import, and modify any reusable component that best fits our business requirements.

We can download the latest release of QlikView Components from GitHub (`https://github.com/RobWunderlich/Qlikview-Components/releases`). We then integrate it with our QDF by copying the `Qvc.qvs` file that is found under the `Qvc_Runtime` folder to `C:\Qlik\SourceData\99.Shared_Folders\3.Include\4.Sub`. We choose to save it to `99.Shared_Folders` so that we can use these subroutines and functions in every container that we create.

In our `load` script, we add the following code after initializing QDF:

```
$(Include=$(vG.SharedSubPath)\Qvc.qvs);
```

We then add the following code to create the master calendar and the calendar-based set-analysis variables:

```
SET Qvc.Calendar.v.CreateSetVariables = 1;
call Qvc.CalendarFromField('_KEY_Date');
```

Every QlikView Components release contains working examples of all its subroutines. We can use these examples to learn the possible parameters and results of each subroutine.

We finish the load script by running a subroutine that eliminates any temporary variables that were used to create the master calendar:

```
CALL Qvc.Cleanup;
```

After running our `load` script, we now have the following master calendar:

_KEY_Date	Day	Weekday	Year	Month	Quarter	_DateSerial	_MonthSerial	_QuarterSerial	_WeekSerial	Year-Month	Year-Quarter
41365	1	Mon	2013	Apr	Q2	41365	1	1	1	2013-Apr	2013-Q2
41382	18	Thu	2013	Apr	Q2	41382	1	1	3	2013-Apr	2013-Q2
41395	1	Wed	2013	May	Q2	41395	2	1	5	2013-May	2013-Q2
41426	1	Sat	2013	Jun	Q2	41426	3	1	9	2013-Jun	2013-Q2
41456	1	Mon	2013	Jul	Q3	41456	4	2	14	2013-Jul	2013-Q3
41463	8	Mon	2013	Jul	Q3	41463	4	2	15	2013-Jul	2013-Q3
41487	1	Thu	2013	Aug	Q3	41487	5	2	18	2013-Aug	2013-Q3

Most of these columns look familiar. However, the columns that end with `Serial` may be new to you. To those of us who have battled with defining date ranges with set analysis, the `Serial` columns help make this an easier task.

For example, we can calculate **year-to-date (YTD)** sales easily with the following expression:

```
sum({$<Year={$(=max(Year))},Month=,_DateSerial={"<=$(=max(
_DateSerial))"},_ActualFlag={1}>}[Net Sales])
```

However, instead of repeating this set analysis in every chart, we can use the calendar-based set-analysis variables to calculate YTD sales. We can improve the preceding expression using the set-analysis variable called `vSetYTDModifier`:

```
sum({$<$(vSetYTDModifier),_ActualFlag={1}>} [Net Sales])
```

We can review all of the available calendar-based set-analysis variables in **Settings | Variable Overview**.

Now that we've reviewed the sales perspective data model and methods in the load script make it support cleaner data visualization and analysis, let's look at our first user story.

Customer stratification.

Many of the user stories that we take into account when we start to use more advanced data analysis and visualization techniques are not new. For example, we have probably already used basic QlikView methods to resolve the following user story.

The simplest way to define customer importance is to base it on how much they've purchased or how much profit they've generated. In its simplest form, we can resolve this user story with a bar chart that ranks customers by sales or gross profit.

However, given our increasing experience with QlikView, we'll take another look at this user story and use a more advanced analysis technique called customer stratification. This method groups customers according to their importance into bins. The number of bins can vary, but for this exercise we will use four bins: A, B, C, and D. We use two techniques to stratify customers. The first technique involves using the Pareto principal, and the second involves using fractiles.

Pareto analysis

Pareto analysis is based on the principle that most of the effects come from a few causes. For example, most sales come from a few customers, most complaints come from a few users and most gross profit come from a few products. Another name for this analysis is the 80-20 rule, which refers to the rule of thumb that, for example, 80% of sales come from 20% of customers. However, it is important to note that the exact percentages may vary.

We can visualize this phenomena using the following visualization. Each bar represents the twelve-month rolling net sales of one customer. The customers are sorted from greatest to least and their names appear along a line that represents the accumulation of their sales. The customers whose names appear below the horizontal reference line called 80% total sales line make up 80% of the total company's twelve-month rolling net sales. These are the customers in which we want to dedicate more of our time to provide great service:

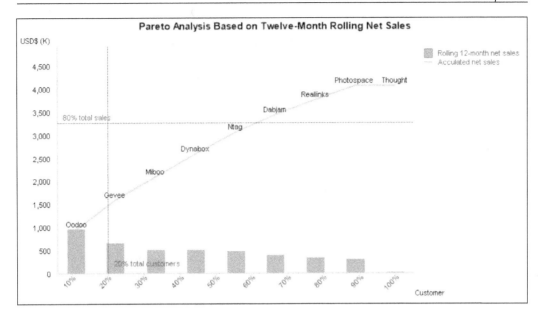

We also confirm that we don't depend on too few customers by including a reference line that represents 20% of the total number of active customers. While the exact percentage depends on the business, we usually hope to have 20% or more of our customers make up 80% of our sales. The preceding chart clearly shows whether this is true by verifying that the accumulated sales line crosses the **80% total sales** reference line to the right of where the **20% total customers** reference line does.

Exercise 12.2

Let's construct this chart in `Sales_Perspective_Sandbox.qvw` using the following chart properties. These are only the principal chart properties that are necessary to create the chart. Adjust the color, number format, font, and text size as you like:

Chart Properties	Value
General / Chart Type	Choose to create a combo chart.

Dimensions / Used Dimensions	Use the following code to create a calculated dimension labeled Customers:
	
	`=aggr(rank(sum({$<$(vSetRolling12Modifier),`
	`_ActualFlag={1}>} [Net Sales]),4)/count({$<$(v`
	`SetRolling12Modifier),_ActualFlag={1}>} Total`
	`Customer),Customer)`

Chart Properties	Value
Expressions	Use the following code to create an expression labeled Rolling 12-Month Net Sales: ``` sum({$<$(vSetRolling12Modifier), _ActualFlag={1}>} [Net Sales]) ``` Choose to display the expression as a bar:
Expressions	Use the following code to create an expression labeled Accumulated Net Sales: ``` sum({$<$(vSetRolling12Modifier), _ActualFlag={1}>} [Net Sales]) ``` Choose to display the expression as a line and enable the Full Accumulation option.

Expressions	Use the following code to create an expression labeled Customer:
	
	``
	if(
	   sum({$<$(vSetRolling12Modifier),
	 _ActualFlag={1}>} [Net Sales])
	   /
	   sum({$<$(vSetRolling12Modifier),
	 _ActualFlag={1}>} Total [Net Sales])
	
	   >=.05,
	
	   Customer,
	   ' '
	)
	``
	
	Choose to display the expression as Values on Data Points.

Axes / Dimension Axis	Choose to Continuous option in the Dimension Axis section.
Presentation / Reference Lines	Use the following code to create a reference line labeled 80% Total Sales: ``` =sum({$<$(vSetRolling12Modifier),_ActualFlag ={1}>} [Net Sales])*.8 ``` Choose the option to Show Label in Chart and the option to locate it on the Primary Y axis.
Presentation / Reference Lines	Use the following code to create a reference line labeled 20% Total Customers: ``` =.2 ``` Choose the option to Show Label in Chart and the option to locate it on the Continuous X axis.

We avoid overlapping labels on the data points by adding some intelligence into the expression called *Customer* and only show the label when the customer's sales participation is greater than 5%.

While this is a powerful visualization, we simplify customer stratification for our sales representatives and assign each customer a particular letter according to how they are ranked as per the Pareto analysis. Those that are assigned the letter A are our most important customers, while those that are assigned the letter D are our least important customers. The following table details how we assign each letter to our customers:

Assigned Letter	Accumulated Sales Percentage
A	0-50%
B	50-80%
C	80-95%
D	95-100%

If we use the chart accumulation options like in the previous exercise or other methods like inter-row chart functions to determine which group each customer belongs to, we are forced to always show every customer. If we select any customer or apply any other filter then we lose how that customer is classified. In order to assign a letter to each customer and view their classification in any context, we use a method that uses alternate states. Let's perform the following tasks to classify our customers based on rolling twelve-month net sales.

This method was first introduced by Christof Schwarz in the Qlik Community (https://community.qlik.com/docs/DOC-6088).

Exercise 12.3

Perform the following steps for this exercise:

1. Create an **Input Box** that contains three new variables: vPctSalesA, vPctSalesB, and vPctSalesC. Assign the values 50%, 80%, and 95% to each variable, respectively.

2. In **Settings -> Document Properties**, click **Alternate States...** in the **General** tab. Add three new alternate states: A_CustomerSales, AB_CustomerSales, and ABC_CustomerSales.

3. Create a button named Calculate Stratification with the following actions:

Actions	Values
Copy State Contents	We leave the Source State empty and use the following Target State: A_CustomerSales
Pareto Select	We will use the following field: Customer We will use the following expression: sum({$<$(vSetRolling12Modifier),_ActualFlag={1}>} [Net Sales]) We will use the following percentage: =vPctSalesA We will use the following alternate state: A_CustomerSales
Copy State Contents	We leave the Source State empty and use the following Target State: AB_CustomerSales
Pareto Select	We will use the following field: Customer We will use the following expression: sum({$<$(vSetRolling12Modifier),_ActualFlag={1}>} [Net Sales]) We will use the following percentage: =vPctSalesB We will use the following alternate state: AB_CustomerSales

Actions	Values
Copy State Contents	We leave the Source State empty and use the following Target State: `ABC_CustomerSales`

Pareto Select	We will use the following field:
	
	`Customer`
	
	We will use the following expression:
	
	`sum({$<$(vSetRolling12Modifier),_ActualFlag={1}>} [Net Sales])`
	
	We will use the following percentage:
	
	`=vPctSalesC`
	
	We will use the following alternate state:
	
	`ABC_CustomerSales`

4. Finally, create a straight table with Customer as the dimension and the following two expressions:

Label	Expression
Rolling 12-month net sales	`=sum({$<$(vSetRolling12Modifier),_ActualFlag={1}>} [Net Sales USD])`

Classif.	`aggr(if(len(only({A_CustomerSales} Customer)) <> 0,`
	`'A',`
	`  if(len(only({AB_CustomerSales} Customer)) <> 0, 'B',`
	`  if(len(only({ABC_CustomerSales} Customer)) <> 0,`
	`'C',`
	`if(len(only(Customer)) <> 0,'D')))`)
	`,Customer)`

5. Optionally, add a background color that corresponds to each letter with the following expression:

```
if(len(only({A_CustomerSales} Customer)) <> 0, blue(100),
  if(len(only({AB_CustomerSales} Customer)) <> 0, blue(75),
  if(len(only({ABC_CustomerSales} Customer)) <> 0,
blue(50),blue(25)))))
```

After some final adjustments to each object's presentation, we should have something similar to the following figure:

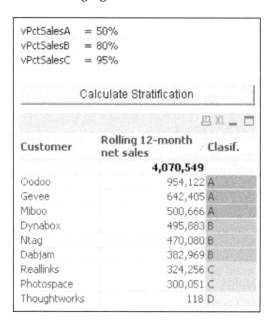

Using this method we can select any customer and still observe how it is classified. We can perform this same stratification technique using other additive metrics, such as gross profit. Also, instead of customers, we can also stratify items or sales representatives.

The second part of stratification involves using nonadditive metrics. For example, we cannot use the Pareto principal to classify customers based on the average number of days they their invoices.

Sales representatives can now easily see which customers have the most impact on sales and dedicate more time to provide them with better service. At the same time, they need to avoid losing these customers. So let's take a look at how we can help them anticipate customer churn.

Customer churn

Customer churn is a measure of the company's tendency to lose customers. Our user story speaks of the need to detect at-risk customers and prevent them from becoming a lost customer.

Surely, there are many variables that we may use to predict customer churn. In this case we expect customers to consistently make a purchase every so many days, so we will use a variable called customer purchase frequency to detect those that we are at risk of losing.

We could calculate the average number of days between purchases and warn sales representatives when the number of days since a customer's last purchase exceeds that average.

However, a simple average may not always be an accurate measure of a customer's true purchasing behavior. If we assume that their purchase frequency is normally distributed then we use the t-test to determine within what range the average is likely to fall. Moreover, we prefer the t-test because it can be used for customers that have made less than thirty or so purchases.

If we want our model to be sensitive to customer inactivity then we send an alert when the days since their last purchase exceeds the average's lower limit. Otherwise, if we don't want to overwhelm the sales representatives with alerts then we use the average's upper limit to determine whether we are at risk of losing a customer. We'll apply the later case in the following example.

Before we calculate the upper limit of a t-distribution, we need to add a table to the data model that contains the number of days that elapse between field the purchases each customer makes. We add the Customer Purchase Frequency with the following code that we add to the load script after having loaded the Facts table:

```
[Customer Purchase Frequency Tmp]:
Load distinct _KEY_Date as [Customer Purchase Date],
    _KEY_Customer
Resident Facts
Where _ActualFlag = 1
  and [Net Sales] > 0;

[Customer Purchase Frequency]:
Load [Customer Purchase Date],
   _KEY_Customer,
     if(_KEY_Customer <> peek(_KEY_Customer),0,[Customer Purchase
Date] - Peek([Customer Purchase Date])) as [Days Since Last Purchase]
Resident [Customer Purchase Frequency Tmp]
Order by _KEY_Customer,[Customer Purchase Date];
DROP Table [Customer Purchase Frequency Tmp];
```

The previous script will produce the following table:

_KEY_Customer	Customer Purchase Date	Days Since Last Purchase
1	4/18/2013	-
1	6/23/2013	66
1	8/16/2013	54
1	9/23/2013	38
1	11/11/2013	49
1	12/19/2013	38

This is a great opportunity to use a histogram to understand the distribution of a customer's purchasing frequency. We can also compare the distribution to a normal or a t-distributions in the same chart. Let's use the following properties to create our histogram:

Exercise 12.4

Chart Properties	Value
General / Chart Type	Choose to create a combo chart.
Dimensions / Used Dimensions	Use the following code to create a calculated dimension called Days Since Last Purchase: `=ValueLoop($(=min([Days Since Last Purchase])),$(=max([Days Since Last Purchase])),1)`

Expressions	Use the following code to create a expression called Number of Purchases:
	
	`sum(if([Days Since Last Purchase]=ValueLoop($(=min([Days Since Last Purchase])),$(=max([Days Since Last Purchase])),1),1))`
	`/`
	`count([Days Since Last Purchase])`
	
	Choose to display the expression as a bar.

Chart Properties	Value
Expressions	Use the following code to create a expression called Normal Distribution: ``` NORMDIST(ValueLoop($(=min([Days Since Last Purchase])),$(=max([Days Since Last Purchase])),1) ,avg([Days Since Last Purchase]),stdev([Days Since Last Purchase]),0) ``` Choose to display the expression as a line.
Expressions	Use the following code to create a expression called t-Distribution: ``` TDIST((fabs(ValueLoop($(=min([Days Since Last Purchase])),$(=max([Days Since Last Purchase])),1) -avg([Days Since Last Purchase]))) / (Stdev([Days Since Last Purchase]) / sqrt(count([Days Since Last Purchase]))) ,count([Days Since Last Purchase]),1) ``` Choose to display the expression as a smooth line.
Axes / Dimension Axis	Choose to Continuous option in the Dimension Axis section.
Presentation / Reference Lines	Use the following code to create a reference line called Mean Days Since Last Purchase: ``` =Avg([Days Since Last Purchase]) ``` We set the following location: Choose the option to Show Label in Chart and the option to locate it on the Continuous X axis.
Presentation / Reference Lines	Use the following code to create a reference line called Upper Limit (95%): ``` =TTest1_Upper([Days Since Last Purchase]-0,(1-(95)/100)/2) ``` Choose the option to locate it on the Continuous X axis.
Presentation / Reference Lines	Use the following code to create a reference line called Lower Limit (95%): ``` =TTest1_Lower([Days Since Last Purchase]-0,(1-(95)/100)/2) ``` Choose the option to locate it on the Continuous X axis.

After additional adjustments to the presentation, we have the following chart. This particular chart compares the actual purchasing frequency distribution for customer *Gevee.* with both a normal and a t-distribution curve:

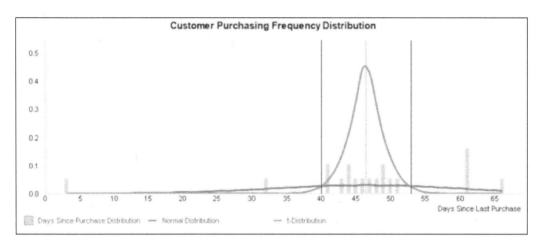

If we alert the sales representatives any time that a customer waits more than the mean number of days, then we could be sending too many false alarms, or in other words false positives. However, if we define at-risk customers as those who wait longer than the upper limit of the 95% confidence level, we have a higher probability of alerting the sales representative about customers that are really at-risk, or true positives.

Let's also keep in mind that not all lost customers have the same effect on the company, so let's combine the stratification that we performed earlier in the chapter with our churn-prediction analysis. In this way, sales representatives know to focus their attention on **A** customers that are at-risk, and not invest too much time to follow-up on **D** customers. The following table shows what this analysis may look like:

Customer	Rolling 12-month net sales	Clasif.	At-risk
	4,070,549		
Oodoo	954,122	A	
Gevee	642,405	A	
Miboo	500,666	A	
Dynabox	495,883	B	
Ntag	470,080	B	
Dabjam	382,969	B	
Reallinks	324,256	C	
Photospace	300,051	C	
Thoughtworks	118	D	

We add the following expression to the customer-stratification table that we created in a previous exercise. The background color expression calculates the days since the last purchase and compares it with the upper limit of the 95% confidence level. Refer the following table for a clear view:

Exercise 12.5

Expressions	Expression for an at-risk customer
	= ' '
	We set the **Background Color** as follows:
| | ```
if(max({$<_ActualFlag={1},Year=,Month=,_
DateSerial={"<=$(=max(_DateSerial))"}>} Total _KEY_
Date)
 - max({$<_ActualFlag={1},Year=,Month=,_
DateSerial={"<=$(=max(_DateSerial))"}>} _KEY_Date)
 >
TTest1_Upper({$<_ActualFlag={1},Year=,Month=,_
DateSerial={"<=$(=max(_DateSerial))"}>} [Days Since
Last Purchase]-0,(1-(95)/100)/2), red(100))
``` |

Customer stratification together with customer-churn prediction is a very powerful business tool. Now, let's take our first look at QlikView extensions and introduce the cycle plot.
```

QlikView extensions and the cycle plot

If we are going to work with advanced data visualization in QlikView, we have to get used to working with extensions. We can either develop the QlikView extension ourselves or use open source extensions that are available in Qlik Branch (http://branch.qlik.com).

For example, we are presented with the challenge to find a better way to visualize **year-over-year (YoY)**, **week-over-week (WoW)**, or any other period-over-period analysis. The following line chart demonstrates how difficult it can be to compare a large number of periods:

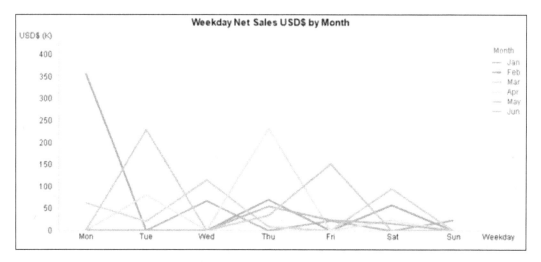

A cycle plot (*Cleveland, Dunn, and Terpenning, 1978*) offers a alternate way to compare a large number of periods. The following cycle plot is a QlikView extension that displays the average sales by weekday in each month and compares it to the total average sales represented by a flat horizontal line:

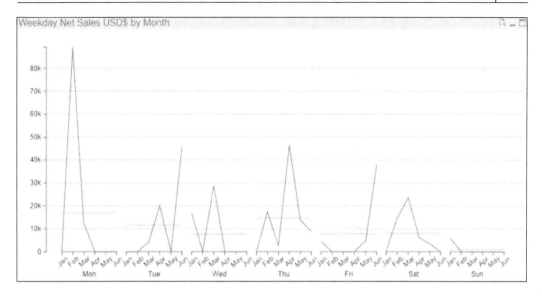

Exercise 12.6

Let's create this cycle plot in `Sales_Perspective_Sandbox.qvw` using the following steps:

1. In the `Ch. 2` folder of the book's exercise files, double-click the `CyclePlot.qar` file. QlikView will automatically open and notify you that the extension has been installed successfully.

2. In `Sales_Perspective_Sandbox.qvw`, activate **WebView**.

3. Right-click over an empty space and select **New Sheet Object**.

4. Click **Extensions Objects** and drag the extension called **Cycle Plot** to a empty place in the sheet.

5. Define the following properties to the cycle plot. The expression is

   ```
   sum({$<_ActualFlag={1}>} [Net Sales])
   /
   count(distinct _KEY_Date)
   ```

The properties of an extension are unique to that extension. We should review the extension's documentation for more information about each option.

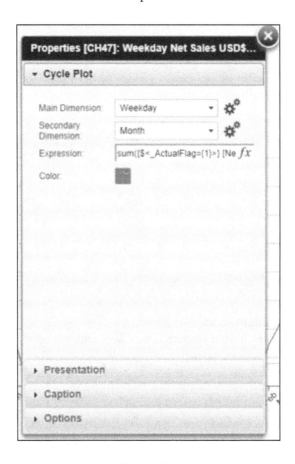

We should now see the cycle plot similar to the one previously shown. We will continue to explore more QlikView extensions in later chapters.

Governance – design template

Although we may think that we should create a design template before creating the first application, it is often better to do so once we've created the first application. After we've made the design adjustments that the business user requests then we can use that application as a template for future ones.

We convert the first QlikView application into a design template by first leaving only the sheets with unique layouts. A layout may include a background, a logo, a sheet title, and lines that separate sections. We may also leave a few example objects, such as list boxes and charts, that serve as references when we create the actual objects that are specific to the each perspective. We save this template into a new QVW file and use a copy of it every time we create a new QlikView application. The following image shows an example layout that we use as a design template:

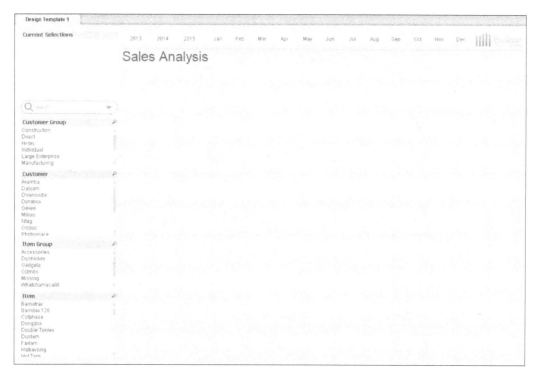

When we create the actual objects for a QlikView application, we can either use the **Format Painter Tool** to transfer the property options of the existing reference objects to the new ones, or we can create a simple QlikView theme based on an existing chart. The key to making an effective theme is to not over fit the design. We should only be concerned with simple properties, such as borders and captions. Let's create a simple theme and enable it to be used to create all new objects from this point on:

1. In the **Properties** dialog of the pareto analysis, let's click **Theme Maker...** in the **Layout** tab.

2. We select **New Theme** and save our theme as `Basic_Theme.qvt` in `C:\Qlik\SourceData\99.Shared_Folders\9.Misc`.

3. We select **Object Type Specific** and **Caption Border**.

4. In the **Object Type Specific** properties, we select only **Axis Thickness, Axis Font, Axis Color**, and **Chart Title Settings**.

5. In the **Caption and border** settings, we leave the default selections.

6. In the last step, select the option to **Set as default theme** for this document. We can also change this setting in the **Presentation** tab of the **Document Properties**.

We will now save a few seconds every time we create a new chart object. We should repeat the same procedure for any other objects we frequently create.Also, if we notice any other repetitive design changes that we are making to new objects, we can update the theme using the same **Theme Maker** wizard.

Summary

Our QlikView sales perspective is a great place to start to use more advanced data visualization and analysis techniques. Sales departments traditionally have both the resources and the data available to continue to improve their QlikView applications.

Apart from the sales data model that we reviewed, we should continue to include additional data. Adding cross-functional data from finance, marketing, and operations gives sales representatives the information that they need to succeed. We can also add external data sources, such as census data or any other government data. When we add this additional data, we should keep in mind the cleaning and standardization tips that we learned in this chapter.

Like customer stratification and customer churn, we can often create minimally viable solutions using basic QlikView. However, we can develop a better solution by understanding and applying more advanced techniques like Pareto analysis and statistical distributions.

We can also add more powerful visualizations and analysis if we use extensions. The cycle plot is an excellent example of a useful visualization that is not available as a native QlikView object. In the next chapter, let's review the data model, user stories, analytical methods and visualization techniques for the financial perspective.

13
Financial Perspective

The financial perspective includes arguably the most important measures of a business. We judge the actions and metrics of all other perspectives based on the effect that they have on the financial situation. Financial reports, such as the balance sheet, the income statement, and the cash flow statement, are universal measures of a company. These reports are used by outside investors, creditors, and the government, and there is a standard way that they are presented.

Accountants use standardized bookkeeping practices to record the financial data. Although we don't have to learn everything that they know about bookkeeping, we do have to understand the basic idea of what it means. For example, we have to understand how to interpret debits and credits in the data that originates from the accounting software. We also have to understand whether a measure is calculated over a certain period or based on an accumulated total. We review a financial data model that will consider these points and makes it easier to calculate financial metrics.

When we develop a QlikView financial perspective, we have to be ready for a challenge. The task is made even more arduous due to the static nature of the reports to which the business users are accustomed. QlikView is a data discovery tool and not a static report builder. Therefore, we need to add metadata to the data model that helps us to format these reports. We also review a few areas where we can take advantage of QlikView to visualize otherwise simple tables.

In this chapter, we will review the following topics:

- The data model for the financial perspective
- Metadata to format reports
- Standard financial reports
- Expenses and other financial indicators

Let's get started and review the data model that we use to create our financial perspective in QlikView.

Financial perspective data model

The data model for our financial perspective is similar to our sales data model.
Let's load the data model and review it.

Exercise 13.1

For this exercise, you need to perform the following steps:

1. In the `Ch. 3` folder of the book's exercise files, copy the container called
   `1002.Financial_Perspective` to the `QDF` folder located on your computer.
   By default, the `QDF` folder will be `C:\Qlik\SourceData`.

2. In the `QDF` folder, open the `VariableEditor` shortcut in the
   `0.Administration` container.

3. Click **Container Map Editor**.

4. In the container map table, go to first empty line, and under the `Container
   Folder Name` column, enter the name of the new container that we just
   copied, `1002.Financial_Perspective`, into the input field.

5. Continue along the row and enter the `Variable Prefix` as `Financial` and
   the `Container Comments` as `Container for Financial Perspective`.

6. Click the **Update Map and create Containers** button located at the top-left of
   the container map table, and when prompted, click **Update Container Map**.

7. Save the QlikView file.

If we open 1.Application\Financial_Analysis_Sandbox.qvw and look at the data
model then we can review the following data model.

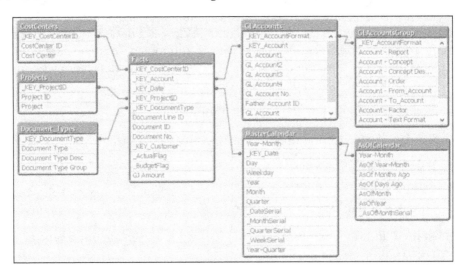

Similar to the data model for the sales perspective, the one that we use for the financial perspective contains a fact table surrounded by dimension tables. In the fact table at the center of the model, we store the following events:

- General journal entries
- Financial budget

General Journal (GJ) entries record all financial information. For example, different GJ entries are created to reflect the financial effects of a sales invoice, a purchase invoice, or a bank deposit. We can also create journal entry directly, without any supporting document.

A GJ entry consists of two types of numeric values: debit, and credit. Each entry assigns a debit or credit amount to two or more **General Ledger (GL)** accounts in such a way that the total debit amount always equals the total credit amount. The following diagram shows a general journal entry for a sales invoice:

GL Account Name	GL Account Number	Debit	Credit
Customer	1-10-1000	114.99	
Value Added Tax (VAT)	2-10-1000		15.00
Sales	4-10-1000		99.99
Total		114.99	114.99

Whether an account is debited or credited depends on the normal balance of the account. For example, GL accounts that measure sales have a normal credit balance. So, if we want to increase the value of sales, then we would credit the account. Inversely, if the customer cancels a sale, we decrease the value of sales by debiting the account.

As keeping track of debits and credits can become confusing, we simplify the handling of debits and credits in the data model and calculate a third field called [GJ Amount]::

    [GJ Amount] = Debit - Credit

The following table shows the [GJ Amount] values for the previous GJ entry. At first it may seem counterintuitive that we increase sales with a negative amount, but we will talk about how to handle the sign of the **Amount** field when we talk about the data model's dimensions tables.

GLAccount	GLAccoutName	Debit	Credit	Amount
1-10-1000	Customer	114.99	0.00	114.99
2-10-1000	Value Added Tax (VAT)	0.00	15.00	-15.00
4-10-1000	Sales	0.00	99.99	-99.99

Similar to the sales data model, a GJ entry is a discrete event. Other than the date dimension, the financial data model does not have many dimensions. Let's take a look at the few dimensions that regularly describe GJ entries in the following table.

Dimensions		
7Ws	**Fields**	**Comments**
What	`GL Account`	This is the most important dimension that describes the GL accounts that correspond to the GJ entry amounts. We use it to identify the GL account type and how we should handle the amount in the reports. Great financial analysis is made easier when accountants precisely define and use a list of GL accounts called a chart of accounts (COA).
Who / Where	`Cost Center`	This is a field that usually defines the business department or unit to which a certain cost or expense can be assigned. The cost centers can be based on segmented numbers that, for example, define the company with the first two numbers, the branch with the next three numbers, and the department with the last three numbers. Revenue is described by a similar dimension called a profit center.
What	`Project`	Project accounting is important to determine the cost and possible income of any business endeavor. Like this field, there may also exist other high-level groupings that are important to the company.
When	`Date`	We record the exact date of the GJ entries. Our financial budgets are defined on a monthly basis, so we assign a budget to the first day of the month.
Metrics		
7Ws	**Fields**	**Comments**
How many	`GJ Amount`	This field is the result of subtracting the credit amount from the debit amount.

The data model for our financial perspective is a slight variation of the *star schema*. As the `AsOfCalendar` dimension table is not directly linked to the `Facts` table, but rather, they are linked to other dimension tables; this data model is called a *snowflake schema*. We prefer to use the star schema, but we've kept two dimensions separate so that we can explain their purpose better in the next two sections. Even though we create an additional link in the data model, the small size of both dimension tables means that there will be no perceivable change to the application's performance.

Financial report metadata

The GLAccountsGroup table contains information on how to organize and format the financial reports. The field called Account - Factor is of particular importance because it helps determine how to handle the sign of the GJ Amount for the reports. For example, if we sum the sales amount directly from the GJ Amount field, we will get a negative number because the GL account for sales has a normal credit balance. However, when we look at this number in a report, we want to see it as a positive number. So, we multiply the sum by the number in Account - Factor in order to change the sign of sales.

In general, the first digit of a GL account number indicates the account type and whether we need to change the sign of the amounts assigned to it. The following diagram shows the normal balance of the principal account types according to a common numbering scheme and the value we will store in Account - Factor:

Example chart of accounts

GL Account Group	First digit in GL Account Number	Debit or Credit Balance	Factor
Asset	1	Debit	1
Liability	2	Credit	-1
Equity or Capital	3	Credit	-1
Revenue	4	Credit	-1
Costs of Sales	5	Debit	1
Expenses	6, 7, 8, or 9	Debit	1

Along with Account - Factor, we also store information about how each financial report groups the GL accounts differently. Unlike customer and product groups in the sales perspective, GL account groups are not only informative, but they are also an essential part of financial analysis. We must take care to verify each account's grouping with an accountant, or else we risk creating erroneous analysis.

Finally, we also include information about how we want to format our financial reports in the same table. We assign a particular format to each group and calculation. By defining that information in this table, we maintain the report's format much easier than if we defined the format directly in the QlikView object:

Report	Concept	Order	From_Account	To_Account	Factor	Format	Indentation	Color	Background Color
Profit_Loss	Income	100	4000	4999	-1	<b>	0	RGB(0,0,0)	RGB(256,256,256)
Profit_Loss	Costs	200	5000	5999	1	<i>	5	RGB(128,128,128)	RGB(256,256,256)
Profit_Loss	Gross Profit	300	4000	5999	-1	<b>	0	RGB(0,0,0)	RGB(256,256,256)
Profit_Loss	Expenses	400	6000	6999	1	<i>	5	RGB(128,128,128)	RGB(256,256,256)
Profit_Loss	EBIT	500	4000	6999	-1	<b>	0	RGB(0,0,0)	RGB(256,256,256)
Profit_Loss	Financial Costs	600	7000	7999	1	<i>	5	RGB(128,128,128)	RGB(256,256,256)
Profit_Loss	Other Income y Expenses	700	8000	8999	1	<i>	5	RGB(128,128,128)	RGB(256,256,256)
Profit_Loss	Net Profit	800	4000	8999	-1	<b>	0	RGB(0,0,0)	RGB(256,256,256)
Balance_Sheet	Assets	100	1000	1999	1	<i>	5	RGB(128,128,128)	RGB(256,256,256)
Balance_Sheet	Total Assets	199	1000	1999	1	<b>	0	RGB(0,0,0)	RGB(256,256,256)
Balance_Sheet	Liabilities	200	2000	2999	-1	<i>	5	RGB(128,128,128)	RGB(256,256,256)
Balance_Sheet	Capital	300	3000	3999	-1	<i>	5	RGB(128,128,128)	RGB(256,256,256)
Balance_Sheet	Net Profit	400	4000	9999	-1	<i>	5	RGB(128,128,128)	RGB(256,256,256)
Balance_Sheet	Total Capital and Liabilities	500	2000	9999	-1	<b>	0	RGB(0,0,0)	RGB(256,256,256)

Let's review the data that we store in our `GLAccountsGroup` table in more detail. Each of the following numbers corresponds to one or more columns in the previous diagram:

1. The first column defines the report that corresponds to the grouping or calculation that define in this row. In this case, we have three reports: an income statement, a balance sheet, and a cash flow statement.

2. In the next column, we include the text description of the account grouping or calculation.

3. Here, we define the order in which each concept must be displayed. We choose numbers in increments of a hundred so that we have room to insert new concepts in between two others without having to reassign the value of every other concept.

4. Account groupings are usually defined by a range of GL accounts. We use `intervalmatch()` in the script to link this table with our `GLAccounts` table. For more information on `intervalmatch()` review the QlikView help documentation where you can find a great example of how it works.

5. We define factor to be negative one (**-1**) for all accounts with a normal credit balance. We also apply a factor of negative one (**-1**) to every calculated group that includes a credit account. For example, we use negative one (**-1**) as a factor for gross profit because it is the sum of income (a normal credit balance) and costs (a normal debit balance). In doing so, we obtain the following results:

        °   If income is greater than costs, we have a profit. As income is a normal credit balance, we first see this as a negative number. As we want to see profit as a positive number, we multiply it by a factor of negative one (**-1**).

        °   Otherwise, if costs are greater than income, we have a loss. As costs are a normal debit balance, we first see this as a positive number. As we want to see loss as a negative number, we multiply it by a factor of negative one (**-1**).

6. We decide whether we want the account group's description and to appear in bold (`<b>`), italic (`<i>`), or bold italic (`<b><i>`) . If we want the text to be normal, we leave the cell blank.

7. We use indentation to help users recognize any group hierarchies. The number represents the amount of spaces that we will use to indent the group's text description.

8. We can color normal text dark grey and important text black. A good dark grey to use is `rgb(128,128,128)` or `DarkGray()`.

9. Finally, we leave the option to highlight certain rows with a background color.

Once we define the financial report metadata in the data model, we can then easily format our financial reports. We can also use this technique to maintain the format of any other legacy report in QlikView. Before we create our first financial report, let's look at one other element in the data model that facilitates financial analysis.

AsOfCalendar

When we perform financial analysis, we have to be able to easily adjust over which period we are going calculate each metric. For example, return on assets is net income divided by total assets. Net income is calculated over the past twelve months while total assets is an accumulated amount calculated over all previous months.

We can use set analysis to calculate these metrics at any one moment in time; however, we also would like to visualize the trend of these metrics. The best way to calculate that trend is to combine set analysis with an `AsOfCalendar`.

An `AsOfCalendar` contains the same months and years as a regular calendar. However, when we select a date in the `AsOfCalendar`, we see everything that is prior to this data in the `Facts` table. For example, in the following diagram if we select **2013-Jun** in the **AsOf Year-Month** field, then we see all months prior to it in the data model as possible values in the **Year-Month** field:

AsOf Year-Month	Year-Month
2013-Jun	2013-Apr
2013-Apr	2013-May
2013-May	2013-Jun
2013-Jul	2013-Jul
2013-Aug	2013-Aug
2013-Sep	2013-Sep
2013-Oct	2013-Oct
2013-Nov	2013-Nov

We use a subroutine, `Qvc.AsOfTable` in QV Components, to create the `AsOfCalendar` and insert the following script after creating the `MasterCalendar` table. We also add the `AsOf Year` and `AsOf Month` fields manually to make the table more useful. The table also contains a field called `AsOf Months Ago` that tells us how many months difference there is between the `AsOf Year-Month` and the `Year-Month`. This field can be quite useful when we need to calculate rolling periods:

```
CALL Qvc.AsOfTable('Year-Month');
AsOfCalendar:
Load *,
  Month([AsOf Year-Month]) as AsOfMonth,
  Year([AsOf Year-Month]) as AsOfYear
Resident [AsOfTable_Year-Month];
Drop table [AsOfTable_Year-Month];
```

In order to take advantage of this calendar, we also need to replace the usual year and month filters with ones that use `AsOf Year` and `AsOf Month`. The filters will look exactly the same as the year and month filters in the sales perspective that uses the master calendar table. However, in the following sections, we see what changes we have to make to accurately calculate the expressions.

Let's start visualizing the financial perspective with the three most important reports.

Income statement

An income statement is an essential report for all the business's stakeholders. We'll take an executive's perspective for our user story.

Financial statements have been around for so long that most business users are going to want to see them in the format that they are accustomed to. As legacy reporting in QlikView involves using advanced methods, let's take the time to create them in their standard format. We will then look at how we can make a report more visual and easier to understand at a glance.

In the following income statement example, we start by calculating the sales that we generated during the course of the year. Proceeding downward through the report, we subtract the costs and expenses that were incurred in these same period. Then at certain moments in the report, we calculate a subtotal. For example, gross profit is sales minus costs, operating profit is gross profit minus expenses, and net profit is operating profit minus other concepts, such as taxes and interest.

Each of these main groups (sales, costs, and expenses) can be divided into further subgroups. These subgroups depend on the business and what the stakeholders want to measure. For example, we want to dissect expenses into various subgroups, such as travel and payroll, and see how each affects whether we make money or not. Let's create an income statement in the following *Exercise 13.2*.

	Jan 2015 Monthly	%	YTD	%
Sales Revenue	1,481,031	100%	1,481,031	100%
Other Revenue	-	-	-	-
Total Revenue	**1,481,031**	**100%**	**1,481,031**	**100%**
COGS - Cost of Goods Sold	1,159,277	78%	1,159,277	78%
Cost Variances	-	-	-	-
Gross Profit	**321,753**	**22%**	**321,753**	**22%**
Travel Expenses	-	-	-	-
Payroll Expenses	-	-	-	-
Bad Debt Expenses	-	-	-	-
Admin Expenses	-	-	-	-
Depreciation and Amorti...	-	-	-	-
Office Expenses	-	-	-	-
Legal Expenses	-	-	-	-
Other Expenses	-	-	-	-
Operating Profit	**321,753**	**22%**	**321,753**	**22%**
Financial Costs	0	0%	0	0%
Other Income y Expenses	-	-	-	-
Net Profit	**321,753**	**22%**	**321,753**	**22%**

Exercise 13.2

In the `Financial_Perspective_Sandbox.qvw` application that is found in the `C:\Qlik\SourceData\1002.Finance_Perspective\1.Application`, let's start by creating a straight table with the following properties:

1. Add the `[Account - Concept]` field as a dimension.

2. Add the following five metrics:

Label	Expression

`=''`	`only({1<[Account - Report]`
	`={'Income_Statement'}>}`
	`[Account - Order])`

`=monthname(`
`max(`
`[AsOf Year-`
`Month]`
`))`
`&`
`chr(10)`
`& 'Monthly'`
	`sum({$<[Account - Report]={'Income_Statement'},`
	`[Month]=, [Year]=,_MonthSerial={'$(=max`
	`(_AsOfMonthSerial))'}>} [GJ Amount])`
	`* only([Account - Factor])`

`%`	`sum({$<[Account - Report]={'Income_Statement'},`
	`[Month]=, [Year]=,_MonthSerial={'$(=max`
	`(_AsOfMonthSerial))'}>} [GJ Amount])`
	`* only([Account - Factor])`
	`/`
	`sum({$<[Account - Report]={'Income_`
	`Statement'},[Account - Concept]={'Total  Revenue'},`
	`[Month]=, [Year]=,_MonthSerial={'$(=max`
	`(_AsOfMonthSerial))'}>} Total [GJ Amount]) * -1`

`=chr(10) &`
`'YTD'`
	`sum({$<[Account - Report]={'Income_Statement'},[Mon`
	`th]=, [Year]={$(=max(AsOfYear))},`
	`_MonthSerial={'<=$(=max(_AsOfMonthSerial))'}>} [GJ`
	`Amount]) * only([Account - Factor])`

`%`	`sum({$<[Account - Report]={'Income_Statement'},`
	`[Month]=, [Year]={$(=max(AsOfYear))},`
	`_MonthSerial={'<=$(=max(_AsOfMonthSerial))'}>} [GJ`
	`Amount])`
	`* only([Account - Factor])`
	`/`
	`sum({$<[Account - Report]={'Income_`
	`Statement'},[Account - Concept]={'Total  Revenue'}`
	`, [Month]=, [Year]={$(=max(AsOfYear))},`
	`_MonthSerial={'<=$(=max(_AsOfMonthSerial))'}>}`
	`Total [GJ Amount])`
	`* -1`

The first expression looks unusual. It doesn't aggregate anything and doesn't even appear in the example income statement. That's because it works as a placeholder for account groups that do not have any GJ entries during the selected period. Unlike QlikView, legacy reports usually show dimensions even when the sum of their corresponding metric is zero. We change the expression's **Text Color** to white() so that it is hidden from the user.

Now that we've added the necessary dimension and expressions let's change a few detailed properties and apply the financial report metadata to the QlikView object:

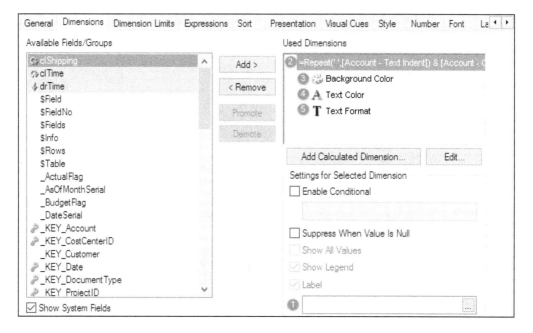

1. In the **Dimensions** tab, select the **Account – Concept** and insert a blank space in the **Label** field.

2. Click **Edit...** and insert the following code to enable the text indentation:

   ```
   =Repeat(' ',[Account - Text Indent]) & [Account - Concept]
   ```

3. Expand the dimension's properties and click **Background Color**. Click **Edit...** and insert the following code:

   ```
   =Only({1} [Account - Background Color])
   ```

4. Click **Text Color** and click **Edit...** and insert the following formula:

   ```
   =Only({1} [Account - Text Color])
   ```

5. Finally, click **Text Format** and then click **Edit...** and insert the following formula:

```
=Only({1} [Account - Text Format])
```

6. In the **Dimensions** tab, there is a little-used option that we can use to adjust the row spacing to make the table more readable and aesthetically pleasing. Click **Advanced...** in the **Dimensions** tab and make the two changes that appear in the following diagram:

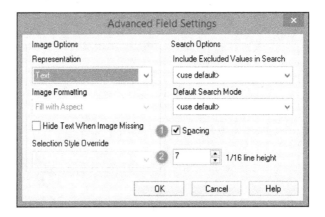

7. Now, let's apply the same formatting changes to the expressions, as follows:

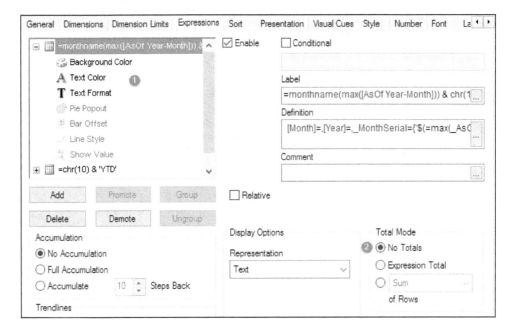

8. In the same way that we defined the properties of the dimension, we define the **Background Color**, **Text Color**, and **Text Format** in the **Definition** field for every expression except for the one we use as a placeholder:

Background Color	=Only({1} [Account - Background Color])
Text Color	=Only({1} [Account - Text Color])
Text Format	=Only({1} [Account - Text Format])

9. Finally, for each expression select the **No Totals** radio button in the **Total Mode** section.

10. Let's move on to the **Sort** tab. Go through the steps in the following diagram to properly sort the report's concepts. The sort expression is =only({1< [Account - Report]={'Income_Statement'}>} [Account - Order]):

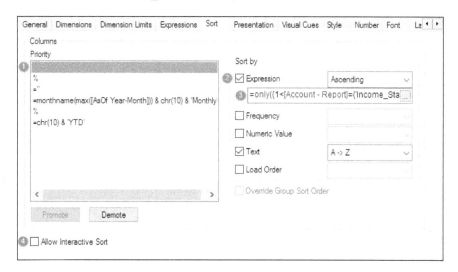

We can reduce the work in this step if we use the dual() function in the script to combine the text description and order number into one field:

dual([Account - Concept], [Account - Order]) as [Account - Sorted Concept]

We would then only need to sort [Account - Sorted Concept] by **Numeric Value**.

11. Now in the **Presentation** tab, let's copy the options that are seen the following diagram:

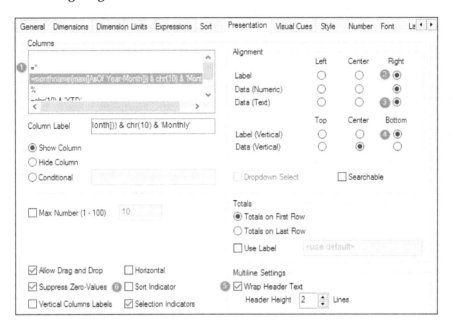

It is good practice to align the column label in the same way that we did to its data. We also keep the label close to the data and vertically align the label on the bottom of a two-line header. Make sure to set these alignments for every expression.

Along with proper formatting, we want to alert users to any negative values. Such values in one of the income statement's calculated groups, such as Gross Profit or Operating Profit, indicate a loss. If found in other groups they may indicate an unusual transaction that affects an account contrary to its normal balance. We enable these alerts in the **Visual Cues** tab.

If we have room enough to only use whitespace to divide columns, let's remove the borders in the **Style** tab in two easy steps:

1. Uncheck **Vertical Dimension Cell Borders**.
2. Uncheck **Vertical Expression Cell Borders**.

Finally, let's perform these last two steps to clean the number format and to hide the caption:

1. In the **Number** tab, define both expressions as integers.
2. In the **Caption** tab, uncheck **Show Caption**.

We should now have a fairly clean income statement, but what if we want to go a little further and change the background of the column header or row borders? We can use a hidden feature called **Custom Format Cell** to make these additional changes.

Custom format cell

Straight tables and pivot tables have an additional properties dialog to further customize a table's style. It is not available by default, so first we go to the **Settings** file menu, and then **User Preference...**.

In the **Design** tab of **User Preferences**, tick the option to **Always Show Design Menu Items**, as shown in the following screenshot:

We now have a new option called **Custom Format Cell** when we right-click over any table:

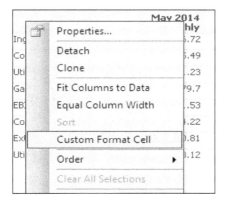

This option opens a window that allows us to define the cell borders, cell backgrounds, text color, text style, and text size of each dimension and expression. Any change that we make to one cell applies to all other cells belonging to the same expression or dimension. In other words, we cannot define a different format for two different cells of the same expression or dimension.

Regardless of this limitation, **Custom Format Cell** does provide us with several options to create a custom table style. Let's go ahead and make our final changes to the format of the income statement as follows:

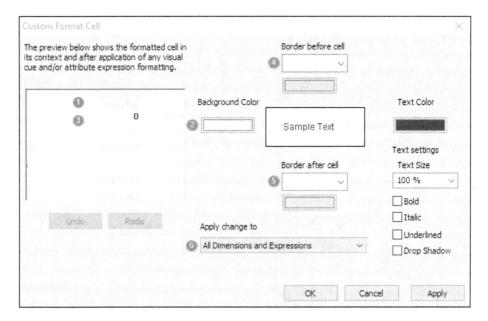

You will notice that on the left-hand side of the window, we can navigate throughout the table and define the style for each dimension and expression without having to close the window and reopen it by right-clicking on a different area of the table. Let's start by clicking on the first expression's column header:

1. Change the **Background Color** to white.
2. Now, click on the first cell with data.
3. Change the **Border before cell** to nothing.
4. Change the **Border after cell** to nothing.
5. Select **All Dimensions and Expression** in the **Apply change to** drop-down box and click OK.

If we add a few more metrics and move the account names to the center of the table, we can achieve a more detailed *winged report* with monthly metrics on one side and year-to-date metrics on the other. You can review the following example in the exercise solution file:

Mar 2015 Monthly	%	LY	%	Var	% Var		YTD	%	LY	%	Var	%Var
3,977,941	100%	2,333,228	100%	1,644,712	70%	Sales Revenue	10,580,068	100%	6,358,645	100%	4,221,424	66%
.	.	.	.	.	.	Other Revenue	.	.	.	.	.	.
3,977,941	100%	2,333,228	100%	1,644,712	70%	**Total Revenue**	10,580,068	100%	6,358,645	100%	4,221,424	66%
3,310,852	83%	2,117,383	91%	1,193,468	56%	COGS - Cost of Goods Sold	10,894,354	103%	6,037,836	95%	4,856,519	80%
.	.	.	.	.	.	Cost Variances	.	.	.	.	.	.
667,089	17%	215,845	9%	451,244	209%	**Gross Profit**	-314,286	-3%	320,809	5%	-635,095	-198%
						Travel Expenses						

Now that we have a well-formatted income statement, let's examine how we can use common visualization techniques to make it more effective. We use a slightly modified version of the previous user story to identify the key points that executives look for in an income statement.

Modern accounting has been around for more than 500 years, and we are probably not going to change how accountants visualize data in our lifetime. The accountant's instinct to use numbers and tables to solve this user story may result in something like the following example, which is a common format to analyze how an income statement is trending:

AsOfMonth									Jan			Feb
	Month	Month LY	Var	% Var	YTD	YTD LY	Var	% Var	Month	Month LY	Var	
Sales Revenue	1,481,031	321,808	1,159,222	360%	1,481,031	321,808	1,159,222	360%	5,121,097	3,703,608	1,417,48	
Total Revenue	**1,481,031**	**321,808**	**1,159,222**	**360%**	**1,481,031**	**321,808**	**1,159,222**	**360%**	**5,121,097**	**3,703,608**	**1,417,489**	
COGS - Cost of Goods Sold	1,159,277	280,221	879,057	314%	1,159,277	280,221	879,057	314%	6,424,225	3,640,231	2,783,99	
Cost Variances	-	-	-	-	-	-	-	- -	-	-	-	
Gross Profit	**321,753**	**41,588**	**280,166**	**674%**	**321,753**	**41,588**	**280,166**	**674%**	**-1,303,128**	**63,376**	**-1,366,50**	
Admin Expenses	-	-	-	-	-	-	-	- -	-	-	-	

Any argument to say that they shouldn't analyze data in this way will cause them to question QlikView's ability to satisfy their reporting needs. Therefore, I recommend that we do it in the way that they are most comfortable with. Luckily, the `AsOfCalendar` table makes this report possible without reverting to methods, such as island tables and if-statements, that can cause the report's calculation time to grow exponentially. You can review the details on how to make the table in the exercise solution file.

Then, in addition to the table, we should propose more abstract ways to view the data more efficiently. Converting a table full of metrics into an abstract visualization is one of the most difficult challenges that we will ever face as data visualization designers. We have to come to terms with the fact that we cannot fit every metric into one chart without making it as hard to read as the originating table. Regardless of whether we use lines, bars, points, or some purportedly omniscient chart, we cannot fit everything into one visualization.

The best solution is to create a group of charts in which each element highlights a different aspect of the income statement. For example, we can create one bar chart to analyze year-to-date amounts and variations, and another graph to analyze monthly amounts and variations. Then we can add a line chart to view the trend of the most important account groups, and another to view the trend of detailed expense accounts.

Another alternative is to use the same familiar table structure to create a grid chart. Again, if we try to fit everything into one chart, we have to sacrifice a certain level of detail, metrics, or dimensions. At the same time, we can use the following grid chart to start a story that will lead us to look at specific charts and tables as we dive deeper into our story:

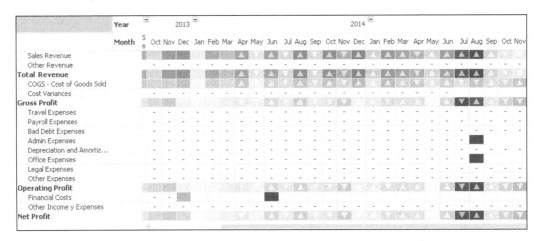

In order to make this chart, we have to sacrifice measuring year-to-date metrics. We've maintained the same number of dimensions, but we've replaced actual numbers with color and year-over-year variation with an arrow.
Even so, we can quickly perceive that we had our highest sales in July and August 2015, while strangely, our cost of goods sold was highest in December 2014. The fact that cost of goods sold is not always correlated to sales is curious. Such an observation may be a great place for a business user to start a story that leads to price and inventory analysis.

Exercise 13.3

In the `Financial_Perspective_Sandbox.qvw` application, let's first create a variable that makes the chart expressions cleaner, as follows:

1. Add the following variables that calculate the GJ amount for the current month and the same month last year:

Name	Definition
vExp_CYMTD_GJAmount	sum({$<[Account - Report]={'Income_Statement'}, [AsOf Months Ago]={0}>} [GJ Amount])
vExp_LYMTD_GJAmount	sum({$<[Account - Report]={'Income_Statement'}, [AsOf Months Ago]={12}>} [GJ Amount])

2. Clone the income statement that we created in *Exercise 13.2* and change the chart type to pivot table.

3. Add the dimensions `AsOfYear` and `AsOfMonth` to the cloned table and pivot them so that they become columns as in the previous figure.

4. Replace the existing metric with the following that creates an up arrow, or `chr(9650)` if the current month is greater than the same month last year and a down arrow otherwise, or chr(9660). This expression also serves as a placeholder for inactive accounts:

Label	Expression

Month	if(
	  $(vExp_CYMTD_GJAmount) * only([Account - Factor])
	  /
	  $(vExp_LYMTD_GJAmount) * only([Account - Factor])
	  -1
	  <0,chr(9660),
	  if(
	    $(vExp_CYMTD_GJAmount) * only([Account - Factor])
	    /
	    $(vExp_LYMTD_GJAmount) * only([Account - Factor])
	    -1
	    >0,chr(9650),
	    if(not isnull(only({1< [Account - Report]={'Income_Statement'}>} [Account - Concept]))
	Statement'}>} [Account - Concept]))
	    ,'')
	    )
	  )

5. Add the following code as a background color of the expression. The `aggr()` function helps define a different range of lightness and darkness for each account. Otherwise, the accounts with the largest numbers like revenue and costs would always be a dark color and every other smaller account a light one:

```
ColorMix2 (
    if($(vExp_CYMTD_GJAmount) * -1  < 0
      ,-Sqrt(($(vExp_CYMTD_GJAmount) * -1)/min(total <[Account
- Concept] > aggr($(vExp_CYMTD_GJAmount)* -1,[Account -
Concept],AsOfMonth,AsOfYear)))
      ,Sqrt(($(vExp_CYMTD_GJAmount)  * -1)/max(total <[Account
- Concept] > aggr($(vExp_CYMTD_GJAmount)* -1,[Account -
Concept],AsOfMonth,AsOfYear))))
    , ARGB(255, 255, 128, 0), ARGB(255, 0, 64, 128), ARGB(255, 255,
255, 255))
```

6. Add `white(150)` as the expression's text color. We make the arrow slightly transparent so that it contrasts less with the background, which makes for easier reading and a more refined look.

We now have an income statement grid chart. We can experiment with the options that we learned earlier in this section to add cell borders and any fine-tuning adjustments. After doing so, let's move on to the next important financial report—the balance sheet.

Balance sheet

We use the following user story to understand the needs of the business users that require a balance sheet.

As an executive, I want to understand the overall financial health of the business so that I can create the necessary strategy to ensure its future.

The balance sheet is a complete analysis of a company's financial situation. It is the sum of all GJ amounts divided into three principal groups: assets, liabilities, and capital. The income statement from the previous section is a small part of the balance sheet that is classified as Retained Earnings in the capital account group. The following is an example balance sheet:

Balance Sheet

	Current Month	%	Last Month	%	Var	%Var
Current Assets	442,873,038	100%	407,692,027	100%	35,181,011	9%
Fixed Assets	-	-	-	-	-	
Long-term Assets	-	-	-	-	-	
Total Assets	**442,873,038**	**100%**	**407,692,027**	**100%**	**35,181,011**	**9%**
Current Liabilities	423,008,636	96%	397,324,153	97%	25,684,483	6%
Long-term Liabilities	-	-	-	-	-	
Total Liabilities	**423,008,636**	**96%**	**397,324,153**	**97%**	**25,684,483**	**6%**
Stock	-	-	-	-	-	
Past Retained Earning	-	-	-	-	-	
Current Retained Earning	19,864,402	4%	10,367,873	3%	9,496,529	92%
Total Capital	**19,864,402**	**4%**	**10,367,873**	**3%**	**9,496,529**	**92%**
Total Capital and Liabilities	**442,873,038**	**100%**	**407,692,027**	**100%**	**35,181,011**	**9%**

Unlike an income statement where we only see financial movements over a certain period of time, a balance sheet shows us an accumulated total of all the financial movements that have occurred prior to the selected month. Another requirement is that total assets must always be equal to the sum of liabilities and capital.

Also, we often divide assets, liabilities, and capital into smaller account groups that permit us to perform a deeper financial analysis of the company. For each group we calculate its percentage contribution with reference to total assets or total capital and liabilities. Finally, variation is calculated between consecutive periods. Year-over-year analysis is less common because seasonality is not as important for the balance sheet as it is for the income statement.

We create a balance sheet in the same way that we create an income statement. Let's create one in the next exercise.

Exercise 13.4

We start to create our balance sheet by cloning the income statement that we created in *Exercise 3.2* and then go through the following steps:

1. Change the placeholder expression to the following code:

```
only({1<[Account - Report]={'Balance_Sheet'}>} [Account - Order])
```

2. Change the expression that calculates the current month to the following code:

```
sum({$<[Account - Report]={'Balance_Sheet'}, [Month]=, [Year]=,
_MonthSerial={'<=$(=max(_AsOfMonthSerial))'}>} [GJ Amount]) *
only([Account - Factor])
```

3. Change the expression that calculates the percentage contribution liabilities to the following code:

```
sum({$<[Account - Report]={'Balance_Sheet'},[Month]=,[Year]=,
_MonthSerial={'<=$(=max(_AsOfMonthSerial))'}>} [GJ Amount])
* only([Account - Factor])
/
sum({$<[Account - Report]={'Balance_Sheet'},[Account -
Concept]={'Total Assets'}
,[Month]=,[Year]=,_MonthSerial={'<=$(=max(_AsOfMonthSerial))'}>}
Total [GJ Amount])
```

4. Replace the remaining two expressions in the cloned chart by repeating steps two and three to calculate the previous month's balances. In doing so, we change the set analysis that refers to `_MonthSerial` from `{'<=$(=max(_AsOfMonthSerial))'}` to `{'<=$(=max(_AsOfMonthSerial)-1)'}`.

5. Add variation and percentage variation columns as shown in the example balance sheet.

6. Change the set analysis in the sort expression so that it refers to `[Account -Report]={'Balance_Sheet'}`.

When we create data visualization that supports a balance sheet, we tend to analyze the ratio between amounts. For example, a metric such as return on assets, which is the net income divided by the average total assets, tells us how well a company uses its assets to earn a profit. Another example is the acid test ratio that divides current assets, such as cash, accounts receivable, and short-term investments, by current liabilities, such as accounts payable. This ratio tells us how well the business can cover short-term liabilities. Similar to these there are numerous other ratios that the accounting department may use to evaluate the current financial situation of a company. You can find out what a certain financial ratio means and how to calculate it at http://www.investopedia.com/.

The actual visualizations for these ratios are often quite simple. In part, this is true because The balance sheet has relatively few dimensions that pertain to it. Fields related to company and time are usually the only applicable dimensions that are available. Even so, it can be difficult to calculate them in QlikView and we often calculate financial ratios for a selected moment in time using set analysis. However, when we add the `AsOfCalendar` to the data model, we have the ability to analyze how they change over time.

In the next exercise, let's make a simple line chart that shows how return on assets behave over time.

Exercise 13.5

1. Add the following variable that includes two parameters that allow us to see the end-of-month balance of any concept. The first parameter defines the concept, and the second determines whether the balance is from the current month or any previous month. Zero (0) is the current month, one (1) is the previous month, two (2) is the month before that, and so on:

Name	Definition
vExp_EOM_ GJBalance	sum({$<[Account - Report]={'Balance_ Sheet'},[Account - Concept]={$1},[AsOf Months Ago]={">=$2"}>} [GJ Amount])

2. Create a bar chart with [AsOf YearMonth] as the dimension and with the following expression. The expression divides the last three months of net income by the three-month average of assets:

```
(sum({$<[Account - Report]={'Balance_Sheet'},[Account
- Concept]={'Current Retained Earning'},[AsOf Months
Ago]={">=1<=3"}>} [GJ Amount LC]))*-1
/
(
RangeSum(
$(vExp_EOM_GJBalance('Current Assets',0))
,$(vExp_EOM_GJBalance('Current Assets',1))
,$(vExp_EOM_GJBalance('Current Assets',2))
)/3
)
```

3. Adjust the bar chart's properties to produce a graph that is similar to the following figure:

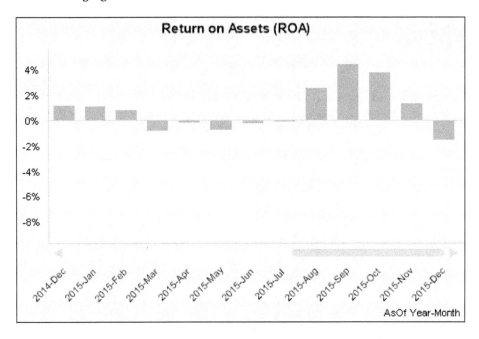

Without the `AsOfCalendar` table, this trend analysis and visualization would be difficult and slow to create. We use the `[AsOf Months Ago]` field in the set analysis to calculate over a rolling period that depends on the value of the `[AsOf YearMonth]` dimension.

Unlike the **Accumulation** option in the **Expression** tab or the `above()` function, we don't have to worry about the first few values of a selected data months being incorrect. Whether the user selects one month or one year, every bar in this chart will show the correct value. Although the final visualization is simple, the data model and calculation that we need to create it is quite elegant.

Cash flow statement

A *cash flow statement* is a report that analyzes the financial movements that affect cash flow.

Cash flow is classified in the following ways:

- Operations can be calculated using a direct or indirect method that is explained as follows:
  - The indirect method starts with the net income from the income statement and adjusts it according to the net changes of accounts receivable (A/R), accounts payable (A/P), and inventory
  - The direct method sums cash transactions between our customers, suppliers, and employees
- Investing includes purchasing and selling assets, such as offices or equipment
- Financing includes receiving or paying a bank loan

Cash Flow Statement		🖫 Xl _ ▢
	Movement	%
Net Income	**903,622**	**33%**
Depreciation and Amortization	0	0%
Inventory Increase (Decrease)	-36,387,104	-1,349%
Accounts Receivable Increase (Decrease)	-6,297,010	-233%
Accounts Payable Increase (Decrease)	44,477,921	1,649%
Cash Flow from Operations	**2,697,428**	**100%**
Capital Expenses	0	0%
Cash Flow from Investing	**0**	**0%**
Notes Payable	0	0%
Cash Flow from Financing	**0**	**0%**
Total Cash Flow	**2,697,428**	**100%**

To create a cash flow statement, we have to find every G/L account that affects the accounts that represent cash assets. In order to be successful at this, we have to team up with an accountant who can help us find and classify these accounts. When the total cash flow in this statement equals the net change of all cash assets then we've successfully found all the accounts.

In the next exercise, we will create a high-level cash flow statement using the more popular indirect method.

Exercise 13.6

We start to create our cash flow statement by cloning the balance statement that we created in *Exercise 13.2* and then go through the following steps:

1. Change the placeholder expression to the following code:
   ```
   only({1<[Account - Report]={'CashFlow'}>} [Account - Order])
   ```

2. Change one of the expressions to calculate net movements across all accounts:

```
sum({$<[Account - Report]={'CashFlow'},[AsOf Months Ago]={0}>} [GJ
Amount] * [Account - Factor])
```

3. Change one of the expressions to calculate the relative percentage between each amount and the total cash flow:

```
sum({$<[Account - Report]={'CashFlow'},[AsOf Months Ago]={0}>} [GJ
Amount] * [Account - Factor])
/
sum({$<[Account - Report]={'CashFlow'},[Account - Concept]={'Total
Cash Flow'},[AsOf Months Ago]={0}>} Total [GJ Amount] * [Account -
Factor])
```

4. Delete all other expressions.

5. Change the set analysis in the sort expression so that it refers to [Account - Report]={'CashFlow'}.

The magic we do to create this report is in the financial report metadata that we reviewed earlier in this chapter. We use the **Factor** field the following table to add or subtract amounts as defined by the accountant. This method of report making is not always easy to grasp at first, so we should take our time to explore and experiment with the metadata.

Report	Concept	From_Account	To_Account	Factor
CashFlow	Net Income	40000000	99999999	-1
CashFlow	Depreciation and Amortization	61500000	61599999	1
CashFlow	Inventory Increase (Decrease)	11300000	11399999	-1
CashFlow	Accounts Receivable Increase (Decrease)	11200000	11299999	-1
CashFlow	Accounts Payable Increase (Decrease)	21100000	21199999	-1
CashFlow	Cash Flow from Operations	40000000	61499999	-1
CashFlow	Cash Flow from Operations	61600000	99999999	-1
CashFlow	Cash Flow from Operations	11300000	11399999	-1
CashFlow	Cash Flow from Operations	11200000	11299999	-1
CashFlow	Cash Flow from Operations	21100000	21199999	-1
CashFlow	Capital Expenses	16100000	16199999	-1
CashFlow	Cash Flow from Investing	16100000	16199999	-1
CashFlow	Notes Payable	21440000	21440000	-1
CashFlow	Cash Flow from Financing	21440000	21440000	-1
CashFlow	Total Cash Flow	40000000	61499999	-1
CashFlow	Total Cash Flow	61600000	99999999	-1
CashFlow	Total Cash Flow	11300000	11399999	-1
CashFlow	Total Cash Flow	11200000	11299999	-1
CashFlow	Total Cash Flow	21100000	21199999	-1
CashFlow	Total Cash Flow	16100000	16199999	-1
CashFlow	Total Cash Flow	21440000	21440000	-1

The most important analysis introduced by the user story in the beginning of the section is to see what percentage of cash is received or spent within each group of activities. The cash flow statement looks distinct for different businesses during each stage in their lives. A start-up will not have much cash flow in operations, but it will have a lot of investment and financing activities. A mature company will have a more balanced cash flow with the greater amount classified as operations. A simple bar chart to that compares these three principal activities over time would be the optimal visualization.

Summary

A QlikView financial perspective is a challenge for any master. The creation of clean, clear, traditional financial reports is just as important as any other way to visualize data. However, we shouldn't stop there. We should strive to go beyond these first reports and create charts that allow financial analysts and executives to discover opportunities that are not so easy to find in a table full of numbers.

Be sure to review the use of the financial report metadata and the as-of calendar as tools to help create the income statement, balance sheet, and cash flow statement. They are also vital to create the supporting data visualization.

In the next chapter, we will leave behind traditional reports and experiment with more advanced data visualization in the QlikView marketing perspective.

14
Marketing Perspective

The most successful businesses understand the market that they serve. They understand that talking with a customer about their needs is more effective than babbling about their own product or service. We can use the marketing perspective to analyze actual customers, potential customers, business competitors, and society at large. Although we have a fair amount of internal data about our own customers, we also look for other data resources to examine other market variables.

One of the internal data sources that we can exploit is the **Customer Relationship Management (CRM)** system. This includes data about current customers that isn't necessarily related to actual sales, such as visits, sales opportunities, and service calls. It also stores sales opportunities with potential customers.

Depending on the company, we may also find data that is useful from external sources. If the business is actively involved in social networks, then we can gather market data from Facebook, Twitter, or LinkedIn. We can also purchase data from market research companies or download free, public data from several governmental and nongovernmental organizations.

In this chapter, we will review the following topics while we create the QlikView marketing perspective:

- Marketing data model
- Customer profiling
- Market analysis
- Social media analysis
- Sales opportunity flow analysis

Let's get started with a look at how we combine the CRM data with the existing sales data model.

Marketing data model

A CRM system serves several functions. Along with keeping track of our sales process and the level of customer service, it also gives us first-hand data about our customers and leads. It contains an evolving event called a sales opportunity that, in itself, contains various discrete events, such as visits, and calls, and sales quotes. All this data is important first-hand information about our market. This is especially true in the case of sales quotes, which are documents that are similar to invoices and give us an idea what customers are interested in buying, how much they plan to purchase, and at what price. An opportunity may also include information about its origins, competing offers, and any reason why we failed to convert it into an actual sale.

A CRM system also tends to add more information to the customer catalog, such as demographic information. If customers are people, then we may gather data about their age, sex, education level, income level, marital status, and so on. Otherwise, if our customers are businesses, then we may gather data about the industry group that they belong to along with the number of employees and annual revenue. We may also add more detailed geographical data, such as latitude and longitude.

Let's load this container into the QDF. Once we've transferred the container, let's open the marketing perspective called `Marketing_Perspective_Sandbox.qvw` in the `1.Application` folder and see how sales opportunities and other marketing data combine with the previous sales data model.

As you can see, the following data model is quite similar to that of the sales perspective. We've added some additional fields in the `Facts` table to help us measure the following events:

- Sales opportunities
- Sales quotes
- Customer-related activities, such as visits and calls

Sales quotes and activities are discrete events that occur on a given date. However, sales opportunities are evolving events that go through several stages. Each stage represents a step that we expect to perform in every sales process. For example, going to the first meeting, sending a sales quote, and negotiating the final sales terms are common steps in a sales process.

In our analysis, we want to know how the process is evolving. More specifically, we want to identify its current step along how it progressed through past steps. We use `intervalmatch()` in the load script to link the start and end dates of each step with the corresponding discrete dates in the `MasterCalendar` table. A side effect of using `intervalmatch()` is the existence of a synthetic key table in the data model. A synthetic table is QlikView's way of linking tables that share more than one key field. Usually, we avoid using these tables as they may affect the performance of the data model, but in this case we leave it in the data model. Any attempt to eliminate the synthetic key table created by `intervalmatch()` often nullifies its purpose or causes the related tables to grow too large.

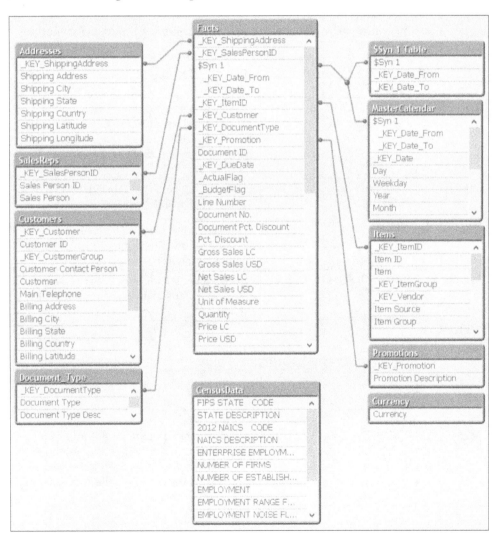

Finally, we add business demographic data and geographical data to the `customer` catalog along with a related table with public census data that helps us look for new markets that share the same attributes as the business's current customers.

 We can download the latest US business census data from `http://www.census.gov/`. The census data that we use in this data model is from `http://www.census.gov/econ/susb/`.

Apart from this additional data, we reuse many of the dimensions and metrics. For example, Customer, Sales Person, and Item also exist in this data model. Let's take a closer look at some of the new dimensions and metrics that pertain to marketing.

Dimensions		
7Ws	**Fields**	**Comments**
Who	`Customer NAICS` `(2-digit)`	This customer attribute comes from the **North American Industry Classification System (NAICS)**, which is a hierarchical group of numbers that classify our customers.
Who	`Customer Employee` `Size`	This attribute helps us determine the demographics of the customer base.
Who	`Competitor`	This market information helps us to examine who we are competing against and measure our success rate against them.
Where	`Sales Opportunity` `Stage`	This is where we identify both the current and closed steps of an evolving sales process.
Metrics		
7Ws	**Fields**	**Comments**
How Many	`Potential Sales`	This is where we estimate how much we will be able to sell to a customer or a prospect.
How Many	`Sale Opportunity` `Close %`	This is a standard practice to calculate a more accurate potential sales amount, which is is to multiply it by the probability that we will succeed in closing the sale. As we progress through the sales process the probability increases.

Now that we have a marketing data model, let's create current customer profiles and discover where we can find similar businesses according to the census data.

Customer profiling

In the marketing data model, we use each customer's NAICS code, employee size, and average revenue to create profiles. We want to look for profitable customers, so we also cross this data with the the gross profit each customer generates. We use a parallel coordinates chart and a Sankey chart to visualize customer profiles.

As a market analyst, I want to discover demographic characteristics of our current customers so that I can search for potential customers among companies with similar attributes.

Parallel coordinates

In `Marketing_Perspective_Sandbox.qvw`, we are going to make the following parallel coordinates chart. This chart helps us analyze multivariate data in a two-dimensional space. We often use metrics that result in numbers to create it and we can find such example at `http://poverconsulting.com/2013/10/10/kpi-parallel-coordinates-chart/`.

However, in the following chart, we use descriptive values for **NAICS**, **Size**, and **Average Revenue** that we can see in detail in the text popup. The highlighted line represents construction companies that have **10-19** employees and **$100,000-$250,000** in annual revenue. The width of the line represents the relative number of customers of this type compared to other types.

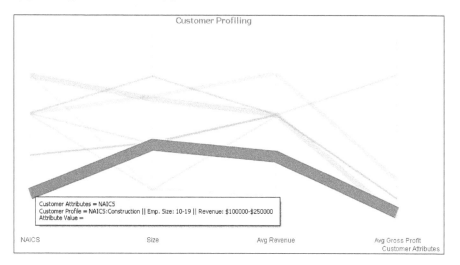

Exercise 14.1

Before we begin to create this chart, let's create the following variable:

Variable	
Label	**Value**
vIgnoreSelectionToHighlight	[Customer NAICS]=,
	[Customer Employment Size]=,
	[Customer Est. Annual Revenue]=

Now, let's create a line chart with the following property options:

Dimensions	
Label	**Value**
Customer Attributes	CustomerProfileAttribute
Customer Profile	='NAICS:' & [Customer NAICS]
	& ' || Emp. Size:' & [Customer Employment Size]
	& ' || Revenue:' & [Customer Est. Annual Revenue]
Expressions	
Label	**Value**

Attribute Value	pick(match(only({$<$(vIgnoreSelectionToHighlig ht)>} CustomerProfileAttribute),'NAICS','Size','A vg Revenue','Avg Gross Profit')
	
	,only({$<$(vIgnoreSelectionToHighlight)>} [Customer NAICS (2digit)])
	    /max({$<$(vIgnoreSelectionToHighlight)>} total
	[Customer NAICS (2digit)])+(Rand()/50-(1/100))
	
	,only({$<$(vIgnoreSelectionToHighlight)>} [Customer Employment Size])
	    /max({$<$(vIgnoreSelectionToHi ghlight)>} total [Customer Employment Size])+(Rand()/50-(1/100))
	
	,only({$<$(vIgnoreSelectionToHighlight)>} [Customer Est. Annual Revenue])
	    /max({$<$(vIgnoreSelectionToHig hlight)>} total [Customer Est. Annual Revenue])+(Rand()/50-(1/100))
	
	,avg({$<$(vIgnoreSelectionToHighlight)>}
	    aggr(sum({$<$(vIgnoreSelectionToHighlight)>} [Gross Profit])
	,Customer,CustomerProfileAttribute,[Customer NAICS],[Customer Employment Size],[Customer Est. Annual Revenue]))
	/max({$<$(vIgnoreSelectionToHighlight)>}
	    total aggr(sum({$<$(vIgnoreSelectionToHighlig ht)>}
	[Gross Profit])
	,Customer,CustomerProfileAttribute,[Customer NAICS],[Customer Employment Size],[Customer Est. Annual Revenue]))
	)

Expression Attributes	**Value**
Line Style	='<w' & (count(Customer)/max(total aggr(count(Cu stomer),CustomerProfileAttribute,[Customer NAICS (2digit)],[Customer Employment Size],[Customer Est. Annual Revenue])) * 7.5 + .5) & '>'

The `CustomerProfileAttribute` dimension is an island table in the data model that includes a list of customer attributes for this chart. We use this island table instead of a `valuelist()` function because we are going to use the `aggr()` function in the metric expression. In a chart, the `aggr()` function works properly only when we include every chart dimension as a parameter, and it doesn't accept a `valuelist()` function as a parameter.

The expression is quite long because it includes a different expression for each attribute. If we are not accustomed to the use of `pick()` or `match()`, we should review their functionality in *QlikView Help*. In the script that loads the data model, we assign a number value behind each attribute. For example, we use the `autonumber()` function to assign a number for each NAICS description. This number's only purpose is to define a space for the description along the Y-Axis. Its magnitude is meaningless.

We then normalize the number by dividing each customer attribute value by the maximum value of that particular attribute. The result is a number between 0 and 1. We do this so that we can compare variables that have different scales of magnitude. We also add a random number to the attribute value expression when it is descriptive, so as to reduce overlapping. Although it is not a perfect solution, a random number that moves the line one-hundredth of a decimal above or below the actual value may help us handle a greater number of lines.

We also dynamically define each line's width in the Line Style expression attribute. A line's width is defined as `<Wn>` where n is a number between .5 and 8. We calculate each line's width by first calculating the percentage of customers each represents, which give us a number between 0 and 1. Then, we multiply that number by 7.5 and add .5 so that we use the line width's full range.

Finally, the numbers along the Y-Axis don't add any value, so we hide the axis and we add dimensional grid lines that are characteristic of parallel coordinate charts. It is likely that this chart will contain myriad lines, so we make every color in the color bucket about 50% transparent, which helps us see overlapping lines, and we disable the option to show the chart legend.

Although this chart is already loaded with features, let's add the ability to dynamically highlight and label the profiles that are most interesting to our analysis. When we are done, we should be able to select a line and have it stand out amongst the others and reveal the detailed profile it represents.

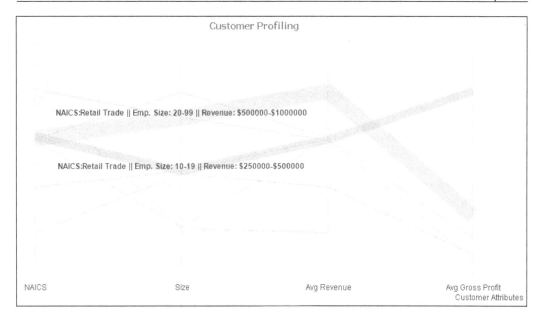

NAICS:Retail Trade || Emp. Size: 20-99 || Revenue: $500000-$1000000

NAICS:Retail Trade || Emp. Size: 10-19 || Revenue: $250000-$500000

NAICS   Size   Avg Revenue   Avg Gross Profit

Customer Attributes

Exercise 14.2

We added the first element of this feature in the previous exercise when we defined
the set analysis of various functions as {$<$(vIgnoreSelectionToHighlight)>}
in the chart's expression. This causes the expression to ignore all selections made
to the profile attributes. The final step to enable dynamic highlighting is to add the
following code to the background color expression attribute of the chart expression:

```
if(
not match(only({1} [Customer NAICS (2digit)]&'_'&[Customer Employment
Size]&'_'&[Customer Est. Annual Revenue]),
    Concat(distinct [Customer NAICS (2digit)]&'_'&[Customer Employment
Size]&'_'&[Customer Est. Annual Revenue],','))
,LightGray(200)
)
```

The next step is to reveal the labels of only the highlighted lines. To do so, we use the
dual() function to mask the line's number values with text. The general layout of the
Attribute Value metric will be dual(text,number). The number parameter will be
the expression that already exists in **Attribute Value** and the text parameter will be
the following code:

```
if(
  count(total distinct [Customer NAICS (2digit)]&'_'&[Customer
Employment Size]&'_'&[Customer Est. Annual Revenue])
  <>
```

```
      count({1} total distinct [Customer NAICS (2digit)]&'_'&[Customer
  Employment Size]&'_'&[Customer Est. Annual Revenue])

      and CustomerProfileAttribute='Size'

      ,'NAICS:' & [Customer NAICS] & ' || Emp. Size:' & [Customer
  Employment Size] & ' || Revenue:' & [Customer Est. Annual Revenue]

      ,''
      )
```

This code only returns a nonempty text when at least one line is filtered and only appears on the data point where the dimension value is equal to Size. We make the text conditional so as to reduce the risk overlapping labels. We also make the label stand out by adding the ='<b>' to the **Text Format** expression attribute. Finally, only when we tick the **Values on Data Points** option for the **Attribute Value** metric will any label appear.

Optionally, we left out the set analysis that contains the vIgnoreSelectionToHighlight variable in the line width expression in the first exercise, so that every line that isn't selected becomes extra thin to let the highlighted lines stand out more. If you want to conserve the line width of the lines that are not highlighted, then we add the set analysis that contains vIgnoreSelectionToHighlight to this expression.

The parallel coordinates chart offers us a native QlikView solution to visualize customer profiles. Let's also look at another powerful visualization that we can add to QlikView by means of an extension.

Sankey

Similar to the parallel coordinates, the Sankey chart is an excellent method to analyze the relationship between dimensional attributes. In the following chart, the width of the bands represents the number of customers that have each attribute value. We can easily see which are the most common at the same time that we see how each attribute value relates to the others.

The order of the attributes is important. For example, we can infer that all construction companies have **10-19** employees using the following chart, but we can't say that all construction companies have 10-19 employees and an annual revenue of $10-25 million. The only thing we can be sure of is that all construction companies have 10-19 employees and an annual revenue of $10-25 million or $25-50 million.

This visual representation may seem inferior to the previous section's parallel coordinates chart where we could follow a continuous line. However, the Sankey is easier to read than a parallel coordinates chart when we are dealing with a large number of customer profiles. In every analytical problem that we encounter, we should respect both the weakness and strengths of type of visualization as we analyze data.

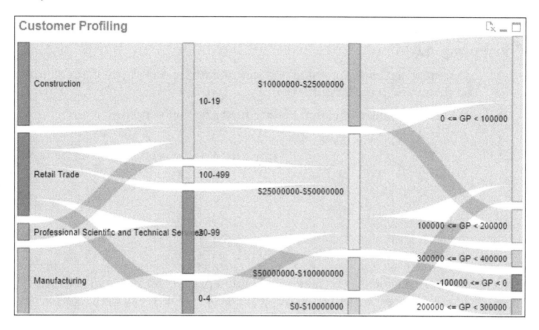

Let's create this chart in our marketing perspective sandbox.

Exercise 14.3

The following steps show you how to create a marketing analysis sandbox:

1. Download and install the Sankey extension created by Brian Munz in Qlik Branch (`http://branch.qlik.com/#/project/56728f52d1e497241 ae69783`).

2. In **Web View**, add the extension to the marketing perspective sandbox and assign the `[Customer Profile Path]` field to **Path**.

3. Add the following expression to **Frequency**:

    ```
    =count(distinct Customer)
    ```

We should now have a Sankey chart with three attributes: NAICS, Employee Size, and Annual Revenue. The [Customer Profile Path] field contains a comma-delimited list of these predefined attributes. We decide to dynamically calculate the fourth attribute that measures the average yearly gross profit that a customer contributes to the business. This allows us to select certain products and see how much gross profit each profile contributes only to these products. Let's go back to the properties of the Sankey and add this dynamic attribute to the path.

Exercise 14.4

1. Navigate to the edit expression window of **Path** by clicking on the cog button and then the expression button.

2. Add the following expression to the edit expression window:

```
=[Customer Profile Path] & ',' &
  class(
    aggr(avg(
      aggr(sum([Gross Profit])
        ,Customer,Year))
    ,Customer)
  ,100000,'GP')
```

We add the dynamic attribute using the class() function over two aggr() functions that calculate each customer's average annual gross profit contribution. The cross between a customer's contribution and its attributes helps us to not only look for new customers, but profitable new customers. Let's take a look at how we can use the census data to look for a new profitable market.

Market size analysis

Now that we can identify profitable customer profiles, we use the census data to look for companies that fit that profile. We begin our search using a layered geographical map that helps us choose which regions to focus our marketing efforts in.

 As a market analyst, I would like to visualize potential markets geographically so that I can execute a more effective advertising campaign.

Even though we have geographical data, such as states, or countries, it doesn't mean that we should use a map to visualize it. Bar charts are usually enough to analyze the top ranking geographical regions. However, maps can be useful when it is important to see both the physical proximity of each entity along with the magnitude of the associated metrics. For example, in the United States, we can expect California and Texas to rank the highest because they have the largest populations. However, the group of smaller states in the northeast may not rank as high as separate states in a bar chart, but, in a map, we can appreciate the proximity of their populations.

QlikView does not have a native map chart object. However, there are multiple third-party software options that are well-integrated with QlikView. QlikMaps (http://www.qlikmaps.com), GeoQlik (http://www.geoqlik.com), and Idevio (http://www.idevio.com) create popular mapping extensions for QlikView.

In this example, we are going to use Idevio to create geographical analysis. You can request an evaluation license and download the extension from http://bi.idevio.com/products/idevio-maps-5-for-qlikview. We install this extension like any other by double-clicking the .qar file. Once you've installed it, let's create the following geographic heat map that reveals the number of companies that are similar to our own customers in each state:

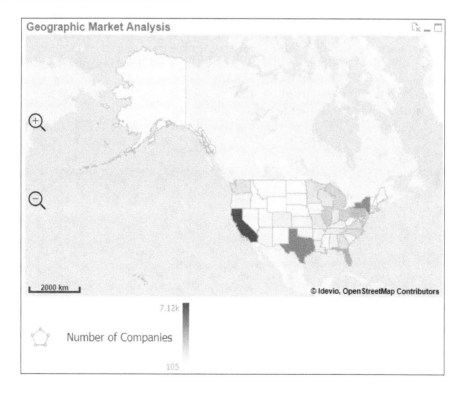

Exercise 14.5

1. In **WebView**, right-click anywhere on the sheet and select **New Sheet Object**.

2. In the **Extension Objects**, add a **Idevio Map 5** object and a **Area Layer** object to the sheet.

3. Open the **Properties** dialog of the **Area Layer** object and set STATE as the **Dimension** and the following expression as the **Color Value**:

   =sum([NUMBER OF FIRMS])

4. Click **More...** and go to the **Location** tab.

5. Make sure **Advanced Location** is not enabled and select United States in the **Country** drop-down box.

6. In the **Legend** tab, disable the **Color Legend Auto** option and add an empty space to the first expression field and Number of Companies in the second expression field. This last step will make the legend clean and simple.

We've used states in this example, but geographic maps that have a greater level of detail, such as counties, or zip codes, have greater analytical value. Also, political or administrative boundaries may not always be the best way to divide a population. Imagine if meteorologists used the previous map to show today's weather forecast. Like weather analysis, we may more easily recognize patterns in human behavior if we were to use heat map that can group data beyond artificial boundaries.

Let's create the following geographical analysis that helps us appreciate the market size of the northeast that is made up of smaller states:

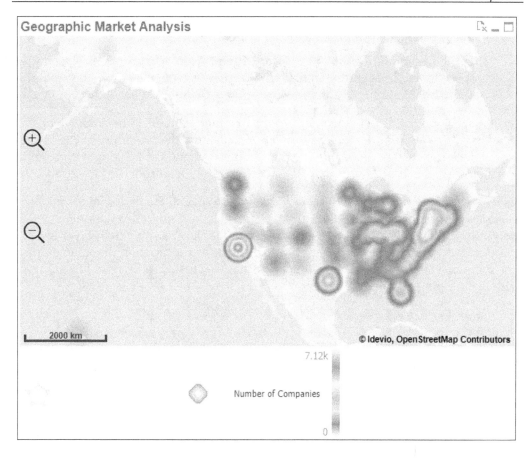

Geographic Market Analysis

2000 km

© Idevio, OpenStreetMap Contributors

7.12k

Number of Companies

0

Exercise 14.6

The following steps help us to create the geographical analysis:

1. In **WebView**, right-click anywhere on the sheet and select **New Sheet Object**.

2. In the **Extension Objects**, add a **Heatmap Layer** object to the sheet.

3. Open the **Properties** dialog of the **Heatmap Layer** object and set STATE as the **Dimension** and the following expression as the **Weight Value**:

   =sum([NUMBER OF FIRMS])

4. Click **More...** and go to the **Location** tab.

5. Make sure that **Advanced Location** is not enabled and select United States in the **Country** drop-down box.

6. In the **Legend** tab, disable the **Color Legend Auto** option and add an empty space to the first expression field and Number of Companies in the second expression field.

At first, we'll see both layers together in the same map. Left-click the **Area Layer** legend and disable **Visible**. We can now appreciate how the proximity of each state's populations can create groups outside their political boundaries. Along with counties and zip codes, this type of heat map also works well with latitude and longitude.

As we saw in the previous exercise, we can overlap several analytical layers in the same geographical map. This multilayering effect can provide a data-dense, insightful chart. For example, we can combine a bubble, area, and chart layer to compare market size, market penetration, and customer location in the same map. The following chart uses the same area layer that we created in *Exercise 14.5* along with overlapping bubble and chart layers:

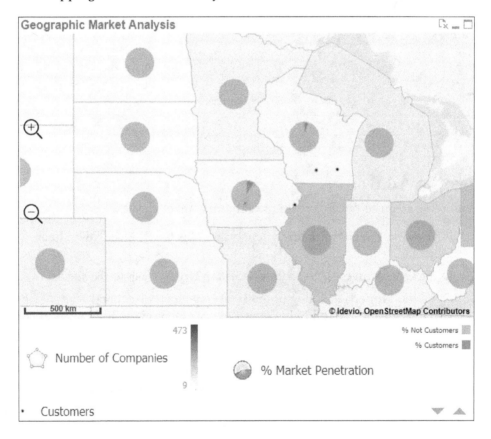

Exercise 14.7

First, let's add the layer of pie charts and then let's add the points that indicate customer locations. Although pie charts are not an ideal data visualization, in this case, they are the best possible solution until we can add other charts, such as bullet graphs:

1. In **WebView**, right-click anywhere on the sheet and select **New Sheet Object**.

2. In the **Extension Objects**, add a **Chart Layer** object to the sheet.

3. Open the **Properties** dialog of the **Chart Layer** object and set STATE as the **ID Dimension**.

4. Define the **Chart Dimension Label** as % Market Penetration and the following expression as the **Chart Dimension**:

    ```
    =ValueList('% Customers','% Not Customers')
    ```

5. Define the **Chart Value Label** as % and the following expression as the **Chart Value**:

    ```
    =round(
    pick(match(ValueList('% Customers','% Not Customers'),'%
    Customers','% Not Customers')

    ,count(DISTINCT if(STATE=[Billing State], Customer)) / sum([NUMBER
    OF FIRMS])*100

    ,(1-count(DISTINCT if(STATE=[Billing State], Customer)) /
    sum([NUMBER OF FIRMS]))*100

    )
    ,.01)
    ```

6. Click **More...** and go to the **Location** tab.

7. Make sure that **Advanced Location** is not enabled and select United States in the **Country** drop-down box.

8. In the **Legend** tab, disable the **Color Legend Auto** option and add an empty space to the first expression field and % Market Penetration in the second expression field.

9. In the **Presentation** tab, adjust the **Radius** to 20.

10. In the **Color** tab, disable the **Auto** option. Select **By Dimension** in **Color Mode** and **Categorized 100** in **Color Scheme**. Adjust **Transparency** to 25.

11. Close the **Properties** dialog of the **Chart Layer** object, and in the **Extension Objects**, add a **Bubble Layer** object to the sheet.

12. Open the **Properties** dialog of the **Bubble Layer** object and set `Customer` as the **ID Dimension**.

13. Define **Latitude / ID** as `= [Billing Latitude]` and **Longitude** as `= [Billing Longitude]`.

14. Define **Size Value** as `1`.

15. Click **More...** and go to the **Legend** tab, disable the **Size Legend Auto** option, and add `Customer` in the first expression field.

16. In the **Shape and Size** tab, define **Min Radius** and **Max Radius** as `2`.

17. In the **Color** tab, disable the **Auto** option. Select **Single Color** in the **Color Mode** and **Black** in the **Color Scheme**. Adjust **Transparency** to `25`.

If we select one of the most common customer profiles (`NAICS: Educational Services || Emp. Size: 100-499 || Revenue: $25000000-$50000000`) and zoom into the central part of the United States around Iowa and Wisconsin, we can reproduce the chart as shown in the previous figure. After creating the maps and its different layers, we organize the legends next to the map, so that the business user can left-click any of the legends at any time to hide or show a layer as they see fit. We also help the user add as many layers as possible by using visual elements such as transparency, as we did in the previous exercise.

Social media analysis

Once we understand the demographics of our current customers and our potential market, we may want to understand what they are saying about our company, products, and services. Over the last decade, social media sites, such as Twitter, Facebook, and LinkedIn, have become an increasingly important source of data to measure market opinion. They can also exert a large amount of influence on a potential customer's decision to do business with us more than any other marketing campaign that we run.

Data from social media sites is often unstructured data. For example, we cannot directly analyze text comments without first using a semantic text analysis tool. Along with several other different types of analysis, these tools apply advanced algorithms over text in order to extract keywords, classify it under certain topics, and determine its sentiment. The last piece of data, text sentiment, is whether the text has a positive, negative, or neutral connotation.

In the following example, we use QlikView's RESTful API to extract tweets containing the hashtag, #qlik, from Twitter. The RESTful API is a free connector from QlikView. You can download the installation file and the documentation that explains how to retrieve data from Twitter at Qlik Market (`http://market.qlik.com/rest-connector.html`).

After extracting the data, we use the same RESTful API to evaluate each tweet's keywords and sentiment using a semantic text analytical tool called AlchemyAPI (`http://www.alchemyapi.com/`). AlchemyAPI is free for up to one thousand API calls per day. If you want to evaluate more than one thousand texts, then they offer paid subscription plans. We've stored the result of this process and the example script in `Twitter_Analysis_Sandbox.qvw` which we can find in the application folder of the marketing perspective container.

In the following exercises, we first use powerful data visualization techniques, such as a histogram and a scatterplot, to analyze text sentiment. Then, we'll use a word cloud to display important keywords extracted from the texts. Although a bar chart is a more effective way to compare keyword occurrence, a word cloud may make for an insightful infographic summary of all the tweets.

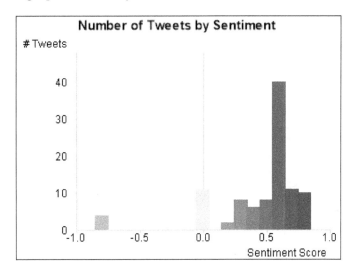

Exercise 14.8

Sentiment is divided into three groups. We represent sentiments that are negative as a negative number, those that are positive as a positive number, and those that are neutral as zero. The closer the number is to -1 or 1, the more negative or positive the sentiment, respectively. Histograms are the best data visualization method to view the distribution of numerical data. In order to create a histogram, we create numerical bins as a calculated dimension and then count how many instances fit into each bin. We also take care to visualize this diverging sequence with a similarly diverging color scheme:

1. Add the following color variables that we will use throughout the next three exercises:

Variable Name	Variable Definition
vCol_Blue_ColorBlindSafePositive	ARGB(255, 0, 64, 128)
vCol_Orange_ColorBlindSafeNegative	ARGB(255, 255, 128, 64)
vCol_Gray_ColorBlindSafeNeutral	ARGB(255, 221, 221, 221)

2. Add a bar chart with the following calculated dimension that creates numerical bins one-tenth of a decimal wide:

   `=class([Sentiment Score],.1)`

3. Add the following expression that counts the number of instances that fit into each bin:

   `=count([Tweet Text])`

4. Open the **Edit Expression** window of the metric's **Background Color** attribute and, in the **File** menu, open the **Colormix Wizard…**.

5. In the wizard, use `avg([Sentiment Score])` as the **Value Expression**.

6. Set the **Upper Limit color** to `$(vCol_Blue_ColorBlindSafePostive)` and the **Lower Limit color** to `$(vCol_Orange_ColorBlindSafePositive)`. Enable the **Intermediate** option, set the value to `0` and the color to `$(vCol_Gray_ColorBlindSafeNeutral)`. Finish the **Colormix Wizard…**.

7. Go to the **Axes** tab and, in the **Dimension Axis** section, enable **Continuous**.

8. In the **Scale** section that is found within **Dimension Axis**, set **Static Min** to `-1` and **Static Max** to `1`.

After cleaning up this presentation, we should now have a chart that is similar to the one pictured before the exercise, which shows how tweets are distributed by sentiment score. We easily note that most of our tweets with the #qlik hashtag are positive. Now, let's compare a tweet sentiment with the number of times that users like that tweet.

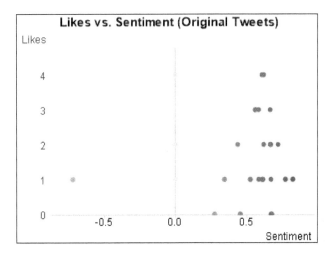

Exercise 14.9

Scatterplots are the best data visualization method to view the relationship between two numerical values. In the previous chart, each dot represents a tweet. Its two-dimensional position depends on its number of likes and its sentiment. We also use the same diverging color scheme as the histogram in order to emphasize the sentiment.

1. Add a scatterplot chart with **Tweet Text** as the dimension and the following two metrics:

Metric Label	Metric Expression
Sentiment	`avg({$<Retweet={0}>} [Sentiment Score])`
Likes	`sum({$<Retweet={0}>} [Like Count])`

2. Similarly to the previous exercise, use the **Colormix Wizard** under the Sentiment metric to determine each dot's color.

The scatterplot shows us that most tweets are positive and that those that are moderately positive tweets are the ones that receive the most likes.

The next step in our social media analysis is to visualize the keywords that are used in these tweets by importance. Although we could compare keyword instance using a bar chart more accurately, a word cloud provides an excellent way to present an executive summary of all tweets:

Exercise 14.10

Word clouds can be a great way to visually analyze unstructured data, such as text. The size of each keyword or phrase is related to its importance, which can be determined by the number of times that it appears in a text or a relevance score. In this case, we've used AlchemyAPI to extract keywords or phrases and give them a relevance score between 0 and 1. In the same way an internet search engine ranks search results according to their relevance to a query, AlchemyAPI ranks a keyword's relevance to each tweets. The higher the relevance value, the larger the text size. We also use a diverging color scheme for the text color so as to determine whether they are more common in tweets with negative or positive sentiments:

1. Download and install the Word Cloud extension created by Brian Munz in Qlik Branch (`http://branch.qlik.com/#/project/56728f52d1e497241 ae69781`).

2. In **Web View**, add this extension to the sheet and assign the Keyword field to **Words**.

3. Add the following expression to **Measurement**:

```
=sum([Keyword Relevance])
```

4. In **Color Expression**, paste the expression created by the **Colormix Wizard** in either of the two previous exercises.

As we would expect, the words QlikView and Qlik Sense are common in our word cloud. These words in the context of training is also quite common. The biggest single keyword trend is the word `Anniversary`. Its relevance in each tweet where it appeared multiplied by the number of times is was retweeted make it the largest word in the cloud. If we want to investigate which tweets are related to Anniversary, we can click on the word.

We also discover that the negative tweets are mistakenly classified by the sentiment analysis tool. The words generic and mixed usually have a negative connotation, but they are neutral words referring to technical subjects in this case. All sentiment analysis tools will occasionally classify words incorrectly and we can use the word cloud to identify these errors.

After all our work to understand our current customers, find potential markets, and analyze our social media presence, we want to figure out the tangible consequences of our work. Let's end this chapter by analyzing sales opportunities.

Sales opportunity analysis

The sales pipeline is the bridge between marketing and sales. Potential customers that are discovered by a market analysis or motivated by a advertising campaign are registered in the CRM system as leads. The sales team then goes through a series of steps to convert the lead into a customer. These steps may include having a first meeting, sending product samples, or sending an initial sales quote.

It is very important to monitor the number of opportunities that we have in the pipeline along with their progress through the steps. An opportunity that doesn't advance consistently through each step is likely to end up as a lost opportunity. It is also important to monitor the potential amount of sales that we currently have in the pipeline. This potential amount not only tells us what we can expect to sell in the immediate future, it also gives us first-hand information about a market's potential.

Let's create a flow chart like the following figure that shows us how each sales opportunity is progressing through the different stages of a sales process. Each line represents a sales opportunity. As it climbs higher, it is advancing to the next step in the sales process.

We can also appreciate the total number of opportunities that are at each stage throughout the month, and how many total opportunities are moving between stages. The lines that come to an end before the final month in the chart are opportunities that are closed.

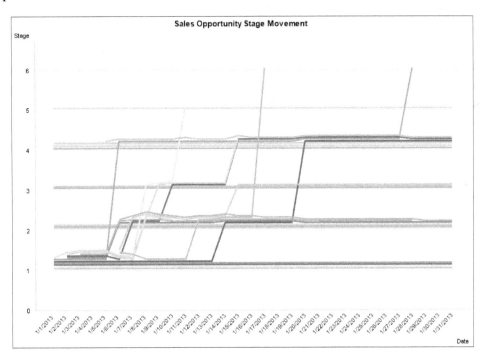

Exercise 14.11

This chart is only possible when we've linked the master calendar with the sales opportunities using `intervalmatch()`, as we did for this data model:

1. Create a line chart with `Date` and `Document ID` as dimensions.

2. Create a metric labeled `Sales Opportunity Stage` with the following expression:

```
dual(
only([Sales Opportunity Stage ID])
,only([Sales Opportunity Stage ID])
+
    aggr(
        rank(
            -only({$<_DocumentType={'Sales Opportunities'}>}
[Document ID])
        ,4,1)
    ,Date,[Sales Opportunity Stage ID],[Document ID])
```

```
/
    max(total
        aggr(
            rank(
                -only({$<_DocumentType={'Sales Opportunities'}>}
[Document ID])
                ,4,1)
            ,Date,[Sales Opportunity Stage ID],[Document ID])
        )
    *.5
    )
```

3. In the **Axes** tab, enable the option to **Show Grid** in the **Expression Axes** section and set the **Scale** with the following values:

Option	Value
Static Min	1
Static Max	6.75
Static Step	1

The text value of the metric returns the sales opportunity stage, while the number is the sales opportunity stage plus a decimal amount that makes each line stack one on top of the other. The decimal amount is calculated by dividing the rank of the Document ID, which is a sequential number by the total number of documents in each stage during each day.

Summary

As we saw in this chapter, the QlikView marketing perspective is filled with opportunities to visualize both internal and external data sources. We should also take advantage of third-party extensions to expand QlikView's analytical capacity. At the same time, we can find different ways to adjust QlikView's native visualizations to perform more advanced analysis. Let's now take a more detailed look at the company's finances and analyze its inventory, accounts receivable, and accounts payable in the next chapter.

15
Working Capital Perspective

A business's financial health depends heavily on its short-term assets, such as inventory and **Accounts Receivable (A/R)**, along with short-term liabilities, such as **Accounts Payable (A/P)**. If these elements are managed well, then the business will have the cash to invest in finding potential customers, developing new products, and hiring new talent. We refer to these three pivotal financial measurements as working capital.

We can find inventory, A/R, and A/P, as separate line items in the balance sheet that we created for our financial perspective in a previous chapter. However, there is also a series of additional analyses that all three have in common. For example, the analysis of the average number of days that a product is in inventory, a customer takes to pay an invoice, or the business takes to pay a vendor invoice requires the same type of data model and formulation. We can also make this information more actionable if we include it in a product, customer, or vendor stratification. As an example, we will complement the customer stratification that we began to create in our sales perspective.

After we examine what each has in common, we also look at the distinct operational analysis of each measurement that helps us maintain a healthy working capital. For example, a customer aging report can help lower the average number of days a customer takes to pay an invoice. Inventory stock level analysis can also help procurement know when to purchase the correct amount of inventory and lower just the right amount of a product.

In this chapter, we review the following topics while we create our QlikView working capital perspective:

- Working capital data model (snapshots)
- Account rotation and cash-to-cash analysis
- A detailed analysis of working capital
- Inventory stock level analysis and customer aging report
- A more complete customer stratification

Let's get started and look at how we combine these three elements of working capital into one data model.

Working capital data model

The working capital data model can be constructed in a variety of ways. The most important feature of the data model is its ability to accumulate account balances over time. We accomplish this by adding an *as-of* calendar. However, we can also create a model that uses periodic snapshots and avoid accumulating individual transactions after every user selection. A periodic snapshot is a recurring event that saves a copy of the data at the end of every day, week, or month.

 Even though we may end up only using monthly snapshots in a QlikView application, it is wise to take a daily snapshot of the data and save it in QVD files in case business requirements change.

In this chapter, we will use a periodic snapshot to measure following events in the data model:

- Month-end inventory balances by item and warehouse over three years
- Day-end inventory balances by item and warehouse over the last the last three months
- Month-end balances of A/R invoices over the last three years
- Month-end balances of A/P invoices over the last three years

Periodic snapshots do not record individual payments or inventory movements, which may be important for some banking or operational analysis. However, such details are not important when we first analyze working capital.

If we've only recently started to create data snapshots, some of the analysis we perform will be deficient as many metrics are calculated over 90-day periods. However, we sometimes have the option to recreate past snapshots using transaction-level data. Even if they are not completely accurate, they are often worth the effort. The decision on whether we wait until we have enough real snapshots or to recreate past snapshots frequently depends on which option takes less time. It also depends on whether the opportunity gained by having them now is greater than the resources spent to recreate the past.

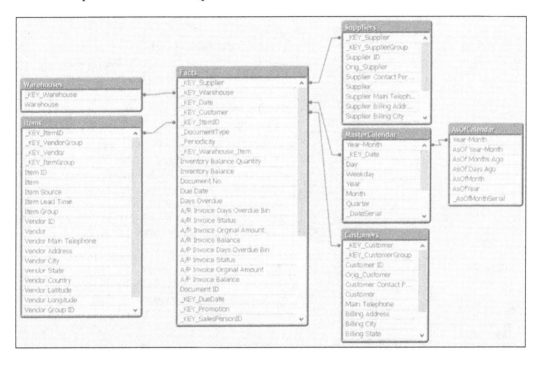

Many of the dimensions that we use to describe these events are the same dimensions that we've used in previous perspectives. We reuse the same tables so that it is easier to maintain the data models and to ensure that everybody in the organization is viewing the same information. Let's take a look at the dimensions and metrics that describe these events:

Dimensions		
7Ws	**Fields**	**Comments**
Who	`Customer`	This is a dimension that we first saw.
Who	`Supplier`	This is who provides products or services to the business. This dimension has similar information to that of the `Customer` dimension.
What	`Item`	This is a dimension that we first saw.
When	`Month, Year`	These are the same dimensions that we've seen in the previous perspectives. However, instead of recording, for example, the date of an invoice or a payment, it records the date when a snapshot was taken of a customer's outstanding balance.
How	`_Periodicity`	This dimension allows periodic snapshots with different frequencies to be loaded into one data model. For example, we load daily inventory snapshots of the past few months and monthly ones of the past few years. We do this so as to only upload the data that is useful. Otherwise, we risk degrading the QlikView application's performance.
Where	`Warehouse`	This dimension describes where we store goods so that they can easily be distributed to the customers who purchase them. We measure inventory levels by Warehouse.
Metrics		
7Ws	**Fields**	**Comments**
How Many	`Item Lead Time`	This is where we store a predefined time that is needed to receive an item in inventory, which helps procurement know when to purchase or produce a product.
How Many	`A/R Invoice Balance`	This is where we measure the outstanding balance of each customer invoice. The outstanding balance is the original invoice amount minus any corresponding payment or credit memo amount. In the ERP system, we link invoices with their related payments and credit memos through a bookkeeping process called reconciliation.

How Many	A/P Invoice Balance	This is the same concept as `A/R Invoice Balance`, but it measures the outstanding balance of purchase invoices.
How Many	`Inventory Balance Quantity` `Inventory Balance`	This is where we measure both the quantity and monetary value of the business's inventory.

While the calendar dimension is related to every event, every other dimension describes only one event. For example, supplier only describes month-end A/P invoices. It is helpful to understand the relationship between dimensions and metrics in a data model in order to know what type of analysis we can perform. However, we cannot obtain this information explicitly from the QlikView table viewer nor the previous 7Ws table.

Therefore, We use the following table to explain the relationship between metrics and dimensions in a data model. We insert all the metrics in the first column and then create a column for each dimension. The x records where a relationship exists and helps us determine how we can visualize the data:

Dimensions Metrics	Month/Year	Date	Customer	Supplier	Item	Warehouse
A/R Invoice Balance	X		X			
A/P Invoice Balance	X			X		
Inventory Balance Quantity	X Past three years	X Past three months			X	X

We maintain the relationship as it is likely to exist in the ERP system. For example, payments do not include information about items. This is not always good enough for the visualizations that we want to create. Even though payments don't include item detail, we may want to know the estimated average number of days that a customer pays for a certain item. We examine how to resolve this problem as we develop the analysis and visualizations for the working capital perspective.

Rotation and average days

At a higher level, we analyze each element of working capital using the same methods. The overall objective is to know the average number of days that it takes for an item in stock to be sold, a customer to pay, or a supplier to be paid.

We can help free up cash for the business if we reduce the number of days that an item is in a warehouse or the number of days that a customer takes to pay an invoice. Inversely, we want to increase the number of days that we can wait to pay our suppliers without any penalty. Let's start our working capital analysis by calculating the average number of days that an item is in a warehouse. We call this key performance indicator **Days Sales of Inventory (DSI)**.

Days Sales of Inventory

If we store inventory for too long, then it takes up space that could be put to better use or sold. If we store inventory for too few days, then we increase the risk of not being able to satisfy customers' needs. **Days Sales of Inventory (DSI)** tells us the average number of days that we store items in inventory based on our average inventory balance and our cost of sales. The following formula calculates DSI over a one-year period:

*Days Sales of Inventory = (Annual Average Inventory Balance / Annual Cost of Sales) * 365*

Let's create a bar chart that displays total DSI by month. We calculate each month's DSI over a rolling one-year period:

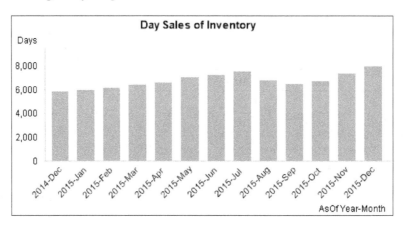

Before beginning the following exercise, we import this chapter's exercise files into the QDF.

Exercise 15.1

Let's create a bar chart with the following property options:

Dimensions	
Label	**Value**
AsOf Year-Month	`AsOf Year-Month`
Expressions	
Label	**Value**

DSI	`avg({$<_Periodicity={'Monthly'}`
	`            ,[AsOf Months Ago]={">0<=12"}>}`
	`        aggr(`
	`            sum({$<_Periodicity={'Monthly'}`
	`                    ,[AsOf Months Ago]={">0<=12"}>}`
	`                [Inventory Balance])`
	`            ,[Year-Month],[AsOf Year-Month])`
	`    )`
	`    /`
	`    sum({$<[AsOf Months Ago]={">0<=12"}>} [Cost])`
	`    *`
	`    365`

Similar to the financial perspective, we use the `[AsOf Months Ago]` field in the set analysis to calculate over twelve rolling months. We first use the `aggr()` function to sum the inventory balance of each `Year-Month` and then calculate the average monthly balance. We are careful to include `[AsOf Year-Month]` in the `aggr()` function because this function only works properly when it contains all fields used as a chart dimension.

We also make sure to use the same set analysis in the `avg()` function outside the `aggr()` as we do in the `sum()` function within the `aggr()` function. A function's set analysis only applies to the fields that are directly located within the function. It is never adopted by a parent function or inherited by a nested one. We, therefore, have to repeat it for every function. Feel free to experiment and remove the set analysis from one of the functions to see how the values in the graph change.

An acceptable DSI varies per industry but a result between 60 and 240 days is common. The previous chart shows that the company has too much inventory in relation to its sales. At one end, it needs to stop purchasing or producing goods and, at the other end, it needs to increase sales. Let's now take a look at how well we collect customer payments.

Days Sales Outstanding

Although sales are important, if we don't collect payment for these sales in a reasonable amount of time, then we won't have the cash necessary to keep the business running. **Days Sales Outstanding (DSO)** is a key performance indicator that measures the average number of days it takes a customer to pay an invoice. Its calculation is quite similar to that of DSI:

*Days Sales of Outstanding = (Annual Average A/R Balance / Annual Net Sales) * 365*

Let's now add DSO to the bar chart that we created in the previous exercise.

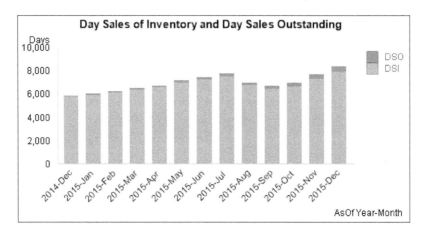

Exercise 15.2

Let's add the following expression to the bar chart from *Exercise 15.1*. We change the bar chart to a stacked bar chart in the **Style** tab:

Expressions	
Label	**Value**

DSO	`avg({$<_Periodicity={'Monthly'}`
	`          ,[AsOf Months Ago]={">0<=12"}>}`
	`     aggr(`
	`        sum({$<_Periodicity={'Monthly'}`
	`                 ,[AsOf Months Ago]={">0<=12"}>}`
	`               [A/R Invoice Balance])`
	`        ,[Year-Month],[AsOf Year-Month])`
	`     )`
	`     /`
	`     sum({$<[AsOf Months Ago]={">0<=12"}>} [Net Sales])`
	`     *`
	`     365`

A healthy DSO depends on the business, but we should expect anything between 15 and 90 days. In the previous chart, we started the year with a DSO that wasn't too far from this range, but, as the year progressed, the DSO grew. As DSO is a ratio that is based on sales and A/R balance, this increase could be caused by an increase in the A/R balance, a decrease in sales, or a mixture of the two. Alongside any DSO analysis, we recommend creating auxiliary charts that can show what is causing the DSO to change. This recommendation also applies to DSI and the final working capital element—Days Payable Outstanding.

Days Payable Outstanding

In order to determine whether we have a healthy DSO and DSI, we compare them with the key performance indicator **Days Payable Outstanding (DPO)**. DPO measures the average number of days before we pay our suppliers and has the same structure as the previous two indicators:

*Days Payable of Outstanding = (Annual Average A/P Balance / Annual Cost of Sales) * 365*

Let's now add DPO to the bar chart that we created in the previous exercise.

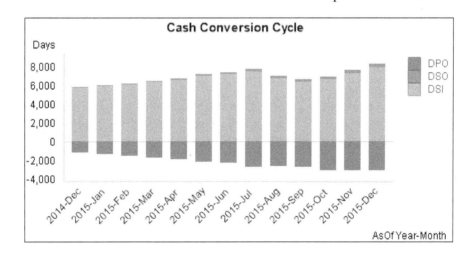

Exercise 15.3

Let's add the following expression to the bar chart from Exercise 15.2:

Expressions	
Label	**Value**
| DPO | ```
-avg({$<_Periodicity={'Monthly'}
            ,[AsOf Months Ago]={">0<=12"}>}
      aggr(
          sum({$<_Periodicity={'Monthly'}
                      ,[AsOf Months Ago]={">0<=12"}>}
                  [A/P Invoice Balance])
          ,[Year-Month],[AsOf Year-Month])
      )
      /
      sum({$<[AsOf Months Ago]={">0<=12"}>} [Cost])
      *
      365
``` |

An ideal DPO is greater than the sum of DSO and DSI. Such a situation means that the business's suppliers finance its operations. Regardless of whether this is really possible, we aim to reduce the time it takes to convert cash spent into cash received, which is called the **Cash Conversion Cycle (CCC)**:

Cash Conversion Cycle = DSO + DSI – DPO

We make a slight change to the previous chart so that we can explicitly analyze CCC.

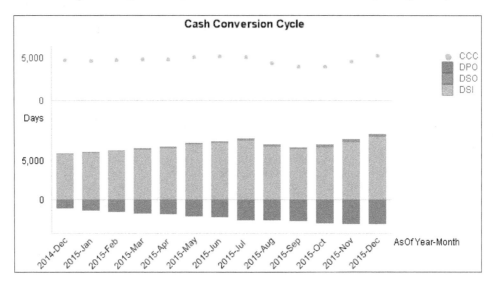
```

Exercise 15.4

Let's go through the following steps to adjust the bar chart from *Exercise 15.3*:

1. Change the bar chart to a combo chart in the **General** tab.

2. In the **Expressions** tab, add the following expression:

Expressions	
Label	Value
CCC	DSO + DSI – DPO

Enable only the **Bar** option for all the expressions except CCC, which should only have the **Symbol** option enabled.

3. In the **Axes** tab, select **CCC** in the **Expressions** list and enable **Right (Top)** in the **Position** section. Enable **Split Axis**.

We can now analyze all the working capital elements in a single chart. In the previous chart, we can see how an increase in DPO has been offset by an even greater increase in DSI. In the next section, let's look at how we can break down and analyze each of the working capital elements. We'll do this using DSI as an example.

Working capital breakdown

We complement the previous section's working capital analysis with a closer look at the elements that make up each measure. In the case of DSI, we analyze **Average Inventory Value** and **Annual Cost of Goods Sold** (**COGS**). This auxiliary analysis helps us understand whether an increasing DSI is the result of rising inventory levels or decreasing sales. It also helps us detect which product is not rotating frequently enough.

Let's combine the related metrics and have them share the same dimension axis, as in the following visualization:

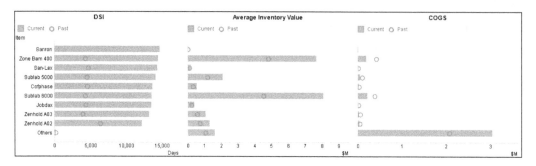

Exercise 15.5

1. Let's create three separate combo charts. We represent the current period with bars and the last period with circles. In each chart, we set the orientation to be horizontal, and move the legend to the top. When we use **Ctrl + Shift** to place the legend on top, we wait until its red outline covers the entire top section so that the labels appear in a row:

Title	DSI
Dimensions	
Labels	**Value**
Item	`Item`
Expressions	
Labels	**Value**

Current	`avg({$<_Periodicity={'Monthly'},[AsOf Months`
	`Ago]={">0<=12"}>}`
	`    aggr(`
	`        sum({$<_Periodicity={'Monthly'},[AsOf Months`
	`Ago]={">0<=12"}>} [Inventory Balance])`
	`    ,[Year-Month],Item)`
	`)`
	`/`
	`sum({$<[AsOf Months Ago]={">0<=12"}>} [Cost])`
	`*365`

Past	This is the same as the Current DSI but replace `[AsOf Months` `Ago]={">0<=12"}` with `[AsOf Months Ago]={">12<=24"}`

Title	Average Inventory Value
Dimensions	
Labels	**Value**
Item	`Item`
Expressions	
Labels	**Value**

Current	`avg({$<_Periodicity={'Monthly'},[AsOf Months Ago]={">0<=12"}>}`
	 `    aggr(`
	 `        sum({$<_Periodicity={'Monthly'},[AsOf Months Ago]={">0<=12"}>} [Inventory Balance])`
	 `    ,[Year-Month],Item)`
	 `    )`

Past	This is the same as the Current Inventory Value but replace `[AsOf Months Ago]={">0<=12"}` with `[AsOf Months Ago]={">12<=24"}`

Title	COGS
Dimensions	
Labels	**Value**
Item	`Item`
Expressions	
Labels	**Value**
Current	`sum({$<[AsOf Months Ago]={">0<=12"}>} [Cost])`
Past	This is the same as the Current COGS but replace `[AsOf Months Ago]={">0<=12"}` with `[AsOf Months Ago]={">12<=24"}`

Create a container object and, in the **Presentation** tab, select **Container Type** as **Grid**. Set **Columns** to **3** and **Rows** to **1**.

2. Drag each chart into the container object.

3. In the **Sort** tab of each chart, enable only **Expression** and select **Descending**. Insert the following code into the expression field:

```
avg({$<_Periodicity={'Monthly'},[AsOf Months Ago]={">0<=12"}>}
    aggr(
        sum({$<_Periodicity={'Monthly'},[AsOf Months
```

```
Ago]={">0<=12"}>} [Inventory Balance])
    ,[Year-Month],Item)
)
/
sum({$<[AsOf Months Ago]={">0<=12"}>} [Cost])
*365
```

4. We cannot scroll through the three charts at the same time, so, in the **Dimension Limits** tab of each chart, let's select the option to **Restrict which values are displayed using the first expression.**

5. In the same tab and under the **Show Only** option, we change the value to **First**.

6. In the Presentation tab, disable the option to Suppress Zero-Values.

7. Finally, after verifying that each row of bars corresponds to the same item, let's remove the dimension labels in the second and third charts by deselecting the **Show Legend** option in the **Dimensions** tab.

Instead of using a common scroll bar, we repeatedly click on the bar that represents **Others** in order to scroll through the charts and review more items. When we analyze all three measures in a single view, it becomes clear that the DSI of most of the items is increasing and that this increase is due to both an increase in the inventory value and a decrease in COGS.

After breaking down each working capital element and analyzing its parts, the next step is to analyze more closely the operations that cause these results. Let's continue to explore the inventory data in more detail and compare each product's inventory levels with their corresponding minimum, reorder, and maximum levels.

Inventory stock levels

The business defines each product's minimum, reorder, and maximum stock levels so as to maintain an adequate quantity in inventory. We often calculate these numbers and insert them into an ERP system that automatically generates purchase orders or work orders every time an item reaches the reorder stock limit In QlikView, we can use sales and purchase cycle data to easily calculate each limit and compare it to historical inventory behavior. We use the following formulas to calculate each stock level:

*Reorder Stock Level = Max Lead Time * Max Daily Sales*

*Minimum Stock Level = Reorder Stock Level – (Avg Lead Time * Avg Daily Sales)*

*Maximum Stock Level = Reorder Stock Level – (Min Lead Time * Min Daily Sales) + Reorder Quantity*

We use a predefined lead time, or the time needed to restock an item, from the item master data table. We also assume that the minimum daily sales amount of any item is 0 and that the reorder quantity is equal to the reorder stock level. Given these assumptions the maximum stock level is the reorder stock level multiplied by two.

Like much of the information at a glance. We therefore use the following trellis chart to compare each item's historical inventory behavior with the calculated stock levels.

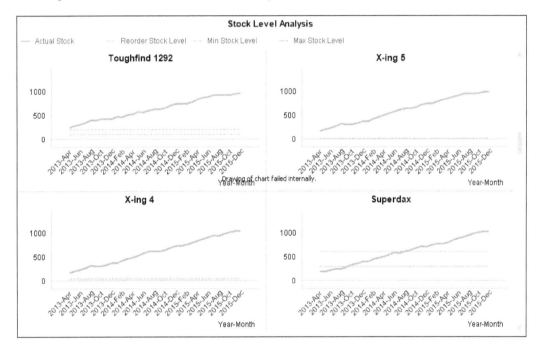

Exercise 15.6

Let's create a line chart with the following dimensions and expressions:

Dimensions	
Labels	**Value**
Item	`Item`
Year-Month	`Year-Month`
Expressions	
Labels	**Value**
Actual Stock	`sum({$<_Periodicity={'Monthly'}>} [Inventory Balance Quantity])`

Reorder Stock Level	`max(Total <Item> {$<$(vSetRolling12Modifier)>}`
	`    aggr(`
	`        sum(Quantity)`
	`    ,_KEY_Date, Item)`
	`    )`
	`*`
	`max([Item Lead Time])`

Min Stock Level	`[Reorder Stock Level]`
	`-`
	`sum({$<$(vSetRolling12Modifier)>}`
	`    Total <Item>`
	`Quantity)`
	`/`
	`networkdays(`
	`    addmonths(max(Total _KEY_Date),-12)`
	`    ,max(Total _KEY_Date)`
	`)`
	`*`
	`avg([Item Lead Time])`

Max Stock Level	`2*[Reorder Stock Level]`

In the **Dimensions** tab, click **Trellis...** and tick the **Enable Trellis Chart** option.

8. Set **Number of Columns** to **Fixed** and **2**. Set **Number of Rows** to **Fixed** and **2**.

9. In the **Expressions** tab, change the **Line Style** properties of **Reorder Stock Level**, **Min Stock Level**, and **Max Stock Level** to a thin, dotted line. For example, use `'<S2><W.5>'`.

10. In the **Sort** tab, select the option to sort by **Y-value**.

The set analysis variable in the previous expression is from Rob Wunderlich's QlikView Component's library and allows us to determine the stock levels based on twelve months of sales data. The actual twelve-month period we use depends on the date that we select in QlikView. In the particular case of Min Stock Level, we use the `networkdays()` function to calculate the average daily sales by working days. We also have the option to calculate the maximum and minimum daily sales using more advanced methods. For example, we can experiment with the fractile() function and use 5% or 95% fractiles to remove outliers. We can also use the same t-distribution functions, to calculate a more conservative daily sales average.

Finally, let's create a customer aging report that helps us monitor the operations that impact DSO.

Aging report

If we are to lower DSO, we need to make sure that customers pay on time. We monitor collections using a customer aging report. The following report shows the customers' total balances and categorizes it into bins based on the original due date of the each payment. As we're mostly interested in the past due payments, it groups these amounts into thirty-day period bins.

The same report structure can be used to monitor suppliers in order to maintain a healthy DPO:

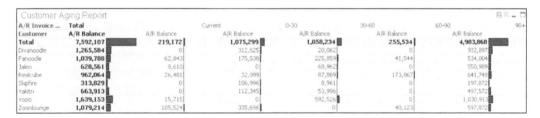

A/R Invoice ...	Total		Current	0-30	30-60	60-90	90+
Customer	A/R Balance	A/R Balance	A/R Balance	A/R Balance	A/R Balance	A/R Balance	
Total	7,592,107	219,172	1,075,299	1,058,234	255,534	4,983,868	
Divanoodle	1,265,584	0	312,625	20,062	0	932,897	
Fanoodle	1,039,788	62,843	175,538	225,859	41,544	534,004	
Jaloo	628,561	8,610	0	68,962	0	550,989	
Realcube	962,064	26,481	32,099	87,869	173,867	641,748	
Skipfire	313,829	0	106,996	8,961	0	197,872	
Yakitri	663,913	0	112,345	53,996	0	497,572	
Yozio	1,639,153	15,715	0	592,526	0	1,030,913	
Zoomlounge	1,079,214	105,524	335,696	0	40,123	597,872	

Exercise 15.7

Let's create a pivot table with the following dimensions and expressions:

Dimensions	
Labels	**Value**
Customer	`Customer`
Status	`[A/R Invoice Days Overdue Bin]`
Expressions	
Labels	**Value**
A/R Balance	`sum({$<_Periodicity={'Monthly'}>} [A/R Invoice Balance])`
<space>	`sum({$<_Periodicity={'Monthly'}>} [A/R Invoice Balance])`
<space>	`=''`

1. Select the second expression and select **Linear Gauge** in **Display Options**.

2. Click **Gauge Setting** and define the **Min** in the **Gauge Settings** section as 0 and **Max** as the following expression:

   ```
   sum({$<_Periodicity={'Monthly'}>} [A/R Invoice Balance])
   ```

3. In the **Segments Setup** section, delete **Segment 2** and change the color of **Segment 1** to blue.

4. In the **Indicator** section, select **Mode Fill to Value**.

5. Disable the **Show Scale** option.

6. Enable the **Hide Segment Boundaries** and **Hide Gauge Outlines** options.

7. In the **Sort** tab, select **Status** and only enable **Numeric Value**.

8. In the **Presentation** tab, enable the option to **Show Partial Sums** for both dimensions and enable the option to show **Subtotals on Top**.

9. Pivot the table as shown in the previous figure.

The creation of the `[A/R Invoice Days Overdue Bin]` field in the script makes this report easy to create. In the script, we subtract the invoice due date by the date of the data snapshot and then use several nested if-statements to assign that result to a bin. As this field is relative to each snapshot's date and not today's date, we can analyze the aging report over time. The field is also a `dual()` data type where **Current** is 0, **0-30** is 1, **31-60** is 2, and so on. This feature allows us to sort the field more easily by selecting only Numeric Value option in the **Sort** tab.

How well a customer pays us, or their DSO is an important indicator of how important that customer is to our business. Let's continue the customer stratification exercise, and see how we use DSO to evaluate a customer's importance.

Customer stratification

We had the following user story:

 As a sales representative, I want to see who my most important customers are so that I can focus my time and effort on them.

A customer's importance is determined by a mixture of measures. In the sales perspective, we started to determine a customer's importance using a Pareto analysis over sales. The following diagram shows the results of a customer stratification based on sales:

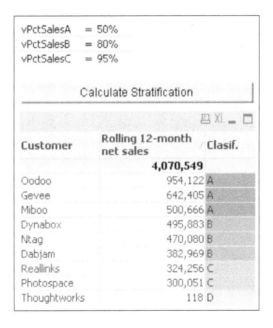

We can use *Pareto analysis* to stratify all measurements whose total is the sum of its parts, such as gross profit and quantity. However, there is another set of customer metrics whose total is an average of its parts. For example, the total company DSO is a weighted average of the DSO of each customer. In this case, we use quartiles to stratify customers.

Finally, once we have more than one measurement that stratifies customers, we look at how to combine them both numerically and visually. Even though we discuss customer stratification, the same principles apply to stratification based on any other dimension, such as item, sales representative, or supplier. The only difference between these is the exact measurements that we use to stratify them.

Stratification by distribution

When the measurement that we want use to stratify customers is based on averages, we use the distribution of the averages to classify them. As we use four letters to stratify customers in the example, we group them by quartiles. Each quartile will contain the same — or nearly the same — number of customers.

Let's create the following chart in the next exercise to see how quartiles group customers by DSO:

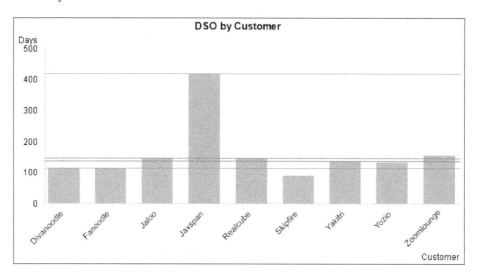

Exercise 15.8

Let's create a bar chart with the following property options:

Dimensions	
Label	**Value**
Customer	Customer
Expressions	
Label	**Value**

| DSO | ```
avg({$<_Periodicity={'Monthly'}
         ,[AsOf Months Ago]={">0<=12"}>}
    aggr(
        sum({$<_Periodicity={'Monthly'}
                     ,[AsOf Months
Ago]={">0<=12"}>}
                        [A/R Invoice Balance])
         ,[Year-Month],[Customer])
    )
    /
    sum({$<[AsOf Months Ago]={">0<=12"}>} [Net
Sales])
    *
    365
``` |
|---|---|

1. In the **Presentation** tab, add the first reference line. This represents the first quartile and uses the following expression:

```
fractile(
    aggr(
        avg({$<_Periodicity={'Monthly'},[AsOf Months
Ago]={">0<=12"}>}
            aggr(
                sum({$<_Periodicity={'Monthly'},[AsOf Months
Ago]={">0<=12"}>} [A/R Invoice Balance])
                ,[Year-Month],Customer)
            )
            /
            sum({$<[AsOf Months Ago]={">0<=12"}>} [Net Sales])
            *365
    ,Customer)
,.25)
```

2. Add three more reference lines for the second, third, and fourth quartile. For each quartile, We use the same expression as in the previous step and change the second parameter in the `fractile` function from `.25` to `.5`, `.75`, and `1`, respectively.

We make slight changes to the `aggr()` function in the expression we used to calculate DSO in *Exercise 15.2*. calculated total DSO by year-month, We replace [AsOf Year-Month] with [Customer] as this is the dimension we use this chart. We also go as far as to use a second `aggr()` function to calculate each fractile as the `fractile()` function only works over a set of numbers. This second `aggr()` function creates a list that contains the DSO of every customer for the `fractile()` function.
```

Stratification by distribution divides the customers into nearly equal-sized bins. The bar belongs to the nearest quartile reference line above it. According to the previous chart, **Divanoodle, Fanoodle,** and **Skipfire** are in the first quartile. Every other quartile has two customers. As the best customers have a low DSO, we classify customers in the first quartile as A, in the second quartile as B, in the third quartile as C, and in the fourth quartile as D.

Let's add DSO to the customer stratification we started in the sales perspective:

Customer	Rolling 12-month net sales	Sales Class	DSO	DSO Class	Total Weighted	Total Class
	4,070,549					
Yozio	954,122	A	404	B	3.6	A
Yakitri	382,969	B	376	A	3.4	B
Divanoodle	642,405	A	414	C	3.2	B
Fanoodle	495,883	B	388	B	3	B
Realcube	500,666	A	522	D	2.8	B
Skipfire	300,051	D	263	A	2.2	C
Zoomlounge	470,080	B	585	D	2.2	C
Jaloo	324,256	C	436	C	2	C
Jaxspan	118	D	420	C	1.4	D

Exercise 15.9

1. Let's create the following variables:

Variable	
Label	**Value**

vExp_DSOCustomer	avg({$<_
	Periodicity={'Monthly'},[AsOf
	Months Ago]={">0<=12"}>}
	    aggr(
	        sum({$<_
	Periodicity={'Monthly'},[AsOf
	Months Ago]={">0<=12"}>} [A/R
	Invoice Balance])
	      ,[Year-Month],Customer)
	)
	/
	sum({$<[AsOf Months
	Ago]={">0<=12"}>} [Net Sales])
	*365

vExp_ DSOCustomerStratificationBoundaries	fractile(Total
	    aggr(
	        $(vExp_DSOCustomer)
	    ,Customer)
	,$1)

2. In the working capital perspective, let's create the same customer stratification table that we created in the sales perspective (*Exercise 12.3*).

3. Let's add the following expressions to the previously created customer stratification table:

Expressions	
Label	**Value**
DSO	`$(vExp_DSOCustomer)`

DSO Class	`if($(vExp_DSOCustomer) < $(vExp_DSOCustomerStratificationBoundaries(.25)),'A'`
	`    ,if($(vExp_DSOCustomer) < $(vExp_DSOCustomerStratificationBoundaries(.5)),'B'`
	`        ,if($(vExp_DSOCustomer) < $(vExp_DSOCustomerStratificationBoundaries(.75)),'C','D'`
	`)))`

Total Weighted	`match([Sales Class],'D','C','B','A') * .6`
	`+`
	`match([DSO Class],'D','C','B','A') * .4`

Total Class	`pick(round([Total Weighted])`
	`,'D'`
	`,'C'`
	`,'B'`
	`,'A'`
	`)`

4. Change the background color of the DSO Class expression to the following expression:

```
if($(vExp_DSOCustomer) < $(vExp_DSOCustomerStratificationBoundarie
s(.25)),blue(100)
    ,if($(vExp_DSOCustomer) < $(vExp_DSOCustomerStratificationBoun
daries(.5)),blue(75)
        ,if($(vExp_DSOCustomer) < $(vExp_DSOCustomerStratification
Boundaries(.75)),blue(50),blue(25))))
```

5. Change the background color of the Total Class expression to the following expression.

```
pick(round([Total Weighted])
,blue(25)
,blue(50)
,blue(75)
,blue(100)
)
```

We create the vExp_DSOcustomerStratification variable with a $1 parameter so that we can calculate different factiles using only one variable. In general, when we encounter several expression variables whose only difference is a number, we reduce them to one variable and add a parameter.

The Total Weighted stratification is calculated by first converting the letters A, B, C, and D of each individually stratified metric into the numbers 1, 2, 3, and 4, respectively. In this example, We use the match() function to efficiently turn the letters into numbers. We then multiple each number by a factor that allows us define how important each metric is to the final customer stratification. Other than the fact that the sum of the factors should be equal to one, they are completely arbitrary and depend on the business's strategy. For example, as we want to put more emphasis on the sales stratification, we multiply it by .6 and the DSO stratification by .4.

As the sum of factors is equal to one, the sum of the all the weighted stratifications is between one and four which makes it possible for us to convert it back to a letter format. In this example, we use the pick() function in Total Class to convert a rounded Total Weight back into letters. In this way, we can combine multiple customer stratifications into one. For many business users, such as sale representatives, this can help them more easily determine a customer's importance according to the business's strategy. Finally, we introduce a way to visualize how individual customer measures influence how they are classified.

Visualizing stratification

We can use a native scatterplot to compare two measures used for stratification. For example, we create the following chart using the expressions we use in the customer stratification table. The legend at the top is a group of eight text objects—one for each dot and letter:

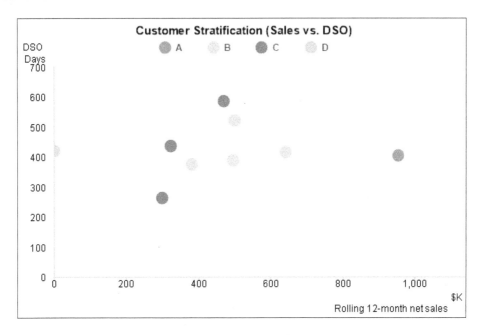

The scatterplot helps us identify whether each classification describes a tight group of closely-related customers or a disparate group of loners. It also helps describe the characteristics of an ideal customer. Although scatterplots appear to be too simple for complex stratifications that use more than two variables, it has the advantage of being easy to read. For most business users, we can add two cyclical expressions to a scatterplot and give them the power to compare any two of a potentially large group of customer stratification metrics. For the more experienced analysts, we can also create a more involved visualization called a scatterplot matrix.

The following figure shows a scatterplot matrix that compares three variables: Sales, DSO, and Gross Profit:

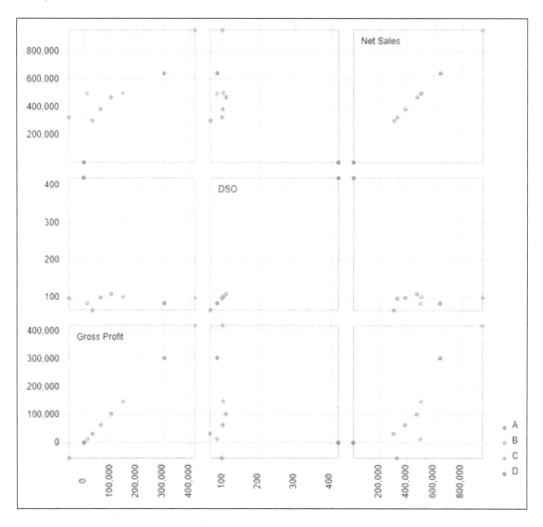

Exercise 15.10

1. Download and install the scatterplot matrix from Qlik Branch (http://branch.qlik.com/#/project/56d99a0a20d00edd11554ea9).

2. Add a third stratification metric based on gross profit. Use the example of the sales stratification, in *Exercise 12.3* to create the gross profit stratification that is based on a Pareto.

3. Add the following variables:

Variable	
Label	Value
vExp_DSOCustomerStratification	if($(vExp_DSOCustomer) < $(vExp_DSOCustomerStratificationBoundaries(.25)),'A' ,if($(vExp_DSOCustomer) < $(vExp_DSOCustomerStratificationBoundaries(.5)),'B' ,if($(vExp_DSOCustomer) < $(vExp_DSOCustomerStratificationBoundaries(.75)),'C', 'D')))
vExp_SalesCustomerStratification	if(len(only({A_CustomerSales} Customer)) <> 0, 'A', if(len(only({AB_CustomerSales} Customer)) <> 0, 'B', if(len(only({ABC_CustomerSales} Customer)) <> 0, 'C', if(len(only({$} Customer)) <> 0,'D'))))
vExp_GrossProfitCustomerStratification	if(len(only({A_CustomerGrossProfit} Customer)) <> 0, 'A', if(len(only({AB_CustomerGrossProfit} Customer)) <> 0, 'B', if(len(only({ABC_CustomerGrossProfit} Customer)) <> 0, 'C', if(len(only({$} Customer)) <> 0,'D'))))

In the **Web View**, add a **New Sheet Object** called **Scatterplot Matrix**:

Dimensions	
Label	**Value**
Customer	Customer

Customer Classification	=aggr(
	   pick(
	     round(
	       match($(vExp_SalesCustomerStratification),'D', 'C', 'B','A') * .35
	
	       +
	
	       match($(vExp_DSOCustomerStratification),'D','C', 'B','A') * .3
	
	       +
	
	       match($(vExp_GrossProfitCustomerStratification), 'D','C','B','A') * .35
	     )
	     ,'D'
	     ,'C'
	     ,'B'
	     ,'A'
	   )
	   ,Customer)

Expressions	
Label	**Value**
Rolling 12-month net sales	=sum({$<$(vSetRolling12Modifier),_ActualFlag={1}>} [Net Sales])
DSO	$(vExp_DSOCustomer)
Rolling 12-month gross profit	=sum({$<$(vSetRolling12Modifier),_ActualFlag={1}>} [Gross Profit])

Multivariate analysis leads to complex data visualization. The scatterplot matrix serves as a tool for more advanced analysts who want a rough idea of correlations and clustering between multiple variables at a glance. For example, we can observe that there is a stronger relationship between gross profit and sales than there is between DSO and either of these two metrics.

In the same way we use DSO for customer stratification, we can also use DSI and DPO for product and supplier stratification. This type of analysis helps us understand each working capital element within the context of other measurements. For example, a top-selling customer with a high DSO may be acceptable. However, we might lower the credit available to customers that buy little and have a high DSO.

Summary

We started analyzing the working capital perspective at a high level and then worked our way through different levels of analysis that empowers the whole business to help raise capital for further development. Additionally, a more complete customer stratification helps sales representatives focus on customers that pay in fewer days. We can also develop item and supplier stratification and help the purchasing or production department.

Finally, we empower warehouse, purchasing, and collection teams to do their jobs more effectively with inventory stock levels and aging reports. Let's continue to make them more productive and create an operations perspective.

16
Operations Perspective

Effective business operations use capital in an efficient way to deliver what the business sells. In other words, we have to discover just the right number of resources needed to deliver the best-possible customer service. In this chapter, we use data to avoid late deliveries and slow responses to our customers' needs without bankrupting our business.

We will start this chapter by examining company-wide indicators and then we will work our way through the data to discover opportunities to improve our internal operations. We will expand on historical analysis and add the ability to use statistics to predict future supplier behavior. We will also add accuracy to our predictive analysis with the help of an integrated planning tool that we will use to confirm future demand.

In this chapter, we will review the following topics while we create our QlikView operations perspective:

- Operations data model (accumulating snapshot)
- On-time in-full analysis
- Predicting supplier lead times
- Supplier and on-time delivery correlation analysis
- Planning in QlikView with KliqPlan

Operations data model

Operations involve multiple discrete events that are represented as documents in the ERP system. For example, our customer selling cycle includes a sales quotation, a sales order, a customer delivery, a sales return, a sales invoice, and a sales credit memo. Our supplier purchasing cycle includes a purchase order, a delivery, a return, a purchase invoice, and a purchase credit memo.

Although we can create a transactional fact table that allows us to analyze each discrete event, we are interested in analyzing the relationship between the events more than the events themselves. For example, we want to know how much time it took to deliver a product after receiving its originating purchase order. It would also be insightful to compare the quantity that we delivered with the quantity of the originating purchase order. We would have to work between multiple rows in a transactional fact table to discover this information; and just like a row-based database, we would find it challenging to work between rows in QlikView.

Therefore, we create a table where one instance of the whole operational process is stored in only one row. Each instance is an evolving event that is updated every time it reaches a milestone in the process. For example, in the beginning a row may only contain a sales order. When this sales order becomes a sales delivery, we update this row with data from the sales delivery. We refer to this fact table as an accumulating snapshot.

We measure the following evolving events in our data model:

- Customer selling cycle
- Supplier purchase cycle

We keep the accumulating snapshot table simple by modeling every cycle as a one-way, linear process. In our ERP system, we can begin this process with any discrete event. For example, we may start the selling cycle with a sales quotation, or we could skip this step and start with a sales order. In the script, we assume that a document created from nothing is a new cycle and concatenate a new row to the accumulating snapshot.

When we generate a document from another document, we assume that we are adding on to an existing cycle. We link this new document's data with an existing row that contains the base document's data. For example, if we generate a sales invoice from a customer delivery, we will insert this invoice into the same row as the base delivery document.

Each event contains multiple dates and amounts that correspond to different discrete events in the process. For example, one row can potentially contain the sales order date, the delivery date, and the sales invoice date. As such, accumulating snapshots tend to have more columns and fewer rows than a transactional fact table.

Although we focus on the number of rows in a fact table when we estimate the size of a QlikView application, the number of columns in a fact table is also important to consider. A large number of columns (>50) in a fact table may cause slow response times.

As sales and purchasing cycles have a similar sequence of events, we use the same columns for each cycle. For example, we use a column called [Order Quantity] to hold the quantity of both sales and purchase orders. We differentiate between each order using a field called [Process Type] that holds a text value that is either Sales or Purchasing. Even with this table optimization, the fact table contains almost one hundred columns.

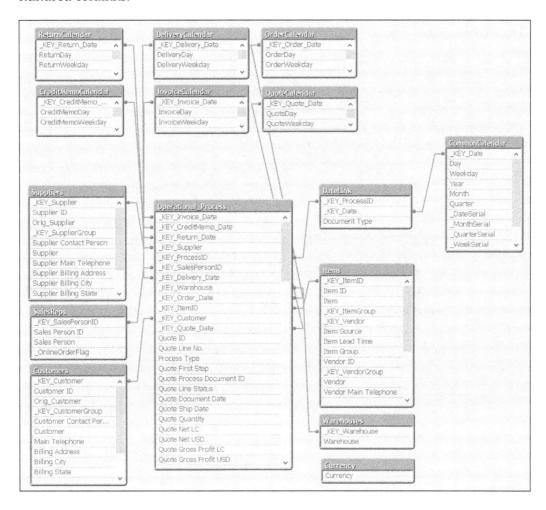

Most of this data model's dimensions are similar to the ones from previous perspectives. The difference is in how it handles dates. Each date has its own master calendar and they all share a common master calendar. We need a bridge table to link this common master calendar to the fact table so that it can handle the multiple date fields that exist in each row. Before we look deeper into this subject in the next section, let's review the 7Ws of our operations data model:

Dimensions		
7Ws	**Fields**	**Comments**
Who	`Customer`	This is a dimension that we first saw.
Who	`Sales Person`	This is a dimension we first saw.
Who	`Supplier`	This is a dimension we first saw.
What	`Item`	This is a dimension we first saw.
What	`[Quote Line Status]`, `[Order Line Status]`, `[Delivery Line Status]`, `[Invoice Line Status]`	This is how we keep track of both finished and pending cycles in the accumulating snapshot. The last step of pending cycles has an `O` as its line status. Otherwise, the line status is `C`.
When	`Month, Year`	This is a common set of calendar fields where we store the dates of multiple discrete events.
When	`[Quote Due Date]`, `[Order Due Date]`, `[Delivery Due Date]`, `[Invoice Due Date]`	This is where we store event-specific due dates.
How	`[Quote First Step]`, `[Order First Step]`, `[Delivery First Step]`, `[Invoice First Step]`	This indicates with a `Yes` or `No` value how the operations cycle was started.
Where	`Warehouse`	`Warehouse` is a dimension that we first saw in *Chapter 15, Working Capital Perspective*.
Metrics		
7Ws	**Fields**	**Comments**

How Many	[Quote Quantity], [Order Quantity], [Delivery Quantity], [Invoice Quantity]	These are the metrics that we measured in our transactional fact table, which are also in an accumulating snapshot. However, all these metrics are on one row and we begin the name of each metric with the name of the discrete event that it measures.

Handling multiple date fields

When we have multiple date fields on one row, we can't just fit every date into one calendar. At the same time that we handle multiple date fields in one common calendar, we also create a master calendar for each important date. The important dates in this case are when we create a new document in a cycle. We use these dates and the same calendar subroutine that we used in previous perspectives to create a separate calendar for each date field for that date. We use calendars that correspond to certain documents in the analysis that we perform in this perspective:

```
call Qvc.CalendarFromField('_KEY_Quote_Date','QuoteCalendar','Quote');
```

We also create a common calendar that helps the user navigate through the data without having to first think about what calendar to filter. This calendar behaves as shown in the following figure. When we select a process cycle that is identified by _KEY_ProcessID, which is equal to 1399, we notice that it contains multiple dates starting from May 15, 2012, until June 9, 2012. As a result, we can see in the common calendar's Year and Month filters that both May and June 2012 are possible values:

We make this behavior possible by creating a bridge or link table between the fact table and the `CommonCalendar` dimension. This link table is called `DateLink` and it stores the date of each cycle's discrete events in individual rows:

_KEY_ProcessID	_KEY_Date	Document Type
1399	5/15/2012	Order
1399	5/15/2012	Quote
1399	5/20/2012	Delivery
1399	6/9/2012	Invoice

The following code is an example of the script to include the dates of the first two discrete events in the `DateLink` table. The other dates can also be added in the same way:

```
DateLink:
Load
    _KEY_ProcessID,
    [Quote Document Date] as _KEY_Date,
    'Quote' as [Document Type]
Resident Operational_Process
Where not isnull([Quote Document Date]);

Concatenate (DateLink)
Load
    _KEY_ProcessID,
    [Order Document Date] as _KEY_Date,
    'Order' as [Document Type]
Resident Operational_Process
Where not isnull([Order Document Date]);
```

Now that we've reviewed the operations data model and how we handle multiple date fields, let's start to analyze our operational cycles.

On-Time and In-Full

Our objective is to help the teams that are in charge of purchasing, production, and shipping, to deliver on the expectations that the sales and marketing teams have built for our customer. We may sell items based on prices or quality, but our customers expect us to deliver what we sell. The first requirement is that we deliver our products **On-Time and In-Full (OTIF)**.

As a logistics manager, I want to analyze what percentage of our orders are OTIF so that I can look for opportunities to improve our operations or adjust the expectations built by the sales team.

We are not only concerned about whether the delivery arrives on time but also whether it is completed without any returns. Although, in some cases, early deliveries may be a problem, we will assume that they are not in this case. We calculate OTIF with the following formula:

OTIF = the number of line items shipped on or before promised delivery and complete divided by the total number of line items shipped

When we use the number of line items, we apply an equal weight to all line items, regardless of whether they represent large or small volumes. If we want to place a bias on deliveries that generate more value for the company, we can replace the number of line items with gross profit, sales, or quantity. We calculate OTIF by line item and by total quantity in the following chart:

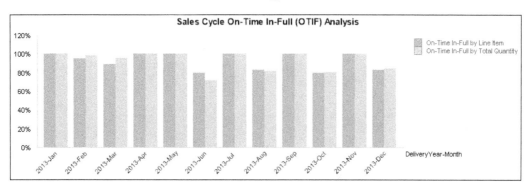

Exercise 16.1

Before beginning the following exercise, we import this chapter's exercise files into the QDF as we did in *Chapter 12, Sales Perspective*. Let's create a bar chart that analyzes OTIF with the following property options in `1.Application\Operations_Perspective_Sandbox.qvw`:

Dimensions	
Label	Value
Delivery Year-Month	DeliveryYear-Month

Expressions	
Label	**Value**
| On-Time In-Full by Line Item | ```
sum({$<[Process Type]={'Sales'},[Delivery First
Step]={'No'}>}
    if([Delivery Document Date]<=[Order Due Date]
        and [Order Quantity]=rangesum([Delivery
Quantity],-[Return Quantity])
        ,1)
)
/
count({$<[Process Type]={'Sales'},[Delivery First
Step]={'No'}>}
    DISTINCT [Delivery Line No.]
)
``` |
| On-Time In-Full by Total Quantity | ```
sum({$<[Process Type]={'Sales'},[Delivery First
Step]={'No'}>}
    if([Delivery Document Date]<=[Order Due Date]
        and [Order Quantity]=rangesum([Delivery
Quantity],-[Return Quantity])
        ,[Delivery Quantity])
)
/
sum({$<[Process Type]={'Sales'},[Delivery First
Step]={'No'}>}
    [Delivery Quantity])
``` |

We use the `Delivery Year-Month` field as a dimension because we specifically want to analyze the deliveries in the month that they were made. In each expression, we use an if-statement within the `sum()` function. For better performance, we can also migrate this logic to the script and create a field in the data model that identifies which line items were OTIF. The conditional expression of the if-statement evaluates whether what we promised in the sales order matches the delivery. Therefore, we filter out delivery documents that start a sales cycle in the set analysis because no promise was ever documented in the ERP system.

An accumulating snapshot tends to contain many null values that represent steps in the cycle that have yet to happen or that never will. In QlikView, binary functions, such as +, -, *, and /, do not work when one of the variables is a null value. For example, the `=8+null()` expression returns a null value instead of eight. On the other hand, the `rangesum()` function treats a null value as if it were zero, so we add we use it to sum `[Delivery Quantity]` and `[Return Quantity]` because they often contain a null value.

We can gather from our OTIF analysis that, for six months in 2013, we delivered 100% of our orders on-time and in-full. The most difficult month in 2013 was June when we delivered 80% of the line items and 72% of the quantity satisfactorily. Assuming that we use a standard unit of measurement for all of our products, this discrepancy between line items and quantity is due to a higher OTIF among lower-quantity deliveries. Let's now analyze how we work through our data to discover opportunities to improve our OTIF.

OTIF breakdown

There are various ways to analyze OTIF in more detail. Just like we did with the DSI calculation in our working capital perspective, we can break up the OTIF calculation into its parts. For example, we can analyze on-time deliveries separately from in full deliveries and also analyze the total absolute number of deliveries per month see its behavior.

We can also analyze the different cycles that support OTIF. For example, we can explore data from the production cycle, the purchasing cycle, or the shipping cycle. As we've added the purchasing cycle to our operations perspective, we can easily analyze our suppliers' OTIF rate in the following chart:

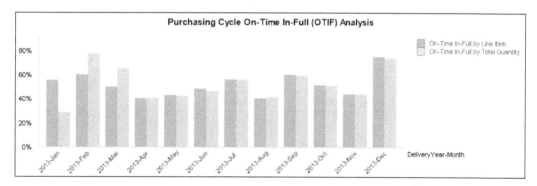

Exercise 16.2

To perform this exercise:

1. Clone the chart that we created in *Exercise 16.1*.
2. Change the code, [Process Type]={'Sales'}, in the metric expressions to [Process Type]={'Purchasing'}.

Finally, we can break down the cycles by their corresponding dimensions, such as supplier, customer, sales person, or item. We notice in the previous chart that our suppliers do not have a high OTIF and we decide to break down the metric by supplier:

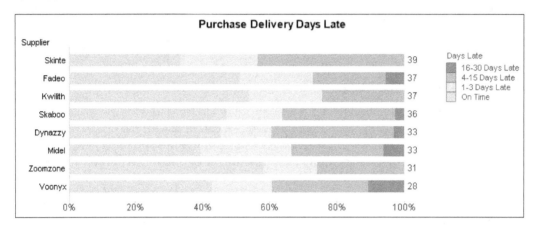

Exercise 16.3

To perform this exercise:

1. We create the following variable so that the code looks cleaner:

Variable	
Label	Value
vSA_PurchaseDelivery_NotFirstStep	{$<[Process Type]={'Purchasing'} ,[Delivery First Step]={'No'}>}

2. Let's create a bar chart with the following dimensions and metrics options:

Dimensions	
Label	**Value**
Supplier	`Supplier`

Days Late	`=aggr(`
	`        if(only($(vSA_PurchaseDelivery_NotFirstStep)`
	`[Delivery Days Late])<=0, dual('On Time',1)`
	`        ,if(only($(vSA_PurchaseDelivery_NotFirstStep)`
	`[Delivery Days Late])<=3, dual('1-3 Days Late',2)`
	`          ,if(only($(vSA_PurchaseDelivery_NotFirstStep)`
	`[Delivery Days Late])<=15, dual('4-15 Days Late',3)`
	`            ,if(only($(vSA_PurchaseDelivery_NotFirstStep)`
	`[Delivery Days Late])<=30, dual('16-30 Days Late',4)`
	
	`       ,dual('>30 Days Late',5)))))`
	`,_KEY_ProcessID)`

Expressions	
Label	**Value**

% of Deliveries	`count($(vSA_PurchaseDelivery_NotFirstStep)`
	`    DISTINCT [Delivery Line No.])`
	`/`
	`count($(vSA_PurchaseDelivery_NotFirstStep)`
	`      Total <Supplier> DISTINCT [Delivery Line No.])`

Number of Deliveries	`count($(vSA_PurchaseDelivery_NotFirstStep)` `      Total <Supplier> DISTINCT [Delivery Line No.])`

3. Change the background color attribute expression for % of deliveries to the following code:

```
=aggr(if(only($(vSA_PurchaseDelivery_NotFirstStep) [Delivery Days
Late])<=0, RGB(171,217,233)
     ,if(only($(vSA_PurchaseDelivery_NotFirstStep) [Delivery Days
Late])<=3, RGB(254,217,142)
     ,if(only($(vSA_PurchaseDelivery_NotFirstStep) [Delivery Days
Late])<=15, RGB(254,153,41)
     ,if(only($(vSA_PurchaseDelivery_NotFirstStep) [Delivery Days
Late])<=30, RGB(217,95,14)
     ,RGB(153,52,4))))),_KEY_ProcessID)
```

4. Select the expression `Number of Deliveries` and, in **Display Options**, disable **Bar** and enable **Values on Data Points**.

5. In the **Sort** tab, sort the `Supplier` by **Expression** in **Descending** order using the following code:

```
count(Total <Supplier> $(vSA_PurchaseDelivery_NotFirstStep)
    DISTINCT [Delivery Line No.])
```

6. Sort `Days Late` using **Numeric Value**.

7. In the **Style** tab, change **Orientation** to horizontal bars and change the **Subtype** to **Stacked**.

We've created the `[Delivery Days Late]` field in the script to make for cleaner code and reduce calculation time. For larger datasets, it may also be necessary to create days late bins in the script instead of using a calculated dimension, as we did in this exercise. Either way, we should create bins using the `dual()` function so that we can easily sort them.

We can use this chart for any step in a cycle that has a due date. We group all on-time instances in one bin and then we divide late instances into bins that represent ranges that are analytically significant. On the other hand, if we simply want to analyze the time that it takes to complete a step, we can use a histogram. Let's take what we've discovered about our suppliers' OTIF and analyze each item's real lead time.

Predicting lead time

Lead time is the time that it takes from the moment that we order an item to the moment that we receive it in inventory. We first saw lead time in our working capital perspective in *Chapter 15, Working Capital Perspective*. In that chapter, we used a predefined lead time to calculate each item's reorder stock level. In this section we look at how to use data to calculate a more accurate lead time. We can also apply these same methods to analyze the time taken to complete any of the steps in a cycle. For example, we can measure how long it takes to generate a customer invoice or convert a quotation into an order.

We begin our analysis by visualizing the average time that it takes from the moment we create a purchase order until we create an inventory delivery receipt. We analyze the trend of average lead times by month.

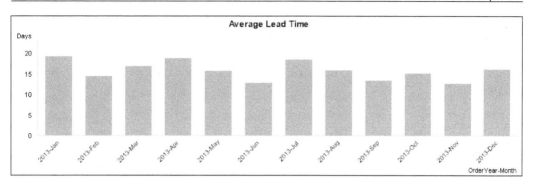

Exercise 16.4

Let's create a bar chart with the following dimensions and metrics options:

Dimensions	
Label	**Value**
OrderYear-Month	`OrderYear-Month`
Expressions	
Label	**Value**
Average Lead Time	`avg({$<[Process Type]={'Purchasing'}>} [Lead Time])`

We create a `[Lead Time]` field in the script that is the difference between `[Delivery Document Date]` and `[Order Document Date]`. The `avg()` function works without the help of *aggr()* because we want the average lead time of each line item, which has the same level of detail as our accumulating snapshot.

If the only statistical measurement that we use is average, then we risk over-simplifying our analysis and failing to define optimal inventory levels. Let's study the time span between a purchase order and its receipt in more detail with a distribution analysis that we first saw in the sales perspective in *Chapter 12, Sales Perspective*:

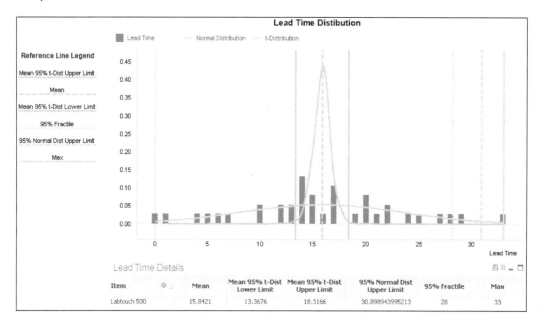

Exercise 16.5

Lead time distribution contains the following three objects:

Let's first create the **Lead Time Details** table:

Dimensions	
Label	**Value**
Item	Item
Expressions	
Label	**Value**
Mean	avg({$<[Process Type]={'Purchasing'}>} [Lead Time])
Mean 95% t-Dist Lower Limit	TTest1_Lower({$<[Process Type]={'Purchasing'}>} [Lead Time], (1-(95)/100)/2)
Mean 95% t-Dist Upper Limit	TTest1_Upper({$<[Process Type]={'Purchasing'}>} [Lead Time], (1-(95)/100)/2)
<empty>	=''

95% Normal Dist Upper Limit	avg({$<[Process Type]={'Purchasing'}>} [Lead Time]) +2*Stdev({$<[Process Type]={'Purchasing'}>} [Lead Time])
97.5% Fractile	Fractile({$<[Process Type]={'Purchasing'}>} [Lead Time],.975)
Max	max({$<[Process Type]={'Purchasing'}>} [Lead Time])

Just as we did in *Chapter 12, Sales Perspective*, we calculate the mean and evaluate its range using a t-distribution. We can use one of these results as the average lead time to calculate our minimum stock level. For example, we can use the upper limit if we want to reduce the risk of any inventory shortage or the lower limit if we want to reduce the risk of purchasing too much stock.

The other set of statistics tells us the maximum lead time that we've recorded and introduces two alternatives that we can use to avoid stocking too many items if the maximum happens to be an outlier. The first alternative, 95% Normal Dist Upper Limit assumes that we have more than thirty lead times in our data sample and that lead times are distributed normally. If this is the case, then we can add the mean and two standard deviations to calculate the upper limit of a 95% confidence level for a standard normal distribution. The result is the lead time that we predict will be larger than 97.5% of past and future lead times.

We can also use fractiles to remove possible outliers. The result of the 97.5% fractile is a number that is larger than 97.5% of past lead times. This fractile works regardless of how lead times is distributed and is easier for the business user to grasp. We can also use it as a test to evaluate whether lead times are normally distributed. If there is a large difference between the 97.5% fractile and the upper limit of the 95% confidence level, then lead times may not be normally distributed.

We may also decide to use the actual maximum lead time even when it is an outlier because the cost of not having an item in stock is greater than the cost of storing too much inventory. Which method we use to determine maximum lead time depends on our strategy and neither is perfect. We should test the accuracy of each and constantly fine tune the calculation according to our findings.

1. Let's create a **Combo Chart** that helps us visualize lead time distribution and the key numbers in our **Lead Time Details** table:

Dimensions	
Label	**Value**
Lead Time	`=ValueLoop($(=min([Lead Time])) ,$(=max([Lead Time])),1)`

Expressions	
Label	**Value**
| Lead Time | ```
sum({$<[Process Type]={'Purchasing'}>}
    if([Lead Time]=
        round(ValueLoop($(=min([Lead Time]))
            ,$(=max([Lead Time]))),.1)),1))
    /
count({$<[Process Type]={'Purchasing'}>} [Lead Time])
``` |
| Normal Distribution | ```
NORMDIST(
    ValueLoop($(=min([Lead Time]))
        ,$(=max([Lead Time]))),1)
    ,avg({$<[Process Type]={'Purchasing'}>} [Lead Time])
    ,stdev({$<[Process Type]={'Purchasing'}>} [Lead
Time])
    ,0)
``` |
| t-Distribution | ```
TDIST(
    (fabs(ValueLoop($(=min([Lead Time])),$(=max([Lead
Time]))),.1)
    -avg({$<[Process Type]={'Purchasing'}>} [Lead Time])))
    /
    (Stdev({$<[Process Type]={'Purchasing'}>} [Lead Time])
    / sqrt(count({$<[Process Type]={'Purchasing'}>} [Lead
Time])))
    ,count({$<[Process Type]={'Purchasing'}>} [Lead Time])
    ,1)
``` |

2. In the **Axes** tab, enable the **Continuous** option in the **Dimension Axis** section.

3. In the **Presentation** tab, add the six metrics in the **Lead Time Details** table as reference lines along the continuous *x* axis. Make the line style and color the same as the previous figure so that we can create a legend in the next step.

4. Finally, let's add a **Line Chart** that serves as our **Reference Line Legend**:

Dimensions	
Label	**Value**
Lead Time	`=ValueLoop(0,2)`
Expressions	
Label	**Value**
Max	`=dual(if(ValueLoop(0,2)=1,'Max',''),sum(.1))`
| 95% Normal Dist Upper Limit | ```
=dual(if(ValueLoop(0,2)=1
    ,'95% Normal Dist Upper Limit',''),sum(.2))
``` |

97.5% Fractile	=dual(if(ValueLoop(0,2)=1 ,'95% Fractile',''),sum(.3))
Mean 95% t-Dist Lower Limit	=dual(if(ValueLoop(0,2)=1 ,'Mean 95% t-Dist Lower Limit',''),sum(.4))
Mean	=dual(if(ValueLoop(0,2)=1,'Mean',''),sum(.5))
Mean 95% t-Dist Upper Limit	=dual(if(ValueLoop(0,2)=1 ,'Mean 95% t-Dist Upper Limit',''),sum(.6))

5. Modify the **Background Color** and **Line Style** in the following way:

Expression	Background Color	Line Style
Max	RGB(178,223,138)	='<s1>'
95% Normal Dist Upper Limit	RGB(178,223,138)	='<s2>'
97.5% Fractile	RGB(178,223,138)	='<s3>'
Mean 95% t-Dist Lower Limit	RGB(192,192,192)	='<s1>'
Mean	RGB(192,192,192)	='<s2>'
Mean 95% t-Dist Upper Limit	RGB(192,192,192)	='<s1>'

6. In the **Expressions** tab, enable **Values on Data Points** in the **Display Options** section.

7. Disable **Show Legend** in the **Presentation** tab.

8. Disable **Show Legend** in the **Dimensions** tab.

9. Enable **Hide Axis** in the **Axes** tab.

10. Resize and adjust each of the objects as necessary.

As in *Chapter 12, Sales Perspective*, we use the valueloop() function as a dimension to create a continuous X-Axis so that we can visualize the distribution curves. We also use it in the **Reference Line Legend** to create a dummy line with three points. We then use the dual() function in each line's expression to add a text data value in the center point.

We've just used advanced statistical methods to create a more complex model to estimate lead time. Let's now use another statistical method called the Chi-squared test of independence to test whether on-time deliveries depend on the supplier.

Supplier and On-Time delivery correlation

When we want to test whether two numeric metrics are correlated, we use scatterplot charts and R-squared. Similarly, we can also test the correlation between two categorical groups using the Chi-squared test of independence.

In this example, we want to confirm that the supplier is not one of the factors that determines a delivery's timeliness. In order to test this hypothesis, we calculate a value called p, which is the probability that supplier and delivery status are independent. Before analyzing the results of the Chi-squared test of independence, we decide that if p is less than .05, then we will reject the assumption that delivery timeliness does not depend on the supplier. This then implies that there is a relationship between them. We call this point (.05) where we would reject the hypothesis of independence as the critical point. Let's analyze and evaluate whether there is a relationship between these two variables:

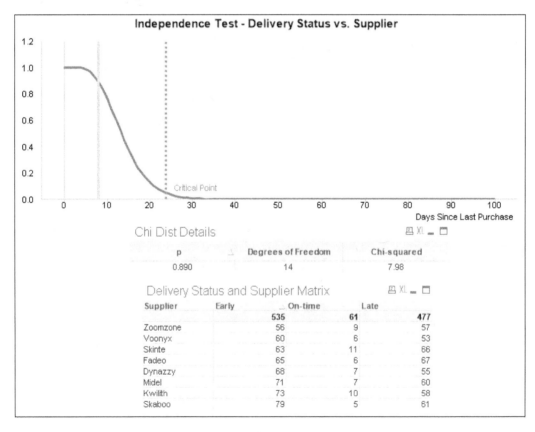

Chi Dist Details

p	Degrees of Freedom	Chi-squared
0.890	14	7.98

Delivery Status and Supplier Matrix

Supplier	Early	On-time	Late
	535	61	477
Zoomzone	56	9	57
Voonyx	60	6	53
Skinte	63	11	66
Fadeo	65	6	67
Dynazzy	68	7	55
Midel	71	7	60
Kwilith	73	10	58
Skaboo	79	5	61

Exercise 16.5

Our independence test contains the following three objects:

1. Let's first create the **Delivery Status and Supplier Matrix** pivot table:

Dimensions	
Label	**Value**
Supplier	Supplier
Status	Status
Expressions	
Label	**Value**
Number of Deliveries	`count({$<[Process Type]={'Purchasing'}>} [Delivery ID])`

> We notice from the table that there are deliveries that have a null status. Upon further investigation, we find that some deliveries do not have originating orders and therefore no due date to evaluate the timeliness of the delivery.
>
> Aside from that observation, it is hard to use this matrix to detect whether the status depends on the supplier or not. Therefore, we use a statistical method to evaluate the numbers.

2. Let's create the **Chi Dist Details** table that contains the statistical results. This straight table has no dimensions and the following expressions:

Expressions	
Label	**Value**

p	`Chi2Test_p(Supplier,Status`
	`,aggr(count({$<[Process Type]={'Purchasing'}>}`
	`[Delivery ID])`
	`,Status,Supplier))`

Degrees of Freedom	`Chi2Test_df(Supplier,Status`
	`,aggr(count({$<[Process Type]={'Purchasing'}>}`
	`[Delivery ID])`
	`,Status,Supplier))`

Chi-squared	`Chi2Test_Chi2(Supplier,Status`
	`,aggr(count({$<[Process Type]={'Purchasing'}>}`
	`[Delivery ID])`
	`,Status,Supplier))`

The *p* value of .89 is much larger than the critical point of .05, so we don't have enough evidence to reject our assumption that [Delivery Status] and Supplier are independent. If the *p* value were below .05, then that would imply that [Delivery Status] and Supplier are correlated in some way.

We use degrees of freedom and Chi-squared to create and build the distribution curve. We can confirm that our chi-squared of 7.98 is far from the chi-squared that crosses the critical point in the distribution curve in the chart.

3. Let's create a **Line Chart** with the following dimensions and expressions:

Dimensions	
Label	**Value**
Lead Time	=ValueLoop(0,100,1)
Expressions	
Label	**Value**
Chi Distribution	CHIDIST(ValueLoop(0,100,1) ,$(=Chi2Test_df(Supplier,Status ,aggr(count({$<[Process Type]={'Purchasing'}>} [Delivery ID]),Status,Supplier))))

4. In the Axes tab, enable the Continuous option in the Dimension Axis section.

5. Add the following reference lines along the continuous x axis of the chart:

Reference Lines	
Label	**Value**
Chi-squared	=Chi2Test_Chi2(Supplier,Status ,aggr(count({$<[Process Type]={'Purchasing'}>} [Delivery ID]),Status,Supplier))
Critical Point	=CHIINV(.05,$(=Chi2Test_df(Supplier,Status ,aggr(count({$<[Process Type]={'Purchasing'}>} [Delivery ID]),Status,Supplier))))

In a Chi-squared distribution curve, the *p* value of .89 is actually the area of the curve to the right of Chi-squared value of 7.98. QlikView draws an accumulated distribution curve that indicates the area that corresponds to a particular Chi-squared value. Therefore, we can see that the Chi-squared reference line crosses the accumulated Chi-squared distribution curve where the *y* value is close to .89. We also note that it is far from the critical point.

We've used advanced statistical methods to perform both relational analysis and predictive analysis. Other than predictive analysis through statistical methods, our business users can also input data into QlikView and help us plan demand.

Planning in QlikView with KliqPlan

Each person in our company is a data source and it is important that they can easily input data that will enrich our analysis. If we combine analysis with planning, then we can be better prepared for the future and support our statistical analysis. In QlikView, business users can simultaneously analyze and input data.

Traditionally, data input in QlikView is limited to what-if scenarios that use variables or input fields. However, when we have a large number of variables, neither of these methods are ideal. A large number of variables is hard to maintain and input fields take up too much RAM. Furthermore, users cannot easily input a large number of values at once and there is a risk they will lose their input that is not directly saved to a database.

Planning tool extensions

As an alternative, we have the option to use an extension that enables us to perform more advanced data input in QlikView. One of these extensions is called KliqPlan (http://www.ktlabs.com) and it allows users to input data directly into a relational database from a QlikView application. It can also read the content from a relational database in real time and allow users to reload a QlikView application from their browser.

In order to implement KliqPlan, you should be familiar with SQL and go through its manual to learn all the property options of its extensions. Although these property options are unique to KliqPlan, it reuses QlikView expression logic to dynamically calculate many property options.

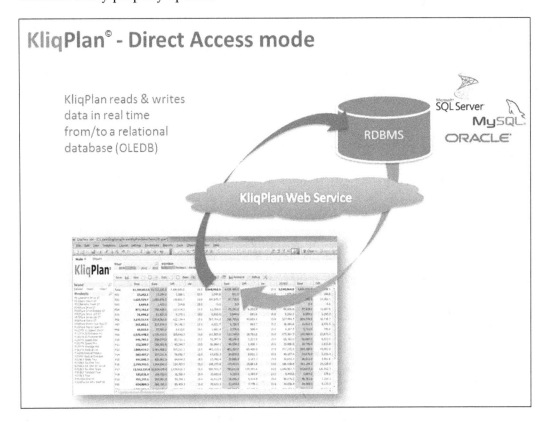

Sales forecasts and purchase planning

If we have a tool like KliqPlan, sales representatives can simultaneously analyze their past sales data and input what they expect to sell over the course of the next month. We can facilitate their planning by using QlikView expressions in a KliqPlan table to propose a future sales amount. For example, we can use a rolling average to predict next month's sales but still allow the sales representatives to adjust it accordingly.

We can then use this information to better plan our purchasing and production activities. We can cross-analyze data from sales representatives with historical data to confirm that it is not exaggerated. We may even experiment with multiple forecast versions as we learn more about our sales process.

It is especially insightful to visualize actual and forecast data side-by-side like in the following figure:

We use `rangesum()` and set analysis to combine actual and forecast data into the same line. Our expression would be similar to the following code:

```
rangesum(
sum({$<_ActualFlag={1},_MonthSerial={'<=$(=max({$<_ActualFlag={1}>}
_MonthSerial))'}>} [Net Sales])
,sum({$<_BudgetFlag={1},_MonthSerial={'>$(=max({$<_ActualFlag={1}>}
_MonthSerial))'}>} [Net Sales])
)
```

We then use the following code for the **Line Style** attribute expression:

```
if(_MonthSerial < max({$<_ActualFlag={1}>} Total _
MonthSerial),'<s1>','<s2>')
```

Along with the use of historical data, new products and customers are an important part of planning. Therefore, KliqPlan includes a component called *KliqTable* that allows users to add new customers and products.

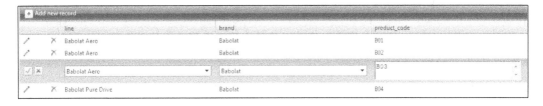

Other applications

KliqPlan is designed as a planning tool, but we can use it for any task that requires us to input data directly in QlikView. We often face analytical tasks that require the user to add information that cannot be found in any other data source. We usually end up using Excel files to input data that is not found anywhere else, but, in some cases, KliqPlan may be the better option, as in the following examples:

Options where KliqPlan is better	Description
Balanced Scorecard	Often, the goals and actual results of some of the indicators do not come from any ERP, CRM, or other formal operational database. For example, we may not have software to manage training and every month somebody has to input the number of employees that are certified QlikView developers. Instead of using Excel a user can input this data directly into Qlikview with KliqPlan.
Formal What-if Scenarios	Before KliqPlan, we used QlikView's native input fields to develop financial what-if scenarios for a customer. They used a series of drivers, such as the daily number of customers and the average amount spent by each customer, to create an estimated profit and loss statement.
	We developed a macro to export the profit and loss statement in XML so that SAP BW could import it into its database. The user then had to wait for QlikView to reload the new information from SAP BW. This functionality can now be developed using KliqPlan.

Summary

This chapter is a great opportunity to improve our internal processes and provide great customer service without bankrupting the company. After we explore the data with basic statistical methods, we should experiment with more predictive and complex analyses that can make our processes more effective.

Our ability to use such methods depends on the people that execute our internal processes. We need talented people to continually innovate how we analyze use data. As such, we will dedicate the next chapter to our human resources perspective.

17
Human Resources

We've created each of our previous perspectives with the objective of becoming a data-driven business. Robert Kaplan and David Norton considered the measurements in the learning and growth of employees as *the infrastructure to enable ambitious objectives in the financial, customer, and internal-business process perspectives.* We need to invest resources in our human capital so that they are capable of using data to help themselves and work at their optimal level. In this chapter, our goal is to learn more about our employees and help them be more effective.

First, we are interested in which factors make our team more productive. We use data from our **Human Resource Management System** (**HRMS**) to calculate metrics, such as headcount, salary, vacation days, sick days, and turnover by pertinent dimensions, such as job function, functional area, and demographics. Then, we compare these measurements with financial metrics, such as sales and gross profit.

Our organization's success is based on how well we develop our human talent. Therefore, we use additional metrics to measure performance and training. Along with our enterprise perspective, we also empower our employees to measure themselves. We look to achieve mutual success in helping them establish their own goals and measure their own performance with their own personal perspective.

We will cover the following topics as we develop our QlikView human resources perspective:

- HR data model
- Personnel productivity
- Personal behavior analysis

Let's begin by reviewing the HR data model that we will create from our HRMS system.

Human resources data model

The HR data model is a transactional fact table with discrete events. This includes the employee-related events along with a few financial events that help us measure productivity. We record the following events in this model:

- Employee payroll

- Employee absences

- Employee training

- Employee hiring and dismissals

- **General Journal (GJ)** entries related to sales, costs, and expenses

Here is a representation of this model:

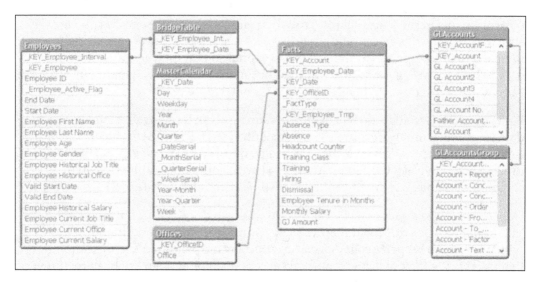

We combine these events into one fact table and use the same type of master calendar as in *Chapter 12, Sales Perspective*. The data model includes a new dimension table called **Employees**. Let's review the 7Ws of our HR data model.

Dimensions		
7Ws	**Fields**	**Comments**
Who	Employee	This is the focus of our HR data model. We include various attributes that are related to their role in the company and general demographic information here.
When	Month, Year	This is where we include a single master calendar that describes the exact date of an event.
Where	Office	We cannot usually measure sales by employee unless they are a sales representative. So, along with describing an employee's geographical location, we also use Office so that we can evaluate the productivity of an employee group.
What	_FactType	We store the event type of each fact table row in order to determine what event it represents. One row could record an absence, a training day, a hiring, a dismissal, or a paid salary.
What	GL Account	This is a dimension that we first saw *Chapter 13, Financial Perspective*.
Why	Absence Type	This is where we store why an employee was absent and whether it was due to sickness, vacation, or unexcused.
Metrics		
7Ws	**Fields**	**Comments**
How Many	[Absence], [Training], [Hiring], [Dismissal]	Several events, such as vacation, training, hiring, and dismissals, are measurements only because of the fact that they occurred on a given date. Therefore, we create a field that measures the event using the number, 1, and use it as a counter in our analysis.

How Much	[Monthly Salary]	We measure how much each employee earns on a monthly basis. We also define our headcount as the number of employees that receive pay. We create a field called [Headcount Counter], which contains the number 1 every time they are paid.
How Much	[Sales], [Costs], [Expenses]	We measure this in the same way as we did in *Chapter 13, Financial Perspective*.

Slowing changing dimensions attributes

Over time, employees will learn and grow and they will earn promotions or transfer to different departments in the company. Some HRMS systems, such as SAP HR, contain tables that conserve history and tell us when an employee has changed their job position or department. Other systems may just contain an employee's current information and not save any record of their past job positions or departments.

Descriptive information that may change over time is called **Slowly Changing Dimensions (SCD)**. Other examples include reassigning customers to new sales representatives, rearranging customers groups, or rearranging product groups. We need to understand the effect that SCDs can have on our analysis and how business users expect to visualize this data. The following are the most common types of SCD's (Kimball and Ross 2013):

SCD Type	SCD Description
Type 0: Retain Original	This dimension attribute value never changes.
Type 1: Overwrite	This is when we erase history and overwrite the old attribute value with the new one in the dimension table.
Type 2: Add New Row	This is when we conserve history and store the new attribute value in a new row in the dimension table.

Often, users need SCD types 1 and 2 in order to answer all of their questions. For example, we may want to assess each office's current employee knowledge. So, we use SCD Type 1 to analyze the amount of training taken by employees regardless of whether some of this training was taken while assigned to other offices. On the other hand, we may want to analyze which office is investing more in training. In this case, we would need to use SCD Type 2 so that we can take into account where employees were working when they were trained.

Therefore, it is worthwhile to allow advanced users the option to compare both types in one application. We'll store Type 1 dimension attributes in fields that contain the word `"Current"` (for example, *Employee Current Job Title*) and Type 2 dimension attributes in fields that contain the word `"Historical"` (for example, *Employee Historical Job Title*).

We can easily create a SCD Type 1 field by assigning the current HRMS attribute value to the appropriate field in the script. The creation of SCD Type 2 is more complicated. We have to link the value in the `_KEY_Date` field in the `Facts` table to the attribute value's valid date interval defined by the `[Valid Start Date]` and `[Valid End Date]` fields in the `Employees` dimension table. We use the same `intervalmatch()` function that we used in *Chapter 14, Marketing Perspective*, to create the relationship between the `Facts` and `Employees` tables in our HR data model. For more information on how to handle SCD in a QlikView data model, read Henric Cronström's blog post on the subject at `https://community.qlik.com/blogs/qlikviewdesignblog/2013/06/03/slowly-changing-dimensions`.

If the ERP or HRMS doesn't save the dates that a dimension attribute is valid and overwrites the values, we can use QVDs to conserve an attribute's history. The start and end dates are created in the script after we detect that a change has been made. A quick way to discover attribute value changes is using the hash function described in Barry Harmsen's blog (`http://www.qlikfix.com/2014/03/11/hash-functions-collisions/`).

Personnel productivity

Human Resources costs can represent up to 70 to 80 percent of the total cost of doing business (Lawler and Boudreau 2012). Our first goal is to analyze headcount, payroll, and how much revenue (or profit) we generate per employee and payroll dollar spent.

[
As an HR analyst, I want to discover who our most productive teams are so that I can share their practices with the rest of company.
]

We start our analysis by comparing headcount and payroll. As these amounts use a different scale, we use the left axis of a dot plot chart for headcount and the right axis for payroll. Before beginning the following exercise, we import this chapter's exercise files into the QDF as we did in *Chapter 12, Sales Perspective*.

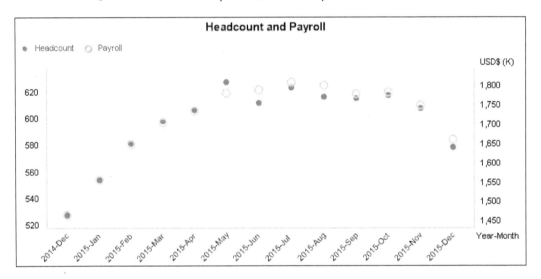

Exercise 17.1

1. In 1.Application\HR_Perspective_Sandbox.qvw, let's create a combo chart that measures headcount and payroll by year-month, as follows:

Dimensions	Details
Label	Value
Year-Month	Year-Month

Expressions	
Label	**Value**
Headcount	`count(distinct [Headcount Counter])`
Payroll	`sum([Monthly Salary])`

2. In the **Expressions** tab, enable only **Symbol** in the **Display Options** section. Define **Headcount** as **Dots** and **Payroll** as **Circles**.

3. In the **Axes** tab, disable the **Forced 0** option for both expressions. Select **Payroll** and enable the **Right (Top)** option in the **Position** section.

4. Adjust the look of the chart accordingly.

When we use a dual axis and remove the **Force the axis to zero** option, QlikView automatically aligns the maximum and minimum values of each metric so that they are at the same height along the Y-axis. We can, therefore, compare the percentage growth of the two metrics. For example, in the **Headcount and Payroll** chart, both **Headcount** and **Payroll** reach their minimum value in December 2014. At the end of 2015, **Payroll** is higher along its axis than **Headcount**, so we can conclude that it grew at a faster rate than **Headcount**. In other words, it implicitly shows an increase in the average payroll per employee.

Also, as we are more interested in the trend of the two metrics than the actual amounts, we can avoid forcing the axis to zero. It is sometimes useful to do this when we are working with a dot plot or a line chart. However, we should be careful to avoid doing the same to bar charts because the length of a bar traditionally represents the total actual value.

Let's apply the same method to compare these two metrics with the company's revenue and determine our personnel's productivity. The first formula compares revenue and headcount:

Revenue per employee = total revenue divided by total headcount

The second formula calculates employee productivity in terms of actual cost:

Employee Productivity = total revenue divided by total payroll

The ideal result of these metrics differ by industry, so we should compare our results with businesses from the same industry. Within our own company, we can also compare the results of different offices or branches. In order to do so, we create a dot plot chart that is similar to the previous example, but use the *Trellis* option so that we can create a series of the same chart by office. Every chart in this series uses the same axis scale so that we can compare the results of different offices as if they were located in only one chart.

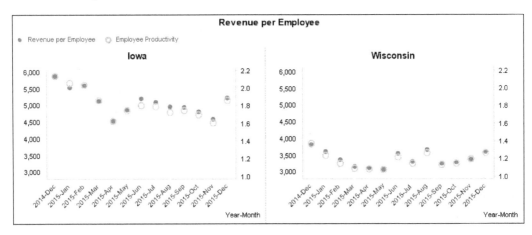

Exercise 17.2

1. Let's create a combo chart that measures headcount and payroll by year-month.

Dimensions	Details
Label	Value
Office	Office
Year-Month	Year-Month
Expressions	
Label	Value
| Revenue per Employee | ```
-sum({$<[Account - Concept]={"Total Revenue"}>}
[GJ Amount])
/
count(distinct [Headcount Counter])
``` |
| Employee Productivity | ```
-sum({$<[Account - Concept]={"Total Revenue"}>}
[GJ Amount])
/
sum([Monthly Salary])
``` |

2. In the **Dimensions** tab, click **Trellis...** and enable the **Enable Trellis Chart** option. Fix the **Number of Columns** to 2 and the **Number of Rows** to 1.

3. In the **Expressions** tab, enable only **Symbol** in the **Display Options** section. Define **Revenue per Employee** as **Dots** and **Employee Productivity** as **Circles**.

4. In the **Axes** tab, disable the **Forced 0** option for both expressions. Select **Payroll** and enable the **Right (Top)** option in the **Position** section.

We can easily see that the office in Iowa is more productive than the one in Wisconsin when the chart uses the same axis scale. Given that the Iowa and Wisconsin offices have equivalent departments and employee functions, the next step is to break down our personnel productivity and analyze why one office may have higher productivity than the other. We begin this process by visualizing our employees' profile and actions.

Personnel productivity breakdown

We begin the analysis of each office's teams by investigating their overall compositions and actions. We have a variety of metrics that may help us understand why one team may perform better than another. The following is a list of common metrics that we can use in our HR perspective:

- Age distribution
- Salary distribution
- Employee-retention rate
- Employee sick and vacation days
- Employee training and performance

Age distribution

Let's begin with our analysis and compare the age distribution between the two offices. Instead of using a histogram, we use a frequency polygon so that we can compare more than one distribution in the same chart.

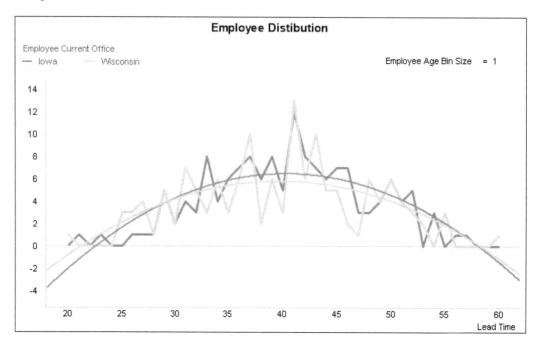

Exercise 17.3

1. Create the following variable:

Variables	Details
Label	Value
vEmployeeAgeBinSize	1

2. Let's create the following line chart:

Dimensions	Details
Label	**Value**
Age	```=ValueLoop(` ` $(=floor(min({$<_Employee_Active_Flag={1}>}` ` [Employee Age]),vEmployeeAgeBinSize))` ` ,$(=floor(max({$<_Employee_Active_` `Flag={1}>}` ` [Employee Age]),vEmployeeAgeBinSize))` ` ,vEmployeeAgeBinSize` `)```
Employee Current Office	Employee Current Office
Expressions	**Details**
Label	**Value**
Number of Employees	```sum({$<_Employee_Active_Flag={1}>}` ` if(floor([Employee Age],vEmployeeAgeBinSize)` ` =ValueLoop(` ` $(=floor(min({$<_Employee_Active_Flag={1}>}` ` [Employee Age]),vEmployeeAgeBinSize))` ` ,$(=floor(max({$<_Employee_Active_Flag={1}>}` ` [Employee Age]),vEmployeeAgeBinSize))` ` ,vEmployeeAgeBinSize` `)` ` ,1,0)` `)```

3. In the **Expressions** tab, enable the **Polynomial of 2nd degree** option in the **Trendlines** section.

4. In the **Presentation** tab, disable the **Suppress Zero-Values** option.

5. In the **Axes** tab, enable the **Continuous** option.

6. Create an `Input Box` to edit the **vEmployeeAgeBinSize** variable.

Normally, we would use the `class()` function to create a histogram; however, the `class()` function generates bins from existing values. A bin without any corresponding value behaves in the same way that missing or null values behaved in *Chapter 12, Sales Perspective*. Although we are not affected by this behavior when we use a bar chart, we are not so lucky when we work with a line chart. The line jumps from one existing bin directly to another without representing the missing bins as zero.

Therefore, we use the `valueloop()` function rather than the `class()` function because `valueloop()` is a list of numbers that have no relationship with the data. We define the range of `valueloop()` dynamically with the `min()` and `max()` functions and the bin size is determined by the value of the `vEmployeeAgeBinSize` variable. The `floor()` function helps to round down *Employee Age* so that we can assign it to the proper bin. We usually use `floor()` to round down to the nearest one, but we can also use it to round down to the nearest five, ten, or thousand.

Finally, we add a second degree polynomial trend line to get a general idea of the shape of the distributions. As both resemble a normal distribution, this trend line does give us a general idea of the distribution. We can observe that the **Wisconsin** office in general has a greater number of young employees and fewer middle-aged ones. If the distribution does not resemble a normal distribution, we can try using trend lines of different degrees or, more simply, enlarge the bin size. Notice how different the distributions look without the trend lines and with **an Employee Age Bin Size** of **5**:

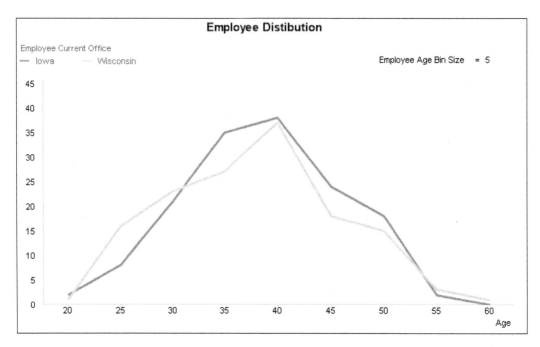

Salary distribution

The next analysis entails comparing how well each office pays their employees. We can analyze salary distribution among various groupings, such as office, job function, age, gender, and performance. In the following exercise, we are going to compare how each office pays each job function. Along with the option to use a frequency polygon trellis chart to compare the **Salary Distribution by Job Function and Office**, we can also use the following box plot chart:

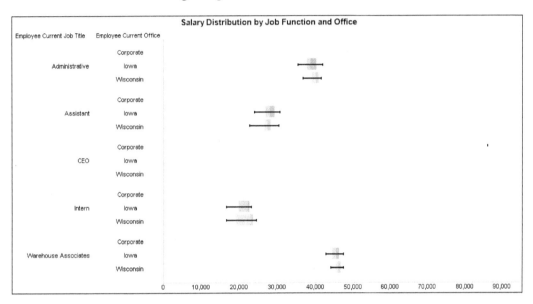

Exercise 17.4

1. Let's create the following combo chart:

Dimensions	Details
Label	Value
Employee Current Job Title	Employee Current Job Title
Employee Current Office	Employee Current Office
Expressions	
Label	Value

| Lower Quartile | ```
Fractile(
      Aggr(only({$<_Employee_Active_Flag={1}>}
            [Employee Current Salary]),[Employee Current
Office],
            [Employee ID],[Employee Current Job Title])
, 0.5)
-
Fractile(
      Aggr(only({$<_Employee_Active_Flag={1}>}
            [Employee Current Salary]),[Employee Current
Office],
            [Employee ID],[Employee Current Job Title])
, 0.25)
``` |
|---|---|
| Upper Quartile | ```
Fractile(
      Aggr(only({$<_Employee_Active_Flag={1}>}
            [Employee Salary]),[Employee Current Office],
            [Employee ID],[Employee Current Job Title])
, 0.75)
-
Fractile(
      Aggr(only({$<_Employee_Active_Flag={1}>}
            [Employee Salary]),[Employee Current Office],
            [Employee ID],[Employee Current Job Title])
, 0.5)
``` |
| Dummy Expression | ```
=0
``` |

2. In the **Expressions** tab, enable the **Bar** option for every expression and the **Has Error Bars** option for **Lower Quartile** in the **Display Options** section.

3. Define the following attribute expression for **Lower Quartile**:

Attribute Expressions	
Label	**Value**
| Background Color | ```
if([Employee Current Office]='Iowa'
      ,ARGB(100,178,171,210)
      ,ARGB(100,253,184,99)
)
``` |
| Bar Offset | ```
Fractile(
      Aggr(only({$<_Employee_Active_Flag={1}>}
            [Employee Current Salary]),[Employee Current
Office],
            [Employee ID],[Employee Current Job Title])
, 0.25)
``` |
```

Error Below	([Lower Quartile])
	-
	Min(
	    Aggr(only({$<_Employee_Active_Flag={1}>}
	        [Employee Current Salary]),[Employee Current
	Office],
	        [Employee ID],[Employee Current Job Title])
	)

Error Above	-([Lower Quartile])
	+
	Max(
	    Aggr(only({$<_Employee_Active_Flag={1}>}
	        [Employee Current Salary]),[Employee Current
	Office],
	        [Employee ID],[Employee Current Job Title])
	)

4. Define the following attribute expression for **Upper Quartile**:

Attribute Expressions	
Label	**Value**

Background Color	if([Employee Current Office]='Iowa'
	   ,ARGB(200,178,171,210)
	   ,ARGB(200,253,184,99)
	)

5. In the **Error Bars** section of the **Presentation** tab, change **Width** to **Narrow**, **Thickness** to **Medium**, and **Color** to a dark gray.

6. In the **Axes** tab, define the **Static Max** with the following code:

```
Max(
Aggr(only({$<_Employee_Active_Flag={1}>}
[Employee Current Salary]),[Employee Current Office]
,[Employee ID],[Employee Current Job Title])
)*1.1
```

We could create a simple box plot using **Box Plot Wizard** in the file menu, **Tools**; however, in this case, we are limited to using one dimension. As a workaround, we use a combo chart with bars and error bars to create a box plot. As a part of this technique, we have to consider the fact that QlikView will draw the same number of error bars as there are expressions. As we have three distinct values in the Employee Current Office field, we add a third, dummy expression that is not visible because the value is zero. If the second dimension has five distinct values, we create a total of three dummy expressions.

Although this trick may seem awkward at first, the chart is not effective when the second dimension has a large number of distinct values. Therefore, we never expect to choose one with more than five or so values and it is not much trouble to create three dummy expressions.

The last adjustment involves the maximum value of the expression axis scale. The maximum that QlikView automatically calculates is unnecessarily large. So, we dynamically calculate the maximum plus a ten percent cushion. This makes it easier to compare the different box plots.

Employee retention rate

As a high-employee turnover can affect a team's productivity, we analyze how many employees leave each month. We also analyze how many people we hire and how our team evolves as they accumulate more years of experience. Along with using histograms, frequency polygons, and box plots to visualize the distribution of experience, we can also show a summarized distribution over time with a stacked bar chart.

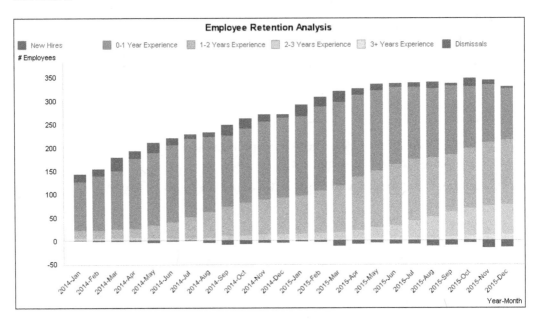

Exercise 17.5

1. Let's create the following bar chart:

Dimensions	
Label	**Value**
Year-Month	Year-Month
Expressions	
Label	**Value**
Dismissals	`-sum(Dismissal)`
3+ Years Experience	`count({$<[Employee Tenure in Months]={">36"}>}` `        distinct [Headcount Counter])`
2-3 Years Experience	`count({$<[Employee Tenure in Months]={">24<=36"}>}` `        distinct [Headcount Counter])`
1-2 Years Experience	`count({$<[Employee Tenure in Months]={">12<=24"}>}` `        distinct [Headcount Counter])`
0-1 Year Experience	`count({$<[Employee Tenure in Months]={">0<=12"}>}` `        distinct [Headcount Counter])`
New Hires	`sum(Hiring)`

2. In the **Style** tab, enable the **Stacked** option in the **Subtype** section.

This chart is simple to create because much of the work is done in the script. We create a new row in the fact table for every dismissal and new hire. The `Dismissal` and `Hiring` fields contain the value, 1, so that we only have to sum them up to discover the total occurrences of each event. Also, every time we add to the employee payroll event, we calculate how many months have passed since they started working for the company.

Employee vacation and sick days

When our employees take too little vacation and too many sick days, this may indicate an overstressed team who may not be as productive as they could be. We can analyze these events with a bar or line chart, but if we want to visualize them on a daily level, it may be more insightful to use a calendar heat map. This heat map was inspired by Julian Villafuerte's blog post at `https://qlikfreak.wordpress.com/2014/03/09/heat-map/`.

Exercise 17.6

1. Let's create the following pivot table chart:

Dimensions	
Label	**Value**
Month	Month
Week	Week
<empty>	Year
<empty>	`=if(wildmatch(Weekday,'s*','t*')` `,left(Weekday,2),left(Weekday,1))`
Expressions	
Label	**Value**

% Absent	`sum({$<[Absence Type]={'Sick Day','Unexcused'}>}`
	`Absence)`
	`/`
	`(count(Total <Month,Year> distinct [Headcount Counter])`
	`*`
	`max(Total <Month,Year> Day))`

2. Pivot this table's dimensions as shown in the following figure:

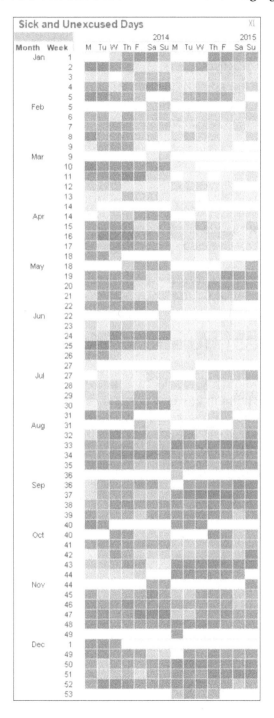

3. In the **Background Color** expression attribute, go through the **Colormix Wizard** found in the **File** menu. Use the same formula in the value expression as we did in the metric expression.

4. Copy the formula generated by **Colormix Wizard** and paste it in the **Text Color** expression attribute.

5. In the **Presentation** tab, disable the **Allow Pivoting** option and enable the **Always Fully Expanded** option. Replace the dashes in **Null Symbol** and **Missing Symbols** with spaces.

6. In the **Style** tab, disable the **Vertical Dimension Cell Borders** option.

7. Open the **Custom Format Cell** dialog window and make all backgrounds and borders white.

Sick days will tend to increase as the team grows; so, instead of basing our heat map on the actual number of sick days, we calculate sick days as a percentage of the total number of employee working days. According to the chart, after a lull in sick days in the beginning of 2015, there seems to have been an increase in the later part of the year. We can also compare the different offices by adding [Employee Current Office] as a dimension and placing it above the Year dimension.

Employee training and performance

Our final break down of employee productivity is to analyze our employee training and the results of this training. We expect employees to have greater success in the company after they are trained; however, sometimes it is inevitable that they leave or transfer to another office. Along with analyzing whether employees stay with the company after training, we also take advantage of the SCD Type 2 in our HR data model to analyze how often employees transfer or earn promotions after their training.

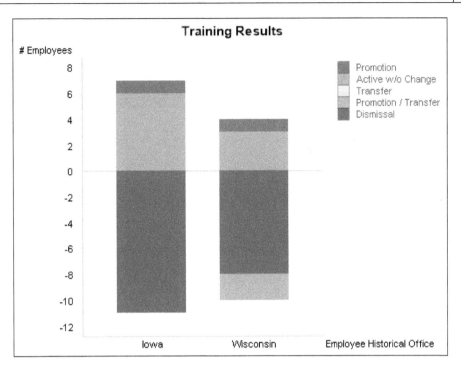

Exercise 17.7

Let's create the following bar chart:

Dimensions	
Label	**Value**
Employee Historical Office	Employee Historical Office
Expressions	
Label	**Value**
Dismissal	`-sum({$<_Employee_Active_Flag={0}>} Training)`

Promotion / Transfer	`-count({$<Training={1},_Employee_Active_Flag={1}>}`
	`distinct`
	`    if([Employee Historical Job Title]`
	`            <> [Employee Current Job Title]`
	`        and [Employee Historical Office]`
	`            <> [Employee Current Office]`
	`, [Employee ID]))`

| Transfer | ```
-count({$<Training={1},_Employee_Active_Flag={1}>}
distinct
    if([Employee Historical Job Title]
            = [Employee Current Job Title]
        and [Employee Historical Office]
            <> [Employee Current Office]
, [Employee ID]))
``` |
|---|---|
| Active w/o Change | ```
sum({$<_Employee_Active_Flag={1}>} Training)
-[Promotion]
+[Promotion / Transfer]
+[Transfer]
``` |
| Promotion | ```
count({$<Training={1},_Employee_Active_Flag={1}>}
distinct
    if([Employee Historical Job Title]
            <> [Employee Current Job Title]
        and [Employee Historical Office]
            = [Employee Current Office]
, [Employee ID]))
``` |

The `Training={1}` set analysis filters the data model, so we only see each employee's historical job title and office at the time he or she was trained. In this data model, we constantly update the current job title and office in every employee record so that we can always compare it with the historical records.

We use an if-statement within the `count()` function in this example in order to highlight how to compare fields of different SCD types. If we are dealing with a large amount of data, then we migrate this if-statement to the script and create a flag in the data model that indicates which dimension attributes have changed. We can then use this flag in the expression's set analysis.

In the chart, we observe that both offices suffer from a large number of dismissals after training employees and employees in the Wisconsin office tend to transfer when they earn a promotion. This example demonstrates why it is important to understand how the data model handles slowly changing dimensions and how we use both SCD Type 1 and SCD Type 2 to create an insightful analysis.

Personal behavior analysis

We collect a huge amount of data about each employee's work habits. Much of this data is located in log files generated when they connect to company servers or work on their own computers. A company that excessively uses this information to evaluate their employee's may be considered intrusive by their employees and the result may be counterproductive.
```

However, if we train employees in such a way as to form a mutually beneficial relationship, then we can rely on the employees themselves to analyze and improve their own productivity. In this case, the responsibility of the company is to give employees the proper tools to be more effective. One such tool may be RescueTime (https://www.rescuetime.com/), which helps a person keep track of which programs and websites he or she uses throughout the day. It also assigns a productivity score to each activity. For example, facebook.com has the minimum productivity score of -2, while MS Word scores the maximum score of 2, and MS Outlook may have a neutral productivity score of 0. The following chart reveals the productivity of a person's computer activities throughout several days:

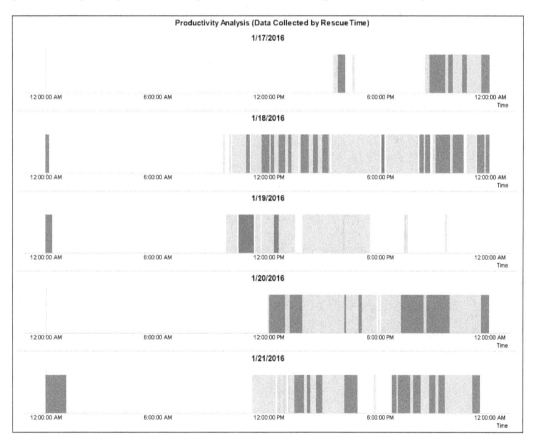

Exercise 17.8

1. Let's create the following bar chart in `1.Application\Personal_
Performance_Analysis.qvw` in the `HR_Perspective` container:

Dimensions	
Label	**Value**
Date	Date
Time	Time
Expressions	
Label	**Value**
<Empty>	=1

2. Place the following code in the **Background Color** expression attribute:

```
=pick(match(round(
      sum([Time Spent (seconds)]*Productivity)
        /sum([Time Spent (seconds)])),-2,-1,0,1,2)
  ,RGB(215,25,28)
  ,RGB(253,174,97)
  ,RGB(255,255,191)
  ,RGB(171,217,233)
  ,RGB(44,123,182)
)
```

3. In the **Axes** tab, enable the **Continuous** option in the **Dimension Axis** section.

4. In the **Dimensions** tab, click **Trellis...** and enable the **Enable Trellis Chart** option with **Number of Columns** set to 1.

In this chart, the colors belong to a typical heat map that uses a diverging color sequence. Red indicates unproductive activity and blue indicates productive activity. The white space in between indicates that no activity was detected.

Summary

This chapter first analyzed the productivity of our personnel. Once we found an opportunity to improve, we explored what may have made one team more productive than the rest. We also proposed the idea that employees can use data that they collect about their own activities to analyze and improve their own personal productivity.

In the same way that we focus on one employee, it is also useful to create reports that focus on one customer, product, supplier, or sales person. Let's take a look at how we can use fact sheets to better execute our day-to-day tasks.

18
Fact Sheets

When sales representatives make customer visits, we want to give them the opportunity to quickly review information about each customer and make every visit as productive as possible. Our proposal to meet this need is to combine the most important measures from several perspectives into one customer fact sheet.

In the same way that we create a customer fact sheet, we can also create a product, an employee, a supplier, or a branch fact sheet. In each fact sheet, we focus on one master data element and include related facts from multiple perspectives. For example, in our customer fact sheet, we include information from our sales, marketing, working capital, and operations perspectives.

Our goal is to discover techniques to best summarize key performance indicators with numbers, spark lines, and bullet charts. We also aim to allow business users to create their own dynamic reports in order to answer any new questions that they may ask.

We will cover the following topics in this chapter as we build a customer fact sheet:

- Consolidated data models
- Agile data visualization design
- Bullet graphs and sparklines
- Customizing the QlikView User Experience

Customer fact sheet consolidated data model

Fact sheet data models combine facts from various perspectives. The customer fact sheet data model combines information from our sales, marketing, working capital, and operations perspectives. However, we don't necessarily include all the facts that are measured in each perspective. In this example, we store the following events in our data model's fact table:

- Sales invoices
- Sales credit memos
- Sales budget
- Sales opportunities
- Sales quotes
- Sales activities like customer meetings and service calls
- Month-end A/R invoice balances
- Customer selling cycle

There are two principal ways to combine all of these events into one data model in QlikView. The first option is to combine all these events into one fact table, while the second option is to create a link table between various fact tables. The link table contains existing key combinations of every fact table, and serves as a bridge between the separate fact tables and a common set of dimensions.

On one hand, the link table creates an additional layer of links in the QlikView data model that often slows the performance of our analysis and data visualization. On the other hand, combining all these separate fact tables into one all-inclusive fact table may drastically increase the application's use of RAM memory if the tables contain a large number of columns.

For this example, we choose to combine all these fact tables into one table. As this consolidated table is directly linked to the dimension tables, it is more likely to have better performance, unless, in the extreme case, it creates an extremely wide fact table with numerous columns. If performance becomes an issue, we test this fact table against the option to create a link table.

According to Qlik, the recent upgrade of QlikView's Associative Data Indexing Engine to the second-generation columnar-based QIX engine in QlikView 12 improves the performance of wide-data tables.

Whether we use one fact table or a link table, we may confront a situation where the data volume is too much to include each detailed transaction. In this case, we only add fields and the level of detail that we know that we are going to use. In our following example, we explore the ideal case of when we can add all customer-related data at the most detailed level.

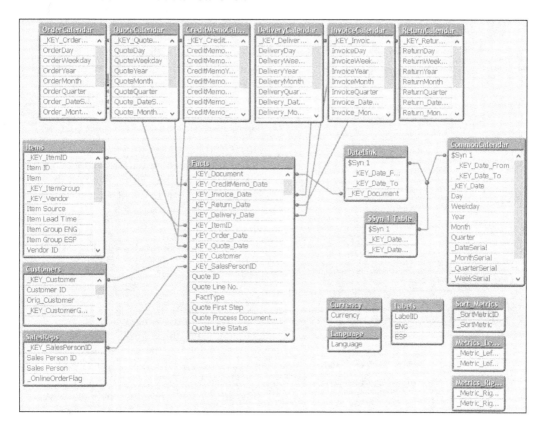

We've already used most of this data model's tables in previous perspectives. We add a few tables called `island tables` that have no relationship to this data model. These tables store data that helps us create certain elements of our user experience. For example, we are going to allow business users to choose the currency and language of the QlikView application. We also allow business users to choose from a list of metrics and dimensions in order to create their own reports on the fly:

Dimensions		
7Ws	**Fields**	**Comments**
Who	`Customer`	This is the central character in this data model. We first saw `Customer` in in *Chapter 12, Sales Perspective.*
Who	`Sales Person`	This plays a supporting role in our customer fact sheet, but we may later use this as the central focal point of a Sales Person fact sheet. We first saw this field in *Chapter 12, Sales Perspective.*

When	`Month, Year`
	
	`OrderMonth, OrderYear`
	
	`QuoteMonth, QuoteYear`
	
	`DeliveryMonth, DeliveryYear`
		These make up a common calendar to know when both transactional facts and snapshots took place. Although the calendar also tells us when an event occurred in an accumulating snapshot, we've also loaded the separate calendars of each step. We saw how to handle multiple calendars in *Chapter 16, Operations Perspective.*

What	`Item`	This is another dimension that plays a supporting role in our customer fact sheet, but which also deserves its own fact sheet. We first saw `Item` in *Chapter 12, Sales Perspective.*
What	`_FactType`	This field is used to help us sift through the large number of different facts that we've added to our customer fact sheet.

Metrics		
7Ws	**Fields**	**Comments**
How Much	`[Net Sales LC]`, `[Net Sales USD]`, `[Gross Profit LC]`, `[Gross Profit USD]`, `Quantity`	These measure discrete events, such as invoices, credit memos, and sales budget, which use the same fields. We use set analysis with the `_FactType`, `_ActualFlag`, and `_BudgetFlag` fields to differentiate the amounts if necessary. We use different fields for LC (local currency) and USD (US Dollars) amounts to support multi-currency analysis.
How Much	`[Customer Activity Counter]`	This is an example of how we measure other discrete events that are related to customers, such as activities that we extract from our CRM system.

How Much	[A/R Invoice Balance LC], [A/R Invoice Balance USD]	These fields measure a recurring event that is the A/R balance monthly snapshot. We must take care to never add more than one month's snapshot.
How Much	[Quote Quantity], [Order Quantity], [Delivery Quantity], [Invoice Quantity]	This data model includes the same metrics that were present in the operation perspective's sales process accumulating snapshot.

We have to be careful when performing analysis over a data model that mixes transactional facts with periodic and accumulating snapshots. For example, the pitfalls that we can avoid here are: while we can sum transactional facts over various months or years, we cannot sum periodic snapshots over time. The sum of several months' balances does not serve any analytical purpose. We can prevent any incorrect summation using set analysis to select the latest month's balance even when the user selects more than one month.

In the case of the accumulating snapshot, the challenge is to determine which date we need to use for our analysis. In the customer fact sheet, we expect the user to select a certain period using fields from the common calendar. In an expression that requires that we analyze the average time delivery for a certain month, we use set analysis to clear the common calendar selection and transfer this selection to the corresponding delivery calendar fields.

In addition to the 7Ws table, we create the following table to clarify how each event is recorded in the fact table. The manner in which we've classified most of the facts should be obvious from the way we've used them in their corresponding perspectives. The one event that is not so clearly defined is a sales opportunity. In other data models, we may handle the sales opportunities like a traditional accumulating snapshot that is similar to the sales operations process. However, in *Chapter 14, Marketing Perspective*, we recorded each stage in our sales pipeline as a separate row instead of a separate column. This treatment is similar to that of a slowly changing dimension, but, instead of a dimension, this is a long-lived event.

Even though each stage is stored by row and not by columns, we treat it the same as any other accumulating snapshot. For example, we cannot sum the amounts between different stages; however, we may want to analyze how the amount changes as we progress through the sales pipeline process:

Facts Fact Type	Sales	Sales Budget	Activities	Sales Opportunities	Sales Operational Process	A/R Invoice Balances
Transactional	X	X	X			
Periodic Snapshot						X
Accumulating Snapshot				X	X	

Finally, when we mix several events together, as we did for our working capital perspective, we tend to have a fact table with mixed granularity. We use the following table to visualize at what level of granularity we can analyze each metric:

Dimensions Events	Month/Year	Date	Customer	Sale Person	Item
Sales	X	X	X	X	X
Sales Budget	X	X	X	X	X
Activities	X	X	X	X	
Sales Opportunities	X	X	X	X	
Sales Operational Process	X	X	X	X	X
A/R Invoice Balances	X		X		

In our example data model, the *A/R Invoice Balances* event is the least detailed and cannot be viewed by the *Date*, *Sales Person*, or *Item* filters. Also, we cannot analyze events, such as activities and sales opportunities by `Item`.

Now that we've reviewed our customer fact sheet data model, let's design how we want to visualize our customer fact sheet.

Customer Fact sheet Agile design

We aim to involve our business users from the beginning of the customer fact sheet design. As a non-technical, collaborative process, we use Agile project tools, such as Post-It notes and a whiteboard to begin the design process. We begin by writing user stories that we think would be important to include in the fact sheet on Post-It notes.

Creating user stories

The user epic we want to solve with our customer fact sheet is as follows:

 As a sales representative, I need an easy way visualize all the information related to a customer and its relationship to the business so that I can plan more productive customer calls and meetings.

This user epic then gets broken down into the following user stories that we can eventually translate into a type of data visualization:

- As a sales representative, I need to compare this year's accumulated sales against last year's sales so that I can detect changes to our customers' buying habits

- As a sales representative, I need to compare this year's accumulated sales against the budget so that I can detect whether I'm going to reach the company's objective

- As a sales representative, I need to know of any outstanding payment that is owed to the company so that I can remind the customer and identify the cause

- As a sales representative, I need to know a customer's available credit and payment performance so that I can be prepared if they ask for more credit

- As a sales representative, I need to know a customer's open opportunities and quotations so that I focus on their closing

- As a sales representative, I need to benchmark this customer against others so that I can identify opportunities to negotiate better terms

- As a sales representative, I need to know how well we have delivered our products or services and of any recent service complaints so that I can be prepared to address such issues

- As a sales representative, I need to know how much a customer is expected to purchase so that I can foresee any abnormal behavior

- As a sales representative, I need to know what products I can recommend to a customer so that I can increase sales

- As a sales representative, I need to be able to create my own visualizations so that I can easily answer any ad-lib questions

User story flow

After we've written out the user stories, let's include a shorter version of each of them on a Post-it note and begin to arrange how we want to organize them in a customer fact sheet. Let's group related user stories together before determining what data visualization satisfies their requirements.

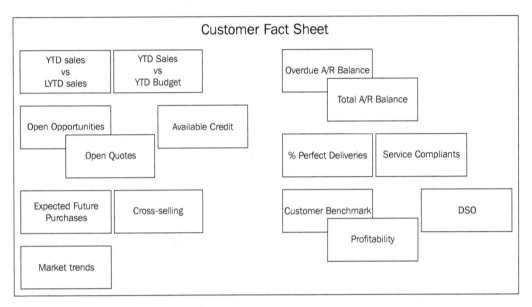

We create a scenario where a sales representative opens the customer fact sheet and reviews the first group of sales-related indicators. They first compare the current status of the YTD sales against last year's sales and the budget. The next information that they review is what is going to fuel the growth in these numbers in the short-term. This data can be found in open sales quotes and opportunities, in addition to the customer's available credit to close these new sales. The final sales indicators predict future sales and make suggestions to sell products that the customer has yet to purchase. We call this last concept *cross-selling* and recommend products based on what similar customers are purchasing.

After reviewing sales, the sales representative reviews post-sales activities that could affect future sales. The first indicator is the customer's A/R Balance and how much of it is overdue. They also analyze how well we as a company have delivered our products and whether there have been any service complaints.

Now that we have a general overview of our customer, we compare it with other customers using the customer stratification method that we've developed as a benchmarking method. We look closely at their profitability and DSO to give us a better idea how we should negotiate pricing and credit terms. Customer stratification also indicates with what priority we should follow up on all the previous indicators.

Converting user stories into visualizations

Once we've logically grouped our user stories and understood how they are interconnected, we convert each element of the story into a visualization. Just like the previous exercise, we design our customer fact sheet in a non-technical and highly collaborative way.

It is quite easy to create an application in QlikView, but it isn't as easy or as inclusive as using Post-it notes and a whiteboard. Although we can begin to design many applications directly in QlikView or develop visualizations in real time in front of the business users, we prefer a non-technical first approach for the following reasons:

- If business users actively participate in an application's design, then they will make it their own at an early stage and avoid asking for frivolous changes later.

- If we design a QlikView application in the presence of the business user, we risk getting hung up by a complex formula or data visualization. Nobody, especially a busy user, likes to wait ten minutes while someone is trying to figure out why their expression doesn't work properly.

- We break the habit of receiving asynchronous feedback about our designs, which can be less productive and create a discouraging 'us against them' attitude.

- We can use this collaborative design as part of our project documentation. A picture of the design may be worth a thousand or more words.

Today's collaborative technology still involves looking at our computer screens more than looking at our peers and, as such, we still do not have the same communication fidelity as a face-to-face activity. While video conference calls and virtual whiteboards may be the best solution for remote teams, it is otherwise better for everyone to gather around a real whiteboard with dry erase markers and Post-it notes.

The following figure shows the layout of our customer fact sheet. As many data-analysis applications use the same set of visualizations, we can save time and paper by breaking down the visual components into smaller, reusable parts. For example, we can reuse the sparklines, bullet charts, tables, monetary numbers, and percentages for other collaborative design exercises.

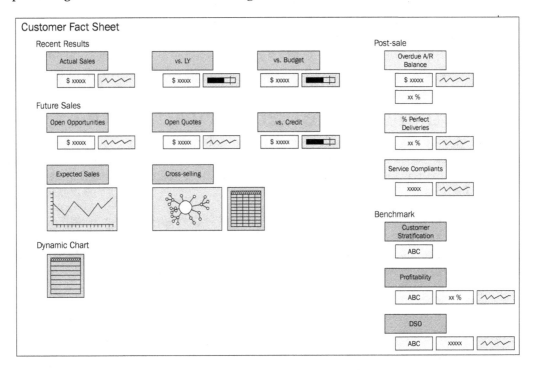

Let's organize our fact sheet in the same way that we broke down the user stories. We start at the upper, left-hand side of the sheet and review the customer's recent sales activity. We propose to use the actual monetary amounts, a *sparkline*, and two bullet charts to show actual sales and compare it with last year's sales and the budget. The next section reveals possible future sales from opportunities and quotes along with these amounts in comparison with the customer's credit limit. We also add a line chart to evaluate expected customer behavior and cross-selling recommendations that may improve sales. We end the main section of the fact sheet with a dynamic chart that the sales representatives can use to do their own visual ad-hoc analysis.

On the upper, right-hand side of the sheet, we include visualizations that fulfill the user story requirements that are related to post-sales activities. We propose using actual and relative numbers along with sparklines to represent the customer's overdue A/R Balance, % perfect deliveries, and the number of service complaints.

Finally, we end the fact sheet by benchmarking our customer using the customer stratification method that we developed in previous perspectives. Along with a general rating, we also include details about profitably and DSO.

This design does a great job of introducing each concept and fulfills the basic requirements of each user story. However, we often cannot fulfill an entire user story requirement with only one visualization.

Going beyond the first visualization

At first glance, the customer fact sheet should pique user curiosity and beg them to investigate each concept in greater detail. We can, of course, create a sheet that is dedicated to each section, but, many times, the user has a quick question that they want answered in one click without changing their context.

Alongside the general layout of the customer fact sheet, we include a second level of more detailed visualizations that users can access with one click. The following figure illustrates how we extend the original design to show how we want to display and visualize the details of several metrics.

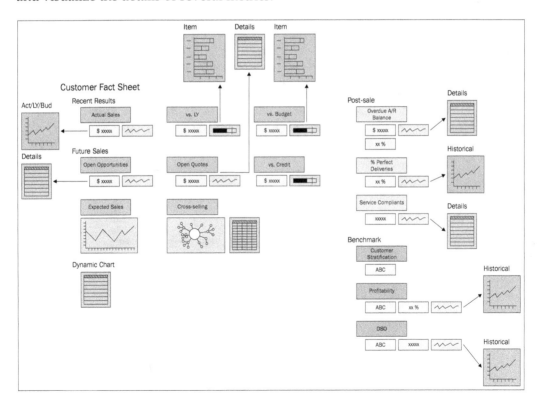

Together with the user, we choose the appropriate visualization for each concept. We also plan to take advantage of *Fast Change* and *Cyclical Dimensions* to make them more dynamic. If a user has more questions that can't be answered will these two levels of visualization, then we can give them the opportunity to navigate to a sheet.

Customer Fact sheet advanced components

Now that we've discussed the business story behind the customer fact sheet, let's review the different visualizations that compose it. We aim to create this perspective in the most precise way possible, so each one of the Post-it notes in our design will be separate objects. The labels and the numbers will be text objects that we align using the design grid tool that we introduced in *Chapter 12, Sales Perspective*.

In the next sections, we will review the following, more advanced components:

- Bullet graphs
- Sparklines

Bullet graph

The bullet chart was invented by Stephen Few to replace the bloated gauge chart in an information dashboard. Its compact design allows us to insert more information into a single view. The following bullet graph definition is from Mr. Few's website (https://www.perceptualedge.com/articles/misc/Bullet_Graph_Design_Spec.pdf) and you can read more about their use in his book *Information Dashboard Design*:

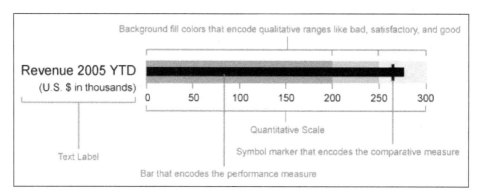

We can find an excellent, easy-to-use bullet graph made by Stefan Walther in Qlik Branch (`http://branch.qlik.com/#/project/56728f52d1e497241ae6980a`). There are also a few means to create a bullet graph using native QlikView objects. Let's explore one way that uses a single object. Before beginning the exercise, let's import this chapter's exercise files into the QDF as we did in *Chapter 12, Sales Perspective*. The following bullet chart compares actual sales YTD against the budget YTD:

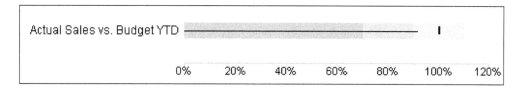

Exercise 18.1

In `1.Application\CustomerFactSheet_Sandbox.qvw`, let's create the following combo chart:

Dimensions	
Label	**Value**
<Empty>	='Actual Sales vs. Budget YTD'
Expressions	
Label	**Value**
0-70%	.7 * 1
70-90%	.2 * 1
90-110%	.2 * 1

1. In the **Expressions** tab, define each expression as a **Bar** in the **Display Options** section. Select the first expression and enable the **Has Error Bars** option in the **Display Options** section.

2. Define the following attribute expressions for **0-70%**:

Attribute Expressions	
Label	**Value**
Error Above	(-.7 * 1) + 1
Error Below	(.7 * 1) - 1

The **Error Below** formula can be confusing because the result is subtracted from the top of the bar in order to calculate the beginning of the error line. For example, if **Error Below** were `.1`, then the error line would start `.1` below the top of the bar and, if it were `-.1`, then the line would start `.1` above the top of the bar. Therefore, we first add the bar expression (`.7`) and then subtract 1 so that the result (`-.3`) will cause the error line to begin `.3` above the bar. The **Error Above** calculation results in `.3` so the error line also ends `.3` above the bar. When the **Error Below** and **Error Above** are the same, then a line is drawn across the width of the bar.

3. In the **Style** tab, enable the **Stacked** option in the **Subtype** section and select the horizontal bars in the **Orientation** section.

4. In the **Presentation** tab, change the **Width** and **Thickness** to **Medium** in the **Error Bars** section.

The next series of steps involves a trick to create a **Stock** expression. Stephen Redmond explained how to add a *Stock* expression in his book, *QlikView for Developers Cookbook*. Before we begin, click **OK** to close the **Chart Properties** window and open it again.

1. In the **Expressions** tab, add a new expression and enter 0 into the **Edit Expression** window. Disable the **Line** option and enable the **Stock** option in the **Display Options** section.

2. Click **OK** to close the **Chart Properties** window and open it again.

3. Define the following attribute expressions for a new stock expression:

Attribute Expressions	
Label	**Value**

Stock High	`sum({$<$(vSetYTDModifier),_ActualFlag={1}>}`
	`    [Net Sales USD])`
	`/`
	`sum({$<$(vSetYTDModifier),_BudgetFlag={1}>}`
	`    [Net Sales USD])`

Stock Low	0

The only fault in this native, one-object bullet graph is the inability to change the width of the line that encodes the performance measurements. We increase the chart's readability by organizing the chart's **Color** tab so that the qualitative ranges are very light and the stock line is black.

The advantage of a one-object bullet graph is that we can easily modify it into a series of bullet graphs that are based on absolute values. The following chart allows us to compare how our sales are performing against the budget in both relative and absolute terms by item. We can easily create this by using the result of the previous exercise.

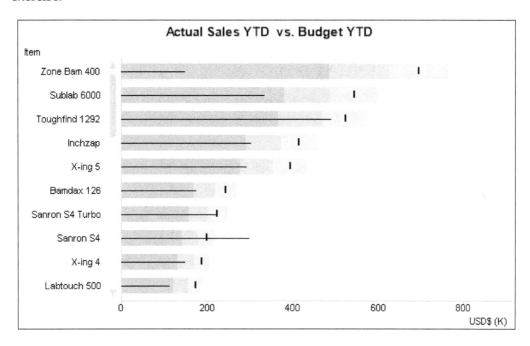

Exercise 18.2

The following exercise tells you how to recreate the chart using the result of the previous exercise:

1. Clone the chart from the previous exercise and replace the calculated dimension with Item.

2. Replace 1 in every expression, including the **Error Below** and **Error Above** attribute expressions, with the following code:

```
sum({$<$(vSetYTDModifier),_BudgetFlag={1}>}
  [Net Sales USD])
```

3. Change the Stock High attribute expression to the following expression:

```
sum({$<$(vSetYTDModifier),_ActualFlag={1}>}
      [Net Sales USD])
```

We now have an excellent alternative to using an extension or overlaying two charts when we create a bullet graph in QlikView. We place the single bullet graphs in the customer fact sheet and open the more detailed ones when the user clicks on that performance indicator. Next, let's review how to create sparklines for our fact sheet.

Sparklines

Sparklines are small, high-resolution graphs that allow users to understand the general trend of a performance indicator. A sparkline can be a line, a bar, or a win/loss chart, and they are drawn without any axes. We can easily create sparklines in a QlikView table using the **Mini Chart Representation** in the **Display Options** section. However, we may occasionally want to create a sparkline from a more customizable QlikView chart object.

In the following sparkline, we can review the percentage of deliveries that were OTIF over the last twelve months. Along with observing the performance indicator's trend, we can also appreciate how often the percentage of perfect deliveries fell below two different ranges. The top, dark-colored range is our preferred target, while the next light-colored range is our minimally acceptable range. Any point below these ranges is unacceptable.

Exercise 18.3

Let's create the following combo chart:

Dimensions	
Label	**Value**
Delivery Year-Month	DeliveryYear-Month
Expressions	
Label	**Value**

OTIF	sum({$<$(vSetRolling12Modifier)
	               ,_FactType={'Sales Process'}
	               ,[Delivery First Step]={'No'}>}
	     if([Delivery Document Date]<=[Order Due Date]
	        and [Order Quantity]
	                     =rangesum([Delivery Quantity]
	                          ,-[Return Quantity])
	    ,1)
	)
	 /
	 count({$<$(vSetRolling12Modifier)
	               ,_FactType={'Sales Process'}
	               ,[Delivery First Step]={'No'}>}
	    DISTINCT [Delivery Line No.])
	   -1

90-100%	-.1
80-90%	-.1

1. In the **Expressions** tab, define **OTIF** as line and the other two expressions as a **Bar** in the **Display Options** section.

2. Insert `'<w.5>'` into the **Line Style** attribute expression for **OTIF**.

3. In the **Style** tab, enable the **Stacked** option in the **Subtype**.

4. In the **Presentation** tab, set the **Bar Distance** and **Cluster Distance** to 0 in the **Bar Settings** section.

5. In the **Presentation** tab, disable the **Suppress Zero-Values** option.

6. In the **Axes** tab, select the expression **OTIF** and disable the option, **Forced 0**.

7. Finally adjust the colors and hide all elements other than the lines and the background created by the bars.

We may also add context to the primary sparkline by adding a second sparkline within the same two-dimensional space. We must be careful to give users more data without distracting their attention from the main information. We do this by making the second line lighter and transparent so that it will never overlap the first. In the following example, we compare this year's actual sales with last year's sales in the same sparkline:

Customizing the QlikView User Experience

Much of the QlikView **User Experience (UX)** is customizable. For example, we can develop ways to guide users through a well-defined series of reports or give them the power to create their own reports. We can also allow them to change the interface's language or the currency. In this section, we will create the following UX components:

- Quick access to supplementary information
- Dynamic data visualization
- Regional settings

Quick access to supplementary information

When users notice something interesting in concise visualizations such as numbers, sparklines, and bullet graphs, they often want to take a glance at the details that compose it. For example, in our customer fact sheet, we want to quickly analyze the detail behind the high-level comparison between actual and budget sales. During the design stage we chose to open a detailed comparison by item when the user clicks on **vs. Budget**, as shown in the following figure:

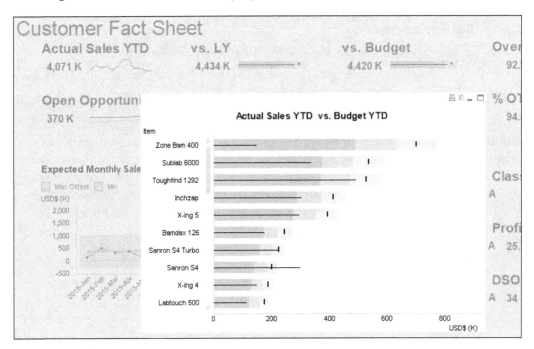

Exercise 18.4

Let's create the following variable:

Variable	
Label	**Value**
vCustomerFactSheetPopUp	None

1. Adjust the position of the detailed bullet graph that we created in exercise 18.2.

2. In the **Layout** tab of the chart's properties, enable **Custom** in the **Layer** section and set it to 3.

3. Also in the **Layout** tab, enable the **Conditional** option in the **Show** section and enter the following code in the expression field:

    ```
    =vCustomerFactSheetPopUp='BudgetDetail'
    ```

4. Create an empty text object that spans the whole fact sheet.

5. In the **General** tab of the text object change the background color to a transparent gray.

6. In the **Layout** tab, enable **Custom** in the **Layer** section and set it to 2.

7. Also in the **Layout** tab, enable the **Conditional** option in the **Show** section and enter the following code in the expression field:

    ```
    =vCustomerFactSheetPopUp<>'None'
    ```

8. In the **Actions** tab, create a **Set Variable** action with the following values:

Action	
Label	**Value**
Variable	vCustomerFactSheetPopUp
Value	None

9. Create a text object that contains the following text:

    ```
    Vs. Budget
    ```

10. In the **Actions** tab, create a **Set Variable** action with the following values:

Action	
Label	**Value**
Variable	vCustomerFactSheetPopUp
Value	BudgetDetail

If everything works correctly, then the detailed bullet graph will appear in front of a transparent, gray background. When we want to close the detail and go back to the general view of our customer fact sheet, we click on the grayed-out background. We could also create a **Close** button, but it is now common UX practice to close a pop-up window by clicking anywhere else on the screen.

As only one pop-up window will appear at any one time, we use one variable to determine which popup is displayed. One variable is obviously easier to maintain than having one for each corresponding popup. However, if we want to give the users the ability to open as many detailed charts as they like, then we would have to create a control variable for each popup.

Dynamic data visualization

It is relatively easy to create a dynamic straight table or pivot table in QlikView and we can find examples in various demos to imitate. However, it can be a challenge to create a simple way for users to make their own attractive graphic charts in a server environment. Qlik Sense is the ultimate tool for users who want to create their own charts and stories, but we can also give users the power to build insightful, ad-hoc data visualization in QlikView. The following chart was created using a few variables that users can readily modify in a server environment:

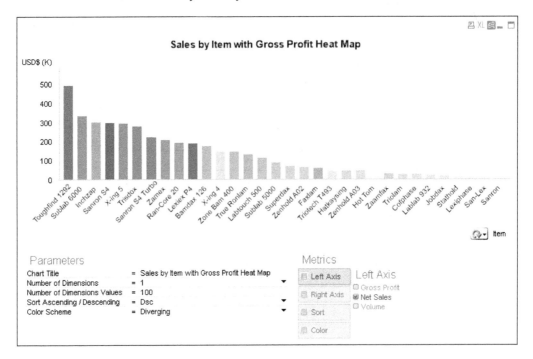

Exercise 18.5

Let's create the following variables:

Variables	
Label	**Value**
vNumDimensions	1
vChartTitle	Please add the chart's title here.

vSortMetric	=pick(match('|' & GetFieldSelections
	(_SortMetric,'|') & '|'
	, '|Net Sales|' , '|Gross Profit|'
	, '|Volume|')
	
	,'sum({$<_ActualFlag={1}>}
	    [Net Sales USD])'
	,'sum({$<_ActualFlag={1}>}
	    [Gross Profit USD])'
	,'sum({$<_ActualFlag={1}>} [Quantity])')

vColorMetric	=pick(match('|' & GetFieldSelections
	(_ColorMetric,'|') & '|'
	, '|Net Sales|' , '|Gross Profit|'
	, '|Volume|')
	
	,'sum({$<_ActualFlag={1}>}
	    [Net Sales USD])'
	,'sum({$<_ActualFlag={1}>}
	    [Gross Profit USD])'
	,'sum({$<_ActualFlag={1}>} [Quantity])'
	
	)

vAscDsc	Dsc
vAscDscNum	=if(vAscDsc='Asc',1,-1)
vColorScheme	Diverging
vNumDimensionValues	10

1. Add vChartTitle, vNumDimensions, vNumDimensionValues, vAscDsc, and vColorScheme to an Input Box.

2. In the **Constraints** tab, set the **Input Constraints** for vNumDimensions, vAscDsc, and vColorScheme to **Predefined Values Only** and disable the **Enable Edit Expression Dialog** option. For the same variables, select the **Value List** as **Predefined Values in Drop-down** and enable **Listed Values** in the **Predefined Values section**. The list values should be the following for each variable:

Variables	
Label	Listed Values
vNumDimensions	0;1;2;3
vAscDsc	Asc;Dsc
vColorScheme	Diverging;Sequential

3. Create four list boxes for the _Metric_LeftAxis, _Metric_RightAxis, _ColorMetric, and _SortMetric fields and insert them in a container.

4. Create a bar chart with the following dimensions and metrics:

Dimensions	
Label	Value
Dimension 1	A cyclical dimension with the following fields: Billing State Customer Item Sales Person Year Month
Dimension 2	A cyclical dimension with the same fields as Dimension 1
Dimension 3	A cyclical dimension with the same fields as Dimension 2
Expressions	
Label	Value
Net Sales	sum({$<_ActualFlag={1}>} [Net Sales USD])
Gross Profit	sum({$<_ActualFlag={1}>} [Gross Profit USD])
Volume	sum({$<_ActualFlag={1}>} Quantity)

5. In the **General** tab, enable all the **Fast Type Change** options except **Gauge Chart**.

6. In the **Dimensions** tab, tick the **Enable Conditional** option for all dimensions and place the following values for each of them:

Dimensions	
Label	**Value**
Dimension 1	`vNumDimensions>=1`
Dimension 2	`vNumDimensions>=2`
Dimension 3	`vNumDimensions=3`

7. In the **Expressions** tab, tick the **Conditional** option for all expressions and place the following values for each of them:

Expressions	
Label	**Value**

Net Sales	`SubStringCount(`
	`  '|' & GetFieldSelections(_Metric_LeftAxis,'|') & '|'`
	`, '|Net Sales|')`

Gross Profit	`SubStringCount(`
	`  '|' & GetFieldSelections(_Metric_LeftAxis,'|') & '|'`
	`, '|Gross Profit|')`

Volume	`SubStringCount(`
	`  '|' & GetFieldSelections(_Metric_LeftAxis,'|') & '|'`
	`, '|Volume|')`

8. In the **Background Color** attribute expression run the **Color Mix Wizard** twice using the expression, `$(vColorMetric)`. In the first run-through select a sequential color scheme from light blue (247, 251, 255) to dark blue (8, 48, 107). In the second run-through select a diverging color scheme from dark red (178, 24, 43) to dark blue (33, 102, 172) passing through a light gray (247, 247, 247) at 0. Place the resulting color mix functions into the following if-statement:

```
if(vColorScheme = 'Diverging'
,ColorMix2 (…)
,ColorMix1 (…)
)
```

Use the same code for the background color of every expression.

9. Copy and paste a duplicate of each expression so that there is a total of six expressions. In the duplicate expression replace `_Metric_LeftAxis` in the **Conditional** expression with `_Metric_RightAxis`.

10. In the **Sort** tab, tick the **Override Group Sort Order** option and then tick the **Expression** option and insert the following code in the expression field:

```
=$(vSortMetric)*vAscDscNum
```

Repeat the same steps for every dimension.

11. In the **Presentation** tab, tick the **Enable X-Axis Scrollbar** option and insert the following code in the expression field:

```
=vNumDimensionValues
```

12. In the **Axes** tab, select the duplicate copy of each expression and enable **Right (Top)** in the **Position** section:

13. In the **Numbers** tab, adjust each expression's number format and symbols, appropriately:

The user now has a way to create custom visualizations using only a few variables. We can continue to create more variables to control the property options defined by an expression field or preconfigure certain properties that can only be modified in the properties windows. However, the result of the previous exercise allows users to create the best possible charts using the fewest variables.

The cyclical dimensions are also more user friendly as they are located next to their axis or legend. We create three of them because graphs may use a maximum of three dimensions. Each should be sorted each dimension alphabetically or numerically by default, but we can easily select an expression by which to sort them in either ascending or descending order. We've also added a variable to limit the number of dimension values as there are often more than those that can fit in a graph at one time.

The metrics are divided by left and right axis as it is common practice to visualize two metrics that do not share the same scale. We also include the ability to add a heat map to the custom visualization to make them more insightful. The heat map can either be sequential, if the metric can only be positive, or it can be diverging if the metric can also be negative.

Although it seems like we use few variables in comparison to the hundreds that exist in the chart properties windows, the users can create a wide variety of different visualizations. Users who want the ability to create even more personalized charts should start working with Qlik Sense, which we will review in *Chapter 21, Mastering Qlik Sense Data Visualization*.

Regional settings

Currency, language, date formats, commas, and decimals can change depending on the region and users often become more engaged in the data discovery process when the effort has been made to respect their regional preferences. Some options, such as currency, are best left to the user to select, while others, such as date formats, should be automatic.

Currency

Contrary to what we may think, the currency used to analyze data does not depend on a user's country. Although some analysis may be done using the local currency, it is common to analyze data using one of the reserve currencies, such as the US dollar or the Euro. For this reason, we often add a currency filter to the user interface.

The values of the currency field correspond to the names given to the monetary amount fields in the data model, such as [Net Sales LC] and [Net Sales USD]. In this way, we can easily make our application multicurrency using the following code:

```
sum({$<_ActualFlag={1}>} [Net Sales $(=Currency)])
```

Language

In a similar way to how we make our application multicurrency, we also make it multilingual. We create a table with one field called Language that contains values that correspond to the field names in another table that contain the texts belonging to each language:

Then, in every multilingual label, we use the following code to calculate a label. We use a descriptive ID, like `Sales`, for our labels so that we can identify expressions and objects without having to manually look up numerical IDs in a table:

```
=only({$<LabelID={'Sales'}>} $(=Language))
```

Along with the labels, we also choose which descriptive field to use for list boxes and dimensions. For example, we have two fields in our `Customer` table that describes customer groups. `[Customer Group ENG]` contains English descriptions and `[Customer Group ESP]` contains Spanish descriptions. We use the following code as an expression in our list box or as a calculated dimension:

```
=[Customer Group $(=Language)]
```

Although we give the user the option to select any language, the application should open in the user's preferred language. One way to do this is to distribute a copy of the QlikView file with

the language prefiltered by the QlikView Publisher. Another way is to use section access to reduce a field that we use to select the preferred language upon opening the QlikView document.

Date and number formats

Date and number formats depend on the country and it should be automatically selected when opening the QlikView document. We use a set of variables that return the preferred formats based on a user's region along with the formatting functions, `num()` and `date()` in order to dynamically format the data.

We can define a user's region using Section Access. The following code is an example of how the dynamically formatted expressions will look:

```
date([Date],$(vRegional_DateFormat))
num(sum(Quantity),$(vRegional_NumberFormat_FixedDecimal)
    ,$(vRegional_Decimal),$(vRegional_Thousand))
```

Customer Fact sheet n QlikView

In the following figure, we bring together text objects, bullet graphs, sparklines, and the dynamic chart to create the customer fact sheet that we designed using Post-it notes and a whiteboard:

Create the pending expected sales chart in the next chapter and review the cross-selling chart extensions in *Chapter 21, Mastering Qlik Sense Data Visualization.*

Summary

Like the customer fact sheet, we can also create item, project, sales representative, or supplier fact sheets. In the next chapter, we will use many of the same visualizations to build a dashboard based on the balanced scorecard methodology. We will also use a more formal design process to help us organize our business strategy and reveal the results of our initiatives.

Balanced Scorecard

19

Over the course of this book, we learned how to analyze business data through various perspectives. We started with the sales perspective and then went on to develop visualizations for financial, marketing, working capital, operations, and human resources perspectives. Then we brought several perspectives together in a fact sheet that analyzed a customer through a sales representative's point of view.

Our next step is to unite the most pertinent perspectives and analyze the business as a whole from a business owner's point of view. This result is often referred to as the company's information dashboard. Stephen Few was the first person to investigate the real purpose of the information dashboard in his book, *Information Dashboard Design*, and he defines dashboards as follows:

> *A dashboard is a visual display of the most important information needed to achieve one or more objectives, consolidated and arranged on a single screen so the information can be monitored at a glance.*

We often design an information dashboard using the same freestyle process that we applied to create our customer fact sheet. However, we can also use a more disciplined approach such as a **Balanced Scorecard** (**BSC**) to unite the business's various perspectives into one consolidated viewpoint. This popular method was first developed by Robert S. Kaplan and David P. Norton to both drive and manage company strategy.

In this chapter, we will create an information dashboard that is based on the Balanced Scorecard method. We will cover the following topics in this chapter:

- The Balanced Scorecard method
- The Balanced Scorecard data model
- The Balanced Scorecard information dashboard design
- Additional QlikView UX customization
- Measuring process change with an XmR chart

The Balanced Scorecard method

The BSC method focuses on the following four perspectives:

- Financial
- Customer
- Internal business process
- Learning and growth

In each perspective, an organization should define a series of objectives, measurements, targets, and initiatives that help align its activities with its vision and strategy.

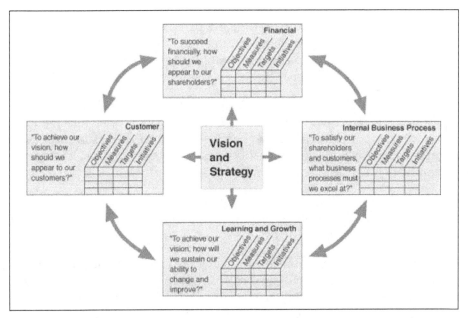

Source: Robert S. Kaplan and David P. Norton, "Using the Balanced Scorecard as a Strategic Management System," Harvard Business Review (January-February 1996):76

The financial perspective is the traditional way to measure an organization, but these measurements tend to tell us more about past events rather than future ones. In other words, the financial perspective uses lagging rather than leading performance indicators. For example, in the financial perspective, sales revenue is a lagging performance indicator that measures the results of a business's past efforts to market, sell, and deliver its products and services. The BSC method helps us to drive and foresee future sales revenue by using leading performance indicators, or we need to use performance drivers, that measure new customer acquisition, customer satisfaction, new product development, and employee retention.

An organization's performance indicators depend on its strategy to accomplish what it envisions as a successful business. The BSC method teaches us how to create a **Strategy Map** through the financial, customer, internal business process, and learning and growth perspectives. This Strategy Map communicates a series of objectives and the cause-and-effect relationships between them.

In our example, our vision of success is to increase the size of our business; therefore, our principal financial objective is to increase revenue. Our strategy to accomplish this is to increase customer retention and customer product mix. We've created the following Strategy Map that breaks down the strategy into objectives that are based on the four BSC perspectives:

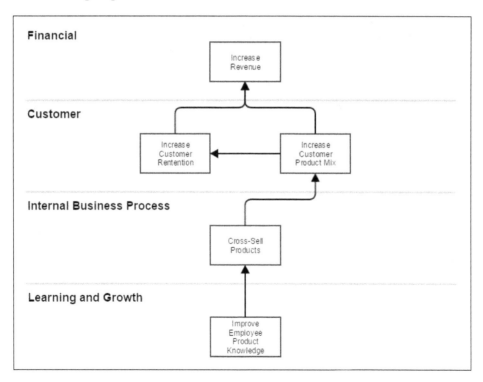

In the following sections, we will review what performance indicators we will use to measure the success of our objectives in each perspective.

The financial perspective

Our financial objective is to increase revenue, so our first financial performance indicator will be revenue growth. We define growth based on **Year-over-Year** (**YOY**) monthly and **Year-to-Date** (**YTD**) growth. We look at growth in terms of monetary amounts and percentages, as both ways can be insightful. Also, given that our strategy involves customer product mix and customer retention, we decide to detail revenue growth by product line and to measure the percentage of revenue that comes from existing customers.

Strategic objective	Strategic measurement
Increase Revenue	• YOY revenue growth • YOY revenue growth of existing customer by product line • Percentage revenue from existing customers

The next step is to review how to measure the customer objectives that are part of our strategy to increase revenue.

The customer perspective

Our customer objectives are to increase customer retention and customer product mix. We measure our customer retention using the customer churn rate or the percentage of customers lost. We are not a business that sells products through a subscription, so we consider a customer as lost if they haven't purchased anything in the last twelve months.

We measure customer product mix by evaluating the average number of product lines that a customer purchases during a given period of time. The exact time period that we use often depends on the type of industry our customers belong to and their buying rhythm. In order to simplify this example, we will use the same time period as we do for the customer churn rate; that is, twelve months. In more complex scenarios, we can use analysis techniques, such as a t-test, to evaluate each customer's purchasing rhythm like we did in *Chapter 12, Sales Perspective*.

We use YOY comparisons on a monthly and YTD basis for both indicators, which is consistent with the financial indicators:

Strategic objective	Strategic measurement
Increase customer retention	YOY change in customer churn rate.
Increase customer product mix	YOY change in average product lines purchased by the customer.

The next step is to review how to measure the internal business process objectives that we will use to drive an increase in customer retention and customer product mix.

The internal business process perspective

In a similar way to how supermarkets grew by providing one place to purchase many products, our plan is to promote cross-selling in order to increase customer product mix and customer retention. Cross-selling is simply the act of selling an additional product or service to a customer. However, it can be a powerful way to increase customer satisfaction and retention.

In the customer perspective, we measure the result of our efforts to increase cross-selling using the indicator *average product lines per customer*. However, in this perspective, we aim to use an indicator that focuses on the sales representatives' efforts to promote cross-selling independent of customer actions.

When we first explained lagging indicators, we referred to financial indicators as lagging and every other indicator as leading. In reality, the terms leading and lagging are relative. Therefore, a measurement such as average product lines per customer can be a leading indicator for future revenue growth, but it can also be a lagging indicator of increased cross-selling. We use another measurement such as the number of cross-selling quotations as the leading indicator of average product lines per customer and a confirmation of sales representatives' efforts to promote cross-selling.

Strategic objective	Strategic measurement
Increase cross-selling	YOY changes in the number of sales quotations with products lines not purchased by customers.

The next step is to review the learning and growth objectives that will enable sales representatives' to be able to promote cross-selling.

The learning and growth perspective

Human talent is often what determines the overall success of our strategies. The investment in employees' knowledge and growth is what drives all the objectives in every other perspective. In our example, we are going to give sales representatives product knowledge training and tools that suggest cross-selling opportunities that they may, otherwise, not recognize.

We measure an increase in product knowledge by evaluating the number of employees that attend each training session this year as compared to the last year. We also evaluate the effectiveness of the training and their behavior outside the classroom by analyzing their usage of the cross-selling analysis tool:

Strategic objective	Strategic measurement
Increase product knowledge	YOY change in number of employees who attended product knowledge training sessions.
	Average number of days that the sales representatives use the cross-selling analysis tool.

Now that we've defined the strategic measurements that we are going to use to evaluate the strategic objectives in our BSC, we will review the necessary data model and its supporting information dashboard.

The Balanced Scorecard consolidated data model

Similarly to the fact sheet data model, the BSC data model combines facts from various perspectives. In accordance with the strategic measures that we defined in the previous section, the BSC data model combines information from our sales, marketing, and human resources perspectives. To be specific, we store the following events in our data model's fact table:

- Sales invoices
- Sales credit memos
- Sales quotes
- Employee training
- Employee QlikView usage

The last event is related to the personal behavior analysis that we performed in the human resources perspective in *Chapter 17, Human Resources*. However, instead of using a data log from RescueTime, we will use QlikView's own session and audit logs to evaluate how employees' use QlikView's applications.

It is also common to add events from the financial, working capital, and operations perspectives. In this example, as we are only measuring revenue in the financial perspective of the BSC, we use the more detailed sales perspective to calculate revenue growth. As this model has the potential to become quite large, we leave the other perspectives out until a new strategic measurement requires their inclusion.

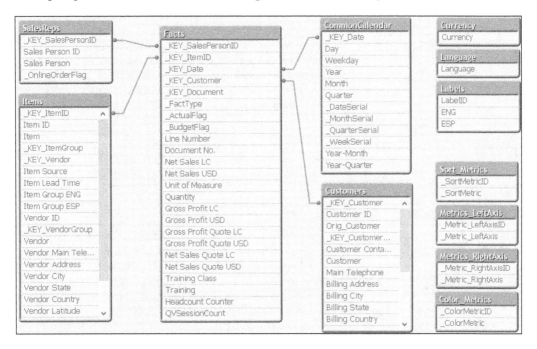

Unlike the customer fact table data model, this one only contains discrete events; therefore, it is far simpler. We only use one calendar table that describes the exact date when each event occurs. The rest of the dimension tables include descriptive information about sales representatives, items, and customers.

As company information dashboards may be used to communicate strategy to the whole company and also to external stakeholders, we include the same regional settings island tables. We also include the option to create dynamic visualizations as we did in the customer fact table. Let's sum up our data model using the 7Ws table:

Dimensions		
7Ws	**Fields**	**Comments**
Who	Customer	We first saw `Customer` *Chapter 12, Sales Perspective.*
Who	Sales Person	We first saw `Sales Person` in *Chapter 12, Sales Perspective.*
When	Month, Year	We use only one common calendar, as all events are discrete. In the case that we have to manage accumulating snapshots and periodic snapshots in one data model, we use the customer fact table data model as an example.
What	Item	We first saw `Item` in *Chapter 12, Sales Perspective.*
What	_FactType	Like the customer fact sheet data model, we use this field to help us distinguish between the different events in a single fact table.
Metrics		
7Ws	**Fields**	**Comments**
How Much	[Net Sales LC], [Net Sales USD], [Net Sales Quotes LC], [Net Sales Quotes USD],	Although the sales quotation and sales invoice share many of the same concepts, we've elected to create a separate set of fields for each document. While this risks creating an extremely wide table, it makes for simpler metric expressions that don't necessarily require set analysis.
How Much	[Headcount Counter]	We count the number of employees that have been in training with this field.
How Much	[QV Session Counter]	We count the number of times an employee has used QlikView with this field.

When we create a data model containing multiple perspectives, we take care to only add data that is necessary to calculate the required measurements. This is ultimately the best way to optimize the QlikView data model. Column-wise, we remove fields that are not used as a dimension, expression, or filter. Row-wise, we filter data that is not pertinent to the analysis. For example, we eliminate many of the fields that we created for our sales perspective, such as [Gross Sales USD] and [Cost USD]. We also reduce the number of rows in the fact table by only including QlikView sessions that pertain to cross-selling analysis.

In the following table, we confirm that all the facts are transactional and that they describe events that take place at a discrete moment in time:

Facts Fact type	Sales invoices	Sales credit memos	Sales quotations	Employee training	Employee QlikView usage
Transactional	X	X	X	X	X

We also describe how each event is related to each dimension table. In our example data model, the facts that represent employee training and QlikView usage cannot be analyzed by customer or item:

Dimensions Events	Month/Year	Date	Customer	Sales Rep	Item
Sales Invoices	X	X	X	X	X
Sales Credit Memos	X	X	X	X	X
Sales Quotations	X	X	X	X	X
Employee Training	X	X		X	
Employee QlikView Usage	X	X		X	

Now that we've reviewed our BSC data model, let's continue to design how we want to visualize a company's information dashboard based on the BSC method.

The Balanced Scorecard information dashboard design

Information dashboards that display BSC-related measures are often designed to replicate the strategy map or the cause-and-effect relationships between each measure. Just as we took a more disciplined approach to combine various perspectives, we will also reflect on a set of formal design rules called the Gestalt principles of perceptual organization to design the information dashboard.

The Gestalt principles of perceptual organization

Molded by human evolution, we are biased in the way that we visually perceive our environment. For example, how do we recognize the form of a tree, based on individual leaves and branches? We recognize the shape of a tree by grouping leaves that are close together, are of similar color and shape, or even by how the leaves are connected to the branches.

In the early twentieth century, a group of researchers called *Gestalt* (the German word for *form* or *shape*) psychologists began to study how we were able to unite individual perceptual inputs into complete objects. The following figure is a nonexhaustive list of visual occurrences that we use to perceive groups of individual elements called the Gestalt principles of perceptual organization:

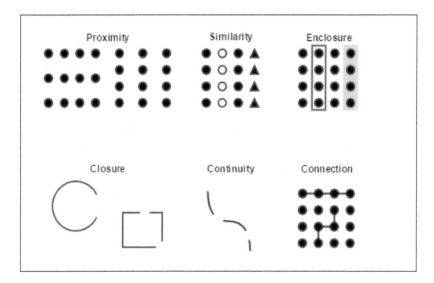

As in the natural world, we use these same principles to organize how we perceive artificial constructs. For example, even though the following sentence is readable, it is less efficient if we don't use proximity to group letters into words:

ThisisatestoftheGestaltprincipleofproximity.

In the same way that we group letters into words with one space, words into sentences with a period, and sentences into paragraphs with a new line, we can also spatially organize the objects of an information dashboard. As it is based on the BSC method, we want to group individual elements into measurements, perspectives, and cause-effect relationships. Along with proximity, we will review the other common principles that we can use to create these three groups.

Proximity

When we work with proximity in an information dashboard, we focus on how white space divides the visual elements on the screen. We often use white space to group information because this does not add any potentially distracting nondata ink. For example, in the following whiteboard design, we use proximity to group nineteen individual visual elements into three groups that represent the three strategic measurements (*YOY Revenue Growth*, *YOY Revenue Growth by Product Line*, and *% Revenue Existing Customers*) in our financial perspective:

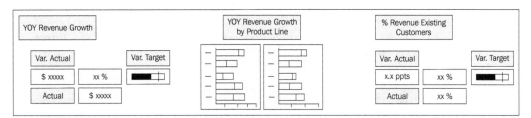

The decision to use proximity to group each measurement leaves us with a greater opportunity to use less obtrusive methods to organize perspectives and relationships. For example, if we were to use the Gestalt principles of closure and and draw a line between each measurement, then we may have to draw a thicker, darker, and more distracting line to separate each perspective. Instead, we are now able to assemble perspectives in subtler ways.

Enclosure

A more explicit way to group elements is to enclose them with a line or a background color. We often use enclosure when we cannot use proximity to group items. For example, when we want to display large amounts of data on a single screen and there is not sufficient white space to separate each visual element, we can use enclosure. In the following whiteboard design, we use a line to draw a box around each perspective:

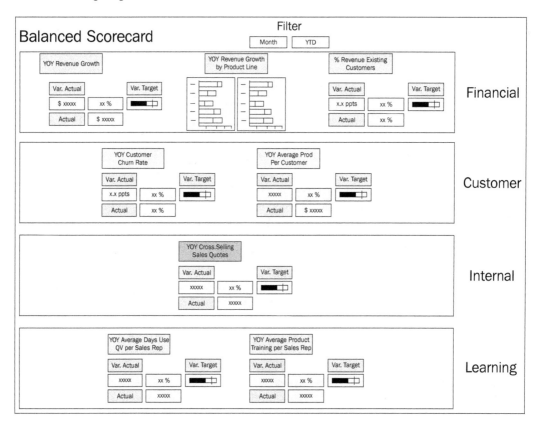

Enclosure is a stronger grouping method than proximity, and we should use it with care so that we do not to interrupt the flow of information in a dashboard. Let's take a look at how we can use the next Gestalt principle, closure, to make enclosure subtler and reduce its nondata ink.

Closure

We don't need a shape to be entirely discovered in order to perceive what form it takes. In the previous whiteboard design, if we draw a single line between each perspective, we still perceive the rectangular enclosures that group each one:

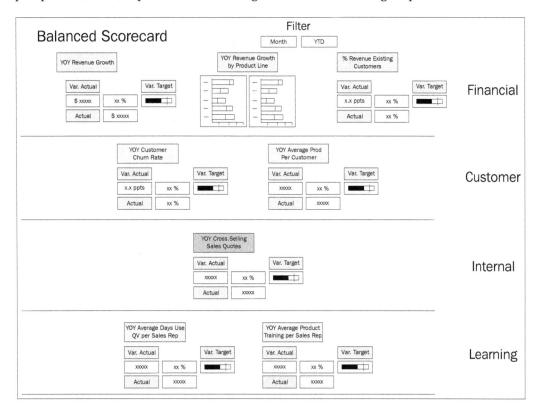

We have now created a subtler way to group different perspectives. An even subtler way would be to replace the lines with the names of each perspective in a very large font size. Sometimes, a simple outdented heading, such as "Balanced Scorecard" in the previous whiteboard design, is enough to perceive an enclosure. However, we elect to use a line so that we avoid overlapping headings with the lines that we will use in the following section to connect related measurements.

Connection

In the previous sections, we used proximity to group measurements, and we used enclosure and closure to group perspectives. In the following sections, we'll use connection, continuity, and similarity to assemble the cause-and-effect relationships. Connection groups elements together more powerfully than proximity but less than enclosure. In the following whiteboard design, we link cause-and-effect measurements in accordance with our strategy map:

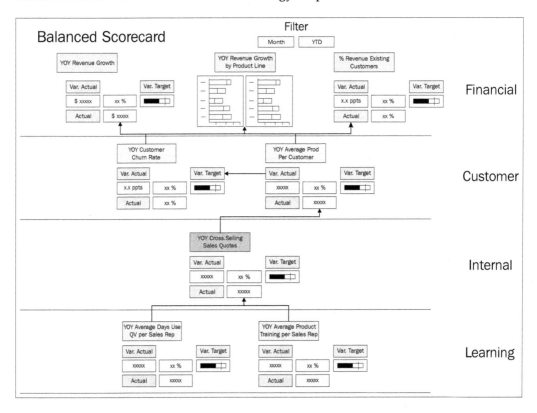

Even though we've now grouped the cause-and-effect measurements, we've also created possible confusion between these new lines and the ones that group each perspective. When we confront conflicting elements, we are often inclined to differentiate them by making one stronger and more explicit than the other. However, for example, if we were to make the lines dividing the perspectives thicker so as to differentiate them from the others, then we risk stealing attention away from what should be the most important element in the dashboard: the data. Let's see how we can use continuity to make sure that our grouping techniques complement rather than supplant the data.

Continuity

Similarly to closure, we don't have to see a complete line in order to perceive one. We can use the Gestalt principle of continuity to create a subtler, dashed line that connects the related measures in the following whiteboard design:

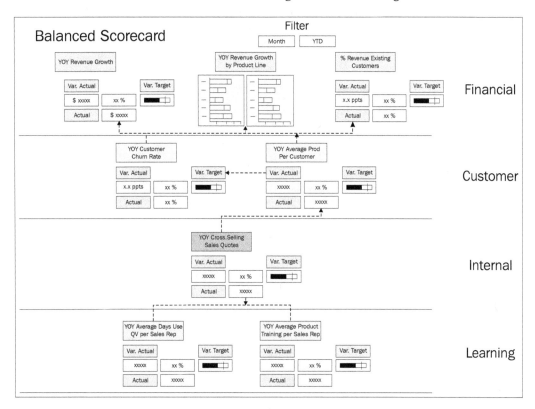

Continuity can also work in a more subtle way when we align objects in the dashboard. For example, the grouping of each perspective is reinforced by the fact that the measurements are vertically aligned. We may also notice that the measurements found in the customer and learning perspectives are also horizontally aligned even though they have no direct relationship. We've aligned them so that the dashboard is symmetric and aesthetically pleasing. In this case, the lines that we've added to enclose each perspective and separate the measurements help lower the risk that they will be interpreted as a meaningful group. We will now review the last Gestalt principle that will help us to further distinguish between the lines that we use to enclose the perspectives and the ones that connect related measurements.

Similarity

Finally, we interpret elements that are alike as part of the same group. Visual likeness can be determined by the elements' color, shape, and size. For example, in the whiteboard design, we've used the principle of similarity to group elements that are alike but dispersed throughout the dashboard. In the previous figure, we can decipher individual bullet charts as neon green and calculated numbers as pale yellow and efficiently identify them during an extremely dynamic agile design exercise.

In the actual dashboard, we use the similarity principle to reaffirm the distinction between the two sets of lines that we use to define two distinct groupings. In the final version of our design that we've migrated to QlikView in the following figure, we use black lines to divide the perspectives and light gray lines to group the cause-and-effect relationships.

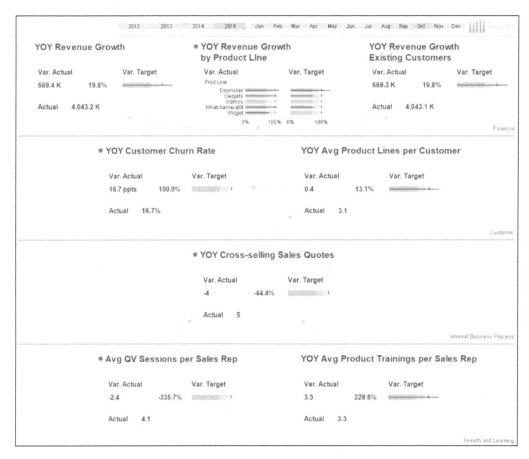

In the same way that we used the continuity principle, we use similarity to differentiate groups by making one subtler rather than making one more explicit. If we were to use a different hue to group the cause-and-effect relationships, then we risk stealing unnecessary attention away from the actual measurements again. In the previous figure, we can appreciate how well the eight BCS measurements stand out at first glance. Then, upon further exploration, we can see how they are first grouped by their perspective and then by their cause-and-effect relationship.

The Gestalt principles of perceptual organization are an important set of rules that help us make user-interface design less an art and more a science. However, they still leave us with plenty of leeway to create unique, aesthetic interfaces. In the next section, we will review how to incorporate a filter pane without changing our original information dashboard design.

Creating the filter pane bubble

The idea that an information dashboard should fit on a single screen is often a design challenge. In QlikView, it is common practice to place the filters to the left and at the top of the screen, where they may take up twenty percent or more of the available screen. Although QlikView list boxes are themselves informative objects that tell us what data is both related and unrelated to the current selection, they aren't always the most important objects on the screen.

This is especially the case with information dashboards, whose principal goal is to provide information that can be monitored at a glance and not necessarily dynamic analysis. However, it would also be a shame to use QlikView to create a fixed information dashboard, so let's allow the user to make data selections in an information dashboard in a way that doesn't take up so much space.

Exercise 19.1

Before beginning the exercise, let's import this chapter's exercise files into the QDF as we did in *Chapter 12, Sales Perspective*. To create a filter pane bubble, let's do the following steps in `1.Application\BalancedScorecard_Sandbox.qvw`:

1. First, let's add the following text object to the top, right-hand side corner of the screen. In this case, we've used explicit enclosure to make it stand out more than just simple text:

2. Next, let's place list boxes for the `[Sales Person]`, `[Customer Group ENG]`, and `[Item Group ENG]` fields in a single object container.

3. Then, let's place the container that we created in a previous step, a current selections object, and a search object in the grid container object. The container should look like the following figure after we align it with the **Other Selections** text object and assign it to the **Top** layer in the **Layout** tab:

4. Create a variable called vToggleFilterPane and define the grid container's **Conditional Show** expression as =vToggleFilterPane.

5. Create a **Set Variable** action in the **Other Selections** text object with vToggleFilterPane as the **Variable** and the following code as the **Value**:

```
=if(vToggleFilterPane = 1, 0, 1)
```

6. Finally, let's use the following code to define the background color of the **Other Selections** text object. We only change the color to green if we make a selection in a field that is neither **Year** nor **Month**, as their selected values are evident in their respective list boxes:

```
if(
  len(
    purgechar(
      replace(
        replace(
          GetCurrentSelections('|')
          , 'Year: '&GetFieldSelections(Year),''
        )
        , 'Month: '&GetFieldSelections(Month),''
      )
      ,'|'
    )
  )
  ,LightGreen()
  ,RGB(232,232,232)
)
```

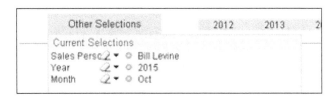

We intentionally use QlikView's native selection color for the background of the **Other Selections** text object. As they review the information dashboard, this helps remind the user of their selection, just like any list box. They can then quickly click **Other Selections** to edit or remove their selection. If they remove their selection, then **Other Selections** turns gray. It would also be reasonable for this to turn white. Although, we've reused QlikView's native color scheme, we may need to create a quick tutorial to help the user understand the application's unique interface.

Creating an interactive tutorial

There are a series of features that users expect to be the same in every application, such as the selection color scheme, bookmarks, cyclical dimensions, fast-type changes, and the ability to export to Excel. However, besides these powerful, generic features, every QlikView application is singular; each has its own data, data model, charts, filters, buttons, and actions. Therefore, if we expect users to get the most out of our applications, then it is often necessary to walk them through the application.

If the application serves one or two users, then the most effective way to show them the application is to give them a short personal tour. However, if we are dealing with an application that has more than a hundred users or has users that are prone to change, then we may want to create more efficient training material. Along with recorded videos lessons, we should also think about something more interactive that forces the user to start playing with the application.

Exercise 19.2

Let's embed a tutorial into our information dashboard and create its first steps in the following exercise:

1. Create variables called `vToggleTutorial` and `vTutorialStepNumber`.

2. Add a text object that uses the following information icon and place it in the upper, right-hand side corner:

   `C:\Qlik\SourceData\1201.Balanced_Scorecard\9.Misc\3.Images\Info_Icon.png`

3. Create a **Set Variable** action in the information icon's text object with `vToggleTutorial` as the **Variable** and the following code as the **Value**:

   `=if(vToggleTutorial = 1, 0, 1)`

4. Create another **Set Variable** action in the information icon with `vTutorialStepNumber` as the **Variable** and with 1 as the **Value**.

5. Let's add *Step 1* and create a text object as it appears in the next figure with this background image and assign it to the **Top** layer in the **Layout** tab, as follows:

```
C:\Qlik\SourceData\1201.Balanced_Scorecard\9.Misc\3.Images\
Bubble_Without_Arrow.png
```

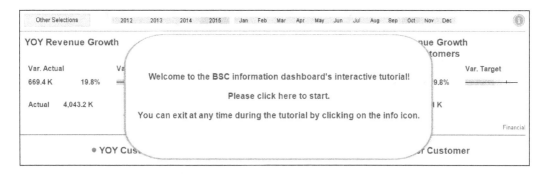

6. Define the text object's **Conditional Show** expression as the following code:

```
=vToggleTutorial and vTutorialStepNumber=1
```

7. In the text object, create a **Set Variable** action with vTutorialStepNumber as the **Variable** and 2 as the **Value**.

8. Let's add *Step 2* and create a text object as it appears in the next figure with this background image and assign it to the **Top** layer in the **Layout** tab, as follows:

```
C:\Qlik\SourceData\1201.Balanced_Scorecard\9.Misc\3.Images\
Bubble_UpperCenter_Arrow.png
```

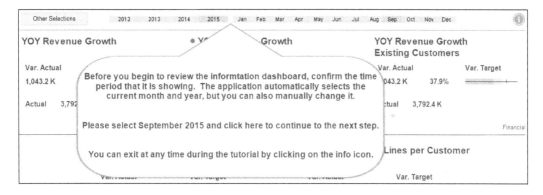

9. Define the text object's **Conditional Show** expression as the following code:

```
=vToggleTutorial and vTutorialStepNumber=2
```

10. In the text object, create a **Set Variable** action with `vTutorialStepNumber` as the **Variable** and the following code as the **Value**:

```
=if(only(Year)=2015 and only(Month) = 9, 3, 2)
```

11. Let's add *Step 3* and create a text object as it appears in the next figure with this background image and assign it to the **Top** layer in the **Layout** tab, as follows:

```
C:\Qlik\SourceData\1201.Balanced_Scorecard\9.Misc\3.Images\
Bubble_UpperLeft_Arrow.png
```

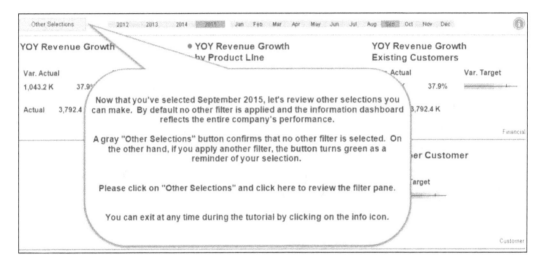

12. Define the text object's **Conditional Show** expression as the following code:

```
=vToggleTutorial and vTutorialStepNumber=3
```

13. In the text object, create a **Set Variable** action with `vTutorialStepNumber` as the **Variable** and the following code as the **Value**:

```
=if(vToggleFilterPane, 4, 3)
```

We stop the exercise at this point as we create all other steps in the same following way:

- Describe to the user what they are seeing from their perspective
- Give the user an action to perform before going on to the next step

The next steps in the interactive tutorial will help the user make a selection in the filter pane and understand that not all the measurements can be filtered by customer or item. It will then describe the measurements and any additional functionality that they may have, such as the detailed pop-ups that we saw in the customer fact sheet, or a link to another sheet or document.

We use the **Set Variable** action in each text object to validate the user's actions and proceed to the next step. We can easily validate user selections and the values in variables, which is what we use to create most custom QlikView UX. We can even validate some native functionality, such as changing a cyclical dimension, with the `GetCurrentField()` function or changing sheets with the `GetActiveSheetID()` function. However, other native functionality, such as exporting to Excel or creating a bookmark cannot be validated through chart functions, so we can only describe their functionality in the tutorial.

In all the other cases, the best practice is to create an interactive tutorial that offers users the chance to learn and remind themselves over and over again through active participation. Just like when somebody shows us how to get somewhere by car and we tend to learn more when we are the driver and not the passenger, we put the user in the driver's seat as we show them how to explore data.

Measuring success with XmR charts

The BSC information dashboards helps us monitor the success or failure of the company's initiatives to reach its objectives and we define this success by creating a target for each measurement. In the dashboard, we've added a series of alerts in the form of dots that only appear when the measurement is below target. For simplicity, we've defined all the targets to be ten percent YOY growth.

> The dots are created using `chr(9679)`.
>
> You can get Unicode geometric shapes at `http://www.alanwood.net/unicode/geometric_shapes.html`.

Along with reaching our targets, we also should analyze the effect on the sales process using statistical process control. Like all measures, monthly sales naturally fluctuates beyond our control. Therefore, how do we differentiate between variations that are natural and those that are caused by a change in the sales process?

In his book, *Understanding Variation: The Key to Managing Chaos*, Donald Wheeler recommends using the *XmR chart*. The X stands for average and the *mR* for moving ranges. It is often used to analyze whether a process is under control or whether process improvement initiatives are successfully reducing process variability. For example, if we were to manufacture bolts, we would notice that each bolt's exact diameter would vary. Some variation is fine as long as the bolt still fits its corresponding screw. However, if the bolts' diameters vary so much so that many have to be scraped and remade, then we confront a costly problem. It is, therefore, important that we monitor the manufacturing process to determine whether its variation is under control. Stephen Redmond includes a recipe to create an XmR chart in QlikView in his book, *QlikView for Developers Cookbook*.

In the previous context, we assumed that a variation is unwanted and that the XmR charts help us eliminate it. However, we can also use it when we want the results of a process to vary. For example, we don't want our sales process to be a controlled process with a predictable result month-in, month-out; but rather, we hope for variation that indicates that our monthly sales average is increasing. We use the XmR chart to eliminate the noise of natural variation and confirm whether this is really happening.

The usage of the XmR chart in this context has been mastered by the *Performance Measure Specialist*, Stacey Barr (`staceybarr.com`). Her book, *Practical Performance Measurement: Using the PuMP Blueprint for Fast, Easy and Engaging KPIs*, helps companies adopt better performance measurement techniques, such as this version of the XmR chart.

The following chart shows the actual sales and its average, or central line, within a range where sales could naturally vary, or the natural process limit. Unlike rolling averages, the central line only changes under certain conditions. In the chart that results from the following exercise, we change the central line and the range under the following conditions:

- If a value is outside of the natural process limit
- If eight consecutive points lie either above or below the central line (we recalculate the central line and the process limit beginning with the point from which the streak began)
- If ten out of twelve points lie either above or below the central line (we recalculate the central line and the process limit beginning with the point from which the streak began)

    The target that we include in the XmR chart is for the central line to reach. In this way, we can be sure that we've reached it due to real process improvement and not because of natural variation. The target is represented by a single dot in the chart:

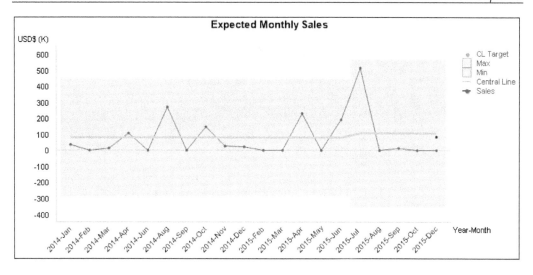

Exercise 19.3

To create an XmR chart, do the following:

1. Let's create the following variables:

Variables	
Label	**Value**
| vPointsGreaterThanCL | ```
if($1=1
 ,Above([Central Line]) >
   Below(Sales,0)
 ,RangeSum(Above([Central Line]) >
   Below(Sales,$(=$1-1))
     ,$(
       $(=if($1=1
         ,'=0'
         ,'vPointsGreaterThanCL($(=$1-1))'
         )
       )
     )
   )
 )
``` |
```

Variables	
Label	**Value**
| vPointsLessThanCL | ```
if($1=1
  ,Above([Central Line]) <
    Below(Sales,0)
  ,RangeSum(Above([Central Line]) <
    Below(Sales,$(=$1-1))
      ,$(
        $(=if($1=1
          ,'=0'
          ,'vPointsGreaterThanCL($(=$1-1))'
          )
        )
      )
    )
  )
``` |

These variables count the number of points above or below the central line within a given set of points. In QlikView, a conditional expression that is true is equal to -1. So, instead of using `if(Above([Central Line]) > Below(Sales,0),1,0)`, we just use `Above([Central Line]) > Below(Sales,0)` and take care of the negative sign later in the chart.

These variables also use a parameter so that we can count the number of points above or below the central line out of the next six, ten, twenty, or fifty points, and we will be able to use the same variable. We also want to avoid calling the variable for each individual point, like in the following code:

```
-sum($(vPointGreaterThanCL(1)) + $(vPointGreaterThanCL(2))
+ $(vPointGreaterThanCL(3)) + $(vPointGreaterThanCL(4))))
```

Therefore, we make the variable recursive so that we can arrive at the same result as the previous code with only one call:

```
-sum($(vPointsGreaterThanCL(4)))
```

This one call will start by evaluating the point four rows down and then call itself to evaluate the point three rows down. It will continue this process until it reaches the current row.

As a final note, we have to be careful to also make the dollar-sign expansion in the recursive function recursive or else it will get stuck in an infinite loop of dollar-sign expansions and cause QlikView and, possibly, the computer to lock-up.
```

2. Next, let's create the following combo chart:

Dimensions	
Label	**Value**
Year-Month	Year-Month
Expressions	
Label	**Value**
Sales	`sum({$<_ActualFlag={1}>} [Net Sales USD])`

Central Line	```//if one of the conditions is met then recalculate CL```
	```//check first row```
	```if(RowNo()=1```
	``` ,RangeAvg(Below(Sales,0,count(Total distinct {$<```
	```_ActualFlag={1}>} [Year-Month]))))```
	``` ,if(```
	```//check if value outside process limit```
	``` (Sales>above([True Max]) or Sales<above(Min))```
	``` or```
	```//check if next 8 values above or below CL```
	``` ((RangeMax(Above([Central Line])```
	``` ,Below(Sales,0,8))=Above([Central Line])```
	``` or RangeMin(Above([Central Line])```
	``` ,Below(Sales,0,8))=Above([Central Line]))```
	``` and```
	``` count(Total distinct {$<_ActualFlag={1}>}```
	``` [Year-Month])-RowNo()+1 >= 8)```
	``` or```
	```//check if next 10 of 12 values above or below CL```
	``` (-1*$(vPointsGreaterThanCL(12))>=10```
	``` or -1*$(vPointsLessThanCL(12))>=10)```
	``` ,RangeAvg(Below(Sales,0,count(Total distinct {$<```
	```_ActualFlag={1}>} [Year-Month])-RowNo()+1))```
	
	```//if none of the conditions are met then use previous```
	```//CL```
	```,Above([Central Line])```
	```))```

Min	`=[Central Line] - 2.66 *  [Moving Range Average]`
Max	`=[True Max] - IF(Min<0,0,Min)`

| CL Target | ```
if(RowNo()=1
    ,RangeAvg(Below(Sales,0,count(Total distinct
        {$<_ActualFlag={1}>} [Year-Month])))*1.1
    ,Above([CL Target])
)
``` |
|---|---|
| True Max | `=[Central Line] + 2.66 *  [Moving Range Average]` |
| Moving Range Average | ```
//if one of the conditions is met then recalculate MR
//check first row
if(RowNo()=1
//check first row
    ,RangeAvg(Below([Moving Range]
        ,0,count(Total distinct
            {$<_ActualFlag={1}>} [Year-Month])))
    ,if(
//check if value outside process limit
    (Sales>above([True Max]) or Sales<above(Min))
        or
//check if next 8 values above or below CL
    ((RangeMax(Above([Central Line])
            ,Below(Sales,0,8))=Above([Central Line])
            or RangeMin(Above([Central Line])
            ,Below(Sales,0,8))=Above([Central Line]))
            and count(Total distinct
            {$<_ActualFlag={1}>}
                [Year-Month])-RowNo()+1 >= 8)
        or
//check if next 10 of 12 values above or below CL
        (-1*$(vPointsGreaterThanCL(12))>=10
        or -1*$(vPointsLessThanCL(12))>=10)
        ,RangeAvg(Below([Moving Range],0,count(Total
            distinct {$<_ActualFlag={1}>}
            [Year-Month])-RowNo()+1))

//if none of the conditions are met then use previous
//CL
    ,above([Moving Range Average])
))
``` |
| Moving Range | `fabs(Above(Sales)-Sales)` |

3. In the **Expressions** tab, define **Sales** as **Line** and **Symbol**, **Central Line** as **Line**, **Min** as **Bar**, **Max** as **Bar**, and **CL Target** as **Symbol** in the **Display Options** section. For the rest of this expression, deselect all the **Display Options** and enable the **Invisible** option.

4. Define the **Background Color** attribute expressions for **Min** as the following code:

```
IF(Min<0,ARGB(100,158,202,225),White())
```

5. Define the **Background Color** attribute expressions for **Max** as the following code:

```
ARGB(100,158,202,225)
```

6. Define the **Background Color** attribute expressions for **CL Target** as the following code:

```
if(
  max(Total [Year-Month]) =
      only([Year-Month])
,black(),black(0))
```

7. In the **Style** tab, enable the **Stacked** option in the **Subtype** section.

8. In the **Presentation** tab, set the **Bar Distance** and **Cluster Distance** to 0 in the **Bar Settings** section.

9. In the **Colors** tab, enable the colors accordingly.

The expressions for **Moving Range Average** and **Moving Range** are invisible, but they help us make cleaner calculations of the natural process limits, **Min** and **Max**. We could also have assigned the expressions to variables and used a dollar-sign expansion. However, we elect to use invisible expressions because they are visual when we export the chart to Excel; therefore, they make the chart easier to debug if we detect any anomaly.

Also, as we use stacked bars to draw the natural process limit's blue background, **Max** only calculates the distance between **Min** and itself. If **Min** is positive, then **Max** will not be equal to the actual maximum process limit. So, we use an invisible expression called **True Max** to evaluate whether any value is beyond the limit. Also, if **Min** is positive, it's background color is white so that only the area between the minimum and maximum limits is blue.

In **Moving Range Average** and **Central Line**, we check the three conditions that indicate the process has changed. If it has changed, then we recalculate these two variables from the point when a streak begins, so we have to be forward looking using the below() function. Also, when we do the recalculation, we do it over all the values from this point onward in the chart. We determine the exact number of values after this point using the following code as the third parameter in the below() function:

```
count(Total distinct {$<_ActualFlag={1}>} [Year-Month])-RowNo()+1)
```

If we were to use a different dimension other than [Year-Month], we would replace it here.

Finally, the explanation for why we use the constant value, 2.66, to calculate the **Min** and **True Max**, and the conditions that indicate a process change can be found in *Understanding Variation: The Key to Managing Chaos, Donald Wheeler*. We can also find a XmR chart recipe in Stephen Redmond's *QlikView for Developers Cookbook* and get a different perspective on how to create one in QlikView. Also, a more detailed explanation about the design and purpose of this chart can be found in Stacey Barr's *Practical Performance Measurement: Using the PuMP Blueprint for Fast, Easy and Engaging KPIs*.

> We incorporate this chart into the customer fact sheet as the expected sales chart. It also serves to align the company's BSC revenue target with the targets for each customer.

Summary

The Balanced Scorecard, the Gestalt principles, and the XmR charts are excellent opportunities to formalize and elevate our level of mastery in QlikView. Like these methods of performance measurement, visualization, and analysis, there are others and there will be more in the future. The XmR chart is the last and most advanced QlikView chart that we will create in this book and it serves as a final example of how far we can go beyond the basics.

Now, it is time for you to go beyond the content of this book and use QlikView in even more advanced and insightful ways. In the next chapter, we will review how to troubleshoot the unknown issues you may encounter in order to help you continue to experiment and lead QlikView into uncharted realms.

20
Troubleshooting Analysis

A paradox development is that we often spend more time troubleshooting QlikView applications than we do developing them. Such is the case that if nobody complains about an incorrect calculation or missing data, then they probably aren't using what we've created. When we become aware of a potential problem, we also tend to invest more time understanding and searching for the anomaly than we do fixing it. Even though this is time well spent when we encounter an issue for the first time, we should avoid repeating the same investigation every time the same issue reoccurs.

In this chapter, we are going to review several common anomalies that occur when we perform data analysis and visualization in QlikView. We document their possible causes and solutions as we would in a knowledge base that we create to help save time when we come across the same issues in the future. Let's cover the following topics to improve our QlikView troubleshooting skills:

- Troubleshooting preparation and resources
- Reporting issues
- Common data model issues
- Common expression issues

Troubleshooting preparation and resources

First, let's go over the general approach that we take when troubleshooting in QlikView and what resources are available to make it easier.

Positive mindset

If we want to create successful QlikView applications, then we have to be prepared to maintain them for many years to come or transfer our knowledge to another person. In reality, we never completely finish great QlikView applications and we continuously transform them when new business questions arise. The troubleshooting, maintenance, corrections, and adjustments that we perform after the initial development is also an excellent opportunity to learn from our mistakes. We also learn what is truly important to business users and constantly improve the quality and value of our work. Therefore, we're better off being positive about post-development work because in the absence of all this feedback, it is hard to master QlikView.

General debugging skills

In addition to a positive mindset, we must possess the basic ability to debug problems. In his book, *Debug It!: Find, Repair, and Prevent Bugs in Your Code (Pragmatic Programmers)*, Paul Butcher proposes the following iterative steps to debug any code:

- Reproduce
- Diagnose
- Fix
- Reflect

These steps also apply to us when we troubleshoot issues in QlikView. Let's take a look at how each applies to QlikView in the following sections.

Reproduce

The first step to debugging any issue is to reproduce it. This allows us to diagnose the anomaly more easily and then confirm that it has been fixed. If we cannot reproduce the issue, then our only recourse is to run a general review of all the components involved and see whether anything stands out as a possible cause. If we don't discover any potential problem, then we could also decide to enable any logging that could help us learn more about the anomaly if it occurs again.

If we can reproduce the issue on our own computer or directly on the server, then it is probable that the issue originates from the QlikView Server, the QlikView document, or the data. Otherwise, if we are only able to recreate the anomaly on the user's own computer, then the problem is usually caused by the network or something in the user's own computer.

For example, QlikView will occasionally not update values that have been cached by the user's web browser. Even though the business user is looking at the same QlikView document with the same selections as those on other computers, they will see different numbers. In this case, we can fix this issue by clearing the user's web browser cache.

Diagnose

Once we reproduce the anomaly, we begin to explore its cause by dividing the problem into smaller parts and independently testing each one. In general, a QlikView document can be broken down into the following parts:

- Script
- Data model
- Expression
- Variable
- Action
- Macro
- Object

In addition to the parts that compose a QlikView document, we also explore the following elements that directly affect it:

- Data
- QlikView Server components
- User's actions

Each of these parts can be recursively divided into smaller and smaller parts. For example, we start by testing an expression and then isolate the problem to its set analysis. We then break this set analysis down into smaller parts and experiment with each set modifier until we find the one that causes the issue.

Also, we often go between various elements in search of the issue's root cause. For example, if we've isolated the issue with an expression to one of its set modifiers but we don't find anything wrong with it, then we look at the set modifier field in the data model. After reviewing the data model, we may need to review the script and, eventually, the source data to find the root cause.

Fix

If we know how to fix an issue's root cause, then we can solve the problem right away. Otherwise, we experiment with possible solutions that we find using the resources that we have available or through our own invention.

We must be careful and take into account that fixing one issue may cause another to appear. Therefore, when we solve our initial problem, we should quickly test anything that may be affected by this fix. We should also define a short list of key tests that we run regardless of whether or not we think that they were affected by the fix. These tests confirm the accuracy and functionality of the most important measurements and charts, along with confirming that the application can successfully reload data.

Reflect

Along with documenting the issue's cause and solution, we reflect on whether the same error could exist in other parts of the application. We also consider whether the same issue may affect other existing QlikView applications or even ones currently being developed. If it does, we analyze if and when to fix them.

We also contemplate on how we can reduce the probability that the same issue will recur. If the mistake is ours, then we should learn from it as soon as we fix it. The issue could also have been caused by some misunderstanding or miscommunication between ourselves and another party. In this case, we work together to find the solution to this issue and continue to work closely to avoid similar ones in the future. In more complex environments, we may also decide to implement tools or processes that help us quickly detect or even prevent future issues.

Resources

There are a number of resources that are available to help us during the whole troubleshooting process, especially when we cannot diagnose or fix the issue. We explore the most popular resources in the next section.

QlikView Help

QlikView Help is filled with examples of both chart and script functions as well as detailed explanations of almost every QlikView property option. This is often the first resource to go to when we have a question about how QlikView works. The sections about set analysis and incremental loads using QVDs are exceptionally well explained.

Local knowledge base

Every QlikView application is unique and we should not just depend on a general QlikView knowledge base to fix our problems. Therefore, we need an efficient way to explore development-related documentation along with past issues and their solutions.

The software that we choose for this job depends on our business's culture. One option is to use a note-taking app, such as Microsoft OneNote (`https://www.onenote.com/`) or Evernote (`https://evernote.com/`) and have the team share a notebook. We can also use a more minimalist notepad approach, such as GitHub Gist (`https://gist.github.com/`). We may also use a wiki, such as Atlassian Confluence (`https://www.atlassian.com/software/confluence`), or a social platform, such as Jive (`https://www.jivesoftware.com/`), which is the same tool that the Qlik Community uses.

Qlik Community

Qlik Community (`https://community.qlik.com/`) is one of Qlik's greatest assets. Developers from various partners, customers, and even Qlik are readily available to help anyone who has a question about QlikView or Qlik Sense. It is also a great repository filled with QlikView tools, templates, and how-to documentation. Let's keep in mind the following tips when we use Qlik Community:

- Search for a solution before asking a question. We rarely ask something that has never been asked before. Our exact data, script, or expression will be different. However, if we diagnose our issue well enough, then we should be able to find a solution to the same problem regardless of the exact example used in the Qlik Community discussion.

- If we don't find an existing solution, then we create a new discussion with a brief explanation of our issue along with a QlikView application that demonstrates the problem. If we can't upload an application, then we should upload one or more of the following artifacts:
    ◦ A screenshot of the issue
    ◦ The current script
    ◦ The current expression code
    ◦ Sample data
    ◦ Our expected results

  An example application or any of these artifacts is far easier to understand than a thousand-word explanation.

- If somebody helps us, then we should mark their answer as either helpful or correct so that they earn points for their contribution. Qlik Community runs on gamification and earning points is like making money. Let's help keep it this way and spend the extra minute that it takes to "pay" those who help us.

- We must avoid the expectation that somebody else will do our work for us. Some so-called QlikView developers create discussions to find people who will develop a report that they themselves are paid to develop. This is an incorrect use of Qlik Community.

- We can't always expect to find answers to our questions in Qlik Community, especially if the issue is related to QlikView Server. We should escalate such issues with Qlik Support.

Qlik Support

If QlikView isn't working as documented in QlikView Help or the issue is related to QlikView Server, then Qlik Support is the best resource to use. Let's keep in mind the following tips when we use Qlik Support:

- Let's not overinflate an issue's priority. If the issue concerns something cosmetic, such as a chart's color, then do not classify it as urgent. Nothing is more annoying or starts a support case on the wrong foot as an overstated priority.

- We can expect the support team to ask us for all sorts of logs, files, and screenshots to help them troubleshoot the issue. Some of the things that they ask us to do or send will appear to be superfluous. However, keep in mind that they are tasked with trying to understand and debug hundreds of issues on remote computers. As this is not any easy job, they do tend to ask for as much information as possible.

- Let's not take advantage of the distance to act overly rude or aggressive. Similar to road rage, technical support rage can be counter-productive. We should promptly and politely answer their inquiries and remain calm.

Reporting issues

An issue that is well-documented is half solved. The fastest, most effective way to report an issue in a QlikView application is to take a screenshot of the anomaly using an image and video screen capture tool like TechSmith's Snagit (`http://www.techsmith.com/snagit.html`). Along with taking an accurate screenshot, it also allows us to easily add annotations that clearly communicate the problem.

In addition to capturing a screenshot, we can also make our troubleshooting process more efficient if we report the anomaly directly into an issue tracking system. BugHerd (`https://www.bugherd.com`) is a bug capturing tool that we can use to track issues or integrate it with other issue trackers, such as Jira or Zendesk. When we capture an issue in BugHerd, it takes an automatic screenshot, records information about the user's system environment, and allows the user to add any additional comment or file.

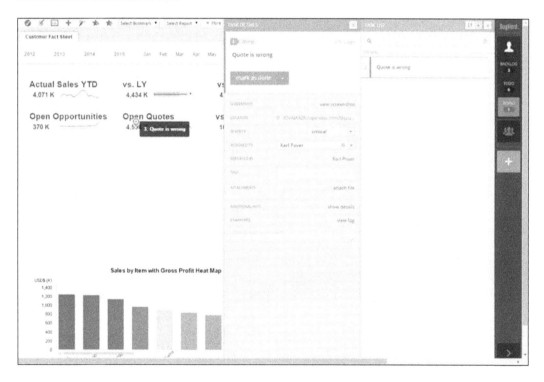

We can create a **BugHerd** project with the hostname, `http://QlikViewServerName/QvAJAXZfc` and use BugHerd's Google Chrome extension in a QlikView Server environment. In case we don't use Google Chrome or we want to report issues directly in the QlikView Desktop WebView, we can use Ralf Becher's BugHerd QlikView document extension (`https://github.com/ralfbecher/QlikView_Extension_BugHerd`). This extension doesn't take an automatic screenshot, but we can easily attach one to the issue.

 In order for the extension to work properly, you may have to add `https://www.bugherd.com` to the list of **Trusted Sites** in the **Security** tab found in **Internet Options**.

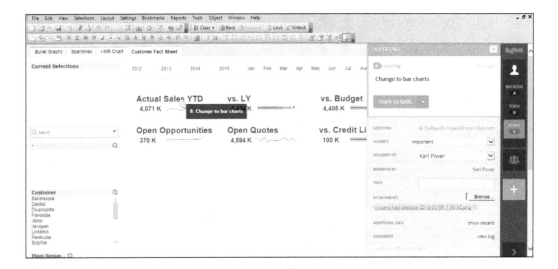

Once we report an issue, we can keep track of its status in a BugHerd project or in one of several issue-tracking tools that integrates with it. The BugHerd project uses the following Kanban board to organize issues:

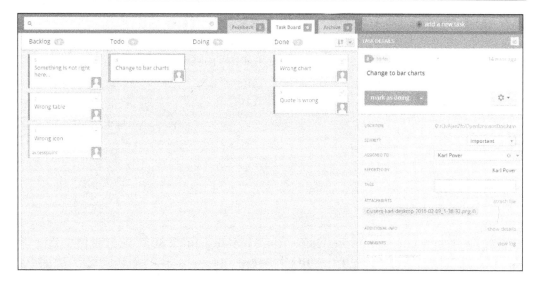

Now that we've reported several issues with help from BugHerd and Snagit, let's review various issues that we commonly encounter in our QlikView applications.

Common QlikView application issues

Along with issues that concern expressions or object properties, we also tend to discover issues related to the data, load script, or model at the moment we create visualizations. Let's review the common issues based on their source in the following sections.

Common QlikView data model issues

We always have to be prepared to review previous steps in the development process when we are diagnosing and fixing a data visualization issue.

All expression values are exactly the same

The following screenshot is an example of what happens when the field that we use as a dimension has no relationship with the field(s) that we use in an expression:

Sales	
Customer	**Sales**
	16,007,472
Avamba	16,007,472
Dabjam	16,007,472
Divanoodle	16,007,472
Dynabox	16,007,472
Gevee	16,007,472
Miboo	16,007,472

This issue is especially common when we are making quick adjustments to a data model and delete a key field or rename it in only one table, thus breaking an existing link. Another reason may also be that we mistakenly add a field from a legitimate island table to a chart.

When we notice the issue illustrated in the previous chart, our first action should be to look at the data model and confirm whether the tables are linked. If they are in fact not linked, then we fix this error by linking the tables in the script. If they shouldn't be linked, we change either the chart's dimension or expression to contain fields that are related to each other.

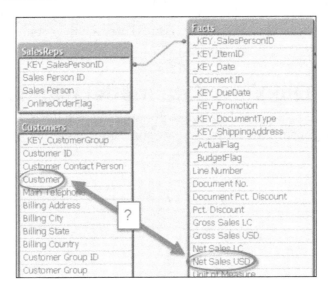

The expression total is not equal to the sum of the rows

When business users export QlikView charts to Excel, they may occasionally report that the sum of the rows in Excel does not match the total in QlikView. For example, the total in the QlikView chart in the following screenshot does not equal the sum of the rows:

Sales	
Item Group	Sales
	16,007,472
Doohickey	1,650,772
Gadgets	2,105,677
Gizmos	483,694
Whatchamacallit	11,248,499
Widget	1,363,206

We can confirm this discrepancy when we export the table to Excel and calculate the sum of the rows.

Item Group	Sales
Doohickey	1,650,772
Gadgets	2,105,677
Gizmos	483,694
Whatchamacallit	11,248,499
Widget	1,363,206
	16,851,846

A common (and incorrect) fix to this error is to change the way that the chart calculates the total. If we change **Total Mode** to **Sum of Rows**, we will fix the problem in this particular chart, but we are most likely ignoring an underlying problem with the data model. We should always use **Expression Total** as **Total Mode**:

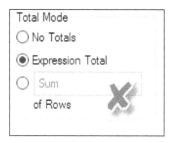

The sum of the rows doesn't equal the expression total because the chart uses fields whose tables have a many-to-many relationship. For example, in the case of the previous example, the error is caused by an item that is assigned to two different item groups. Therefore, two rows in the **Items** table are linked to the same multiple rows in the **Facts** table.

Sales		🖳 XL ⬍ ⬜
Item Group	**Item** ⬙ ⬤	**Sales**
		844,374
Whatchamacallit	Bamdax 126	844,374
Widget	Bamdax 126	844,374

If the item is supposed to be in two groups, then we may need to add a business rule to prorate the amount between the two groups. For example, we could prorate the total sales amount so that 40% is assigned to Widgets and 60% to Whatchamacallits. However, in most cases, this issue is caused by poor data quality or an error in the load script.

Duplicate values in a list box

List boxes always show a list of unique values. However, as in the following list box, we sometimes come across ones that appear to contain repeat values. Before we start proclaiming that we've found a bug in QlikView, let's review how QlikView handles data types.

CreateDate 🔎
12/31/2013
12/31/2013
12/31/2013
12/31/2013
12/31/2013
12/31/2013
12/31/2013
12/31/2013
12/31/2013
12/31/2013

We rarely have to worry about data types in QlikView. For example, we don't declare fields to be a varchar, nvarchar, int, double, or text data type like we do in SQL. In QlikView, the only thing that we have to remember is that every field value is a dual data type or, in other words, it has two values: a string, and a number.

The string value is the one that is displayed in a list box and it's possible that the same string represents different numbers. Even if the numbers have the same string, the list box will not group them into one entry. We force the list box to show the number values that are paired with each string using the following options in the **Number** tab of the list box's property dialog window.

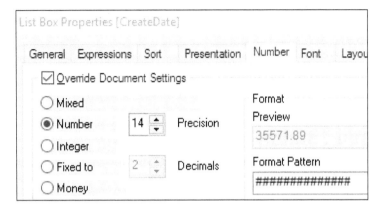

 We maximize the precision of the number in order to avoid scientific notation (e) from appearing when the number is too big or too small.

We can now confirm that the dates represent distinct numbers. We expect the number, 41639, to correspond to the string, 12/31/2013. However, the fractional part of each number is different because it represents a particular time during the day.

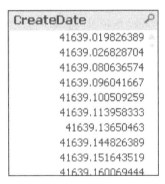

The source of this issue is in the load script and this is where we should fix it. In this case, the `Date()` function, which manipulates the string part of a field value, is used to format a field value that contains a timestamp. Although the string part of the values is formatted as expected, the number part of the value remains the same. If we want to convert a timestamp into a date, then we first need to convert the number part from a decimal into an integer using the `Floor()` function and then format the string using the `Date()` function. For example, we use the following code in the load script to fix our example:

```
...
Date(Floor(CreateDate),'MM/DD/YYYY') as CreateDate,
...
```

Data doesn't match user expectation

Business users often report that the numbers in QlikView don't match their expectations or their own manual reporting. Given QlikView is where they visualize data, this is going to be where they detect numerous data-related issues even if the problem originates in the data source.

When business users report data discrepancies in a stable QlikView application, our first step should be to follow the data's lineage to its source. If the source is correct, then we break down the problem into the different steps of the same path that the data follows until it reaches the user—extraction, transform, model, and visualization.

Along with creating a well-designed folder structure for our QlikView applications, there are a couple of tools that can help us understand the exact path that data takes from its source until its visualization. The first tool is QlikView Governance Dashboard, which you can download from Qlik Market (`https://market.qlik.com/qlikview-governance-dashboard.html`).

QlikView Governance Dashboard offers a complete overview of a QlikView deployment. Once we've entered in the necessary information in the **Configuration** tab and then reloaded the application, we can review data lineage in the **Lineage** tab:

In the **Lineage** tab, we can select a source table in the **Sources** table and take a look at which QlikView files use this table in the **Processes** table. We can also review whether it is used to create a QVD in the **Generated QVDs/QVXs** table. In the same way that we navigate from the source table to its target, we can also begin our analysis by selecting a target table in **Generated QVDs/QVXs** and investigating which process generates it from which possible sources.

The second tool is the `DataLineage` subroutine in **QlikView Components** (QVC) (`https://github.com/RobWunderlich/Qlikview-Components`). In the same way that we used a QVC subroutine to create a master calendar, we first include the QVC library in the load script of the QlikView application whose data lineage we want to analyze:

```
$(Include=..\qvc_runtime\qvc.qvs)
```

Then, we call the `DataLineage` subroutine:

```
CALL Qvc.DataLineage;
```

Finally, we call the `Cleanup` subroutine to clean up any global variables:

```
CALL Qvc.Cleanup;
```

Once we reload the application, we can create the following table that details the application's data lineage:

These two tools can help us discover data lineage at the table level. Once we understand it at this level, we analyze it at the field level by reviewing the load scripts of each QlikView application involved in the process.

Once we have an idea of the data lineage, we walk through the following steps to diagnose the issue:

1. Confirm that the source QVDs are being updated properly.

2. Review the data in the QVDs at the extraction level and confirm that it shows the same values as the data source.

3. Review the data in the QVDs at the transform level and confirm that it shows the values we expect. The majority of data issues caused by QlikView will be found at this stage.

4. Review the raw data in the data model and confirm that it shows the values that we expect.

5. Test the visualization that shows the incorrect result in the QlikView application. If the result is calculated by a complex expression or a calculated dimension, then we begin to test it without any set analysis or conditional statements. We then add, bit by bit, the components that were left out and confirm that we see the values that we expect after each change.

Hopefully, we will find the cause of the issue in the first few steps and fix the problem quickly. If not, then at least by the time we get to the visualization, we can be confident that the problem is there.

> In many cases, we can review QVD data more efficiently by opening it in EasyQlik QViewer (`http://easyqlik.com/`) rather than by creating a temporary Qlikview application to load it.

Common QlikView expression issues

Complex analysis can make for complex expressions and potential issues. Let's review the common issues caused by erroneous expressions.

The expression does not calculate every row

The following table shows the total sales and average monthly sales by customer and item group. However, common sense tells us that if a customer has an amount in **Total Sales**, then there should also be an amount listed in **Monthly Sales Avg** and not a null value. It also seems strange that the **Monthly Sales Avg** values that do appear are larger than the **Total Sales** amounts on the same row.

Total Sales			
Customer	Item Group	Total Sales	Monthly Sales Avg
		16,007,472	1,627,689
Dabjam	Doohickey	81,409 -	
Dabjam	Gadgets	315,073 -	
Dabjam	Whatchamacallit	1,014,710	1,698,327
Dabjam	Widget	236,594 -	
Dynabox	Doohickey	354,863 -	
Dynabox	Gadgets	479,882 -	
Dynabox	Whatchamacallit	1,418,850 -	
Dynabox	Widget	165,172 -	
Gevee	Doohickey	287,672 -	

In the **Monthly Sales Avg** column, we used the following code with an `aggr()` function to calculate the average monthly sales of each customer and item group:

```
avg(aggr(sum(Amount),Month))
```

However, the dimensions in the `aggr()` function should always include the same fields that are defined as the chart's dimensions. If we change the expression to include `Customer` and `[Item Group]` as parameters to the `aggr()` function, then we get a table with the correct numbers.

```
avg(aggr(sum(Amount),Month,Customer,[Item Group]))
```

Total Sales			🖳 XL ▬ ☐
Customer	Item Group	Total Sales	Monthly Sales Avg
		16,007,472	119,517
Dabjam	Doohickey	81,409	81,409
Dabjam	Gadgets	315,073	157,536
Dabjam	Whatchamacallit	1,014,710	101,471
Dabjam	Widget	236,594	78,865
Dynabox	Doohickey	354,863	118,288
Dynabox	Gadgets	479,882	159,961
Dynabox	Whatchamacallit	1,418,850	118,238
Dynabox	Widget	165,172	55,057
Gevee	Doohickey	287,672	95,891

The amounts in the table are not accumulating

Set analysis is a powerful tool, but it is not a panacea for every analytical need. The following table is an example of a chart that cannot be created using set analysis:

Sales - Rolling Accumulation											🖳 XL ▬ ☐
Month		Jan		Feb		Mar		Apr		May	
Customer	Monthly Sales	Accumulated Sales	Monthly Sales	Accumulated Sales	Monthly Sales	Accumulated Sales	Monthly Sales	Accumulated Sales	Monthly Sales	Accumulated Sales	
Thoughtworks	-	-	-	-	-	-	-	-	-	-	
Reallinks	9,190	9,190	69,779	78,969	224,949	303,918	141,925	445,843	78,232	524,075	
Photospace	-	-	83,157	83,157	62,452	145,609	0	145,609	100,039	245,648	
Oodoo	73,838	73,838	0	73,838	32,097	105,934	447,278	553,212	0	553,212	
Ntag	23,260	23,260	217,224	240,484	57,654	298,138	0	298,138	20,411	318,549	
Miboo	-	-	206,563	206,563	22,000	228,563	69,198	297,761	77,856	375,617	
Gevee	-	-	635,424	635,424	114,700	750,124	399,328	1,149,452	157,690	1,307,143	
Dynabox	22,082	22,082	277,233	299,315	215,190	514,506	157,272	671,778	36,382	708,160	
Dabjam	66,857	66,857	0	66,857	20,149	87,006	318,495	405,501	0	405,501	

The false belief that set analysis may be the way to create this chart is born from its ability to create the following chart that contains the same monthly and accumulated sales columns:

Month		Monthy and Accumulated Sales	🖳 Xl _ ☐
Jan	Customer	Monthly Sales	Accumulated Sales
Feb	Reallinks	224,949	303,918
Mar	Photospace	62,452	145,609
Apr	Oodoo	32,097	105,934
May	Ntag	57,654	298,138
Jun	Miboo	22,000	228,563
Jul	Gevee	114,700	750,124
Aug	Dynabox	215,190	514,506
Sep	Dabjam	20,149	87,006
Oct			
Nov			
Dec			

In this chart, we used the following code to calculate **Accumulated Sales**:

```
sum({$<Month={"<=$(=max(Month))"}>} [Net Sales])
```

When we use a chart dimension in the set modifier of an expression, we have to understand that this expression can only calculate over the data that corresponds to the dimension value in that row , or in the case of a pivot table, that column. For example, the following chart uses the previous expression in a table with Month as a chart dimension and we can see what happens when we select **March**, as follows:

Month		Sales - Rolling Accumulation (Incorrect)					🖳 Xl _ ☐	
Jan	Month		Jan		Feb		Mar	
Feb								
Mar	Customer		Monthly Sales	Accumulated Sales	Monthly Sales	Accumulated Sales	Monthly Sales	Accumulated Sales
Apr								
May	Reallinks		0	9,190	0	69,779	224,949	224,949
Jun	Photospace	-		-		0	83,157	62,452	62,452
Jul	Oodoo		0	73,838	-		32,097	32,097
Aug	Ntag		0	23,260	0	217,224	57,654	57,654
Sep	Miboo	-		-		0	206,563	22,000	22,000
Oct	Gevee	-		-		0	635,424	114,700	114,700
Nov	Dynabox		0	22,082	0	277,233	215,190	215,190
Dec	Dabjam		0	66,857	-		20,149	20,149

Accumulated Sales does not accumulate because set analysis is not an inter-row function or, in other words, it does not see data outside the data slice defined by the dimension values. Even if we use the `Total` keyword to allow the previous expression to calculate overall data, we still don't get the result that we expect because the maximum `Month` in the set modifier (**March**) is the same for every value in the `Month` chart dimension:

Month		Sales - Rolling Accumulation (Incorrect)					🖳 XL _ ☐
Jan Feb	**Month**			Jan		Feb	Mar
Mar Apr	**Customer**	Monthly Sales	Accumulated Sales	Monthly Sales	Accumulated Sales	Monthly Sales	Accumulated Sales
May	Reallinks	0	303,918	0	303,918	224,949	303,918
Jun	Photospace	0	145,609	0	145,609	62,452	145,609
Jul	Oodoo	0	105,934	0	105,934	32,097	105,934
Aug	Ntag	0	298,138	0	298,138	57,654	298,138
Sep	Miboo	0	228,563	0	228,563	22,000	228,563
Oct	Gevee	0	750,124	0	750,124	114,700	750,124
Nov	Dynabox	0	514,506	0	514,506	215,190	514,506
Dec	Dabjam	0	87,006	0	87,006	20,149	87,006

The solution in order to create the table at the beginning of this section is to use inter-row functions, such as `above()` or `below()`, in combination with range functions, such as `rangesum()`. We use the following code for **Accumulated Sales**:

```
rangesum(before(sum([Net Sales]),0,ColumnNo(Total)+1))
```

We can also use the **Accumulation** section in the **Expressions** tab if we use a straight table and only one dimension, or we can use a more robust solution such as the **As Of Calendar** we used in *Chapter 13, Financial Perspective*.

Summary

There will always be new issues to investigate and resolve and we have a whole host of resources available to help us troubleshoot them. However, as we resolve more issues and become more experienced, the most important resource will be our own local knowledge base. If we haven't started one yet, then we can start one with the short list of common issues that we reviewed in this chapter.

In the next and final chapter, we will take a look at Qlik Sense, which in some ways allows us to build on the experience that we've gained by working with QlikView. However, in others ways, it challenges us to forget what we know and learn something new.

21
Mastering Qlik Sense Data Visualization

In 2014, Qlik released the first version of its next-generation data visualization and discovery tool, Qlik Sense. Once thought to be a revamped QlikView, it has instead turned out to be part of something larger. Let's take a quick look at what Qlik Sense means to QlikView developers, especially in the area of data visualization.

Let's review the following topics as we devise a plan to master Qlik Sense data visualization:

- Qlik Sense and what it means for QlikView developers
- Qlik Sense visualization extension examples for cross-selling
- Plans and resources to master Qlik Sense data visualization

Qlik Sense and QlikView developers

In short, Qlik Sense is an application to help nontechnical users perform data visualization, analysis, and storytelling, within a governed environment. In this self-service BI tool, users can create simple data models and metric calculations without writing, or even seeing, one line of code. Also, Qlik Sense automatically generates cleaner, more intuitive visualizations without the need to memorize a myriad of property options.

As each new version is released, more and more features will be added to simplify tasks that were once only possible through coding. However, there will still be the need to code the more advanced data models and metric calculations. For example, users with technical aptitude will still be needed to facilitate the advanced analysis that we've seen in this book.

How we develop the load script and chart expressions remains largely unchanged between Qlik Sense and QlikView. Therefore, many data visualization tips and tricks that depend on manipulating the script, a calculated dimension, or a measure expression will work in both tools. On the other hand, Qlik Sense's chart objects have been built anew from the ground up, and they have no direct relationship to the ones in QlikView. Therefore, any tips or tricks that involve a particular chart property option in QlikView will most likely not work in Qlik Sense.

Even though Qlik Sense's chart objects currently offer fewer customizable properties than QlikView's, we can expect more property options to be added with each new version. However, as Qlik Sense's design intent is to be one that nontechnical users can easily manipulate, it would be unlikely that its property dialogs will reach QlikView's complexity or flexibility. Therefore, if we limit ourselves to employ only what is natively available in Qlik Sense, we will fail take full advantage of the opportunities that it offers.

For this reason, it is important that we change how we approach Qlik Sense. There won't be many opportunities to resolve our challenges by playing with an object's property options. So, the primary solution to most of our problems will be to develop a new, or edit an existing *visualization extension*. If we are not familiar with JavaScript, HTML5, and CSS, then we will need to invest time to learn these web programming skills. Such investment is more worthwhile when we see how it can also create opportunities to use Qlik-supported data analytics outside of Qlik Sense.

Qlik Sense is, in fact, only an example of what one could build on top of the **Qlik Analytics Platform** (**QAP**), a developer platform that gives us the opportunity to use Qlik's associative data model to address any data analytics need. We can use QAP to embed custom data analytics into existing applications or create our own personalized analytical tools. For example, we can embed data analytics in our customer or supplier portals, our ERP, or our CRM.

Although we can also create extensions in QlikView, we can never make them as powerful as native chart objects. However, QAP gives us access to the same APIs that Qlik uses to develop Qlik Sense, so visualization extensions can be just as robust. In the following section, let's take a look at an example of how we can use a visual extension to help sales representatives discover cross-selling opportunities.

Visualization extension examples for cross-selling

As part of our balanced scorecard in *Chapter 19, Balanced Scorecard*, we purposed giving sales representatives a tool that allowed them to analyze cross-selling opportunities. We've decided to deliver this tool using Qlik Sense for the following two reasons:

- Nontechnical users, such as sales representatives, can create their own analysis
- Developers can create more powerful visualization extensions to help sales representatives discover cross-selling opportunities

The following three Qlik Sense data visualizations were created by Ralf Becher (`http://irregular-bi.tumblr.com/`). The first chart is a table that contains a numerical interpretation of how different items or item sets are related. It was created using a data mining algorithm called Apriori (`https://en.wikipedia.org/wiki/Apriori_algorithm`), which is used to discover associations between items or item sets and is a popular method to perform basket analysis.

Although we can use native QlikView and Qlik Sense to analyze individual associations, a visualization extension using the **Apriori algorithm** offers a more robust solution to discover the statistical correlation of every possible association. Similarly to how we use R-squared along with a scatterplot to understand correlations, we use confidence, support, and lift to understand association rules.

The first row in the table in the next figure evaluates the association rule, "If **Toughfind 1292** and **True Ronlam** are purchased, then **Stathold** is purchased by the same customer." According to this table, **Toughfind 1292**, **True Ronlam**, and **Stathold** are purchased by 22.2% of all customers (**Support**). Also, if a customer purchases **Toughfind 1292**, **True Ronlam**, they are 100% likely to purchase **Stathold** (**Confidence**).

The final column, called **Lift**, takes **Confidence** and divides it by the overall probability that a customer purchases **Stathold**. For example, if **Stathold** was purchased by 50% of all customers, then **Lift** would be 2.00 (100%/50%). This would imply that there is a relationship between purchasing **Stathold**, given that a customer purchases **Toughfind 1292**, and **True Ronlam**. In short, a **Lift** greater than 1.00 implies an association between the item sets, and the greater the lift, the stronger the relationship. In the case of **Toughfind 1292**, **True Ronlam**, and **Stathold**, a lift of 4.5 indicates a strong association:

Start Apriori Calculation

| 0 Baskets | 6.400 Rules found | Calc. Time: 89.114 ms |

#	LHS	RHS	Confidence	Support	Lift
1	Toughfind 1292, True Ronlam	Stathold	1,0000	0.2222	4.50
2	Stathold	Sublab 6000, True Ronlam	1,0000	0.2222	4.50
3	True Ronlam, Zenhold A82	Stathold	1,0000	0.2222	4.50
4	Stathold	True Ronlam, Zenhold A82	1,0000	0.2222	4.50
5	Stathold	Labtouch 500, True Ronlam	1,0000	0.2222	4.50
6	Labtouch 500, True Ronlam	Stathold	1,0000	0.2222	4.50
7	Stathold	Toughfind 1292, True Ronlam	1,0000	0.2222	4.50
8	Superdax, True Ronlam	Stathold	1,0000	0.2222	4.50
9	Stathold	Superdax, True Ronlam	1,0000	0.2222	4.50
10	Sublab 6000, True Ronlam	Stathold	1,0000	0.2222	4.50
11	Jobdax, Zaamfax	X-ing 4	1,0000	0.3333	3.00
12	San-Lex, X-ing 5	Ran-Core 20	1,0000	0.2222	3.00
13	Ran-Core 20, San-Lex	X-ing 5	1,0000	0.2222	3.00
14	X-ing 5	Ran-Core 20, San-Lex	0.6667	0.2222	3.00
15	Ran-Core 20	San-Lex, X-ing 5	0.6667	0.2222	3.00
16	Labtouch 500, Triotech T493	Stathold	0.6667	0.2222	3.00

The table in the previous figure alone is powerful, but there are also a couple of visualizations that we can use to detect any customer purchase behavior that would otherwise be difficult to discover. We can also use them to give us a general overview of the data. Again, we use extensions to visualize this complex dataset that would otherwise be laborious, if not impossible, to create through native objects.

The first chart is a network chart that connects customer nodes to the product nodes that they purchase. Along with the *Gestalt principle* of connection to perceive the general connectivity between products and customers, we also use the principle of proximity to detect clusters that may indicate stronger relationships. For example, the remoteness of the customer **Wordtune** indicates how little their purchasing behavior has in common with that of other customers:

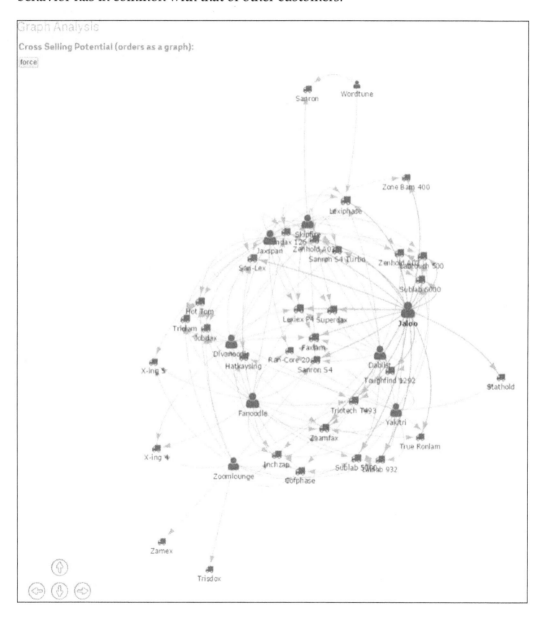

Another example is the cluster of product nodes that comprises the products, **Hot Tom**, **Triolam**, and **Jobdax**, that indicates a strong relationship between them. Upon further investigation, we confirm that all three products are purchased by the same customers. We can find cross-selling opportunities by zooming in on these product clusters to see which customers have yet to purchase one of the related products. We could also do the inverse and zoom in on related customer clusters and look for products which have not been purchased by every related customer.

We could also make cross-selling recommendations based on the length of the path between customer and product nodes. For example, Customer A's path to *Product Y* is three nodes long if *Customer A* purchases the same *Product X* as *Customer B*, who, in turn, also purchases Product Y. Therefore, we may have an opportunity to sell Product Y to Customer A:

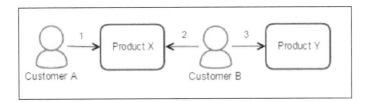

In order to create a list of opportunities based on path distance, we calculate the shortest path between customer and product nodes using the *Dijkstra algorithm* (https://en.wikipedia.org/wiki/Dijkstra's_algorithm) and define the maximum path length that we will interpret as an opportunity. As a longer path implies a weaker relationship between a product and its potential buyer, we create our recommendations using paths of three or fewer nodes. Using the path shown in the previous figure as an example, we will see both Product Y (3-node path) and Product X (1-node path) being recommended for sale to Customer A.

Finally, we visualize these cross-selling recommendations using a Sankey chart that is similar to the one we use in the marketing perspective in *Chapter 14, Marketing Perspective*. In the chart, we can visualize the general extent of the cross-selling opportunities through the connections between customer and product. We can also perceive the number of opportunities per customer and per product through the size of the bar that represents them. For example, the outlier, **Wordtune**, has the most cross-selling recommendations. On the other hand, there are few opportunities to cross-sell the **Zamex** and **Trisdox** products:

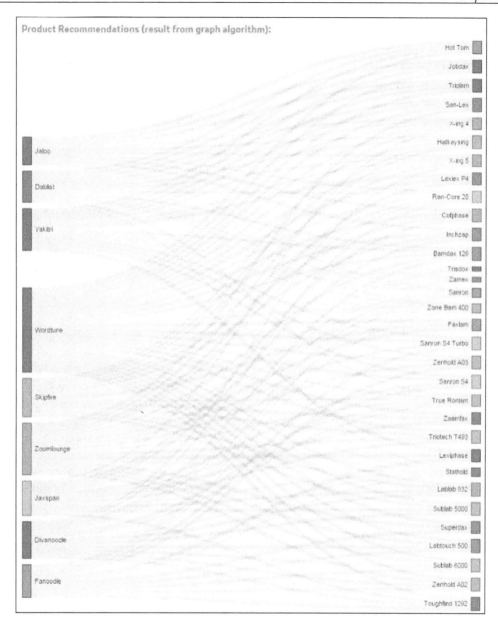

The Qlik Sense visualization extensions that Ralf Becher created are an example of what we can expect from those who want to also become masters in Qlik Sense data visualization. For those of us who have mastered QlikView and are excited to meet this new challenge, let's go over the top-ten list of things that will be important to us during the next year as we learn to master Qlik Sense.

Plan to master Qlik Sense data visualization

For those of us who are QlikView developers with little or no web development experience, developing visualization extensions can seem like a daunting task. However, if we've mastered QlikView's load script and chart expressions and we've learned how to effectively use data visualization and analysis to solve numerous business problems, then this is the most obvious next step forward into growth. Let's review our top-ten list of activities and resources that we need to consider to make this next step successful:

1. Take care of the fundamentals and learn HTML5, CSS, and JavaScript.

    If you have no web development experience or it's been a while since you've actively used HTML, CSS or JavaScript, then brush up on the fundamentals using the free tutorials available at `http://www.w3schools.com/`. If you want something with even more structure, you can also try `http://www.asmarterwaytolearn.com/`.

2. Go through Qlik Sense developer's help documentation and create your first extensions.

    Qlik's online help documentation contains a simple tutorial that will help you get familiar with the development environment called the Dev Hub, and the available APIs, as you create your first extension. As of Qlik Sense 2.2, you can find documentation to create visualization extensions, and the tutorial at `https://help.qlik.com/en-US/sense-developer/2.2/Content/extend.htm`. Make sure that you are looking at the latest version of the documentation by selecting the most current version in the top section of the page. You can also find a similar tutorial by Stefan Walther at GitHub (`https://github.com/stefanwalther/qliksense-extension-tutorial`).

3. Get updated information and insight from the Qlik-related blogs.

    Review the Qlik Branch blog (`http://branch.qlik.com/`) and search for `extensions` at `http://www.askqv.com/` to get the latest news about how to use extensions.

4. Get live advice from the experts.

    There is nothing like live advice from an expert to make sure that you are on the right path. Ralf Becher, who created the extensions used in this chapter, gives online classes on the subject through Q-On Training Center at `http://www.q-on.bi/`.

5. Learn to use a data visualization JavaScript library.

   Keep it simple and learn to use the most popular open source data visualization JavaScript library D3 (`https://d3js.org/`). Along with online examples and documentation, you can also find plenty of books on the subject.

6. Find a visualization to develop and just get started.

   Again, keep it simple and choose a D3 chart that looks fun, and then get started developing it. Even if it's an animated chart that ends up being useless in the end, pick something that will motivate you to show it off.

7. Fail fast and look for answers in the work done by others.

   Although it is important that you try to do it yourself first, when you do get stuck, don't hesitate to look over the example extensions found in `C:\Users\<username>\Documents\Qlik\Examples\Extensions`, or the extensions created by fellow developers in Qlik Branch (`http://branch.qlik.com/`).

8. Contribute to the Qlik Branch.

   Now that you've created the first extension on your own, it's time to give back to the community. As you now know what kind of work is out there in the Qlik Branch (`http://branch.qlik.com/`), choose your next extension based on what you think would be useful to others and upload it. As well as helping others enrich their data visualization, they help you by testing your extension in different environments and giving you feedback.

9. Take the time to learn what will make you better (sharpen the saw).

   Once you have mastered the fundamentals and become a contributor to Qlik Branch, go back to learn anything that you feel would make your development better, such as jQuery, Angular JS, other data visualization JavaScript libraries, or even a predicative analysis JavaScript library.

10. Create an extension to solve a real business need.

    Find a data analysis need that you cannot directly resolve using Qlik Sense and develop a solution using an extension. This could be a user requirement for a visualization that cannot be created using native chart objects, or a data mining example, such as basket analysis. Once you have a customer that demands certain functionality and you are challenged to deliver a solution, you will quickly become a proficient Qlik Sense developer.

Summary

Just as Qlik invested time and resources to rebuild a new, deeper foundation, we also need to take the time to sharpen the saw and become more capable developers. We need to learn web development skills in order to extend Qlik Sense's ability to provide self-service analytics, and make insightful data analysis and visualization ubiquitous using the Qlik Analytics Platform.

Amid all these new developments, QlikView will persist to address the needs of organizations which require analytical applications with a personalized UX. As such, it will continue to be the backbone analytics tools for many customers, and as such, we need to continue to push the limits of what is possible in QlikView.

Other Books You May Enjoy

If you enjoyed this book, you may be interested in these other books by Packt:

Mastering QlikView

QlikView Essentials

Chandraish Sinha

ISBN: 978-1-78439-728-9

- ▸ Learn the complete QlikView workflow – from loading data, to visualization and analytics
- ▸ Learn how to Load data from different sources, including QVD files and how to optimize data models for accuracy and precision
- ▸ Discover solutions to common data modeling problems, so you can respond quickly to changing situations
- ▸ Create accessible dashboards and quality data visualizations to share insights effectively
- ▸ Learn how to deploy your BI application for optimal availability

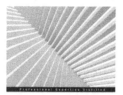

QlikView Unlocked

QlikView Unlocked

Roger Stone, Andrew Dove

ISBN: 978-1-78528-512-7

- ▸ Build the QlikView environment correctly so that it is flexible and robust
- ▸ Deliver a successful QlikView Project
- ▸ Understand and implement QlikView best practices
- ▸ Discover the best way to prototype, develop and deploy applications
- ▸ Overcome data modelling challenges
- ▸ Explore the in's and out's of Section Access
- ▸ Solve post-deployment issues in Server and Publisher

Leave a review – let other readers know what you think

Please share your thoughts on this book with others by leaving a review on the site that you bought it from. If you purchased the book from Amazon, please leave us an honest review on this book's Amazon page. This is vital so that other potential readers can see and use your unbiased opinion to make purchasing decisions, we can understand what our customers think about our products, and our authors can see your feedback on the title that they have worked with Packt to create. It will only take a few minutes of your time, but is valuable to other potential customers, our authors, and Packt. Thank you!

Index

A

Above function 221

Access Document Properties (Users),
user privilege 460

ACCESS field 452

Access Restriction Table Wizard
dialog 452, 457

Access Sheet Object Properties,
user privilege 462

Access Sheet Properties (Users),
user privilege 462

Access Tab row Properties,
user privilege 460

Accounts Payable (A/P) 565

Accounts Receivable (A/R) 565

Accumulation option

Accumulation optionabout 350

actions

actionsadding, to text object 375

additive facts 93

Add new tab button 439

Add Sheet Objects, user privilege 462

Add Sheets, user privilege 460

Admin Override Security,
user privilege 461

advanced aggregations

Aggr, used for calculating control chart 227

calculated dimensions 228

creating, with Aggr 225, 226, 227

nodistinct option, avoiding 229, 230

Advanced Color Map dialog window 330

advanced search 189

advanced Table File Wizard options

Crosstable wizard, using 282, 283, 284

examining 278

transformation step, enabling 278

After function 221

Aggr

advanced aggregations, creating
with 225, 226, 227

used, for calculating control chart 227

Aggregate operator 174

aggregation functions

aggregation functionsConcat() function 421

aggregation functionsCount() function 421

aggregation functionsMax() function 421

aggregation functionsMaxString()
function 421

aggregation functionsMin() function 421

aggregation functionsMinString()
function 421

aggregation functionsOnly() function 421

aggregation functionssum() function 421

Aggr function 225

agile development

about 474, 475

minimum viable product (MVP) 475

user story 475

Airline Operations

Airline OperationsDAR principle,
adding to 336

Airline Operationsdocument
requisites 337, 338, 360

Air Time % gauge

Air Time % gaugecreating 370

AlchemyAPI

URL 557

alignment option 320

Allow Copy/Clone option 322

Allow Export, user privilege 460

Allow Maximize option 323

B

www.ingramcontent.com/pod-product-compliance
Lightning Source LLC
LaVergne TN
LVHW081504050326
832903LV00025B/1387